January 24–25, 2011
Austin, Texas, USA

Association for
Computing Machinery

Advancing Computing as a Science & Profession

PEPM'11

Proceedings of the 20th ACM SIGPLAN Workshop on

Partial Evaluation and Program Manipulation

Sponsored by:

ACM SIGPLAN

Association for
Computing Machinery

Advancing Computing as a Science & Profession

The Association for Computing Machinery
2 Penn Plaza, Suite 701
New York, New York 10121-0701

ISBN: 978-1-4503-0485-6

Additional copies may be ordered prepaid from:

ACM Order Department
PO Box 30777
New York, NY 10087-0777, USA

Phone: 1-800-342-6626 (USA and Canada)
+1-212-626-0500 (Global)
Fax: +1-212-944-1318
E-mail: acmhelp@acm.org
Hours of Operation: 8:30 am – 4:30 pm ET

Printed in the USA

Foreword

It is our great pleasure to welcome you to the *20th ACM SIGPLAN Workshop on Partial Evaluation and Program Manipulation – PEPM'11.* This year's workshop program maintains PEPM's tradition of being the premier forum for presentation of research results and experience reports on partial evaluation and semantics-based manipulation of programs. We continue to base the call for papers on a broad interpretation of program manipulation and carry on the efforts of recent years to expand the scope of PEPM significantly beyond the traditionally covered areas of partial evaluation and specialization.

The call for papers attracted 35 submissions. The reviewing process and program committee discussions were handled by the *EasyChair* conference management system. Each submission received at least three reviews, on average 4.1 reviewers, by program committee members assisted by external reviews from over 30 external reviewers. After thorough discussion the program committee accepted 14 regular research papers and 1 tool demonstration. We are excited that the program includes invited talks by Charles Consel, Olivier Danvy and Martin Rinard. Both Consel and Danvy were founders of *PEPM*, and it is an honor to have them returned to celebrate the 20th anniversary of *PEPM.*

Many people worked hard and offered their valuable time so generously to make *PEPM'11* successful. First of all, we would like to thank the authors and invited speakers for providing the content of the program. We would like to express our gratitude to the program committee and external reviewers, who worked very hard in reviewing papers and providing suggestions for their improvements. The *PEPM'11* website was developed with help of Eelco Visser, to whom we express our appreciation. We thank Anh Cuong Nguyen and Narcisa Andreea Milea for their help in sending call-for-paper announcement to past participants of *PEPM.* We also thank ACM for its continued support of *PEPM.* Last, but not least, many thanks to Matthew Might (POPL'11 Workshops Chair) and to the local arrangements committee of POPL'11 for their work on the local arrangements of this affiliated event.

We hope that you will find this program interesting and thought-provoking and that the workshop will provide you with a valuable opportunity to share ideas with other researchers and practitioners from institutions around the world.

Siau-Cheng Khoo
PEPM'11 Co-Chair
National University of Singapore, Singapore

Jeremy Siek
PEPM'11 Co-Chair
University of Colorado at Boulder USA

Table of Contents

Session 8: Functional-Logic Programming

Session 9: Functional Programming

PEPM 2011 Workshop Organization

Program Chairs:	Siau-Cheng Khoo *(National University of Singapore, Singapore)*
	Jeremy Siek *(University of Colorado at Boulder, USA)*
Program Committee:	Jacques Carette *(McMaster University, Canada)*
	Kung Chen *(National Chengchi University, Taiwan)*
	Évelyne Contejean *(CNRS & Université Paris-Sud XI, France)*
	Francisco J. López Fraguas *(Universidad Complutense de Madrid, Spain)*
	Ronald Garcia *(Carnegie Mellon University, USA)*
	Jurriaan Hage *(Utrecht University, The Netherlands)*
	Zhenjiang Hu *(National Institute of Informatics, Japan)*
	Shan Shan Huang *(LogicBlox, Inc., USA)*
	Yukiyoshi Kameyama *(University of Tsukuba, Japan)*
	Ralf Lämmel *(University of Koblenz-Landau, Germany)*
	Michael Leuschel *(University of Düsseldorf, Germany)*
	Andrew Moss *(University of Bristol, UK)*
	Maurizio Proietti *(IASI-CNR, Italy)*
	Peter Sestoft *(IT University of Copenhagen, Denmark)*
	Chung-chieh Shan *(Rutgers, USA)*
	Scott D. Stoller *(Stony Brook University, USA)*
	Peter Thiemann *(University of Freiburg, Germany)*
	Simon Thompson *(Kent University, UK)*
	Germán Vidal *(Universidad Politecnica de Valencia, Spain)*
	Edwin Westbrook *(Rice University, USA)*
Steering Committee Chair:	Germán Puebla *(Technical University of Madrid, Spain)*
Steering Committee:	John Gallagher *(Roskilde University, Denmark)*
	John Hatcliff *(Kansas State University, USA)*
	Annie Liu *(State University of New York at Stony Brook, USA)*
	Janis Voigtländer *(University of Bonn, Germany)*
	Germán Vidal *(Universidad Politecnica de Valencia, Spain)*

Additional reviewers:

Kenichi Asai
Max Bolingbroke
Carl Friedrich Bolz
Rafael Caballero
Qichang Chen
Fabio Fioravanti
Sebastian Fischer
Marc Fontaine
Raul Gutierrez
Miguel Gómez-Zamalloa
Joxan Jaffar
Wolfram Kahl
Emanuel Kitzelmann
Sean Leather
Jos Pedro Magalhes
Enrique Martin-Martin
Arie Middelkoop
Jorge A. Navas
Naoki Nishida
Hugo Pacheco
Alberto Pettorossi
Tom Rothamel
Fernando Saenz-Perez
Jaime Sanchez-Hernandez
Andrew Santosa
Valerio Senni
Salvador Tamarit
Tuncay Tekle
Teck Bok Tok
Razvan Voicu
Meng Wang
Shu-Chun Weng
Dana N. Xu

Sponsor: ACM SIGPLAN

A Walk in the Semantic Park

Olivier Danvy
Department of Computer Science
Aarhus University
Aabogade 34, 8200 Aarhus N
Denmark
danvy@cs.au.dk

Jacob Johannsen
School of Computing
University of Kent
Canterbury, Kent CT2 7NF
United Kingdom
jj80@kent.ac.uk

Ian Zerny
Department of Computer Science
Aarhus University
Aabogade 34, 8200 Aarhus N
Denmark
zerny@cs.au.dk

Abstract

To celebrate the 20th anniversary of PEPM, we are inviting you to a walk in the semantic park and to inter-derive reduction-based and reduction-free negational normalization functions.

Categories and Subject Descriptors D.1.1 [*Software*]: Programming Techniques—applicative (functional) programming; D.3.2 [*Programming Languages*]: Language Classifications—applicative (functional) languages; F.3.1 [*Logics and Meanings of Programs*]: Specifying and Verifying and Reasoning about Programs—Specification techniques; F.4.1 [*Mathematical Logic and Formal Languages*]: Mathematical Logic—Lambda calculus and related systems.

General Terms Algorithms, Languages, Theory

Keywords reduction-based normalization, reduction-free normalization, negational normal forms, De Morgan laws, reduction semantics, abstract machines, reduction contexts, evaluation contexts, continuations, continuation-passing style (CPS), CPS transformation, defunctionalization, refunctionalization, refocusing

1. Introduction

The De Morgan laws provide conversion rules between Boolean formulas, where negations float up or down an abstract syntax tree:

$$\begin{aligned} \neg(\neg t) &\leftrightarrow t \\ \neg(t_1 \wedge t_2) &\leftrightarrow (\neg t_1) \vee (\neg t_2) \\ \neg(t_1 \vee t_2) &\leftrightarrow (\neg t_1) \wedge (\neg t_2) \end{aligned}$$

where $t ::= x \mid \neg t \mid t \wedge t \mid t \vee t$. These conversion rules can be oriented into reduction rules. For example, the following reduction rules make negations float down the abstract syntax tree of a given formula:

$$\begin{aligned} \neg(\neg t) &\rightarrow t \\ \neg(t_1 \wedge t_2) &\rightarrow (\neg t_1) \vee (\neg t_2) \\ \neg(t_1 \vee t_2) &\rightarrow (\neg t_1) \wedge (\neg t_2) \end{aligned}$$

Any Boolean formula can be reduced into a negational normal form, where only variables are negated:

$$t_{nf} ::= x \mid \neg x \mid t_{nf} \wedge t_{nf} \mid t_{nf} \vee t_{nf}$$

PEPM'11, January 24–25, 2011, Austin, Texas, USA.

Negational normalization can be equivalently viewed as a *small-step process*, where the De Morgan reduction rules are repeatedly applied until a normal form is obtained, and as a *big-step process*, where a given Boolean formula is recursively traversed in one fell swoop. On the occasion it is also specified with an abstract machine, which can itself be equally viewed as a small-step process and as a big-step one [6].

The goal of this article is to inter-derive these normalization processes using the program transformations used in Reynolds's functional correspondence between evaluators and big-step abstract machines [1, 16] and in the syntactic correspondence between calculi and small-step abstract machines [2], to which we add a new prelude. In the rest of this introduction, we specify the abstract syntax of Boolean formulas and of negational normal forms. We then successively consider two reduction strategies: leftmost outermost (Section 2) and leftmost innermost (Section 3). For emphasis, the presentations of Sections 2 and 3 are deliberately parallel, so that the reader can easily identify what is generic to the methodology and what is specific to each example. Throughout, we use pure ML as a functional meta-language. We have tried to make this article self-contained, but in case of doubt, the reader should consult the first author's lecture notes at the Sixth International School on Advanced Functional Programming [3].

Terms: A Boolean formula is either a variable, a negated formula, a conjunction of two formulas, or a disjunction of two formulas. We implement Boolean formulas with the following ML data type:

```
datatype term = VAR of ide
              | NEG of term
              | CONJ of term × term
              | DISJ of term × term
```

The fold functional associated to this data type abstracts its recursive descent by parameterizing what to do in each case:

```
fun term_foldr (var, neg, conj, disj) t
    = let fun visit (VAR x)
              = var x
            | visit (NEG t)
              = neg (visit t)
            | visit (CONJ (t1, t2))
              = conj (visit t1, visit t2)
            | visit (DISJ (t1, t2))
              = disj (visit t1, visit t2)
      in visit t
      end
```

Normal forms: A normal form is a formula where only variables are negated. Since ML does not support subtyping, we implement normal forms with the following specialized data type:

```
datatype term_nf = POSVAR_nf of ide
                 | NEGVAR_nf of ide
                 | CONJ_nf of term_nf × term_nf
                 | DISJ_nf of term_nf × term_nf
```

The fold functional associated to this data type abstracts its recursive descent by parameterizing what to do in each case:

```
fun term_nf_foldr (posvar, negvar, conj, disj) t
    = let fun visit (POSVAR_nf x)
                = posvar x
            | visit (NEGVAR_nf x)
                = negvar x
            | visit (CONJ_nf (t1_nf, t2_nf))
                = conj (visit t1_nf, visit t2_nf)
            | visit (DISJ_nf (t1_nf, t2_nf))
                = disj (visit t1_nf, visit t2_nf)
      in visit t
      end
```

For example, a normal form is dualized by recursively mapping positive occurrences of variables to negative ones, negative occurrences of variables to positive ones, conjunctions to disjunctions, and disjunctions to conjunctions:

```
val dualize = term_nf_foldr (NEGVAR_nf,
                             POSVAR_nf,
                             DISJ_nf,
                             CONJ_nf)
```

A normal form is embedded into a Boolean formula by mapping every specialized constructor into the corresponding original constructor(s):

```
val embed = term_nf_foldr (VAR,
                           fn x => NEG (VAR x),
                           CONJ,
                           DISJ)
```

2. Leftmost outermost negational normalization

In this section, we go from a leftmost-outermost *reduction* strategy to the corresponding leftmost-outermost *evaluation* strategy. We first implement the reduction strategy (Section 2.1) as a prelude to implementing the corresponding reduction semantics (Section 2.2). We then turn to the syntactic correspondence between reduction semantics and abstract machines (Section 2.3) and to the functional correspondence between abstract machines and normalization functions (Section 2.4).

2.1 Prelude to a reduction semantics

The reduction strategy induces a notion of value and of potential redex (i.e., of a term that is an actual redex or that is stuck); we are then in position to state a compositional search function that implements the reduction strategy and maps a given term either to the corresponding value, if it is in normal form, or to a potential redex (Section 2.1.1). From this search function we derive a decomposition function mapping a given term either to the corresponding value, if it is in normal form, or to a potential redex and its reduction context (Section 2.1.2). As a corollary we can then state the associated recomposition function that maps a reduction context and a contractum to the corresponding reduct (Section 2.1.3).

2.1.1 The reduction strategy

The reduction strategy consists in locating the leftmost-outermost negation of a term which is not a variable. A value therefore is a term where only variables are negated, i.e., a normal form:

```
type value = term_nf
```

A potential redex is the negation of a term that is not a variable:

```
datatype potential_redex = PR_NEG of term
                         | PR_CONJ of term × term
                         | PR_DISJ of term × term
```

The following compositional search function implements the reduction strategy. It searches a potential redex depth-first and from left to right:

```
datatype found = VAL of value
               | POTRED of potential_redex

(*  term → found  *)
fun search_term_neg (VAR x)
    = VAL (NEGVAR_nf x)
  | search_term_neg (NEG t)
    = POTRED (PR_NEG t)
  | search_term_neg (CONJ (t1, t2))
    = POTRED (PR_CONJ (t1, t2))
  | search_term_neg (DISJ (t1, t2))
    = POTRED (PR_DISJ (t1, t2))


(*  term → found  *)
fun search_term (VAR x)
    = VAL (POSVAR_nf x)
  | search_term (NEG t)
    = search_term_neg t
  | search_term (CONJ (t1, t2))
    = (case search_term t1
         of (VAL v1)
            => (case search_term t2
                  of (VAL v2)
                     => VAL (CONJ_nf (v1, v2))
                   | (POTRED pr)
                     => POTRED pr)
          | (POTRED pr)
            => POTRED pr)
  | search_term (DISJ (t1, t2))
    = (case search_term t1
         of (VAL v1)
            => (case search_term t2
                  of (VAL v2)
                     => VAL (DISJ_nf (v1, v2))
                   | (POTRED pr)
                     => POTRED pr)
          | (POTRED pr)
            => POTRED pr)

(*  term → found  *)
fun search t
    = search_term t
```

When a negation is encountered, the auxiliary function `search_term_neg` is called to decide whether this negation is a value or a potential redex.

2.1.2 From searching to decomposing

Let us transform the search function of Section 2.1.1 into a decomposition function for the reduction semantics of Section 2.2. The only difference between searching and decomposing is that given a non-value term, searching yields a potential redex whereas decomposing yields a potential redex *and its reduction context*. This reduction context is the defunctionalized continuation of the search function, and we construct it as such, by (1) CPS-transforming the search function (and simplifying it one bit) and (2) defunctionalizing its continuation.

CPS transformation: The search function is CPS-transformed by naming its intermediate results, sequentializing their computation, and introducing an extra functional argument, the continuation, that maps an intermediate result to a final answer:

```
(*  term × (found → α) → α  *)
fun search_term_neg (VAR x, k)
    = k (VAL (NEGVAR_nf x))
  | search_term_neg (NEG t, k)
    = k (POTRED (PR_NEG t))
  | search_term_neg (CONJ (t1, t2), k)
    = k (POTRED (PR_CONJ (t1, t2)))
  | search_term_neg (DISJ (t1, t2), k)
    = k (POTRED (PR_DISJ (t1, t2)))
```

```
(*  term × (found → α) → α  *)
fun search_term (VAR x, k)
    = k (VAL (POSVAR_nf x))
  | search_term (NEG t, k)
    = search_term_neg (t, k)
  | search_term (CONJ (t1, t2), k)
    = search_term (t1,
        fn (VAL v1)
           ⇒ search_term (t2,
                fn (VAL v2)
                   ⇒ k (VAL (CONJ_nf (v1, v2)))
                 | (POTRED pr)
                   ⇒ k (POTRED pr))
         | (POTRED pr)
           ⇒ k (POTRED pr))
  | search_term (DISJ (t1, t2), k)
    = search_term (t1,
        fn (VAL v1)
           ⇒ search_term (t2,
                fn (VAL v2)
                   ⇒ k (VAL (DISJ_nf (v1, v2)))
                 | (POTRED pr)
                   ⇒ k (POTRED pr))
         | (POTRED pr)
           ⇒ k (POTRED pr))

(*  term → found  *)
fun search t
    = search_term (t, fn f ⇒ f)
```

Simplifying the CPS-transformed search: The search is completed as soon as a potential redex is found. It can thus be simplified by only applying the continuation when a value is found:

```
(*  term × (value → found) → found  *)
fun search_term_neg (VAR x, k)
    = k (NEGVAR_nf x)
  | search_term_neg (NEG t, k)
    = POTRED (PR_NEG t)
  | search_term_neg (CONJ (t1, t2), k)
    = POTRED (PR_CONJ (t1, t2))
  | search_term_neg (DISJ (t1, t2), k)
    = POTRED (PR_DISJ (t1, t2))

(*  term × (value → found) → found  *)
fun search_term (VAR x, k)
    = k (POSVAR_nf x)
  | search_term (NEG t, k)
    = search_term_neg (t, k)
  | search_term (CONJ (t1, t2), k)
    = search_term (t1, fn v1 ⇒
        search_term (t2, fn v2 ⇒
          k (CONJ_nf (v1, v2))))
  | search_term (DISJ (t1, t2), k)
    = search_term (t1, fn v1 ⇒
        search_term (t2, fn v2 ⇒
          k (DISJ_nf (v1, v2))))

(*  term → found  *)
fun search t
    = search_term (t, fn v ⇒ VAL v)
```

Potential redexes are now returned directly and the `VAL` constructor is relegated to the initial continuation.

Defunctionalization: To defunctionalize the continuation, we first enumerate the inhabitants of its function space. These inhabitants arise from the initial continuation in the definition of `search` and in the 4 intermediate continuations in the definition of `search_term`. We therefore represent the continuation as a data type with 5 constructors, together with a function `apply_cont` dispatching upon these 5 summands:

```
datatype cont = C0
              | C1 of value × cont
              | C2 of cont × term
              | C3 of value × cont
              | C4 of cont × term

(*  cont → value → found  *)
fun apply_cont C0
    = (fn v ⇒ VAL v)
  | apply_cont (C1 (v1, k))
    = (fn v2 ⇒ apply_cont k (CONJ_nf (v1, v2)))
  | apply_cont (C2 (k, t2))
    = (fn v1 ⇒ search_term (t2, C1 (v1, k)))
  | apply_cont (C3 (v1, k))
    = (fn v2 ⇒ apply_cont k (DISJ_nf (v1, v2)))
  | apply_cont (C4 (k, t2))
    = (fn v1 ⇒ search_term (t2, C3 (v1, k)))

(*  term × cont → found  *)
and search_term_neg (VAR x, k)
    = apply_cont k (NEGVAR_nf x)
  | search_term_neg (NEG t, k)
    = POTRED (PR_NEG t)
  | search_term_neg (CONJ (t1, t2), k)
    = POTRED (PR_CONJ (t1, t2))
  | search_term_neg (DISJ (t1, t2), k)
    = POTRED (PR_DISJ (t1, t2))

(*  term × cont → found  *)
and search_term (VAR x, k)
    = apply_cont k (POSVAR_nf x)
  | search_term (NEG t, k)
    = search_term_neg (t, k)
  | search_term (CONJ (t1, t2), k)
    = search_term (t1, C2 (k, t2))
  | search_term (DISJ (t1, t2), k)
    = search_term (t1, C4 (k, t2))

(*  term → found  *)
fun search t
    = search_term (t, C0)
```

This data type of defunctionalized continuations is that of reduction contexts.

We have defined `apply_cont` in curried form to emphasize that it maps each summand to a continuation. In the following, we consider its uncurried definition.

Decomposition: We are now in position to extend the search function to not only return a potential redex (if one exists) *but also its reduction context*. The result is the decomposition function of a reduction semantics, where `value_or_decomposition`, `decompose`, `decompose_term`, `decompose_term_neg`, and `decompose_cont` are the respective clones of `found`, `search`, `search_term`, `search_term_neg`, and `apply_cont`:

```
datatype value_or_decomposition
  = VAL of value
  | DEC of potential_redex × cont

(*  cont × value → value_or_decomposition  *)
fun decompose_cont (C0, v)
    = VAL v
  | decompose_cont (C1 (v1, k), v2)
    = decompose_cont (k, CONJ_nf (v1, v2))
  | decompose_cont (C2 (k, t2), v1)
    = decompose_term (t2, C1 (v1, k))
  | decompose_cont (C3 (v1, k), v2)
    = decompose_cont (k, DISJ_nf (v1, v2))
  | decompose_cont (C4 (k, t2), v1)
    = decompose_term (t2, C3 (v1, k))

(*  term × cont → value_or_decomposition  *)
and decompose_term_neg (VAR x, k)
    = decompose_cont (k, NEGVAR_nf x)
  | decompose_term_neg (NEG t, k)
    = DEC (PR_NEG t, k)
  | decompose_term_neg (CONJ (t1, t2), k)
    = DEC (PR_CONJ (t1, t2), k)
  | decompose_term_neg (DISJ (t1, t2), k)
    = DEC (PR_DISJ (t1, t2), k)

(*  term × cont → value_or_decomposition  *)
and decompose_term (VAR x, k)
    = decompose_cont (k, POSVAR_nf x)
```

```
  | decompose_term (NEG t, k)
    = decompose_term_neg (t, k)
  | decompose_term (CONJ (t1, t2), k)
    = decompose_term (t1, C2 (k, t2))
  | decompose_term (DISJ (t1, t2), k)
    = decompose_term (t1, C4 (k, t2))
(*  term → value_or_decomposition  *)
fun decompose t
    = decompose_term (t, C0)
```

2.1.3 Recomposing

A reduction context is recomposed around a term with a left fold over this context:

```
(*  cont × term → term  *)
fun recompose (C0, t)
    = t
  | recompose (C1 (v1, k), t2)
    = recompose (k, CONJ (embed v1, t2))
  | recompose (C2 (k, t2), t1)
    = recompose (k, CONJ (t1, t2))
  | recompose (C3 (v1, k), t2)
    = recompose (k, DISJ (embed v1, t2))
  | recompose (C4 (k, t2), t1)
    = recompose (k, DISJ (t1, t2))
```

2.2 A reduction semantics

We are now fully equipped to implement a reduction semantics for negational normalization.

2.2.1 Notion of contraction

The contraction rules implement the De Morgan laws:

```
datatype contractum_or_error = CONTRACTUM of term
                             | ERROR of string

(*  potential_redex → contractum_or_error  *)
fun contract (PR_NEG t)
    = CONTRACTUM t
  | contract (PR_CONJ (t1, t2))
    = CONTRACTUM (DISJ (NEG t1, NEG t2))
  | contract (PR_DISJ (t1, t2))
    = CONTRACTUM (CONJ (NEG t1, NEG t2))
```

In the present case, all potential redexes are actual ones, i.e., no terms are stuck.

2.2.2 One-step reduction

Given a non-value term, a one-step reduction function (1) decomposes this non-value term into a potential redex and a reduction context, (2) contracts the potential redex if it is an actual one, and (3) recomposes the reduction context with the contractum. If the potential redex is not an actual one, reduction is stuck. Given a value term, reduction is also stuck:

```
datatype reduct_or_stuck = REDUCT of term
                         | STUCK of string

(*  term → reduct_or_stuck  *)
fun reduce t
    = (case decompose t
         of (VAL v)
            => STUCK "irreducible term"
          | (DEC (pr, k))
            => (case contract pr
                  of (CONTRACTUM t')
                     => REDUCT (recompose (k, t'))
                   | (ERROR s)
                     => STUCK s))
```

This one-step reduction function is the hallmark of a reduction semantics [10].

2.2.3 Reduction-based normalization

A reduction-based normalization function is one that iterates the one-step reduction function until it yields a value or becomes stuck. If it yields a value, this value is the result of evaluation, and if it becomes stuck, evaluation goes wrong:

```
datatype result_or_wrong = RESULT of value
                         | WRONG of string
```

The following definition uses `decompose` to distinguish between value and non-value terms:

```
(*  value_or_decomposition → result_or_wrong  *)
fun iterate (VAL v)
    = RESULT v
  | iterate (DEC (pr, k))
    = (case contract pr
         of (CONTRACTUM t')
            => iterate
                 (decompose
                    (recompose (k, t')))
          | (ERROR s)
            => WRONG s)

(*  term → result_or_wrong  *)
fun normalize t
    = iterate (decompose t)
```

2.3 From reduction-based to reduction-free normalization

In this section, we transform the reduction-based normalization function of Section 2.2.3 into a family of reduction-free normalization functions, i.e., functions that do not enumerate the reduction sequence and where no intermediate reduct is ever constructed. We first refocus the reduction-based normalization function to deforest the intermediate reducts [9], and we obtain a small-step abstract machine implementing the iteration of the refocus function (Section 2.3.1). After inlining the contraction function (Section 2.3.2), we transform this small-step abstract machine into a big-step one [6] (Section 2.3.3). This machine exhibits a number of corridor transitions, and we compress them (Section 2.3.4). We also opportunistically specialize its contexts (Section 2.3.5). The resulting abstract machine is in defunctionalized form [8], and we refunctionalize it [7] (Section 2.4.1). The result is in continuation-passing style and we re-express it in direct style [4] (Section 2.4.2). The resulting direct-style function is a traditional conversion function for Boolean formulas; in particular, it is compositional. We express it with one recursive descent using `term_foldr` (Section 2.4.3).

Modus operandi: In each of the following subsections, we derive successive versions of the normalization function, indexing its components with the number of the subsection.

2.3.1 Refocusing

The normalization function of Section 2.2.3 is reduction-based because it constructs every intermediate term in the reduction sequence. In its definition, `decompose` is always applied to the result of `recompose` after the first decomposition. In fact, a vacuous initial call to `recompose` ensures that in all cases, `decompose` is applied to the result of `recompose`:

```
fun normalize t
    = iterate (decompose (recompose (C0, t)))
```

We can factor out these composite calls in a function, `refocus0`, that maps a contractum and its reduction context to the next potential redex and the next reduction context, if such a pair exists, in the reduction sequence:

```
(*  term × cont → value_or_decomposition  *)
fun refocus0 (t, k)
    = decompose (recompose (k, t))
```

```
(*  value_or_decomposition → result_or_wrong  *)
fun iterate0 (VAL v)
    = RESULT v
  | iterate0 (DEC (pr, k))
    = (case contract pr
         of (CONTRACTUM t')
            ⇒ iterate0 (refocus0 (t', k))
          | (ERROR s)
            ⇒ WRONG s)

(*  term → result_or_wrong  *)
fun normalize0 t
    = iterate0 (refocus0 (t, C0))
```

Refocusing, extensionally: The refocus function goes from a redex site to the next redex site, if there is one.

Refocusing, intensionally: As investigated by Nielsen and the first author [9], the refocus function can be deforested to avoid constructing any intermediate reduct. Such a deforestation makes the normalization function reduction-free. The deforested version of `refocus` is optimally defined as continuing the decomposition of the contractum in the current context, i.e., as `decompose_term`:

```
(*  term × cont → value_or_decomposition  *)
fun refocus1 (t, k)
    = decompose_term (t, k)
```

The refocused evaluation function therefore reads as follows:

```
(*  value_or_decomposition → result_or_wrong  *)
fun iterate1 (VAL v)
    = RESULT v
  | iterate1 (DEC (pr, k))
    = (case contract pr
         of (CONTRACTUM t')
            ⇒ iterate1 (refocus1 (t', k))
          | (ERROR s)
            ⇒ WRONG s)

(*  term → result_or_wrong  *)
fun normalize1 t
    = iterate1 (refocus1 (t, C0))
```

This refocused normalization function is reduction-free because it is no longer based on a (one-step) reduction function and it no longer enumerates the successive reducts in the reduction sequence.

In the rest of this section, we mechanically transform this reduction-free normalization function into an abstract machine.

2.3.2 Inlining the contraction function

We first unfold the call to `contract` in the definition of `iterate1`, and name the resulting function `iterate2`. Reasoning by inversion, there are three potential redexes and therefore the `DEC` clause in the definition of `iterate1` is replaced by three `DEC` clauses in the definition of `iterate2`:

```
(*  term × cont → value_or_decomposition  *)
fun refocus2 (t, k)
    = decompose_term (t, k)

(*  value_or_decomposition → result_or_wrong  *)
fun iterate2 (VAL v)
    = RESULT v
  | iterate2 (DEC (PR_NEG t, k))
    = iterate2
        (refocus2 (t, k))
  | iterate2 (DEC (PR_CONJ (t1, t2), k))
    = iterate2
        (refocus2 (DISJ (NEG t1, NEG t2), k))
  | iterate2 (DEC (PR_DISJ (t1, t2), k))
    = iterate2
        (refocus2 (CONJ (NEG t1, NEG t2), k))

(*  term → result_or_wrong  *)
fun normalize2 t
    = iterate2 (refocus2 (t, C0))
```

2.3.3 Lightweight fusion: from small-step abstract machine to big-step abstract machine

The refocused normalization function is a small-step abstract machine in the sense that `refocus2` (i.e., `decompose_term`, `decompose_term_neg` and `decompose_cont`) acts as an inner transition function and `iterate2` as an outer transition function. The outer transition function (also known as a 'driver loop' and as a 'trampoline' [11]) keeps activating the inner transition function until a value is obtained. Using Ohori and Sasano's 'lightweight fusion by fixed-point promotion' [6, 12], we fuse `iterate2` and `refocus2` (i.e., `decompose_term`, `decompose_term_neg` and `decompose_cont`) so that the resulting function `iterate3` is *directly* applied to the result of `decompose_term`, `decompose_term_neg` and `decompose_cont`. The result is a big-step abstract machine [15] consisting of four (mutually tail-recursive) state-transition functions:

- `normalize3_term` is the composition of `iterate2` and `decompose_term` and a clone of `decompose_term`;
- `normalize3_term_neg` is the composition of `iterate2` and `decompose_term_neg` and a clone of `decompose_term_neg`;
- `normalize3_cont` is the composition of `iterate2` and `decompose_cont` that directly calls `iterate3` over a value or a decomposition instead of returning it to `iterate2` as `decompose_cont` did;
- `iterate3` is a clone of `iterate2` that calls the fused function `normalize3_term`.

```
(*  cont × value → result_or_wrong  *)
fun normalize3_cont (C0, v)
    = iterate3 (VAL v)
  | normalize3_cont (C1 (v1, k), v2)
    = normalize3_cont (k, CONJ_nf (v1, v2))
  | normalize3_cont (C2 (k, t2), v1)
    = normalize3_term (t2, C1 (v1, k))
  | normalize3_cont (C3 (v1, k), v2)
    = normalize3_cont (k, DISJ_nf (v1, v2))
  | normalize3_cont (C4 (k, t2), v1)
    = normalize3_term (t2, C3 (v1, k))

(*  term × cont → result_or_wrong  *)
and normalize3_term_neg (VAR x, k)
    = normalize3_cont (k, NEGVAR_nf x)
  | normalize3_term_neg (NEG t, k)
    = iterate3 (DEC (PR_NEG t, k))
  | normalize3_term_neg (CONJ (t1, t2), k)
    = iterate3 (DEC (PR_CONJ (t1, t2), k))
  | normalize3_term_neg (DISJ (t1, t2), k)
    = iterate3 (DEC (PR_DISJ (t1, t2), k))

(*  term × cont → result_or_wrong  *)
and normalize3_term (VAR x, k)
    = normalize3_cont (k, POSVAR_nf x)
  | normalize3_term (NEG t, k)
    = normalize3_term_neg (t, k)
  | normalize3_term (CONJ (t1, t2), k)
    = normalize3_term (t1, C2 (k, t2))
  | normalize3_term (DISJ (t1, t2), k)
    = normalize3_term (t1, C4 (k, t2))

(*  value_or_decomposition → result_or_wrong  *)
and iterate3 (VAL v)
    = RESULT v
  | iterate3 (DEC (PR_NEG t, k))
    = normalize3_term (t, k)
  | iterate3 (DEC (PR_CONJ (t1, t2), k))
    = normalize3_term (DISJ (NEG t1, NEG t2), k)
  | iterate3 (DEC (PR_DISJ (t1, t2), k))
    = normalize3_term (CONJ (NEG t1, NEG t2), k)
```

```
(*  term → result_or_wrong  *)
fun normalize3 t
    = normalize3_term (t, C0)
```

2.3.4 Hereditary transition compression

In the abstract machine of Section 2.3.3, many of the transitions are 'corridor' ones in that they yield configurations for which there is a unique further transition. Let us hereditarily compress these transitions. To this end, we cut-and-paste the transition functions above, renaming their indices from 3 to 4. We consider each of their clauses in turn:

Clause `normalize4_cont (C0, v)`:

```
normalize4_cont (C0, v)
= (* by inlining normalize4_cont *)
iterate4 (VAL v)
= (* by inlining iterate4 *)
RESULT v
```

Clause `normalize4_term_neg (NEG t, k)`:

```
normalize4_term_neg (NEG t, k)
= (* by inlining normalize4_term_neg *)
iterate4 (DEC (PR_NEG t, k))
= (* by inlining iterate4 *)
normalize3_term (t, k)
```

Clause `refocus4_term_neg (CONJ (t1, t2), k)`:

```
normalize4_term_neg (CONJ (t1, t2), k)
= (* by inlining normalize4_term_neg *)
iterate4 (DEC (PR_CONJ (t1, t2), k))
= (* by inlining iterate4 *)
normalize4_term (DISJ (NEG t1, NEG t2), k)
= (* by inlining normalize4_term *)
normalize4_term (NEG t1, C4 (k, NEG t2))
= (* by inlining normalize4_term *)
normalize4_term_neg (t1, C4 (k, NEG t2))
```

Clause `refocus4_term_neg (DISJ (t1, t2), k)`:

```
normalize4_term_neg (DISJ (t1, t2), k)
= (* by inlining normalize4_term_neg *)
iterate4 (DEC (PR_DISJ (t1, t2), k))
= (* by inlining iterate4 *)
normalize4_term (CONJ (NEG t1, NEG t2), k)
= (* by inlining normalize4_term *)
normalize4_term (NEG t1, C2 (k, NEG t2))
= (* by inlining normalize4_term *)
normalize4_term_neg (t1, C2 (k, NEG t2))
```

As a corollary of the compressions, the definition of `iterate3` is now unused and can be omitted. The resulting abstract machine reads as follows:

```
(*  cont × value → result_or_wrong  *)
fun normalize4_cont (C0, v)
    = RESULT v
  | normalize4_cont (C1 (v1, k), v2)
    = normalize4_cont (k, CONJ_nf (v1, v2))
  | normalize4_cont (C2 (k, t2), v1)
    = normalize4_term (t2, C1 (v1, k))
  | normalize4_cont (C3 (v1, k), v2)
    = normalize4_cont (k, DISJ_nf (v1, v2))
  | normalize4_cont (C4 (k, t2), v1)
    = normalize4_term (t2, C3 (v1, k))

(*  term × cont → result_or_wrong  *)
and normalize4_term_neg (VAR x, k)
    = normalize4_cont (k, NEGVAR_nf x)
  | normalize4_term_neg (NEG t, k)
    = normalize4_term (t, k)
  | normalize4_term_neg (CONJ (t1, t2), k)
    = normalize4_term_neg (t1, C4 (k, NEG t2))
  | normalize4_term_neg (DISJ (t1, t2), k)
    = normalize4_term_neg (t1, C2 (k, NEG t2))

(*  term × cont → result_or_wrong  *)
and normalize4_term (VAR x, k)
    = normalize4_cont (k, POSVAR_nf x)
  | normalize4_term (NEG t, k)
    = normalize4_term_neg (t, k)
  | normalize4_term (CONJ (t1, t2), k)
    = normalize4_term (t1, C2 (k, t2))
  | normalize4_term (DISJ (t1, t2), k)
    = normalize4_term (t1, C4 (k, t2))

(*  term → result_or_wrong  *)
fun normalize4 t
    = normalize4_term (t, C0)
```

2.3.5 Context specialization

To symmetrize the definitions of `refocus4_term` and `refocus4_term_neg`, we introduce two specialized contexts for `C2` and `C4`, and we specialize `normalize4_cont` to directly call `normalize5_term_neg` for the new contexts `C2NEG` and `C4NEG`:

```
datatype cont = C0
              | C1 of value × cont
              | C2 of cont × term
              | C2NEG of cont × term
              | C3 of value × cont
              | C4 of cont × term
              | C4NEG of cont × term

(*  cont × value → result_or_wrong  *)
fun normalize5_cont (C0, v)
    = RESULT v
  | normalize5_cont (C1 (v1, k), v2)
    = normalize5_cont (k, CONJ_nf (v1, v2))
  | normalize5_cont (C2 (k, t2), v1)
    = normalize5_term (t2, C1 (v1, k))
  | normalize5_cont (C2NEG (k, t2), v1)
    = normalize5_term_neg (t2, C1 (v1, k))
  | normalize5_cont (C3 (v1, k), v2)
    = normalize5_cont (k, DISJ_nf (v1, v2))
  | normalize5_cont (C4 (k, t2), v1)
    = normalize5_term (t2, C3 (v1, k))
  | normalize5_cont (C4NEG (k, t2), v1)
    = normalize5_term_neg (t2, C3 (v1, k))

(*  term × cont → result_or_wrong  *)
and normalize5_term_neg (VAR x, k)
    = normalize5_cont (k, NEGVAR_nf x)
  | normalize5_term_neg (NEG t, k)
    = normalize5_term (t, k)
  | normalize5_term_neg (CONJ (t1, t2), k)
    = normalize5_term_neg (t1, C4NEG (k, t2))
  | normalize5_term_neg (DISJ (t1, t2), k)
    = normalize5_term_neg (t1, C2NEG (k, t2))

(*  term × cont → result_or_wrong  *)
and normalize5_term (VAR x, k)
    = normalize5_cont (k, POSVAR_nf x)
  | normalize5_term (NEG t, k)
    = normalize5_term_neg (t, k)
  | normalize5_term (CONJ (t1, t2), k)
    = normalize5_term (t1, C2 (k, t2))
  | normalize5_term (DISJ (t1, t2), k)
    = normalize5_term (t1, C4 (k, t2))

(*  term → result_or_wrong  *)
fun normalize5 t
    = normalize5_term (t, C0)
```

2.4 From abstract machines to normalization functions

In this section, we transform the compressed abstract machine of Section 2.3.4 into two compositional normalization functions, one in continuation-passing style (Section 2.4.1) and one in direct style (Section 2.4.2).

2.4.1 Refunctionalization

Like many other big-step abstract machines [1, 3], the abstract machine of Section 2.3.5 is in defunctionalized form [8]: the reduction contexts, together with `normalize5_cont`, are the first-order counterpart of a function. This function is introduced with the data-type constructors `C0`, etc., and eliminated with calls to the dispatching function `normalize5_cont`. The higher-order counterpart of this abstract machine reads as follows:

```
(*  term × (value → α) → α  *)
fun normalize6_term_neg (VAR x, k)
    = k (NEGVAR_nf x)
  | normalize6_term_neg (NEG t, k)
    = normalize6_term (t, k)
  | normalize6_term_neg (CONJ (t1, t2), k)
    = normalize6_term_neg (t1, fn v1 =>
        normalize6_term_neg (t2, fn v2 =>
          k (DISJ_nf (v1, v2))))
  | normalize6_term_neg (DISJ (t1, t2), k)
    = normalize6_term_neg (t1, fn v1 =>
        normalize6_term_neg (t2, fn v2 =>
          k (CONJ_nf (v1, v2))))

(*  term × (value → α) → α  *)
and normalize6_term (VAR x, k)
    = k (POSVAR_nf x)
  | normalize6_term (NEG t, k)
    = normalize6_term_neg (t, k)
  | normalize6_term (CONJ (t1, t2), k)
    = normalize6_term (t1, fn v1 =>
        normalize6_term (t2, fn v2 =>
          k (CONJ_nf (v1, v2))))
  | normalize6_term (DISJ (t1, t2), k)
    = normalize6_term (t1, fn v1 =>
        normalize6_term (t2, fn v2 =>
          k (DISJ_nf (v1, v2))))

(*  term → result_or_wrong  *)
fun normalize6 t
    = normalize6_term (t, fn v => RESULT v)
```

This normalization function is compositional over source terms.

2.4.2 Back to direct style

The refunctionalized definition of Section 2.4.1 is in continuation-passing style since it has a functional accumulator and all of its calls are tail calls [4]. Its direct-style counterpart reads as follows:

```
(*  term → value  *)
fun normalize7_term_neg (VAR x)
    = NEGVAR_nf x
  | normalize7_term_neg (NEG t)
    = normalize7_term t
  | normalize7_term_neg (CONJ (t1, t2))
    = DISJ_nf (normalize7_term_neg t1,
               normalize7_term_neg t2)
  | normalize7_term_neg (DISJ (t1, t2))
    = CONJ_nf (normalize7_term_neg t1,
               normalize7_term_neg t2)

(*  term → value  *)
and normalize7_term (VAR x)
    = POSVAR_nf x
  | normalize7_term (NEG t)
    = normalize7_term_neg t
  | normalize7_term (CONJ (t1, t2))
    = CONJ_nf (normalize7_term t1,
               normalize7_term t2)
  | normalize7_term (DISJ (t1, t2))
    = DISJ_nf (normalize7_term t1,
               normalize7_term t2)

(*  term → result_or_wrong  *)
fun normalize7 t
    = RESULT (normalize7_term t)
```

This normalization function is compositional over source terms.

2.4.3 Catamorphic normalizers

The compositional normalizer of Section 2.4.2 features two mutually recursive functions from terms to values. These two functions can be expressed as one, using the following type isomorphism:

$$(A \to B) \times (A \to B) \;\simeq\; A \to B^2$$

Representationally, this isomorphism can be exploited in two ways: by representing B^2 as $2 \to B$ and by representing B^2 as $B \times B$. Let us review each of these representations.

Representing B^2 as $2 \to B$: We first need a two-element type to account for the "polarity" of the current sub-term, i.e., whether the number of negations between the root of the given term and the current sub-term is even (in which case the polarity is positive) or it is odd (in which case the polarity is negative):

```
datatype polarity = P   (* P like Plus  *)
                  | M   (* M like Minus *)
```

We are now in position to express the normalizer with one recursive descent over the given term, threading the current polarity in an inherited fashion, and returning a term in normal form:

```
(*  term → (polarity → value)  *)
fun normalize8_term (VAR x)
    = (fn P => POSVAR_nf x
        | M => NEGVAR_nf x)
  | normalize8_term (NEG t)
    = let val c = normalize8_term t
      in fn P => c M
          | M => c P
      end
  | normalize8_term (CONJ (t1, t2))
    = let val c1 = normalize8_term t1
          val c2 = normalize8_term t2
      in fn P => CONJ_nf (c1 P, c2 P)
          | M => DISJ_nf (c1 M, c2 M)
      end
  | normalize8_term (DISJ (t1, t2))
    = let val c1 = normalize8_term t1
          val c2 = normalize8_term t2
      in fn P => DISJ_nf (c1 P, c2 P)
          | M => CONJ_nf (c1 M, c2 M)
      end

(*  term → result_or_wrong  *)
fun normalize8 t
    = RESULT (normalize8_term t P)
```

Initially, the given term has a positive polarity.

To make it manifest that this normalizer is (1) compositional and (2) singly recursive, let us express it as a catamorphism, i.e., as an instance of `term_foldr`:

```
(*  term → (polarity → value)  *)
val normalize9_term
    = term_foldr
        (fn x =>
          (fn P => POSVAR_nf x
            | M => NEGVAR_nf x),
         fn c =>
           (fn P => c M
             | M => c P),
         fn (c1, c2) =>
           (fn P => CONJ_nf (c1 P, c2 P)
             | M => DISJ_nf (c1 M, c2 M)),
         fn (c1, c2) =>
           (fn P => DISJ_nf (c1 P, c2 P)
             | M => CONJ_nf (c1 M, c2 M)))

(*  term → result_or_wrong  *)
fun normalize9 t
    = RESULT (normalize9_term t P)
```

Representing B^2 as $B \times B$: We use a pair holding a term in normal form and its dual. This pair puts us in position to express the normalizer with one recursive descent over the given term, returning a pair of terms in normal form in a synthesized fashion:

```
(*  term → value × value *)
fun normalize10_term (VAR x)
    = (POSVAR_nf x, NEGVAR_nf x)
  | normalize10_term (NEG t)
    = let val (tp, tm) = normalize10_term t
      in (tm, tp)
      end
  | normalize10_term (CONJ (t1, t2))
    = let val (t1p, t1m) = normalize10_term t1
          val (t2p, t2m) = normalize10_term t2
      in (CONJ_nf (t1p, t2p), DISJ_nf (t1m, t2m))
      end
  | normalize10_term (DISJ (t1, t2))
    = let val (t1p, t1m) = normalize10_term t1
          val (t2p, t2m) = normalize10_term t2
      in (DISJ_nf (t1p, t2p), CONJ_nf (t1m, t2m))
      end

(*  term → result_or_wrong   *)
fun normalize10 t
    = let val (tp, tm) = normalize10_term t
      in RESULT tp
      end
```

The final result is the positive component of the resulting pair.

To make it manifest that this normalization function is (1) compositional and (2) singly recursive, let us express it as a catamorphism, i.e., as an instance of `term_foldr`:

```
(*  term → value × value   *)
val normalize11_term
    = term_foldr
        (fn x ⇒
          (POSVAR_nf x, NEGVAR_nf x),
         fn (tp, tm) ⇒
          (tm, tp),
         fn ((t1p, t1m), (t2p, t2m)) ⇒
          (CONJ_nf (t1p, t2p), DISJ_nf (t1m, t2m)),
         fn ((t1p, t1m), (t2p, t2m)) ⇒
          (DISJ_nf (t1p, t2p), CONJ_nf (t1m, t2m)))

(*  term → result_or_wrong   *)
fun normalize11 t
    = let val (tp, tm) = normalize11_term t
      in RESULT tp
      end
```

2.5 Summary and conclusion

We have refocused the reduction-based normalization function of Section 2.2.3 into a small-step abstract machine, and we have exhibited a family of corresponding reduction-free normalization functions that all are inter-derivable.

3. Leftmost innermost negational normalization

In this section, we go from a leftmost-innermost *reduction* strategy to the corresponding leftmost-innermost *evaluation* strategy. We first implement the reduction strategy (Section 3.1) as a prelude to implementing the corresponding reduction semantics (Section 3.2). We then turn to the syntactic correspondence between reduction semantics and abstract machines (Section 3.3) and to the functional correspondence between abstract machines and normalization functions (Section 3.4).

3.1 Prelude to a reduction semantics

The reduction strategy induces a notion of value and of potential redex (i.e., of a term that is an actual redex or that is stuck); we are then in position to state a compositional search function that implements the reduction strategy and maps a given term either to the corresponding value, if it is in normal form, or to a potential redex (Section 3.1.1). From this search function we derive a decomposition function mapping a given term either to the corresponding value, if it is in normal form, or to a potential redex and its reduction context (Section 3.1.2). As a corollary we can then state the associated recomposition function that maps a reduction context and a contractum to the corresponding reduct (Section 3.1.3).

3.1.1 The reduction strategy

The reduction strategy consists in locating the leftmost-innermost negation of a term which is not a variable. A value therefore is a term where only variables are negated, i.e., a normal form:

```
type value = term_nf
```

A potential redex is the negation of a term in negational normal form which is not a variable:

```
datatype potential_redex = PR_NEG of value
                         | PR_CONJ of value × value
                         | PR_DISJ of value × value
```

The following compositional search function implements the reduction strategy: it searches a potential redex depth-first and from left to right:

```
datatype found = VAL of value
               | POTRED of potential_redex

(*  term → found   *)
fun search_term_neg t
    = (case search_term t
         of (VAL v)
            ⇒ (case v
                  of (POSVAR_nf x)
                     ⇒ VAL (NEGVAR_nf x)
                   | (NEGVAR_nf x)
                     ⇒ POTRED (PR_NEG (POSVAR_nf x))
                   | (CONJ_nf (v1, v2))
                     ⇒ POTRED (PR_CONJ (v1, v2))
                   | (DISJ_nf (v1, v2))
                     ⇒ POTRED (PR_DISJ (v1, v2)))
          | (POTRED pr)
            ⇒ POTRED pr)

(*  term → found   *)
and search_term (VAR x)
    = VAL (POSVAR_nf x)
  | search_term (NEG t)
    = search_term_neg t
  | search_term (CONJ (t1, t2))
    = (case search_term t1
         of (VAL v1)
            ⇒ (case search_term t2
                 of (VAL v2)
                    ⇒ VAL (CONJ_nf (v1, v2))
                  | (POTRED pr)
                    ⇒ POTRED pr)
          | (POTRED pr)
            ⇒ POTRED pr)
  | search_term (DISJ (t1, t2))
    = (case search_term t1
         of (VAL v1)
            ⇒ (case search_term t2
                 of (VAL v2)
                    ⇒ VAL (DISJ_nf (v1, v2))
                  | (POTRED pr)
                    ⇒ POTRED pr)
          | (POTRED pr)
            ⇒ POTRED pr)

(*  term → found   *)
fun search t
    = search_term t
```

When a negation is encountered, the auxiliary function `search_term_neg` is called to decide whether this negation is a value or a potential redex.

3.1.2 From searching to decomposing

As in Section 2.1.2, we transform the search function of Section 3.1.1 into a decomposition function for the reduction semantics of Section 3.2. We do so by (1) CPS-transforming the search function, (2) defunctionalizing its continuation,

```
datatype cont = C0
              | C1 of value × cont
              | C2 of cont × term
              | C3 of value × cont
              | C4 of cont × term
              | C5 of cont
```

and (3) returning a potential redex (if one exists) and its reduction context:

```
datatype value_or_decomposition
  = VAL of value
  | DEC of potential_redex × cont

(*  cont × value → value_or_decomposition  *)
fun decompose_cont (C0, v)
    = VAL v
  | decompose_cont (C1 (v1, k), v2)
    = decompose_cont (k, CONJ_nf (v1, v2))
  | decompose_cont (C2 (k, t2), v1)
    = decompose_term (t2, C1 (v1, k))
  | decompose_cont (C3 (v1, k), v2)
    = decompose_cont (k, DISJ_nf (v1, v2))
  | decompose_cont (C4 (k, t2), v1)
    = decompose_term (t2, C3 (v1, k))
  | decompose_cont (C5 k, v)
    = (case v
         of (POSVAR_nf x)
            => decompose_cont (k, NEGVAR_nf x)
          | (NEGVAR_nf x)
            => DEC (PR_NEG (POSVAR_nf x), k)
          | (CONJ_nf (v1, v2))
            => DEC (PR_CONJ (v1, v2), k)
          | (DISJ_nf (v1, v2))
            => DEC (PR_DISJ (v1, v2), k))

(*  term × cont → value_or_decomposition  *)
and decompose_term_neg (t, k)
    = decompose_term (t, C5 k)

(*  term × cont → value_or_decomposition  *)
and decompose_term (VAR x, k)
    = decompose_cont (k, POSVAR_nf x)
  | decompose_term (NEG t, k)
    = decompose_term_neg (t, k)
  | decompose_term (CONJ (t1, t2), k)
    = decompose_term (t1, C2 (k, t2))
  | decompose_term (DISJ (t1, t2), k)
    = decompose_term (t1, C4 (k, t2))

(*  term → value_or_decomposition  *)
fun decompose t
    = decompose_term (t, C0)
```

3.1.3 Recomposing

Recomposing a reduction context around a term is simply done with a left fold over the reduction context:

```
(*  cont × term → term  *)
fun recompose (C0, t)
    = t
  | recompose (C1 (v1, k), t2)
    = recompose (k, CONJ (embed v1, t2))
  | recompose (C2 (k, t2), t1)
    = recompose (k, CONJ (t1, t2))
  | recompose (C3 (v1, k), t2)
    = recompose (k, DISJ (embed v1, t2))
  | recompose (C4 (k, t2), t1)
    = recompose (k, DISJ (t1, t2))
  | recompose (C5 k, t)
    = recompose (k, NEG t)
```

3.2 A reduction semantics

We are now fully equipped to implement a reduction semantics for negational normalization.

3.2.1 Notion of contraction

The contraction rules implement the De Morgan laws:

```
datatype contractum_or_error = CONTRACTUM of term
                             | ERROR of string

(*  potential_redex → contractum_or_error  *)
fun contract (PR_NEG v)
    = CONTRACTUM (embed v)
  | contract (PR_CONJ (v1, v2))
    = CONTRACTUM (DISJ (NEG (embed v1),
                        NEG (embed v2)))
  | contract (PR_DISJ (v1, v2))
    = CONTRACTUM (CONJ (NEG (embed v1),
                        NEG (embed v2)))
```

In the present case, all potential redexes are actual ones, i.e., no terms are stuck.

3.2.2 One-step reduction

Given a non-value term, a one-step reduction function (1) decomposes this non-value term into a potential redex and a reduction context, (2) contracts the potential redex if it is an actual one, and (3) recomposes the reduction context with the contractum. If the potential redex is not an actual one, reduction is stuck. Given a value term, reduction is also stuck:

```
datatype reduct_or_stuck = REDUCT of term
                         | STUCK of string

(*  term → reduct_or_stuck  *)
fun reduce t
    = (case decompose t
         of (VAL v)
            => STUCK "irreducible term"
          | (DEC (pr, k))
            => (case contract pr
                  of (CONTRACTUM t')
                     => REDUCT (recompose (k, t'))
                   | (ERROR s)
                     => STUCK s))
```

This one-step reduction function is the hallmark of a reduction semantics [10].

3.2.3 Reduction-based normalization

A reduction-based normalization function is one that iterates the one-step reduction function until it yields a value or becomes stuck. If it yields a value, this value is the result of evaluation, and if it becomes stuck, evaluation goes wrong:

```
datatype result_or_wrong = RESULT of value
                         | WRONG of string
```

The following definition uses decompose to distinguish between value and non-value terms:

```
(*  value_or_decomposition → result_or_wrong  *)
fun iterate (VAL v)
    = RESULT v
  | iterate (DEC (pr, k))
    = (case contract pr
        of (CONTRACTUM t')
           => iterate
                (decompose
                   (recompose (k, t')))
         | (ERROR s)
           => WRONG s)

(*  term → result_or_wrong  *)
fun normalize t
    = iterate (decompose t)
```

3.3 From reduction-based to reduction-free normalization

In this section, we transform the reduction-based normalization function of Section 3.2.3 into a family of reduction-free normalization functions, i.e., functions that do not enumerate the reduction sequence and where no intermediate reduct is ever constructed. We first refocus the reduction-based normalization function [9] to deforest the intermediate terms, and we obtain a small-step abstract machine implementing the iteration of the refocus function (Section 3.3.1). After inlining the contraction function (Section 3.3.2), we transform this small-step abstract machine into a big-step one [6] (Section 3.3.3). This machine exhibits a number of corridor transitions, and we compress them (Section 3.3.4). The resulting abstract machine is in defunctionalized form [8], and we refunctionalize it [7] (Section 3.4.1). The result is in continuation-passing style and we re-express it in direct style [4] (Section 3.4.2). The resulting direct-style function is a traditional conversion function for Boolean formulas; in particular, it is compositional. We express it with one recursive descent using `term_foldr` (Section 3.4.3).

Modus operandi: In each of the following subsections, we derive successive versions of the normalization function, indexing its components with the number of the subsection.

3.3.1 Refocusing

As in Section 2.3.1, we isolate the recomposition of a reduction context with a contractum and its subsequent decomposition in one refocus function. In this refocus function, we short-cut the construction of every reduct in the reduction sequence, turning normalization from being reduction-based to being reduction-free.

3.3.2 Inlining the contraction function

As in Section 2.3.2, we inline `contract` in the definition of `iterate1`. The result is a small-step abstract machine.

3.3.3 Lightweight fusion: from small-step abstract machine to big-step abstract machine

As in Section 2.3.3, we fuse the outer and inner transition functions of the small-step abstract machine of Section 3.3.2. The result is a big-step abstract machine.

3.3.4 Hereditary transition compression

As in Section 2.3.4, many of the transitions of the abstract machine of Section 2.3.3 are 'corridor' ones. We compress them hereditarily, and we also exploit the property that decomposing the term representation of a value in a context is the same as continuing the decomposition of this value in this context.

3.3.5 Context specialization

As in Section 2.3.5, for symmetry, we introduce two specialized contexts for `C2` and `C4`, and we specialize `normalize4_cont` to directly call `normalize5_cont_neg` for the new contexts `C2NEG` and `C4NEG`:

```
datatype cont = C0
              | C1 of value × cont
              | C2 of cont × term
              | C2NEG of cont × value
              | C3 of value × cont
              | C4 of cont × term
              | C4NEG of cont × value
              | C5 of cont

(*  cont × value → result_or_wrong  *)
fun normalize5_cont (C0, v)
    = RESULT v
  | normalize5_cont (C1 (v1, k), v2)
    = normalize5_cont (k, CONJ_nf (v1, v2))
  | normalize5_cont (C2 (k, t2), v1)
    = normalize5_term (t2, C1 (v1, k))
  | normalize5_cont (C2NEG (k, v2), v1)
    = normalize5_cont_neg (C1 (v1, k), v2)
  | normalize5_cont (C3 (v1, k), v2)
    = normalize5_cont (k, DISJ_nf (v1, v2))
  | normalize5_cont (C4 (k, t2), v1)
    = normalize5_term (t2, C3 (v1, k))
  | normalize5_cont (C4NEG (k, v2), v1)
    = normalize5_cont_neg (C3 (v1, k), v2)
  | normalize5_cont (C5 k, v)
    = normalize5_cont_neg (k, v)

(*  cont × value → result_or_wrong  *)
and normalize5_cont_neg (k, POSVAR_nf x)
    = normalize5_cont (k, NEGVAR_nf x)
  | normalize5_cont_neg (k, NEGVAR_nf x)
    = normalize5_cont (k, POSVAR_nf x)
  | normalize5_cont_neg (k, CONJ_nf (v1, v2))
    = normalize5_cont_neg (C4NEG (k, v2), v1)
  | normalize5_cont_neg (k, DISJ_nf (v1, v2))
    = normalize5_cont_neg (C2NEG (k, v2), v1)

(*  term × cont → result_or_wrong  *)
and normalize5_term (VAR x, k)
    = normalize5_cont (k, POSVAR_nf x)
  | normalize5_term (NEG t, k)
    = normalize5_term (t, C5 k)
  | normalize5_term (CONJ (t1, t2), k)
    = normalize5_term (t1, C2 (k, t2))
  | normalize5_term (DISJ (t1, t2), k)
    = normalize5_term (t1, C4 (k, t2))

(*  term → result_or_wrong  *)
fun normalize5 t
    = normalize5_term (t, C0)
```

3.4 From abstract machines to normalization functions

In this section, we transform the compressed abstract machine of Section 3.3.4 into two compositional normalization functions, one in continuation-passing style (Section 3.4.1) and one in direct style (Section 3.4.2).

3.4.1 Refunctionalization

Like many other big-step abstract machines [1, 3], the abstract machine of Section 3.3.4 is in defunctionalized form [8]: the reduction contexts, together with `normalize4_cont`, are the first-order counterpart of a function. We refunctionalize this big-step abstract machine into a higher-order normalization function. As in Section 2.4.1, this normalization function is compositional over source terms.

3.4.2 Back to direct style

The refunctionalized definition of Section 3.4.1 is in continuation-passing style since it has a functional accumulator and all of its calls are tail calls [4]. Its direct-style counterpart reads as follows:

```
(*  value → value  *)
fun normalize7_cont_neg (POSVAR_nf x)
    = NEGVAR_nf x
  | normalize7_cont_neg (NEGVAR_nf x)
    = POSVAR_nf x
  | normalize7_cont_neg (CONJ_nf (v1, v2))
    = DISJ_nf (normalize7_cont_neg v1,
               normalize7_cont_neg v2)
  | normalize7_cont_neg (DISJ_nf (v1, v2))
    = CONJ_nf (normalize7_cont_neg v1,
               normalize7_cont_neg v2)

(*  term → value  *)
and normalize7_term (VAR x)
    = POSVAR_nf x
  | normalize7_term (NEG t)
    = normalize7_cont_neg (normalize7_term t)
```

```
  | normalize7_term (CONJ (t1, t2))
    = CONJ_nf (normalize7_term t1,
               normalize7_term t2)
  | normalize7_term (DISJ (t1, t2))
    = DISJ_nf (normalize7_term t1,
               normalize7_term t2)

(*  term → result_or_wrong  *)
fun normalize7 t
    = RESULT (normalize7_term t)
```

This normalization function is compositional over source terms, and uses an auxiliary function which is compositional over normal forms.

3.4.3 Catamorphic normalizer

To make it manifest that the normalizer of Section 3.4.2 is (1) compositional and (2) singly recursive, let us express it as a catamorphism, i.e., as an instance of `term_foldr`. By the same token, since the auxiliary function is also compositional and singly recursive, we also express it as an instance of `term_nf_foldr`:

```
(*  value → value  *)
val normalize8_cont_neg = term_nf_foldr (NEGVAR_nf,
                                         POSVAR_nf,
                                         DISJ_nf,
                                         CONJ_nf)

(*  term → value  *)
val normalize8_term = term_foldr (POSVAR_nf,
                                  normalize8_cont_neg,
                                  CONJ_nf,
                                  DISJ_nf)

(*  term → result_or_wrong  *)
fun normalize8 t
    = RESULT (normalize8_term t)
```

NB: In effect, `normalize8_cont_neg` dualizes normal forms. This dualization captures the essence of the innermost normalization strategy.

3.5 Summary and conclusion

We have refocused the reduction-based normalization function of Section 3.2.3 into a small-step abstract machine, and we have exhibited a family of corresponding reduction-free normalization functions that all are inter-derivable.

4. Conclusion and perspectives

The inter-derivations illustrated here witness a striking unity of computation, be this for reduction semantics, abstract machines, and normalization function: they all truly define the same elephant. The structural coincidence between reduction contexts and evaluation contexts as defunctionalized continuations, in particular, plays a key rôle to connect reduction strategies and evaluation strategies, a connection that was first established by Plotkin [14]. As for Ohori and Sasano's lightweight fusion [12], it provides the linchpin between the functional representations of small-step and big-step operational semantics [6]. Overall, the inter-derivations illustrate the conceptual value of semantics-based program manipulation, as promoted over the past two decades in PEPM.

Acknowledgments: We are grateful to Jeremy Siek and Siau-Cheng Khoo for the invitation to present this work at the 20th anniversary of PEPM. The example of negational normalization originates in a joint work of the first and second authors [5]. The two preludes to a reduction semantics originate in a joint work of the first and third authors, who benefited from Kenichi Asai's gracious hospitality at Ochanomizu University to complete this article.

References

[1] M. S. Ager, D. Biernacki, O. Danvy, and J. Midtgaard. A functional correspondence between evaluators and abstract machines. In D. Miller, editor, *Proceedings of the Fifth ACM-SIGPLAN International Conference on Principles and Practice of Declarative Programming (PPDP'03)*, pages 8–19, Uppsala, Sweden, Aug. 2003.

[2] M. Biernacka and O. Danvy. A syntactic correspondence between context-sensitive calculi and abstract machines. *Theoretical Computer Science*, 375(1-3):76–108, 2007. Extended version available as the research report BRICS RS-06-18.

[3] O. Danvy. From reduction-based to reduction-free normalization. In P. Koopman, R. Plasmeijer, and D. Swierstra, editors, *Advanced Functional Programming, Sixth International School*, number 5382 in Lecture Notes in Computer Science, pages 66–164, Nijmegen, The Netherlands, May 2008. Springer. Lecture notes including 70+ exercises.

[4] O. Danvy. Back to direct style. *Science of Computer Programming*, 22 (3):183–195, 1994. A preliminary version was presented at the Fourth European Symposium on Programming (ESOP 1992).

[5] O. Danvy and J. Johannsen. Inter-deriving semantic artifacts for object-oriented programming. *Journal of Computer and System Sciences*, 76:302–323, 2010.

[6] O. Danvy and K. Millikin. On the equivalence between small-step and big-step abstract machines: a simple application of lightweight fusion. *Information Processing Letters*, 106(3):100–109, 2008.

[7] O. Danvy and K. Millikin. Refunctionalization at work. *Science of Computer Programming*, 74(8):534–549, 2009. Extended version available as the research report BRICS RS-08-04.

[8] O. Danvy and L. R. Nielsen. Defunctionalization at work. In H. Søndergaard, editor, *Proceedings of the Third International ACM SIGPLAN Conference on Principles and Practice of Declarative Programming (PPDP'01)*, pages 162–174, Firenze, Italy, Sept. 2001. Extended version available as the research report BRICS RS-01-23.

[9] O. Danvy and L. R. Nielsen. Refocusing in reduction semantics. Research Report BRICS RS-04-26, Department of Computer Science, Aarhus University, Aarhus, Denmark, Nov. 2004. A preliminary version appeared in the informal proceedings of the Second International Workshop on Rule-Based Programming (RULE 2001), Electronic Notes in Theoretical Computer Science, Vol. 59.4.

[10] M. Felleisen. *The Calculi of λ-v-CS Conversion: A Syntactic Theory of Control and State in Imperative Higher-Order Programming Languages*. PhD thesis, Computer Science Department, Indiana University, Bloomington, Indiana, Aug. 1987.

[11] S. E. Ganz, D. P. Friedman, and M. Wand. Trampolined style. In P. Lee, editor, *Proceedings of the 1999 ACM SIGPLAN International Conference on Functional Programming*, SIGPLAN Notices, Vol. 34, No. 9, pages 18–27, Paris, France, Sept. 1999.

[12] A. Ohori and I. Sasano. Lightweight fusion by fixed point promotion. In M. Felleisen, editor, *Proceedings of the Thirty-Fourth Annual ACM Symposium on Principles of Programming Languages*, SIGPLAN Notices, Vol. 42, No. 1, pages 143–154, Nice, France, Jan. 2007.

[13] G. D. Plotkin. The origins of structural operational semantics. *Journal of Logic and Algebraic Programming*, 60-61:3–15, 2004.

[14] G. D. Plotkin. Call-by-name, call-by-value and the λ-calculus. *Theoretical Computer Science*, 1:125–159, 1975.

[15] G. D. Plotkin. A structural approach to operational semantics. Technical Report FN-19, Department of Computer Science, Aarhus University, Aarhus, Denmark, Sept. 1981. Reprinted in the Journal of Logic and Algebraic Programming 60-61:17-139, 2004, with a foreword [13].

[16] J. C. Reynolds. Definitional interpreters for higher-order programming languages. In *Proceedings of 25th ACM National Conference*, pages 717–740, Boston, Massachusetts, 1972. Reprinted in Higher-Order and Symbolic Computation 11(4):363-397, 1998, with a foreword [17].

[17] J. C. Reynolds. Definitional interpreters revisited. *Higher-Order and Symbolic Computation*, 11(4):355–361, 1998.

Ordering Multiple Continuations on the Stack

Dimitrios Vardoulakis Olin Shivers
Northeastern University
dimvar@ccs.neu.edu shivers@ccs.neu.edu

Abstract

Passing multiple continuation arguments to a function in CPS form allows one to encode a wide variety of direct-style control constructs, such as conditionals, exceptions, and multi-return function calls. We show that, with a simple syntactic restriction on the CPS language, one can prove that these multi-continuation arguments can be compiled into stack frames in the traditional manner. The restriction comes with no loss in expressive power, since we can still encode the same control mechanisms.

In addition, we show that tail calls can be generalized efficiently for many continuations because the run-time check to determine which continuation to pop to can be avoided with a simple static analysis. A prototype implementation in Scheme48 shows that our analysis is very precise.

Categories and Subject Descriptors F.3.2 [*Semantics of Programming Languages*]: Program Analysis

General Terms Languages, Performance

Keywords flow analysis, continuation-passing style, tail recursion

1. Introduction

Continuation-passing style (CPS) has a long history as a compiler intermediate representation [1, 5, 7, 11], going back to Steele's Rabbit compiler [14]. More recently, Kennedy studied the engineering benefits afforded by CPS-based intermediate representations [4]. When used in compilers, CPS is usually extended in two ways from the simple form we see in more foundational developments [8].

First, every element of a CPS term (lambdas, variable references, and calls) is statically marked as either a "user" or a "continuation" term. There is a similar user/continuation partition among dynamic values, which respects the static partition: continuation values are produced only from "continuation" λ terms, bound only to "continuation" variables, and invoked only at "continuation" call sites; likewise for "user" values. This partition enables the compiler to produce code that uses a stack to manage procedure calls. Continuations are simply procedures whose environment record is a stack frame.

Second, CPS-based compilers often pass many continuations across function calls:

- The SML/NJ compiler implements exceptions by passing two continuations to each function: one for the normal return point and one for the current exception handler.
- ORBIT [5] encodes conditionals as primitives that take two continuations. Instead of having special syntax for if/then/else, ORBIT employs a primitive procedure, `%if`, with three arguments, a boolean and two continuations:
  (`%if` *bool* $cont_{\text{then}}$ $cont_{\text{else}}$)
  Control branches to $cont_{\text{then}}$ if the boolean argument is true, and to $cont_{\text{else}}$ if it is false. By representing control operators as functions, the compiler can wring even more utility out of its general capabilities for reasoning about functions. This technique has been explored in detail in the literature [5].
- The "multi-return λ calculus" (λ_{MR}) [12] can be considered a generalization of the aforementioned Orbit technique. Where Orbit uses this technique internally, in λ_{MR} the mechanism is exported to the language level: the direct-style term language is designed to provide the power of passing multiple return points to user procedures, yet ensure that these return points can be stack allocated. The multi-return mechanism was specifically designed to fit naturally with an IR that uses multiple continuations to represent the multiple return points.
- Finally, multiple-continuation function calls can be used to implement "stream processing" computations, such as DSP pipelines [13].

These two extensions are a standard part of the lore of engineering compilers using CPS. However, they raise issues that have yet to be addressed. First, compiler writers work on the assumption that statically partitioned CPS allows continuation closures to be treated as stack frames. The question arises: why is this a safe assumption?

If we only have single-continuation calls, then it is fairly simple to show that the continuation environment records can be managed with a LIFO policy. But what happens when, as is often the case in practice, we pass multiple continuations across procedure calls? The compiler assumes that the continuations being passed all lie on the same stack, and so can all be passed as pointers into that stack. Is this in fact always true? Does it remain true when one lifts the idea of multiple return points from a limited, compiler-internal technique to a general user mechanism, as in λ_{MR}?

Further, when a function call is made, tail recursion requires that the compiler clear the stack back to the caller's continuation. Even if it is safe to suppose that all continuation arguments point into the same stack, the compiler must now pop the stack back to the most recent of these continuations. At a fixed call site, the continuation that is the "high-water" one can vary dynamically from call to call; in these cases, the compiler must emit code to compare the continuations at run time, in order to correctly adjust the stack.

This paper addresses the issues raised by the demands of stack-managing procedure calls in a CPS setting that permits multiple continuations to be passed across function calls.

PEPM'11, January 24–25, 2011, Austin, Texas, USA.

- First, we describe a reasonable static restriction on CPS that ensures that multiple continuations can be safely passed across function calls as pointers into a single stack (sections 2-5).
- Second, we describe a higher-order flow analysis that resolves the order of various continuations on a common stack, permitting a program to avoid computing the "high water" continuation at run time. This helps to make complex multi-return-point program structure a more pay-as-you-go feature (section 6).
- Third, we develop $\lambda_{\rm MR}$ as a motivating example: it can be naturally converted into our Restricted CPS form using multiple continuations; these continuations can be safely represented as stack frames; and $\lambda_{\rm MR}$ programs that call procedures with many return points can be analyzed by our flow analysis.

  It's worth noting that, while Fisher and Shivers developed $\lambda_{\rm MR}$ with an eye towards representing programs written in it with multi-continuation CPS, they did not exhibit a CPS conversion algorithm for their language. The conversion we show is interesting in that it handles the issue of "control polymorphism" that arises by means of a simple type system; the CPS conversion is thus type-directed (section 7).
- Fourth, we report on experimental results from a prototype implementation of our analysis in Scheme48. Our findings show that the analysis can find the youngest continuation in most cases, and it requires little increase in compilation time and implementation effort over k-CFA (section 8).

These results are obtained in a setting that permits continuations to be captured by operators such as `call/cc`, which can force the run-time stack to be copied to, and restored from, the heap. The net result is to put CPS intermediate representations as they are employed in practice onto a more solid footing, and to make multi-continuation function calls more efficient, in a general setting.

2. Restricted CPS

We propose Restricted CPS as a variant of Partitioned CPS [7]. Partitioned CPS splits the variables, lambdas and calls of a CPS program into disjoint sets, the "user" and the "continuation" set, so that it is easy to distinguish the two syntactically. Elements of the direct-style source program end up in the "user" set in CPS. Continuations and calls added by the CPS transform end up in the "continuation" set.

We begin with a brief description of Partitioned CPS (Fig. 1). The partitioning between the user and the continuation world happens by assigning labels to CPS terms from two disjoint sets; user elements get labels from $ULab$ and continuation elements get labels from $CLab$. Hence, $UVar$, $ULam$ and $UCall$ refer to user variables, lambdas and calls respectively. Similarly, $CVar$, $CLam$ and $CCall$ refer to continuation variables, lambdas and calls.

We assume that all variables in a program have distinct names and all labels are unique. In such a program, the function $VL(v)$ returns the label of the lambda that binds the variable v and $LV(l)$ returns the list of *continuation* parameters of the $ulam$ labeled l. The function $\text{fcv}(h)$ returns the set of free $cvar$s of the term h. Concrete syntax enclosed in $[\![\cdot]\!]$ denotes an item of abstract syntax.

We use two notations for tuples, $(e_1, \ldots, e_n)$ and $\langle e_1, \ldots, e_n \rangle$, to avoid confusion when tuples are deeply nested. We use the latter for lists as well; ambiguities are resolved by the context. Lists are also described by a head-tail notation, *e.g.*, $3 :: \langle 1, 3, -47 \rangle$.

User functions take any number of user arguments and one or more continuation arguments. Continuation functions take only user arguments. In CPS, "returning" happens by calling a continuation. Hence, only $ulam$s can be returned, not $clam$s. Thus, a continuation can only escape when it is bound to a $cvar$ that occurs free in a $ulam$.

$pr \in PR$	$::=$	$[\![(\lambda\,(halt)\,call)]\!]$
$v \in Var$	$=$	$UVar + CVar$
$u,\ uvar \in UVar$	$=$	a set of identifiers
$k,\ cvar \in CVar$	$=$	a set of identifiers
$lam \in Lam$	$=$	$ULam + CLam$
$ulam \in ULam$	$::=$	$[\![(\lambda_l\,(u^*\,k^+)\,call)]\!]$
$clam \in CLam$	$::=$	$[\![(\lambda_\gamma\,(u^*)\,call)]\!]$
$call \in Call$	$=$	$UCall + CCall$
$UCall$	$::=$	$[\![(f\,e^*\,q^+)^l]\!]$
$CCall$	$::=$	$[\![(q\,e^*)^\gamma]\!]$
$h \in Exp$	$=$	$UExp + CExp$
$f, e \in UExp$	$=$	$UVar + ULam$
$q \in CExp$	$=$	$CVar + CLam$
$\psi \in Lab$	$=$	$ULab + CLab$
$l \in ULab$	$=$	a set of labels
$\gamma,\ \zeta \in CLab$	$=$	a set of labels

Figure 1. Partitioned CPS

$$
\begin{aligned}
&RCPS(x) = true\\
&RCPS([\![(\lambda_l\,(u_1 \ldots u_n\ k_1 \ldots k_m)\,call)]\!]) =\\
&(\text{fcv}(call) \subseteq \{k_1, \ldots, k_m\} \wedge RCPS(call)) \vee\\
&([\![(\lambda_l\,(u^*\,k^+)\,call)]\!] \equiv_\alpha [\![(\lambda\,(f\ cc)\,(f\ \ (\lambda\,(x\ k)\,(cc\ x))\ \ cc))]\!])\\
&RCPS([\![(\lambda_\gamma\,(u_1 \ldots u_n)\,call)]\!]) = RCPS(call)\\
&RCPS([\![(h_1 \ldots h_n)^\psi]\!]) = RCPS(h_1) \wedge \cdots \wedge RCPS(h_n)
\end{aligned}
$$

Figure 2. The RCPS predicate defines Restricted-CPS terms

```
(define (square n cc h)
  (number? n (λ1(test)
               (%if test
                 (λ2() (* n n cc))
                 (λ3() (h "not a number"))))))
```

Figure 3. Non-local exit

Many applications of multiple continuations use them in a "downward" fashion: after its creation, a continuation closure is passed as an argument to a number of $ulam$s and then called – it is never captured in a user closure.

This led us to observe that we can impose a syntactic constraint to Partitioned CPS and still maintain all its benefits; a $ulam$ can refer only to continuations from its list of formals, it cannot have free $cvars$.[1] The only $ulam$ that is allowed to have a free $cvar$ appears in the CPS translation of `call/cc`, which is $(\lambda\,(f\ cc)\,(f\ \ (\lambda\,(x\ k)\,(cc\ x))\ \ cc))$. We refer to this variant of CPS as "Restricted Continuation-Passing Style" (RCPS, Fig. 2).

By placing this restriction we permit more effective reasoning about the stack behavior of continuations. In section 5 we show that even in the presence of `call/cc` the continuation arguments of a $ulam$ are still on the stack.

The simple function in Fig. 3 takes two continuations. It computes the square of its argument and passes it to the current continuation, or it calls the handler continuation if it is passed a non-number. The program is in RCPS since the user functions can only refer to continuations that are passed to them.[2]

[1] Sabry and Felleisen also proposed this constraint to forbid first-class control in single-continuation CPS [9].

[2] Note that although we use the λ-calculus to develop our theory, we add constants and primitives in the examples to keep them short and clear.

3. Stack management in RCPS

Might and Shivers [7] generalized ORBIT's stack policy to handle multiple continuations. Here, we give an outline of this stack policy.

At run time, continuations are closures whose environments live on the stack. A continuation is represented as a pair (c, s) where c is a pointer to its code and s a pointer into the stack. Continuations access their free variables from a pointer into the stack, never from the heap. To ensure this in the presence of first-class continuations, we have to copy the stack when a continuation escapes and restore it later when it is called.

Before a call to a user function $[\![(f\, e_1 \ldots e_n\ q_1 \ldots q_m)]\!]$, we want to retain the frames needed for $q_1 \ldots q_m$ and remove any redundant frames. There are two possibilities:

- In a *tail call*, all q_js are variables, so they are bound to closures already born. The frames pushed after the birth of the youngest closure are not needed. We pop these frames to restore the stack to the environment of the youngest closure. This way, all continuations are retained when we enter f.
- In a *non tail call*, some q_js are lambdas. These are newly born continuation closures, closed over the current stack pointer. Thus, all frames are needed and we leave the stack intact.

After this adjustment, the environment of the youngest continuation is at the top of the stack. We push a frame for f's arguments and jump to f. Generally, this policy maintains the following invariant: when a $ulam$ is executing, the second frame is the youngest live continuation.

In the same spirit, before calling a continuation $[\![(q\ e^*)]\!]$, its environment must be on the top of the stack, so we reset the stack to the stack of its birth.[3] We then push a frame for its arguments and jump to q. The invariant maintained here is that during q's execution the second frame points to its environment.

Returning to our example, if we run `(square 5 halt err)` the actions on the stack are $\langle$`square`$|$ $\langle$`number?`$|$ $|$`number?`$\rangle$ $\langle 1|$ $\langle$`%if`$|$ $|$`%if`$\rangle$ $\langle 2|$ $|2\rangle$ $|1\rangle$ $|$`square`$\rangle$ $\langle$`*`$|$ $|$`*`$\rangle$ $\langle$`halt`$|$. The notation $\langle \psi|$ means pushing a frame for λ_ψ, and $|\psi\rangle$ pops it. Initially we push frames for `square` and `number?`. When we evaluate λ_1 we pop a frame to restore the stack of its birth and then push a frame for its argument. The execution continues along these lines. The only thing to note is the evaluation of `(* n n cc)`; `cc` is bound to `halt`, so to maintain the stack invariant we have to pop to the stack at the time of `halt`'s birth. Thus, we pop three frames before pushing $\langle$`*`$|$.

4. Frame strings

In order to formally express stack properties and prove them, we must have a way to describe actions on the stack. In languages without tail calls, these push and pop actions correspond to sequences of calls and returns that nest properly. The call-string mechanism [10] can be used to describe these sequences. However, in properly tail-recursive languages calls and returns no longer nest, because iterative functions perform many calls and a single return. First-class continuations break call-return nesting even more. However, *stack operations* (that is, pushes and pops) still nest in these languages, of course. Might and Shivers adapted the call-string mechanism to create frame strings [7], an abstraction that works well for languages with exotic calling behavior.

We already gained some intuition about the use of frame-strings in the last section; *stack actions* are pushes/pops and they contain the label of the procedure being pushed/popped. We also mark stack actions with timestamps *e.g.*, $|{}^{\gamma_3}_{t_4}\rangle$ means popping the frame that holds the arguments of a call to λ_{γ_3} and was first pushed on time t_4.[4] A *frame-string* is a sequence of stack actions.

$$p \in F ::= \varepsilon \,\big|\, F \langle {}^{\psi}_{t} | \,\big|\, F\, | {}^{\psi}_{t} \rangle$$

Let's return to our example and see how the stack looks after we push $\langle 2|$. Since the frames for **number**? and %**if** have been popped, the stack is $\langle square|\langle 1|\langle 2|$. So, by repeatedly cancelling adjacent push/pop actions for the same frame, we get a picture of the stack. We call this *netting* the frame-string:

$$\lfloor p \rfloor = \begin{cases} \lfloor p_1\, p_2 \rfloor & \exists p_1, p_2 . (p \equiv p_1 \langle {}^{\psi}_{t} || {}^{\psi}_{t} \rangle p_2) \vee (p \equiv p_1 | {}^{\psi}_{t} \rangle \langle {}^{\psi}_{t} | p_2) \\ p & \text{otherwise} \end{cases}$$

In our example, if we net the frame string that starts with $|2\rangle$ and ends with $\langle halt|$ we get $|2\rangle|1\rangle|square\rangle\langle halt|$. This gives us the *change* to the stack after $\langle 2|$.

The associative operator $+$ concatenates two frame-strings. Might and Shivers showed that frame-strings modulo netting form a group with respect to concatenation. So, for every frame-string p there exists another one p^{-1} such that $\lfloor p + p^{-1} \rfloor = \lfloor p^{-1} + p \rfloor = \varepsilon$. Intuitively, the inverse string undoes the actions p did to the stack. When inverting the concatenation of two frame strings, we know that $(p_1 + p_2)^{-1} = {p_2}^{-1} + {p_1}^{-1}$.

To summarize, if the execution of a program is at time t and we net the frame string from the initial time t_0 to t, we will calculate the stack at time t. Also, if we net the frame string from some past time t_p to t, we will see the stack change since t_p. The ability to use frame strings both for recording all stack actions and for finding net stack change makes them a particularly helpful mechanism to reason about the stack.

5. Concrete semantics and stack properties

In this section, we prove that the continuations passed to a user function live on the stack, even in the presence of first-class control (*cf.* item 2 of theorem 2). To do this, we use the concrete semantics of the ΔCFA analysis [7]. This semantics extends k-CFA with a log that records frame strings. ΔCFA uses the log only for recording frame strings, not for variable binding or return-point information; these are accomplished using environments, like k-CFA. The log shows the stack actions that would happen at runtime if the program was compiled using ORBIT's stack policy. Here, we use the log to study the stack behavior of continuations in RCPS.

The semantics and the relevant domains are shown in Fig. 4. At every transition, ς refers to the state on the left of the arrow. Boldface letters indicate tuples of values. Execution traces alternate between $Eval$ and $Apply$ states. At an $Eval$ state, we evaluate the subexpressions of a call site before performing a call. At an $Apply$ state, we perform the call.

The last component of each state is a unique timestamp, taken from the set $Time$. The function $succ$ increments the time at every transition. By $t_1 \preceq t_2$ we mean that t_2 is a later time than t_1. Times indicate points in the execution when variables are bound. The binding environment β is a partial function from variables to their binding times. The variable environment ve maps variable-time pairs to values. To find the value of a variable v, we look up the time v was put in β, and use that to search for the value in ve.

Let's look at the transitions more closely. At a $UEval$ state, we evaluate the operator and the arguments using function $\mathcal{A}$ (rule [UEA]). Lambdas evaluate to closures, which contain the binding environment and also the time of creation. Variables are looked up in ve using β. Note that in the resulting $UApply$ state, we use $\mathbf{d}$ and $\mathbf{c}$ to refer to the user and continuation arguments respectively,

[3] Without `call/cc` this is just popping, with `call/cc` it might also include pushing some frames.

[4] First-class continuations allow the same frame to be pushed more than once.

$$
\begin{aligned}
\varsigma \in \mathit{State} &= \mathit{Eval} + \mathit{Apply} \\
\mathit{Eval} &= \mathit{UEval} + \mathit{CEval} \\
\mathit{UEval} &= \mathit{UCall} \times \mathit{BEnv} \times \mathit{VEnv} \times \mathit{Log} \times \mathit{Time} \\
\mathit{CEval} &= \mathit{CCall} \times \mathit{BEnv} \times \mathit{VEnv} \times \mathit{Log} \times \mathit{Time} \\
\mathit{Apply} &= \mathit{Proc} \times \mathit{Proc}^* \times \mathit{VEnv} \times \mathit{Log} \times \mathit{Time} \\
\beta \in \mathit{BEnv} &= \mathit{Var} \rightharpoonup \mathit{Time} \\
ve \in \mathit{VEnv} &= \mathit{Var} \times \mathit{Time} \rightharpoonup \mathit{Proc} \\
c, d, proc \in \mathit{Proc} &= \mathit{Clo} + \mathit{halt} \\
clo \in \mathit{Clo} &= \mathit{Lam} \times \mathit{BEnv} \times \mathit{Time} \\
\delta \in \mathit{Log} &= \mathit{Time} \rightharpoonup F \\
t \in \mathit{Time} &= \text{a countably infinite, totally ordered set}
\end{aligned}
$$

$$
\begin{aligned}
&[\text{UEA}]\ ([\![(f\, e^*\, q^+)]\!], \beta, ve, \delta, t) \longrightarrow (proc, \mathbf{d}\,\mathbf{c}, ve, \delta', t') \\
&\quad t' = succ(\varsigma) \\
&\quad proc = \mathcal{A}(f, \beta, ve, t) \\
&\quad d_i = \mathcal{A}(e_i, \beta, ve, t) \\
&\quad c_j = \mathcal{A}(q_j, \beta, ve, t) \\
&\quad p_\Delta = \delta(youngest(c_j))^{-1} \\
&\quad \delta' = (\lambda\,(t)\,(\delta(t) + p_\Delta))[t' \mapsto \varepsilon]
\end{aligned}
$$

$$
\begin{aligned}
&[\text{CEA}]\ ([\![(q\, e^*)]\!], \beta, ve, \delta, t) \longrightarrow (proc, \mathbf{d}, ve, \delta', t') \\
&\quad t' = succ(\varsigma) \\
&\quad proc = \mathcal{A}(q, \beta, ve, t), \quad \text{of the form } (clam, \beta_\gamma, t_\gamma) \\
&\quad d_i = \mathcal{A}(e_i, \beta, ve, t), \\
&\quad p_\Delta = \delta(t_\gamma)^{-1} \\
&\quad \delta' = (\lambda\,(t)\,(\delta(t) + p_\Delta))[t' \mapsto \varepsilon]
\end{aligned}
$$

$$
\begin{aligned}
&[\text{AE}]\ (([\![(\lambda_\psi\,(v^*)\,call)]\!], \beta, t_\psi), \mathbf{d}, ve, \delta, t) \longrightarrow (call, \beta', ve', \delta', t') \\
&\quad t' = succ(\varsigma) \\
&\quad \beta' = \beta[\overline{v_i \mapsto t'}] \\
&\quad ve' = ve[\overline{(v_i, t') \mapsto d_i}] \\
&\quad p_\Delta = \langle^{\psi}_{t'}| \\
&\quad \delta' = (\lambda\,(t)\,(\delta(t) + p_\Delta))[t' \mapsto \varepsilon]
\end{aligned}
$$

$$
\mathcal{A}(h, \beta, ve, t) \triangleq \begin{cases} ve(h, \beta(h)) & h \in \mathit{Var} \\ (h, \beta, t) & h \in \mathit{Lam} \end{cases}
$$

Figure 4. Semantics of ΔCFA

although formally there is only one tuple of arguments in *Apply* states. This harmless pattern matching helps us distinguish the two easily. The *CEval*-to-*CApply* transition is similar (rule [CEA]).

From an *Apply* to an *Eval* state, we bind the formals of a procedure $\langle lam, \beta, t_\psi \rangle$ to the arguments and jump to its body. The new binding environment β' is an extension of β, with the formals mapped to the current time. The new variable environment ve' maps each (v_i, t') to the corresponding closure d_i.

States use a log to keep track of the actions they would perform on the stack. We write δ_t for the log of the state with timestamp t (we omit t when it is clear from the context). Then, $\delta_t(t')$ returns a frame string of all the pushes and pops performed from time t' to time t. Also, we write $\delta(t)^{-1}$ to mean $(\delta(t))^{-1}$.

At each transition from ς to ς', p_Δ records the stack change. To find the stack actions from a time t_p in the past to t', we concatenate the actions from t_p to t with p_Δ. Thus, the log δ' of ς' is $(\lambda\,(t)\,(\delta(t) + p_\Delta))[t' \mapsto \varepsilon]$. Naturally, $\delta'(t')$ is ε because some time must elapse for stack change to happen.

The stack policy dictates the stack actions p_Δ at each transition. At [UEA], we must undo all actions that happened since the creation of the youngest continuation argument. We use the function *youngest*, which takes a set of closures, compares their creation times and returns the most recent time. Then, the stack change should be $\delta(youngest(c_j))^{-1}$. We compute p_Δ for the other transitions in a similar way. Before calling a continuation, we must reset the stack to the stack of its birth (rule [CEA]). Before entering a function, we push a frame for its arguments (rule [AE]).

We use *halt* to denote the top-level continuation of a program pr. The initial state $\mathcal{I}(pr)$ is $(\langle pr, \emptyset, t_0 \rangle, \langle halt \rangle, \emptyset, [t_0 \mapsto \varepsilon], t_0)$.

With the formal machinery in place, we can now show that in a *UEval* state ς, the frames that make up the environments for the continuation arguments $q_1 \ldots q_m$ are still on the stack. When a continuation q_j is born, its environment is on the top of the stack, so it suffices to show that the net stack change from q_j's birth to ς is push-monotonic (written $\langle^{\cdot}_{\cdot}|^*$, to mean a frame string that contains just pushes). In this case, the stack adjustment $\delta(youngest(c_j))^{-1}$ in [UEA] transitions consists solely of pops.

By observing the CPS translation of `call/cc` you can see why our claim holds even when we allow first-class control: when a continuation is captured by a *ulam*, it can only be called later on, it cannot be passed as an argument to another *ulam*.

To prove push-monotonicity, we will show that each state satisfies a tighter set of constraints (*cf.* theorem 2). The first constraint is arguably the most important because it talks about stack properties of *any* continuation closure in ve. The stack motion between the birth of such a closure and the current state can be arbitrary. The constraint guarantees that when a continuation closure is created, it captures continuations that are still on the stack.

Let's look more closely at the creation of continuation-closures. For every continuation lambda λ_γ, there is an innermost user lambda λ_l that contains it. Because of RCPS, λ_γ can only refer to continuation variables bound by λ_l. To create a closure c over λ_γ, we must first call λ_l. Assume that at the time of the call we pass continuations $c_1 \ldots c_m$ that are still on the stack. Then, if the net stack motion p from the call to λ_l to the creation of c is push-monotonic, $c_1 \ldots c_m$ will still be on the stack when c is created. There are two cases for λ_γ: it can appear directly under λ_l, *e.g.*,

```
(λl(u k1 k2) (u 15 (λγ(res) (+ 4 res k1))))
```

or after a series of *CEval*s whose operators are lambdas, *e.g.*,

```
(λl(k1)((λγ1(u1)
          ((λγ2(u2) ((λγ(u)(k1 u)) "hello"))
           "foo"))
         "bar"))
```

In both cases, p is push-monotonic.

DEFINITION 1 (Continuation ordering).
Ord$(\{q_1, \ldots, q_n\}, \beta, ve, \delta, t)$ *is true iff:*

- *Let* $k \in \bigcup \mathrm{fcv}(q_i)$ *and* $ve(k, \beta(k)) = (clam, \beta', t')$. *Then, we have that* $\lfloor \delta(t') + \delta(t)^{-1} \rfloor$ *is* $\langle^{\cdot}_{\cdot}|^*$
- *Let* $k_1, k_2 \in \bigcup \mathrm{fcv}(q_i)$ *and* $ve(k_1, \beta(k_1)) = (clam_1, \beta_1, t_1)$ *and* $ve(k_2, \beta(k_2)) = (clam_2, \beta_2, t_2)$ *and* $t_1 \preceq t_2$. *Then, we have that* $\lfloor \delta(t_1) + \delta(t_2)^{-1} \rfloor$ *is* $\langle^{\cdot}_{\cdot}|^*$

THEOREM 2. *Let* ς *be a state of the form* $(\ldots, ve, \delta, t)$

- *If* $(clam, \beta, t') \in \mathrm{range}(ve)$ *then* $Ord(\{clam\}, \beta, ve, \delta, t')$
- *If* $\varsigma \in UEval$, $([\![(f\, e^*\, q_1 \ldots q_m)]\!], \beta, ve, \delta, t)$ *then* $Ord(\{q_1, \ldots, q_m\}, \beta, ve, \delta, t)$
- *If* $\varsigma \in CEval$, $([\![(q\, e^*)]\!], \beta, ve, \delta, t)$ *and* $q \in clam$ *then* $Ord(\{q\}, \beta, ve, \delta, t)$
- *If* $\varsigma \in UApply$, $((ulam, \beta, t'), \mathbf{d}\, c_1 \ldots c_n, ve, \delta, t)$ *and* $c_i = (clam_i, \beta_i, t_i)$ *then* $Ord(\{clam_i\}, \beta_i, ve, \delta, t_i)$ *and* $\lfloor \delta(t_i) \rfloor$ *is* $\langle^{\cdot}_{\cdot}|^*$ *and for each* $t_a, t_b \in \{t_1, \ldots, t_n\}$ *such that* $t_a \preceq t_b$ *we have that* $\lfloor \delta(t_a) + \delta(t_b)^{-1} \rfloor$ *is* $\langle^{\cdot}_{\cdot}|^*$
- *If* $\varsigma \in CApply$, $((clam, \beta, t'), \mathbf{d}, ve, \delta, t)$ *then* $Ord(\{clam\}, \beta, ve, \delta, t)$

Proof. We show that the constraints hold for $\mathcal{I}(pr)$ and are maintained by transition. □

Note that in a *CEval* state, if q is a variable we can guarantee nothing about it; it may be bound to a continuation that has escaped. Therefore, q's environment may be popped.

However, in a program without `call/cc` we can guarantee that continuation environments are never popped because *CEval* states satisfy $Ord(\{q\}, \beta, ve, \delta, t)$ even if q is a variable.

6. Continuation-Age analysis

We now know that continuation environments are still on the stack in *UEval* states. This means that we never need to push frames to restore environments in *UEval*. Also, it means that the environments are totally ordered on the stack at run time. Put formally, if t_1 and t_2 are the birthdays of two continuations then either $\lfloor \delta(t_1) \rfloor$ is a suffix of $\lfloor \delta(t_2) \rfloor$ or vice versa. So, if t_y is the birthday of the youngest continuation then $\lfloor \delta(t_y) \rfloor$ is a suffix of $\lfloor \delta(t_c) \rfloor$ where t_c is the birthday of any other continuation.

So far there has not been an analysis that finds the youngest continuation, and one would have to resort to dynamic checks. We present Continuation-Age analysis (*abbrev. Cage* analysis) that can find the youngest continuation statically in most cases. We first show the workings of the analysis by example and then proceed to develop a formal semantics for it. Consider the following snippet of some RCPS program pr:

$$(\lambda(u_1 \;\ldots\; u_5\; k_1\; k_2\; k_3)$$
$$\ldots\; (u_2\; k_1\; k_3\; (\lambda_\gamma(u_6)\, call)\; (\lambda_\varsigma(u_7)\, call'))^l \ldots)$$

Assume that we let pr run and execution reaches the call site l. We know that k_1, k_2 and k_3 are bound to closures whose environments are totally ordered, *e.g.*, with k_3 being the youngest and k_2 the oldest. Also, assume that u_2 is bound to a closure over $[\![(\lambda_{l_2}(k_4\; k_5\; k_6\; k_7)\, call'')]\!]$. To find the ordering of the environments at l we first observe that k_2 is not used at the call site, so we do not take it into account. Also, λ_γ and λ_ς will evaluate to newly born closures, so the ordering after control enters l_2 will be "k_6 and k_7 followed by k_5 followed by k_4". Because of RCPS, this is the only information we need to keep to decide the order of continuations inside $call''$; remember that $\mathrm{fcv}(call'') \subseteq \{k_4, k_5, k_6, k_7\}$. For this reason, our analysis can simply record total orders of *cvars* bound by the same *ulam*.[5] It can forget which closures these *cvars* are bound to.

6.1 Concrete semantics

The concrete semantics of *Cage* and some auxiliary definitions are shown in Fig. 5. To remove elements from lists we use the set-difference operator, with its meaning adapted in the obvious way. We use $map(f, lst)$ to apply a function f to all elements of lst. The function $ind(elm, lst)$ finds the 1-based index of elm in lst and $get(i, lst)$ returns the element at index i in lst. We also lift *get* and *ind* to sets of elements/indices respectively.

The semantic domains are the same as k-CFA with the addition of two domains to record the ordering of continuations.

$$ages,\ tor \in Tor = (Pow(CVar))^*$$
$$ce \in CEnv = ULab \times Time \rightharpoonup Tor$$

We represent a total order as a list of sets of *cvars*, rather than just a list of *cvars*, because we want to make explicit the case when two closures are born at the same time. In our example, the order will be $\langle\{k_6, k_7\}, \{k_5\}, \{k_4\}\rangle$. The continuation environment ce maps pairs of user-labels and times to total orders. We write $k \preceq_{tor} k'$ to mean that the index of k is smaller than or equal to the index of k' in tor, *i.e.*, k is younger than k'.

$$k \preceq_{tor} k' = \exists\, S, S'.\, k \in S \wedge k' \in S' \wedge ind(S, tor) \leqslant ind(S', tor)$$

In *UEval*, we gather order information about the *ulam* we are in, and use it to compute order information about the *ulam* we are about to enter. Since the new bindings in ce take place in *UApply*, *ages* serves as the carrier of that information between states.

Let's see how to find the order for the next *ulam* using the order of the current *ulam*. If there are any lambdas among $q_1 \ldots q_m$, the variables they will be bound to will be the youngest. So $rename(CLam)$ gathers the indices of lambdas among $q_1 \ldots q_m$, and uses them to index in the list of formals of λ_l. If every q_j is a variable, $rename(CLam)$ returns the empty set. If there are variables among $q_1 \ldots q_m$, they are bound by the same *ulam*, and $ce(VL(q_j), \beta(q_j))$ gathers the order information for that *ulam*. Then, we filter out variables that are not among $q_1 \ldots q_m$ and index the rest in the list of formals of λ_l. In our example, $ce(VL(k_3), \beta(k_3))$ returns $\langle\{k_3\}, \{k_1\}, \{k_2\}\rangle$ and $map(rename, \langle\{k_3\}, \{k_1\}, \{k_2\}\rangle)$ returns $\langle\{k_5\}, \{k_4\}, \emptyset\rangle$. We remove possible empty sets from our list and we have the new *ages*.

Since only user states can influence the ordering, the semantics for *CEval* and *CApply* are the same as k-CFA. Note that we can compute continuation ages without using information about the stack actions, thus we do not need a log in the *Cage* semantics.

[UEA] $([\![(f\, e^*\, q_1 \ldots q_m)]\!], \beta, ve, ce, t) \longrightarrow (d_0, \mathbf{d}\,\mathbf{c}, ve, ce, ages, t')$

$$t' = succ(\varsigma)$$
$$d_0 = \mathcal{A}(f, \beta, ve, t), \text{ of the form } ([\![(\lambda_l(v^+)\, call)]\!], \ldots)$$
$$d_i = \mathcal{A}(e_i, \beta, ve, t)$$
$$c_j = \mathcal{A}(q_j, \beta, ve, t)$$
$$tor = \begin{cases} ce(VL(q_j), \beta(q_j)) & \exists\, 1 \leqslant j \leqslant m\,.\, q_j \in Var \\ \langle\rangle & \forall\, 1 \leqslant j \leqslant m\,.\, q_j \in Lam \end{cases}$$
$$rename(S) = Get(Ind(S, \langle q_1 \ldots q_m\rangle), LV(l))$$
$$ages = (rename(CLam) :: map(rename, tor)) \setminus \{\emptyset\}$$

[UAE] $(d_0, \mathbf{d}, ve, ce, ages, t) \longrightarrow (call, \beta', ve', ce', t')$

$$d_0 \equiv ([\![(\lambda_l(v^+)\, call)]\!], \beta, t_l)$$
$$t' = succ(\varsigma)$$
$$\beta' = \beta[\overline{v \mapsto t'}]$$
$$ve' = ve[\overline{(v, t') \mapsto d_i}]$$
$$ce' = ce[(l, t') \mapsto ages]$$

[CEA] $([\![(q\, e_1 \ldots e_n)]\!], \beta, ve, ce, t) \longrightarrow (proc, \mathbf{d}, ve, ce, t')$

$$t' = succ(\varsigma)$$
$$proc = \mathcal{A}(q, \beta, ve, t)$$
$$d_i = \mathcal{A}(e_i, \beta, ve, t)$$

[CAE] $(([\![(\lambda(u^*)\, call)]\!], \beta, t_\gamma), \mathbf{d}, ve, ce, t) \longrightarrow (call, \beta', ve', ce, t')$

$$t' = succ(\varsigma)$$
$$\beta' = \beta[\overline{u_i \mapsto t'}]$$
$$ve' = ve[\overline{(u_i, t') \mapsto d_i}]$$

$$ind(elm, lst) = \begin{cases} i & lst = \langle e_1, \ldots, e_m\rangle,\ elm = e_i \\ \bot & \text{otherwise} \end{cases}$$

$$Ind(S, lst) = \{\, ind(s, lst) \mid s \in S \,\} \setminus \{\bot\}$$

$$get(i, lst) = \begin{cases} e_i & lst = \langle e_1, \ldots, e_m\rangle,\ 1 \leqslant i \leqslant m \\ \bot & \text{otherwise} \end{cases}$$

$$Get(I, lst) = \{\, get(i, lst) \mid i \in I \,\} \setminus \{\bot\}$$

Figure 5. Concrete semantics of *Cage* Analysis

[5] Even though the CPS translation of `call/cc` contains the term $[\![(\lambda(x\ k)(cc\ x))]\!]$ with a free *cvar*, this is not a problem since this *ulam* does not contain a user call site. Thus, we do not need to find the age of continuations while in $[\![(\lambda(x\ k)(cc\ x))]\!]$.

$$
\begin{array}{ll}
[\widehat{\mathrm{UEA}}] & (\llbracket (f\, e^*\, q_1 \ldots q_m) \rrbracket, \hat\beta, \widehat{ve}, \widehat{ce}, \hat t) \rightsquigarrow (\hat{\mathrm{d}}_0, \hat{\mathbf{d}}\, \hat{\mathbf{c}}, \widehat{ve}, \widehat{ce}, \widehat{ages}, \hat t') \\
 & \hat t' = \widehat{succ}(\hat\varsigma) \\
 & \hat{\mathrm{d}}_0 \in \hat{\mathcal{A}}(f, \hat\beta, \widehat{ve}, \hat t), \text{ of the form } (\llbracket (\lambda_l\, (v^+)\, call) \rrbracket, \ldots) \\
 & \hat d_i = \hat{\mathcal{A}}(e_i, \hat\beta, \widehat{ve}, \hat t) \\
 & \hat c_j = \hat{\mathcal{A}}(q_j, \hat\beta, \widehat{ve}, \hat t) \\
 & tors = \begin{cases} \widehat{ce}(\mathit{VL}(q_j), \hat\beta_l(q_j)) & \exists 1 \leqslant j \leqslant m \,.\, q_j \in \mathit{Var} \\ \langle\rangle & \forall 1 \leqslant j \leqslant m \,.\, q_j \in \mathit{Lam} \end{cases} \\
 & ren(S) = \mathit{Get}(\mathit{Ind}(S, \langle q_1 \ldots q_m \rangle), \mathit{LV}(l)) \\
 & \widehat{ages} = \{\, (ren(\mathit{CLam}) :: map(ren, tor)) \setminus \{\emptyset\} \mid tor \in tors \}
\end{array}
$$

$$
\begin{array}{ll}
[\widehat{\mathrm{UAE}}] & (\hat{\mathrm{d}}_0, \hat{\mathbf{d}}, \widehat{ve}, \widehat{ce}, \widehat{ages}, \hat t) \rightsquigarrow (call, \hat\beta', \widehat{ve}', \widehat{ce}', \hat t') \\
 & \hat{\mathrm{d}}_0 \equiv (\llbracket (\lambda_l\, (v^+)\, call) \rrbracket, \hat\beta, \hat t_l) \\
 & \hat t' = \widehat{succ}(\hat\varsigma) \\
 & \hat\beta' = \hat\beta[\,\overline{v \mapsto \hat t'}\,] \\
 & \widehat{ve}' = \widehat{ve} \sqcup [\,\overline{(v, \hat t') \mapsto \hat d_i}\,] \\
 & \widehat{ce}' = \widehat{ce} \sqcup [(l, \hat t') \mapsto \widehat{ages}]
\end{array}
$$

$$
\begin{array}{ll}
[\widehat{\mathrm{CEA}}] & (\llbracket (q\, e_1 \ldots e_n) \rrbracket, \hat\beta, \widehat{ve}, \widehat{ce}, \hat t) \rightsquigarrow (\widehat{proc}, \hat{\mathbf{d}}, \widehat{ve}, \widehat{ce}, \hat t') \\
 & \hat t' = \widehat{succ}(\hat\varsigma) \\
 & \widehat{proc} \in \hat{\mathcal{A}}(q, \hat\beta, \widehat{ve}, \hat t) \\
 & d_i = \hat{\mathcal{A}}(e_i, \hat\beta, \widehat{ve}, \hat t)
\end{array}
$$

$$
\begin{array}{ll}
[\widehat{\mathrm{CAE}}] & ((\llbracket (\lambda\, (u^*)\, call) \rrbracket, \hat\beta, \hat t_\gamma), \hat{\mathbf{d}}, \widehat{ve}, \widehat{ce}, \hat t) \rightsquigarrow (call, \hat\beta', \widehat{ve}', \widehat{ce}, \hat t') \\
 & \hat t' = \widehat{succ}(\hat\varsigma) \\
 & \hat\beta' = \hat\beta[\,\overline{u_i \mapsto \hat t'}\,] \\
 & \widehat{ve}' = \widehat{ve} \sqcup [\,\overline{(u_i, \hat t') \mapsto \hat d_i}\,]
\end{array}
$$

Figure 6. Abstract semantics for *Cage* Analysis

6.2 Abstract semantics

Abstracting the semantics of *Cage* raises no difficulty. Like k-CFA, making the set $\widehat{Time}$ finite ensures computability of the abstract state-space. The abstract counterparts of Tor and $CEnv$ are

$$
\begin{array}{rl}
\widehat{ages},\ tors \in \widehat{Tor} = & Pow(Tor) \\
\widehat{ce} \in \widehat{CEnv} = & ULab \times \widehat{Time} \rightharpoonup \widehat{Tor}
\end{array}
$$

Since one abstract state corresponds to many concrete states, we have to fold many total orders to one element of $\widehat{Tor}$. Thus, the elements of $\widehat{Tor}$ are sets of total orders, with set-union being the join operation. For a $cvar$ to be the youngest in $tors$, it has to be the youngest in every total order contained in $tors$. This happens because different elements of $tors$ correspond to different flows of control in the abstract semantics. Some of these flows may have occurred due to imprecision introduced by the static analysis, but most of them will have a concrete counterpart, so we make sure that all concrete flows agree on the age of $cvars$. We also define maps from the concrete to the abstract domains.

$$
\begin{array}{rl}
|tor| = & \{tor\} \\
|ce| = & (\lambda\, (l\, \hat t)\ \bigsqcup_{|t| = \hat t} |ce(l, t)|\,)
\end{array}
$$

The abstract semantics is shown in Fig. 6. Contrary to the concrete semantics, it is non-deterministic. Also, when we add new elements to $\widehat{ve}$ and $\widehat{ce}$ we join them instead of doing a destructive update. The two semantics are otherwise similar.

6.3 Soundness

There are two results we need to establish for our analysis to be sound. We first show that a total order of $cvars$ "agrees" with the birthdays of the closures to which these variables are bound.

$$
\begin{array}{l}
\lhd 2\quad (\lambda\,(x)\; x{+}1)\; (\lambda\,(x)\; x{+}2) \rhd \longrightarrow ((\lambda\,(x)\; x{+}1)\; 2) \longrightarrow 3 \\[1em]
\lhd\lhd 2\;\; \#2 \rhd\;\; (\lambda\,(x)\; x{+}1)\; (\lambda\,(x)\; x) \rhd \longrightarrow \lhd 2\quad (\lambda\,(x)\; x) \rhd \longrightarrow 2
\end{array}
$$

$$
\begin{array}{l}
((\lambda(\mathtt{f})\ \mathtt{if}\ \ test \\
\quad\quad \lhd(f\quad 2)\quad (\lambda\,(x)\; x+1)\quad (\lambda\,(x)\; x-1) \rhd \\
\quad\quad \lhd(f\quad 3)\quad \#1 \rhd) \\
\;\; (\lambda\,(y)\; y\ *\ y))
\end{array}
$$

Figure 7. Examples of λ_{MR}

THEOREM 3. *Let ς be any state of the form $(\ldots, ve, ce, \ldots)$ and $ce(l, t) = tor$. If $k_i \preceq_{tor} k_j$ and $ve(k_i, t) = (clam, \beta_\gamma, t_\gamma)$ and $ve(k_j, t) = (clam', \beta_\varsigma, t_\varsigma)$ then $t_\varsigma \preceq t_\gamma$ i.e., $ve(k_i, t)$ was born later than $ve(k_j, t)$.*

Secondly, we show that the abstract semantics simulates the concrete semantics, which means that our approximation is safe.

THEOREM 4 (Soundness of *Cage* analysis). *If $|\varsigma| \sqsubseteq \hat\varsigma$ and $\varsigma \longrightarrow \varsigma'$ then there exists $\hat\varsigma'$ such that $\hat\varsigma \rightsquigarrow \hat\varsigma'$ and $|\varsigma'| \sqsubseteq |\hat\varsigma'|$.*

Regarding the time complexity of *Cage*: since n elements can be totally ordered in $n!$ ways, and the range of $\widehat{CEnv}$ records sets of total orders, the analysis is exponential in $\mathit{max\text{-}len}_{l \in ULab}\, LV(l)$. This is not a problem in practice, since the number of continuation arguments is usually small. A factor that can influence the speed of *Cage* more dramatically is the choice of $\widehat{Time}$, since for k greater than zero k-CFA is exponential in the size of the program [15].

Alternatively, there is a less precise lattice we can use for $\widehat{CEnv}$. $\widehat{CEnv}$ can record partial orders of $cvars$ and the join would be set-intersection. Then, k_i would be younger than k_j in $\widehat{ce}_1 \sqcup \widehat{ce}_2$ iff $(k_i, k_j) \in \widehat{ce}_1$ and $(k_i, k_j) \in \widehat{ce}_2$. However, join introduces more approximation than we would like. For example, consider $\widehat{ce}_1 = \{(k_1, k_2), (k_1, k_3), (k_2, k_3)\}$ and $\widehat{ce}_2 = \{(k_3, k_2), (k_3, k_1), (k_2, k_1)\}$.[6] Then, $\widehat{ce}_1 \sqcup \widehat{ce}_2$ is $\emptyset$ even though we know that k_2 is never the youngest. In other words, this representation cannot express properties like "either k_1 or k_3 is younger than k_2."

6.4 *Cage* vs ΔCFA for age analysis

Theoretically, we could use ΔCFA to find the youngest continuation. Since ΔCFA tracks stack change, we would check if the change between the birthdays of two closures is push monotonic. In practice, this does not work well for the following reasons.

First, variables in the abstract are bound to sets of closures. So, if we want to compare the age of two $cvars$ at a call site, we must check that every closure in one set is younger than every closure in the other set. But then we would end up comparing closures from different flows, which causes imprecision. *Cage* decouples variables from their bindings and remembers distinct flows as distinct total orders, thus avoiding these problems.

Second, the stack information ΔCFA computes in the abstract can be imprecise in the presence of recursion. It does roughly the following: it can remember exactly one push or one pop action for some λ_ψ, but if we push two (or more) frames for λ_ψ, ΔCFA will record this as $\langle\psi|^*$. Therefore, if we enter a recursive procedure and later return, ΔCFA will not net the pushes and pops. *Cage* does not suffer from this problem because it does not use the stack to compute continuation age.

7. From λ_{MR} to RCPS

The multi-return λ-calculus [12] is a variant of the λ-calculus in which functions may have many return points. Return points are not first-class continuations, hence they give the programmer the ability to express a wide variety of algorithms without paying the cost of general-purpose, heap-allocated continuations. Search algorithms that take a success and a failure continuation, functional tree transformations and LR-parsers are typical examples of programs that are naturally and efficiently expressed with this mechanism.

The multi-return form $\lhd e \quad r_1 \ldots r_m \rhd$ is how we get contexts with many return points. The expression e is evaluated with m return points in scope. If e does not use the multi-return form internally, it will always return to the first one, as in the first example of Fig. 7. However, if e is of the form $\lhd e' \quad \#i \rhd$ then the result of e' will be passed to r_i, as in the second example. A return point $\#i$ passes its input to the ith return point of its own context.

Restricted CPS, with the restrictions it places on continuations, would seem like a natural target for λ_{MR}. However, a subtlety of λ_{MR} is that functions are polymorphic in the number of return points that they expect, they do not specify it explicitly in their syntax. The last snippet of Fig. 7 is one such example. Depending on the result of the test, the square function will be evaluated in a context with one or two return points, even though it always returns to the first. Since in RCPS a *ulam* has to specify the number of continuations it expects, we cannot translate this code to RCPS.

A control-monomorphic variant however has a simple transform to RCPS. We require that a function take a specific number of return points, which we pass when we apply the function. We change the syntax and semantics of λ_{MR} slightly to reflect this (section 7.1). We provide a type system that rejects control-polymorphic λ_{MR} programs and prove it sound (section 7.2). Then, we give a type-directed transform from λ_{MR} to RCPS (section 7.3).

7.1 Syntax and semantics

Expressions in control-monomorphic λ_{MR} include variables, numbers, functions, applications with a specified number of return points and multi-return forms. Numbers and functions are values:

$$\begin{aligned}
&lam \in Lam ::= (\lambda\,(x)\; e)\\
&e \in Exp ::= x \mid n \mid lam \mid \lhd(e_1\; e_2) \quad r_1 \ldots r_m \rhd \mid \lhd e \quad r_1 \ldots r_m \rhd\\
&r \in RP ::= lam \mid \#i
\end{aligned}$$

The semantics is call-by-value (Fig. 8). To evaluate $\lhd e \quad r_1 \ldots r_m \rhd$, we first evaluate e in a context with m return points (multi-prog). If it reduces to a value v and there is a single return point which is a function, we apply it to v (fst-lam). If the single return point is $\#1$ we return v to the context (fst-sharp). When there are multiple return points, v is returned to the first one (multi-drop). If e evaluates to $\lhd v \quad \#i \rhd$ in a context with i or more return points then we pass v to r_i (multi-select).

In an application we start with the operator (rator), then the operand (rand) and then the body of the function (app). These rules highlight the difference from control-polymorphic λ_{MR}. Unlike the last example of Fig. 7, we have to mention the return points when applying a function. Our type system checks that a function is always applied in contexts with the same number of return points.

A note about the stack behavior of λ_{MR} deserves a mention. When a return point is a function, it requires a frame to be pushed, while a $\#i$ return point just points to an older frame. Thus, when all return points of $\lhd e \quad r_1 \ldots r_m \rhd$ are not functions, the stack does not grow, and it might even shrink. This is essentially the tail call mechanism applied to λ_{MR}.[7]

[6] For readability, we omitted the reflexive pairs from the relations.

[7] For details, see [12] where semi-tail calls and super-tail calls are explained.

7.2 Types for control-monomorphism

We modify the original type system of λ_{MR} to annotate function types with the number of return points that a function expects.

Each expression e is assigned a type vector $\langle \tau_1, \ldots, \tau_n \rangle$ meaning that if e returns a value v to its ith return point, v has type τ_i. Placing $\perp$ instead of a type at index i means that e never returns to that return point. For example, $\lhd 11 \quad \#2 \rhd$ has type $\langle \perp, \text{int} \rangle$. But $\lhd 11 \quad \#2 \rhd$ never returns to any return point r_i for $i > 2$. Hence it can also have type $\langle \perp, \text{int}, \perp \rangle$, $\langle \perp, \text{int}, \perp, \perp \rangle$, *etc.* Moreover, $\langle \text{int}, \text{int} \rangle$ is also a possible type since the requirement "if $\lhd 11 \quad \#2 \rhd$ returns to its first return point it gives back an integer" is vacuously true. To model these, our type system has a notion of subtyping.

Types include integers and functions, and type vectors $\vec{\tau}$ are finite maps from natural numbers to types. Then, $\vec{\tau}[i] = \perp$ means that $i \notin \text{dom}(\vec{\tau})$.

$$\begin{aligned}
\tau \in T \quad &::= \quad \text{int} \mid (\tau,\, n) \rightarrow \vec{\tau}\\
\vec{\tau} \in \vec{T} \quad &= \quad \mathbb{N} \overset{\text{fin}}{\rightarrow} T
\end{aligned}$$

Function types include a natural number n, meaning that n return points must be provided when a function f is applied. Obviously, we run into trouble if f tries to return to r_i for $i > n$. Therefore, we require that $|\vec{\tau}| \leqslant n$ where $|\vec{\tau}|$ is $\min\{\, i \mid \forall j > i.\ \vec{\tau}[j] = \perp \}$. The subtyping rules for types and vectors are

$$\text{int} \sqsubseteq \text{int} \qquad \frac{\tau_b \sqsubseteq \tau_a \qquad \vec{\tau}_a \,\vec{\sqsubseteq}\, \vec{\tau}_b}{(\tau_a,\, n) \rightarrow \vec{\tau}_a \sqsubseteq (\tau_b,\, n) \rightarrow \vec{\tau}_b}$$

$$\frac{\forall\, i \in \text{dom}(\vec{\tau}_a).\; i \in \text{dom}(\vec{\tau}_b) \;\wedge\; \vec{\tau}_a[i] \sqsubseteq \vec{\tau}_b[i]}{\vec{\tau}_a \,\vec{\sqsubseteq}\, \vec{\tau}_b}$$

The type system is shown in Fig. 9. It assigns type vectors to expressions under an environment Γ which is a partial map from variables to types.

The rules for numbers and variables are standard (num, var). To typecheck a function $(\lambda\,(x)\; e)$, we typecheck its body in an environment extended with x. The side condition states that if the function uses $|\vec{\tau}|$ return points then it must request at least as many in its type.

For an application $\lhd(e_1\; e_2) \quad r_1 \ldots r_m \rhd$ we require that e_1 have a function type with exactly m return points (appl). The type of the argument must be a subtype of what the function expects (side condition 1). If the jth return point is a *lam* with type $\langle\, (\tau_j,\, m_j) \;\rightarrow\; \vec{\tau}_j \,\rangle$, then anything that e_1 returns to it must be a subtype of τ_j. Additionally, anything that r_j returns to the context must be consistent with what the whole expression returns. For this, we require $\vec{\tau}_j \vec{\sqsubseteq} \vec{\tau}_{app}$ (side condition 2). On the other hand, if the return point is of the form $\#i$ then whatever e_1 returns to its jth return point will be sent to the context's i^{th} return point, which is why we require $\vec{\tau}[j] \sqsubseteq \vec{\tau}_{app}[i]$ (side condition 3).

For a $\lhd e \quad r_1 \ldots r_m \rhd$ expression (multi) the typing constraints required from return points are the same as in the application case (side conditions 2, 3). We also require that e only try to return to $r_1 \ldots r_m$ (side condition 1).

We can now see why the type system rejects control-polymorphic λ_{MR} programs. The operator of our last example is

$$\begin{aligned}
&(\lambda(\mathtt{f})\ \mathtt{if}\ \textit{test}\\
&\quad \lhd(f \quad 2) \quad (\lambda\,(x)\, x + 1) \quad (\lambda\,(x)\, x - 1) \rhd\\
&\quad \lhd(f \quad 3) \quad \#1 \rhd)
\end{aligned}$$

The true-branch requires f to have a type of the form $\langle\, (\text{int},\, 2) \rightarrow \vec{\tau}_a \,\rangle$ and the false-branch requires f to have a type of the form $\langle\, (\text{int},\, 1) \;\rightarrow\; \vec{\tau}_b \,\rangle$. Since none of these types is a subtype of the other, the body cannot be typechecked with a unique type for f.

$$[\text{multi}-\text{prog}]\quad \frac{e \rightarrow e'}{\triangleleft e \quad r_1 \ldots r_m \triangleright \rightarrow \triangleleft e' \quad r_1 \ldots r_m \triangleright}$$

$$[\text{fst}-\text{lam}]\quad \frac{}{\triangleleft v \quad (\lambda\,(x)\; e) \triangleright \rightarrow [v/x]e}$$

$$[\text{fst}-\text{sharp}]\quad \frac{}{\triangleleft v \quad \#1 \triangleright \rightarrow v}$$

$$[\text{multi}-\text{drop}]\quad \frac{}{\triangleleft v \quad r_1 \ldots r_m \triangleright \rightarrow \triangleleft v \quad r_1 \triangleright}$$

$$[\text{multi}-\text{select}]\quad \frac{1 < i \leqslant m}{\triangleleft \triangleleft v \quad \#i \triangleright \quad r_1 \ldots r_m \triangleright \rightarrow \triangleleft v \quad r_i \triangleright}$$

$$[\text{rator}]\quad \frac{e_1 \rightarrow e_1'}{\triangleleft(e_1\; e_2) \quad r_1 \ldots r_m \triangleright \rightarrow \triangleleft(e_1'\; e_2) \quad r_1 \ldots r_m \triangleright}$$

$$[\text{rand}]\quad \frac{e_2 \rightarrow e_2'}{\triangleleft((\lambda\,(x)\; e)\; e_2) \quad r_1 \ldots r_m \triangleright \rightarrow \triangleleft((\lambda\,(x)\; e)\; e_2') \quad r_1 \ldots r_m \triangleright}$$

$$[\text{app}]\quad \frac{}{\triangleleft((\lambda\,(x)\; e)\; v) \quad r_1 \ldots r_m \triangleright \rightarrow \triangleleft [v/x]e \quad r_1 \ldots r_m \triangleright}$$

Figure 8. Operational Semantics of λ_{MR}

$$[\text{num}]\quad \Gamma \vdash n : \langle \text{int} \rangle \qquad [\text{var}]\quad \frac{}{\Gamma \vdash x : \langle \Gamma(x) \rangle}\; x \in \text{dom}(\Gamma) \qquad [\text{abs}]\quad \frac{\Gamma[x \mapsto \tau] \vdash e : \vec{\tau}}{\Gamma \vdash (\lambda\,(x)\; e) : \langle (\tau, n) \rightarrow \vec{\tau} \rangle}\; n \geqslant |\vec{\tau}|$$

$$[\text{appl}]\quad \frac{\Gamma \vdash e_1 : \langle (\tau, m) \rightarrow \vec{\tau} \rangle \quad \Gamma \vdash e_2 : \vec{\tau_2} \qquad \Gamma \vdash r_j : \langle (\tau_j, m_j) \rightarrow \vec{\tau_j} \rangle (\forall r_j \in \mathit{Lam})}{\Gamma \vdash \triangleleft(e_1\; e_2) \quad r_1 \ldots r_m \triangleright : \vec{\tau}_{app}} \qquad \begin{array}{ll} (1) & \vec{\tau_2}\, \vec{\sqsubseteq}\, \langle \tau \rangle \\ (2) & \forall r_j \in \mathit{Lam}.\, (\vec{\tau}[j] = \perp \vee \vec{\tau}[j] \sqsubseteq \tau_j) \wedge \vec{\tau_j}\, \vec{\sqsubseteq}\, \vec{\tau}_{app} \\ (3) & \forall r_j = \#i.\, \vec{\tau}[j] = \perp \vee \vec{\tau}[j] \sqsubseteq \vec{\tau}_{app}[i] \end{array}$$

$$[\text{multi}]\quad \frac{\Gamma \vdash e : \vec{\tau}_e \qquad \Gamma \vdash r_j : \langle (\tau_j, m_j) \rightarrow \vec{\tau_j} \rangle (\forall r_j \in \mathit{Lam})}{\Gamma \vdash \triangleleft e \quad r_1 \ldots r_m \triangleright : \vec{\tau}} \qquad \begin{array}{ll} (1) & |\vec{\tau}_e| \leqslant m \\ (2) & \forall r_j \in \mathit{Lam}.\, (\vec{\tau}_e[j] = \perp \vee \vec{\tau}_e[j] \sqsubseteq \tau_j) \wedge \vec{\tau_j}\, \vec{\sqsubseteq}\, \vec{\tau} \\ (3) & \forall r_j = \#i.\, \vec{\tau}_e[j] = \perp \vee \vec{\tau}_e[j] \sqsubseteq \vec{\tau}[i] \end{array}$$

Figure 9. Types

Trivial Term:

$\mathscr{T}[\![x]\!] = x$

$\mathscr{T}[\![n]\!] = n$

$\mathscr{T}[\![(\lambda\,(x)\; e)]\!] = (\lambda\,(x\; k_1 \ldots k_m) \mathscr{S}[\![e]\!]\; k_1 \ldots k_m)$ where $(\lambda\,(x)\; e)$ has type $\langle (\tau, m) \rightarrow \vec{\tau} \rangle$

Return Point:

$\mathscr{R}[\![\#i]\!]\; k_1 \ldots k_l = k_i$

$\mathscr{R}[\![(\lambda\,(x)\; e)]\!]\; k_1 \ldots k_l = (\lambda\,(x) \mathscr{S}[\![e]\!]\; k_1 \ldots k_l)$

Serious Term:

$\mathscr{S}[\![t_0]\!]\; k_1 \ldots k_l = (k_1\; \mathscr{T}[\![t_0]\!])$

If every k_i is a variable,

$\mathscr{S}[\![\triangleleft(t_0\; t_1) \quad r_1 \ldots r_m \triangleright]\!]\; k_1 \ldots k_l = (\mathscr{T}[\![t_0]\!]\; \mathscr{T}[\![t_1]\!]\; (\mathscr{R}[\![r_1]\!] k_1 \ldots k_l) \ldots (\mathscr{R}[\![r_m]\!] k_1 \ldots k_l))$

$\mathscr{S}[\![\triangleleft(t_0\; s_1) \quad r_1 \ldots r_m \triangleright]\!]\; k_1 \ldots k_l = \mathscr{S}[\![s_1]\!]\; (\underline{\lambda}(x) (\mathscr{T}[\![t_0]\!]\; x\; (\mathscr{R}[\![r_1]\!] k_1 \ldots k_l) \ldots (\mathscr{R}[\![r_m]\!] k_1 \ldots k_l)))$

$\mathscr{S}[\![\triangleleft(s_0\; t_1) \quad r_1 \ldots r_m \triangleright]\!]\; k_1 \ldots k_l = \mathscr{S}[\![s_0]\!]\; (\underline{\lambda}(x) (x\; \mathscr{T}[\![t_1]\!]\; (\mathscr{R}[\![r_1]\!] k_1 \ldots k_l) \ldots (\mathscr{R}[\![r_m]\!] k_1 \ldots k_l)))$

$\mathscr{S}[\![\triangleleft(s_0\; s_1) \quad r_1 \ldots r_m \triangleright]\!]\; k_1 \ldots k_l = \mathscr{S}[\![s_0]\!]\; (\underline{\lambda}(f) \mathscr{S}[\![s_1]\!]\; (\underline{\lambda}(x) (f\; x\; (\mathscr{R}[\![r_1]\!] k_1 \ldots k_l) \ldots (\mathscr{R}[\![r_m]\!] k_1 \ldots k_l))))$

If there exists a *lam* among $k_1 \ldots k_l$,

$\mathscr{S}[\![\triangleleft(e_0\; e_1) \quad r_1 \ldots r_m \triangleright]\!]\; k_1 \ldots k_l = ((\lambda\,(k_1 \ldots k_l) \mathscr{S}[\![\triangleleft(e_0\; e_1) \quad r_1 \ldots r_m \triangleright]\!]\; k_1 \ldots k_l) \quad k_1 \ldots k_l)$

If every k_i is a variable,

$\mathscr{S}[\![\triangleleft e \quad r_1 \ldots r_m \triangleright]\!]\; k_1 \ldots k_l = \mathscr{S}[\![e]\!]\; (\mathscr{R}[\![r_1]\!] k_1 \ldots k_l) \ldots (\mathscr{R}[\![r_m]\!] k_1 \ldots k_l)$

If there exists a *lam* among $k_1 \ldots k_l$,

$\mathscr{S}[\![\triangleleft e \quad r_1 \ldots r_m \triangleright]\!]\; k_1 \ldots k_l = ((\lambda\,(k_1 \ldots k_l) \mathscr{S}[\![e]\!]\; (\mathscr{R}[\![r_1]\!] k_1 \ldots k_l) \ldots (\mathscr{R}[\![r_m]\!] k_1 \ldots k_l)) \quad k_1 \ldots k_l)$

Figure 10. Transformation of λ_{MR} to Restricted CPS

We split the type-soundness proof in the progress and preservation theorems.

THEOREM 5 (Progress).
If $\Gamma \vdash e : \vec{\tau}$ *and e is closed then either e is a value, or e is of the form* $\triangleleft v \quad \#i\triangleright$ *where* $i > 1$*, or* $e \rightarrow e'$.

THEOREM 6 (Preservation).
If $\Gamma \vdash e : \vec{\tau}$ *and* $e \rightarrow e'$ *then* $\Gamma \vdash e' : \vec{\tau}'$ *where* $\vec{\tau}' \vec{\sqsubseteq} \vec{\tau}$.

Both proofs proceed by structural induction on e. In the progress theorem, note that a well-typed expression does not always reduce to a value. It might evaluate to a multi-return form that cannot take any steps. The proofs require the following lemmas.

LEMMA 7 (Weakening).
If $\Gamma[x \mapsto \tau] \vdash e : \vec{\tau}$ *and* $x \notin FV(e)$ *then* $\Gamma \vdash e : \vec{\tau}$.

LEMMA 8 (Substitution).
If $\Gamma[x \mapsto \tau] \vdash e : \vec{\tau}_1$, e' *is closed and has type* $\vdash e' : \vec{\tau}'$, *and* $\vec{\tau}' \vec{\sqsubseteq} \langle\tau\rangle$ *then* $\Gamma \vdash [e'/x]e : \vec{\tau}_2$ *such that* $\vec{\tau}_2 \vec{\sqsubseteq} \vec{\tau}_1$.

7.3 Transformation of λ_{MR} to RCPS

In this section, we describe a CPS transformation from λ_{MR} to RCPS (Fig. 10). Fisher and Shivers have shown that multi-return functions are cheap to implement and do not require novel compilation techniques. By translating λ_{MR} to RCPS, it becomes amenable to *Cage* Analysis which can further improve performance.

The transform relies on information provided by the type system to add the correct number of continuation parameters to *ulams*. We use standard techniques [3] to make the transform compositional and first-order. Last, some effort is spent on making sure that the transform does not duplicate code.

The transform uses three mutually recursive functions, for trivial terms, serious terms and return points. Variables and values are trivial terms and the rest are serious. The metavariables t and s range over trivial and serious terms respectively. Underlined lambdas $\underline{\lambda}$ generate fresh identifiers to avoid variable capture. We apply the transform to a λ_{MR} program e by calling $\mathscr{S}[\![e]\!]\mathit{halt}$.

The translation of variables and numbers is straightforward. When translating a *ulam*, we look at its type to find out how many continuations it takes in CPS.

A $\#i$ return point becomes a reference to the ith continuation of its context. A $(\lambda\,(x)\;e)$ return point becomes a *clam* in CPS. Here, there is possible code duplication that we want to avoid. Assume that one of $k_1 \ldots k_l$ is a *clam*. Then, if e refers to the corresponding return point more than once, this *clam* will be duplicated. For this reason, the rest of the rules call $\mathscr{R}$ with *cvar* arguments only.

If $\mathscr{S}$ is applied to a trivial term then we return the term to the first continuation.

Application is split in four cases depending on the operator and the operand. Note how the continuations $k_1 \ldots k_l$ are passed to all return points, which is why we require that they all be *cvars* to prevent duplication. If there is a *clam* among $k_1 \ldots k_l$ we create a new *ulam* and transform the application using the new *cvars*.[8]

For $\triangleleft e \quad r_1 \ldots r_m \triangleright$, we have to translate e in a context with m continuations. Here again we split in two cases to avoid duplication.

It is simple to see why our transformation generates RCPS code. The only place where a *ulam* is generated is the rule $\mathscr{T}[\![(\lambda\,(x)\;e)]\!]$, and we pass only the newly-created *cvars* to e.

The duplication of code is best seen in an example. Assume that we omit the rules that take care of *clams* in $k_1 \ldots k_l$. Then, all continuation arguments are treated the way variables are now treated. In the following transform, the return point $(\lambda\,(y)\;e')$ will be duplicated in the RCPS output:

$$
\begin{aligned}
&\mathscr{S}[\![\triangleleft\triangleleft((\lambda\,(x)\,e)\quad 42)\quad \#1\quad \#1\triangleright\quad (\lambda\,(y)\,e')\triangleright]\!]\;\mathit{halt}\\
=\;&\mathscr{S}[\![\triangleleft((\lambda\,(x)\,e)\quad 42)\quad \#1\quad \#1\triangleright]\!]\;(\lambda\,(y)\;\mathscr{S}[\![e']\!]\;\mathit{halt})\\
=\;&((\lambda\,(x\;k_1\;k_2)\;\mathscr{S}[\![e]\!]\;k_1\;k_2)\;\;42\\
&\qquad\qquad\qquad\qquad (\lambda\,(y)\;\mathscr{S}[\![e']\!]\;\mathit{halt})\\
&\qquad\qquad\qquad\qquad (\lambda\,(y)\;\mathscr{S}[\![e']\!]\;\mathit{halt})
\end{aligned}
$$

On the other hand, our transformation yields the more compact:

$$
\begin{aligned}
&((\lambda\,(k)\;((\lambda\,(x\;\;k_1\;\;k_2)\;\mathscr{S}[\![e]\!]k_1k_2)\;\;42\;\;k\;\;k))\\
&\;(\lambda\,(y)\;\mathscr{S}[\![e']\!]\mathit{halt}))
\end{aligned}
$$

8. Evaluation of *Cage*

We implemented *Cage* in Scheme48. Our compiler takes a multi-return Scheme program to RCPS, on which it runs *Cage*. It does not go all the way down to machine code. We measured the precision by counting the multiple-continuation call sites for which the analysis can find the youngest continuation statically. The results are encouraging, since the analysis is very precise, with little additional cost in running time and implementation effort over k-CFA.

Our analysis handles a purely functional subset of Scheme with numbers, booleans, lists, explicit recursion, and multi-return functions. We changed the front end of Scheme48 to accept a multi-return construct. After the front end takes care of parsing and macro-expansion, *every* call in the AST is represented as a multi-return call, *e.g.*, $(+\;1\;2)$ becomes $\triangleleft(+\;1\;2)\quad \#1\triangleright$. This makes the conversion to RCPS more uniform. The compiler then runs *Cage*, followed by a final linear pass that computes the results per call site (since ages in $\widehat{ce}$ are grouped by *ulam* labels). For instance, assume that, for the lambda expression `(`λ_l`(f k1 k2) (f '(1 2 3) k2 k1)`$^\gamma$`)`, *Cage* finds that `k1` is younger than `k2` in every total order contained in $\bigsqcup_{\hat{t} \in \widehat{Time}} \widehat{ce}(l, \hat{t})$. Then, the final pass will deduce that `k1` is always younger than `k2` at γ. Our current implementation spots the opportunity for optimization and stops. However, this information could be passed to a code-generation phase, which would avoid emitting code to check the ages of continuations at γ.

Fisher and Shivers suggested that LR-parsers can be compiled to λ_{MR}, with considerable speed gains [12]. Each state of the parser's automaton is represented as a function; a shift is a function call. Reductions do not return to a state function's immediate caller; but to points higher in the stack. This is handled with multiple return points to point to the necessary frames; a simple analysis determines how these return points represent the target reduction states. Such parsers contain an abundance of multi-continuation calls, which makes them attractive benchmarks for *Cage*.

We ran *Cage* (with $k = 0$) on a parser for a medium-sized, Pascal-like language. Out of the 973 calls to *ulams*, 152 pass two continuations and 32 pass three. If there is a *clam* argument, it is trivially the youngest continuation. This happens in 20 calls. The remaining 164 pass only *cvars*. *Cage* found the youngest continuation in 142, and in 22 calls it narrowed the youngest down to two choices instead of three. There was *no* call site for which the analysis failed to gain at least partial information. *Cage* amounts to 19.8% of the total running time of the abstract interpretation (the rest is spent on flow analysis), and 32.2% of the code size.

The effectiveness of the analysis is also illustrated by tail-recursive programs that can throw exceptions. The RCPS program of Fig. 11 sums all numbers in a list `l` and returns to `cc`, or throws an exception by calling `h` if it finds a non-number in `l`. It could have been written originally in any language with exceptions, or in a multi-return language. Placed in some code that computes the sum of a list of lists of numbers, this essentially becomes the inner

[8] This rule may appear to break compositionality at first glance, because the right hand side does not call $\mathscr{S}$ on a proper subexpression of the left hand side. However, it can be expanded to four rules as in the all-variable case, which is compositional. We use one rule only for readability.

```
(define (suml l acc cc h)
  ...
  (number? fst)
    (λ(test2)
      (%if test2
        (λ()
          (cdr l
            (λ(rest)
              (+ acc fst
                (λ(sum) (suml rest sum cc h))))))
        (λ() (h "not a number")))))
```

Figure 11. Tail recursion with exceptions

loop, so optimizing it is crucial. *Cage* statically figures out that the continuations in the recursive call have the same age.

In the following program, *Cage* fails to figure out the youngest continuation passed to λ_{l1} when k is 0. That is because in $l2$ the first continuation is the youngest, and in $l3$ the second. Similar examples can be written for any k:

```
((λ(f k) (%if some-test
            (λ() (f (λ(x) (k x)) k)^l2)
            (λ() (f k (λ(y) (k y)))^l3)))
 (λ(k1 k2) ...)^l1
 halt)
```

Overall, we are satisfied with the precision of *Cage*. It remains to be seen how useful it is in practice. More experience with multi-return code and multi-continuation CPS is needed to see if *cvar*-only call sites show up as often as in the programs presented here.

9. Related work

CPS was first formalized by Plotkin [8] and was used as an IR in Rabbit [14] and ORBIT [5], which were early and influential compilers for Scheme. Shivers used CPS to solve the control-flow problem in higher-order functional languages [11].

The starting point for the present work has been ΔCFA [6, 7]. ΔCFA is a static analysis that can reason about stack change in functional languages with first-class control. To date, ΔCFA has been primarily used to show environment equivalence and related optimizations, but it enables, in principle, many stack-related transformations. We use several elements of ΔCFA in this paper. First, we base our Restricted CPS on Partitioned CPS. More importantly, we use frame strings and the concrete semantics of ΔCFA to prove that continuation arguments of *ulams* are still on the stack.

Kennedy [4] proposed a variant of CPS which, like ORBIT, provides a variety of choices for procedures. He argues that CPS is preferable over ANF and monadic languages because function inlining does not require renormalization steps or the use of commuting conversions. Also, he advocates CPS as a suitable IR even in the absence of first-class control in the source language. Kennedy's CPS satisfies some syntactic restrictions similar to Restricted CPS. The main differences are that his CPS does not deal with first-class control and that user lambdas can take up to two continuation arguments, the current continuation and a handler continuation. If a *ulam* can throw many exceptions, the handler must be polymorphic; in RCPS we can pass as many continuations as needed.

There has been significant work done on efficient run-time implementations of first-class continuations, that is, continuations that outlive their dynamic extent and so require the stack to be saved in the heap [2]. Our work here, however, focusses on demonstrating the circumstances under which we may safely assume that continuations need not be copied, and on reasoning about the relationships between different continuations that are known to live on the stack.

10. Conclusions

In this paper, we show how a simple syntactic constraint on a CPS intermediate representation enables efficient use of the stack in the presence of multiple continuations. We prove that when we pass many continuations to a user function their environments are still on the stack. The generalization of the tail-call mechanism dictates that we pop to the most recent of these frames before control enters a user function.

We proceed to develop *Cage*, an analysis that finds the youngest frame at compile time in most cases. The main idea behind *Cage* is that inside a function $[\![(\lambda\,(u_1 \ldots u_m\ k_1 \ldots k_n)\ call)]\!]$ we only need to remember age information about $k_1 \ldots k_n$, we can *forget* which closures these variables are bound to. This decoupling between variables and bindings is possible because of Restricted CPS.

A prototype implementation of *Cage* in Scheme48 shows that it is a precise analysis with little extra overhead in compilation time over k-CFA. Therefore, control constructs that require passing many continuations, like exceptions and multi-return functions, can be compiled to fast native code.

Acknowledgements We would like to thank Mike Sperber for his help with Scheme48, David Fisher for insightful discussions on the control-polymorphic nature of λ_{MR} and the anonymous referees, whose helpful comments greatly improved this paper.

References

[1] A. Appel. *Compiling with Continuations.* Cambridge Univ. Press, 1992.

[2] W. Clinger, A. Hartheimer, and E. Ost. Implementation Strategies for First-Class Continuations. *Higher-Order and Symbolic Computation*, 12(1):7–45, 1999.

[3] O. Danvy and L. R. Nielsen. A first-order one-pass CPS transformation. *Theoretical Comp. Science*, 308(1-3):239–257, November 2003.

[4] A. Kennedy. Compiling with continuations, continued. In *International Conference on Functional Programming*, pages 177–190, 2007.

[5] D. Kranz. *ORBIT: An Optimizing Compiler for Scheme.* PhD thesis, Yale University Department of Computer Science, New Haven, Connecticut, February 1988.

[6] M. Might. *Environment Analysis of Higher-Order Languages.* PhD thesis, Georgia Institute of Technology, June 2007.

[7] M. Might and O. Shivers. Analyzing the environment structure of higher-order languages using frame strings. *Theoretical Computer Science*, 375(1–3):137–168, May 2007.

[8] G. Plotkin. Call-by-Name, Call-by-Value and the λ-Calculus. *Theoretical Computer Science*, 1:125–159, 1975.

[9] A. Sabry and M. Felleisen. Reasoning About Programs in Continuation-Passing Style. In *LISP and Functional Programming*, pages 288–298, 1992.

[10] M. Sharir and A. Pnueli. Two approaches to interprocedural data flow analysis. In Muchnick and Jones, editors, *Program Flow Analysis, Theory and Application*. Prentice Hall International, 1981.

[11] O. Shivers. *Control-Flow Analysis of Higher-Order Languages.* PhD thesis, Carnegie-Mellon University, May 1991.

[12] O. Shivers and D. Fisher. Multi-return function call. *Journal of Functional Programming*, 16(4):547–582, July/September 2006.

[13] O. Shivers and M. Might. Continuations and transducer composition. In *Prog. Language Design and Implementation*, pages 295–307, 2006.

[14] G. Steele. Rabbit: A compiler for Scheme. Technical Report 474, Massachusetts Institute of Technology, 1978.

[15] D. Van Horn and H. Mairson. Deciding k-CFA is complete for EXPTIME. In *International Conference on Functional Programming*, pages 275–282, 2008.

Partial Evaluation of the Reversible Language Janus

Torben Ægidius Mogensen
University of Copenhagen, Denmark
torbenm@diku.dk

Abstract

A reversible programming language is a programming language in which you can only write reversible programs, i.e., programs that can be run both forwards (computing outputs from inputs) and backwards (computing inputs from outputs). It is interesting to study reversible programs and languages because computations on reversible computers (computers that only allow reversible programs) in theory can be done using less energy than computations on traditional irreversible computers. Janus is a reversible, structured imperative programming language.

We present a partial evaluator for the full Janus language with the exception of procedure calls. The partial evaluator converts Janus programs into reversible flowcharts, specialises these using polyvariant specialisation and converts the result back to structured form. Reversibility adds some complications, which we address in the paper. We demonstrate the results by some small examples.

We believe this to be the first partial evaluator for a deterministic reversible programming language.

Categories and Subject Descriptors D.3.4 [*Programming languages*]: Processors—Optimization

General Terms Languages

Keywords Partial evaluation, Janus, Reversible computation

1. Introduction

Reversible computation [3, 4, 9, 14, 19] can theoretically be done using less energy than irreversible computation, as erasure of information necessarily dissipates energy in the form of thermodynamic entropy [14]. Most studies use low-level computational models such as reversible Turing machines [3, 18], but some studies use structured reversible programming languages[1, 16, 22–24].

Partial evaluation [11, 13] is a technique for generating specialised programs by fixing the value of some of the inputs to more general programs. The intent is that the specialised programs are more efficient than the originals, and this has often been observed in practise. Specialised programs perform fewer computations (and, hence, use less energy), so they can be of interest to further reduce energy consumption.

The partial evaluator presented in this paper handles all of the Janus language except procedure calls, which we address in a follow-up paper.

PEPM '11 January 24-25, Austin, Texas.

2. The reversible language Janus

Janus is a structured reversible programming language originally designed for a class at Caltech [16]. A Janus program starts with a declaration of variables divided into inputs, outputs and other variables. Variables are either integer variables or arrays of integers. The size of an array is either a constant number or given by a previously declared input variable. The main part of a Janus program is a list of parameter-less procedure declarations and a sequence of reversible statements that can use conditionals, loops and procedure calls. A special feature is that procedures can be run backwards by calling them with the keyword `uncall` instead of `call`. A grammar for Janus is shown in figure 1 and figure 2 shows a few examples of Janus programs:

(a) Fibonacci. This Janus program takes a number n and returns both the nth and the $(n+1)$th Fibonacci numbers.

(b) Multiplication. This program takes two odd numbers `a` and `b` and returns both their product and `b` (unchanged) as outputs. Running this in reverse divides the product by `b`.

(c) Postfix interpreter. This program reads a postfix expression (represented as an array of numbers) and an array of input values and then outputs the expression and its result. Outputting the expression with the result is required for reversibility. Evaluation uses two stacks: An evaluation stack `stack` and a stack `garbage` that is used to ensure reversibility. Uncalling `calc` undoes the stack operations, so the stacks are, again, empty.

2.1 Informal semantics of Janus

We will only describe Janus informally and refer to [22] for a formal semantics.

Variables and array elements that are not inputs are initialised to 0 and variables and array elements that are not outputs are verified to be 0 when the program ends. A variable or array can be both input and output. Statements can take the following forms:

Update. The left-hand side of an update is either an integer variable or an element of an array. The update can either add or subtract the value of the right-hand side to this. The right-hand side can be any expression that does *not* contain the variable or array used on the left-hand side and if the left-hand side is an array element, the array can not be used in the expression specifying the index into the array. For example, the update `a[a[i]] += 1` is not legal. These restrictions ensures that the update can be reversed. Expressions can use the operators +, - and /2.

Swap. A statement of the form lv_1 `<=>` lv_2 swaps the contents of lv_1 and lv_2, which can be integer variables or array elements. It is possible to swap two elements of the same array, but the index expression of an array can contain none of the arrays or integer variables used in the swap statement. For example, while `a[i] <=> a[j]` is legal, `a[i] <=> i` is not. Again, the restriction is required for reversibility.

Prog	→	*Dec** `->` *Dec** (`with` *Dec**)? ; *Stat* *Proc**
Dec	→	**id**
Dec	→	**id** [**size**]
Stat	→	*Lval* `+=` *Exp*
Stat	→	*Lval* `-=` *Exp*
Stat	→	*Lval* `<=>` *Lval*
Stat	→	*Stat* ; *Stat*
Stat	→	`skip`
Stat	→	`if` *Cond* `then` *Stat* `else` *Stat* `fi` *Cond*
Stat	→	`from` *Cond* `do` *Stat* `loop` *Stat* `until` *Cond*
Stat	→	`call` **id**
Stat	→	`uncall` **id**
Lval	→	**id**
Lval	→	**id** [*Exp*]
Exp	→	**num**
Exp	→	*Lval*
Exp	→	*Exp* + *Exp*
Exp	→	*Exp* - *Exp*
Exp	→	*Exp* /2
Exp	→	(*Exp*)
Cond	→	*Exp* < *Exp*
Cond	→	*Exp* == *Exp*
Cond	→	`odd`(*Exp*)
Cond	→	! *Cond*
Cond	→	*Cond* `&&` *Cond*
Cond	→	*Cond* || *Cond*
Cond	→	(*Cond*)
Proc	→	`procedure` **id** *Stat*

Figure 1. Syntax of Janus

Sequence. Statements separated by ; are executed in sequence.

Skip. No effect.

Conditional. A statement of the form `if` c_1 `then` s_1 `else` s_2 `fi` c_2 is executed by first evaluating c_1. If this is true, s_1 is executed and it is verified that c_2 is true. If c_1 is false, s_2 is executed and it is verified that c_2 is false. If the exit-assertion c_2 does not have the expected value, the program stops with an error message. A condition can compare numbers for equality (==), inequality (<) and test if a number is odd. Conditions can be combined by conjunction, disjunction and negation. The construction can be illustrated by the flowchart in figure 3(a), where a two-entry assertion is shown as a circle with two entry arrows marked with the expected truth value.

Loop. A statement of the form `from` c_1 `do` s_1 `loop` s_2 `until` c_2 is executed by first evaluating the assertion c_1. If this is false, the program stops with an error message, otherwise s_1 is executed and the c_2 is evaluated. If this is true, the loop terminates. Otherwise, s_2 is executed and c_1 is evaluated (again). If c_1 is true, the program stops with an error message, otherwise the loop repeats from s_1. The construction can be illustrated with the flowchart in figure 3(b).

Procedure call. A procedure call is either of the form `call` *p* or `uncall` *p*, where *p* is a procedure name. `call` *p* executes the body of *p* and returns to the place of the call. `uncall` *p* executes the body of *p in reverse* and then returns to the place of the call. The sequence `call` *p*; `uncall` *p* has no net effect, as `uncall` *p* will undo all the state changes done by `call` *p*.

Note that a Janus program can either terminate normally, fail or be nonterminating. We regard all failures as equivalent, i.e., we do not differentiate between failing an assertion in a loop or conditional or failing due to a non-zero non-output variable.

```
n -> a b;

a += 0; b += 1;
from a==0 do
  n -= 1; a <=> b; b += a
loop skip
until n==0
```

(a) Fibonacci

```
a b -> b prod with t v;

from 0==prod do
  if odd(a) then
    prod += b; t += a/2;
    a -= t+1; t -= a
  else
    t += a/2; a -= t; t -= a
  fi !(prod<b)
loop
  v += b; b += v; v -= b/2
until a==0;

from prod<b+b do
  v += b/2; b -= v; v -= b
loop skip
until odd(b)
```

(b) Multiplication

```
     sz exp[sz] i ins[i]
->   sz exp[sz] i ins[i] result
with pc sp stack[sz] gp garbage[sz];

call calc;
result += stack[0];
uncall calc

procedure calc
from pc==0 do
  if exp[pc]==0 then
    stack[sp] += exp[pc+1];
    sp += 1
  else
    if exp[pc]==1 then
      stack[sp] += ins[exp[pc+1]]; sp += 1
    else // exp[pc]==2
      sp -= 1; garbage[gp] <=> stack[sp];
      if exp[pc+1]==0 then
        stack[sp-1] += garbage[gp]
      else
        stack[sp-1] -= garbage[gp]
      fi exp[pc+1]==0;
      gp += 1
    fi exp[pc]==1
  fi exp[pc]==0;
  pc += 2
loop skip
until pc==sz
```

(c) Postfix interpreter

Figure 2. Janus programs

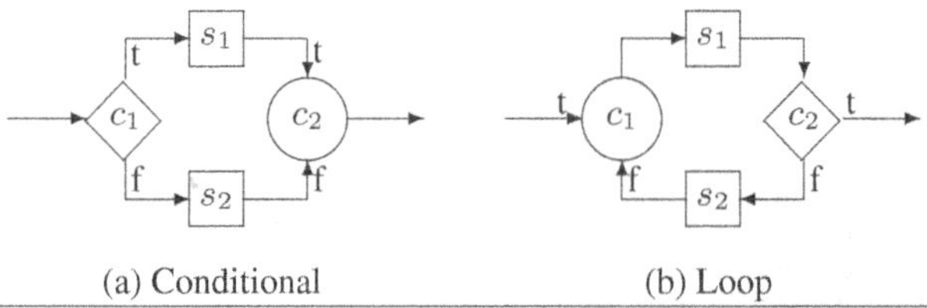

(a) Conditional (b) Loop

Figure 3. Flowchart diagrams for conditional and loop

2.2 Reverse execution

Statements can be executed both forwards and backwards (when a procedure is called with `uncall`). Backwards execution can be realised by syntactically reversing the statement and then executing it forwards. A program can be reversed by swapping input and output variables and reversing the body statement. The function R below shows how statements can be reversed.

$$
\begin{array}{rcl}
R(lv \texttt{ += } e) & = & lv \texttt{ -= } e \\
R(lv \texttt{ -= } e) & = & lv \texttt{ += } e \\
R(lv_1 \texttt{ <=> } lv_2) & = & lv_1 \texttt{ <=> } lv_2 \\
R(s_1;\ s_2) & = & R(s_2);\ R(s_1) \\
R(\texttt{call}\ p) & = & \texttt{uncall}\ p \\
R(\texttt{uncall}\ p) & = & \texttt{call}\ p \\
R(\texttt{skip}) & = & \texttt{skip}
\end{array}
$$

$$
\begin{array}{l}
R(\texttt{if}\ c_1\ \texttt{then}\ s_1\ \texttt{else}\ s_2\ \texttt{fi}\ c_2) \\
= \texttt{if}\ c_2\ \texttt{then}\ R(s_1)\ \texttt{else}\ R(s_2)\ \texttt{fi}\ c_1
\end{array}
$$

$$
\begin{array}{l}
R(\texttt{from}\ c_1\ \texttt{do}\ s_1\ \texttt{loop}\ s_2\ \texttt{until}\ c_2) \\
= \texttt{from}\ c_2\ \texttt{do}\ R(s_1)\ \texttt{loop}\ R(s_2)\ \texttt{until}\ c_1
\end{array}
$$

3. Partial evaluation

Partial evaluation has been studied for many languages. Good overviews can be found in [13] and [11].

Briefly stated, partial evaluation is about producing residual programs. If a program p takes two inputs and a r takes one input, r is a residual program of p with respect to a value s if, for any value d, running p with s and d as inputs yields the same result as running r with d as input. I.e., either both terminate and produce the same result, both fail with an error or both are nonterminating. A partial evaluator is a program that given (representations of) a program p and a value s can produce (a representation of) a program r that is residual to p with respect to s. Often, the definition of a partial evaluator is relaxed, so it is allowed to be nonterminating for some p and s. In this relaxed definition, the always nonterminating program is a partial evaluator, just not a very useful one.

These definitions generalise to cases where p has more inputs.

We will focus on *offline* partial evaluation: Inputs are classified in advance as known (static) or unknown (dynamic), and it is determined which parts of the program depend only on the static inputs and which parts may depend on the remaining (dynamic) inputs. When values for the static inputs are given, this classification is used to determine which parts of the program can be executed during specialisation and which parts must be included in specialised form in the residual program. Thus, the specialisation process is divided into the following steps:

1. Classify input variables as static (to be specialised away) or dynamic (to remain in the residual program).
2. Given the input classification, automatically classify all parts of the program as static or dynamic. This is called a *binding-time analysis*. Input variables that in step 1 were classified as static may be reclassified as dynamic. The binding-time analysis can ensure that all residual programs obey certain properties. We will use it to ensure that residual programs are reversible.
3. Given the full program classification and the values of the inputs classified as static, produce the specialised (residual) program by executing the static parts and copying instances of the dynamic parts into the residual program. The dynamic parts of the program may contain static values as constants, so the residual program can contain several copies of the same dynamic program part with different static values as constants. This phase is called *specialisation*.

The residual program can now be run with the remaining (dynamic) input values and will produce the same result as running the original program with all inputs. You can run the residual program repeatedly with different dynamic input values.

As an example of offline specialisation, consider the multiplication program shown in figure 2(b). We might want to specialise the program with the value 11 for `a` to get a one-input program that takes `b` and returns `b` and the product of 11 and `b`.

In this example, all outputs depend on the dynamic input and are, hence, outputs of the residual program. But in other programs there can be outputs that only depend on static inputs. If we follow the usual definition of a residual program, the residual program must return *all* outputs of the original program, including outputs that don't depend on the dynamic inputs and are, hence, the same every time. We will relax this requirement, so the partial evaluator will return both a residual program and the values of the outputs that depend only on static inputs, i.e., the static outputs. The residual program will, then, only return the outputs that depend on dynamic inputs, i.e., the dynamic outputs. The reason for this relaxation is that reversibility often requires a Janus program to return parts of its input along with the "interesting" output. For example, an interpreter written in Janus usually returns both the interpreted program and the result of running it. If we specialise the interpreter to a program, we don't want the residual program to return this program as part of its output. Hence, we define the following correctness criterion for offline partial evaluation for Janus:

Given a a program p and an initial classification of inputs as static or dynamic, the binding-time analysis must produce an annotated program where inputs and outputs are classified as static or dynamic. Some variables that were initially classified as static may now be classified as dynamic.

When, given the annotated program and values s of the static inputs, specialisation terminates with static output s' and a residual program r, the following must hold:

- If running p with inputs s and d terminates with outputs o, the part of o that was classified as static must have the value s' and if the part of the output that was classified as dynamic has the value d', then running r with d as input must terminate and return d' as output.
- If running p with inputs s and d stops with a failed assertion or does not terminate, running r with d as input must do the same.

These requirements can easily be fulfilled either by the binding-time analysis classifying all inputs and outputs as dynamic and let $r = p$ or by making the specialiser not produce any output. While we characterise such behaviours as correct, they are not desirable. But they are not always possible to avoid: Consider a program with one input and one output. It is undecidable if the program will terminate without failure, so if we classify the output as static we risk nontermination or failure during specialisation. So to ensure termination, we must reclassify the output as dynamic, which may unnecessarily postpone computations until the residual program is executed. Analyses can determine if specialisation of a given program is guaranteed to terminate [6, 10, 12], but since this is undecidable, such analyses must necessarily be imprecise. We will not address this issue further in this paper but simply allow specialisation to sometimes not terminate.

4. Polyvariant partial evaluation

The standard approach to partial evaluation of imperative languages is polyvariant partial evaluation [5, 11, 13]. Polyvariant partial evaluation allows the same portion of the original program to be specialised to multiple different static states. This can completely change the structure of the program, so unless severe restrictions are imposed, it works best with programs that use unstructured control, i.e., programs that consist of basic blocks that each start with a label and end with a (possibly conditional) jump.

In polyvariant specialisation of basic blocks, the label of a basic block and the values of the static variables (the static state) are combined to make a new residual label. The statements in the basic block are then specialised with respect to this static state and a new static state is obtained. The jump at the end of the basic block is specialised in the following way:

- An unconditional jump to l is made into a residual jump to a residual label made by combining l with the static state.
- A jump with a static condition is made into a residual unconditional jump to a residual label made by combining the selected label with the static state.
- A jump with a dynamic condition is made into a residual conditional jump by specialising the condition to the static state and making two residual labels by combining the original labels with the static state.

If there are not already specialised basic blocks for the residual labels constructed above, these are now produced. When there are specialised basic blocks for all residual labels, the residual program is complete. It is possible that this process will not terminate.

4.1 Translation into flowchart form

A reversible flowchart language similar to Janus is described in [24]. We will convert the body of a Janus program and all the procedure bodies into lists of basic blocks. Each basic block consists of three parts: An entry point, a body and a jump. An entry point can be one of the following:

- `start`, that indicates the block where execution starts.
- A named label.
- A two-entry assertion consisting of a condition c and two named labels l_1 and l_2. This is written as `if` c `from` l_1 l_2. The condition c must be true if the basic block is entered by a jump to l_1 and false if the basic block is entered by a jump to l_2.

No label nor `start` can occur more than once in the entry points of all the basic blocks. The body of a basic block is either empty or any statement that does not contain structured control statements (conditionals and loops). The jump can be:

- `return`, that indicates the end of the program or procedure.
- An unconditional jump `goto` l.
- A conditional jump consisting of a condition c and two named labels l_1 and l_2. This is written as `if` c `goto` l_1 l_2. If c is true, the jump goes to l_1, otherwise to l_2.

No label nor `return` can occur more than once in the jumps of all the basic blocks. A basic block e: s; j, where e is an entry point, s a statement and j a jump is reversed into $R(j)$: $R(s)$; $R(e)$, where R is the statement-reversing function shown in section 2.2 extended to handle entry points and jumps:

$$\begin{array}{rclrcl} R(\texttt{start}) & = & \texttt{return} & R(\texttt{return}) & = & \texttt{start} \\ R(l) & = & \texttt{goto}\, l & R(\texttt{goto}\, l) & = & l \\ \multicolumn{3}{r}{R(\texttt{if}\ c\ \texttt{from}\ l_1\ l_2) \ =} & \multicolumn{3}{l}{\texttt{if}\ c\ \texttt{goto}\ l_1\ l_2} \\ \multicolumn{3}{r}{R(\texttt{if}\ c\ \texttt{goto}\ l_1\ l_2) \ =} & \multicolumn{3}{l}{\texttt{if}\ c\ \texttt{from}\ l_1\ l_2} \end{array}$$

A structured program is translated by first making the body statements of the program and procedures into single basic blocks by adding the entry point `start` and the jump `return`. These basic

```
a b  -> b prod with t v ;

start:
goto f_2

if 0==prod from f_2 a_2:
if odd(a) goto t1_3 e1_3

t1_3:
prod += b; t += a/2; a -= t+1; t -= a
goto t2_3

e1_3:
t += a/2; a -= t; t -= a
goto e2_3

if !(prod<b) from t2_3 e2_3:
if a==0 goto f_11 l_2

l_2:
v += b; b += v; v -= b/2
goto a_2

if prod<b+b from f_11 a_11:
v += b/2; b -= v; v -= b
if odd(b) goto u_11 a_11

u_11:
return
```

Figure 4. Multiplication program as flowchart

blocks may contain structured statements, so we translate them using the function T that translates a basic block that may contain structured statements into a set of basic blocks that do not:

$$T(e:\ s;\ j) = \{e:\ s;\ j\} \quad \text{if } s \text{ does not contain structured statements}$$

$$T(e:\ s_1;\ \ s_2;\ j) = T(e:\ s_1;\ \texttt{goto}\ l) \cup T(l:\ s_2\ j) \quad \text{where } l \text{ is a new label}$$

$$\begin{aligned} T(e:\ &\texttt{if}\ c_1\ \texttt{then}\ s_1\ \texttt{else}\ s_2\ \texttt{fi}\ c_2;\ j) = \\ &\{e:\ \texttt{if}\ c_1\ \texttt{goto}\ l_1\ l_2\} \\ &\cup T(l_1:\ s_1;\ \texttt{goto}\ l_3) \cup T(l_2:\ s_2;\ \texttt{goto}\ l_4) \\ &\cup \{\texttt{if}\ c_2\ \texttt{from}\ l_3\ l_4\texttt{:}\ j\} \\ &\text{where } l_1,\ l_2,\ l_3 \text{ and } l_4 \text{ are new labels} \end{aligned}$$

$$\begin{aligned} T(e:\ &\texttt{from}\ c_1\ \texttt{do}\ s_1\ \texttt{loop}\ s_2\ \texttt{until}\ c_2;\ j) = \\ &\{e:\ \texttt{goto}\ l_1\} \\ &\cup T(\texttt{if}\ c_1\ \texttt{from}\ l_1\ l_2\texttt{:}\ s_1\texttt{;}\ \texttt{if}\ c_2\ \texttt{goto}\ l_3\ l_4) \\ &\cup T(l_4:\ s_2;\ \texttt{goto}\ l_2) \cup \{l_3:\ j\} \\ &\text{where } l_1,\ l_2,\ l_3 \text{ and } l_4 \text{ are new labels} \end{aligned}$$

After the translation, there can be trivial basic blocks of the form $(l_1 : \texttt{goto}\ l_2)$. We can eliminate such a block by making the jump to l_1 jump to l_2 instead. The program in figure 2(b) is translated into the flowchart program in figure 4.

4.2 Binding-time analysis

We will, in this paper, not handle procedure calls, so we assume that the body of a basic block is a sequence of updates and swaps. For simplicity, we use one global binding time for each variable. so binding time analysis is fairly straightforward:

1. A statement, expression or condition that contains a dynamic variable is dynamic.
2. If an update statement is dynamic, then the variable or array element on the left-hand side is dynamic.
3. If a swap statement is dynamic, the variables or array elements on both sides are dynamic.
4. If one element of an array is dynamic, all elements of the array are dynamic.

```
a ~b  -> ~b ~prod  with t ~v ;

start:
~goto f_2

~if ^0~=prod from f_2 a_2:
if odd(a) goto t1_3 e1_3

t1_3:
prod ~+= b~; t += a/2; a -= t+1; t -= a
~goto t2_3

e1_3:
t += a/2; a -= t; t -= a
~goto e2_3

~if ~!(prod~<b) from t2_3 e2_3:
if a==0 goto f_11 l_2

l_2:
v ~+= b~;~ b ~+= v~;~ v ~-= b~/2
~goto a_2

~if prod~<b~+b from f_11 a_11:
v ~+= b~/2~;~ b ~-= v~;~ v ~-= b
~if ~odd(b) goto u_11 a_11

~u_11:
return
```

Figure 5. Annotated multiplication program

5. An array indexed by a dynamic index expression is dynamic.
6. An `if-goto` or `if-from` with dynamic condition is dynamic.
7. A label used in a dynamic `if-goto` or `if-from` is dynamic.
8. An `if-from` with a dynamic label is dynamic.
9. An unconditional jump to a dynamic label is dynamic.
10. `start` and `return` are dynamic.
11. Static subexpressions of dynamic expressions or conditions are enclosed in "lift" operators that indicate that the static values will be inserted as constants during specialisation.

Note that there are three cases for arrays: A fully static array has static elements and is always indexed using static index expressions. A dynamic array has dynamic element values and is always indexed by dynamic index expressions (if not, a lift operator is used to make it so). But we may also have arrays that are statically indexed but contains dynamic element values. We explain specialisation of these in section 4.5

We start binding-time analysis from an initial classification of the input variables as static or dynamic and everything else as static. We then iterate applying the rules above until no changes occur.

We will later need to add extra rules to ensure reversibility of residual programs, but we need to describe the specialisation process first to identify the issues.

The multiplication program shown in figure 4 with `a` classified as static and `b` as dynamic results in the binding-time-annotated program shown in figure 5. A ~ indicates a dynamic declaration or operation and ^ is the lift operator.

4.3 Specialisation of flowchart programs

As mentioned in section 4, the basic idea is to create specialised basic blocks by combining labels with static state and specialising the statements of the basic block according to the static state (and updating the static state when static variables are changed). Additionally, static jumps can be unfolded. We use the following rules for specialisation:

- Static statements are executed to update the static state.
- Dynamic statements are made into residual statements by evaluating static subexpressions and inserting their values as constants in place of the expressions.
- `start` is specialised to `start`.
- An unconditional dynamic label is specialised by combining it with the static state to construct a new residual label. This is done by hashing the static state to a number and adding this number as a suffix to the label.
- A dynamic `if-from` is specialised into a residual `if-from` consisting of a residual condition and two residual labels constructed like above.
- Static labels and assertions are targets of static jumps, so we describe their treatment there.
- `return` is specialised to `return`. It is verified that all static variables that are not output variables have the value zero. If not, an error message is issued.
- An unconditional dynamic jump is specialised by combining its label with the static state to construct a new residual label, as described above for entry points. The specialised label is used to make a residual unconditional jump. If there is not already a specialised basic block for the specialised label, one is made.
- A dynamic `if-goto` is specialised into a residual `if-goto` consisting of a residual condition and two residual labels constructed like above. If there are not already specialised basic blocks for the specialised labels, these are made.
- An static unconditional jump is specialised by finding the basic block that has this label in its entry point. If the target basic block has an unconditional label as entry, the jump is unfolded by specialising the body of the target basic block and adding it to the body of the specialised basic block that contains the static jump and then specialising the jump of the target basic block. If the target basic block has a two-way assertion as entry, this will be static (by rules 8 and 9 of the binding-time analysis), so its condition will be evaluated and checked. If the assertion fails, an error is reported. Otherwise, the jump is unfolded in the same way a jump to an unconditional label is unfolded.
- A static `if-goto` is specialised by first evaluating the condition and selecting the label that corresponds to the result. It is then unfolded like an unconditional static or dynamic jump to this label, depending on whether the label is static or dynamic.

Specialisation starts by reading the values of the static input variables and setting the static state accordingly. Then the block with the `start` entry point is specialised with this state. This may trigger specialisation of more basic blocks with different static states. If this eventually terminates, there will be residual basic blocks for all residual jumps.

4.4 Making the residual program reversible

It is not hard to see that residual statements are reversible, but it is not clear that jumps and entry points are reversible. We will look at the requirements from section 4.1 in turn:

1. There must be exactly one entry point of the form `start`.

   There can be no jumps to `start`, so only one residual basic block can have the `start` entry point. So this property is preserved.

2. There must be exactly one jump of the form `return`.

   If the basic block that contains the `return` jump is specialised to two or more different static states, creating two or more residual basic blocks, there will be two or more `return` jumps in the residual program. So we need to remedy this.

3. Each named label must occur in exactly one entry point.

   When we make a residual jump to a specialised label, we check if a specialised basic block for this label already exists, so we will not produce multiple basic blocks with the same label. Also, if no specialised basic block exists for a residual jump, we will make one. Hence, each residual label will occur in exactly one entry point.

4. Each named label must occur in exactly one jump.

   This requirement forbids two situations: **No jumps to a label:** This may, actually happen: When we specialise a dynamic two-way assertion, we produce two residual labels even though we have seen only a residual jump to one of these. We may eventually see a jump to the other label, but there is no guarantee of this. So we may end up with a two-way assertion that has a jump to only one of its labels. **Two jumps to the same label:** This might occur if a basic block is specialised to two different static states but the updates to static variables make the static states at the end of these basic blocks identical. But since all static updates and swaps are reversible and a basic block is just a sequence of updates and swaps, this can not happen: Identical static end-states imply identical static start states.

Hence, we have two problems to fix: There may be several `return` jumps, and there may be a two-way assertion that has a jump to only one of its labels.

Multiple `return` jumps can occur only if the basic block containing the original `return` jump is specialised to several different static states. Since a basic block is reversible, this implies that there are several possible static states at the `return` jump itself, i.e., at the end of the program execution. So if we can ensure that there is only one possible static state at the end of program execution, we can avoid multiple `return` jumps.

All variables and array elements that are not part of the program output must, according to the Janus semantics, be 0 at the end of program execution. So for these, there is only one possible state at the end of execution. Output variables and arrays can, however, potentially have several possible values at the end program execution. If a static output variable or array can have several possible values, we get multiple specialised `return` jumps.

We avoid this by classifying all output variables that are modified anywhere in the program as dynamic, so no static output variables are ever updated. Static output variables will, hence, have the same value throughout execution.

It is common in partial evaluation to classify *all* outputs as dynamic, so even severe restrictions on static outputs is a relaxation compared to the usual case.

The issue of having a two-way entry with a jump to only one of its labels is not so easy to solve. The obvious solution would be to reduce the two-way assertion to an unconditional label, hence eliminating the label to which there is no jump. However, this will also eliminate the assertion, which may be required to preserve semantics (otherwise we might replace a failing execution by successful termination or nontermination). Another solution is to add a jump to the label that has none. This can be done in the following way: A residual basic block of the form `if` c `from` l_1 l_2`:` s`;` j where there is a jump only to l_1 is replaced by the two basic blocks l_1`: if true goto` l_3 l_2 and `if` c `from` l_3 l_2`:` s`;` j where l_3 is a new label. The case where there is a jump only to l_2 is handled in a symmetric way.

Introducing extra jumps may make residual programs slower than the original programs, so to avoid this we extend the Janus language with statements of the form `assert` c (with the obvious semantics). If there is a jump only to l_1, we replace the basic block `if` c `from` l_1 l_2`:` s`;` j by the basic block l_1`: assert` c`;` s`;` j. If there is a jump only to l_2, we replace `if` c `from` l_1 l_2`:` s`;` j with l_2`: assert !`c`;` s`;` j.

```
b  -> b prod with v ;

start:
assert 0==prod; prod += b;
assert !(prod<b); v += b; b += v; v -= b/2;
assert !(0==prod); prod += b;
assert !(prod<b); v += b; b += v; v -= b/2;
assert !(0==prod);
assert prod<b; v += b; b += v; v -= b/2;
assert !(0==prod); prod += b;
assert !(prod<b)
goto f_11_92636

if prod<b+b from f_11_92636 a_11_92636:
v += b/2; b -= v; v -= b
if odd(b) goto u_11_92636 a_11_92636

u_11_92636:
return
```

Figure 6. Specialised multiplication program

The statement `assert` c reverses to itself and it is simple to specialise: It is classified as static if the condition is static, and a dynamic `assert` it is made into a residual `assert` by replacing the static subexpressions of c by constants.

We can eliminate unconditional jumps to unconditional labels by unfolding the jumps: The basic blocks e`:` s_1`; goto` l and l`:` s_2`;` j are combined to the single basic block e`:` s_1`;` s_2`;` j.

The program in figure 5 can be specialised to `a=11` to yield the residual program shown in figure 6. Note that some two-way assertions have been converted to one-way assertion statements and unconditional jumps to unconditional labels have been eliminated.

4.5 Partially static arrays

We specialise a array `a` of size n with dynamic elements and static indices into n integer variables named `a_0` ... `a_`m where $m = n-1$. The l-value `a[`e`]` is specialised by evaluating the static expression e to the value i and returning the residual l-value `a_`i.

This technique is an instance of partially static data structures [17] and is well known from, e.g., C-mix as described in section 11.4.1 of [13]. It is useful for, among other things, specialising interpreters where a single array is used to hold the values of individual variables in the interpreted program. By splitting the array into scalar variables, the variables of the interpreted program become individual variables in the residual program obtained by specialising the interpreter to the interpreted program. For example, the arrays `ins[i]`, `stack[sz]` and `garbage[sz]` in the postfix interpreter in figure 2(c) will be partially static.

5. Recovering structured control

The residual program shown in figure 6 is not a Janus program, as it uses unstructured control where Janus uses structured control statements. In [24] it is shown that any reversible flowchart can be translated into a program that uses only the reversible control structures shown in section 2. The translation works by first numbering all labels from 1 to $n-1$. A flowchart program

in `->` *outs* `with` *others*`;` *blocks*

is translated into the structured program

in `->` *outs* `with` *others* `control;`
`from control==0 do` $S(blocks)$
`loop skip until control==`n`;`
`control -=` n

```
a -> b;

start: goto x

if b==0 from x y
a -= 1; b += 1
if a==0 goto z y

z: return
```

(a) Simple flowchart program

```
a -> b with control;

from control==0 do
  if control==0 then
    control+=1
  else
    if control==1 || control==2 then
      if control==1 then skip else control-=1 fi b==0;
      a -= 1; b += 1;
      if a==0 then control+=2 else control+=1 fi control==3
    else
      control+=1
    fi control==2 || control==3
  fi control==1
loop skip
until control==4;
control-=4
```

(b) Structured with `control` variable

```
a -> b;

from b==0
  a -= 1; b += 1
loop skip
until a==0
```

(c) Natural structure

Figure 7. Two ways of structuring a flowchart program

where S takes a set of basic blocks and returns a statement:

$$
\begin{array}{lll}
S(\emptyset) & = \texttt{skip} & \\
S(\{e\colon s;\ j\} \cup B) & = E\ s;\ C\ \texttt{else}\ S(B)\ \texttt{fi}\ J & \\
 & \quad \text{where} \quad (E,\ l) \ = \ S_E(e) & \\
 & \quad \phantom{\text{where}} \quad (C,\ J) \ = \ S_J(j,\ l) & \\
\\
S_E(\texttt{start}) & = (\texttt{if control==0 then},\ 0) & \\
S_E(l) & = (\texttt{if control==}l\ \texttt{then},\ l) & \\
S_E(\texttt{if}\ c\ \texttt{from}\ l_1\ l_2) & = (\texttt{if control==}l_1\ \texttt{||}\ \texttt{control==}l_2\ \texttt{then} & \\
 & \quad \texttt{if control==}l_1\ \texttt{then skip} & \\
 & \quad \texttt{else control += }l_1\texttt{-}l_2\ \texttt{fi}\ c;\ , & \\
 & \quad l_1) & \\
\\
S_J(\texttt{return},\ l) & = (\texttt{control += }n\texttt{-}l,\ \texttt{control==}n) & \\
S_J(\texttt{goto}\ l_1,\ l) & = (\texttt{control += }l_1\texttt{-}l,\ \texttt{control==}l_2) & \\
S_J(\texttt{if}\ c\ \texttt{goto}\ l_1\ l_2,\ l) & = (\texttt{if}\ c\ \texttt{then control += }l_1\texttt{-}l & \\
 & \quad \texttt{else control += }l_2\texttt{-}l & \\
 & \quad \texttt{fi control==}l_1\ , & \\
 & \quad \texttt{control==}l_1\ \texttt{||}\ \texttt{control==}l_2) &
\end{array}
$$

As an example, the flowchart program in figure 7(a) is translated into the structured program in figure 7(b). This structure is, however, not natural and the addition of the extra `control` variable and the branching on this adds overhead. The flowchart program shown in figure 7(a) has a much simpler and more efficient structured equivalent shown in figure 7(c)

Ideally, we would like to have a translation that can find a structured program such that the sequences of variable updates and tests made by the structured program is the same as the sequence made by the flowchart program when both are executed with the same inputs. Intuitively, this means that no overhead is introduced by structuring the program.

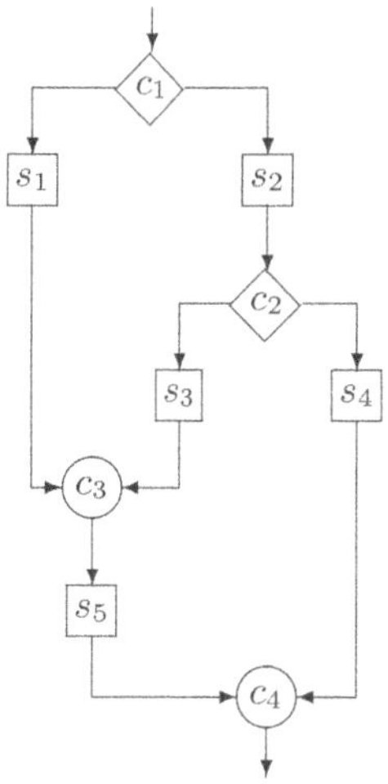

Figure 8. Unstructured flowchart

There has (in the context of decompilation) been some work on recovering structured control from flowcharts [2, 7, 8, 21], but this has been done in a non-reversible setting. To our knowledge, there is no similar work on recovering reversible control.

It has been shown [2] that general control flow can not always be translated into structured control without adding extra variable updates, but again, this result is for general, irreversible control. Since reversible flowcharts are quite restricted compared to general flowcharts, it is not obvious that the result carries over: Unrestricted flowcharts that can not be structured might not be realisable as reversible flowcharts. We will, however, below show a similar result for reversible programs.

We first define evaluation equivalence of flowchart programs.

DEFINITION 1. *Two reversible flowchart programs are evaluation equivalent if they both execute the same sequence of tests and state modifiers when run on the same inputs. We only consider terminating executions, so the sequences are finite. A state modifier is an update or swap. A test is a condition in an* `assert` *statement, a conditional jump or a two-way entry point. If a condition* c *evaluates to false, it is shown as* $\overline{c}$ *in the sequence. We consider* $\overline{c}$ *equivalent to* `!`c *and* $\overline{!c}$ *equivalent to* c*, so it is possible to swap the two branches of a conditional jump.*

A structured program is deemed to be evaluation equivalent to the flowchart program obtained by the translation shown in section 4.1 and, by transitivity, to all flowchart programs evaluation equivalent to this.

The proof in [2] that not all control flow can be made structured shows that a specific unstructured control-flow graph has no structured evaluation equivalent program (using a somewhat different notion of evaluation equivalence).

Consider the reversible flowchart in figure 8. The true exits/entries of conditional jumps and entry-points are to the left. There are three possible paths through this flowchart:

$$
\begin{array}{rl}
1: & c_1,\ s_1,\ c_3,\ s_5,\ c_4 \\
2: & \overline{c_1},\ s_2,\ c_2,\ s_3,\ \overline{c_3},\ s_5,\ c_4 \\
3: & \overline{c_1},\ s_2,\ \overline{c_2},\ s_4,\ \overline{c_4}
\end{array}
$$

Let us see which structured programs can realise the above sequences.

Since all sequences start with c_1 or $\overline{c_1}$, c_1 must be the initial condition of an `if-then-else-fi` construct: An `assert` statement or the entry condition of a loop might have both outcomes, but would terminate execution after one of these. An `if-then-else-fi` construct must have a closing condition (assertion). The only condition (apart from c_1) that occurs in all the above sequences is c_4, so this must be it. So, the structured program must be of the form `if` c_1 `then` T `else` E `fi` c_4, though with the possibility that one or both of c_1 and c_4 is negated. We can without loss of generality assume that c_1 is not negated (we could swap the branches if it was), so E must be able to realise the rest of sequence 1. It ends in c_4, so the exit assertion must be c_4 (without negation). Sequence 2 and 3 start with $\overline{c_1}$, so they both go to the false branch. They, however, end with different values for the c_4 condition, which contradicts the assumption that they are in the same branch of the conditional.

So if we can find actual conditions and statements such that all three sequences can be realised, we have an example of a flowchart that has no structured evaluation equivalent using the control structures of Janus. If we use the following instances of the tests and conditions:

c_1	=	`a == 0`	s_1	=	`a += 1`
c_2	=	`a == 0`	s_2	=	`a -= 1`
c_3	=	`a == 1`	s_3	=	`a += 2`
c_4	=	`a < 2`	s_4	=	`a += 2`
			s_5	=	`a -= 1`

then sequence 1 is followed when `a` is 1 initially, sequence 2 is followed when `a` is 2 initially and sequence 3 is followed when `a` is 3 initially. Hence, we have a flowchart that is not evaluation equivalent to any structured program.

The above is just one example of a flowchart that has no evaluation equivalent structured program.

So we may sometimes need to introduce extra state modifiers or tests when re-structuring residual programs. But we want to avoid this whenever we can.

We use a restructuring methods based on recognising subsets of basic blocks that correspond to structured statements and then replace these subsets by basic blocks that use structured statements.

The following rules do this for 17 different patterns of basic blocks. We apply these until no rule applies to the remaining set of basic blocks.

1. If the set of basic blocks contains two blocks:
   (e: s_1; `goto` l)
   (l: s_2; j)
   combine these to the single basic block
   (e: s_1; s_2; j)
2. If the set of basic blocks contains four blocks:
   (e: s_1; `if` c_1 `goto` l_1 l_2)
   (l_1: s_2; `goto` l_3)
   (l_2: s_3; `goto` l_4)
   (`if` c_2 `from` l_3 l_4: s_4; j)
   combine these into the single basic block
   (e: s_1; `if` c_1 `then` s_2; `else` s_3; `fi` c_2; s_4; j)
3. If the set of basic blocks contains three blocks
   (e: s_1; `if` c_1 `goto` l_1 l_2)
   (l_1: s_2; `goto` l_3)
   (`if` c_2 `from` l_3 l_2: s_3; j)
   combine these into a single basic block
   (e: s_1; `if` c_1 `then` s_2; `else skip fi` c_2; s_3; j)
4. If the set of basic blocks contains three blocks
   (e: s_1; `if` c_1 `goto` l_1 l_2)
   (l_2: s_2; `goto` l_3)
   (`if` c_2 `from` l_1 l_3: s_3; j)
   combine these into a single basic block
   (e: s_1; `if` c_1 `then skip else` s_2; `fi` c_2; s_3; j)
5. If the set of basic blocks contains two blocks
   (e: s_1; `if` c_1 `goto` l_1 l_2)
   (`if` c_2 `from` l_1 l_2: s_2; j)
   combine these into a single basic block
   (e: s_1; `if` c_1 `then skip else skip fi` c_2; s_2; j)
6. If the set of basic blocks contains four blocks
   (e: s_1; `if` c_1 `goto` l_1 l_2)
   (l_1: s_2; `goto` l_3)
   (l_2: s_3; `goto` l_4)
   (`if` c_2 `from` l_4 l_3: s_4; j)
   combine these into a single basic block
   (e: s_1; `if` c_1 `then` s_2; `else` s_3; `fi !`c_2; s_4; j)
7. If the set of basic blocks contains three blocks
   (e: s_1; `if` c_1 `goto` l_1 l_2)
   (l_1: s_2; `goto` l_3)
   (`if` c_2 `from` l_2 l_3: s_3; j)
   combine these into a single basic block
   (e: s_1; `if` c_1 `then` s_2; `else skip fi !`c_2; s_3; j)
8. If the set of basic blocks contains three blocks
   (e: s_1; `if` c_1 `goto` l_1 l_2)
   (l_2: s_2; `goto` l_3)
   (`if` c_2 `from` l_3 l_1: s_3; j)
   combine these into a single basic block
   (e: s_1; `if` c_1 `then skip else` s_2; `fi !`c_2; s_3; j)
9. If the set of basic blocks contains two blocks
   (e: s_1; `if` c_1 `goto` l_1 l_2)
   (`if` c_2 `from` l_2 l_1: s_2; j)
   combine these into a single basic block
   (e: s_1; `if` c_1 `then skip else skip fi !`c_2; s_2; j)
10. If the set of basic blocks contains two blocks
    (`if` c_1 `from` l_1 l_2: s_1; `if` c_2 `goto` l_3 l_4)
    (l_4: s_2;`goto` l_2)
    combine these into a single basic block
    (l_1: `from` c_1 `do` s_1 `loop` s_2 `until` c_2; `goto` l_3)
11. If the set of basic blocks contains a block
    (`if` c_1 `from` l_1 l_2: s; `if` c_2 `goto` l_3 l_2)
    replace this by the basic block
    (l_1: `from` c_1 `do` s `loop skip until` c_2; `goto` l_3)
12. If the set of basic blocks contains two blocks
    (`if` c_1 `from` l_1 l_2: s_1;`if` c_2 `goto` l_4 l_3)
    (l_4: s_2;`goto` l_2)
    combine these into a single basic block
    (l_1: `from` c_1 `do` s_1 `loop` s_2 `until !`c_2; `goto` l_3)
13. If the set of basic blocks contains a block
    (`if` c_1 `from` l_1 l_2: s; `if` c_2 `goto` l_2 l_3)
    replace this by the basic block
    (l_1: `from` c_1 `do` s `loop skip until !`c_2; `goto` l_3)
14. If the set of basic blocks contains two blocks
    (`if` c_1 `from` l_2 l_1: s_1; `if` c_2 `goto` l_3 l_4)
    (l_4: s_2;`goto` l_2)

```
b  -> b prod with v ;

assert 0==prod; prod += b;
assert !(prod<b); v += b; b += v; v -= b/2;
assert !(0==prod); prod += b;
assert !(prod<b); v += b; b += v; v -= b/2;
assert !(0==prod);
assert prod<b; v += b; b += v; v -= b/2;
assert !(0==prod); prod += b;
assert !(prod<b);
from prod<b+b do
  v += b/2; b -= v; v -= b
loop
  skip
until odd(b)
```

Figure 9. Restructured specialised multiplication program

combine these into a single basic block

(l_1: `from !`c_1 `do` s_1 `loop` s_2 `until` c_2; `goto` l_3)

15. If the set of basic blocks contains a block

    (`if` c_1 `from` $l_2\,l_1$: s; `if` c_2 `goto` $l_3\,l_2$)

    replace this by the basic block

    (l_1: `from !`c_1 `do` s `loop skip until` c_2; `goto` l_3)

16. If the set of basic blocks contains two blocks

    (`if` c_1 `from` $l_2\,l_1$: s_1; `if` c_2 `goto` $l_4\,l_3$)
    (l_4: s_2;`goto` l_2)

    combine these into a single basic block

    (l_1: `from !`c_1 `do` s_1 `loop` s_2 `until !`c_2; `goto` l_3)

17. If the set of basic blocks contains a block

    (`if` c_1 `from` $l_2\,l_1$: s; `if` c_2 `goto` $l_2\,l_3$)

    replace this by the basic block

    (l_1: `from !`c_1 `do` s `loop skip until !`c_2; `goto` l_3)

The important rules are 1, 2 and 10, which are essentially inverses of the translation from section 4.1. The remaining rules are special cases where one branch of a conditional or part of a loop is empty or where labels in `if-goto` or `if-from` are swapped (so conditions need to be negated).

It is easy to see that these rules preserve (strong) evaluation equivalence. Since we negate some conditions, we need the equivalence of c and $\overline{!c}$ and of $!c$ and $\bar{c}$ that we allowed in the definition of evaluation equivalence.

The reversibility requirement actually makes some things simpler than in the irreversible case, as we know that there can not be multiple jumps to the same label. In the irreversible case we would, for example, need a side condition to rule 1 saying that there are no other jumps to l. Also, since there are exactly two occurrences of each label, it is easy to verify that the rules do not overlap, so they can be applied in any order.

If application of the rules reduces the set of basic blocks to a single basic block (`start`: s; `return`), we have a single structured Janus statement s. If not, we can either declare failure to structure the program or add the extra `control` variable as described above. Currently, we admit failure and return a partially unstructured program, as our (extended) Janus compiler allows programs to mix structured and unstructured control. This is easy enough to change if we need to use an unextended Janus compiler.

As an example, figure 9 shows a restructured version of the residual program in figure 6. Also, if we translate any of the programs in figure 2 into flowchart form and restructure the result, we get the original structure back.

Program	Source lines	Flowchart lines	Residual lines
fib	9	12	33
multiply	23	30	28
encrypt	15	23	171
postfix	46	74	16
control	17	39	6
dfa	26	29	48

Program	Original steps	Residual steps
fib	147	95
multiply	160	108
encrypt	442	354
postfix	998	70
control	558	145
dfa	510	216

Figure 10. Size and speed

5.1 Replacing jumps by procedure calls

In [8], it is suggested that unstructured control that can not be reduced to structured control without adding variables can instead be replaced by mutually recursive procedure calls. The idea is that a tail call is very much like an unstructured `goto`. The method replaces every remaining basic block with a procedure and all remaining jumps by tail calls to these procedures. This works well because basic blocks in irreversible languages are headed by unconditional labels (that translate easily into procedure names) and both unconditional and conditional jumps can be translated into tail calls. In our reversible flowchart language, we have two issues not present in irreversible languages:

1. Basic blocks can be headed by two-way assertions.
2. In Janus, the branches of an `if-then-else-fi` are not in tail-call position, even if the whole conditional statement is. This is because the `fi`-condition needs to be tested after the chosen branch completes.

Two-way assertions are not difficult to handle: We just make two procedures that each test the condition (positively and negatively) and call a procedure for the common body. But we can not translate `if` c `goto` $l_1\,l_2$ into `if` c `then call` p_1 `else call` p_2 `fi` c' because there might be no suitable condition c', and even if there is, there is no obvious way to find it.

Hence, we believe that it is not workable to translate unstructured control flow into tail-recursive procedure calls.

6. Experiments

We have implemented (in Standard ML) a partial evaluator using the methods described in this paper.

We have used the partial evaluator to specialise a few Janus programs. For each of these, the table in figure 10 shows the number of non-blank lines in the original Janus program, the flowchart form of the program and the residual program.

`fib` is the program from figure 2(a). It is specialised to `n`=10, so the residual program is run without inputs. `encrypt` is a simple encryption program. The program is specialised to the key (which is used both for encryption and decryption). During specialisation, a loop is unrolled, so the residual program is quite large. `postfix` is the program from figure 2(c) with the procedure calls manually unfolded (as the specialiser doesn't handle procedure calls yet). `postfix` uses a partially static array for the input values, so the residual program has individual variables for these. The stacks are also partially static, so the stack elements become individual variables. The interpreter is specialised with respect to a postfix expression with two inputs and five operations. `control` is the program from figure 7(b). This is specialised with no static inputs, but the `control` variable is static. The residual program is identical to the program in figure 7(c). The difference in running time show the overhead of structuring a program using a `control` variable. `dfa` is an interpreter for reversible DFAs. It is specialised to a DFA that recognises bit strings that are divisible by 3. The restructurer was not able to restructure the residual program, so the numbers for the residual program are for the flowchart form.

We compile Janus programs to MIPS code that is run on the simulator MARS [20]. Figure 10 show the instruction counts of the original and residual programs. As usual with partial evaluation, the most dramatic speedups are found when specialising interpreters.

7. Conclusion and future work

We have made a partial evaluator for the reversible language Janus with the exception of procedure calls. It is to our knowledge the first partial evaluator for a deterministic reversible programming language.[1]

Polyvariant program-point specialisation can be applied to Janus, but the reversibility requirement added some complications, which we have solved.

The residual programs produced by the specialiser use unstructured control flow where Janus uses structured control flow, so we have devised a method to restructure residual programs from flowchart form to using the reversible control structures of Janus. This is not always possible to do without introducing extra variables. Currently, the specialiser will return partially unstructured programs in such cases, but it is easy to add an extra pass to structure these using a `control` variable. Since this adds overhead and our Janus compiler can handle unstructured programs, we have not done so.

We have in this paper not handled procedure calls. It is, as such, not difficult to specialise procedure calls: Procedures must, like the program, have a single `return` jump. For the program, we ensured this by disallowing modification of static output variables, so there is only one possible static state at program end (all non-output variables are zero at program end). There is no requirement that variables are zero at the end of a procedure, so to ensure that there is only one possible static state at procedure end, the equivalent solution is to disallow modification of `all` static variables inside a procedure. This means that a procedure call can not change static state, which makes specialisation easy. The restriction against modifying static state makes this of limited use, though. We will look at better ways of handling procedure calls in a future paper.

References

[1] S. Abramsky. A structural approach to reversible computation. Manuscript, Oxford University Computing Laboratory, 2001.

[2] E. A. Ashcroft and Z. Manna. The translation of "go to" programs to "while" programs. Technical report, Stanford University, Stanford, CA, USA, 1971.

[3] C. H. Bennett. Time/space trade-offs for reversible computation. *SIAM Journal on Computing*, 18(4):766–776, 1989.

[4] H. Buhrman, J. Tromp, and P. Vitányi. Time and space bounds for reversible simulation. In F. Orejas, P. G. Spirakis, and J. van Leeuwen, editors, *Automata, Languages and Programming. Proceedings*, LNCS 2076, pages 1017–1027. Springer-Verlag, 2001.

[5] M. A. Bulyonkov. Polyvariant mixed computation for analyzer programs. *Acta Informatica*, 21:473–484, 1984.

[1] Pure logic languages can be considered reversible and partial evaluators for such exist [15].

[6] N. H. Christensen, R. Glück, and S. Laursen. Binding-time analysis in partial evaluation: one size does not fit all. In D. Bjørner, M. Broy, and A. V. Zamulin, editors, *Perspectives of System Informatics. Proceedings*, LNCS 1755, pages 80–92. Springer-Verlag, 2000.

[7] C. Cifuentes. Reverse compilation techniques. PhD thesis, Queensland University of Technology, http://www.itee.uq.edu.au/~cristina/dcc.html#thesis, 1994.

[8] C. Cifuentes. Structuring decompiled graphs. In *Proceedings of the International Conference on Compiler Construction*, pages 91–105. Springer Verlag, 1996.

[9] R. P. Feynman. *Feynman Lectures on Computation*, chapter 5 Reversible computation and the thermodynamics of computing, pages 137–184. Addison-Wesley, 1996.

[10] A. J. Glenstrup and N. D. Jones. BTA algorithms to ensure termination of off-line partial evaluation. In D. Bjørner, M. Broy, and I. V. Pottosin, editors, *Perspectives of System Informatics. Proceedings*, LNCS 1181, pages 273–284. Springer-Verlag, 1996.

[11] J. Hatcliff, T. Æ. Mogensen, and P. Thiemann, editors. *Partial Evaluation. Practice and Theory*. LNCS 1706. Springer-Verlag, Berlin, Heidelberg, New York, 1999.

[12] N. D. Jones and A. Glenstrup. Program generation, termination, and binding-time analysis. In D. Batory, C. Consel, and W. Taha, editors, *Generative Programming and Component Engineering. Proceedings*, LNCS 2487, pages 1–31. Springer-Verlag, 2002.

[13] N. D. Jones, C. K. Gomard, and P. Sestoft. *Partial Evaluation and Automatic Program Generation*. Prentice-Hall, 1993.

[14] R. Landauer. Irreversibility and heat generation in the computing process. *IBM Journal of Research and Development*, 5(3):183–191, 1961.

[15] M. Leuschel. Logic program specialisation. In *Partial Evaluation - Practice and Theory, DIKU 1998 International Summer School*, pages 155–188, London, UK, 1999. Springer-Verlag. ISBN 3-540-66710-5.

[16] C. Lutz. Janus: a time-reversible language. A letter to Landauer. http://www.cise.ufl.edu/~mpf/rc/janus.html, 1986.

[17] T. Æ. Mogensen. Partially static structures in a self-applicable partial evaluator. In D. Bjørner, A. P. Ershov, and N. D. Jones, editors, *Partial Evaluation and Mixed Computation*, pages 325–347. North-Holland, 1988.

[18] K. Morita, A. Shirasaki, and Y. Gono. A 1-tape 2-symbol reversible turing machine. *IEICE Transactions*, E72(3):223–228, 1989.

[19] T. Toffoli. Reversible computing. In J. W. de Bakker and J. van Leeuwen, editors, *Automata, Languages and Programming*, volume 85 of *Lecture Notes in Computer Science*, pages 632–644. Springer-Verlag, 1980.

[20] K. Vollmar and P. Sanderson. MARS: An education-oriented MIPS assembly language simulator. *ACM SIGCSE Bulletin*, 38(1):239–243, 2006.

[21] M. H. Williams. Generating structured flow diagrams: the nature of unstructuredness. *Computer Journal*, 20(1):45–50, 1977. doi: 10.1093/comjnl/20.1.45.

[22] T. Yokoyama and R. Glück. A reversible programming language and its invertible self-interpreter. In *PEPM '07: Proceedings of the 2007 ACM SIGPLAN symposium on Partial evaluation and semantics-based program manipulation*, pages 144–153, New York, NY, USA, 2007. ACM. ISBN 978-1-59593-620-2. doi: http://doi.acm.org/10.1145/1244381.1244404.

[23] T. Yokoyama, H. B. Axelsen, and R. Glück. Principles of a reversible programming language. In *Proceedings of the 5th conference on Computing frontiers*, CF '08, pages 43–54, New York, NY, USA, 2008. ACM. ISBN 978-1-60558-077-7. doi: http://doi.acm.org/10.1145/1366230.1366239.

[24] T. Yokoyama, H. B. Axelsen, and R. Glück. Reversible flowchart languages and the structured reversible program theorem. In A. L. et al., editor, *Automata, Languages and Programming (ICALP)*, LNCS 5126, pages 258–270. Springer-Verlag, 2008. doi: 10.1007/978-3-540-70583-3-22.

Taming Code Explosion in Supercompilation

Peter A. Jonsson Johan Nordlander
Luleå University of Technology
{pj, nordland}@csee.ltu.se

Abstract

Supercompilation algorithms can perform great optimizations but sometimes suffer from the problem of code explosion. This results in huge binaries which might hurt the performance on a modern processor. We present a supercompilation algorithm that is fast enough to speculatively supercompile expressions and discard the result if it turned out bad. This allows us to supercompile large parts of the imaginary and spectral parts of nofib in a matter of seconds while keeping the binary size increase below 5%.

Categories and Subject Descriptors D.3.4 [*Programming Languages*]: Processors – Compilers, Optimization; D.3.2 [*Programming Languages*]: Language Classifications – Applicative (functional) languages

General Terms Algorithms, Performance

Keywords supercompilation, deforestation, Haskell

1. Introduction

Supercompilation is an automatic program transformation that subsumes several program transformations which are available in production compilers [29]. It is well known that the transformation is correct [22] and terminates [25]. We also know that supercompilation gives remarkable optimization results on small examples: a textbook example of word counting in Haskell performs better than a low level implementation written in C [16].

Given these accomplishments, why does not your favorite compiler include a supercompiler? The two main problems are scalability of the supercompiler and the risk for code explosion. Existing implementations of supercompilers trade compilation time against great optimization and do not take the resulting program size into account. Closer investigation reveals that it is the test for non-termination, the homeomorphic embedding, that takes up to 50% of the transformation time [16]. We suggest sacrificing some optimization in exchange for faster compilation by revising the design of the supercompilation algorithm.

The faster algorithm allows us to control code explosion by speculatively supercompile expressions and discard bad results. Even incredibly cheap and simple tests can get a long way towards the goal: a surprising discovery is that comparing the number of syntactic nodes of the resulting expression with a well-chosen constant is a remarkably accurate predictor of "bad optimizations" that should be discarded. Except this size threshold our measurements use a simple comparison of the size of the resulting expression versus the number of reduction steps performed by the supercompiler.

The performance of our algorithm rests on two important design choices:

Term Representation: We represent terms as zippers [4] during the transformation, which gives efficient and convenient implementations of tests for non-termination and splitting of terms. As a side effect this representation also makes it easy to reduce the number of terms to test for non-termination: only test against those terms who have the same head as the current term.

Term Size in Focus: By decreasing the size of the term that our supercompiler focuses on we can effectively decrease the cost of testing for non-termination. This shows in our compilation times: they are less than 3 seconds on a modern desktop computer for all the small examples from the nofib suite [18].

Our design allows us to supercompile most programs from the spectral part of nofib in less than three seconds. Some of these programs are 10 times larger than previously supercompiled Haskell programs. We do not believe that an ordinary programmer will turn on the supercompiler for his development builds, but it is certainly reasonable to do so for testing and nightly builds.

Our contributions are:

- A mechanism that is parametric with respect to a metric that allows us to control code explosion (Section 3.2 and Section 4.6).
- A practical supercompilation algorithm (Section 4)
- Measurements on the imaginary and spectral parts of nofib (Section 5).
- Implementation tricks to speed up the actual implementation (Section 6).

2. Language

Our language of study is a higher-order functional language with let-bindings, case-expressions and primitive values. Its syntax for expressions, values and patterns is shown in Figure 1.

Let F range over a set $\mathcal{F}$ of global function definitions, where all functions have a specific arity and contain no free variables. This is not a severe restriction on the programmer since the input can be lambda lifted [5].

The language contains integer values n and arithmetic operations $\oplus$, although these meta-variables can preferably be understood as ranging over primitive values in general and arbitrary operations on these. We let $+$ denote the semantic meaning of $\oplus$.

A list of expressions $e_1 \ldots e_n$ is abbreviated as $\overline{e}$, and a list of variables $x_1 \ldots x_n$ as $\overline{x}$.

We denote the free variables of an expression e by $fv(e)$ and a program is an expression with no free variables and all function

PEPM'11, January 24–25, 2011, Austin, Texas, USA.

Expressions

$$\begin{array}{lcl} e & ::= & n \mid x \mid F \mid K \mid e\,e' \mid \lambda x.e \mid e \oplus e' \\ & \mid & \texttt{case}\, e\, \texttt{of}\, \{p_i \to e_i\} \mid \texttt{let}\, x = e\, \texttt{in}\, e' \end{array}$$

$$p \quad ::= \quad n \mid K\,\overline{x}$$

Weak Head Normal Form

$$w \quad ::= \quad n \mid \lambda x.e \mid K\,\overline{e}$$

Figure 1. The language

Reduction contexts

$$\mathcal{E} \quad ::= \quad \Box \mid \mathcal{E}\,e \mid \mathcal{E} \oplus e \mid n \oplus \mathcal{E} \mid \texttt{case}\ \mathcal{E}\ \texttt{of}\ \{p_i \to e_i\}$$

Evaluation relation

$$\begin{array}{llr} [F]\mathcal{E} & \mapsto [e]\mathcal{E}, \text{if } F \stackrel{\text{def}}{=} e & \text{(Global)} \\ [(\lambda x.e)\,e']\mathcal{E} & \mapsto [[e'/x]e]\mathcal{E} & \text{(Beta)} \\ [\texttt{let}\, x = e\, \texttt{in}\, e']\mathcal{E} & \mapsto [[e/x]e']\mathcal{E} & \text{(Let)} \\ [\texttt{case}\, K\,\overline{e}\, \texttt{of}\, \{K_i\,\overline{x}_i \to e_i\}]\mathcal{E} & \mapsto [[\overline{e}/\overline{x}_j]e_j]\mathcal{E} & \text{(KCase)} \\ & \quad \text{if } K = K_j & \\ [\texttt{case}\, n\, \texttt{of}\, \{n_i \to e_i\}]\mathcal{E} & \mapsto [e_j]\mathcal{E}, \text{if } n = n_j & \text{(NCase)} \\ [n_1 \oplus n_2]\mathcal{E} & \mapsto [n]\mathcal{E}, \text{if } n = n_1 + n_2 & \text{(Arith)} \end{array}$$

Figure 2. Reduction semantics

names defined in $\mathcal{F}$. The operational semantics is call-by-name as defined in Figure 2. Capture free substitution expressions $\overline{e}$ for variables $\overline{x}$ in e' is denoted by $[\overline{e}/\overline{x}]e'$.

A reduction context $\mathcal{E}$ is a term containing a single hole $\Box$, which indicates the next expression to be reduced. The expression $[e]\mathcal{E}$ is the term obtained by replacing the hole in $\mathcal{E}$ with e.

3. Design Choices

This section describes a number of important design choices and how they contribute to our goal of making a practical supercompiler for program optimization.

Our guiding principle has been simple: sacrifice optimization opportunities if it significantly improves the performance or simplifies the implementation of the supercompiler. Our only concern is soundness of the supercompiler, we do not have to worry about completeness properties that could be important in theorem proving or similar domains. We therefore design a positive supercompiler, but these choices should be straightforward to transfer to other more powerful supercompilers.

There is some overlap between what problem each design choice helps to protect against.

Code Explosion The primary mechanism to tame code explosion is described in Section 3.2. Section 3.1, Section 3.3, and Section 3.4 contain design choices that help reduce the code size.

Compiler Performance Avoiding code explosion helps compilation performance, but this is not enough: Section 3.5 contains a mechanism to avoid performing work that is unlikely to give any benefit.

We have also made a lot of minor non-controversial design choices in our supercompiler which we describe in Section 3.6.

3.1 Boring Contexts

There are sometimes function calls that have no static information in their argument, making it impossible to improve them by supercompiling them in their context. By using a simple approximation of such function calls we save compilation time and avoid creating specializations that do not improve the performance. We say that such functions are in a boring context. A boring expression is an expression of the form:

$$b ::= x \mid b\,b \mid n \oplus b \mid b \oplus n \mid b \oplus b$$

A context $\mathcal{R}$ is defined as boring iff $\mathcal{R} = \epsilon$ or $\mathcal{R} = \Box\ b : \mathcal{R}'$ and $\mathcal{R}'$ is boring.

3.2 Discarding Expressions

The initial function call to reverse with an accumulating parameter, *reverse xs* [], is an example that will pass the test for boring expressions since the second argument is a known constructor. Despite this there is not much the supercompiler can do with this expression and the end result will be a new function with one unfolding of reverse and a second function that is isomorphic to reverse.

Designing an algorithm that approximates what the result and how much savings were achieved from supercompiling an arbitrary expression is difficult. We can completely avoid to solve this problem by speculatively supercompile the expression, have the supercompiler keep track of the reduction steps taken, and look at the output of the supercompiler. If the number of reduction steps taken is small or the code size is deemed too large we discard the supercompiled expression and supercompile the subexpressions of the current expression instead.

3.3 Normalization of Expressions

We perform a simple normalization of expressions, as specified in Section 4.5, before comparing them for folding possibilities. This makes the supercompiler significantly faster. The big win is the removal of identity coercions in expressions, which makes the memoization list a lot shorter.

3.4 Sharing New Function Definitions

It is quite common for the case of case-rule to fire. A typical case looks something like this:

$$\begin{array}{l} \textbf{case}\ (\ \textbf{case}\ x\ \textbf{of} \\ \qquad\qquad p_1 \to x_1 \\ \qquad\qquad \ldots \\ \qquad\qquad p_n \to x_n)\ \textbf{of} \\ \quad [] \to [] \\ \quad (x' : xs') \to \mathit{append}\ xs'\ zs \end{array}$$

Once the case of case-rule is done the code is:

$$\begin{array}{l} \textbf{case}\ x\ \textbf{of} \\ \quad p_1 \to \textbf{case}\ x_1\ \textbf{of} \\ \qquad\qquad [] \to [] \\ \qquad\qquad (x' : xs') \to \mathit{append}\ xs'\ zs \\ \quad \ldots \\ \quad p_n \to \textbf{case}\ x_n\ \textbf{of} \\ \qquad\qquad [] \to [] \\ \qquad\qquad (x' : xs') \to \mathit{append}\ xs'\ zs \end{array}$$

The driving algorithm will transform the call to append twice, and create two functions that are both isomorphic to append. Creating the functions at the top level and calling the same function from both branches saves both transformation work and reduces code size.

Using a state monad for the driving algorithm, and have that monad store a memoization list augmented with the function definitions will allow the second branch to just insert a call to this new function created in the first branch, thereby saving a lot of transformation effort.

However, if we fold too eagerly this will miss out on specialization opportunities and this will make the final program perform worse than necessary. An example is $append\ (append\ xs\ ys)\ zs$, which when transformed will create a function isomorphic to append itself in the first branch. After the supercompiler has transformed the second branch it will find a recursive call to $append\ (append\ xs'\ ys)\ zs$, which can fold against both the call in the first branch, $append\ ys\ zs$, and the initial call that the transformation started from. If the former is chosen no fusion will occur.

We therefore only look for renamings, not instances, when trying to fold against things stored in the monad. If there exists a specialised version of our current function the algorithm will use that, and otherwise it will create a new specialised copy. Our algorithm will only generalize expressions against their ancestors, never across branches of case-expressions.

3.5 Tainting Functions

If the same function, regardless of context, is supercompiled in different parts of the program and the result is discarded more than a certain number of times we make the unfolding for the function unavailable. This prevents future attempts of specializing the function. The concrete mechanism is that we add a special triple on the form $(*,\ \emptyset,\ F)$ to the store each time we discard a result from supercompiling a function F in some context, and the number of such triples in the store is checked for before inlining a function.

One might ask whether innocent functions will be tainted when trying to supercompile complex expressions, for example $id\ e$ where e is an expression that will be discarded after supercompilation, which will prevent other callsites from benefiting of supercompilation. Since the supercompiled e is discarded the supercompiler will compare e and $id\ e$ with the extra information that the transformation has saved one beta-reduction. Whether this is a worthwhile saving is a question of balancing the acceptable-predicate.

We used being discarded 3 times as threshold for our measurements.

3.6 Miscellaneous Design Choices

When supercompiling a function call $const\ x\ y$ our supercompiler blindly emits a call to a fresh function $h\ x\ y$ whose body is defined as $(\lambda x\ y.x)\ x\ y$. It is safe to directly inline the body of $const$ at the call-site but we can increase the code sharing by allowing the supercompiler to fold against this definition from other parts of the program.

If it turns out that there is only one call to h in the entire supercompiled program the ordinary simplifier of the compiler will inline it.

The reason we use evaluation contexts in our algorithm is that there is a chance that good things can happen in the interaction between evaluation contexts and an expression in the hole. There are no such possibilities with an arbitrary context that has the hole outside the focus for evaluation.

4. Supercompilation

This section contains the definition of our supercompilation algorithm and its dependencies.

4.1 Preliminaries

We replace our nested evaluation context $\mathcal{E}$ with a list of shallow reduction contexts for our supercompiler as defined in Figure 3. It will turn out to be convenient for the implementation to pattern match on the context if it is a list of single level contexts. We let $\overline{\Box\ e}$ denote a list of application contexts.

If a variable appears no more than once in an expression, that expression is said to be *linear* with respect to that variable. Like Wadler [31], we extend the definition slightly for linear case ex-

The outer context:

$$\mathcal{R} ::= \epsilon \mid \mathcal{G} : \mathcal{R}$$

Each frame:

$$\mathcal{G} ::= \Box\, e \mid \Box \oplus e \mid n' \oplus \Box \mid \texttt{case}\ \Box\ \texttt{of}\ \{p_i \rightarrow e_i\}$$

Memoization element:

$$\nu ::= (h, \overline{x}, [F]\mathcal{R})$$

Memoization list and store:

$$\rho \ ::= \ \epsilon \mid \nu : \rho$$
$$\sigma \ ::= \ \epsilon \mid (\nu, e') : \sigma$$

Figure 3. Context definition

pressions: no variable may appear in both the selector and a branch, although a variable may appear in more than one branch.

4.2 Algorithm Definition

Our supercompiler is defined as two mutually recursive functions that pattern-match on expressions and contexts in order to rewrite expressions. The first algorithm is called the *driving* algorithm, used to perform evaluation steps, and the second algorithm is called the *building* algorithm, which reassembles the transformed expression. These algorithms are defined in Figure 4. Both algorithms take five parameters: 1) an expression; 2) a memoization list ρ; 3) the context $\mathcal{R}$; 4) the store σ; and 5) the savings from the supercompiler so far. New function definitions are put in the store. The memoization list holds information about expressions already traversed and is used to guarantee termination. A notational convention is to use e' to denote expressions that are already transformed.

There is an ordering between rules; i.e., all rules must be tried in the order they appear. Rules R11-R13 are the default focusing rules that extend the given driving context $\mathcal{R}$ and zoom in on the next expression to be transformed. If no other rule matches, such as for a single variable, rule R14 will match and call build to rebuild the expression.

The program is turned "inside-out" by moving the surrounding context $\mathcal{R}$ into all branches of the case-expression through rules R19 and R20. Rule R10 has a similar mechanism for let-expressions. Rule R9 is only allowed to match if the variable y is not freshly generated by the splitting mechanism described in the Section 4.4. This side condition ensures that the expression splitting and reassembly performed by $\mathcal{D}_{app}(\,)$ will not cause arbitrary code and work duplication.

Rules R3 and R4 refer to $\mathcal{D}_{app}(\,)$ and $\mathcal{D}_{varapp}(\,)$, both defined in Figure 5. They can both be inlined in the definition of the driving algorithm, they are merely given a separate name for improved clarity of the presentation.

The fifth parameter to the supercompiler, the savings, is there to track how many reduction steps the supercompiler has performed. This is currently represented as a tree in our implementation to aid us in the design of when to discard expressions, but a production compiler should use a more efficient representation. We assign the value 1 to ordinary evaluation steps in rules R1, R2, R6, R8, R9 and R10. Rule R5, the case reduction with a known constructor, is assigned the value 5 since it both decreases code size and removes a memory allocation.

We need some more arithmetic operations on our savings beyond plain addition: # indicates that a saving was under a lambda, ? combines branches of savings such as in rule R10 and max of all savings in rules R19 and R20. The most important saving, folding, is denoted by the exclamation mark (!). These abstract savings need to be interpreted to a concrete number in order to make deci-

General form:

$\mathcal{D}[\![e]\!]\,\rho\,\mathcal{R}\,\sigma\,s = (e', \sigma', s')$

Evaluation Rules

$$\mathcal{D}[\![n_j]\!]\,\rho\,(\texttt{case}\ \square\ \texttt{of}\ \{n_i \to e_i\} : \mathcal{R})\,\sigma\,s = \mathcal{D}[\![e_j]\!]\,\rho\,\mathcal{R}\,\sigma\,(s+1) \qquad \text{(R1)}$$

$$\mathcal{D}[\![n]\!]\,\rho\,(n_1 \oplus \square : \mathcal{R})\,\sigma\,s = \mathcal{D}[\![n_2]\!]\,\rho\,\mathcal{R}\,\sigma\,(s+1), \text{ where } n_2 = n_1 + n \qquad \text{(R2)}$$

$$\mathcal{D}[\![F]\!]\,\rho\,\mathcal{R}\,\sigma\,s \mid F \text{ not tainted and } \mathcal{R} \text{ not boring} = \mathcal{D}_{app}(F)\,\rho\,\mathcal{R}\,\sigma\,s \qquad \text{(R3)}$$

$$\mathcal{D}[\![x]\!]\,\rho\,\mathcal{R}\,\sigma\,s = \mathcal{D}_{varapp}(x)\,\rho\,\mathcal{R}\,\sigma\,s \qquad \text{(R4)}$$

$$\mathcal{D}[\![K_j]\!]\,\rho\,(\overline{\square\,e} : \texttt{case}\ \square\ \texttt{of}\ \{K_i\,\overline{x}_i \to e_i\} : \mathcal{R})\,\sigma\,s = \mathcal{D}[\![\texttt{let}\,\overline{x}_j = \overline{e}\,\texttt{in}\,e_j]\!]\,\rho\,\mathcal{R}\,\sigma\,(s+5) \qquad \text{(R5)}$$

$$\mathcal{D}[\![\lambda\overline{x}.e_1]\!]\,\rho\,(\overline{\square\ e_2} : \mathcal{R})\,\sigma\,s = \mathcal{D}[\![\texttt{let}\,\overline{x} = \overline{e_2}\,\texttt{in}\,e_1]\!]\,\rho\,\mathcal{R}\,\sigma\,(s+1) \qquad \text{(R6)}$$

$$\mathcal{D}[\![\lambda x.e]\!]\,\rho\,\mathcal{R}\,\sigma\,s = \text{let}\,(e', \sigma_1, s') = \mathcal{D}[\![e]\!]\,\rho\,\epsilon\,\sigma\,0 \;\; \text{in}\,\mathcal{B}[\![\lambda x.e']\!]\,\rho\,\mathcal{R}\,\sigma_1\,(s + \#s') \qquad \text{(R7)}$$

$$\mathcal{D}[\![\texttt{let}\,x = n\,\texttt{in}\,e]\!]\,\rho\,\mathcal{R}\,\sigma\,s = \mathcal{D}[\![[n/x]e]\!]\,\rho\,\mathcal{R}\,\sigma\,(s+1) \qquad \text{(R8)}$$

$$\mathcal{D}[\![\texttt{let}\,x = y\,\texttt{in}\,e]\!]\,\rho\,\mathcal{R}\,\sigma\,s \mid y \text{ not freshly generated} = \mathcal{D}[\![[y/x]e]\!]\,\rho\,\mathcal{R}\,\sigma\,(s+1) \qquad \text{(R9)}$$

$$\mathcal{D}[\![\texttt{let}\,x = e_1\,\texttt{in}\,e_2]\!]\,\rho\,\mathcal{R}\,\sigma\,s \mid \text{linear } x\,e_2 = \mathcal{D}[\![[e_1/x]e_2]\!]\,\rho\,\mathcal{R}\,\sigma\,(s+1) \qquad \text{(R10)}$$

$$\mid \text{otherwise} = \text{let}\,(e_1', \sigma_1, s_1) = \mathcal{D}[\![e_1]\!]\,\rho\,\epsilon\,\sigma\,0 \;\; (e_2', \sigma_2, s_2) = \mathcal{D}[\![e_2]\!]\,\rho\,\mathcal{R}\,\sigma_1\,s \;\; \text{in}\,(\texttt{let}\,x = e_1'\,\texttt{in}\,e_2', \sigma_2, ?s_1 + s_2)$$

Focusing Rules

$$\mathcal{D}[\![e_1 \oplus e_2]\!]\,\rho\,\mathcal{R}\,\sigma\,s = \mathcal{D}[\![e_1]\!]\,\rho\,(\square \oplus e_2 : \mathcal{R})\,\sigma\,s \qquad \text{(R11)}$$

$$\mathcal{D}[\![e_1\,e_2]\!]\,\rho\,\mathcal{R}\,\sigma\,s = \mathcal{D}[\![e_1]\!]\,\rho\,(\square\ e_2 : \mathcal{R})\,\sigma\,s \qquad \text{(R12)}$$

$$\mathcal{D}[\![\texttt{case}\,e\ \texttt{of}\ \{p_i \to e_i\}]\!]\,\rho\,\mathcal{R}\,\sigma\,s = \mathcal{D}[\![e]\!]\,\rho\,(\texttt{case}\ \square\ \texttt{of}\ \{p_i \to e_i\} : \mathcal{R})\,\sigma\,s \qquad \text{(R13)}$$

Fallthrough

$$\mathcal{D}[\![e]\!]\,\rho\,\mathcal{R}\,\sigma\,s = \mathcal{B}[\![e]\!]\,\rho\,\mathcal{R}\,\sigma\,s \qquad \text{(R14)}$$

Rebuilding Expressions

$$\mathcal{B}[\![n]\!]\,\rho\,(\square \oplus e_2 : \mathcal{R})\,\sigma\,s = \mathcal{D}[\![e_2]\!]\,\rho\,(n \oplus \square : \mathcal{R})\,\sigma\,s \qquad \text{(R15)}$$

$$\mathcal{B}[\![e']\!]\,\rho\,(\square \oplus e_2 : \mathcal{R})\,\sigma\,s = \text{let}\,(e_2', \sigma_1, s') = \mathcal{D}[\![e_2]\!]\,\rho\,\epsilon\,\sigma\,s \;\; \text{in}\,\mathcal{B}[\![e' \oplus e_2']\!]\,\rho\,\mathcal{R}\,\sigma_1\,s' \qquad \text{(R16)}$$

$$\mathcal{B}[\![e']\!]\,\rho\,(e_1' \oplus \square : \mathcal{R})\,\sigma\,s = \mathcal{B}[\![e_1' \oplus e']\!]\,\rho\,\mathcal{R}\,\sigma\,s \qquad \text{(R17)}$$

$$\mathcal{B}[\![e']\!]\,\rho\,(\square\,e : \mathcal{R})\,\sigma\,s = \text{let}\,(e'', \sigma_1, s') = \mathcal{D}[\![e]\!]\,\rho\,\epsilon\,\sigma\,s \;\; \text{in}\,\mathcal{B}[\![e'e'']\!]\,\rho\,\mathcal{R}\,\sigma_1\,s' \qquad \text{(R18)}$$

$$\mathcal{B}[\![x']\!]\,\rho\,(\texttt{case}\ \square\ \texttt{of}\ \{p_i \to e_i\} : \mathcal{R})\,\sigma\,s = \text{let}\,(e_i', \sigma_i, s_i) = \mathcal{D}[\![[p_i/x]e_i]\!]\,\rho\,([p_i/x]\mathcal{R})\,\sigma_{i-1}\,s \;\; \text{in}\,(\texttt{case}\,x'\ \texttt{of}\ \{p_i \to e_i'\}, \sigma_i, max(s_i)) \qquad \text{(R19)}$$

$$\mathcal{B}[\![e']\!]\,\rho\,(\texttt{case}\ \square\ \texttt{of}\ \{p_i \to e_i\} : \mathcal{R})\,\sigma\,s = \text{let}\,(e_i', \sigma_i, s_i) = \mathcal{D}[\![e_i]\!]\,\rho\,\mathcal{R}\,\sigma_{i-1}\,s \;\; \text{in}\,(\texttt{case}\,e'\ \texttt{of}\ \{p_i \to e_i'\}, \sigma_i, max(s_i)) \qquad \text{(R20)}$$

$$\mathcal{B}[\![e']\!]\,\rho\,\epsilon\,\sigma\,s = (e', \sigma, s) \qquad \text{(R21)}$$

Figure 4. Driving algorithm and building algorithm

sions on them. For our measurements we used regular addition of savings both under lambdas and in branches such as rule R10, and gave folding an extremely high constant value (500). Our design principle was that foldings should trump all other kinds of savings, but this is an extremely coarse design that leaves plenty of room for future improvements.

We use the operator $\rho|_F$ to extract all expressions with the head F from ρ. Our implementation stores the partitioned ρ's to avoid repeating the partitioning. Partitioning the memoization list gives significant time savings, but it can only be applied on the outermost level.

$\mathcal{D}_{varapp}()$ will try to fold against expressions with a variable in the head. This is convenient and reduces code size in general. A good example is supercompiling the right hand sides of append in a module:

$$\begin{array}{l}
append\ xs\ ys\ = \mathcal{D}[\![\ \texttt{case}\ xs\ \texttt{of}\ \{\ldots\}\ ]\!] \\
\{\ \textit{Create a fresh function and transform its body}\ \} \\
append\ xs\ ys\ = \ h\ xs\ ys \\
h\ xs\ ys\ = \ \textbf{case}\ xs\ \textbf{of} \\
\qquad [\,] \to ys \\
\qquad (x' : xs') \to x' : \mathcal{D}[\![\ append\ xs'\ ys]\!] \\
\{\ \textit{Inline append}\ \} \\
append\ xs\ ys\ = \ h\ xs\ ys \\
h\ xs\ ys\ = \ \textbf{case}\ xs\ \textbf{of} \\
\qquad [\,] \to ys \\
\qquad (x' : xs') \to x' : \mathcal{D}[\![\ \texttt{case}\ xs'\ \texttt{of}\ \{\ldots\}]\!] \\
\{\ \textit{Fold against}\ h\ \} \\
append\ xs\ ys\ = \ h\ xs\ ys \\
h\ xs\ ys\ = \ \textbf{case}\ xs\ \textbf{of} \\
\qquad [\,] \to ys \\
\qquad (x' : xs') \to x' : h\ xs'\ ys
\end{array}$$

Without variable folding this example would give one more unrolling of the recursion which would have increased the code size.

$$
\begin{array}{llll}
\mathcal{D}_{app}(F)\,\rho\,\mathcal{R}\,\sigma\,s & |\,\exists(h,\overline{y},e_1)\in(\sigma|_F\cup\rho|_F)\,.\,[\overline{x}/\overline{y}]e_1=e_2 & = & (h\,\overline{x},\sigma,!s) & (1)\\
 & |\,\exists(h,\overline{y},e_i)\in(\rho|_F)\,.\,e_1 \trianglelefteq^* e_2 & = & \mathbf{let}\,(f_g,[\overline{f}/\overline{y}]) = divide(e_2,e_1) & (2)\\
 & & & \quad(\overline{f}',\sigma_i,s_i) = \mathcal{D}[\![\overline{f}]\!]\,\rho\,\epsilon\,\sigma_{i-1}\,s_{i-1} & \\
 & & & \quad(f'_g,\sigma_2,s_2) = \mathcal{D}[\![f_g]\!]\,\rho\,\epsilon\,\sigma_i\,s_i & \\
 & & & \mathbf{in}\,([\overline{f}'/\overline{y}]f'_g,\sigma_2,max(s_i,s_2)) & \\
 & |\,acceptable(e_2,e',s_1) & = & (h\,\overline{x},((h,\overline{x},e_2),e'):\sigma_1,s_1) & (3)\\
 & |\,\text{otherwise} & = & \mathcal{B}[\![F]\!]\,\rho\,\mathcal{R}\,((*,\emptyset,F):\sigma)\,s & (4)
\end{array}
$$

$$
\begin{array}{l}
\text{where } (e',\sigma_1,s_1) = \mathcal{D}[\![e]\!]\,\rho'\,\mathcal{R}\,\sigma s\\
\quad F \stackrel{\text{def}}{=} e,\ \rho' = (h,\overline{x},e_2):\rho,\ \overline{x} = \mathit{fv}(e_2),\ h \text{ fresh},\ e_2 = normalize([F]\mathcal{R})
\end{array}
$$

$$
\begin{array}{llll}
\mathcal{D}_{varapp}(x)\,\rho\,\mathcal{R}\,\sigma\,s & |\,\exists(h,\overline{y},e_1)\in(\sigma\cup\rho)\,.\,[\overline{x}/\overline{y}]e_1=e_2 & = & (h\,\overline{x},\sigma,!s) & (5)\\
 & |\,acceptable(e_2,e',s_1) & = & (h\,\overline{x},((h,\overline{x},e_2),e'):\sigma_1,s_1) & (6)\\
 & |\,\text{otherwise} & = & \mathcal{B}[\![x]\!]\,\rho\,\mathcal{R}\,\sigma\,s & (7)
\end{array}
$$

$$
\begin{array}{l}
\text{where } (e',\sigma_1,s_1) = \mathcal{B}[\![x]\!]\,\rho'\,\mathcal{R}\,\sigma\,s\\
\quad e_2 = normalize([x]\mathcal{R}),\ \rho' = (h,\overline{x},e_2):\rho,\ \overline{x} = \mathit{fv}(e_2),\ h \text{ fresh}
\end{array}
$$

Figure 5. Driving of applications

4.3 Termination Checking

Folding by itself is not sufficient to ensure termination of the driving algorithm. We therefore define a predicate which is commonly referred to as "the whistle" in literature on supercompilation. Whenever the whistle blows, our algorithm splits the input expression into strictly smaller expressions that are transformed separately in the empty context. This might expose new folding opportunities, and allows the algorithm to remove intermediate structures in subexpressions.

The design of the predicate is inspired by the homeomorphic embedding relation [26] but adjusted to work on our zipper representation and to admit more expressions. A specific design criterion was that *append xs ys* must not be embedded in *append xs xs*. It is easy to construct infinite chains of expressions that will be admitted by this predicate by itself, *append xs ys*, *append xs ys*, ... is one example. However, non-termination is still avoided because the folding mechanism will prevent such chains to build up in ρ.

Definition 4.1 ($\trianglelefteq^*$).

$$
\frac{sizeof([e_1]\mathcal{R}) < sizeof([e_2]\mathcal{R}')}{[e_1]\mathcal{R} \trianglelefteq^* [e_2]\mathcal{R}' = [e_1]\mathcal{R} \trianglelefteq [e_2]\mathcal{R}'}
$$

Definition 4.2 ($\trianglelefteq$).

$$
x \trianglelefteq y,\ \ n_1 \trianglelefteq n_2,\ \ \frac{e_1,e_2 \neq \lambda x.e,\ \ e_1 = e_2,\ \ \mathcal{R} \trianglelefteq \mathcal{R}'}{[e_1]\mathcal{R} \trianglelefteq [e_2]\mathcal{R}'}
$$

$$
\epsilon \trianglelefteq \epsilon,\ \ \frac{\mathcal{R} \trianglelefteq \mathcal{R}'\ \ \mathcal{G} \trianglelefteq \mathcal{G}'}{\mathcal{G}:\mathcal{R} \trianglelefteq \mathcal{G}':\mathcal{R}'},\ \ \frac{\mathcal{R} \trianglelefteq \mathcal{R}'}{\mathcal{R} \trianglelefteq \mathcal{G}':\mathcal{R}'}
$$

$$
\frac{e \trianglelefteq e'}{\Box\, e \trianglelefteq \Box\, e'},\ \ \frac{e \trianglelefteq e'}{\Box \oplus e \trianglelefteq \Box \oplus e'},\ \ \frac{e \trianglelefteq e'}{e \oplus \Box \trianglelefteq e' \oplus \Box},
$$

$$
\frac{e_i \trianglelefteq e'_i}{\mathtt{case}\ \Box\ \mathtt{of}\{p_i \to e_i\} \trianglelefteq \mathtt{case}\ \Box\ \mathtt{of}\{p_i \to e'_i\}},
$$

We postpone dealing with the problem of non-termination of the supercompiler in the case of recursive data types that appear contravariantly in their own definition. As an aside, we note that the inliner in GHC will also loop on such programs [19].

4.4 Expression Splitting

When the whistle has blown it is necessary to stop transforming the current expression. It is safe to just leave it in place, but by splitting the expression and transforming the parts separately it is possible to achieve more optimization.

Divide tries to preserve as much structure between its first input argument and output by first calling an adaptation of the most specific generalisation (msg) [26] to the zipper representation. Our adaption is a bit unconventional in that it returns an expression and a substitution rather than the standard of an expression and two substitutions. Should the call to msg fail, *divide* instead calls split which will always return a valid result under the conditions ensured by the driving algorithm: *divide* is always called on two expressions on the form $[F]\mathcal{R}$ and $[F]\mathcal{R}'$. Divide, split and msg are defined in Figure 6. For the presentation we ignore the issues concerned with splitting under binders in expressions since binders are treated in the same way as described by Pfenning [20].

The msg can return an expression which is of greater size than its input because of binders: when splitting the two expressions $\mathtt{case}\ x\ \mathtt{of}\ \{\ (a,\ b) \to a\ \}$ and $\mathtt{case}\ x\ \mathtt{of}\ \{\ (a,\ b) \to b\ \}$ the result will be $(\mathtt{case}\ x\ \mathtt{of}\ \{\ (a,\ b) \to z\ a\ \},\ [(\lambda\, a.a)/z])$.

4.5 Normalization of Expressions

Finding renamings of an expression is a syntactical check, and sometimes this will miss out opportunities to fold because expressions that are semantically equivalent have different forms.

Consider the two expressions $F\ x\ (1\ +\ 2)$ and $F\ y\ (2\ +\ 1)$ – it is obvious to a human that these two expressions should be foldable against each other. By performing some kind of limited normalization on these expressions the second parameter will turn out to be 3 in both cases and they can fold. We can not hope to find a normal form for our expressions in general, but performing ordinary evaluation except inlining of function calls on all subexpressions will get a long way towards our goal. It is of course important to have a normalization that terminates.

A word of caution about making the normalization too powerful: many common optimizations change the structure of expressions. One example is changing the expression $(x+1)+1$ to $x+2$ which is semantically correct and clearly saves computations, but chances are that in practice the first expression came from an expression $y\ +\ 1$ in a recursive call with an increasing parameter. Both $(y+1)$ will be homeomorphically embedded in both $(x\ +\ 1)\ +\ 1$ and $x\ +\ 2$, but the former will be generalized to $(z\ +\ 1,\ [(x+1)/z])$ and which in turn will fold nicely against $y\ +\ 1$. The normalization scheme we use is the following rewrite rules applied exhaustively on all parts of expressions:

$$
\begin{array}{rcl}
n_1 \oplus n_2 & \leadsto & n, \text{ where } n = n_1 + n_2\\
\mathtt{case}\ K_j\ \overline{e}\ \mathtt{of}\ \{p_i \to e_i\} & \leadsto & \mathtt{let}\ \overline{x_j} = \overline{e}\ \mathtt{in}\ e_j\\
\mathtt{case}\ n_j\ \mathtt{of}\ \{p_i \to e_i\} & \leadsto & e_j\\
\mathtt{let}\ x = n\ \mathtt{in}\ e & \leadsto & [n/x]e
\end{array}
$$

$divide([e_1]\mathcal{R}, [e_2]\mathcal{R}') = (e, \theta)$	iff $(e, \theta) = msg([e_1]\mathcal{R}, [e_2]\mathcal{R}')$ and $sizeof(e) < sizeof([e_1]\mathcal{R})$
$divide([e_1]\mathcal{R}, [e_2]\mathcal{R}') = split([e_1]\mathcal{R})$	
$split([F]\mathcal{G}_1 : \ldots : \mathcal{G}_n : \epsilon) = ([x]\mathcal{G}_n : \epsilon, [([F]\mathcal{G}_1 : \ldots : \mathcal{G}_{n-1} : \epsilon)/x])$	x fresh
$msg([e_1]\mathcal{R}_1, [e_2]\mathcal{R}_2) = ([e]\mathcal{R}, \theta\theta')$	if $\mathcal{R}' = \epsilon$
$\quad = ([x]\mathcal{R}', \theta\theta'[[e]\mathcal{R}/x])$	otherwise
$\quad$ if $(e, \theta) = msg(e_1, e_2)$ and $(\mathcal{R}, \mathcal{R}', \theta') = msg(\mathcal{R}_1, \mathcal{R}_2)$	
$msg(\Box\, e_1, \Box\, e_2) = (\Box\, e', \theta)$	iff $(e', \theta) = msg(e_1, e_2)$
$msg(\Box \oplus e_1, \Box \oplus e_2) = (\Box \oplus e', \theta)$	iff $(e', \theta) = msg(e_1, e_2)$
$msg(e_1 \oplus \Box, e_2 \oplus \Box) = (e' \oplus \Box, \theta)$	iff $(e', \theta) = msg(e_1, e_2)$
$msg(\texttt{case}\ \Box\ \texttt{of}\ \{p_i \rightarrow e_{1i}\}, \texttt{case}\ \Box\ \texttt{of}\ \{p_i \rightarrow e_{2i}\}) = (\texttt{case}\ \Box\ \texttt{of}\ \{p_i \rightarrow e'_i\}, \theta_1 \ldots \theta_i)$	iff $(e'_i, \theta_i) = msg(e_{1i}, e_{2i})$
$msg(\lambda x.e_1, \lambda x.e_2) = (\lambda x.e', \theta)$	iff $(e', \theta) = msg(e_1, e_2)$
$msg(F, F) = (F, \emptyset)$	
$msg(K, K) = (K, \emptyset)$	
$msg(n, n) = (n, \emptyset)$	
$msg(x, x) = (x, \emptyset)$	
$msg(e_1, e_2) = (x, [e_1/x])$	x fresh
$msg(\mathcal{G}_1 : \mathcal{R}_1, \mathcal{G}_2 : \mathcal{R}_2) = (\mathcal{G} : \mathcal{R}, \mathcal{R}', \theta\theta')$,	if $(\mathcal{G}, \theta) = msg(\mathcal{G}_1, \mathcal{G}_2)$ and $(\mathcal{R}, \mathcal{R}', \theta') = msg(\mathcal{R}_1, \mathcal{R}_2)$
$msg(\mathcal{R}_1, \mathcal{R}_2) = (\epsilon, \mathcal{R}_1, \emptyset)$	(default)

Figure 6. Divide, split and msg in zipper form

4.6 Discarding Expressions

The savings that are propagated by the supercompiler are used as input to a predicate *accept* which decides whether to discard or keep transformed functions. Our current implementation is remarkably simple and unconditionally discards expressions that are deemed too large, admit size reductions if they are accompanied with some reduction savings and require size increases to be accompanied by more reduction savings:

```
acceptable before after savings
  | sizeof(after) > 40 = False
  | sizeof(after) > 20 = savings - 100 <= 29
  | sizeof(before) >= sizeof(after) = s - 3 <= 0
  | otherwise = s - 50 <= 29
```

The reason this function works at all is that our algorithm will by construction emit a lot of small functions. If a function body contains many syntactic nodes it is a sign that optimization was not very successful. This typically happens in code that contains a lot of FFI-calls which are opaque to the supercompiler.

5. Measurements

The results supported by this section can be summarized with a single sentence: we can supercompile most programs from the spectral and imaginary part of nofib in less than two seconds of compile time while keeping the maximum binary size increase below 5%.

We start by establishing a base line against ghc -O2 on a small set of examples from the imaginary part of nofib as shown in Table 1. The table uses output from *nofib-analyse*, where each column indicates the difference between the baseline (O2 in this case) and the optimization. Absolute numbers without a sign, such as the runtime for rfib, means that the absolute numbers were too small to give reliable information. The size column is the size of the binary produced by ghc, which includes the runtime system and libraries. By turning off the features normalization of expressions, boring contexts, discarding expressions and tainting expressions in our supercompiler we get to something that is close to an ordinary positive supercompiler [27]. The compilation times range from 2.5 seconds to almost 10 seconds.

We suffer from the same problem that Bolingbroke and Peyton Jones [3] report: the supercompiler can sometimes prevent GHC from applying other important optimizations such as unboxing of arithmetics. Since that is a slightly different algorithm it is not exactly the same programs that get staggering increases in memory allocations. A particular example is *tak*, which our supercompiler slightly optimizes, whereas their get an 18,000-fold increase in memory allocations.

The situation is the reverse with *rfib*, where we get +1599532.1% in allocations and their supercompiler does not change memory allocations at all. The optimized *rfib* program has a recursive function taking an unboxed double and returning an unboxed double, making the program run in constant memory and nearly constant allocations regardless of input size. The supercompiled program is not unboxed and the short recursive function that appears in the ordinary program is stretched out through numerous other function calls making the actual program flow very hard to follow for the human eye.

Looking closer at what happens inside the supercompiler when it produces this program is interesting: the whistle blows and the expression currently transformed is split into two parts. This split forces the inner part of the expression, which is the tight loop, to get a return type that is boxed. It is important to notice that even if our supercompiler used the standard versions of the homeomorphic embedding and the msg, the whistle and the split would produce the same results.

Integrate and *wheel-sieve2* are two other examples that shows the problem with our supercompiler preventing GHC from performing unboxing. The symptom is the same: a vast amount of increase in allocations for the supercompiled program.

There are two examples that show a rather hefty increase in binary size: *digits-of-e1* and *integrate*. One might argue that a 20%

Program	Size (%)	Allocs (%)	Runtime (%)	Elapsed (%)	TotalMem (%)	Compilation Time (s)
bernouilli	+8.0	-1.5	+0.0	+1.5	+0.0	3.52
digits-of-e1	+16.6	-20.3	-19.2	-16.0	+0.0	8.67
exp3_8	+6.0	-16.7	-17.6	-17.3	+0.0	2.58
integrate	+20.4	+65230.5	+104925.9	+93051.6	+30.4	9.02
primes	+6.0	+0.2	-13.9	-16.0	+0.0	2.46
rfib	+6.0	+1599532.1	0.18	0.18	+0.0	2.45
tak	+6.0	-12.5	-2.6	-2.8	+0.0	2.42
wheel-sieve2	+7.3	+307.0	0.54	+195.2	+252.1	3.15

Table 1. ghc -O2 compared with Supercompilation

reduction in runtime is worth a size increase of 16.6% for *digits-of-e1*. This is obviously not the case with *integrate*, a massive slowdown combined with more than 20% size increase of the resulting binary.

By turning on normalization of expressions (Table 2) there is a slight decrease of binary size, a small decrease of compilation time and no changes to the performance of the output programs. This is a small but worthwhile improvement over regular positive supercompilation.

Table 3 shows that by turning on boring contexts it is possible to further shrink the binary size and reduce compilation time. Two benchmarks are affected by this performance wise: *digits-of-e1* is optimized with another 20% reduction in memory allocations giving a slight performance improvement while *tak* goes back to the same amount of memory allocations as without supercompilation and a slight performance decrease.

By discarding expressions (Table 4) there is a further decrease of binary size and the performance loss *wheel-sieve2* suffered from plain supercompilation is somewhat mitigated. The compilation times are all shorter except for *digits-of-e1* which supercompiles several expressions and discards them only to find them in a slightly different context at a later time and repeating this work.

Tainting expressions (Table 5) gives an additional decrease of binary size and compilation with two benchmarks showing speedups: the performance of integrate is improved compared to ordinary optimization and *wheel-sieve2* is back to the same performance as without supercompilation. *Digits-of-e1* becomes slightly worse, but there is still a 16% reduction of memory compared to ordinary optimization and the compilation time is reduced to less than two seconds.

We finally give the full table with a greater selection of benchmarks from both the spectral and imaginary parts of nofib in Table 6. *Integrate* is the benchmark with the biggest size increase at 4.3%, but the supercompiler also manages to remove nearly one fifth of the total allocations.

Circsim is another interesting example, because it consists of about 400 lines of code and compiles in 1.12 seconds with the supercompiler turned on. The supercompiler manages to reduce the memory allocations slightly and give 0.6% binary size increase.

We saw that before adding the tainting of functions it was possible for the supercompiler to perform a lot of unnecessary work by speculatively supercompiling an expression, discard the result, supercompile the subexpressions, discard those results, and so on. One possible strategy to mitigate this further is to keep the supercompiled result around as a cache that successive supercompilation of subexpressions can fold against, thereby avoiding to repeat work.

Our experience so far is that the discarding of functions is not preventing optimizations, on the contrary: programs that were optimized by the supercompiler without discarding expressions are actually slightly faster when discarding the large useless specializations that ended up in the program previously.

6. Implementation Notes

This section contains an outline of the most obvious issues and areas for improvement that any programmer will come across when implementing a supercompiler.

6.1 Parallelism

The supercompiler is currently defined in a very sequential way: it is not possible to inspect the store unless the previous parts of the expression is supercompiled and the store contains all the new definitions. Beyond a lot of infrastructure hacking it appears that lifting this restriction while preserving code sharing is an interesting algorithmic problem that probably requires some research.

There are however some parts of the supercompiler as it is currently defined that are inherently parallel: the testing for folding and non-termination in $\mathcal{D}_{app}()$ can easily be done in parallel since the common case is that there are several possible candidates to test against. This gave a measurable speedup in an an earlier version of our prototype but had to be removed because other parts of GHC are not threadsafe.

6.2 Name Capture

Avoiding name capture can cause significant churn and make the supercompiler dreadfully slow. Bolingbroke and Peyton Jones [3] report that for a particular example 42% of their supercompilation time is spent on managing names and renaming.

Our current implementation uses eager substitutions with the scheme outlined by Peyton Jones and Marlow [19]. There are two obvious improvements to this: using a lazy substitution that the supercompiler applies as it traverses the expression would avoid some churn, and this could be further reduced by allowing some shadowing during supercompilation.

6.3 Representation Improvements for the Homeomorphic Embedding

Our implementation stores expressions annotated with their size in the memoization list. These annotations can be used for avoiding some testing altogether: an expression can only fold against an expression of equal size and an expression can never be homeomorphically embedded in a smaller expression. A similar representation was also independently suggested by Ilya Klyuchnikov in a personal conversation so this seems to be a well known optimization in the supercompilation community.

6.4 Splitting Typed Terms

The most obvious difference between our implementation and the algorithm described in this paper is that the intermediate language of GHC is a typed language [28]. This brings additional complexity when generalizing similar terms of different type against eachother.

Pfenning [20] has already identified our problems: the presence of binders in expressions and the presence of types in binders. There are two advantages for our particular setting: 1) type vari-

Program	Size (%)	Allocs (%)	Runtime (%)	Elapsed (%)	TotalMem (%)	Compilation Time (%)
bernouilli	-1.6	+0.0	+0.0	-2.2	+0.0	-27.8
digits-of-e1	-1.6	+0.0	-0.5	+0.5	+0.0	-10.5
exp3_8	-1.6	+0.0	-0.9	+1.6	+0.0	-33.7
integrate	-1.5	+0.1	-0.3	-0.4	-3.0	-6.8
primes	-1.8	+0.0	+0.0	+0.0	+0.0	-32.9
rfib	-1.6	+0.0	0.18	0.18	+0.0	-37.5
tak	-1.6	+0.0	+0.0	+0.5	+0.0	-38.8
wheel-sieve2	-1.7	+0.0	-0.4	-1.3	+0.0	-29.5

Table 2. Supercompilation compared with Supercompilation+normalization

Program	Size (%)	Allocs (%)	Runtime (%)	Elapsed (%)	TotalMem (%)	Compilation Time (%)
bernouilli	-2.1	+0.0	+0.8	-1.5	+0.0	-30.3
digits-of-e1	-1.5	-22.6	-4.9	-7.4	+0.0	-10.7
exp3_8	-1.6	+0.0	+0.9	-3.2	+0.0	-40.3
integrate	-3.9	+0.3	+0.9	+1.0	+2.3	-21.2
primes	-1.5	+0.0	+0.0	+5.1	+0.0	-40.6
rfib	-1.6	+0.0	0.16	0.17	+0.0	-38.6
tak	-1.6	+13.9	+16.0	+15.6	+0.0	-37.8
wheel-sieve2	-1.6	+0.0	+0.0	+0.0	+0.0	-33.4

Table 3. Supercompilation+normalization compared with Supercompilation+normalization+boring expressions

Program	Size (%)	Allocs (%)	Runtime (%)	Elapsed (%)	TotalMem (%)	Compilation Time (%)
bernouilli	-1.7	+0.0	-0.8	-0.8	+0.0	-35.0
digits-of-e1	-1.0	+0.0	-2.6	+0.5	+0.0	+78.6
exp3_8	-2.1	+0.0	+0.0	+0.0	+0.0	-43.1
integrate	-4.0	-0.1	-0.2	-0.2	+0.8	-9.5
primes	-1.9	+0.0	+0.0	-4.8	+0.0	-42.9
rfib	-2.0	+0.0	0.18	0.18	+0.0	-46.8
tak	-2.0	+0.0	-21.8	-21.8	+0.0	-45.7
wheel-sieve2	-1.9	-73.6	-64.8	-65.0	-72.2	-33.1

Table 4. Supercompilation+normalization+boring expressions compared with Supercompilation+normalization+boring expressions+discarding expressions

Program	Size (%)	Allocs (%)	Runtime (%)	Elapsed (%)	TotalMem (%)	Compilation Time (%)
bernouilli	-1.2	-0.8	+0.0	+3.1	+0.0	-44.3
digits-of-e1	-8.9	+8.7	+2.6	-0.5	+0.0	-89.6
exp3_8	-0.3	+0.0	+0.0	+0.0	+0.0	-32.8
integrate	-4.7	-99.9	-99.9	-99.9	-23.3	-64.8
primes	-0.4	+0.0	-3.2	+0.0	+0.0	-35.7
rfib	-0.4	+0.0	0.18	0.19	+0.0	-36.0
tak	-0.4	+0.0	+5.9	+5.9	+0.0	-36.0
wheel-sieve2	-1.5	-6.9	0.19	-1.9	+2.1	-52.5

Table 5. Supercompilation+normalization+boring expressions+discarding expressions compared with Supercompilation+normalization+boring expressions+discarding expressions+tainting functions

ables are the top element for types; and 2) it is safe to fail during generalization and call split on the term instead.

After having implemented the type generalization we noticed that it was not performed very often in practice on our examples from nofib. The main cost related to this feature appears to be the implementation cost.

7. Related Work

Turchin [29] invented supercompilation in the context of the functional language Refal. The supercompiler Scp4 [17] is implemented in Refal and is the most well-known implementation from this line of work. Sørensen et al. [27] and Secher [23], Secher and Sørensen [24] presented supercompilers formulated for pure first order functional languages but never reported anything about the performance of the algorithms or the resulting programs.

More recently there has been a spur of activity in actual implementations of supercompilers:

Supero Supero [14, 16] could optimize a text book example of word counting written in Haskell to the same performance as a C program performing the same task. The latest version has changed the design significantly in order to improve performance of the supercompiler and Mitchell [15] report compilation times below 4 seconds for all examples.

Program	Size (%)	Allocs (%)	Runtime (%)	Elapsed (%)	TotalMem (%)	Compilation Time (s)
bernouilli	+1.0	-2.3	+0.0	-2.9	+0.0	0.64
digits-of-e1	+1.9	-32.9	-23.5	-21.9	+0.0	1.29
exp3_8	+0.1	-16.7	-17.6	-19.8	+0.0	0.39
integrate	+4.3	-18.7	-0.6	-2.6	+0.0	2.11
primes	+0.1	+0.2	-17.1	-17.4	+0.0	0.36
rfib	+0.1	+1599533.0	0.18	0.19	+0.0	0.32
tak	+0.1	-0.3	-6.5	-6.5	+0.0	0.32
wheel-sieve2	+0.1	+0.0	0.19	+0.0	+0.0	0.47
atom	+3.0	-32.3	-49.8	-49.4	-33.3	1.50
circsim	+0.6	-1.5	-2.3	-2.6	-4.8	1.12
clausify	+0.6	-1.9	-0.7	-0.7	+0.0	0.71
constraints	+0.7	+14.3	-33.7	-33.9	-96.9	0.80
cryptarithm1	+0.3	-7.5	-5.6	-3.4	+0.0	0.38
eliza	+1.2	-40.8	0.00	0.00	+0.0	1.09
fish	+2.1	-4.9	0.01	0.01	+0.0	0.92
gcd	+0.6	-5.8	0.09	0.10	+0.0	0.51
lcss	+1.4	+10.3	+8.8	+10.2	-11.1	0.82
life	+0.4	+1.2	0.13	0.14	+0.0	0.52
mandel2	+1.3	+4.5	0.00	0.00	+0.0	0.99
minimax	+0.1	+0.0	0.00	0.00	+0.0	0.30
pretty	+0.6	-3.3	0.00	0.00	+0.0	0.54
primetest	+3.6	-0.2	+0.0	+0.0	+0.0	1.58

Table 6. ghc -O2 compared with Supercompilation with all features enabled

CHSC Bolingbroke and Peyton Jones [3] presented a supercompiler with call-by-need semantics that did not require its input to be lambda lifted.

HOSC Klyuchnikov and Romanenko [9, 10] have implemented HOSC in Scala and used it for proving equivalence of terms.

Others Riech et al. [21] use supercompilation to optimize programs intended to run on the Reduceron, an FPGA-based soft processor for executing lazy functional programs. They report average performance boosts on a set of programs of 40%. Supercompilation has also been investigated in a call-by-value setting and can give good speedups there too [6, 8].

Narrowing-driven partial evaluation [1, 2] is the functional logic programming equivalent of positive supercompilation but formulated as a term rewriting system. Partial evaluators such as Ecce and Logen [13] seem to be more popular approaches in the logic programming community and more recent work has focused on scaling partial evaluation so that it can be applied to large programs [12, 30].

8. Future Work

Supercompilation is still a rather expensive optimization, but it can undoubtedly produce great results on high level Haskell programs. The major obstacle we see at the moment is that supercompilation might prevent the compiler from applying other optimizations, which in turn can increase the runtime of the final executable by several orders of magnitude. There are several possible ways to tackle this problem:

- Integrate other optimizations into the supercompiler
- Make the supercompiler output programs that are friendly to other optimizations
- Strengthen other optimizations so that they can optimize the output from the supercompiler

The approximation of boring expressions could be extended in several ways to avoid transforming expressions that will give bad results. One observation is that the first call to reverse with an accumulating parameter (*reverse xs* []) is not boring since it has a known constructor in the parameter, but by inspecting the body of *reverse* it is obvious that this parameter is never used. One idea is to extend boring expressions to utilize strictness information so that it would discard this example because the static information present in the context is never used. This idea is related to the concept of "deterministic unfolding" in logic programming.

There is certainly room to improve the decision whether to discard supercompiled expressions. The constants currently used could be tuned further, and there is also the possibility to use other information that is present in the program.

A route that we have not explored is to use different acceptable-predicates for different parts of the supercompiler. Rule R19 and R20 could be extended with a similar test which could allow that only some parts of $\mathcal{R}$ was pushed down.

We observed that there are sometimes several candidates in the memoization list that the supercompiler could generalize the current expression against. Our current implementation selects the first one which is not necessarily the best candidate. A ranking function between different candidates would be useful.

Bolingbroke and Peyton Jones [3] have presented a call-by-need algorithm for supercompilation. We believe that the algorithm presented in this paper could be adjusted to call-by-need semantics as well.

Leuschel [11] has investigated interesting variations of the homeomorphic embedding and we are currently investigating whether similar proof techniques can be used for our whistle.

The focus in this paper has been on a practical algorithm that can supercompile programs without risking code explosion. We believe that our previous proofs of correctness of a closely related algorithm [7] should go through without much adjustment for the algorithm presented.

9. Conclusions

We have presented a supercompilation algorithm and shown that it can give significant speedups on programs from the nofib suite even under a tight code budget constraint. We have also shown that larger programs are supercompiled in reasonable time and also benefits from the aggressive inlining and specialization that our supercompiler performs.

Acknowledgments

This work was partly funded by an internship at Microsoft Research. The authors would like to thank Simon Peyton Jones for both ideas and many suggestions to improve the presentation. We would also like to thank Colin Runciman, Neil Mitchell, Max Bolingbroke, and Ilya Klyuchnikov for valuable discussions about supercompilation. Simon Marlow and Ian Lynagh answered countless questions about GHC which helped realize our prototype implementation. The anonymous referees provided many insightful comments that helped improve both the presentation and technical content.

References

[1] E. Albert and G. Vidal. The narrowing-driven approach to functional logic program specialization. *New Generation Comput*, 20(1):3–26, 2001.

[2] M. Alpuente, M. Falaschi, and G. Vidal. Partial Evaluation of Functional Logic Programs. *ACM Transactions on Programming Languages and Systems*, 20(4):768–844, 1998.

[3] M. Bolingbroke and S. L. Peyton Jones. Supercompilation by evaluation. In *Proceedings of the third ACM Haskell symposium on Haskell*, pages 135–146. ACM, 2010.

[4] G. Huet. The zipper. *Journal of Functional Programming*, 7(05): 549–554, 1997.

[5] T. Johnsson. Lambda lifting: Transforming programs to recursive equations. In *FPCA*, pages 190–203, 1985.

[6] P. A. Jonsson and J. Nordlander. Positive supercompilation for a higher-order call-by-value language. In *POPL*, pages 277–288, 2009.

[7] P. A. Jonsson and J. Nordlander. Positive supercompilation for a higher-order call-by-value language. *Logical Methods in Computer Science*, 6(3), 2010.

[8] P. A. Jonsson and J Nordlander. Strengthening Supercompilation for Call-By-Value Languages. In *Second International Workshop on Metacomputation in Russia*, pages 64–81, 2010.

[9] I. Klyuchnikov and S. Romanenko. Proving the equivalence of higher-order terms by means of supercompilation. In *PSI '09: Proceedings of the Seventh International Andrei Ershov Memorial Conference*, 2009.

[10] I. Klyuchnikov and S. Romanenko. Towards Higher-Level Supercompilation. In *Second International Workshop on Metacomputation in Russia*, pages 82–101, 2010.

[11] M. Leuschel. Homeomorphic embedding for online termination of symbolic methods. In T. Æ. Mogensen, D. A. Schmidt, and I. Hal Sudborough, editors, *The Essence of Computation, Complexity, Analysis, Transformation. Essays Dedicated to Neil D. Jones*, volume 2566 of *Lecture Notes in Computer Science*, pages 379–403. Springer, 2002. ISBN 3-540-00326-6.

[12] M. Leuschel and G. Vidal. Fast Offline Partial Evaluation of Large Logic Programs. In *Logic-based Program Synthesis and Transformation (revised and selected papers from LOPSTR'08)*, pages 119–134. Springer LNCS 5438, 2009.

[13] M. Leuschel, D. Elphick, M. Varea, S-J Craig, and M. Fontaine. The ecce and logen partial evaluators and their web interfaces. In *PEPM*, pages 88–94, New York, NY, USA, 2006. ACM. ISBN 1-59593-196-1.

[14] N. Mitchell. *Transformation and Analysis of Functional Programs*. PhD thesis, University of York, June 2008.

[15] N. Mitchell. Rethinking supercompilation. In *ICFP '10: Proceedings of the 15th ACM SIGPLAN International Conference on Functional Programming*, pages 309–320. ACM, September 2010. ISBN 978-1-60558-794-3.

[16] N. Mitchell and C. Runciman. A supercompiler for core haskell. In O. Chitil et al., editor, *Selected Papers from the Proceedings of IFL 2007*, volume 5083 of *Lecture Notes in Computer Science*, pages 147–164. Springer-Verlag, 2008.

[17] A. P. Nemytykh. The supercompiler SCP4: General structure. In M. Broy and A. V. Zamulin, editors, *Perspectives of Systems Informatics, 5th International Andrei Ershov Memorial Conference, PSI 2003, Revised Papers*, volume 2890 of *LNCS*, pages 162–170. Springer, 2003. ISBN 3-540-20813-5.

[18] W. Partain. The nofib benchmark suite of haskell programs. In J. Launchbury and P. M. Sansom, editors, *Functional Programming*, Workshops in Computing, pages 195–202. Springer, 1992. ISBN 3-540-19820-2.

[19] S. L. Peyton Jones and S. Marlow. Secrets of the glasgow haskell compiler inliner. *J. Funct. Program*, 12(4&5):393–433, 2002.

[20] F. Pfenning. Unification and anti-unification in the calculus of constructions. In *LICS*, pages 74–85. IEEE Computer Society, 1991.

[21] J. S Riech, M. Naylor, and C. Runciman. Supercompilation and the Reduceron. In *Second International Workshop on Metacomputation in Russia*, pages 159–172, 2010.

[22] D. Sands. Proving the correctness of recursion-based automatic program transformations. *Theoretical Computer Science*, 167(1–2):193–233, 30 October 1996.

[23] J. P. Secher. Perfect supercompilation. Technical Report DIKU-TR-99/1, Department of Computer Science (DIKU), University of Copenhagen, February 1999.

[24] J.P. Secher and M.H. Sørensen. On perfect supercompilation. In D. Bjørner, M. Broy, and A. Zamulin, editors, *Proceedings of Perspectives of System Informatics*, volume 1755 of *Lecture Notes in Computer Science*, pages 113–127. Springer-Verlag, 2000.

[25] M.H. Sørensen. Convergence of program transformers in the metric space of trees. *Sci. Comput. Program*, 37(1-3):163–205, 2000.

[26] M.H. Sørensen and R. Glück. An algorithm of generalization in positive supercompilation. In J.W. Lloyd, editor, *International Logic Programming Symposium*, pages 465–479. Cambridge, MA: MIT Press, 1995.

[27] M.H. Sørensen, R. Glück, and N.D. Jones. A positive supercompiler. *Journal of Functional Programming*, 6(6):811–838, 1996.

[28] M. Sulzmann, M. M. T. Chakravarty, S. Peyton Jones, and K. Donnelly. System F with type equality coercions. In *TLDI '07: Proceedings of the 2007 ACM SIGPLAN international worksh op on Types in languages design and implementation*, pages 53–66, New York, NY, USA, 2007. ACM. ISBN 1-59593-393-X.

[29] V.F. Turchin. The concept of a supercompiler. *ACM Transactions on Programming Languages and Systems*, 8(3):292–325, July 1986.

[30] G. Vidal. A Hybrid Approach to Conjunctive Partial Deduction. In *Proc. of the 21th Int'l Symp. on Logic-based Program Synthesis and Transformation (LOPSTR'10)*, 2010. Available from `http://users.dsic.upv.es/~gvidal/german/papers.html`.

[31] P. Wadler. Deforestation: transforming programs to eliminate trees. *Theoretical Computer Science*, 73(2):231–248, June 1990. ISSN 0304-3975.

Allocation Removal by Partial Evaluation in a Tracing JIT

Carl Friedrich Bolz[a] Antonio Cuni[a] Maciej Fijałkowski[b] Michael Leuschel[a]
Samuele Pedroni[c] Armin Rigo[a]

[a]Heinrich-Heine-Universität Düsseldorf, STUPS Group, Germany
[b]merlinux GmbH, Hildesheim, Germany
[c]Open End, Göteborg, Sweden

cfbolz@gmx.de anto.cuni@gmail.com fijal@merlinux.eu leuschel@cs.uni-duesseldorf.de
samuele.pedroni@gmail.com arigo@tunes.org

Abstract

The performance of many dynamic language implementations suffers from high allocation rates and runtime type checks. This makes dynamic languages less applicable to purely algorithmic problems, despite their growing popularity. In this paper we present a simple compiler optimization based on online partial evaluation to remove object allocations and runtime type checks in the context of a tracing JIT. We evaluate the optimization using a Python VM and find that it gives good results for all our (real-life) benchmarks. [1]

Categories and Subject Descriptors D.3.4 [*Programming Languages*]: Processors—code generation, interpreters, run-time environments

General Terms Languages, Performance, Experimentation

Keywords Tracing JIT, Partial Evaluation, Optimization

1. Introduction

The objective of a just-in-time (JIT) compiler for a dynamic language is to improve the speed of the language over an implementation of the language that uses interpretation. The first goal of a JIT is therefore to remove the interpretation overhead, i.e. the overhead of bytecode (or AST) dispatch and the overhead of the interpreter's data structures, such as operand stack etc. The second important problem that any JIT for a dynamic language needs to solve is how to deal with the overhead of boxing primitive types and of type dispatching. Those are problems that are usually not present or at least less severe in statically typed languages.

Boxing of primitive types is necessary because dynamic languages need to be able to handle all objects, even integers, floats, booleans etc. in the same way as user-defined instances. Thus those primitive types are usually *boxed*, i.e., a small heap-structure is allocated for them that contains the actual value. Boxing primitive types can be very costly, because a lot of common operations, particularly all arithmetic operations, have to produce new boxes, in addition to the actual computation they do. Because the boxes are allocated on the heap, producing many of them puts pressure on the garbage collector.

Type dispatching is the process of finding the concrete implementation that is applicable to the objects at hand when performing a generic operation on them. An example would be the addition of two objects: For addition the types of the concrete objects need to be checked and the suiting implementation chosen. Type dispatching is a very common operation in modern[2] dynamic languages because no types are known at compile time. Therefore all operations need it.

A recently popular approach to implementing just-in-time compilers for dynamic languages is that of a tracing JIT. A tracing JIT works by observing the running program and recording its commonly executed parts into *linear execution traces*. Those traces are optimized and turned into machine code.

One reason for the popularity of tracing JITs is their relative simplicity. They can often be added to an existing interpreter, reusing a lot of the interpreter's infrastructure. They give some important optimizations like inlining and constant-folding for free. A tracing JIT always produces linear pieces of code, which simplifies many of the hard algorithms in a compiler, such as register allocation.

The use of a tracing JIT can remove the overhead of bytecode dispatch and that of the interpreter data structures. In this paper we want to present a new optimization that can be added to a tracing JIT that further removes some of the overhead more closely associated to dynamic languages, such as boxing overhead and type dispatching. Our experimental platform is the PyPy project, which is an environment for implementing dynamic programming languages. PyPy and tracing JITs are described in more detail in Section 2. Section 3 analyzes the problem to be solved more closely.

The core of our trace optimization technique can be viewed as partial evaluation: the partial evaluation performs a form of escape analysis [4] on the traces and makes some objects that are allocated in the trace *static,* which means that they do not occur any more in the optimized trace. This technique is informally described in Section 4; a more formal description is given in Section 5. The introduced techniques are evaluated in Section 6 using PyPy's Python interpreter.

The contributions made by this paper are:

[1] This research is partially supported by the BMBF funded project PyJIT (nr. 01QE0913B; Eureka Eurostars).

[2] For languages in the LISP family, basic arithmetic operations are typically not overloaded; even in Smalltalk, type dispatching is much simpler than in Python or JavaScript.

PEPM'11, January 24–25, 2011, Austin, Texas, USA.

1. A description of a practical, efficient and effective algorithm for removing object allocations in a tracing JIT.
2. A characterization of this algorithm as partial evaluation.
3. Performance benchmarks for this algorithm.

2. Background

2.1 PyPy

The work described in this paper was done in the context of the PyPy project[3] [26]. PyPy is an environment where dynamic languages can be implemented in a simple yet efficient way. When implementing a language with PyPy one writes an *interpreter* for the language in *RPython* [1]. RPython ("restricted Python") is a subset of Python chosen in such a way that type inference becomes possible. The language interpreter can then be compiled ("translated") with PyPy's tools into a VM on C level. During translation to C, many low-level aspects of the final VM, such as object layout, garbage collection and memory model, are woven into the generated code. Therefore the interpreter itself can remain at a relatively high level of abstraction.

A number of languages have been implemented with PyPy. The project was initiated to get a better Python implementation, which inspired the name of the project and is still the main focus of development. In addition a number of other languages were implemented, among them a Prolog interpreter [7], a Smalltalk VM [6] and a GameBoy emulator [8].

The feature that makes PyPy more than a compiler with a runtime system is its support for automated JIT compiler generation [5]. During the translation to C, PyPy's tools can generate a tracing just-in-time compiler for the language that the interpreter is implementing. This process is mostly automatic; it only needs to be guided by the language implementer using a small number of source-code hints in the interpreter. Mostly-automatically generating a JIT compiler has many advantages over writing one manually, an error-prone and tedious process. By construction, the generated JIT has the same semantics as the interpreter. Optimizations can be shared between different languages implemented with PyPy.

Moreover, thanks to the internal design of the JIT generator, it is very easy to add new *backends* for producing the actual machine code. Examples of JIT backends that are implemented are those for Intel x86 and x86-64 and an experimental one for the CLI .NET Virtual Machine [12].

2.2 Tracing JIT Compilers

Tracing JITs are a recently popular approach to write just-in-time compilers for dynamic languages. Their origins lie in the Dynamo project, which used a tracing approach to optimize machine code using execution traces [2]. Tracing JITs have then be adapted to be used for a very light-weight Java VM [15] and afterwards used in several implementations of dynamic languages, such as JavaScript [13], Lua[4] and now Python (and other languages) via PyPy.

The core idea of tracing JITs is to focus the optimization effort of the JIT compiler on the commonly executed, i.e., *hot* paths of the core loops of the program and to just use an interpreter for the less commonly executed parts. VMs that use a tracing JIT are mostly mixed-mode execution environments, they contain both an interpreter and a JIT compiler. By default the interpreter is used to execute the program, doing some light-weight profiling at the same time. This profiling is used to identify the hot loops of the program. If a hot loop is found in that way, the interpreter enters a special *tracing mode*. In this tracing mode, the interpreter tries to record all operations that it is executing while running one iteration of the hot loop. This history of executed operations of one loop is called a *trace*. Because the trace corresponds to one iteration of a loop, it always ends with a jump to its own beginning. The trace also contains all operations that are performed in functions that were called in the loop, thus a tracing JIT automatically performs inlining. This trace of operations subsequently forms the basis of the generated code. The trace is first optimized, and then turned into machine code. Both optimization and machine code generation are simple, because the traces are linear. This linearity makes many optimizations a lot more tractable, and the inlining that happens gives the optimizations automatically more context to work with.

Since the trace corresponds to one concrete execution of a loop, the code generated from it is only one possible path through the loop. To make sure that the trace maintains the correct semantics, it contains a *guard* at all places where the execution could have diverged from the path. Those guards check the assumptions under which execution can stay on the trace. As an example, if a loop contains an if-statement, the trace will contain the execution of one of the paths only, which is the path that was taken during the production of the trace. The trace will also contain a guard that checks that the condition of the if-statement is the same as during tracing, because if it isn't, the rest of the trace would not be valid.

When generating machine code, every guard is turned into a quick check to see whether the assumption still holds. When such a guard is hit during the execution of the machine code and the assumption does not hold, the execution of the machine code is stopped, and interpreter continues to run from that point on. These guards are the only mechanism to stop the execution of a trace, the loop end condition also takes the form of a guard.

If one specific guard fails a lot (i.e., more than some threshold), the tracing JIT will generate a new trace that starts exactly at the position of the failing guard [14]. The existing assembler is patched to jump to the new trace when the guard fails. This approach guarantees that all the hot paths in the program will eventually be traced and compiled into efficient code.

2.3 Running Example

For the purpose of this paper, we are going to use a tiny interpreter for a dynamic language with a very simple object model, that just supports an integer and a float type. The objects support only two operations, `add`, which adds two objects (promoting ints to floats in a mixed addition) and `is_positive`, which returns whether the number is greater than zero. The implementation of `add` uses classical Smalltalk-like double-dispatching. The classes can be seen in Figure 1 (written in RPython).

Using these classes to implement arithmetic shows the basic problem of a dynamic language implementation. All the numbers are instances of either `BoxedInteger` or `BoxedFloat`, therefore they consume space on the heap. Performing many arithmetic operations produces lots of garbage quickly, putting pressure on the garbage collector. Using double dispatching to implement the numeric tower needs two method calls per arithmetic operation, which is costly due to the method dispatch.

Let us now consider a simple "interpreter" function `f` that uses the object model (see the bottom of Figure 1). The loop in `f` iterates `y` times, and computes something in the process. Simply running this function is slow, because there are lots of virtual method calls inside the loop, one for each `is_positive` and even two for each call to `add`. These method calls need to check the type of the involved objects repeatedly and redundantly. In addition, a lot of objects are created when executing that loop, many of these objects are short-lived. The actual computation that is performed by `f` is simply a sequence of float or integer additions.

[3] `http://pypy.org`

[4] `http://luajit.org/`

```
class Base(object):
   pass

class BoxedInteger(Base):
   def __init__(self, intval):
      self.intval = intval

   def add(self, other):
      return other.add__int(self.intval)

   def add__int(self, intother):
      return BoxedInteger(intother + self.intval)

   def add__float(self, floatother):
      floatvalue = floatother + float(self.intval)
      return BoxedFloat(floatvalue)

   def is_positive(self):
      return self.intval > 0

class BoxedFloat(Base):
   def __init__(self, floatval):
      self.floatval = floatval

   def add(self, other):
      return other.add__float(self.floatval)

   def add__int(self, intother):
      floatvalue = float(intother) + self.floatval
      return BoxedFloat(floatvalue)

   def add__float(self, floatother):
      return BoxedFloat(floatother + self.floatval)

   def is_positive(self):
      return self.floatval > 0.0


def f(y):
   res = BoxedInteger(0)
   while y.is_positive():
      res = res.add(y).add(BoxedInteger(-100))
      y = y.add(BoxedInteger(-1))
   return res
```

Figure 1. An "Interpreter" for a Tiny Dynamic Language Written in RPython

If the function is executed using the tracing JIT, with y being a BoxedInteger, the produced trace looks like the one of Figure 2 (lines starting with a hash "#" are comments). The trace corresponds to one iteration of the while-loop in f.

The operations in the trace are indented corresponding to the stack level of the function that contains the traced operation. The trace is in single-assignment form, meaning that each variable is assigned a value exactly once. The arguments p_0 and p_1 of the loop correspond to the live variables y and res in the while-loop of the original function.

The operations in the trace correspond to the operations in the RPython program in Figure 1:

- new creates a new object.
- get reads an attribute of an object.
- set writes to an attribute of an object.
- guard_class is a precise type check and precedes an (inlined) method call and is followed by the trace of the called method.
- int_add and int_gt are integer addition and comparison ("greater than"), respectively.
- guard_true checks that a boolean is true.

```
# arguments to the trace: p0, p1
# inside f: res.add(y)
guard_class(p1, BoxedInteger)
    # inside BoxedInteger.add
    i2 = get(p1, intval)
    guard_class(p0, BoxedInteger)
        # inside BoxedInteger.add__int
        i3 = get(p0, intval)
        i4 = int_add(i2, i3)
        p5 = new(BoxedInteger)
            # inside BoxedInteger.__init__
            set(p5, intval, i4)

# inside f: BoxedInteger(-100)
p6 = new(BoxedInteger)
    # inside BoxedInteger.__init__
    set(p6, intval, -100)

# inside f: .add(BoxedInteger(-100))
guard_class(p5, BoxedInteger)
    # inside BoxedInteger.add
    i7 = get(p5, intval)
    guard_class(p6, BoxedInteger)
        # inside BoxedInteger.add__int
        i8 = get(p6, intval)
        i9 = int_add(i7, i8)
        p10 = new(BoxedInteger)
            # inside BoxedInteger.__init__
            set(p10, intval, i9)

# inside f: BoxedInteger(-1)
p11 = new(BoxedInteger)
    # inside BoxedInteger.__init__
    set(p11, intval, -1)

# inside f: y.add(BoxedInteger(-1))
guard_class(p0, BoxedInteger)
    # inside BoxedInteger.add
    i12 = get(p0, intval)
    guard_class(p11, BoxedInteger)
        # inside BoxedInteger.add__int
        i13 = get(p11, intval)
        i14 = int_add(i12, i13)
        p15 = new(BoxedInteger)
            # inside BoxedInteger.__init__
            set(p15, intval, i14)

# inside f: y.is_positive()
guard_class(p15, BoxedInteger)
    # inside BoxedInteger.is_positive
    i16 = get(p15, intval)
    i17 = int_gt(i16, 0)
# inside f
guard_true(i17)
jump(p15, p10)
```

Figure 2. An Unoptimized Trace of the Example Interpreter

Method calls in the trace are preceded by a guard_class operation, to check that the class of the receiver is the same as the one that was observed during tracing.[5] These guards make the trace specific to the situation where y is really a BoxedInteger. When the trace is turned into machine code and afterwards executed with BoxedFloat, the first guard_class instruction will fail and execution will continue using the interpreter.

The trace shows the inefficiencies of f clearly, if one looks at the number of new, set/get and guard_class operations. The number of guard_class operation is particularly problematic, not only because of the time it takes to run them. All guards also have additional information attached that makes it possible to return to

[5] guard_class performs a precise class check, not checking for subclasses.

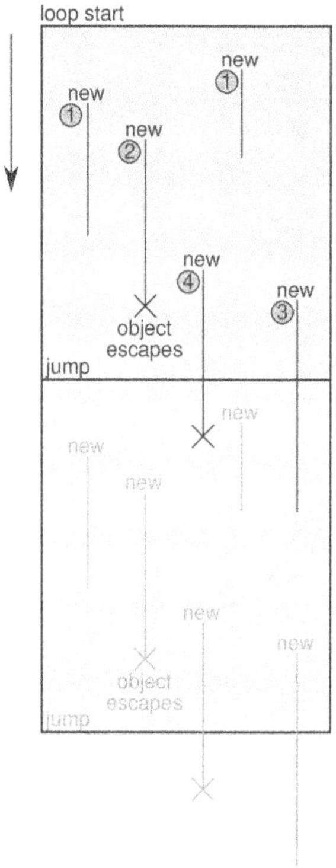

Figure 3. Object Lifetimes in a Trace

the interpreter, should the guard fail. This means that too many guard operations also consume a lot of memory.

In the rest of the paper we will see how this trace can be optimized using partial evaluation.

3. Object Lifetimes in a Tracing JIT

To understand the problems that this paper is trying to solve in more detail, we first need to understand various cases of object lifetimes that can occur in a tracing JIT compiler.

Figure 3 shows a trace before optimization, together with the lifetime of various kinds of objects created in the trace. It is executed from top to bottom. At the bottom, a jump is used to execute the same loop another time (for clarity, the figure shows two iterations of the loop). The loop is executed until one of the guards in the trace fails, and the execution is aborted and interpretation resumes.

Some of the operations within this trace are `new` operations, which each create a new instance of some class. These instances are used for some time, e.g., by calling methods on them (which are inlined into the trace), reading and writing their fields. Some of these instances *escape*, which means that they are stored in some globally accessible place or are passed into a non-inlined function via a residual call.

Together with the `new` operations, the figure shows the lifetimes of the created objects. The objects that are created within a trace using `new` fall into one of several categories:

1. Objects that live for some time, and are then just not used any more afterwards.
2. Objects that live for some time and then escape.
3. Objects that live for some time, survive across the jump to the beginning of the loop, and are then not used any more.
4. Objects that live for some time, survive across the jump, and then escape. To these we also count the objects that live across several jumps and then either escape or stop being used.

The objects that are allocated in the example trace in Figure 2 fall into categories 1 and 3. Objects stored in p_5, p_6, p_{11} are in category 1, objects in p_{10}, p_{15} are in category 3.

The creation of objects in category 1 is removed by the optimization described in Sections 4 and 5. Objects in the other categories are partially optimized by this approach as well.[6]

4. Allocation Removal in Traces

The main insight to improve the code shown in Section 2.3 is that objects in category 1 do not survive very long – they are used only inside the loop and there is no other outside reference to them. The optimizer identifies objects in category 1 and removes the allocation of these objects, and all operations manipulating them.

This is a process that is usually called *escape analysis* [18]. In this paper we will perform escape analysis by using partial evaluation. The use of partial evaluation is a bit peculiar in that it receives no static input arguments for the trace, but it is only used to optimize operations within the trace. This section will give an informal account of this process by examining the example trace in Figure 2. The final trace after optimization can be seen in Figure 4 (the line numbers are the lines of the unoptimized trace where the operation originates).

To optimize the trace, it is traversed from beginning to end and an output trace is produced. Every operation in the input trace is either removed or copied into the output trace. Sometimes new operations need to be produced as well. The optimizer can only remove operations that manipulate objects that have been allocated within the trace, while all other operations are copied to the output trace unchanged.

Looking at the example trace of Figure 2, the operations in lines 1–9 are manipulating objects which existed before the trace and that are passed in as arguments: therefore the optimizer just copies them into the output trace.

The following operations (lines 10–17) are more interesting:

```
p5 = new(BoxedInteger)            10
set(p5, intval, i4)               12
p6 = new(BoxedInteger)            15
set(p6, intval, -100)             17
```

When the optimizer encounters a `new`, it removes it optimistically, and assumes that the object is in category 1. If later the optimizer finds that the object escapes, it will be allocated at that point. The optimizer needs to keep track of the state of the object that the operation would have created. This is done with the help of a *static object*[7]. The static object describes the shape of the object that would have been allocated, i.e., the type of the object and where the values that would be stored in the fields of the allocated object come from.

In the snippet above, the two `new` operations are removed and two static objects are constructed. The `set` operations manipulate static objects, therefore they can be removed as well; their effect is remembered in the static objects.

After the operations the static object associated with p_5 would store the knowledge that it is a `BoxedInteger` whose `intval` field contains i_4; the one associated with p_6 would store that it is a `BoxedInteger` whose `intval` field contains the constant -100.

[6] We also started to work on optimizing objects in category 3, which will be the subject of a later paper.

[7] Here "static" is meant in the sense of partial evaluation, i.e., known at partial evaluation time, not in the sense of "static allocation" or "static method".

The subsequent operations (line 20–26) in Figure 2, which use p_5 and p_6, can then be optimized using that knowledge:

```
20 guard_class(p5, BoxedInteger)
22 i7 = get(p5, intval)
23 guard_class(p6, BoxedInteger)
25 i8 = get(p6, intval)
26 i9 = int_add(i7, i8)
```

The `guard_class` operations can be removed, since their arguments are static objects with the matching type `BoxedInteger`. The `get` operations can be removed as well, because each of them reads a field out of a static object. The results of the get operation are replaced with what the static object stores in these fields: all the occurences of i_7 and i_8 in the trace are just replaced by i_4 and -100. The only operation copied into the optimized trace is the addition:

```
26 i9 = int_add(i4, -100)
```

The rest of the trace from Figure 2 is optimized in a similar vein. The operations in lines 27–35 produce two more static objects and are removed. Those in line 36–39 are just copied into the output trace because they manipulate objects that are allocated before the trace. Lines 40–42 are removed because they operate on a static object. Line 43 is copied into the output trace. Lines 44–46 produce a new static object and are removed, lines 48–51 manipulate that static object and are removed as well. Lines 52–54 are copied into the output trace.

The last operation (line 55) is an interesting case. It is the `jump` operation that passes control back to the beginning of the trace. The two arguments to this operation at this point are static objects. However, because they are passed into the next iteration of the loop they live longer than the trace and therefore cannot remain static. They need to be turned into dynamic (runtime) objects before the actual `jump` operation. This process of turning a static object into a dynamic one is called *lifting*.

Lifting a static object puts `new` and `set` operations into the output trace. Those operations produce an object at runtime that has the shape described by the static object. This process is a bit delicate, because the static objects could form an arbitrary graph structure. In our example it is simple, though:

```
44 p15 = new(BoxedInteger)
46 set(p15, intval, i14)
27 p10 = new(BoxedInteger)
29 set(p10, intval, i9)
55 jump(p15, p10)
```

Observe how the operations for creating these two instances have been moved to a later point in the trace. This is worthwhile even though the objects have to be allocated in the end because some `get` operations and `guard_class` operations on the lifted static objects could be removed.

More generally, lifting needs to occur if a static object is used in any operation apart from `get`, `set`, and `guard`. It also needs to occur if `set` is used to store a static object into a non-static one.

The final optimized trace of the example can be seen in Figure 4. The optimized trace contains only two allocations, instead of the original five, and only three `guard_class` operations, compared to the original seven.

5. Formal Description of the Algorithm

In this section we want to give a formal description of the semantics of the traces and of the optimizer and liken the optimization to partial evaluation. We focus on the operations for manipulating heap allocated objects, as those are the only ones that are actually optimized. We also consider only objects with two fields L and R in this section, generalizing to arbitrary many fields is straightforward. Traces are lists of operations. The operations considered here are `new`, `get`, `set` and `guard_class`.

```
1  # arguments to the trace: p0, p1
3  guard_class(p1, BoxedInteger)
5  i2 = get(p1, intval)
6  guard_class(p0, BoxedInteger)
8  i3 = get(p0, intval)
9  i4 = int_add(i2, i3)
26 i9 = int_add(i4, -100)

37 guard_class(p0, BoxedInteger)
39 i12 = get(p0, intval)
43 i14 = int_add(i12, -1)

52 i17 = int_gt(i14, 0)
54 guard_true(i17)

44 p15 = new(BoxedInteger)
46 set(p15, intval, i14)
27 p10 = new(BoxedInteger)
29 set(p10, intval, i9)

55 jump(p15, p10)
```

Figure 4. Resulting Trace After Allocation Removal

The values of all variables are locations (i.e., pointers). Locations are mapped to objects, which are represented by triples (T, l_1, l_2) of a type T, and two locations that represent the fields of the object. When a new object is created, the fields are initialized to null, but we require that they are initialized to a real location before being read, otherwise the trace is malformed (this condition is guaranteed by how the traces are generated in PyPy).

We use some abbreviations when dealing with object triples. To read the type of an object, $\text{type}((T, l_1, l_2)) = T$ is used. Reading a field F from an object is written $(T, l_1, l_2)_F$ which either is l_1 if $F = L$ or l_2 if $F = R$. To set field F to a new location l, we use the notation $(T, l_1, l_2)!_F l$, which yields a new triple (T, l, l_2) if $F = L$ or a new triple (T, l_1, l) if $F = R$.

Figure 5 shows the operational semantics for traces. The interpreter formalized there executes one operation at a time. Its state is represented by an environment E and a heap H, which may be changed by the execution of an operation. The environment is a partial function from variables to locations and the heap is a partial function from locations to objects. Note that a variable can never be null in the environment, otherwise the trace would have been malformed. The environment could not directly map variables to objects, because several variables can point to the *same* object, because of aliasing.

We use the following notation for updating partial functions: $E[v \mapsto l]$ denotes the environment which is just like E, but maps v to l.

The `new` operation creates a new object $(T, \text{null}, \text{null})$ on the heap under a fresh location l and adds the result variable to the environment, mapping it to the new location l.

The `get` operation reads a field F out of an object, and adds the result variable to the environment, mapping it to the read location. The heap is unchanged.

The `set` operation changes field F of an object stored at the location that variable v maps to. The new value of the field is the location in variable u. The environment is unchanged.

The `guard_class` operation is used to check whether the object stored at the location that variable v maps to is of type T. If that is the case, then execution continues without changing heap and environment. Otherwise, execution is stopped.

5.1 Optimizing Traces

To optimize the simple traces of the last section, we use online partial evaluation. The partial evaluator optimizes one operation

$$\textit{new}\quad \frac{l \text{ fresh}}{v = \texttt{new}(T), E, H \overset{\text{run}}{\Longrightarrow} E\left[v \mapsto l\right], H\left[l \mapsto (T, \text{null}, \text{null})\right]}$$

$$\textit{guard}\quad \frac{\text{type}(H(E(v)) = T}{\texttt{guard\_class}(v, T), E, H \overset{\text{run}}{\Longrightarrow} E, H}$$

$$\textit{get}\quad \frac{}{u = \texttt{get}(v, F), E, H \overset{\text{run}}{\Longrightarrow} E\left[u \mapsto H\left(E\left(v\right)\right)_F\right], H}$$

$$\frac{\text{type}(H(E(v)) \neq T}{\texttt{guard\_class}(v, T), E, H \overset{\text{run}}{\Longrightarrow} \bot, \bot}$$

$$\textit{set}\quad \frac{}{\texttt{set}\left(v, F, u\right), E, H \overset{\text{run}}{\Longrightarrow} E, H\left[E\left(v\right) \mapsto \left(H\left(E\left(v\right)\right)!_F E(u)\right)\right]}$$

Object Domains:

$u, v \in V$	variables in trace
$T \in \mathfrak{T}$	runtime types
$F \in \{L, R\}$	fields of objects
$l \in L$	locations on heap

Semantic Values:

$E \in V \rightharpoonup L$	Environment
$H \in L \rightharpoonup \mathfrak{T} \times (L \cup \{\text{null}\}) \times (L \cup \{\text{null}\})$	Heap

Figure 5. The Operational Semantics of Simplified Traces

of a trace at a time. Every operation in the unoptimized trace is replaced by a list of operations in the optimized trace. This list is empty if the operation can be optimized away. The optimization rules can be seen in Figure 6. Lists are written using angular brackets $<$ ... $>$, list concatenation is expressed using two colons: $l_1 :: l_2$.

The state of the optimizer is stored in an environment E and a *static heap* S. Each step of the optimizer takes an operation, an environment and a static heap and produces a list of operations, a new environment and a new static heap.

The environment is a partial function from variables in the unoptimized trace V to variables in the optimized trace V^* (which are themselves written with a * for clarity). The reason for introducing new variables in the optimized trace is that several variables that appear in the unoptimized trace can turn into the same variables in the optimized trace. The environment of the optimizer serves a function similar to that of the environment in the semantics: to express sharing.

The static heap is a partial function from V^* into the set of static objects, which are triples of a type and two elements of V^*. The object referenced by a variable v^* is static, if v^* is in the domain of the static heap S. The object $S(v^*)$ describes what is statically known about the object, i.e., its type and its fields. The fields of objects in the static heap are also elements of V^* (or null, for short periods of time).

When the optimizer sees a new operation, it optimistically removes it and assumes that the resulting object can stay static. The optimization for all further operations is split into two cases. One case is for when the involved variables are in the static heap, which means that the operation can be performed at optimization time and can be removed from the trace. These rules mirror the execution semantics closely. The other case is for when not enough is known about the variables, and the operation has to be residualized.

If the argument v of a `get` operation is mapped to something in the static heap, the `get` can be performed at optimization time. Otherwise, the `get` operation needs to be residualized.

If the first argument v to a `set` operation is mapped to something in the static heap, then the `set` can be performed at optimization time (which updates the static heap). Otherwise the `set` operation needs to be residualized. This needs to be done carefully, because the new value for the field, from the variable u, could itself be static, in which case it needs to be lifted first.

If a `guard_class` is performed on a variable that is in the static heap, the type check can be performed at optimization time, which means the operation can be removed if the types match. If the type check fails statically or if the object is not in the static heap, the `guard_class` is residualized. This also needs to lift the variable on which the `guard_class` is performed.

Lifting takes a variable and turns it into a dynamic variable. If the variable is already dynamic, nothing needs to be done. If it is in the static heap, operations are emitted that construct an object with the shape described there, and the variable is removed from the static heap.

Lifting a static object needs to recursively lift its fields. Some care needs to be taken when lifting a static object, because the structures described by the static heap can be cyclic. To make sure that the same static object is not lifted twice, the `liftfield` operation removes it from the static heap *before* recursively lifting its fields.

As an example for lifting, consider the static heap

$$\{v^* \mapsto (T_1, w^*, v^*), w^* \mapsto (T_2, u^*, u^*)\}$$

which contains two static objects. If v^* needs to be lifted, the following residual operations are produced:

```
v* = new(T1)
w* = new(T2)
set(w*, L, u*)
set(w*, R, u*)
set(v*, L, w*)
set(v*, R, v*)
```

After the lifting the static heap is the empty set, because both static objects were lifted. If we had lifted w^* instead of v^*, then the following operations would have been produced:

```
w* = new(T2)
set(w*, L, u*)
set(w*, R, u*)
```

In this case, the static heap afterwards would be:

$$\{v^* \mapsto (T_1, w^*, v^*)\}$$

5.2 Analysis of the Algorithm

While we do not offer a formal proof of it, it can argue informally that the algorithm presented above is sound: it works by delaying (and often completely removing) some operations. The algorithm *new*

$$\frac{v^* \text{ fresh}}{v = \texttt{new}(T), E, S \overset{\text{opt}}{\Longrightarrow} \langle\,\rangle, E[v \mapsto v^*], S[v^* \mapsto (T, \text{null}, \text{null})]}$$

get

$$\frac{E(v) \in \text{dom}(S)}{u = \texttt{get}(v, F), E, S \overset{\text{opt}}{\Longrightarrow} \langle\,\rangle, E[u \mapsto S(E(v))_F], S}$$

$$\frac{E(v) \notin \text{dom}(S), \quad u^* \text{ fresh}}{u = \texttt{get}(v, F), E, S \overset{\text{opt}}{\Longrightarrow} \langle u^* = \texttt{get}(E(v), F)\rangle, E[u \mapsto u^*], S}$$

set

$$\frac{E(v) \in \text{dom}(S)}{\texttt{set}(v, F, u), E, S \overset{\text{opt}}{\Longrightarrow} \langle\,\rangle, E, S[E(v) \mapsto (S(E(v))!_F E(u))]}$$

$$\frac{E(v) \notin \text{dom}(S), (E(v), S) \overset{\text{lift}}{\Longrightarrow} (\text{ops}, S')}{\texttt{set}(v, F, u), E, S \overset{\text{opt}}{\Longrightarrow} \text{ops} :: \langle \texttt{set}(E(v), F, E(u))\rangle, E, S'}$$

guard

$$\frac{E(v) \in \text{dom}(S), \text{type}(S(E(v))) = T}{\texttt{guard\_class}(v, T), E, S \overset{\text{opt}}{\Longrightarrow} \langle\,\rangle, E, S}$$

$$\frac{E(v) \notin \text{dom}(S) \vee \text{type}(S(E(v))) \neq T, (E(v), S) \overset{\text{lift}}{\Longrightarrow} (\text{ops}, S')}{\texttt{guard\_class}(v, T), E, S \overset{\text{opt}}{\Longrightarrow} \text{ops} :: \langle \texttt{guard\_class}(E(v), T)\rangle, E, S'}$$

lifting

$$\frac{v^* \notin \text{dom}(S)}{v^*, S \overset{\text{lift}}{\Longrightarrow} \langle\,\rangle, S}$$

$$\frac{v^* \in \text{dom}(S), (v^*, S) \overset{\text{liftfields}}{\Longrightarrow} (\text{ops}, S')}{v^*, S \overset{\text{lift}}{\Longrightarrow} \langle v^* = \texttt{new}(\text{type}(S(v^*)))\rangle :: ops, S'}$$

$$\frac{\left(S(v^*)_L, S \setminus \{v^* \mapsto S(v^*)\}\right) \overset{\text{lift}}{\Longrightarrow} (\text{ops}_L, S'), \left(S(v^*)_R, S'\right) \overset{\text{lift}}{\Longrightarrow} (\text{ops}_R, S'')}{v^*, S \overset{\text{liftfields}}{\Longrightarrow} \text{ops}_L :: \text{ops}_R :: \left\langle \texttt{set}\left(v^*, L, S(v^*)_L\right), \texttt{set}\left(v^*, R, S(v^*)_R\right)\right\rangle, S''}$$

Object Domains:

$u, v \in V$	variables in trace
$u^*, v^* \in V^*$	variables in optimized trace
$T \in \mathfrak{T}$	runtime types
$F \in \{L, R\}$	fields of objects

Semantic Values:

$E \in V \rightharpoonup V^*$	Environment
$S \in V^* \rightharpoonup \mathfrak{T} \times (V^* \cup \{\text{null}\}) \times (V^* \cup \{\text{null}\})$	Static Heap

Figure 6. Optimization Rules

runs in a single pass over the list of operations. We can check that although recursively lifting a static object is not a constant-time operation, the algorithm only takes a total time linear in the length of the trace. The algorithm itself is not particularly complex; our focus is rather that *in the context of tracing JITs* it is possible to find a simple enough algorithm that performs well.

Note in particular that objects in category 1 (i.e., those that do not escape) are completely removed; moreover, objects in category 2 (i.e., escaping) are still partially optimized: all the operations in between the creation of the object and the point where it escapes that involve the object are removed. Objects in category 3 and 4 are also partially optimized, their allocation is delayed till the end of the trace.

The optimization is particularly effective for chains of operations. For example, it is typical for an interpreter to generate sequences of writes-followed-by-reads, where one interpreted opcode writes to some object's field and the next interpreted opcode reads it back, possibly dispatching on the type of the object created just before. A typical example would be a chain of arithmetic operations.

6. Implementation and Evaluation

The allocation removal techniques described in this paper were implemented in the optimizer of PyPy's tracing JIT. The optimization is independent of which interpreter a JIT is generated for. There are some practical issues beyond the techniques described in this paper. The actual implementation needs to deal with more operations than described in Section 5, e.g., to also support static arrays in addition to static objects. The implementation of this optimization is about 400 lines of RPython code.

A further complication is that most interpreters written with PyPy use heap-allocated frame objects to store local variables. Those severely hinder the effectiveness of allocation removal, because every time an object is stored into a local variable, it is stored into the frame-object, which makes it escape. We implemented a technique to treat such frames objects in a special way to solve this problem. This is a common approach in VM implementations [13, 22]; the novelty of our approach is that we generalized it enough to be usable for different interpreters.

To evaluate our allocation removal algorithm, we look at the effectiveness when used in the generated tracing JIT of PyPy's Python interpreter. This interpreter is a full implementation of Python 2.5 language semantics and is about 30,000 lines of RPython code.

The benchmarks we used are small-to-medium Python programs, some synthetic benchmarks, some real applications.[8]

Some of them are from the Computer Language Benchmark Game[9]: **fannkuch**, **nbody**, **meteor-contest**, **spectral-norm**.

Furthermore there are the following benchmarks:

- **crypto_pyaes**: An AES implementation.
- **django**: The templating engine of the Django web framework[10].
- **go**: A Monte-Carlo Go AI[11].
- **html5lib**: An HTML5 parser.
- **pyflate-fast**: A BZ2 decoder.
- **raytrace-simple**: A ray tracer.
- **richards**: The Richards benchmark.
- **spambayes**: A Bayesian spam filter[12].
- **telco**: A Python version of the Telco decimal benchmark[13], using a pure Python decimal floating point implementation.
- **twisted_names**: A DNS server benchmark using the Twisted networking framework[14].

We evaluate the allocation removal algorithm along two lines: first we want to know how many allocations could be optimized away. On the other hand, we want to know how much the run times of the benchmarks is improved.

The benchmarks were run on an otherwise idle Intel Core2 Duo P8400 processor with 2.26 GHz and 3072 KB of cache on a machine with 3GB RAM running Linux 2.6.35. We compared the performance of various Python implementations on the benchmarks. As a baseline, we used the standard Python implementation in C, CPython 2.6.6[15], which uses a bytecode-based interpreter. Furthermore we compared against Psyco[25] 1.6, a (hand-written) extension module to CPython which is a just-in-time compiler that produces machine code at run-time. It is not based on traces. Finally, we used two versions of PyPy's Python interpreter (revision 77823 of SVN trunk[16]): one including the JIT but not optimizing the traces, and one using the allocation removal optimizations (as well as some minor other optimizations, such as constant folding).

As the first step, we counted the occurring operations in all generated traces before and after the optimization phase for all benchmarks. The resulting numbers can be seen in Figure 7. The optimization removes between 4% and 90% and of allocation operations in the traces of the benchmarks. All benchmarks taken together, the optimization removes 70% percent of allocation operations. The numbers look similar for reading and writing of attributes. There are even more `guard` operations that are removed, however there is an additional optimization that removes guards, so not all the removed guards are an effect of the optimization described here (for technical reasons, it would be very hard to separate the two effects).

In addition to the count of operations we also performed time measurements. All benchmarks were run 50 times in the same process, to give the JIT time to produce machine code. The arithmetic mean of the times of the last 30 runs were used as the result. The errors were computed using a confidence interval with a 95% confidence level [16]. The results are reported in Figure 8. For each implementation the table also reports the speedup that PyPy with optimization achieves over it.

With the optimization turned on, PyPy's Python interpreter outperforms CPython in all benchmarks except spambayes (which heavily relies on regular expression performance and thus is not helped much by our Python JIT) and meteor-contest. All benchmarks are improved by the allocation removal optimization, by at least 20% and by as much as a factor of 6.95.

Psyco is able to outperform PyPy's JIT in five out of 14 benchmarks. We hope to overtake Psyco (which is no longer being actively developped) by adding some further optimizations.

[8] All the source code of the benchmarks can be found at `http://codespeak.net/svn/pypy/benchmarks/`. There is also a website that monitors PyPy's performance nightly at `http://speed.pypy.org/`.

[9] `http://shootout.alioth.debian.org/`

[10] `http://www.djangoproject.com/`

[11] `http://shed-skin.blogspot.com/2009/07/disco-elegant-python-go-player.html`

[12] `http://spambayes.sourceforge.net/`

[13] `http://speleotrove.com/decimal/telco.html`

[14] `http://twistedmatrix.com/`

[15] `http://python.org`

[16] `http://codespeak.net/svn/pypy/trunk`

	num loops	new	removed	get/set	removed	guard	removed	all ops	removed
crypto_pyaes	78	3088	50%	57148	25%	9055	95%	137189	80%
django	51	673	54%	19318	18%	3876	93%	55682	85%
fannkuch	43	171	49%	886	63%	1159	81%	4935	45%
go	517	12234	76%	200842	21%	53138	90%	568542	84%
html5lib	498	14432	68%	503390	11%	71592	94%	1405780	91%
meteor-contest	59	277	36%	4402	31%	1078	83%	12862	68%
nbody	13	96	38%	443	69%	449	78%	2107	38%
pyflate-fast	162	2278	55%	39126	20%	8194	92%	112857	80%
raytrace-simple	120	3118	59%	91982	15%	13572	95%	247436	89%
richards	87	844	4%	49875	22%	4130	91%	133898	83%
spambayes	314	5608	79%	117002	11%	25313	94%	324125	90%
spectral-norm	38	360	64%	5553	20%	1122	92%	11878	77%
telco	46	1257	90%	37470	3%	6644	99%	98590	97%
twisted-names	214	5273	84%	100010	10%	23247	96%	279667	92%
total	2240	49709	70%	1227447	14%	222569	93%	3395548	89%

Figure 7. Number of Operations and Percentage Removed By Optimization

	CPython [ms]	×	Psyco [ms]	×	PyPy w/o optim. [ms]	×	PyPy w/ optim. [ms]	×
crypto_pyaes	2757.80 ± 0.98	10.33	67.90 ± 0.47	0.25	1652.00 ± 4.00	6.19	266.86 ± 5.94	1.00
django	993.19 ± 0.50	3.83	913.51 ± 4.22	3.52	694.73 ± 2.86	2.68	259.53 ± 1.79	1.00
fannkuch	1987.22 ± 2.02	4.26	944.44 ± 0.61	2.02	566.99 ± 1.06	1.21	466.87 ± 1.85	1.00
go	947.21 ± 1.58	3.00	445.96 ± 0.68	1.41	2197.71 ± 25.21	6.95	316.15 ± 9.33	1.00
html5lib	13987.12 ± 19.51	1.39	17398.25 ± 36.50	1.72	27194.45 ± 46.62	2.69	10092.19 ± 23.50	1.00
meteor-contest	346.98 ± 0.35	0.88	215.66 ± 0.23	0.55	433.04 ± 1.45	1.10	392.85 ± 0.87	1.00
nbody_modified	637.90 ± 1.82	6.14	256.78 ± 0.18	2.47	135.55 ± 0.33	1.30	103.93 ± 0.25	1.00
pyflate-fast	3169.35 ± 1.89	1.74	1278.16 ± 3.13	0.70	3285.89 ± 8.51	1.80	1822.36 ± 11.52	1.00
raytrace-simple	2744.60 ± 51.72	4.24	1072.66 ± 1.08	1.66	2778.27 ± 15.13	4.29	647.24 ± 5.44	1.00
richards	354.06 ± 1.00	4.01	63.48 ± 0.15	0.72	383.93 ± 3.28	4.35	88.32 ± 0.91	1.00
spambayes	299.16 ± 0.35	0.75	338.68 ± 3.14	0.85	580.90 ± 24.68	1.46	397.37 ± 10.60	1.00
spectral-norm	478.63 ± 0.80	4.27	139.83 ± 1.54	1.25	353.51 ± 1.39	3.15	112.10 ± 1.17	1.00
telco	1207.67 ± 2.03	2.44	730.00 ± 2.66	1.47	1296.08 ± 4.37	2.62	495.23 ± 2.14	1.00
twisted_names	9.58 ± 0.01	1.34	10.43 ± 0.01	1.46	17.99 ± 0.27	2.52	7.13 ± 0.09	1.00

Figure 8. Benchmark Times in Milliseconds, Together With Factor Over PyPy With Optimizations

7. Related Work

There exists a large number of works on escape analysis, which is a program analysis that tries to find an upper bound for the lifetime of objects allocated at specific program points [4, 11, 18, 24]. This information can then be used to decide that certain objects can be allocated on the stack, because their lifetime does not exceed that of the stack frame it is allocated in. The difference to our work is that escape analysis is split into an analysis and an optimization phase. The analysis can be a lot more complex than our simple one-pass optimization. Also, stack-allocation reduces garbage-collection pressure but does not optimize away the actual accesses to the stack-allocated object. In our case, an object is not needed at all any more.

Chang *et al.* describe a tracing JIT for JavaScript running on top of a JVM [10]. They mention in passing an approach to allocation removal that moves the allocation of an object of type 1 out of the loop to only allocate it once, instead of every iteration. No details are given for this optimization. The fact that the object is still allocated and needs to be written to means that only the allocations are optimized away, but not the reads out of and writes into the object.

SPUR, a tracing JIT for C# seems to be able to remove allocations in a similar way to the approach described here, as hinted at in the technical report [3]. However, no details for the approach and its implementation are given.

Psyco [25] is a (non-tracing) JIT for Python that implements a more ad-hoc version of the allocation removal described here. Our static objects could be related to what are called *virtual* objects in Psyco. Historically, PyPy's JIT can be seen as some successor of Psyco for a general context (one of the authors of this paper is the author of Psyco).

The original SELF JIT compiler [9] used an algorithm for forward-propagating the types of variables as part of its optimizations. This makes it possible to remove all type checks on a variable but the first one. The optimization does not deal with removing the full object, if it is short-lived, but the type check removals are similar to what our optimization achieves.

Partially known data structures are built directly into Prolog (via unbound logic variables) and thus the treatment of partially static data structures was part of partial evaluation of Prolog programs from the early stages [21]. One effect of unfolding in Prolog is that terms that are constructed and immediately matched again, completely disappear in the residual program. This is similar to what our optimization does for an imperative language. In functional programming this idea was introduced as constructor specialisation by Mogensen [23].

A related optimization is also that of deforestation [17, 27] which removes intermediate lists or trees in functional languages. A more general approach is boxing analysis [20] which optimizes pairs of calls to box/unbox in a functional language. Similarly, "dynamic typing" [19] tries to remove dynamic type coercions in a dynamically typed lambda-calculus. All these optimizations work by analyzing the program before execution, which makes them unsuitable for dynamic languages like Python, where almost nothing can be inferred purely by looking at the source code.

8. Conclusion and Future Work

In this paper, we used an approach based on online partial evaluation to optimize away allocations and type guards in the traces of a tracing JIT. In this context a simple approach based on partial evaluation gives good results. This is due to the fact that the tracing JIT itself is responsible for all control issues, which are usually the hardest part of partial evaluation: the tracing JIT selects the parts of the program that are worthwhile to optimize, and extracts linear paths through them, inlining functions as necessary. What is left to optimize are only those linear paths.

We expect a similar result for other optimizations that usually require a complex analysis phase and are thus normally too slow to use at runtime. A tracing JIT selects interesting linear paths by itself; therefore, a naive version of many optimizations on such paths should give mostly the same results. For example, we experimented with (and plan to write about) store-load propagation with a very simple alias analysis.

Acknowledgements

The authors would like to thank Stefan Hallerstede, David Schneider and Thomas Stiehl for fruitful discussions and detailed feedback during the writing of the paper. We thank the anonymous reviewers for the valuable comments.

References

[1] D. Ancona, M. Ancona, A. Cuni, and N. D. Matsakis. RPython: a step towards reconciling dynamically and statically typed OO languages. In *Proceedings of the 2007 symposium on Dynamic languages*, pages 53–64, Montreal, Quebec, Canada, 2007. ACM.

[2] V. Bala, E. Duesterwald, and S. Banerjia. Dynamo: a transparent dynamic optimization system. *ACM SIGPLAN Notices*, 35(5):1–12, 2000.

[3] M. Bebenita, F. Brandner, M. Fahndrich, F. Logozzo, W. Schulte, N. Tillmann, and H. Venter. SPUR: a trace-based JIT compiler for CIL. In *Proceedings of the ACM international conference on Object oriented programming systems languages and applications*, pages 708–725, Reno/Tahoe, Nevada, USA, 2010. ACM.

[4] B. Blanchet. Escape analysis for Java: Theory and practice. *ACM Trans. Program. Lang. Syst.*, 25(6):713–775, 2003.

[5] C. F. Bolz, A. Cuni, M. Fijałkowski, and A. Rigo. Tracing the meta-level: PyPy's tracing JIT compiler. In *Proceedings of the 4th workshop on the Implementation, Compilation, Optimization of Object-Oriented Languages and Programming Systems*, pages 18–25, Genova, Italy, 2009. ACM.

[6] C. F. Bolz, A. Kuhn, A. Lienhard, N. Matsakis, O. Nierstrasz, L. Renggli, A. Rigo, and T. Verwaest. Back to the future in one week — implementing a Smalltalk VM in PyPy. In *Self-Sustaining Systems*, pages 123–139. 2008.

[7] C. F. Bolz, M. Leuschel, and D. Schneider. Towards a jitting VM for Prolog execution. In *Proceedings of the 12th international ACM SIGPLAN symposium on Principles and practice of declarative programming*, pages 99–108, Hagenberg, Austria, 2010. ACM.

[8] C. Bruni and T. Verwaest. PyGirl: generating Whole-System VMs from High-Level prototypes using PyPy. In W. Aalst, J. Mylopoulos, N. M. Sadeh, M. J. Shaw, C. Szyperski, M. Oriol, and B. Meyer, editors, *Objects, Components, Models and Patterns*, volume 33 of *Lecture Notes in Business Information Processing*, pages 328–347. Springer Berlin Heidelberg, 2009. 10.1007/978-3-642-02571-6_19.

[9] C. Chambers, D. Ungar, and E. Lee. An efficient implementation of SELF a dynamically-typed object-oriented language based on prototypes. *SIGPLAN Not.*, 24(10):49–70, 1989.

[10] M. Chang, M. Bebenita, A. Yermolovich, A. Gal, and M. Franz. Efficient just-in-time execution of dynamically typed languages via code specialization using precise runtime type inference. Technical Report ICS-TR-07-10, Donald Bren School of Information and Computer Science, University of California, Irvine, 2007.

[11] J. Choi, M. Gupta, M. Serrano, V. C. Sreedhar, and S. Midkiff. Escape analysis for Java. *SIGPLAN Not.*, 34(10):1–19, 1999.

[12] A. Cuni. *High performance implementation of Python for CLI/.NET with JIT compiler generation for dynamic languages.* PhD thesis, Dipartimento di Informatica e Scienze dell'Informazione, University of Genova, 2010. Technical Report DISI-TH-2010-05.

[13] A. Gal, B. Eich, M. Shaver, D. Anderson, B. Kaplan, G. Hoare, D. Mandelin, B. Zbarsky, J. Orendorff, M. Bebenita, M. Chang, M. Franz, E. Smith, R. Reitmaier, and M. Haghighat. Trace-based just-in-time type specialization for dynamic languages. In *PLDI*, 2009.

[14] A. Gal and M. Franz. Incremental dynamic code generation with trace trees. Technical Report ICS-TR-06-16, Donald Bren School of Information and Computer Science, University of California, Irvine, Nov. 2006.

[15] A. Gal, C. W. Probst, and M. Franz. HotpathVM: an effective JIT compiler for resource-constrained devices. In *Proceedings of the 2nd international conference on Virtual execution environments*, pages 144–153, Ottawa, Ontario, Canada, 2006. ACM.

[16] A. Georges, D. Buytaert, and L. Eeckhout. Statistically rigorous Java performance evaluation. *SIGPLAN Not.*, 42(10):57–76, 2007.

[17] A. Gill, J. Launchbury, and S. L. P. Jones. A short cut to deforestation. In *Proceedings of the conference on Functional programming languages and computer architecture*, FPCA '93, page 223–232, New York, NY, USA, 1993. ACM.

[18] B. Goldberg and Y. G. Park. Higher order escape analysis: optimizing stack allocation in functional program implementations. In *Proceedings of the third European symposium on programming on ESOP '90*, pages 152–160, Copenhagen, Denmark, 1990. Springer-Verlag New York, Inc.

[19] F. Henglein. Dynamic typing: syntax and proof theory. *Sci. Comput. Program.*, 22:197–230, June 1994.

[20] J. Jørgensen. *A Calculus for Boxing Analysis of Polymorphically Typed Languages.* Ph.D. Thesis, University of Copenhapen, 1996. TR 96/28.

[21] J. W. Lloyd and J. C. Shepherdson. Partial evaluation in logic programming. *J. Log. Program.*, 11(3-4):217–242, 1991.

[22] E. Miranda. Context management in VisualWorks 5i. Technical report, ParcPlace Division, CINCOM, Inc., 1999.

[23] T. Mogensen. Constructor specialization. In *Proceedings of the 1993 ACM SIGPLAN symposium on Partial evaluation and semantics-based program manipulation*, pages 22–32, Copenhagen, Denmark, 1993. ACM.

[24] Y. G. Park and B. Goldberg. Escape analysis on lists. *SIGPLAN Not.*, 27(7):116–127, 1992.

[25] A. Rigo. Representation-based just-in-time specialization and the Psyco prototype for Python. In *Proceedings of the 2004 ACM SIGPLAN symposium on Partial evaluation and semantics-based program manipulation*, pages 15–26, Verona, Italy, 2004. ACM.

[26] A. Rigo and S. Pedroni. PyPy's approach to virtual machine construction. In *Companion to the 21st ACM SIGPLAN conference on Object-oriented programming systems, languages, and applications*, pages 944–953, Portland, Oregon, USA, 2006. ACM.

[27] P. Wadler. Deforestation: transforming programs to eliminate trees. In *Proceedings of the Second European Symposium on Programming*, page 231–248, Amsterdam, The Netherlands, The Netherlands, 1988. North-Holland Publishing Co.

A Generative Geometric Kernel

Jacques Carette
Department of Computing and Software
McMaster University
1280 Main Street West
Hamilton, Ontario L8S 4K1
Canada
carette@mcmaster.ca

Mustafa Elsheikh
PhD Student
Cheriton School of Computer Science
University of Waterloo
Canada
melsheik@uwaterloo.ca

Spencer Smith
Department of Computing and Software
McMaster University
1280 Main Street West
Hamilton, Ontario L8S 4K1
Canada
smiths@mcmaster.ca

Abstract

We present the design and implementation of a generative geometric kernel[1]. The kernel generator is generic, type-safe, parametrized by many design-level choices and extensible. The resulting code has minimal traces of the design abstractions. We achieve genericity through a layered design deriving concepts from affine geometry, linear algebra and abstract algebra. We achieve parametrization and type-safety by using OCaml's module system, including higher order modules. The cost of abstraction is removed by using MetaOCaml's support for code generation coupled with some annotations atop the code type.

Categories and Subject Descriptors D.3.4 [*Programming Languages*]: Processors—Code generation; D.2.2 [*Software Engineering*]: Design Tools and Techniques; I.1.3 [*Symbolic and Algebraic Manipulation*]: Languages and Systems—Evaluation strategies

General Terms Code Generation, Geometric Kernel, Methodology, Generic Programming

Keywords MetaOCaml, Geometry, Generative, Generic

1. Introduction

Our work developed from a simple observation [12, 39, 40]: mesh generation and computational geometry software forms a family of programs. Furthermore, generative programming [6], especially when coupled with domain-specific simplifications [7], can be an effective method for "coding" such families. There are however some well-known drawbacks to the most common implementation languages, to wit C++ templates [8]. We instead chose a typed methodology, using MetaOCaml [29, 45] for higher assurance.

More precisely, a past case-study on using typed metaprogramming for capturing a program family of Gaussian Elimination algorithms [2, 4] was rather promising. But there was still a serious doubt: was Gaussian Elimination somehow especially well-suited to such an approach? We needed to know if the previously developed techniques (from the above papers as well as those of [5, 24, 44] for example) would really be transferable. Furthermore, we were interested in moving beyond case-studies of feasibility requiring the invention of new techniques, and rather extend the methodological work of [4] towards a real recipe for typed metaprogramming, at least in the context of scientific computation software.

Thus we embarked on another case study, but this time, we were quite careful to *not* invent new techniques, but rather to reuse existing techniques, or at worst to adapt them slightly. Furthermore, we always tried to use the simplest possible technique for solving each problem, even when we were aware of more powerful techniques, which could definitely solve the problem. Throughout the design and development process we paid close attention to our design decisions and the rationale behind each of them. This has allowed us to compare the current decisions and their rationale with previous work, and document the common ideas.

Motivating Example

First we need to establish that geometric computations are indeed a good topic for such a case study. Consider the following problem: Let $\{p_i\}_{i\in[1..n]}$ be n points in an n-dimensional Euclidean space equipped with an orthogonal coordinate system. Let H be the hyperplane defined by these points. That is, H is a line in 2D, a plane in 3D, or in general, a subspace of codimension 1. Let the coordinates of a point p_i be $(p_{i1}, p_{i2}, \cdots, p_{in})$. The relative position of a point $x = (x_1, \cdots, x_n)$ with regard to H is called the *orientation* of x and H. The orientation test is a fundamental geometric primitive in many computational geometry algorithms (such as computing the convex hull and triangulations [18]). The usual method for the orientation test relies on computing the following determinant:

$$\begin{vmatrix} p_{11} & p_{12} & \cdots & p_{1n} & 1 \\ p_{21} & p_{22} & \cdots & p_{2n} & 1 \\ \vdots & \vdots & \ddots & \vdots & \vdots \\ p_{n1} & p_{n2} & \cdots & p_{nn} & 1 \\ x_1 & x_2 & \cdots & x_n & 1 \end{vmatrix}$$

From a software point of view, a dimension-generic implementation of the orientation test requires computing this determinant at runtime, which is an expensive operation. If the dimension is known before runtime, then a straightforward optimization is to use the expanded closed-form expression instead. For example, for $n = 2$, the determinant simplifies to

$$(p_{22} - x_2)p_{11} - (p_{12} - x_2)p_{21} + (p_{12} - p_{22})x_1,$$

[1] The code is available from http://www.cas.mcmaster.ca/~carette/ggk/

PEPM '11 January 24–25, 2011, Austin, Texas, USA.

which can be implemented with a fairly small number of arithmetic operations. For $n = 1$, this simplifies to a subtraction of two numbers $p_{11} - x_1$. It is also noticeable that the constant (1 in this case) no longer appears. This is a seemingly trivial difference, but in the context of larger computations, we cannot assume that all compilers will be able to reduce to such "trivial" computations. This means that writing an *efficient* generic orientation test requires writing and maintaining n different specialized versions for n different variations. Our goal is to write and maintain one abstract version, which can then be specialized *optimally* for each n.

In other words, in our human-maintained source code, we want the most mathematically meaningful version of the "orientation test" to appear, but in the code that we will ultimately compile (for each dimension), we want the most simplified expression. Most geometric computations have a similar character, where the abstract mathematical definition is simple and elegant, but can be computationally inefficient.

One note on efficiency: our aim is to produce *source code* which is comparable to hand-written code for the same task. Our efficiency goals are that we are no slower than hand-written (but not micro-optimized) code. Some modern compilers, which do aggressive inlining, may well produce very efficient code for highly generic algorithms; our aim is to guarantee this, rather than hope that the compiler is "sufficiently smart".

Contribution

We provide the first typed geometric kernel generator. But, more importantly, we clearly document our design decisions and their rationale, which allows us to compare to our previous work on typed generators, and extract some further methodological aspects. We have explicitly not used "new" techniques, so as to enable a cleaner extraction of methodological aspects.

We have made a very explicit design decision to encapsulate "code generation". This is the key for showing that for high-level algorithms, "generic" and "generative" can be done with the same code – and in fact resemble pseudo-code versions of mathematical algorithms. To achieve this, we need to abstract away all issues of "code generation", by localizing *all* uses of code construction operations (i.e. the features added by MetaOCaml to OCaml) to a single module.

In particular, the software architecture for our generator is mostly driven by mathematical clarity, elegance and generality. This leads to an unusually modular design, whilst the code we generate is essentially free of abstraction overheads. In fact, we achieve more inlining than what is found in many geometric kernels, from code that is written at a much more generic and abstract level.

Plan of the paper

We start with some necessary background, covering some of the basic techniques we need. Then in section 3, we cover the global design of the geometric kernel generator, in a top-down manner. Sections 4–8 then give more details of each layer, in a bottom-up manner. In section 9, we first give an illustrative example of our methodology, before providing a higher-level description of the steps we successfully followed. After this we provide further general discussion, which also covers future work. In section 11, we cover some of the related work that is not otherwise covered in the main text, before wrapping up with some conclusions in section 12.

2. Background

We give a quick overview of the basic tools that we use for all of our work. Throughout we assume the reader is familiar with Objective Caml [21].

2.1 Metaprogramming

Meta-programming involves writing programs that manipulate programs [36]. The programs being manipulated are called *object-programs*. Our use is of the simplest kind: we want to write program generators. Our generators are parametrized by *design decisions*, in the context of *program families* [32, 48]. Since this is a difficult task at the best of times, we wanted to have as many "free" correctness guarantees as possible. Currently, this means using MetaOCaml, the only language in which a type-safe code generator also guarantees that all object-programs will also be type-safe (as well as being syntactically well-formed) [42].

2.2 Programming in MetaOCaml

MetaOCaml is an extension of Objective Caml [21] (henceforth abbreviated to OCaml). It provides mechanisms for constructing and combining code expressions, which can be executed in future stages. MetaOCaml extends OCaml's syntax with three new concepts: *Bracket*, *Escape*, and *Run*. It also extends the type system by an additional type: `code`. Although MetaOCaml allows arbitrarily many stages, we only use 2, which we will sometimes refer to as the *generation* stage and the *run-time* stage.

The Bracket operator (syntax: `.<e>.`) delays the computation of an expression `e`, which is referred to as a *future-stage computation*. If `e` is an OCaml expression of type `t`, then `.<e>.` has type `('a, t) code`[2]. The execution of this expression is delayed to a future stage. However, both the syntax and the type of this expression are checked at the current stage (generation stage in our case). This gives a static guarantee that the generated code will have the appropriate type when executed at a future stage. This means that well-typed code generators will produce only syntactically well-formed and well-typed code.

The Escape operator (syntax: `.~e`) allows running of code-producing expressions in the current stage, in the context of a (future) stage code expression. When evaluating `.~e`, MetaOCaml first evaluates `e` in the current stage, then splices the resulting code expression inside a later stage expression. The power of the Escape operator lies in the fact that the expression `e` gets evaluated *before* splicing. This allows *arbitrary* computations over code expressions at generation time.

The Run operator (syntax: `.!e`) forces the execution of a code expression in the current stage; in other words, if `e` has type `('a, t) code`, `.!e` has type `t`. This is very useful for run-time code generation – which is a feature we do not in fact need here. For our purposes, it would be sufficient for there to be a perfect printer from `('a, t) code` to strings or files, albeit with the guarantee that the results are syntactically well-formed, type-safe OCaml programs. In practice, we end up using Run on code values that always evaluate to functions (at generation time).

As MetaOCaml is a strict superset of OCaml, this gives us an extremely powerful language to use at *generation* time. If we are careful which language features we use inside future-stage (generated) code, we insure that most abstraction costs are at generation time [4].

2.3 Annotations

By design, MetaOCaml treats values of type `code` as black boxes, i.e., they cannot be examined[3]. Naïve code generation will produce sub-optimal code, which we want to avoid. As we cannot optimize code post facto, we need to make sure that we gener-

[2] The polymorphic type parameter `'a` is called the *environment classifier*. The reasons and details behind environment classifiers are outside the scope of this paper. Interested readers are advised to consult [43] for more details.

[3] This is a mechanism that helps preserve the type-safety of generated code in the presence of effects, see [41] for details.

Geometric Objects
Affine Space
Linear Algebra
Number Types
Code

Figure 1. Overview of the layers

ate optimal code on the first (and only) pass. Kiselyov et al. [24] tackle this problem by using abstract interpretation. We use simple annotations (via algebraic types) that capture enough information about future-stage computations to allow us to perform some computations at generation time, so that we may generate the code "just right". Optimizations such as algebraic simplification, constant folding, let insertion and constant propagation are all performed before any code is generated. More precisely, we guarantee that expressions like `x+0` will never be generated [47].

In fact, we indeed use *abstract interpretations* for this purpose, but since the lattices involved are quite trivial, we prefer to refer to them simply as "annotations" here.

2.4 Modules and Functors

Our main goal is to realize a program family of geometric computations with a high degree of parametricity. Following [4], we use OCaml's module system for encoding the domain concepts and the parametrizations. The abstract concepts are encoded as module types (interfaces), with modules being instances of those concepts. The type checker can then reject invalid implementations of these concepts. To express variabilities, we use Functors. Functors are parametrized modules. By adding appropriate type constraints, we can enforce that certain relations must hold between parameters of Functors. This allows us to encode certain domain information into the type system, and leverage the type checker's ability to inform us of improper compositions of variabilities.

3. The Design of the Geometric Kernel

Our original motivation was to be able to experiment with differing meshing algorithms, in the context of solving partial differential equations. All meshing algorithms rely on a core foundation of geometric objects and computations [27]. To be able to conduct such experiments, we need a whole family of (implementations of) geometric objects and computations. The abstraction cost of making all of these choices at run-time, through whatever dispatching mechanism we may choose, is simply too high – we could never hope to be competitive with existing meshing software.

It thus seemed reasonable for us to design a *geometric kernel* that was both parametric and efficient; previous work told us that this could be achieved via code generation. We also knew that we needed to find "the right abstractions" to be able to be properly modular and achieve the desired parametricity.

The problem of finding a proper set of abstractions that allows expressing geometric computations independently of the underlying coordinate space and its dimensions is a thorny one, but study of the literature made it clear that this was key. If this can be achieved, then a *family* of geometric computations can be expressed using essentially the same abstract code. As a positive side-effect, this would also scale to higher dimensions. In other words, if we can find a proper interface for the lower-level implementation details, we could then provide different implementations (aka *variabilities*) for those details. It is important to remember that we have put ourselves in a generative context, so we need to make choices that allow us to specialize the generator, rather than directly specializing the program. However, the partial evaluation literature tells us that, through staging, we can turn programs directly into their own *generating extensions* [22] by hand-writing a `cogen`.

Orientation	Inside	Simplex
Vertex	Sidedness	Hypersphere
Insphere	Hyperplane Operations	Hyperplane

Vector	Affine Transforms	Point

Tuple	Matrix	Determinant

RealField	Order	Field
Set	Ring	Monoid

Staged Types
Base Types

Figure 2. Details of the layers.

We first sought to proceed as in [2], and "reverse engineer" the commonalities and variabilities from a sample set of geometric kernels, which embodied different design choices. This did not work. These kernels where much too highly optimized, thereby completely obscuring the abstract structures involved. The choice of Gaussian Elimination in [2] was *lucky* in that the mathematical structure was still visible in the code.

We thus turned away from the literature describing implementations of geometric algorithms, and started exploring abstract geometric computations instead. Mann et al. [26] propose using a geometric algebra as a basis for geometric abstractions. This approach results in generic higher-dimensional geometric kernels [28], and coordinate-free computations [20]. A comparison of the different types of geometric algebras can be found in [14, 19]. Among these different geometric algebras, affine geometry treats n-dimensional spaces through the same set of abstract concepts. In effect, geometric primitives that are based on affine geometry scale to higher dimensions. However, the affine geometry does not allow a straightforward extension to different coordinate systems other than the orthogonal coordinate systems [10]. A promising alternative geometric algebra can be found in [14] that can address this problem. For simplicity, we chose to follow the route of basing our geometric kernel on affine algebra.

Once we decided that we would not worry about non-Cartesian coordinate systems, the rest of the design became simpler. The final design (see figure 1) was completely motivated by top-down functionality requirements, in other words the implementation needs of the upper-layers drove the requirements for the lower layers.

Briefly, our geometric objects are encoded in terms of concepts from affine spaces, which are encoded using linear algebra (and containers), which itself is parametric over the underlying "number types" of the entries of matrices. And, at the bottom, the very representation of the programming language primitives (data-types and functions) are themselves abstracted into staged versions – which we will detail later.

Each layer is designed to be generic and parametric, however our current implementation only covers those parts that are necessary to implement variations on our geometric kernel.

Details of the Layers

The layers' contents are further detailed in Figure 2. The purpose and functionality of each of the layers is described as follows:

- The *geometric objects layer*: Geometric objects and computations are exposed in sufficient detail to allow writing geometric algorithms independently from the underlying geometric space representations. Choices such as the coordinate system, the coordinate number types, or dimensions are not exposed. Examples of objects at this layer are hyperplanes, hyperspheres, and operations on them.

- The *affine space layer* provides the basic functionality for computing with geometric primitives of affine spaces. The concepts here are those for points, vectors, orientation, sidedness and general affine transforms.
- The *linear algebra layer*: A straightforward implementation of affine geometric primitives uses linear algebra. The scope of this layer is motivated by the needs of the affine geometry, not by the general scope of linear algebra. We only require a (representation of) vectors, which we call tuple, a (representation of) linear transformation – matrices, and the computation of determinants. However, obtaining "good" code for this was challenging, and drove a lot of our design for facilities in lower layers.
- The *number types layer*: Proper abstractions in geometric computation include identifying a "number type" for the underlying coordinate system. Traditionally this has been seen in a narrow fashion as being entirely determined by the carrier type – but here when we speak of "number type", we really mean an algebraic approach to these. So this layer exposes *algebraic structures* in their entirety, rather than leaving this implicit. This in turn allows us to place certain simplifications in the "right" place (i.e. in this layer) instead of being ad hoc; for example, constant folding can be done here, as can simplifications based on algebraic properties.
- The *code layer* provides code generation facilities. It provides abstractions for "staging" values and functions, as well as some code combinators.

In the next sections, we will describe, from the bottom up, each one of these layers in more detail.

4. The Code Layer

The code layer offers abstractions for building and manipulating staged types, as well as code generation combinators.

We have made a very explicit design decision to encapsulate "code generation". Our goal is to provide the "right" primitives so that, at the higher levels, generic algorithms and generative algorithms are identical – and in fact resemble pseudo-code versions of mathematical algorithms. To achieve this, we need to abstract away all issues of "code generation", by localizing all uses of Escape and Bracket to a single module in the code layer.

4.1 Abstracting code

We could proceed by simply abstracting the code type and the operations on it. However, we noticed that a fair amount of information is available statically, as generation-time values. We want to be able to take advantage of this to simplify the generated code (e.g. by constant folding), yet still have the higher layers of our code be unaware of such issues. We now explain how we provide a unified view of code and values.

Code Expressions

As is by now well-understood [4, 24], it is important not to duplicate computations. To facilitate let insertion, we need to know if a code value can be duplicated or not; rather than encoding at the type-level like the `maybeValue` type of [24], we use the value-level at generation time. This is naturally isomorphic, but allows for more elegant code. We define the type `code_expr` as

```
type ('a,'b) code_expr =
  { c : ('a,'b) code; a : bool }
```

where the boolean represents whether the code expression can be duplicated or not (we call such expressions *atomic*). An expression `e` is atomic if and only if it is either an immediate value or (the code for) a variable.

Staged Expressions

Expressions can be classified in terms of evaluation time into two categories:

1. *Now expressions*. This category comprises immediate values and constants. The value of a Now expression is known at code generation time.
2. *Later expressions*. Values in this category are known at run-time. At generation time, the values in this category are represented by code expressions whose execution is delayed to a further stage, i.e., run-time.

As we want to abstract away from these considerations, we combine these into a single type of `staged` values:

```
type ('a,'b) staged =
  | Now of 'b
  | Later of ('a,'b) code_expr
```

4.2 Staging Functions

Once we have staged values, we need to build functions over these, which we will naturally call staged functions. Our mechanism is general, and only depends on the arity of the function.

4.2.1 Staging Unary Functions

A straightforward way to lift a function of type `'b -> 'c` to a staged one would be

```
let lift_unary f = function
  | Now x -> Now (f x)
  | Later x -> Later { a = false;
                       c = .< f .~(x.c) >. }
```

but this inlining could cause code duplication. This can be improved to

```
let lift_unary' f = function
  | Now x -> Now (f x)
  | Later x -> Later ({ a = false; c =
      if x.a then .< f .~(x.c) >.
      else .< let t = .~(x.c) in f t >. })
```

This solution is still not entirely satisfactory, as function composition now generates rather unnatural code. Furthermore, we are residualising a call to `f`, even though we might possess a version of `f` that does inlining. The problem is that we do not have enough contextual information at hand to deal with this case properly.

A better solution then is to *delegate* the handling of the `Later` case to the caller. That is, rather than asking for a single function f working on values as input, we rather ask for f_n working on values and f_l which works on code expressions. We bundle these up into a record, and a straightforward implementation of the application for these generalized unary functions is

```
type ('a,'b,'c) unary = {
  unow: 'b -> 'c ;
  ulater: ('a,'b) code_expr -> ('a, 'c) code_expr
}
let mk_unary f = function
  | Now x -> Now (f.unow x)
  | Later x -> Later (f.ulater x)
```

4.2.2 Staging Binary Functions

If we apply the above scheme to binary functions in a naïve manner, we would require 4 cases for a generalized binary functions, which does not seem quite "right". What we would prefer would be to give only 2 cases, and use lifting for the other cases.

To achieve this, we need a simple auxiliary function to lift atomic values (in this case, constants). Then we can define a type for generalized binary functions and its application function.

```
let lift_const x = {c = .<x>.; a = true}
type ('a,'b,'c,'d) binary = {
  bnow : 'b -> 'c -> 'd ;
  blater : ('a,'b) code_expr ->
             ('a, 'c) code_expr ->
               ('a,'d) code_expr
}
let mk_binary bop = fun x y -> match x, y with
  | (Now x), (Now y) -> Now (bop.bnow x y)
  | (Now x), (Later y) ->
       Later (bop.blater (lift_const x) y)
  | (Later x), (Now y) ->
       Later (bop.blater x (lift_const y))
  | (Later x), (Later y) -> Later (bop.blater x y)
```

It is important to note that the above is still sub-optimal: the knowledge of one of the static arguments could sometimes be useful for simplifications, but is not used. We will rectify this in section 5.1.

4.3 Generating Let Statements

Straightforward inlining can easily result in code duplication. The usual solution [3, 24] involves writing the generator in continuation passing style (CPS). However, in the cases we treat here, we do not need to use such high-powered tools. We can instead use a simpler `let` generator.

The principal usage is to express sharing in *non-linear expressions*, which are expressions where a value is used more than once (for example, in the expression `x+(x+y)`, `x` is used non-linearly). We want to rewrite this as `let v=x in v+(v+y)`. To achieve this, we need the "body" `v+(v+y)` to be expressed as a function (of `v`). This can be done in two ways, either as a staged function, or as a generalized unary function. In each case, we can write a let generator over staged values – which we call `let_` for the staged case and `letp` for the generalized unary function case.

```
let lift_atom x = {c=x;a=true}
let let_ ce exp = match ce with
  | Now _ -> exp ce
  | Later c when c.a -> exp ce
  | Later c ->
     of_comp .< let v = .~(c.c) in
       .~ (to_code (exp (lift_atom .<v>.))) >.
let letp ce exp = match ce with
  | Now v -> Now (exp.unow v)
  | Later c when c.a ->
     Later (exp.ulater (lift_atom c.c))
  | Later c -> Later
     { c = .< let v = .~(c.c) in
         .~((exp.ulater (lift_atom .<v>.)).c) >.;
         a = false }
```

In practice, we frequently use `let_` as it gives us the same behaviour as `letp` in simple situations.

4.4 Base Types and code combinators

We also provide some simple facilities for generating code involving boolean predicates (as well as for String, but it is not used). Some code combinators (like sequencing and choice) are likewise provided.

5. The Number Types Layer

The number types layer provides generic abstractions of the number types. It is probably misnamed: it should properly be called the "single-sorted universal algebra" layer. But as that is rather a mouthful, and our uses are largely for algebras of "numbers", we have decided to remain with our early name. Its purpose remains the same: encapsulating the right properties so that we may implement a *family* of algorithms with the number type as a *variability*. Thus we introduce a hierarchy of abstractions based on traditional algebraic structures, such as rings and fields. However, we do not strive for completeness, but rather only define those structures that naturally appear in our algorithms.

In retrospect, this layer really should be divided into two layers: we have a first part that directly uses the low-level code layer objects (like `unary` and `binary`) for building simplifiers for algebraic structures, encoded using records. The second part uses the `staged` types to create "staged" versions of algebraic structures – encoded using module types.

5.1 Building Simplifiers

Monoids Although monoids, as a mathematical structure, are rather uninteresting (they support very few theorems), they are a pervasive structure in computer science. We recall that a monoid consists of a carrier set M, an associative binary operation $\star$ over M, and a special element $u \in M$ such that u is a left and right unit for $\star$. We can take advantage of staging and build *better* staged operators that respect the identity laws of the base operators. That is, the resulting staged operator can generate code that does not contain unnecessary operations, for all "types" that support a monoidal structure. In particular, we can generically simplify $x + 0$ and $1 * x$ to x in the monoids $(\mathbb{B}, +, 0)$ and $(\mathbb{Q}, *, 1)$, respectively.

Concretely, we can create a type for monoids, and then create a special evaluator for the monoid's binary operation that takes advantage of the monoidal structure to perform simplification whenever possible. When no simplification applies, we just dispatch to the generic case of staged binary operations, covered in the previous section.

```
type ('a,'b) monoid = {
  bop : ('a, 'b, 'b, 'b) binary;
  uelem : 'b
}
let mk_monoid mon x y = match x, y with
  | (Now x), y when x = (mon.uelem) -> y
  | x, (Now y) when y = (mon.uelem) -> x
  | x,y -> mk_binary mon.bop x y
```

Rings Mathematically, a *ring* consists of a carrier set R, a commutative associative binary operator $+$ with two-sided unit $0 \in R$, and an associative binary operator $*$ with two-sided unit $1 \in R$, where $*$ distributes over $+$ and 0 acts as an annihilator for $*$. Seen another way, a ring consists of 2 monoidal structures over the same carrier set R which satisfy some compatibility laws. As with a monoid, we can make a type `ring` and a simplifier:

```
type ('a,'b) ring = {
  monp : ('a,'b) monoid;
  mont : ('a,'b) monoid;
}
let mult_ring rng x y = match x, y with
  | (Now x), (Later y) when
      x = (rng.monp.uelem) -> Now rng.monp.uelem
  | (Later x), (Now y) when
      y = (rng.monp.uelem) -> Now rng.monp.uelem
  | x, y -> mk_monoid rng.mont x y
```

Note how we take definite advantage of the multiplicative monoid structure when simplifying the multiplicative aspect of a ring. The additive aspect is exactly covered by the additive monoid structure.

5.2 Staged Structures

We use Ocaml's module types to encode concepts such as sets, orderings, monoid, normed set, ring, field and real field. Each interface (aka module type) specifies a minimal set of (typed) operations for each concept. To minimize duplication of code at this level as well, we use OCaml's module inclusion for extension among types. The following *types* are ordered by the inclusion relation ($A \sqsubseteq B$ if module B includes module A):

$$\texttt{SET} \sqsubseteq \texttt{RING} \sqsubseteq \texttt{FIELD} \sqsubseteq \texttt{REALFIELD}.$$

By writing generators that are independent of the choice of representation, we obtain genericity. However, since we are in a generative context, the code generated is specific to the choices made. The principal reason for using modules (rather than records) here is sub-typing.

6. The Linear Algebra Layer

An abstract implementation of affine geometry uses matrices. But since we will always be generating code for fixed, usually very small, dimensions, the overhead associated with matrices (both in terms of time and space) are prohibitive. But this is not a problem: our linear algebra layer uses matrices at *generation time* only. We have made sure that all linear algebra operations are always computed strictly at generation time.

On the other hand, linear algebra provides an extremely useful, and generic, formalism for expressing all the important operations in affine geometry. We thus use this formalism, in the generator, as a convenient abstraction between the affine geometry layer and the "algebra" layer.

The most important function in this layer is the computation of *determinants*. Most of the affine geometry operations which we are interested in, are defined in terms of special determinants. However, these determinants are performed on structured matrices, with many statically known entries, many of which are in fact 0 and 1. By doing a careful expansion of the determinant used in the definition of each concept at generation-time, we can produce "efficient" computation sequences for them.

7. The Affine Space Layer

This layer encapsulates the concepts from affine geometry, and drawn from both the literature on the mathematics of geometry as well as computational geometry [1, 9, 17, 34]. We selected concepts that were n-dimensional, abstract but specializable, and that were required for mesh generation computations [15, 18].

Our design follows the mathematical abstraction in the affine geometry domain. For example, an affine space is defined as a triple $(\mathcal{D}, \mathcal{V}, \mathcal{P})$, where $\mathcal{D}$ is a division ring, $\mathcal{V}$ is a set of free vectors over $\mathcal{D}$, and $\mathcal{P}$ is a set of points (also over $\mathcal{D}$). In a sense, an affine space is a vector space without a marked "origin". This abstract definition says little about the dimension of the space or the coordinate systems. However, certain concepts can be extracted from the definition such as number types, vectors, and points. At this level, the interfaces corresponding to those objects should make no assumptions about dimensions or coordinate system. In other terms, the API for these module types should be dimensionless and coordinate-free.

Matrix Representation of Affine Transforms

An affine transform T on a vector x can be represented as $Tx = Ax + b$ where A is an n by n matrix, and b and x are both n-dimensional vectors. A is called the *linear transformation matrix*. x is the column vector representing the affine coordinates of the object subject to transformation. b is the additive part of the transformation, normally called the *translation* part. If we denote by a bold font symbol (such as $\mathbf{a}$) an n-dimensional column vector, then $T\mathbf{x} = \mathbf{y} = A\mathbf{x} + b$ can equivalently be written as

$$\begin{pmatrix} \mathbf{y} \\ 1 \end{pmatrix} = \begin{pmatrix} A & \mathbf{b} \\ \mathbf{0}^T & 1 \end{pmatrix} \begin{pmatrix} \mathbf{x} \\ 1 \end{pmatrix}$$

The expressive power that we get from the linear algebra layer allows us to implement the affine transforms following the formulation above.

8. The Geometric Objects Layer

Here we finally get geometric computations, with our selection driven by the prevalence of the objects and computations in mesh generation systems. There are challenges in designing such a layer: in typical texts on mesh generation, as well as on computational geometry, most primitive operations are given in special forms for 2 and 3 dimensions only. For example, a 2D in-circle test is usually defined as testing whether a point x is inside the circle circumscribing a particular triangle t, while in 3D the circle becomes a sphere and the triangle, a tetrahedron. All too frequently, 2 separate expressions are given for each of these computations, with no formal link between them. More abstract presentations define the in-circle test as testing whether a point is inside a hypersphere circumscribing a simplex – and then proceed to give a general constructive definition via the computation of the determinant of a particular matrix built in terms of the coordinates of the point x and simplex t. At this point, all our work on the lower layers pays off immediately: this abstract definition can directly be used in our generator, and furthermore the code it generates in special cases is identical to the special form found in textbooks. Note that we do not have to specialize the dimension – our generator can also produce dimension-generic forms of the in-circle test.

We give a quick overview of the fundamental geometric objects we have implemented.

Hyperplanes A hyperplane is an n-dimensional generalization of a point in 1D, a line in 2D, and a plane 3D. More specifically, it is a codimension 1 linear subspace of an n-dimensional space. It is frequently defined by giving $n - 1$ non-colinear points that lie on the hyperplane. The implementation of a hyperplane is free to choose whatever "container" representation it wishes for storing those points. The interface for hyperplanes leaves the representation completely abstract. Hyperplanes are parametrized by (representations for) a normed set, a vector and a point and some compatibility constraints. All of these are dimensionless and coordinate-free.

The interface to hyperplanes exposes functions for their construction, extracting the dimension, the normal vector and offset, as well as operations for 'frames' and local coordinates. Above this, one can then generically build functions for computing the distance between a point and hyperplane, computing whether a point is "above" or "below" (or on) a hyperplane, as well as projecting a point onto a hyperplane.

For example, given a hyperplane implementation `H`, we can compute the distance between a point p and a hyperplane h, as $\hat{n} \cdot (p - o)$, where $\hat{n}$ is a vector normal to h and o is an arbitrary point on h. In code, this is

```
let dist h p =
  H.V.dot (H.normal h) (H.P.sub p (H.orig h))

val dist:'a H.h ->'a H.P.point ->'a H.V.N.n=<fun>
```

We can see the delegation of duties – we ask the underlying vector space representation for the computation of a dot product, and the point presentation for the computation of "subtraction" of 2 points (which returns a vector).

Hyperspheres A hypersphere is a generalization of circle and sphere to any dimension. The implementation of a hypersphere is quite similar to that of a hyperplane – both are defined in terms of points, as we are interested in circumscribing spheres defined by points on the circumference, rather than general spheres defined by radius-center. Currently, the interface for hyperspheres is less extensive than that for a hyperplane, but they have a number of commonalities, as they are both orientable surface that can be closed (hypersphere) or open (hyperplane). The interface exposes functions for construction, and getting an arbitrary point on the hypersphere. From this one can provide generic implementations of getting the center point, the content (volume), the "surface", and defining an in-sphere predicate. The formulas are much more complicated than the formula for distance seen above, but nevertheless all reduce to operations from layers below this one.

Simplex A simplex is a generalization of the concept of a triangle to any dimension. The interface `SIMPLEX` provides functionality for construction of simplices, retrieval of vertices and faces, and accessing neighbourhood information. Then one can generically build an is-inside predicate for testing whether a point is inside a simplex.

9. Methodology

We first demonstrate the bottom-up part of our methodology for building code generators through a simple example. Although we were sorely tempted to use the `power` function for this purpose (as it actually demonstrates many of our ideas rather well), we will use ℓ^1 vector norm instead.

9.1 Example: ℓ^1 norm

The simplest implementation is for a `list` of `floats`:

```
let rec norm = function
    | [] -> 0.
    | x::xs -> abs_float x +. norm xs
val norm : float list -> float = <fun>
```

We achieve the task of building a generator for the above function via the following six steps:

(1) Generalize the type of numbers. What we really need is a 'normed set'. Our "numbers" can come from an arbitrary set as long as we have a function from that set into a commutative additive monoid as the 'target' of the norm function. Let us use `NS` for a normed set, over a normed commutative monoid `R`. Then we can write

```
let rec norm = function
    | [] -> NS.R.zero
    | x::xs -> NS.R.plus (NS.norm x) (norm xs)
val norm : NS.n list -> NS.R.n = <fun>
```

(2) Staging `norm`. We now lift from the normed set type `NS` to a staged version

```
let rec norm = function
    | [] -> Staged.of_immediate NS.R.zero
    | x::xs -> NS.R.plus_s (NS.norm_s x) (norm xs)
val norm : 'a NS.ns list -> 'a NS.R.ns = <fun>
```

where we use the staged version of `NS.R.plus` and `NS.norm`.

(3) Parametrizing `norm`. The function `norm` is parametric in `R`. By using a Functor, we can better express this parametricity. So we can lift this to use a Functor:

```
module GenericNorm (NS : NORMED_SET) =
struct
  let rec norm = function
    | [] -> Staged.of_immediate NS.R.zero
    | x::xs -> NS.R.plus_s (NS.norm_s x) (norm xs)
end
```

(4) Abstracting the container. Vectors do not have to be represented by lists - any container which implements a fold will do. We can repeat steps (1)-(3) above, but for the type of lists generalized to any type with a fold. Since it is frequent to first do a 'map' then a 'fold', an optimized version is provided. The most general code would then be

```
module GenericNorm(NS : NORMED_SET)
                  (C: FOLDABLE with t = R.n) =
struct
  let norm = C.mapfold(NS.norm_s)(NS.R.plus_s)
                (Staged.of_immediate NS.R.zero)
end
```

(5) Collecting variabilities. The generator `GenericNorm` has two variabilities: the normed set, and the container. These variabilities can be collected in the (module) type:

```
module type NORM_VAR =
sig
  module NS : NORMED_SET
  module C : FOLDABLE with t = NS.n
end
```

which becomes the input for the generator.

(6) Building the generator. The generator, `GenNorm`, is defined as:

```
module GenNorm (NV : NORM_VAR) =
struct
 let gen_norm () =
  let module GP = GenericNorm(NV.NS)(NV.C) in
   .< fun x -> .~(Staged.to_code
        (GP.norm (Staged.of_atom .<x>.))) >.
end

module GenNorm :
 functor (NV : NORM_VAR) ->
  sig
   val gen_norm :
    unit -> ('a, NV.NS.n NV.C.t -> NV.NS.R.n) code
  end
```

The generator `gen_norm` is put in a functor which takes as input the module `NV` of variabilities. In other words, `NV` is the configuration for the generator.

In fact, all of our containers are fixed-length. This is another variability which can be exposed (but we have chosen not to do so in this example to try to keep things relatively simple).

We can instantiate our norm function with different number type implementations as well as different containers. If we choose say `Float_Ring` as our instantiation of a normed set (where floats are elements of the set and floats are also used as the commutative monoid), and a 2-tuple for the container, the result is:

```
.<fun x_1 -> abs_float(fst x_1) +.
            (abs_float(snd x_1))>.
```

Choosing `IntegerRing` and a 1 dimensional container represented using a record (with single entry `x`), we get:

```
 .<fun x_1 -> abs (x_1.x) >.
```

The code has no traces of `norm` or `mapfold`. Furthermore, there are no traces of the "zero" of the monoid, since it always occurs statically and operations with it can always be optimized out at generation time.

9.2 Aspects of the Methodology

The bottom-up aspects of our methodology are well-known in the generic programming [30, 37] world. From pieces of working code, one finds the minimal assumptions necessary for ensuring the operational semantics and the correctness properties, and then abstracts out every other aspect. As shown above, this can frequently be done incrementally. There are two difficult aspects of this task: recognizing the minimal assumptions, and abstracting out "the rest". Recognizing minimal assumptions is a very mathematical endeavour, which requires a thorough knowledge of abstract algebra, geometry, topology, etc. The abstracting step on the other hand is difficult because one must use the facilities available for abstraction in the host programming language. Finding appropriate encodings of structures to enable parametrization can be quite challenging in a typed environment.

The top-down aspects were somewhat counter-intuitive to us, when we first encountered them:

1. The *code generation* aspects need to be abstracted out *first*, and integrated at the very base of the hierarchy.
2. Very abstract mathematical formulations help produce the best code. Our reasoning here is that the abstract formulation captures the core knowledge of each concept. Once this is captured, then it becomes quite clear where to put in particular optimizations (like algebraic simplifications), which are otherwise done in an ad hoc manner.
3. More layers produces better code than fewer layers. In normal code, more layers produces slower programs – although it does improve modularity. In the generative setting, more layers helps expose more opportunities for attaching meta-knowledge (in other words, static invariants), and they are then used for generating better code.
4. Separating out operational concepts (like arrays) from mathematical concepts (like matrices) is crucial. An array is really a memory arrangement, while a matrix is a representation of a linear operator with respect to a certain basis. The "natural" operations on matrices have completely different interfaces than those of arrays.
5. Separating out concepts (like points and vectors) that are usually stored the same way, but whose semantics is quite different.

There is a real tension between the bottom-up and the top-down aspects of the methodology. For example, when we first attempted what amounts to a pure bottom-up approach to "reverse engineer" abstract mathematical structures from a collection of existing geometry kernels, we failed. This is because we did not, at that point, know about *geometric algebra*. This was the key abstraction we were missing to proceed. From that point on, we actively looked for more such abstractions, and used them as appropriate.

10. Discussion

Here we discuss a few more items we learned while performing this work.

10.1 Infrastructure

At first, the additional infrastructure seems rather heavyweight. However the most complex parts are actually the bottom 3 layers, and the upper layers end up actually being much simpler than "normal". This is because the code in the upper layers is essentially identical to the abstract mathematical formulation of the concepts. Furthermore, as more variabilities are added, the payoff becomes increasingly clear, as the amount of extra effort necessary is very small. And since these lower layers are quite generic, they should be shared amongst any program families of scientific computation software, thus lowering the overall development costs.

10.2 Linear algebra

We want to remark again that our linear algebra layer performs all of its computations at generation-time. The computations performed here are the generation of *simplified closed-form expressions* for determinant expansions. This hints that other computations that are essentially symbolic *computer algebra* may become an important part of code generators.

10.3 Eliminating Code Duplication

We already covered the generation of let bindings in section 4.3. But it is easy to get the impression that this is a feature only used in the lower layers, which is not at all the case. For example, consider the function `length` for computing the Euclidean length of a vector. For `N` a `REALFIELD`, a naive implementation of `length` is:

```
let length v = N.sqrt_s (dot v v)
```

However, if `v` is an non-atomic expression, the resulting code will contain duplications. We can do this via

```
let length v = N.sqrt_s(let_ v (fun x->dot x x))
```

which avoids the duplication.

10.4 Optimizations

By leveraging techniques originally developed for partial evaluation, we are able to write a code generator that performs both *constant folding* and *constant propagation*. By tracking which (code) values are non-atomic, we can use known let-insertion techniques to make sure that these computations are not duplicated. We do this not only for "base" values, but also for compound data-structures (like vectors), where the gain is even more noticeable[4].

While many have implemented algebraic simplifications before us, we believe that we have exploited the underlying mathematical *structures* in a novel manner. In other words, rather than using the mathematical structures only in (generally paper) proofs of the correctness of our algebraic simplifications, we use the structures directly in the code. This also serves to structure our own code, as well as making these simplifications generic.

10.5 Future Work

While we achieved our goals with respect to what we set out to learn, based on that knowledge, there are a number of items we would like to do.

1. *Expand the staging layer.* Many refinements can be done in the staging layer.
   (a) Modifying the type `staged` to accommodate more complex types such as staged pairs and records. In particular, apply the techniques from [11].
   (b) Employing the monadic techniques from [4], to improve the generation of control structures, and let-bindings.
   (c) Implementing more code optimizations such as loop unrolling and other code transformations from [5].

[4] At the source code level. We encourage the reader to run the tests included (directory `ctest`) in our distribution, and to inspect the generated code.

2. *Expand the abstract algebra layer.* For example, the current abstractions do not differentiate between concepts such as division rings and commutative rings. Such a finer set of abstractions will allow expressing the geometric algorithms in terms as close as possible to the domain concepts and hence, reduce the gap between program code and domain concepts. This will also be reusable for many other projects.
3. *Experiment with different geometric algebras.* Affine algebra is not the only choice of "geometric algebra." Other algebras should also be considered in future experiments. For example, the algebra in [14] looks promising for handling different coordinate systems.
4. Rework our implementation of mesh generation (not presented here) to use our geometric kernel.
5. Determine how to best encode domain-specific constraints. Some of these are implemented via types, while others are done via generation-time values. The advantage of encoding this information in the type system is that the compiler will automatically track this for us; the disadvantage is that the resulting error messages can be generously described as cryptic. Using generation-time values requires more initial effort from the generator-writer, but the benefit to the user of the generator is that we can output precise, domain-specific error messages.

11. Related Work

Previous work on the geometric core of mesh generation and computational geometry has focused on obtaining genericity, flexibility, or performance, but rarely attempting all three simultaneously.

Simpson [38] presents an attempt to decouple mesh generators from the underlying geometry by using object-oriented programming techniques to dynamically bind computations to different local coordinate representations. However, object-oriented programming can introduce run-time overhead because of dynamic dispatch. XYZ GeoBench [35] offers a programming environment for implementing geometric algorithms by relying on object-oriented programming and virtual functions to implement genericity – for example their geometric algorithms are implemented in an arithmetic-independent manner. However, here again, the use of dynamic binding for achieving flexibility can result in performance penalties. By avoiding dynamic dispatch, we believe we can achieve the same level of genericity as these libraries, but better performance.

LEDA [28] is a comprehensive library of data types and algorithms focused on geometry. LEDA makes use of C++ templates to achieve genericity. The library has a layered design that decouples geometric algorithms from number types. The independence from coordinate systems is achieved by having two sets of geometric kernels: one for Cartesian coordinates, and another for the homogeneous coordinates. This duplication is a challenge to the extensibility and maintainability of the overall library. Our current work covers but a small fraction of their extensive library; however, we believe our design will scale better than theirs. We also have the advantage of the stronger abstraction mechanisms available in OCaml over those of C++.

Another large C++ library for geometry, also using templates is CGAL [13]. They achieve extensibility by parametrizing each geometric object by the geometric kernel type and the number type. For vector mathematics, Blitz++ [46] pioneered many of the C++ template meta-programming technologies used in LEDA and CGAL. As with LEDA, we believe that our design and use of OCaml's abstraction mechanisms will allow us to scale further.

The work on using MetaOCaml for scientific computation has already been cited several times throughout this paper.

Generative programming in the context of numeric computation has a very long history: the 1953 work of Kahrimanian [23] on what is now called automatic differentiation is a personal favourite. By 1972 (see for example the beautiful work of A. Norman [31] on code generation for the solution of ODEs), the techniques were already quite advanced. Outside the C++ libraries already mentioned, modern work would include FFTW [16] and Spiral [33].

12. Conclusion

Our eventual goal is to have a rich program family of mesh generators, implemented as a generator. Here we report on the foundations of this, which is the implementation and design of a program family of geometric kernels, implemented generatively, using typed meta-programming. By cleanly separating run-time from generation-time, we are able to create a much more modular program family (for geometry) than has previously been done, without paying the abstraction cost associated with traditional modularity mechanisms. More precisely, the source code which we obtain from our generator is comparable to the human-written source code for the same specialized situation.

We believe that typed generative programming is relatively successful for the implementation of program families because it allows extremely modular code as well as the use of advanced abstraction techniques (in the generator) without sacrificing efficiency of the generated code. It does impose an extra burden on the generator writer: being conversant with a level of abstract mathematics that is not commonly seen in computer science education. There is also an extra design effort consisting in capturing some invariants (like being either "atomic" or a computation) which are only obvious post-facto. But, in the end, since the generator's higher layers are based on abstractions that are natural to the domain itself, we believe this makes correctness much easier to verify, as well as improving maintainability.

Furthermore, for well-understood domains, we have developed a methodology for writing (typed) generators based on leveraging the most abstract mathematical formalization of that domain for structuring modules. As this methodology is compatible with the successive generalization of existing code, it can be applied to existing (OCaml) codes.

References

[1] Michele Audin. *Geometry.* Springer-Verlag, Inc., New York, NY, USA, 2003.

[2] Jacques Carette. Gaussian elimination: a case study in efficient genericity with MetaOCaml. *Sci. Comput. Program.*, 62(1):3–24, 2006.

[3] Jacques Carette and Oleg Kiselyov. Multi-stage programming with functors and monads: Eliminating abstraction overhead from generic code. In Robert Glück and Michael Lowry, editors, *Generative Programming and Component Engineering*, volume 3676 of *Lecture Notes in Computer Science*, pages 256–274. Springer Berlin / Heidelberg, 2005.

[4] Jacques Carette and Oleg Kiselyov. Multi-stage programming with functors and monads: Eliminating abstraction overhead from generic code. *Science of Computer Programming*, In Press, Corrected Proof, 2008.

[5] Albert Cohen, Sébastien Donadio, Maria-Jesus Garzaran, Christoph Herrmann, Oleg Kiselyov, and David Padua. In search of a program generator to implement generic transformations for high-performance computing. *Sci. Comput. Program.*, 62(1):25–46, 2006.

[6] Krzysztof Czarnecki and Ulrich W. Eisenecker. *Generative programming: methods, tools, and applications.* ACM Press/Addison-Wesley Publishing Co., New York, NY, USA, 2000.

[7] Krzysztof Czarnecki, Ulrich W. Eisenecker, Robert Gluck, David Vandevoorde, and Todd L. Veldhuizen. Generative programming and active libraries. In *Selected Papers from the International Seminar on*

Generic Programming, pages 25–39, London, UK, 2000. Springer-Verlag.

[8] Krzysztof Czarnecki, John T. O'Donnell, Jörg Striegnitz, and Walid Taha. DSL implementation in MetaOCaml, Template Haskell, and C++. In Lengauer et al. [25], pages 51–72.

[9] Mark de Berg, Marc van Kreveld, Mark Overmars, and Otfried Schwarzkopf. *Computational Geometry: Algorithms and Applications*. Springer, 1st edition, 1997.

[10] T. D. DeRose. A coordinate-free approach to geometric programming. *Theory and practice of geometric modeling*, pages 291–305, 1989.

[11] Iavor Diatchki and Tim Sheard. Staging algebraic datatypes. `http://web.cecs.pdx.edu/~sheard/papers/stagedData.ps`.

[12] A. H. ElSheikh, S. Smith, and S. E. Chidiac. Semi-formal design of reliable mesh generation systems. *Adv. Eng. Softw.*, 35(12):827–841, 2004.

[13] Andreas Fabri, Geert-Jan Giezeman, Lutz Kettner, Stefan Schirra, and Sven Schönherr. On the design of CGAL a computational geometry algorithms library. *Softw. Pract. Exper.*, 30(11):1167–1202, 2000.

[14] Daniel Fontijne and Leo Dorst. Modeling 3D Euclidean geometry. *IEEE Comput. Graph. Appl.*, 23(2):68–78, 2003.

[15] Pascal Jean Frey and Paul-Louis George. *Mesh Generation: Application to Finite Elements*. ISTE, 2007.

[16] Matteo Frigo and Steven G. Johnson. FFTW: An adaptive software architecture for the FFT. In *Proc. 1998 IEEE Intl. Conf. Acoustics Speech and Signal Processing*, volume 3, pages 1381–1384. IEEE, 1998.

[17] Jean Gallier. *Geometric methods and applications: for computer science and engineering*. Springer-Verlag, London, UK, 2000.

[18] P.L. George and H. Borouchaki. *Delaunay Triangulation and Meshing: Application to Finite-Elements*. Hermes, New York, NY, 1998.

[19] Ron Goldman. On the algebraic and geometric foundations of computer graphics. *ACM Trans. Graph.*, 21(1):52–86, 2002.

[20] Philip W. Grant, Magne Haveraaen, and Michael F. Webster. Coordinate free programming of computational fluid dynamics problems. *Sci. Program.*, 8(4):211–230, 2000.

[21] Objective Caml home page. `http://caml.inria.fr/ocaml/`.

[22] Neil D. Jones, Carsten K. Gomard, and Peter Sestoft. *Partial evaluation and automatic program generation*. Prentice-Hall, Inc., Upper Saddle River, NJ, USA, 1993.

[23] H. G. Kahrimanian. Analytical differentiation by a digital computer. Master's thesis, Temple University, May 1953.

[24] Oleg Kiselyov, Kedar N. Swadi, and Walid Taha. A methodology for generating verified combinatorial circuits. In *EMSOFT '04: Proceedings of the 4th ACM international conference on Embedded software*, pages 249–258, New York, NY, USA, 2004. ACM.

[25] Christian Lengauer, Don S. Batory, Charles Consel, and Martin Odersky, editors. *Domain-Specific Program Generation, International Seminar, Dagstuhl Castle, Germany, March 23-28, 2003, Revised Papers*, volume 3016 of *Lecture Notes in Computer Science*. Springer, 2004.

[26] Stephen Mann, Nathan Litke, and Tony Derose. A Coordinate Free Geometry ADT. Technical Report CS-97-15, Computer Science Dept., University of Waterloo, 1997.

[27] Kurt Mehlhorn, Michael Müller, Stefan Näher, Stefan Schirra, Michael Seel, Christian Uhrig, and Joachim Ziegler. A computational basis for higher-dimensional computational geometry and applications. In *SCG '97: Proceedings of the thirteenth annual symposium on Computational geometry*, pages 254–263, New York, NY, USA, 1997. ACM.

[28] Kurt Mehlhorn and Stefan Näher. *LEDA: a platform for combinatorial and geometric computing*. Cambridge University Press, New York, NY, USA, 1999.

[29] MetaOCaml Home Page. `http://www.metaocaml.org/`.

[30] D. R. Musser and A. A. Stepanov. Generic programming. In P. (Patrizia) Gianni, editor, *Symbolic and algebraic computation: International Symposium ISSAC '88, Rome, Italy, July 4–8, 1988: proceedings*, volume 358 of *Lecture Notes in Computer Science*, pages 13–25. Springer Verlag, 1989.

[31] Arthur C. Norman. A system for the solution of initial and two-point boundary value problems. In *Proceedings of the ACM annual conference - Volume 2*, ACM '72, pages 826–834, New York, NY, USA, 1972. ACM.

[32] David Lorge Parnas. On the design and development of program families. *IEEE Trans. Software Eng.*, 2(1):1–9, 1976.

[33] Markus Püschel, José M. F. Moura, Jeremy Johnson, David Padua, Manuela Veloso, Bryan Singer, Jianxin Xiong, Franz Franchetti, Aca Gacic, Yevgen Voronenko, Kang Chen, Robert W. Johnson, and Nicholas Rizzolo. SPIRAL: Code generation for DSP transforms. *Proceedings of the IEEE, special issue on "Program Generation, Optimization, and Adaptation"*, 93(2):232– 275, 2005.

[34] Philip J. Schneider and David Eberly. *Geometric Tools for Computer Graphics*. Elsevier Science Inc., New York, NY, USA, 2002.

[35] Peter Schorn. Implementing the XYZ GeoBench: A programming environment for geometric algorithms. In *CG '91: Proceedings of the International Workshop on Computational Geometry – Methods, Algorithms and Applications*, pages 187–202, London, UK, 1991. Springer-Verlag.

[36] Tim Sheard. Accomplishments and research challenges in meta-programming. In *Proceedings of the Second International Workshop on Semantics, Applications, and Implementation of Program Generation*, pages 2–44, London, UK, 2001. Springer-Verlag.

[37] Jeremy G. Siek and Andrew Lumsdaine. The matrix template library: A generic programming approach to high performance numerical linear algebra. In *ISCOPE '98: Proceedings of the Second International Symposium on Computing in Object-Oriented Parallel Environments*, pages 59–70, London, UK, 1998. Springer-Verlag.

[38] R. Bruce Simpson. Isolating geometry in mesh programming. In *Proc. of the 8th Int'l Meshing Roundtable*, pages 45–54, South Lake Tahoe, California, October 1999.

[39] S. Smith and C. H. Chen. Commonality analysis for mesh generating systems. Technical Report CAS-04-10-SS, McMaster University, 2004.

[40] S. Smith, J. McCutchan, and F. Cao. Program families in scientific computing. In J. Sprinkle, J. Gray, M. Rossi, and J.-P. Tolvanen, editors, *7th OOPSLA Workshop on Domain Specific Modelling*, pages 39–47, Montreal, Quebec, 2007.

[41] Walid Taha. *Multi-stage programming: its theory and applications*. PhD thesis, Oregon Graduate Institute of Science and Technology, 1999.

[42] Walid Taha. A gentle introduction to multi-stage programming. In *Domain-specific Program Generation, LNCS*, pages 30–50. Springer-Verlag, 2004.

[43] Walid Taha and Michael Florentin Nielsen. Environment classifiers. *SIGPLAN Not.*, 38(1):26–37, 2003.

[44] Walid Taha and Tim Sheard. MetaML and multi-stage programming with explicit annotations. *Theor. Comput. Sci.*, 248(1-2):211–242, 2000.

[45] Walid Mohamed Taha. *Multistage programming: its theory and applications*. PhD thesis, Oregon Graduate Institute of Science and Technology, 1999. Supervisor-Sheard, Tim.

[46] Todd L. Veldhuizen. Arrays in Blitz++. In *ISCOPE '98: Proceedings of the Second International Symposium on Computing in Object-Oriented Parallel Environments*, pages 223–230, London, UK, 1998. Springer-Verlag.

[47] Todd L. Veldhuizen. Guaranteed optimization for domain-specific programming. In Lengauer et al. [25], pages 307–324.

[48] David M. Weiss. Commonality analysis: A systematic process for defining families. In *Proceedings of the Second International ESPRIT ARES Workshop on Development and Evolution of Software Architectures for Product Families*, pages 214–222, London, UK, 1998. Springer-Verlag.

An Embedded Language for Programming Protocol Stacks in Embedded Systems *

Yan Wang and Verónica Gaspes
CERES, Halmstad University, Sweden
yan.wang, veronica.gaspes@hh.se

Abstract

Protocol stack specifications are well-structured documents that follow a number of conventions and notations that have proven very useful for the design and dissemination of communication protocols. Protocol stack implementations on the other hand, are done in low-level languages, using error-prone programming techniques resulting in programs that are difficult to relate to the specifications, difficult to maintain, modify, extend and reuse. To overcome these problems we propose a domain-specific language that provides abstractions close to the notations used in protocol specifications. From descriptions in our language we generate C programs that can be integrated with other systems software. The language provides constructs to describe packet formats, including physical layout, constraints and dependencies. It also provides constructs for state machines and for layering protocols into stacks. Experiments show that the C programs we generate are comparable in performance and binary size to hand-crafted C programs.

Categories and Subject Descriptors D.1.1 [*Programming techniques*]: Applicative (Functional) Programming; C.2.2 [*Computer Communication Networks*]: Network Protocols/Protocol Architecture; D.3.2 [*Programming languages*]: Specialized Application Languages

General Terms Languages, Design

Keywords Domain-Specific Language, Embedded Compilation, Embedded Network Software

1. Introduction

As embedded systems increase in number and ubiquity, embedded network software, most notoriously protocol stack implementation, plays a central role in their development. New communication services with new demands lead to the design of new protocols that have to be implemented. Also, new hardware platforms require re-implementations of well-known infrastructure protocols. Network software has an impact on time-to-market, scalability, maintainability and on the possibility of making fair comparisons when selecting a protocol.

* A very brief description of this approach was described previously in a short paper [23].

PEPM'11, January 24–25, 2011, Austin, Texas, USA.


```
0                   1                   2                   3
0 1 2 3 4 5 6 7 8 9 0 1 2 3 4 5 6 7 8 9 0 1 2 3 4 5 6 7 8 9 0 1
+-+-+-+-+-+-+-+-+-+-+-+-+-+-+-+-+-+-+-+-+-+-+-+-+-+-+-+-+-+-+-+-+
|Version|  IHL  |Type of Service|          Total Length         |
+-+-+-+-+-+-+-+-+-+-+-+-+-+-+-+-+-+-+-+-+-+-+-+-+-+-+-+-+-+-+-+-+
|         Identification        |Flags|      Fragment Offset    |
+-+-+-+-+-+-+-+-+-+-+-+-+-+-+-+-+-+-+-+-+-+-+-+-+-+-+-+-+-+-+-+-+
                        ... ...
Version: The Version field indicates the format of the internet
         header. This document describes version 4.
IHL: Internet Header Length is the length of the internet header
     ... Note that the minimum value for a correct header is 5.
           +------+     +------+     +------+
           | TCP  |     | UDP  | ... | ...  |
           +------+     +------+     +------+
              |            |            |
           +---------------------------+-----+
           |    Internet Protocol & ICMP     |
           +---------------------------------+
```

Figure 1. IP specification (excerpt from RFC791)

```
00581 len=(BUF->len[0]<<8)+BUF->len[1]-(BUF->vhl&0x0f)*4;
00582 offset=(((BUF->ipoffset[0]&0x3f)<<8)+BUF->ipoffset[1])*8;

00819   goto udp_send;

00840 /* Check validity of the IP header. */
00841 if(BUF->vhl != 0x45) { /* IP version and header length. */
...
00844   UIP_LOG("ip: invalid version or header length.");
00845   goto drop;
00846 }
...
00915       goto udp_input;
...
00952     goto tcp_input;
...
00957     goto udp_input;
...
01379   goto tcp_send;
```

Figure 2. Code fragments from uIP: *uip.c* (abstracted)

1.1 Problem

Implementing protocol stacks is tedious, error-prone and time-consuming. There is a characteristic gap between how protocol stacks are specified and how they are implemented: well-established protocol specification techniques and notations contrast with error-prone low-level programming techniques in the implementations, typically written using C and in tight connection to the platform.

As an example, consider fragments of the well-known IPv4 (Internet Protocol version 4) specification [18] (Figure 1), and fragments of corresponding C code taken from uIP [4], a well-written TCP/IP implementation for micro-controllers (Figure 2). Figure 1 shows the *packet specification*. The physical layout is given as the bit-length for the header fields. For instance, the **Total Length** field takes 16 bits and the **Fragment Offset** field takes 13 bits. In the implementation, these values are established using bit-shifts and bit-masks on a raw buffer which stores incoming packets (line 00581 and line 00582 in Figure 2). Constraints and field dependencies are specified by accompanying text in the specification. For instance, in the implementation of IPv4, the **Version** field must be 4. Furthermore, the value of IHL must be 5 when no options field is used. Both values are checked in one operation in line 00841. In Figure 1, an intuitive graph shows the relationships between IP and other protocols, i.e., TCP and UDP. Corresponding code in the implementation consists of goto-statements in various locations: lines 00819, 00915, 00952, 00957 and 01379.

The example above illustrates three problems that we have identified in typical protocol stack implementations:

P1. Packet specifications turn into cumbersome code fragments that use type casts, offsets, bitmasks and other low-level operations that implement packet processing. Programming in this style is tedious and a common source of errors that are very difficult to spot.

P2. Code fragments reached via goto-statements and packet processing fragments that occur all over the program make it extremely difficult to update an implementation following modifications or extensions in a specification.

P3. Protocol stacks are designed and specified in a modular fashion, but are commonly implemented as a monolithic unit for sake of speed and code size. Code can hardly be reused when new requirements are added; it is common practice to rewrite large parts.

1.2 A Language Based Approach

To address these problems and enable a faster and more sustainable development, we propose a domain-specific compilation-based approach. We have developed a domain-specific language Protege (*Prot*ocol Impl*e*mentation *Ge*nerator) embedded in Haskell with the following features:

F1. Protege provides a high-level language with domain-specific abstractions which are syntactically close to the notations used in specifications. Instead of writing packet processing code with bit patterns, the programmer can provide abstract packet descriptions from which bit-oriented packet processing code will be generated.

F2. Protocol stacks become easy to maintain. The Protege programmer uses packet combinators and protocol combinators to construct packets and to layer the individual protocols. Changes or extensions in a specification have a direct correspondence to changes in the implementation.

F3. Code for the individual protocols can be reused without much ado. Protocols within a stack can be developed in isolation, and the stack is compiled as a whole to enable cross-layer optimizations.

Other features of Protege include type safe arithmetic operations and header declarations. Protege programs are easy to integrate to other systems programs due to the fact that we use the language to generate C. The compilation scheme guarantees certain good implementation disciplines, e.g. memory usage can be predicted during code generation and semantic checks can detect implementation errors such as cyclic protocol graphs.

This paper presents the language Protege in detail (Section 2) and focuses on describing its embedding (Section 3) and implementation (Section 4). In Section 5, we describe the supporting runtime system. Section 6 briefly evaluates Protege, Section 7 discusses the related work, and the final section concludes.

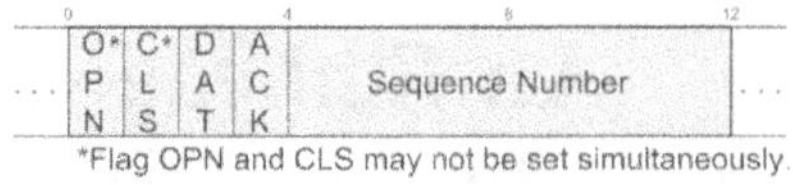

Figure 3. p1's packet specification

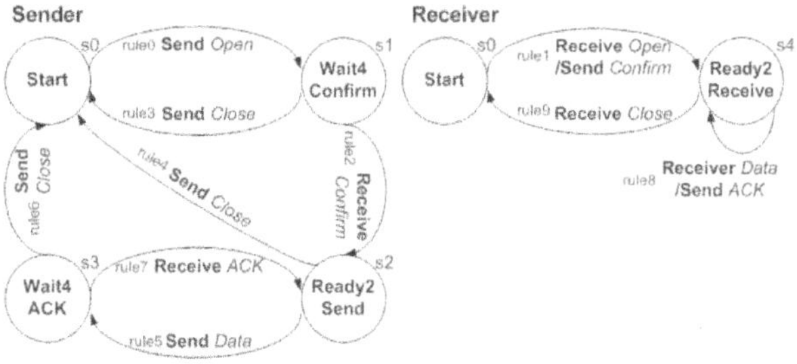

Figure 4. p1's protocol logic specification

2. The Protege Language

Network software is typically organized according to a layered architecture to make design, implementation, evaluation and reuse easier. Complex functionality of network software is divided into smaller individual pieces, called *protocols*, which are specified by two aspects: the packet format and the protocol logic. Single protocols can then be hierarchically layered into *a protocol stack* to realize more complex functionality [17].

Protege is designed to retain a close correspondence to this hierarchical and modular specification style in the implementation, to encourage reuse and achieve good readability and maintainability. Each protocol is described in isolation and then integrated into a stack using combinators. In turn, each protocol is also described in a modular way: packet specifications are separate from protocol logic. This similarity with how protocol specifications are organized makes our language accessible to network engineers. Since packet processing code is automatically generated, protocol logic implementation is liberated from low-level data manipulation related to the wire format of packet, which substantially reduces the complexity of such implementations.

Changes in protocol specifications directly carry over to the Protege descriptions. These descriptions become in fact specification documents and the generated code is, by construction, consistent with the specification. Typical problems like forgetting to change one of the possibly many code fragments of the protocol logic referring to a packet field are thus avoided. In what follows we illustrate these different parts using an example and providing details on the way.

2.1 An Example Using Protege

The packet layout of our example protocol p1 is depicted in Figure 3. The packet header of a p1 packet contains four one-bit flag fields, OPN (open), CLS (close), DAT (data), and ACK (acknowledgement), followed by an eight-bit field **Sequence Number**. One constraint on the values is that the flags OPN and CLS should not be both set at the same time.

The protocol logic is defined as a finite state machine (FSM), describing the different actions taken by the protocol software over time. Figure 4 shows how data exchange progresses through five states during the lifetime of a p1 connection. For example, **Start** represents waiting for a connection. After a **Send *Open*** event (sending out a request to open a connection), `p1` changes to state `Wait4Confirm`, and waits for an acknowledgment. The protocol logic specifies rules of operation for interactions between communication peer protocols as *Sender* and *Receiver* (left and right side of the Figure). The protocol logic specification also includes how a protocol interacts with adjacent protocols in a stack. For example, as shown in Figure 6, `p1` is situated between its upper protocol `p2` and the lower protocol `p0`.

```
p1 :: Protocol
p1 = protocol{
  name    = "p1",
  packet  = packetheader<:>opn<:>cls<:>dat<:>ack<:>seqn,
  variables  = declareVariable <.> seqn_v,
  send    = __builtFSM (fsm<+>rule0<+>...<+>rule6),
  receive = __builtFSM (fsm<+>rule1<+>...<+>rule9)}
opn  = header 0 (uint8h bit_1)
cls  = header 1 (uint8h bit_1)|* not1togetherwith opn
...
seqn = header 4 (uint8h bit_8)
not1togetherwith x y = (y.==.1).?.(x.==.0, true)
seqn_v = variable 0 typeUint8
s0 = state "Start"
s1 = state "Wait4Confirm"
... ...
rule1 = rule s0 (__receive) (opn.==.1) s4
                (do ack*:=*1;__send)
rule5 = rule s2 (do dat*:=*1;seqn*:=*seqn_v;
                    seqn_v*:=*(seqn_v+1);__send) true s3
                __donothing
```

Figure 5. A Protege example: protocol definition

The implementation of `p1` in Protege is shown in Figure 5. P1's packet layout is specified as a sequence of header fields (`opn`, `cls`, `dat`, etc.). Both their syntactic and semantic properties can be specified. For example, `opn` is the header field with id 0 and size 1 (bit), type unsigned char (`uint8h`). The field `seqn` has the same type, id 4 and size 8 (bits). Constraints are specified by header field predicates on the right of the operator `(|*)`. In our example, the constraints on `opn` and `cls` are constructed using the helper function `not1togetherwith`, a test that fails when the respective header field parameters are both set to `1`.

The protocol logic has to specify how to transmit packets via its lower-layer protocols (`send`), and how to pass incoming packets to the upper-layer protocols (`receive`). Both are specified in the form of a FSM with output. For example, the possible protocol states for `p1` are `Start(s0)`, `Wait4Confirm(s1)`, etc. Transitions are defined by rules including the old state, the input event, the transition condition that must be satisfied, the new state and the generated output event. For instance, `rule1` describes the receiver's transition from the `Start` state (s0) into state `Ready2Receive` (s4), when it receives (`__receive`) a packet `Open` (with `opn.==.1`), and the corresponding output is to send a `Confirm` packet (`do ack*:=*1;__send`).

```
stack0 =
  stack 0
    (protocol p2)
    <|>
    (protocol p1)
    <|>
    (protocol p0)<&&>[(P0.field0.==.0)])
stack1 = ...
graph = stack0<->stack1
```

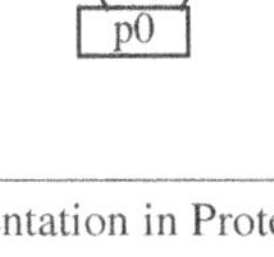

Figure 6. A protocol graph implementation in Protege

Figure 6 shows how Protege uses a set of combinators to overlay individually developed protocols into protocol stacks (graphs) in a structured manner. The basic combinator `<|>` overlays several protocols in a top-down protocol stack. In our example, a stack `stack0` is constructed which overlays protocol `p2` above `p1`, and `p1` above `p0`. Additional assumptions of packet encapsulation are declared in the constraints on field values using `<&&>`. Here, a `p0` packet should have value `0` in `field0` indicating that the upper-layer protocol is `p1`. Finally, combinator `<->` combines two of these protocol stacks, merging duplicate instances of the same protocol (in our example, `p0` at the bottom).

2.2 Specifying Packets

Packets are fundamental components of protocols. They are messages that computers on the network use for communication, including information to be sent to the receiver, e.g., the address of the sender, and how the message is encoded, e.g., the first byte of the message is used to store the sender's address. Packets are semi-structured data including the physical layout of the fields as well as the dependencies and constraints on the values of the fields. A packet specification describes the physical layout in terms of the packet format. Figures are used to provide a bit-length for each of the header fields. Dependencies and constraints are usually provided via informal explanations written in natural language (as we did in Figure 3).

Protege provides a data description language based on the Data Description Calculus [10] that uses types for describing packets. A packet format is defined as a sequence of header fields put together using the combinator `<:>` to resemble the packet specification figure.

packet ::= **packetheader** [<:> *field*]*
field ::= **header** *id ftype*
ftype ::= *B e* | *ftype* |* *p* | **orh** *ftype ftype*
| **andh** *ftype ftype* | **seqh** *e ftype*

A field introduces its index (`id`) within the packet and its field type (`ftype`), which can be one of the following:

- *Base type.* B stands for a primitive C type and e is a numerical expression that indicates the size in bits needed for its representation. The advanced field type's primitive type depends on its base type. The numerical expression could be another field in the header thus introducing depedencies.
- *Constrained type.* For a field type `ftype`, a predicate `p` on the field value may be added using the combinator `(|*)`. This constraint can also make use of other fields in the header.
- *Sum type.* Given two field types `ft1` and `ft2`, an alternative field type `orh ft1 ft2` can be constructed where `ft1` and `ft2` have to have the same primitive type, but may vary in bit size.
- *Intersection type.* Given the field types `ft1` and `ft2`, a field type `andh ft1 ft2` has both type `ft1` and `ft2`.
- *Array type.* From a field type `ft` and a numerical expression `e`, a field type `seqh e ft` describes a sequence of length `e` with elements of field type `ft`.

A field can be referred to from various Protege expressions, provided that the field type can be used in the respective context. For example, in

```
headlen = header 3 (inth bit_32)
```

the type of field `headlen` is `int` (specified as its primitive field type `inth`, "int header field"). Usage of the header field in Protege expressions is type-checked during compilation, and the resulting type in the generated code for a field depends on its primitive type (we give details in a later section). Protege also allows the specification of variable sized fields as a dependency between fields. For example, in the specification

```
option = header 15 (seqh (headlen*4-20) (uint8h bit_8))
```

the `option` field is an array of unsigned char, and the number of elements in this array depends on the value of the `headlen` field.

2.3 Specifying Protocol Logic

The protocol specification includes a description of the operations to be performed when sending or receiving packets – the protocol logic. Header fields and protocol properties could be updated or set, and a protocol instance could go through several states in the life-cycle. In Protege, these actions and reactions are described using a simple imperative language including some specialized statements and finite state machines:

program ::= *statement* | **do** [*statement*]+
statement ::= **__send** | **__receive**
| (*field* | *var*) ***:=*** *e*
| **__if** *e statement statement*
| *var* <- **__call_n** *fun* [*e*]*n*
| **__builtFSM** (**fsm** [<+> *rule*]+)
| *special_protocol_statement*

A Protege program consists of a series of simple statements. Elementary statements are to **__send** or to **__receive** a packet, and assignments for fields or protocol local variables. Along with conditional branches and calls to helper functions (where the number of arguments must match the respective **__call** keyword), Protege provides features aimed specifically at protocol implementation. It provides a number of primitives for specific protocol functionality. Examples include packet reassembly for network protocols, and routing table access for routing protocols. Furthermore, a Protege statement can be constructed from a finite state machine which runs to completion.

Finite State Machines The execution of a protocol often consists of a sequence of actions which depend both on the operated data and on previous actions. This view of a protocol is usually specified as a finite state machine, more precisely, a Mealy machine, in order to express the exact operation in all aspects. For example, TCP [19] uses a FSM to describe the "life stages" of a connection. Formalizing a protocol into a finite state machine also makes it accessible for formal reasoning, validation and conformance test.

Protege provides an intuitive FSM-model for protocol logic specification. The FSM is built up from its *transition rules*, specified in the following form:

r ::= **rule** *state event condition state event*

Each rule has five parameters, where the first three describe what must be satisfied for the transition rule to be executed. A rule applies to a protocol in a particular *state*, labeled with a suggestive name and represented as ordinary Haskell strings. The *input event* can be a sequence of Protege statements, e.g., sending out a packet, or a system timeout occurring. The *condition* is a boolean-valued expression that examines the environment upon an input event, to determine if the transition should be performed. Finally, the last two parameters define the effect of the transition on the protocol: the next state and the output event (a sequence of statements).

2.4 Specifying Protocols

Protocol stacks are usually designed in a modular fashion, each of which provides particular functionality independent of others. Protege enforces a strict layered and fully modular structure where protocols are implemented in individual Haskell modules. Each protocol is a particular instance of a protocol type, e.g. `Protocol` or `NetworkProtocol`, which are instances of class `ProtocolClass`. A protocol definition is introduced by a descriptive keyword, e.g. `protocol`, followed by comma-separated component definitions enclosed by curly brackets (shown in Figure 5). The protocol specification consists of the protocol identifier (`name`), packet description (`packet`), local variable declarations (e.g. `variables`) and handler definitions for processing events passed from adjacent layers (e.g., `send` and `receive`).

Protege facilitates code reuse by allowing to overwrite part of a specification. As an example, let protocol `p3` work in a similar way as protocol `p1` but instead of using two-way handshake to build a connection, use one-way handshake. This can be realized by reusing the existing `p1` implementation and only overwriting the protocol's `name`, `send` and `receive`:

```
import P1(p1)
p3 = p1{
    name    = "p3",
    send    = __builtFSM (fsm<+>rule0<+>...),
    receive = __builtFSM (fsm<+>rule1<+>...)
    }
```

2.5 Specifying Protocol Stacks (Graphs)

In Protege, protocol stacks (graphs) can be constructed by overlaying separately developed protocol modules. As all protocol abstractions have the uniform interfaces which satisfy `ProtocolClass`, it allows almost arbitrary composition. Protege provides a basic combinator `<|>` to build protocol stacks. It allows to overlay protocols in a strictly linear way, as a proper *stack*. Introduced by the keyword `stack`, a number of protocols are enumerated to form a top-down stack. The encapsulation relationship between protocols is also specified in the constraints on field values of their packets by field constraints using `<&&>`. For instance, the field `Protocol` of an IP packet can have value `4` or `17`, indicating that the upper-layer protocol is either TCP or UDP. The second combinator `<->`, with similar intuition, merges two stacks together into a protocol graph. The syntax of the combinators is:

graph ::= *stack* [<-> *stack*]*
stack ::= **stack** *id prot* [<|> *prot*]*
prot ::= **protocol** *p* (<&&> *constraints*)?

where *p* is an identifier bound to a protocol that is imported from its definition file. *Constraints* specify a list of conditions in one given stack where the header fields of protocol *p* are involved (see Figure 6 for an example).

3. The Embedding

We used Haskell for embedding our domain-specific language. By following well-documented techniques, we were able to concentrate on the design of the essential parts of our language, and experiment with different designs without having to implement parsers, type checkers and other language infrastructure. We compile Protege descriptions to C.

3.1 Deep and Shallow Embedding

Embedded languages can be developed using two styles known as *deep* and *shallow*.

A language embedding is called *deep* when the syntax of the embedded language is directly represented by data types in the host language, i.e. each language construct has its own representation in a data structure. This representation can then be interpreted in many different ways. A deep embedding is thus necessary when the main task is to generate another type of source code (in our case, C code). The deeply embedded elements of Protege are packet field representations, statements, and the entire expression sublanguage. The Haskell data types for this deep embedding are shown in Figure 7. Syntax trees constructed from these types will be translated to corresponding C code.

```
data RawHeader = Layout Raw RawType
               | Or RawHeader RawHeader
               | And RawHeader RawHeader
               | Constrain RawHeader Raw
               | Seq Raw RawHeader
               | Element Raw RawHeader

data Statement =  Assign Raw Raw
                | Fsm Id [FsmRule]
                | Reassembly Id Id [Id] Raw
                | Timeout Id Raw Statement
                | ... ...

data Raw = INT Int | UINT8 Int | UINT16 Int | ...
         | ADD Raw Raw | MUL Raw Raw | NEGATE Raw | ...
         | VAR Ide | LAM Ide Raw | APP Raw Raw | ...
         | HEADER Id RawHeader | ...
```

Figure 7. Data types to represent deeply embedded Protege parts (shortened)

```
class ProtocolClass a where
  getName :: a -> String
  getPacket :: a -> Message
  ... ...
class ProtocolClass a => NetworkProtocolClass a where
  getConnect :: a ->  State Env ()

data Protocol = MkProtocol {
  name :: String,
  packet :: Message,
  ... ...
data NetworkProtocol = MkNetworkProtocol {
  parentprotocol_ne :: Protocol,
  connect :: State Env ()

instance ProtocolClass NetworkProtocol where ...
instance NetworkProtocolClass NetworkProtocol where ...
```

Figure 8. Some type classes in the Protege embedding

In a *shallow* language embedding, the language constructs themselves perform an interpretation of the language, and their semantics, not their syntax, is represented in a host language data type. New constructs can be added independently of each other, thus the language can be extended easily. Since we expect Protege to grow essentially by supporting and classifying new protocol variants, it is crucial to retain the flexibility of a shallow embedding for this Protege part.

We use a hierarchy of type classes to classify protocols with different types of functionality and for further extension. As shown in Figure 8, `NetworkProtocolClass` is a subclass of the base class `ProtocolClass` with an extra operation `getConnect`. For each of these classes we provide type instances. The basic protocol type is included as a parent type when new protocol type variants are added. For example, `NetworkProtocol` is an instance of both `ProtocolClass` and `NetworkProtocolClass`. Protocols are then values of these types. A shallow embedding is used to construct protocols by a construction which simulates sub-typing in Haskell. Each protocol in Protege needs to specify the basic information for the base type `Protocol` together with the extra specific information for its own type. For instance, a protocol of type `NetworkProtocol` should specify how to establish a `connection`, as well as `name`, `packet` and other basic fields.

The combinators to construct the protocol stack from its components is also realized as a shallow embedding. Rather than having a direct correspondence to the resulting C code, the stack overlay requires a semantic analysis, for instance, to ensure that the resulting protocol graph is acyclic. The combinators compute the required interfaces of a protocol (to its upper and lower protocols), needed

```
-- Phantom type t for expressions (represented as Raw later)
newtype Exp t = E ([Ide] -> Raw)

type Ide = String

int :: Int -> Exp Int
int i = E (\ns -> INT i)

bool :: Bool -> Exp Bool
bool b = E (\ns -> BOOL b)

header :: Id -> Header a -> Exp a
header index (H h) = E (\ns ->  HEADER index h)

raw :: Exp a -> Raw
```

Figure 9. Expression type in Protege, using a phantom type

when generating shared header files and common code for the entire protocol stack.

3.2 Phantom Types

The development of Protege, as well as the language itself, benefited from Haskell's various well-established techniques for embedding compilers. In particular, we use *phantom types* [8] as shown in Figure 9 to achieve type-safe arithmetic expressions in Protege programs. A computation can refer directly to fields in the packet header, so these need to be typed accordingly as well. This type-safe arithmetics can detect the simple yet so typical errors in C programs, like using = instead of == or using the overloaded division (/) with two integer constants when a float is expected as result.

We have implemented the syntactic elements of Protege in one single data type `Raw` (see Figure 7), created by function `raw`. While `Raw` is untyped, we use higher-level expression types `Exp t` with phantom type `t` to give types to expressions. By instantiating type class `Num`, Haskell functions can be used in a Protege program, especially all polymorphic numerical functions are in scope. Functions are explicitly represented in the abstract syntax of Protege. The following example illustrates typing and polymorphic helper function usage in Protege. In Figure 5 earlier, header field `seqn` was declared as having type `Exp Uint8` (unsigned 8 bit char). As an instance of `Num`, we can use it as an argument to function `f` together with a numeric literal 2, which is then interpreted as a `Exp Uint8` to match `seqn`'s type, yielding a result of type `Exp Uint8` again.

```
f :: Num a => a -> a -> a
f x y = (x+y)*2

welltyped = f seqn 2        -- seqn :: Exp Uint8 (Figure 5)
illtyped  = f seqn (int 2)
```

Protege provides integer types of different precision and signedness, but does not allow any conversion between them. For instance, the second argument of `f` cannot be the Protege numeral `int 2`, which has type `Exp Int`. The definition of `illtyped` causes a Haskell type error at load time (before the translation process).

```
Couldn't match expected type 'Exp Uint8' against inferred
type 'Exp Int'
In the second argument of 'illtyped', namely '(int 2)'
```

4. Translating Protege to C

Figure 10 provides an overview of the architecture of Protege. Packet descriptions are used both to generate packet processing code and to generate packet representations that can be used by auxiliary functions and protocol logic implementation. In addition to the code for the individual protocols, the compiler generates

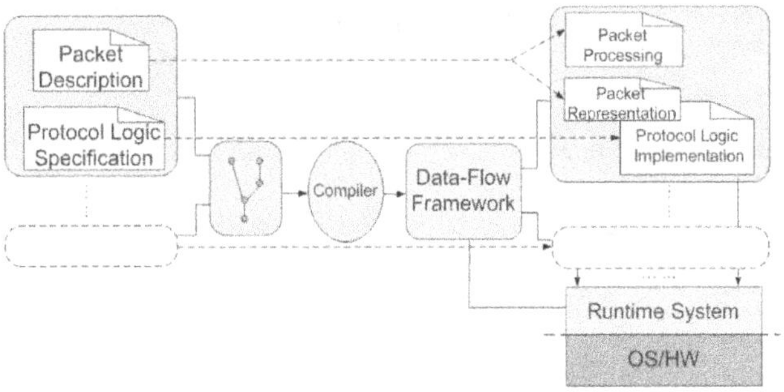

Figure 10. Architecture of Protege system.

a data-flow framework which is specific to the overlaid protocol stack in the Protege program. This framework integrates the different protocols into shared header files and provides necessary global shared code fragments, e.g., the library of generated helper functions.

We compile Protege descriptions to C. This makes it easier to integrate protocol stacks implemented in Protege with the rest of the software in a networked embedded system. Also, we avoid making language implementation choices that might lead to arguments about the efficiency of our language. By generating C we can always improve the quality of our implementation by choosing new programming techniques designed for network software [22].

4.1 Compiling Packets

The data description language to describe packet fields in Protege is based on the Data Description Calculus (DDC) [10]. However, its representation semantics and parsing (marshalling) semantics are more focused on the protocol domain.

$$\frac{}{\texttt{Layout}\ r\ t\ :\ t} \qquad \frac{h\ :\ t}{\texttt{Constrain}\ h\ r\ :\ t}$$

$$\frac{h_1\ :\ t\quad h_2\ :\ t}{\texttt{Or}\ h_1\ h_2\ :\ t} \qquad \frac{h\ :\ t}{\texttt{Seq}\ r\ h\ :\ [t]}$$

$$\frac{h_1\ :\ t\quad h_2\ :\ t}{\texttt{And}\ h_1\ h_2\ :\ t} \qquad \frac{h\ :\ [t]}{\texttt{Element}\ r\ h\ :\ t}\ \text{(protocol logic only)}$$

Figure 11. Protege rules to derive the C type for header fields

A packet description, i.e., a sequence of well-formed header fields, is first translated into a list of type declarations in C. The C types of the fields are obtained from Protege field types by erasing information, e.g., type dependencies and constraints. The translation process unwinds all these type "decorations" to the inner-most basic type (see Figure 11), and uses the field ID to generate a unique name. For instance, a field definition `f3` in Protege

```
f3 = header 3 (inth bit_6) |* (.>. 1)
```

with abstract syntax tree (AST)

```
HEADER 3 (Constrain (Layout (INT 6) INTType)
                    (LAM ''x'' (GREAT (Var ''x'') (Int 1)))
```

is translated into the declaration `int field3`. In the protocol logic implementation, we are only interested in identifying the fields, so fields are simplify represented by their name.

For packet processing, a field declaration translates to a code fragment which constructs the respective value by reading it from the packet buffer (we only present parsing code, marshaling code works vice-versa). Packet layout in Protege is *globally bit-oriented*, i.e. all fields of all protocols in a protocol stack are bitwise adjacent in a global packet buffer (described in Section 5). The generated

```
int field3;                              // type is int
offset = 6;                              // size is 6 bit

field3_p = FieldMake(self->in_buffer, index, offset);
index += offset;
FieldRead(field3_p, &field3);            // read the value

int flag_field3_1=1;                     // constraint
flag_field3_1 = (field3>1);
if((flag_field3_1)==0) return -1; // signal constraint violation
```

Figure 12. Generated C code for field `f3` with constraint

code therefore uses a bit offset value and a dedicated runtime library for addressing, reading and writing values. Generated C code for our previous example `f3` is shown in Figure 12. The size of `field3` was declared to be 6 bits, so this amount of bits will be read from the packet buffer. The generated code uses `FieldMake` to create a bit-oriented address `field3_p`, which is then used to read a value into `field3` (using `FieldRead`). The global `index` gives the current parsing position in bits, and is updated accordingly after reading the field.

Our example already shows a case of constraint on header fields: If `field3` is not greater than 1, the entire parse fails and the packet will be dropped (indicated by an immediate `return -1`). Besides constraints, Protege allows to combine packet layout in sum and intersection types (`Or` and `And`) and arrays (`Seq`). The corresponding parsing functions are constructed using the following rules:

- For fields of *Sum type*, if the attempt to parse the first underlying type fails, the second underlying type will be used (i.e. the first alternative takes precedence, as in DDC).
- For fields of *Intersection type*, both underlying types are processed, starting at the same starting bit. The parse will fail if one of the branches fails, and the `index` will be incremented by the maximum of the two `offsets`.
- For fields of *Array type*, the indicated number of elements is parsed according to the underlying types. The `index` will be updated by the sum of all fields `offsets`. Note that the element offsets can be different, in case of sum or intersection types.

4.2 Compiling Protocols

Protege-generated C represents protocols in an object-oriented style. As the example in Figure 13 shows, each protocol is represented with a structure grouping together buffers, a block of en-

```
typedef struct protocol_block *Protocol;

struct variables_block {
  int intv0;
  int intv1;
  unsigned short u16v0;
};
struct protocol_block {
    unsigned char   *out_buffer;
    unsigned char   *in_buffer;
    unsigned char   *out_data;
    unsigned char   *in_data;
    ... ...
    struct variables_block variables;
    Method init;
    MethodConcurrent send;
    MethodConcurrent receive;
    ... ...
    Protocol up;
    Protocol down;
};
```

Figure 13. A generated protocol header file

capsulated protocol variables and the protocol methods (essentially `init`, `send`, and `receive`). The buffers are shared among all protocols within one stack, so buffer addresses are chosen when constructing the stack. In contrast, the variable block is private to the individual protocol, accessible only by its methods. In the example, two variables in the block have type `int` and one variable has type `short`.

The translation of Protege `send` and `receive` methods is relatively straightforward: basic statements like assignment and conditionals map directly to C syntax, and special protocol statements use dedicated runtime support. Protocols rarely use many state machines in a hierarchical structure. A state machine is compiled into a single level of C switch statements which describe the transition table.

4.3 Compiling Helper Functions

By virtue of the deep embedding, function declarations in Protege are just Haskell function declarations. Protege statements can thus freely use Haskell functions, e.g., compute required field values. Protege supports two kinds of translations for helper functions: by global inlining or by identifying the function calls and generating corresponding C code. Global inlining is achieved by calling the function in the Protege source, which is an easy strategy for the compiler. However, generating corresponding C code for a helper function can substantially increase the program's memory footprint when this function is called from many different places. Frequently used helper functions should therefore not be inlined, but the choice is left to the programmer. Functions which should not be inlined but separately generated have to be called using special operators, e.g., `fun_call_1`, which are provided for functions of up to four arguments in Protege. We call this an *identified* function call. To illustrate the difference, consider an example for an inlined function call `g field3` where field3 has type `int` and g is defined as:

```
f x = x*x+2*x+1
g x = f x + f (x+1)
```

The inlined function in generated C is:

```
field3*field3+2*field3+1+(field3+1)*(field3+1)+2*(field3+1)+1
```

If we identify the function calls as `fun_call_1 g` and `fun_call_1 f`, the generated code is `g(field3)` and two functions:

```
int f(int x){return(x*x+2*x+1);}
int g(int x){return(f(x)+f(x+1));}
```

Protege inherits Haskell's polymorphism, especially all polymorphic numerical functions are in scope. When several identified function calls use a polymorphic function, the translation in the source code can lead to several generated functions, depending on the concrete function usage in the program. Continuing the example, if e.g. the function `g` is called with arguments of type `short` as `fun_call_1 g (short 1)`, Protege will generate two new functions corresponding to `f` and `g`.

```
short f'(short x){return(x*x+2*x+1);}
short g'(short x){return(f'(x)+f'(x+1));}
```

The translation uses a global function dictionary for identified function calls. This means, if two functions used in identified function calls are observationally identical (have the same AST), they are unified into one definition.

A note about translating recursive helper functions Obviously, *recursive* helper functions can only be used in identified function calls in Protege. A recursive function cannot be inlined, since compilation would go into an infinite loop: the base case cannot be checked at compile time. Assume a recursive function `h` defined as follows:

```
h x = (x.==.0) .?. (0, (x + h (x-1)))
```

An inlined function call `h field3` would result in

```
field3+(field3-1)+((field3-1)-1)+...
```

In Protege, recursive functions should be identified as being recursive by a special call syntax, e.g., `self_call_1 h field3`. Then such a function call can be translated into `h(field3)` together with a recursive function `h` as one would expect:

```
int h(int x){return((x==0)?0:(x + h (x-1)));}
```

4.4 Compilation of the Protocol Stack Framework

As explained, the combinators for protocol overlay specification have a shallow embedding in Protege. They evaluate to a directed acyclic protocol graph, described in a data structure: `ProtocolGraph`.

```
data Idx = N Int | Nil
type ProtocolGraph = [(AProtocol, [(Idx, Constraint, Ap)])]
```

Each node in the graph is a protocol (`AProtocol`), with a list of edges to the adjacent lower-layer protocols. Edges in the graph, implying a possible data flow to another protocol, are represented by an index (`Idx`) to the target protocol in the graph, together with a *field constraint* (`Constraint`) and the *A*ccess *P*oint (`Ap`). An edge with index `Nil` indicates that the current protocol can interface to the outside, e.g. other system applications. The *field constraint* specifies the encapsulated relationship of two protocol packets. The *A*ccess *P*oint (`Ap`), an integer, is a helper variable indicating which protocol stack is being used.

According to the information provided by edges, additional code for each protocol is generated to specify its interaction with the corresponding upper and lower layers. A hash table is used for each protocol to store the links to all its lower-layer protocols. For an outgoing packet, the next lower-layer protocol is determined from the *A*ccess *P*oint (`Ap`), and *field constraint* is used to multiplex incoming packets to one of the next upper-layer protocols. As every protocol satisfies type class `ProtocolClass`, its common operations (e.g. `getName`) can be used to access protocol information. For example, in Figure 6 `p0` has two possible upper-layer protocols which are represented by two edges in the graph, i.e., `p1` for `stack0`. As the *field constraint* is `field0 .==. 0`, and the name of `p1` is `"p1"`, the generated code for guiding the incoming `p0` packet is:

```
int receive_p0(Protocol self, ...){
  ... ...
  if(p0_f0==1){
    self->up = protocolpool_get(&p2protocolpool, "p1");
  ... ...
```

Protocol graphs most commonly have tree shape, i.e. no protocol has more than one lower-layer protocol. This can be exploited by a compilation scheme which enables a *fast path*, an often-used technique [2, 5] to achieve more efficient composition of protocol layers. In a tree-shaped overlay, the compilation becomes a path search problem in acyclic graphs: starting from each leaf protocol and going through all its paths. For example, `p1` only has `p0` at its lower-layer (see Figure 6). We first poll an anonymous protocol from protocol pool, and link it to `p1`'s down protocol, then we initialize it. The generated code is as follow.

```
void build_p1(Protocol self, ...){
  ... ...
  /*build lower-layer protocol*/
  self->down = protocolpool_poll(&p2protocolpool, ...);
  build_p0(self->down, ...);
  ... ...
```

Since each protocol has a fixed lower-layer protocol, outgoing packets can be directly passed to this lower layer (stored as `self->down`), without requiring a complicated neighbor search or condition checks. A further optimization could be to inline `send` functions within a stack (trading function call overhead for code size). For now, we keep the general object-oriented style and leave this as part of future work.

5. Runtime System

5.1 Concurrency Models

Real world embedded systems normally allow concurrent execution of multiple tasks, and protocols naturally execute concurrently with each other. Memory-constrained embedded systems often use an event-driven concurrency model (e.g. TinyOS [13], Contiki [5] and TinyTimber [14]). The protocol stack has to be integrated with the rest of the systems software and has to follow its concurrency model and central control mechanisms. So far, Protege has been integrated with *Protothreads* [6], a lightweight stackless implementation of threads, and with *Posix threads*. To avoid the overhead of context switches when crossing layers, Protege employs a thread-per-message model: each message is guided through the entire protocol stack by one dedicated thread.

Protege encodes protocols in an object-oriented style in order to make the implementations fit into different concurrency models such as threads with blocking operations or reactive objects [14]. Most of the generated code does not depend on any OS-specific functionality. With small modifications of the library (for example, header files and small changes in the object declarations), Protege implementations will be portable to a wide range of embedded operating systems.

5.2 Bit-Oriented Packet Processing

Energy consumption is an important issue for resource constrained embedded system. The size of packet headers matters for the energy consumption because larger packet headers require more transmission and reception time and thus have higher energy consumption. Studies have found that the ratio of the energy consumption to send one bit compared to computing a single instruction is between 1500 to 2700 [12] for certain hardware platforms. Therefore, packet headers within a stack are commonly compressed manually before being sent out. For example, protocols for sensor networks are typically very lightweight and only have a few bits of packet header, e.g. flag fields. Short bit-sized header fields belonging to individually developed protocols would need to be held in separate byte-sized fields first, and then be copied and compressed into a compacted packet.

The Protege runtime includes a library of generic functions for bitwise access to a global input or output buffer (including the explained `FieldMake` and `FieldRead`). Packet fields are freely constructed and extracted across byte boundaries, and the quantities can be aligned arbitrarily. Since both the parsing and marshaling functions access the buffer directly, the packet can remain in the buffer and will not be copied for processing.

While the Protege specifications are broken up in modules, the code generator can profit from a global view on the complete protocol stack. It enables *bit-sized header field packing* between layers, compressing small header fields into the same byte, even when they belong to different protocols. The bit-oriented implementation efficiently uses all available bits in a transmitted byte, and considerably reduces the size of the header.

5.3 Timer Scheme

Timers are needed by protocols that require certain actions to be executed after a given time interval has elapsed. So far, Protege implements one timer scheme [22], a linear list of timers. Timers are stored in a list, sorted by the absolute time when the timer expires (with the earliest expiration at the head of the list). Using the system clock and interrupts, this timer list is checked with a certain timer granularity, e.g., 200 msec. If the timer at the head of the list has a time equal or less than the current time, it calls its timeout event handler and is removed from the list. The time comparison and handler execution proceeds until the timer at the head of the list has a time strictly greater than the current time. In the Protege implementation, care has been taken to separate the platform dependent part from the main implementation, thus only the small fraction that uses platform specific features has to be modified when porting to other platforms.

5.4 Memory Management

A crucial requirement for memory-constrained embedded systems is that memory consumption (buffer space) should be bounded. Protege has its own memory management instead of using platform dependent dynamic memory allocation. Memory consumption of the runtime system is determined at compile time with fixed size, reserved for two purposes.

One usage is to store temporary variables in packet processing or protocol logic code in a pre-allocated *byte pool* (operating in units of one byte). The amount of memory required for packet processing can be statically unknown, for example when a variable-length sequence of constrained fields is parsed. The amount of constraint flags to check the validity of each field cannot be declared statically in this case. These required flags will be allocated from the internal byte pool, and automatically released when packet processing is complete.

Another use is to store temporary packets, e.g. for packet retransmission, in the *packet pool*. The packet pool's unit is the fixed *maximum packet size*, calculated when constructing the protocol stack. Protege uses region-based memory management [21] for the packet pool to increase safety while avoiding runtime cost. A region is a per-session packet pool: every buffer used by an open session of a protocol stack has to be allocated from this packet pool. The session-related packet pool will be automatically released when its associated session terminates. This scheme not only guarantees certain resource bounds of the implementation, but also improves the code quality.

All allocation and deallocation statements are automatically generated by the Protege compiler, thereby memory allocation is out of the programmer's reach and memory fragmentation is avoided. If predefined memory limitations are exceeded, the runtime system will handle this exception gracefully and, for example, drop incoming packets instead of halting the entire program with a segmentation fault.

6. Evaluation

Developing embedded network software requires particular attention on resource limits and performance. To demonstrate that Protege is able to reduce the implementation complexity of protocol stacks while showing competitive resource usage and performance, we have compared a Protege implementation to the hand-crafted C code written by specialists, for the Rime [7] protocol stack for sensor networks.

6.1 Complexity of Protocol Implementations

One of the design goals of Protege is to facilitate the implementation of protocol stacks. To substantiate that Protege reduces the complexity of protocol stack implementation, we use lines of code as an approximation to estimate the amount of effort that will be required to develop a program (although, we have noticed that this measurement is affected by aspects not only inherent to the programming language, but also to programming style). The statements are counted as lines of code, excluding comments, header files and module specification statements. As Figure 14 shows, the numbers for Protege are considerably smaller than the ones for Rime's original implementation, generally less than 50 % of the lines of C code. In addition, we can see that the code for the two protocols `ipolite` and `rmh` is extremely short because they are identical to previously defined protocol `polite` and `mh`, only situated in other place in the protocol graph. While the C implementation duplicates a considerable amount of code, Protege can reuse the previous code and only overwrites the protocol name.

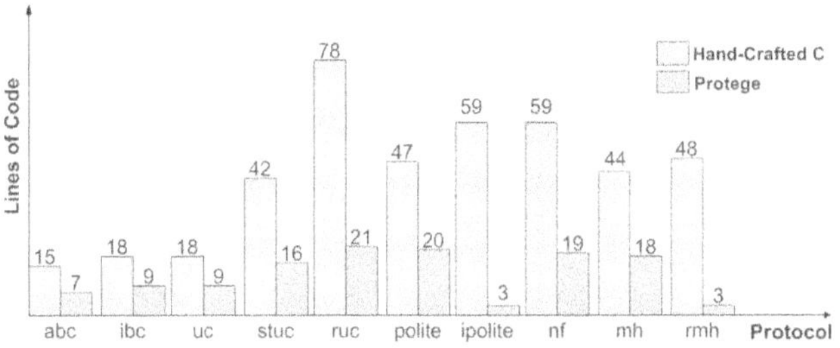

Figure 14. Lines of code for Rime implementations

6.2 Memory Footprint

The memory footprint depends on the code footprint of compiled code and the dynamically allocated buffers at runtime. Figure 15 lists the compiled code memory footprint of the Rime implementations in hand-crafted C code and Protege, both compiled for the Netsim simulator [20]. We see that the compiled code footprint resulting from our implementation is comparable to the one from the hand-crafted implementation. On average, Protege's code footprint is 0.5% bigger. In Protege, the runtime memory footprint is limited within a certain boundary at compile time. This size depends on implementation decisions by the programmer, therefore we do not provide numbers for it here.

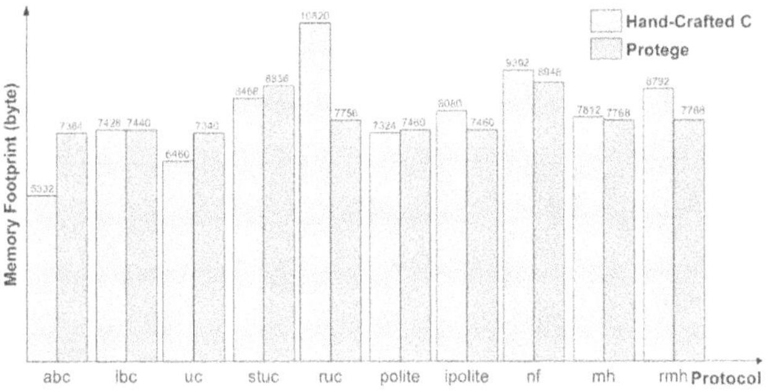

Figure 15. Static memory footprint of Rime implementations

6.3 Performance

At the protocol level, the time to transfer a complete packet involves the time taken for processing a packet (*latency*), plus the time it takes for the remaining bits to be sent/received (data length of the packet divided by the *throughput*). As the *throughput* mainly depends on the hardware, we only measure the *latency* to compare performance.

The application scenario is a sensor network with 25 sensor nodes in a square lattice. Each node runs a single-hop unicast protocol stack of Rime, exchanging four bytes of application data with its neighbors. We simulate our test scenario by NetSim, and measure the amount of time that is needed to process 500 packets for sending/receiving, by taking timestamps before calling and after returning from the Rime stack. Figure 16 reports the average time for sending/receiving packets in the test setup for the Protege and the hand-crafted implementation. We see that the execution time resulting from the generated and the hand-crafted code are approximately the same. This is not surprising, since the C code resulting from our code generation uses techniques similar to the hand-crafted implementation, e.g., bit-oriented packet packing.

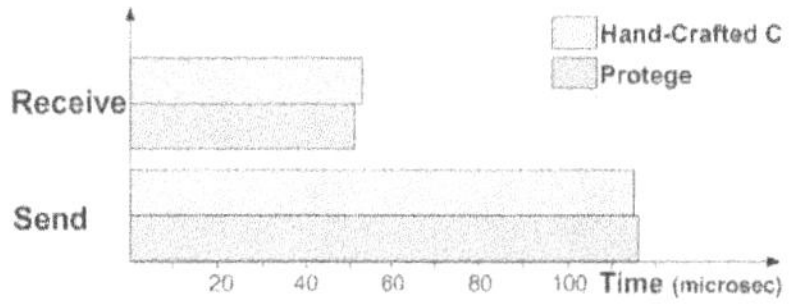

Figure 16. Average time for processing packets

7. Related Work

In the past two decades, there has been continuous research on improving protocol implementation techniques, often using a paradigm of high-level descriptions and language technology.

Packet format specification has been a research focus for tool developers. To our knowledge PACKETTYPES [15] was the first approach that uses dependent types for packet specifications. Types are used externally, and a compiler generates parsing functions that can be rapidly adapted to implement packet filters. It provides a way for *overlaying* a packet in the payload field of another packet. In our work, we replace the ad-hoc notion of attributes from PACKETTYPES with a richer system of dependent types. In this way we can deal with more semantic constraints and consistency conditions that are beyond the scope of PACKETTYPES. Data description languages such as PADS [9] promote the idea of using dependent types to express constraints and physical representations for ad-hoc data processing in a more general setting, and DDC [10] proposes a general semantics of dependent types as a formalization of ad-hoc data formats. However, being more general-purpose, these data description languages do not express *overlays* as they typically occur in packet formats. Protege adapted the DDC semantics for the specific case of packets for parsing and representation, and extends it to also generate marshalling code.

Domain-specific languages for *protocol logic and overlaying* have been studied extensively for a long time. Languages are sometimes tailored to just one particular protocol category, focusing on both verification and code generation. For example, TAP [16] has been designed for asynchronous message-passing network protocols. Due to the focus on one specific layer, protocol stack construction is out of scope for this work. Other approaches put more focus on the layering itself, and use language technology and compilation to reduce the performance penalty of protocol layering. Morpheus [1] has been designed specifically for fast and flexible development through a modular architecture. By enforcing its design philosophy through specific language constructs, Morpheus enables some protocol-oriented compiler optimizations. For example, it uses a specialized tail-call optimization (called *short-circuit return*) which saves one jump instruction per protocol layer. However, the language has largely remained a mere design, its realization was not completed. Promela++ [2] is a more closely related work, which provides explicit language mechanisms to encapsulate and compose protocol layers where the adjacent layers communicate neatly using FIFO message queues to achieve more efficient composition of multiple protocol layers. An essential and important inspiration of both is the idea of cross-layer optimization, which has been adopted in the design of Protege.

Our work Protege is unique in that none of the mentioned systems has integrated support for all aspects of protocol implementation: packet specification and processing, protocol logic implementation and protocol overlaying. Furthermore, Protege specifically targets resource constrained platforms. To achieve low resource consumption for the *Protege runtime system*, we took inspirations from several existing systematic software architectures for constructing protocol stacks. These systems seek to clearly express the modular structures and protocol layer composition, while enabling particular specific protocol stack optimizations. For instance, Integrated Layer Processing [3] advocates rewriting of existing protocol stacks such that the processing done by the different layers is pipelined, avoiding message copies every time a layer boundary is crossed. Protege is using a global packet buffer shared by all protocols in different layers within a stack. The threading model of Protege follows the idea which was proposed in *x*-kernel [11]: one reserved thread per message is used across all layers. The bit-oriented cross-layer packet compaction in Protege follows an idea which was presented in Chameleon [7], a protocol stack architecture for sensor networks which isolates low-level packet processing from other implementation aspects.

8. Conclusions and Future Work

With Protege, we have presented a language based approach to improve network software development. Protocols can be programmed using domain abstractions for packet layout specification and constraints, protocol logic in state machines, and protocol overlays, at the same level of abstraction as in the protocol specifications. Protege provides maintainable implementations and good modularity for combining existing protocols into new protocol stacks. The compilation based approach of Protege allows one to easily integrate the resulting C code with other system software, and delivers good portability and competitive performance.

In this paper, we have given details on the implementation of Protege, outlined how it is embedded in Haskell, and described our techniques for generating well-performing C code. The technique of deep embedding which we use for the packet handling sublanguage of Protege is particularly well-suited for a compilation based approach. Other parts of Protege (protocol types and overlay specification) use a shallow embedding which is more flexible for later extensions. We have illustrated the phantom types of Protege and how to systematically derive corresponding C types during code generation. Polymorphic Haskell helper functions can be used and, depending on the calling convention used by the programmer, will be either inlined or compiled to C functions, thereby also allowing (a limited form of) recursion. Bit-oriented packet layout, flexible concurrency model and memory management are distinctive features of the Protege runtime system to meet the resource constraints of embedded systems. Our experiences with Haskell as a host language for the Protege embedding are overall positive: Haskell's smooth syntax and expressiveness allowed us to experiment with several versions of the language without spending too much time maintaining parsers and type checkers.

In the future, we plan to improve on the techniques used in the generated code, using a number of novel techniques for programming network devices [22]. We also plan to use Protege together with tools to generate application specific instruction set processors. Finally, we plan to conduct experiments with network engineers to evaluate Protege in detail.

References

[1] M. B. Abbott and L. L. Peterson. A Language-Based Approach to Protocol Implementation. *IEEE/ACM Transactions on Networking*, 1 (1):4–19, 1993.

[2] A. Basu, J. G. Morrisett, and T. von Eicken. Promela++: A Language for Constructing Correct and Efficient Protocols. In *INFOCOM*, pages 455–462, 1998.

[3] D. D. Clark and D. L. Tennenhouse. Architectural Considerations for a New Generation of Protocols. In *SIGCOMM '90*. ACM Press, 1990.

[4] A. Dunkels. Full TCP/IP for 8-bit Architectures. In *MobiSys '03*. ACM, 2003.

[5] A. Dunkels, B. Gronvall, and T. Voigt. Contiki - A Lightweight and Flexible Operating System for Tiny Networked Sensors. In *LCN '04*. IEEE Computer Society, 2004.

[6] A. Dunkels, O. Schmidt, T. Voigt, and M. Ali. Protothreads: Simplifying Event-Driven Programming of Memory-Constrained Embedded Systems. In *SenSys '06*. ACM, 2006.

[7] A. Dunkels, F. Österlind, and Z. He. An Adaptive Communication Architecture for Wireless Sensor Networks. In *SenSys '07*. ACM, 2007.

[8] C. Elliott, S. Finne, and O. de Moor. Compiling Embedded Languages. *Journal of Functional Programming*, 13(2), 2003.

[9] K. Fisher and R. Gruber. PADS: A Domain-Specific Language for Processing Ad Hoc Data. *SIGPLAN Not.*, 40(6), 2005.

[10] K. Fisher, Y. Mandelbaum, and D. Walker. The Next 700 Data Description Languages. *SIGPLAN Not.*, 57(2):1–51, 2010.

[11] N. C. Hutchinson and L. L. Peterson. The X-Kernel: An Architecture for Implementing Network Protocols. *IEEE Trans. Softw. Eng.*, 17(1): 64–76, 1991.

[12] H. Karl and A. Willig. *Protocols and Architectures for Wireless Sensor Networks*. Wiley, 2005.

[13] P. Levis, S. Madden, D. Gay, J. Polastre, R. Szewczyk, A. Woo, E. Brewer, and D. Culler. The Emergence of Networking Abstractions and Techniques in TinyOS. In *NSDI '04*, Berkeley, CA, USA, 2004. USENIX Association.

[14] P. Lindgren, J. Eriksson, S. Aittamaa, and J. Nordlander. TinyTimber, Reactive Objects in C for Real-Time Embedded Systems. In *DATE '08*. ACM, 2008.

[15] P. J. McCann and S. Chandra. Packet Types: Abstract Specification of Network Protocol Messages. In *SIGCOMM '00*. ACM, 2000.

[16] T. M. Mcguire. *Correct Implementation of Network Protocols*. PhD thesis, The University of Texas at Austin, 2004. Supervisor-Mohamed G. Gouda.

[17] L. L. Peterson and B. S. Davie. *Computer Networks: A Systems Approach, 3rd Edition*. Morgan Kaufmann Publishers Inc., San Francisco, CA, USA, 2003.

[18] RFC791. IP. http://www.rfc-editor.org/rfc/rfc791.html. [Online; accessed 20-Oct-2010].

[19] RFC793. TCP. http://www.faqs.org/rfcs/rfc793.html. [Online; accessed 20-Oct-2010].

[20] Tetcos. NetSim. http://www.tetcos.com/software.html. [Online; accessed 20-Oct-2010].

[21] M. Tofte and J.-P. Talpin. Region-Based Memory Management. *Information and Computation*, 132, 1997.

[22] G. Varghese. *Network Algorithmics: An Interdisciplinary Approach to Designing Fast Networked Devices*. Elsevier/Morgan Kaufmann, San Francisco, CA, USA, 2005.

[23] Y. Wang and V. Gaspes. A Domain-Specific Language Approach to Protocol Stack Implementation. In M. Carro and R. Peña, editors, *PADL'10*, LNCS 5937. Springer, 2010.

Verified Resource Guarantees using COSTA and KeY

Elvira Albert
Complutense University of Madrid
elvira@sip.ucm.es

Richard Bubel
Chalmers University of Technology
bubel@chalmers.se

Samir Genaim
Complutense University of Madrid
samir.genaim@fdi.ucm.es

Reiner Hähnle
Chalmers University of Technology
reiner@chalmers.se

Germán Puebla
Technical University of Madrid
german@fi.upm.es

Guillermo Román-Díez
Technical University of Madrid
groman@fi.upm.es

Abstract

Resource guarantees allow being certain that programs will run within the indicated amount of resources, which may refer to memory consumption, number of instructions executed, etc. This information can be very useful, especially in real-time and safety-critical applications. Nowadays, a number of automatic tools exist, often based on type systems or static analysis, which produce such resource guarantees. In spite of being based on theoretically sound techniques, the implemented tools may contain bugs which render the resource guarantees thus obtained not completely trustworthy. Performing full-blown verification of such tools is a daunting task, since they are large and complex. In this work we investigate an alternative approach whereby, instead of the *tools*, we formally verify the *results* of the tools. We have implemented this idea using COSTA, a state-of-the-art static analysis system, for producing resource guarantees and KeY, a state-of-the-art verification tool, for formally verifying the correctness of such resource guarantees. Our preliminary results show that the proposed tool cooperation can be used for automatically producing verified resource guarantees.

Categories and Subject Descriptors F3.2 [*Logics and Meaning of Programs*]: Program Analysis; F2.9 [*Analysis of Algorithms and Problem Complexity*]; D3.0 [*Programming Languages*]

General Terms Languages, Theory, Verification, Reliability

Keywords Static Analysis, Resource Guarantees, Java

1. Introduction

There is a growing awareness, both in industry and academia, of the crucial role of formally proving the correctness of systems. Verifying the correctness of modern static analyzers is rather challenging, among other things, because of the sophisticated algorithms used in them, their evolution over time, and, possibly, proprietary considerations. A simpler alternative is to construct a validating tool [7] which, after every run of the analyzer, formally confirms that the results are correct and, optionally, generates correctness proofs. Such proofs could then be translated to *resource certificates* [5, 6].

PEPM'11, January 24–25, 2011, Austin, Texas, USA.

In this work, we are interested in *resource guarantees* obtained by static analysis. An essential aspect of programs is that resources be used effectively. This is especially true in the current programming trends, which provide us with mechanisms for code reuse by means of components and services: not only functionality, but also resource consumption (or *cost*) must be taken into consideration.

COSTA is a state-of-the-art COSt and Termination Analyzer for Java bytecode (and hence Java). It receives as input the bytecode of a Java program, the signature of the method whose cost is to be inferred, a choice of one among several available cost models (termination [1], number of bytecode instructions [3], memory consumption, or calls to certain method) and automatically infers an *upper bound* (UB for short) on the cost as a function of the method's input arguments. The most challenging step is to infer UBs for the loops in the program [2]. Intuitively, this requires (1) bounding the number of iterations of each loop and (2) finding the worst-case cost among all iterations. *Ranking functions* [8] give us safe approximations for requirement (1). To infer the maximal cost in requirement (2), we need to track how the values of variables change in the loop iterations and the inter-relations between (the values of) variables. As we will see, this information is obtained in COSTA by means of *loop invariants* and *size relations*. The analysis algorithms used in COSTA for inferring the main components of the UB generation were proven correct at a theoretical level. However, there is no guarantee that correctness is preserved in the actual implementation which is rather involved.

KeY [4] is a state-of-the-art source code verification tool for the Java programming language. Its coverage of Java is comparable to that of COSTA (nearly full sequential Java, plus a simplified concurrency model). KeY implements a logic-based setting of symbolic execution that allows deep integration with aggressive first-order simplification. While the degree of automation of KeY is very high on loop- and recursion-free programs, the user must in general supply suitable invariants to deal with loops and recursion. In general, invariants that are sufficient to prove complex functional properties cannot be inferred automatically. However, simpler invariants that are sufficient to establish UBs *can* be automatically derived in many cases and this is exactly COSTA's forte. Our work is based on the insight that the static analysis tool COSTA and the formal verification tool KeY have complementary strengths: COSTA is able to derive UBs of Java programs including the invariants needed to obtain them. This information is enough for KeY to *prove* the validity of the bounds and provide a certificate. The main contribution of this work is to show that, using KeY, it is possible to formally and automatically verify the correctness of the UBs obtained by COSTA.

2. Inference of Upper Bounds in COSTA

In this section, we briefly describe the techniques used in COSTA for automatically inferring UBs, and we identify the proof obligations that need to be verified using KeY.

2.1 Main Components of an Upper Bound

Consider the following (JML annotated) program that implements the insert sort algorithm.

```
1  void insert_sort (int A[]) {
2   int i, j, v;
3   //@ ghost int i0=i; int j0=j; int a0=a;
4   i =A.length−2;
5   //@ assert (i=i0−2 ∧ j=j0 ∧ a=a0)
6   //@ ghost int i1=i; int j1=j; int a1=a;
7   //@ loop_invariant i≤i1
8   //@ decreases i>0 ? i : 0
9   while ( i>=0 ) {
10    //@ ghost int i2=i; int j2=j; int a2=a;
11    j =i+1;
12    v=A[i];
13    //@ assert j=i2+1 ∧ i2 ≥ 0
14    //@ ghost int i3=i; int j3=j; int a3=a;
15    //@ loop_invariant j≤a3
16    //@ decreases a − j>0 ? a − j : 0
17    while ( j <A.length && A[j]<v) {
18      A[j −1]=A[j];
19      j++; }
20    A[j −1]=v;
21    i −−; } }
```

COSTA receives a non-annotated version of the above program and, for the cost model that counts the number of executed bytecode instructions, produces the (asymptotic) UB insert_sort$(a)=a^2$, where a refers to A.**length**. The underlying analysis used in COSTA infers UBs for each iterative and recursive constructs (loops) and then composes the results in order to obtain an UB for the method of interest. Intuitively, in order to infer an UB for a single loop, it first infers an UB A on the cost of a single execution of its body, an UB I on the number of iterations that it can make, and then $A * I$ is an UB for the loop. In order to infer A and I COSTA relies on several program analysis components that provide essential information:

Ranking functions. For each loop, COSTA infers a linear function from the loop variables to $\mathbb{N}$ which is decreasing at each iteration. For example, for the loop at line 17, it infers function $f(a,j) = \mathsf{nat}(a-j)$ where $\mathsf{nat}(\ell) = \max(0,\ell)$. This function can be safely used to bound the number of iterations. In the example, if a_3 and j_3 are the initial values of a and j, then it is guaranteed that $f(a_3, j_3)$ is an UB on the number of iterations of the loop.

Loop invariants. For each loop in the program, COSTA infers an invariant that involves the loop's variables and their initial values (i.e., their values before entering the loop). Let us denote by i_1 the initial value of i when entering the loop at line 9. COSTA infers the invariant $i \leq i_1$, which states that i is always smaller than or equal to its initial value when the program reaches the loop condition. This information, together with the size relations below, is needed to compute the worst-case cost of executing one loop iteration.

Size relations. Given a fragment of code or a scope (details below), COSTA infers relations between the values of the program variables at a certain program point of interest within the scope and their initial values when entering the scope. For example, at program point 13, it infers that $j = i_2 + 1$, where i_2 is the value of i when entering the scope that contains line 13 (i.e., the scope here is the loop body). In this case the relation is a simple consequence of the instruction at line 11. In general, however, it may not be trivial to infer such relations nor to prove that they are correct.

Upper Bounds. Once the above information has been inferred, it is straightforward to compute an UB for the method. Let us show this process on the running example:

Inner loop. The process starts from the innermost loops. Thus, we start with the loop at line 17. Assuming that executing the condition costs (at most) c_1 instructions, and that the cost of each iteration (i.e., the loop body) is c_2 instructions, then it is clear that $\mathsf{nat}(a_3 - j_3) * (c_1 + c_2) + c_1$ is an UB on the cost of this loop (because c_1 and c_2 are constant).

Outer loop. Next, we move to the outer loop at line 9. Let us assume that the cost of the comparison is c_3 instructions, the code at lines 11–12 are c_4 instructions, and the code at lines 20–21 are c_5 instructions. Then, the cost of each iteration of this loop is $c_3 + c_4 + \mathsf{nat}(a_3 - j_3) * (c_1 + c_2) + c_1 + c_5$, where the highlighted subexpression corresponds to the cost of the inner loop computed above. Note that in this case, each iteration might have a different cost, since $a_3 - j_3$ is not the same for all iterations. Simply multiplying the number of iterations $\mathsf{nat}(i_1)$ by such a cost is unsound. The solution is to find an expression U in terms of the initial values of a_1, i_1, j_1 which does not change during the loop such that $U \geq a_3 - j_3$ in all iterations. Then, $\mathsf{nat}(i_1) * [c_3 + c_4 + \mathsf{nat}(U) * (c_1 + c_2) + c_1 + c_5] + c_3$ is an UB for the loop. In order to find such a U, COSTA uses the loop invariant (line 7) and the size relations (line 13) as follows: it solves the parametric integer programming (PIP) problem of maximizing the objective function $a_3 - j_3$ w.r.t. the loop invariant and the size relations where i_1, a_1, j_1 are the parameters. This produces an expression in terms of i_1, a_1, j_1 which is greater than or equal to $a_3 - j_3$ in all iterations of the loop. In our example, it is $U = a_1 - 1$.

Method. We finally can compute the cost of the insert_sort method. Assume that the cost of line 4 is c_6, then the cost of the method is $c_6 + \mathsf{nat}(i_1) * [c_3 + c_4 + \mathsf{nat}(a_1 - 1) * (c_1 + c_2) + c_1 + c_5] + c_3$. We need to express this UB in terms of the input parameter a. For this, COSTA maximizes (using PIP) i_1 and $a_1 - 1$ w.r.t. the size relation at line 5 and, respectively, obtains $a-2$ and $a-1$. Therefore, $c_6 + \mathsf{nat}(a-2) * [c_3 + c_4 + \mathsf{nat}(a-1) * (c_1 + c_2) + c_1 + c_5] + c_3$ is the UB for insert_sort.

2.2 COSTA Claims as JML Annotations

To justify that the UBs obtained by COSTA are correct, we need to provide formal correctness proofs for all the claims above. This includes the ranking functions, invariants, size relations, the cost model that provides all c_i, and the underlying PIP solver.

Correctness of the cost model is trivial as it is a simple mapping from each instruction to a number. Correctness of the underlying PIP solver is also straightforward if we use the maximization procedure defined in [2], which is based only on the Gaussian elimination algorithm. Therefore, we concentrate on verifying the correctness of the ranking functions, size relations and invariants. They are inferred by large software components whose correctness has not been verified. We now briefly describe the translation of the different pieces of information generated by COSTA to JML annotations on the Java program, which will allow their verification in KeY.

Ranking functions. For a given loop, when COSTA infers a ranking function of the form $\mathsf{nat}(\ell)$, we translate it to the JML annotation "//@ decreasing $\ell > 0\ ?\ \ell : 0$", since $\mathsf{nat}(\ell)$ can be defined as an if-then-else. COSTA might provide also ranking functions of the form $\log(\mathsf{nat}(\ell) + 1)$, which are handled similarly.

Invariants. COSTA infers an invariant φ for each loop. This invariant involves the loop variables $\bar{v}$ and auxiliary variables $\bar{w}$ such that each w_i represents the initial value of v_i. The JML annotation for this invariant consists of one line defining all $\bar{w}$ as ghost variables ("//@ ghost int $w_1 = v_1$;...; int $w_n = v_n$") and one line for declaring the loop invariant ("//@ loop_invariant φ").

Size relations. Size relations are linear constraints between the values of a set of variables of interest between two program points. As we have seen, this allows composing the cost of the different program fragments. For each loop (or method call), COSTA infers the relation φ between the values before the loop entry (or the call) and the entry of its parent scope. Suppose that the loop (or the call) is at line L_l, its parent scope starts at line L_p, and that $\bar{v}$ are the variables of interest at L_l and $\bar{w}$ represent their values at L_p. Then we add the JML annotation "//@ ghost int $w_1 = v_1$;... ; int $w_n = v_n$;" immediately after line L_p to capture the values of $\bar{v}$ at line L_p, and the JML annotation "//@ assert φ" immediately before line L_l to state that the relation φ must hold at the program point. Additional size relations inferred by COSTA are input-output size relations. These are linear constraints that relate the return value of a given method to its input values. For example, suppose that we replace "i −−" in line 21 of the insert_sort program by "i =decrement(i)" where decrement is defined by "**int** decrement(**int** x) {**return** x−1;}". Then COSTA infers the relation "$\varphi \equiv$\result= x−1" which is used to bound the number of iterations of that loop. In order to verify this relation in KeY we add the JML annotation "//@ ensures φ" to the contract of decrement.

3. Verification of Upper Bounds using KeY

We now describe the verification techniques used in KeY to prove program correctness, focusing on those relevant to UB verification.

3.1 Verification by Symbolic Execution

The program logic used by KeY is *JavaCard Dynamic Logic* (JavaDL) [4], a first-order dynamic logic with arithmetic. Programs are first-class citizens similar to Hoare logics but, in dynamic logic, correctness assertions can appear arbitrarily nested. JavaDL extends sorted first-order logic by a program modality $\langle\cdot\rangle\cdot$ (read "diamond"). Let p denote a sequence of executable Java statements and ϕ an arbitrary JavaDL formula, then $\langle \mathsf{p} \rangle \phi$ is a JavaDL formula which states that program p terminates and in its final state ϕ holds. A typical formula in JavaDL looks like

$$\mathsf{i} \doteq i0 \wedge \mathsf{j} \doteq j0 \rightarrow \langle \overbrace{\mathsf{i{=}j{-}i;j{=}j{-}i;i{=}i{+}j;}}^{\mathsf{p}} \rangle (\mathsf{i} \doteq j0 \wedge \mathsf{j} \doteq i0)$$

where i, j are program variables represented as *non-rigid* constants. Non-rigid constants and functions are state-dependent: their value can be changed by programs. The *rigid* constants $i0, j0$ are state-independent: their value cannot be changed. The formula above says that if program p is executed in a state where i and j have values $i0$, $j0$, then p terminates *and* in its final state the values of the variables are swapped. To reason about JavaDL formulas, KeY employs a sequent calculus whose rules perform *symbolic execution* of the programs in the modalities. Here is a typical rule:

$$\mathsf{ifSplit}\ \frac{\Gamma, b \Longrightarrow \langle \{\mathsf{p}\}\mathsf{rest}\rangle\phi, \Delta \quad \Gamma, \neg b \Longrightarrow \langle \{\mathsf{q}\}\mathsf{rest}\rangle\phi, \Delta}{\Gamma \Longrightarrow \langle \mathsf{if\ (b)\ \{p\}\ else\ \{q\}\ rest}\rangle\phi, \Delta}$$

As values are symbolic, it is in general necessary to split the proof whenever an implicit or explicit case distinction is executed. It is also necessary to represent the *symbolic* values of variables throughout execution. This becomes apparent when statements with side effects are executed, notably assignments. The assignment rule in JavaDL looks as follows:

$$\mathsf{assign}\ \frac{\Gamma \Longrightarrow \{\mathsf{x} := \mathsf{val}\}\langle \mathsf{rest}\rangle\phi, \Delta}{\Gamma \Longrightarrow \langle \mathsf{x} = \mathsf{val;\ rest}\rangle\phi, \Delta}$$

The expression in curly braces in the premise is called *update* and is used in KeY to represent symbolic state changes. An *elementary* update $loc := val$ is a pair of a location (program variable, field, array) and a value. The meaning of updates is the same as that of an assignment, but they can be composed in different ways to represent complex state changes. Updates u_1, u_2 can be composed into *parallel updates* $u_1 \| u_2$. In case of clashes (updates u_1, u_2 assign different values to the same location) a last-wins semantics resolves the conflict. This reflects left-to-right sequential execution. Apart from that, parallel updates are applied simultaneously, i.e., they do not depend on each other. Update application to a formula/term e is denoted by $\{u\}e$ and forms itself a formula/term. Application of updates is similar to explicit substitutions, but is aware of aliasing.

Loops and recursive method calls give rise to infinitely long symbolic executions. Invariants are used in order to deal with unbounded program structures (an example is given below). Exhaustive application of symbolic execution and invariant rules results in formulas of the form $\{u\}\langle\rangle\phi$ where the program in the modality has been fully executed. At this stage, symbolic updates are applied to the postcondition ϕ resulting in a first-order formula that represents the weakest precondition of the executed program wrt ϕ.

3.2 Proof-Obligation for Verifying Upper Bounds

To verify UBs in KeY the annotated source code files provided by COSTA are loaded. For methods where COSTA did not generate a contract, KeY provides the following default contract:

```
/*@ public behavior
  @ requires true;
  @ ensures true;
  @ signals_only Exception;
  @ signals (Exception) true; @*/
```

This contract requires to prove termination for any input and ensures that all possible execution paths are analyzed. Abrupt termination by uncaught exceptions is allowed (signals clauses). To prove that a method m satisfies its contract, a JavaDL formula is constructed which is valid iff m satisfies its contract. Slightly simplified, for insert_sort this formula (using the default contract) is:

$$\forall o; \forall a0; \{\mathsf{a} := a0 \ \| \ \mathsf{self} := o\}(\neg(\mathsf{a} \doteq \mathsf{null}) \wedge \neg(\mathsf{self} \doteq \mathsf{null}) \rightarrow \langle\ \mathsf{try\ \{\ self.insert\_sort(a)@NestedLoops;\ \}\ catch(Exception\ e)\{\ exc{=}e;\ \}}\rangle(\ \mathsf{exc} \doteq \mathsf{null} \vee \mathsf{instance}_{\mathsf{Exception}}(\mathsf{exc}))$$

The above formula states that for any possibly value o of self and any value $a0$ of the argument a which satisfy the implicit JML preconditions (self and a are not null), the method invocation self.insert_sort(a) *terminates* (required by the use of the diamond modality) and in its final state no exception has been thrown or any thrown exception must be of type Exception.

3.3 Verification of Proof-Obligations

The proof obligation formula must be proven valid by executing the method insert_sort symbolically starting with the execution of the variable declarations. Ghost variable declarations and assignments to ghost variables (//@ set var=val;) are symbolically executed just like Java assignments.

Verifying Size Relations. If a JML assertion assert φ; is encountered during symbolic execution, the proof is split: the first branch must prove that the assertion formula φ holds in the current symbolic state; the second branch continues symbolic execution. In the insert_sort example, a proof split occurs exactly before entering each loop. This verifies the size relations among variables as derived by COSTA and encoded in terms of JML assertion statements (see Sect. 2.2). Input-output size relations encoded in terms of method contracts are proven correct as outlined in Sect. 3.2.

Verifying Invariants and Ranking Functions. Verification of the loop invariants and ranking functions obtained from COSTA is achieved with a tailored loop invariant rule that has a variant term to ensure termination:

$$\text{loopInv}\ \frac{\begin{array}{ll}(i) & \Gamma \Longrightarrow Inv \wedge dec \geq 0, \Delta \\ (ii) & \Gamma, \{\mathcal{U}_A\}(b \wedge Inv \wedge dec \doteq d0) \Rightarrow \\ & \quad \{\mathcal{U}_A\}\langle \mathsf{body} \rangle (Inv \wedge dec < d0 \wedge dec \geq 0), \Delta \\ (iii) & \Gamma, \{\mathcal{U}_A\}(\neg b \wedge Inv) \Longrightarrow \{\mathcal{U}_A\}\langle \mathsf{rest} \rangle \phi, \Delta \end{array}}{\Gamma \Longrightarrow \langle \mathsf{while\ (b)\ \{\ body\ \}\ rest} \rangle \phi, \Delta}$$

Inv and dec are obtained, respectively, from the loop_invariant and decreasing JML annotations generated by COSTA. Premise (i) ensures that invariant Inv is valid just before entering the loop and that the variant dec is non-negative. Premise (ii) ensures that Inv is preserved by the loop body and that the variant term decreases strictly monotonic while remaining non-negative. Premise (iii) continues symbolical execution upon loop exit. The integer-typed variant term ensures loop termination as it has a lower bound (0) and is decreased by each loop iteration. Using COSTA's derived ranking function as variant term obviously verifies that the ranking function is correct. The update $\mathcal{U}_A$ assigns to all locations whose values are potentially changed by the loop a fixed, but unknown value. This allows using the values of locations that are unchanged in the loop during symbolic execution of the body.

Generated Proofs. A single proof for each method is sufficient to verify the correctness of the derived loop invariants, ranking functions and size relations. The reason is that the contracts capturing the input-output size relations are not more restrictive w.r.t. the precondition than the default contracts are. Hence, with the verification of the input-output size relation contracts, we analyze all feasible execution paths and prove correctness of all loop invariants, ranking functions and JML assertion annotations. We stress that the proofs run fully automatic. Much of the time is needed to derive specific instances of arithmetic properties. As future work, we plan to do proof profiling and to reduce the search time by hashing frequently occuring normalisation steps.

4. Implementation and Experiments

The implementation of our approach has required the following non-trivial extensions to COSTA and KeY (note that COSTA works on Java bytecode, and KeY on Java source): (1) output the proof obligations using the original variable names (at the bytecode level, operand stack variables are often used); (2) place the obligations in the Java source at the precise program points where they must be verified (entry points of loops); (3) finding a suitable JML format for representing proof obligations on UBs has required a considerable number of iterations (defining ghost variables, introducing assert constructs, etc.); (4) implement the JML assert construct in KeY which was not supported hitherto. To express assertions which have to hold before a method call but after parameter binding support for a second assertion construct invocAssert has been added.

Eclipse plugins for both the extended COSTA and KeY systems are available from `http://pepm2011.hats-project.eu`. Source code for the tools (under GPL) is planned in the near future.

Table 1 shows some preliminary experiments using a set of representative programs, available from the above website, which include sorting algorithms, namely bubble sort (*bubsort*), insert sort (*inssort*), and selection sort (*selsort*); a method to generate a Pascal Triangle (*pastri*); simple (*slm*) and nested loops (*nlf*). Columns $\mathbf{T}_{size}$, $\mathbf{T}_{inv}$, $\mathbf{T}_{rf}$, $\mathbf{T}_{ana}$ and $\mathbf{T}_{jml}$ show, respectively, the times taken by COSTA to obtain the size relations, loop invariants, ranking functions, the whole analysis (which includes the previous times) and generate the JML annotations. Column $\mathbf{T}_{ver}$ shows the time taken by KeY in order to verify the JML annotations generated

Bench	COSTA					KeY			**Total**
	$\mathbf{T}_{size}$	$\mathbf{T}_{inv}$	$\mathbf{T}_{rf}$	$\mathbf{T}_{ana}$	$\mathbf{T}_{jml}$	**Nodes**	**Branches**	$\mathbf{T}_{ver}$	
slm	22	20	26	112	4	3641	36	6700	6816
nlf	30	16	24	106	6	5665	37	2800	2912
bubsort	38	24	144	296	14	14890	230	57800	58110
inssort	30	12	46	142	6	9875	167	29300	29448
selsort	40	20	112	232	8	12564	209	40700	40940
pastri	66	38	138	394	14	29723	337	110100	110508

Table 1. Statistics about the Analysis and Verification Process

by COSTA. As time measurements for Java are imprecise we state in addition the number of nodes and branches of the generated proof to provide some insight on the proof complexity. Column **Total** shows the time taken by the whole process. All times are measured in ms and were obtained using an Intel Core2 Duo P8700 at 2.53GHz with 4Gb of RAM running a Linux 2.6.32 (Ubuntu Desktop). A notable result of our experiments is that KeY was able to spot a bug in COSTA, as it failed to prove correct one invariant which was incorrect. In addition, KeY could provide a concrete counterexample that helped understand, locate and fix the bug, which was related to a recently added feature of COSTA.

5. Conclusions and Future Work

We have demonstrated that automatic verification of the upper bounds inferred by COSTA using KeY is feasible. Instead of verifying the correctness of the underlying static analysis, we take the alternative approach of verifying the correctness of their results. Interestingly, this approach, though weaker in principle than verification of the analyzer, has advantages in the context of mobile code. Following proof-carrying-code [6] principles, code originating from an untrusted *producer* can be bundled together with the proof generated by KeY for its declared resource consumption. This way, the code *consumer* can check locally and automatically using KeY whether the claimed resource guarantees are verified. As future work, we plan to extend our approach to support programs that manipulate data structures other than arrays.

Acknowledgments

This work was funded in part by the Information Society Technologies program of the European Commission, Future and Emerging Technologies under the IST-231620 *HATS* project, by TIN-2008-05624 *DOVES*, by UCM-BSCH-GR58/08-910502 (GPD-UCM) and S2009TIC-1465 *PROMETIDOS* project.

References

[1] E. Albert, P. Arenas, M. Codish, S. Genaim, G. Puebla, and D. Zanardini. Termination Analysis of Java Bytecode. In *FMOODS'08*, volume 5051 of *LNCS*, pages 2–18. Springer, 2008.

[2] E. Albert, P. Arenas, S. Genaim, and G. Puebla. Closed-Form Upper Bounds in Static Cost Analysis. *Journal of Automated Reasoning*, 2010. To appear.

[3] E. Albert, P. Arenas, S. Genaim, G. Puebla, and D. Zanardini. Cost Analysis of Java Bytecode. In *ESOP'07*, volume 4421 of *LNCS*, pages 157–172. Springer, 2007.

[4] B. Beckert, R. Hähnle, and P. Schmitt, editors. *Verification of Object-Oriented Software: The KeY Approach*, volume 4334 of *LNCS*. Springer, 2006.

[5] K. Crary and S. Weirich. Resource Bound Certification. In *POPL'05*, pages 184–198. ACM Press, 2000.

[6] G. Necula. Proof-Carrying Code. In *POPL 1997*. ACM Press, 1997.

[7] A. Pnueli, M. Siegel, and E. Singerman. Translation Validation. In *TACAS'98*, volume 1384 of *LNCS*, pages 151–166. Springer, 1998.

[8] A. Podelski and A. Rybalchenko. A Complete Method for the Synthesis of Linear Ranking Functions. In *VMCAI'04*, LNCS. Springer, 2004.

DiaSuite:
A Paradigm-Oriented Software Development Approach

Charles Consel
University of Bordeaux / INRIA, France
Charles.Consel@inria.fr

Abstract

We present a software development approach, whose underlying paradigm goes beyond programming. This approach offers a language-based design framework, high-level programming support, a range of verifications, and an abstraction layer over low-level technologies. Our approach is instantiated with the Sense-Compute-Control paradigm, and uniformly integrated into a suite of declarative languages and tools.

Categories and Subject Descriptors D.2.11 [*Software Engineering*]: Software Architectures—Domain-specific architectures, Languages, Patterns; D.3.4 [*Programming Languages*]: Processors

General Terms Design, Language

Keywords Declarative Languages, Programming Support, Program Analysis, Program Generation

Introduction

A software development process inherently relies on some form of development paradigm to help structure, program and compose the building blocks of a software system. A development paradigm is most commonly concretized in the form of a programming language (*e.g.*, functional or object-oriented), associated with a range of techniques and tools to facilitate programming (*e.g.*, editing, verification, and debugging). However, a development paradigm involves multiple dimensions, besides programming, whose integration incurs both a conceptual and programming overhead. Further downstream from programming are dimensions such as middleware, which may impose a specific control flow on the program, as is done by event-based middlewares. Further upstream from programming are architectural styles and patterns [10] that guide the decomposition of a software system into components and define their interactions.

Interestingly, the partial evaluation community has been contributing to this multi-dimension approach by promoting the interpreter style [10] and introducing related techniques and tools. In the interpreter style, a program must implement a processing driven by the interpretation of a key input argument, whose binding time is assumed early. The structure of the resulting program allows a static analysis phase to determine binding-time invariants. These invariants are used by a transformation phase to specialize the program, given a value for the key input argument. The static analysis and the transformation phase form the partial evaluation process [5]. This process is most commonly used as an optimization strategy dedicated to removing the interpretation layer. The interpreter paradigm, coupled with partial evaluation, has been successfully applied to a wide range of areas, besides programming language implementations, including string matching [1], networking [2] and operating systems [7]. Although limited in the dimensions covered, this form of a paradigm-oriented software development approach has demonstrated its effectiveness for optimization purposes.

Realizing that the scope of development paradigm goes beyond programming is a key to improve the software production process, and it suggests to integrate the multiple dimensions of software development into a uniform approach.

This talk. We report on research results showing that a paradigm-oriented approach covers many more dimensions than program optimization. We introduce a paradigm-oriented development approach that offers a language-based design framework, high-level programming support, a range of verifications, and an abstraction layer over underlying technologies, going beyond a contemplative approach. We have developed a paradigm inspired by the *Sense-Compute-Control* (SCC) architecture pattern [10]; it is realized by a suite of languages and tools, named DiaSuite [4].

Our Approach

In our approach, an SCC software system gathers data about an environment via sensors (whether hardware or software). Sensed data are used by *context components* to compute refined, application-specific values. These values are then provided to *control components*; they define the control logic aimed to issue orders to the actuators, impacting the environment. The architecture of an SCC software system is depicted in Figure 1.

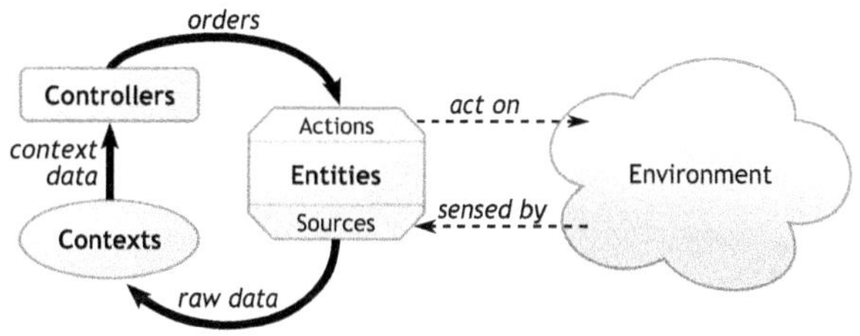

Figure 1. The architecture of an SCC software system

The SCC paradigm has a wide spectrum of applicability; we have used it successfully in the domains of home/building automation, multimedia, avionics and networking.

PEPM'11, January 24–25, 2011, Austin, Texas, USA.
ACM 978-1-4503-0485-6/11/01.

Let us now examine how this paradigm guides the design of a software system, provides dedicated programming support, and enables verifications.

Software design. Our SCC-oriented development approach relies on an SCC-specific description language. This language provides syntax and semantics to define a conceptual framework, and is supported by processing tools.

Specifically, our approach revolves around a description language, named DiaSpec, dedicated to describing an SCC software system. To do so, DiaSpec consists of two language layers: (1) one layer is for declaring a software system at the functional level, decomposing it into context and control components, and defining how these components are connected to each other; (2) another layer is for declaring the sensors and actuators to be used by the SCC software system.

Programming support. A DiaSpec description is processed to generate a customized programming framework. This framework provides high-level support to implement sensors, actuators, and components, abstracting away from the underlying technologies (*e.g.,* hardware, networking and middleware). Furthermore, the generated programming support guides and constrains programming, leveraging the underlying programming language. For example, DiaSuite generates an abstract class for each DiaSpec declaration. An abstract class implements methods, hiding low-level mechanisms such as communications, and declares abstract methods, delimiting where the application logic is to be introduced.

Verification. At declaration time, a DiaSpec description is verified independently of an implementation for consistency properties. For example, every component, sensor and actuator must be connected. At development time, a DiaSpec description is used to reason about an implementation to check its conformance. For example, a component implementation only communicates directly with another component if they are connected in the DiaSpec description. In doing so, we ensure the *communication integrity* property [9]. At runtime, the generated programming framework includes code to preserve this conformance. For example, if a class of sensors has no running instance, an error can be raised and a repair strategy performed.

Non-Functional Properties

Beyond offering a conceptual framework, our language-based approach provides an ideal setting to address non-functional properties (*i.e.,* performance, reliability, security...). A description language can be extended with non-functional declarations, expanding further the type of conformance that can be checked between the description of a software system and its implementation, and enabling additional programming support and guidance.

We have investigated this idea by extending DiaSpec with non-functional declarations to address error handling [8], component flow behavior [3], and quality of service constraints [6].

Following our approach to paradigm-oriented software development, non-functional declarations are verified at declaration time, they generate support that guides and constrains programming, they produce a runtime system that preserves invariants.

Let us instantiate our approach with error handling [8].

Software design. First, declarations are introduced to provide a conceptual framework to express how errors should be treated. Specifically, declarations specify what errors are raised by sensors and actuators, and what types of treatment are provided by context and control components. For example, a declaration may require a component to fully handle sensor-related errors, shielding client components from these concerns.

Programming support. A DiaSpec description, extended with error-handling declarations, is used to generate a programming framework that guides and supports the implementation of error handling, besides the application logic. In doing so, the paradigm-oriented development makes the programming of error handling more rigorous and systematic.

Verification. Verification at declaration time aims to ensure that components define appropriate treatment types along the flow of errors. Conformance of the component implementation with respect to error-handling declarations is checked statically.

Conclusion

Our initial work on the paradigm-oriented software development approach suggests a number of future research directions. It would be insightful to go beyond the SCC paradigm. What other style could cover a range of application domains and give rise to a dedicated description language, and dedicated framework generation and verification phases? Another direction is to explore other non-functional properties of a software system, such as security and performance.

Acknowledgements

The author is indebted to the members of the Phoenix Group, who contributed to the research results that enabled this work. Special thanks to Emilie Balland for insightful discussions and helpful comments.

References

[1] T. Amtoft, C. Consel, O. Danvy, and C. Malmkjær. The Abstraction and Instantiation of String-Matching Programs. In *The Essence of Computation*, number 2566, pages 367–390. Lecture Notes in Computer Science, 2002.

[2] S. Bhatia, C. Consel, A.-F. Le Meur, and C. Pu. Automatic Specialization of Protocol Stacks in OS kernels. In *Proceedings of the 29th Annual IEEE Conference on Local Computer Networks*, Tampa, Florida, Nov. 2004. Awarded best paper.

[3] D. Cassou, E. Balland, C. Consel, and J. Lawall. Leveraging Architectures to Guide and Verify Development of Sense/Compute/Control Applications. In *Proceedings of the 33rd International Conference on Software Engineering (ICSE'11)*. ACM, 2011.

[4] D. Cassou, B. Bertran, N. Loriant, and C. Consel. A Generative Programming Approach to Developing Pervasive Computing Systems. In *Proceedings of the Eighth International Conference on Generative Programming and Component Engineering*, pages 137–146. ACM, 2009.

[5] C. Consel and O. Danvy. Tutorial Notes on Partial Evaluation. In *Proceedings of the 20th ACM SIGPLAN-SIGACT Symposium on Principles of Programming Languages*, pages 493–501. ACM, 1993.

[6] S. Gatti, E. Balland, and C. Consel. A Step-wise Approach for Integrating QoS throughout Software Development. Technical report, INRIA, 2010.

[7] D. McNamee, J. Walpole, C. Pu, C. Cowan, C. Krasic, A. Goel, P. Wagle, C. Consel, G. Muller, and R. Marlet. Specialization Tools and Techniques for Systematic Optimization of System Software. *ACM Transactions on Computer Systems*, 19(2):217–251, May 2001.

[8] J. Mercadal, Q. Enard, C. Consel, and N. Loriant. A Domain-Specific Approach to Architecturing Error Handling in Pervasive Computing. In *Proceedings of the ACM international conference on Object Oriented Programming Systems Languages and Applications (OOPSLA'10)*. ACM, 2010.

[9] M. Moriconi, X. Qian, and R. Riemenschneider. Correct Architecture Refinement. *IEEE Transactions on Software Engineerin*, 21(4):356–372, 2002.

[10] R. N. Taylor, N. Medvidovic, and E. M. Dashofy. *Software Architecture: Foundations, Theory, and Practice*. Wiley, 2009.

Probabilistic Accuracy Bounds for Perforated Programs

A New Foundation for Program Analysis and Transformation

Martin Rinard
Massachusetts Institute of Technology
rinard@mit.edu

Categories and Subject Descriptors F.3.2 [*Semantics of Programming Languages*]: Program Analysis; I.2.2 [*Automatic Programming*]: Program Transformation; D.3.4 [*Processors*]: Optimization

General Terms Performance, Reliability, Accuracy, Verification, Program Analysis, Program Transformation

Keywords Loop Perforation, Program Analysis

1. Motivation

Traditional program transformations operate under the onerous constraint that they must preserve the exact behavior of the transformed program. But many programs are designed to produce approximate results. Lossy video encoders, for example, are designed to give up perfect fidelity in return for faster encoding and smaller encoded videos [10]. Machine learning algorithms usually work with probabilistic models that capture some, but not all, aspects of phenomena that are difficult (if not impossible) to model with complete accuracy [2]. Monte-Carlo computations use random simulation to deliver inherently approximate solutions to complex systems of equations that are, in many cases, computationally infeasible to solve exactly [5].

For programs that perform such computations, preserving the exact semantics simply misses the point. The underlying problems that these computations solve typically exhibit an inherent performance versus accuracy trade-off — the more computational resources (such as time or energy) one is willing to spend, the more accurate the result one may be able to obtain. Conversely, the less accurate a result one is willing to accept, the less resources one may need to expend to obtain that result. Any specific program occupies but a single point in this rich trade-off space. Preserving the exact semantics of this program abandons the other points, many of which may be, depending on the context, more desirable than the original point that the program happens to implement.

2. Loop Perforation

Loop perforation can automatically generate variants of a given computation, with the variants occupying a rich set of points spread across the underlying perfomance versus accuracy trade-off space [3, 6–8]. Systems can build on the availability of this range of different computations to, for example, produce acceptably accurate results more quickly or with less energy [3, 7, 8], dynamically adapt to changes in the underlying computational platform [3], eliminate barrier idling [7], identify promising opportunities for manual optimization [6], or survive failures [3, 8].

2.1 Loop Perforation Transformation

Loop perforation transforms loops to perform a subset of their original iterations. For example, given the following loop:

```
for (i = 0; i < n; i++) { sum += a[i]; }
```

loop perforation can produce the following transformed loop:

```
for (i = 0; i < n; i += k) { sum += a[i]; }
sum = sum * k;
```

The transformed loop simply executes every `k`th iteration of the original loop, then extrapolates `sum` to obtain an approximation to the result that the original loop produces (of course, other policies such as skipping an initial or final block of iterations or skipping a psuedorandomly selected set of iterations are also possible). For many such loops, perforation produces a computation that executes in significantly less time (for our set of benchmark programs chosen from the PARSEC benchmark suite [1] typically between three to five times faster than the original computation) with modest accuracy losses (the result differs by less than 10% from the result that the original program produces).

3. Probabilistic Reasoning

How can one justify the application of loop perforation? We model the effect of perforation on the above loop by modeling the values `a[i]` as independent random samples from the same probability distribution with mean μ and finite variance σ^2. The expected value of `sum` is $\mathtt{n}\mu$ for both the original and perforated loops. The probability that the absolute difference between the two values of `sum` is greater than d is less than or equal to $(\mathtt{n}(\mathtt{k}-1)\sigma^2)/d^2$ for d at least $\sigma\sqrt{\mathtt{n}(\mathtt{k}-1)}$. If we further assume that the `a[i]` are drawn from a Gaussian distribution, the expected value of the absolute difference between the two values of `sum` is $\sigma\sqrt{(k-1)2\mathtt{n}/\pi}$.

If adjacent values of `a[i]` are positively correlated (this can be the case, for example, if they come from a spatially sampled domain such as an image or geographic data whose adjacent values tend to change slowly or if they come from computations on overlapping sets of numbers), it is possible to improve the estimate of the expected difference.

For example, assume the `a[i]` are a Gaussian random walk with step size variance σ^2 (i.e., the `a[i]` are a Markov chain where `a[i+1]-a[i]` is Gaussian distributed with mean 0 and variance σ^2). For `k=2`, the expected absolute difference between the two values of `sum` is $\sigma\sqrt{\mathtt{n}/\pi}$. If we drop the Gaussian assumption and sim-

PEPM'11, January 24–25, 2011, Austin, Texas, USA.
ACM 978-1-4503-0485-6/11/01.

ply assume independent increments between adjacent `a[i]` with finite variance σ^2, the probability that the absolute difference between the two values of `sum` is greater than d is less than $\mathtt{n}\sigma^2/2d^2$ for d at least $\sigma\sqrt{\mathtt{n}/2}$.

It is often possible to generalize such analyses to model arbitrary linear combations of the input data followed by nonlinear operations such as `min`, `max`, division, and multiplication. It is possible to validate such analyses by running the program on representative inputs and either performing statistical tests on the values that the program manipulates, observing how well the analytic model (conservatively) predicts the observed differences in the results that the original and perforated computations produce, or both. In the absence of an accurate analytic model of the computation (this can happen if the computation is too complex to model analytically), simulation may provide an effective way to model the effect of perforation on the accuracy of the computation [9].

4. A New Foundation

This probabilistic approach provides a new foundation for program analysis and transformation. Traditional analyses use discrete logic to reason about the behavior of the program and justify transformations that are guaranteed to preserve the exact semantics. We instead propose analyses that probabilistically bound the accuracy loss that the transformation may introduce. Potentially in combination with desirable-accuracy specifications, such probabilistic analyses provide the justification required to transform the computation in a principled way with guarantees about the effect of the transformation on the result that the computation produces. To the best of our knowledge, this is a fundamentally new paradigm for program analysis and transformation and the first to deliver program transformations that change the result that the program produces in predictable ways with analytically justified guarantees.

5. Building on the Foundation

So how can one use this new foundation? A first step is to identify patterns that interact in guaranteed ways with accuracy-preserving transformations such as loop perforation [9]. Systems can then recognize such patterns as they occur in the program and transform them appropriately. It is possible to generalize this approach to programs that compute arbitrary linear functions (potentially composed with nonlinear operations at the end of the computation) Profiling may help the program transformation system identify time-consuming computations that are appropriate optimization targets.

Probabilistic reasoning can also justify new transformations such as approximate memoization (returning previously computed values for function invocations that are close in time, parameter values, and/or the function itself to previous invocations) or targeted linear thinning (approximating or eliminating computations of terms in linear expressions with small coefficients).

6. Propagating Transformed Results

In many cases transformed computations are invoked by larger client applications. A common scenario, for example, is the use of loop perforation to obtain more efficient heuristic search metrics [3]. When it is possible to trace the effects through the client to the result that the application produces, analytic models can accurately predict the global consequences of applying the transformation. When the client is too complex to model analytically, we propose the use of empirical propagation analysis (systematically exploring the effect of changing the result that the transformed computation returns back to the client) to predict the global effect of the transformation and justify the transformation of selected subcomputations.

7. Potential Uses

As with traditional optimizations, it is possible to apply the transformation policy (for example, the choice of loop perforation factors `k`) statically before the program runs. It is also usually straightforward to generate code that can dynamically change the transformation policy. This capability enables the construction of systems that measure various aspects of the interaction of the program with the underlying computational platform, then dynamically adapt the transformation policy to realize goals such as eliminating idling at barriers placed at the end of parallel loops [7], reducing the fixed cost of provisioning for peak load in clusters of servers [4], or maximizing accuracy while meeting real-time deadlines in the face of phenomena (for example, voltage scaling, processor failures, or load fluctations) that cause fluctuations in the amount of computational resources that the underlying computing platform delivers to the program [3].

8. Conclusion

Since the inception of the field, researchers developing analyses and transformations have operated under the onerous constraint of preserving the exact program semantics. Given the broad (and increasing) range of programs designed to perform inherently approximate computations, this constraint is no longer appropriate. We present a fundamentally new paradigm that is appropriate for such computations. This paradigm uses probabilistic analysis to justify transformations that change, within guaranteed probabilistic accuracy bounds, the result that the transformed program produces.

Acknowledgments

Dan Roy performed the analysis presented in Section 3. Hank Hoffman, Sasa Misailovic, Stelios Sidiroglou, and Anant Agarwal all contributed to various aspects of the loop perforation project.

References

[1] C. Bienia, S. Kumar, J. P. Singh, and K. Li. The PARSEC benchmark suite: Characterization and architectural implications. In *PACT-2008: Proceedings of the 17th International Conference on Parallel Architectures and Compilation Techniques*, Oct 2008.

[2] J. Hartigan and M. Wong. A k-means clustering algorithm. *JR Stat. Soc., Ser. C*, 28:100–108, 1979.

[3] H. Hoffman, S. Misailovic, S. Sidiroglou, A. Agarwal, and M. Rinard. Using Code Perforation to Improve Performance, Reduce Energy Consumption, and Respond to Failures. Technical Report TR-2009-042, Computer Science and Artificial Intelligence Laboratory, MIT, Sept. 2009.

[4] H. Hoffmann, S. Sidiroglou, M. Carbin, S. Misailovic, A. Agarwal, and M. Rinard. Power-Aware Computing with Dynamic Knobs. Technical Report TR-2010-027, MIT CSAIL, May 2010.

[5] M. Kalos and P. Whitlock. *Monte carlo methods*. Wiley-VCH, 2008. ISBN 352740760X.

[6] S. Misailovic, S. Sidiroglou, H. Hoffmann, and M. Rinard. Quality of service profiling. In *Proceedings of the 32nd ACM/IEEE International Conference on Software Engineering-Volume 1*. ACM, 2010.

[7] M. Rinard. Using early phase termination to eliminate load imbalancess at barrier synchronization points. In *Proceedings of the 2007 ACM SIGPLAN Conference on Object-Oriented Programming Systems, Languages, and Applications*, Oct. 2007.

[8] M. Rinard. Probabilistic accuracy bounds for fault-tolerant computations that discard tasks. In *Proceedings of the 20th Annual International Conference on Supercomputing*, 2006.

[9] M. Rinard, H. Hoffmann, S. Misailovic, and S. Sidiroglou. Patterns and statistical analysis for understanding reduced resource computing. In *Proceedings of Onward! 2010*, Oct. 2010.

[10] x264. http://www.videolan.org/x264.html.

Adaptation-Based Programming in Java

Tim Bauer Martin Erwig Alan Fern Jervis Pinto

School of EECS
Oregon State University
{bauertim,erwig,afern,pinto}@eecs.oregonstate.edu

Abstract

Writing deterministic programs is often difficult for problems whose optimal solutions depend on unpredictable properties of the programs' inputs. Difficulty is also encountered for problems where the programmer is uncertain about how to best implement certain aspects of a solution. For such problems a mixed strategy of deterministic programming and machine learning can often be very helpful: Initially, define those parts of the program that are well understood and leave the other parts loosely defined through default actions, but also define how those actions can be improved depending on results from actual program runs. Then run the program repeatedly and let the loosely defined parts adapt.

In this paper we present a library for Java that facilitates this style of programming, called *adaptation-based programming*. We motivate the design of the library, define the semantics of adaptation-based programming, and demonstrate through two evaluations that the approach works well in practice. Adaptation-based programming is a form of program generation in which the creation of programs is controlled by previous runs. It facilitates a whole new spectrum of programs between the two extremes of totally deterministic programs and machine learning.

Categories and Subject Descriptors D [*3*]: 3

General Terms Languages

Keywords Java, Reinforcement Learning, Partial Programming, Program Adaptation

1. Introduction

Programs written in traditional programming languages are typically deterministic, that is, at every step they specify exactly which action to take next. In contrast, there are many problems that do not lend themselves easily to such a deterministic implementation. This is particularly the case for applications that involve decisions for which the best choice depends on aspects of the program input that are unpredictable. Consider, for example, the implementation of an intelligent agent for a real-time strategy game. If the choices are to retreat or attack, to wait or advance, to move toward or away from an object, etc., the best course of action depends on many aspects of the current game state. It is practically impossible to anticipate all the situations such an agent can be faced with and program a specific strategy for each and every case. The programmer is left with considerable uncertainty about how to write deterministic code that makes good choices across all possibilities. Note, however, that even in these situations a programmer is still often able to specify a numeric reward/penalty function that distinguishes good program behavior from poor behavior. For example, in a real-time strategy game this reward might relate to the damage inflicted on an enemy versus the damage taken.

In situations like these, it would be nice if a programmer could leave specific decisions that they are uncertain about as open and instead provide "reward" signals that indicate whether the program is performing well or not. Of course, this would only be useful if the program could automatically "figure out" how to select actions at the open decision points in order to maximize the reward obtained during program executions. One approach to achieve this behavior is to provide functionality for the program to learn, over repeated runs of the program, to optimize the selection of actions at open decision points. This learning functionality should not be visible for the programmer, who needs only to specify their uncertainty about decisions and provide the reward signal.

We call this approach to programming *adaptation-based programming* (ABP) because programs are written in a way that defines their own adaptation based on the situations encountered at runtime. In this paper we describe the realization of ABP as a library for Java. The design of this library [4] has to address many questions. For example:

- How can program decisions be made adaptable? We need constructs to mark parts of a program as adaptable, and we must be able to specify default and adaptive behaviors as well as rewards and the allocation of rewards to behaviors.
- What granularity of adaptation should be supported? How can rewards be shared among different decisions, and how can they be kept separate if needed? How can adaptation be properly scoped with respect to program time and locality?
- What mechanisms do programmers need for controlling the adaptation process? Under which conditions can a decision be considered fully adapted as opposed to still adapting? How can adaptations be made persistent?

Answers to these questions determine the design of a library for adaptation-based programming, and will be addressed in Section 2 by discussing variations of a small ABP example. Specifically, this section provides a programmer's point of view on the library design, which is an important aspect since ease of use and clarity of concepts is an essential precondition for a widespread adoption of a library.

Our library is designed to be used by regular programmers, not machine-learning experts. Hence this work is distinct from Java reinforcement learning libraries (e.g. [20]). In fact, the user is insulated from the details of the RL algorithm used and they need not understand its implementation to use our library. By design the library interface and concepts necessary to use it are minimal.

Before we describe the details we briefly discuss the question regarding the scope of program adaptation supported by our ABP library. One could certainly envision the adaptation of, say type

PEPM'11, January 24–25, 2011, Austin, Texas, USA.

definitions, in response to repeated program executions to optimize data representations. Similarly, the change of control structures could be a response to feedback gathered from runtime information. However, one practical problem with such an approach is that it generally requires recompilation of programs after adaptation, which leads to a more complicated framework compared to a system that only works completely within a single compiled program. Moreover, if the adaptation system does not require recompilation, this will certainly lead to a more efficient runtime behavior of adaptation, which is a very important aspect since problems that are amenable to ABP often require an enormous number of program runs to successfully adapt, see also Section 4. The design of our Java ABP library is therefore based on compilation-invariant adaptations.

The remainder of this paper is structured as follows. After illustrating the use of our Java ABP library in the next section, we will provide a more formal description of the semantics of ABP in Section 3. In particular, we will describe the meaning of an ABP program as an optimization problem and then define the meaning through the learning of good (or optimal) policies. Section 4 provides an evaluation of our library using a dice game and a real-time strategy game. We discuss related work in Section 5, future work in Section 6, and conclude with Section 7.

2. Library Support for ABP in Java

To illustrate our program generation approach suppose we are implementing a simple hunting simulation involving two wolves hunting a rabbit. Our goal is to write a program where the wolves work together to trap the rabbit.

In Section 2.1 we provide some implementation details about the example application to set the stage for the application of ABP. In Section 2.2 we then illustrate how to realize the application using our ABP library. We will also use the example to motivate the design of the library components. In Section 2.3 we discuss some additional aspects regarding the programmer's control over the machine learning process. In particular, we show how a programmer can improve (that is, speed up) the adaptation process by coding insights about the domain. Finally, we discuss in Section 2.4 the flexibility and safety that our library design offers for working with multiple adaptations.

2.1 Example Scenario

Our game world's state is represented by a two-dimensional grid as in the class given below.

```
class Grid {
  Grid moveWolf1(Move m);
  Grid moveWolf2(Move m);
  Grid moveRabbit(Move m);

  boolean rabbitCaught();

  ...

  static Grid INITIAL;
}
```

This class maintains the coordinate positions of each animal on the grid and implements game logic and rules. We omit some of the details that are not important for the following discussion. Changes to the state are made via three move methods `moveWolf1`, `moveWolf2`, and `moveRabbit`. Each of these methods returns a new `Grid` with the move applied. Additionally, a method `rabbitCaught` is given that checks to see if the rabbit has been captured in the current game grid. The static constant `INITIAL` corresponds to the instance of the world with the wolves at the top-left and the rabbit at the bottom right. This is used for the game's initial configuration.

Permissible moves for each animal are described via a `Move` enumeration.

```
enum Move {
  STAY,LEFT,RIGHT,UP,DOWN;

  static final Set<Move> SET =
    unmodifiableSet(EnumSet.allOf(Move.class));
}
```

For our example the `Rabbit` class given below is an interface for any number of fixed strategies that the rabbit may take.

```
abstract class Rabbit {
  abstract Move pickMove(Grid g);
  static Rabbit random();
}
```

The static method `random` returns a rabbit that moves randomly.

A game proceeds as follows. First, the rabbit may observe the location of the wolves and then move one square in any direction. Next, the first wolf gets to observe the rabbit's move and move itself. After that the second wolf gets to observe both prior moves and then move itself. If at the end of a round either wolf has landed on the rabbit's square, the rabbit is captured. Otherwise, the hunt continues.

To make the problem more interesting we allow the x-coordinate of the world to wrap. Hence an animal at the left end of the grid can wrap around to the right end and vice versa. In this way, the rabbit could always escape if the wolves close from the same direction. Hence, the wolves must be smart enough to cooperate and close from opposite directions.

A programmer solving this problem with the above definitions might initially sketch out pseudocode such as that given below.

```
Rabbit rabbit = Rabbit.random();
Grid g0 = Grid.INITIAL;
while (true) {
  Move rabbitMove = rabbit.pickMove(g0);
  Grid g1 = g0.moveRabbit(rabbitMove);

  // ... pick move for wolf 1
  Move wolf1Move = ???
  Grid g2 = g1.moveWolf1(wolf1Move);

  // ... pick move for wolf 2
  Move wolf2Move = ???
  Grid g3 = g2.moveWolf2(wolf2Move);

  if (g3.rabbitCaught()) {
    ... raise our score a large amount
    break;
  }

  g0 = g3;
  ... lower our score a small amount
}
```

The grid `g0` represents the world state at the beginning of the loop each iteration. Again this includes the location of each animal. We move each animal as described before in the rules. The `Grids` `g1`, `g2`, and `g3` correspond to the game state after each animal's move.

For now, we are uncertain about how to select the wolf moves, so we indicate that with question marks. Near the end of the loop, we check to see if the rabbit has been captured. If not, we reassign `g0` and perform another round.

This pseudocode motivates some observations.

- There is a natural sense of constrained uncertainty when our wolves select their moves. They have to pick one of a small finite set of moves.
- We can consider the score as a reward or indicator of success or failure. It can be used as a metric telling us how successful our wolves are. Moreover, it suggests that it is easier to classify good and bad solutions than to generate them.

- There is an inherent dependency between each wolf's strategy. They must work together. Moreover, the reward or score applies to both as they share a common goal.

2.2 Adaptation Concepts

The coupling between choice and reward suggests that some sort of abstraction could automatically select sequences of moves and then evaluate those moves by checking the score. Over time, this abstraction could identify better and better sequences of choices so as to optimize their average reward. Implementing these notions is the goal of our ABP library which we now describe.

We define an *adaptive variable* (*adaptive* for short) as one of these points of uncertainty in a program where we must make some decision amongst a small discrete set of choices. A value generated by one of these variables is called an adaptive value. We call the location of this uncertain selection a *choice point*.

An adaptive can suggest a potential action at a choice point. But in order to do so, it requires some unique descriptor that identifies the state of the world. In our above example, there are two points of uncertainty, namely the wolf move selection indicated with `???`. In our library we represent adaptive variables via the `Adaptive` class shown below.

```
public class Adaptive<C,A> {
  public A suggest(C context, Set<A> actions);
}
```

Adaptive values are parameterized by two type variables. The first (`C`) corresponds to the context or world state, and the second (`A`) corresponds to the type of permissible actions that the adaptive can take.

The context parameter `C` gives the library a clean and efficient description of what the world looks like at any given point. In our hunting example, this will initially be the `Grid` class.

The `suggest` method is our way of asking the adaptive for an appropriate value for some context. Moreover, we pass a set of permissible actions for the adaptive to choose from. We are asking the adaptive value, "If the state of the world is `context`, what is a good move from the set of `actions`?"

In our wolf hunt example, each of our wolves could be represented by an adaptive. The context type parameter would be the world state `Grid`, and the action type would simply be a `Move`. We illustrate this shortly.

The dependency between the moves we select for our wolves elicits another important observation: multiple adaptives might share a common goal. Under this view our adaptive wolves must share a common reward stream. The score in the game (the reward) applies to both wolves, not just one. This sharing of rewards asks for a scoping mechanism that allows the grouping of multiple adaptive variables.

We define this common goal as an *adaptive process*. It represents a goal that all its adaptives share, it distributes rewards (or penalties) to its adaptives, and it manages various history information that its adaptive variables learn from.

We show the basic interface in our ABP framework defining an adaptive process below.

```
public class AdaptiveProcess {
  static AdaptiveProcess init(File status);
  public <C,A> Adaptive<C,A>
          initAdaptive(Class<C> contextClass,
                       Class<A> actionClass);

  public void reward(double r);
  public void disableLearning();
}
```

A new adaptive process is created via the class's `init` method. The source file argument permits the `AdaptiveProcess` to automatically be persisted between runs. The first time the program is run, a new file is created to save all information about adaptives. When the program terminates, the process and all its adaptives are automatically saved. Successive program invocations will reload the learning process information from the given file. This persistence permits the adaptive variables contained in the process to evolve more effective strategies over multiple program runs.

Individual adaptives are created with the `initAdaptive` method. The context and action type parameters are passed in as arguments, typically as class literals. This permits us to dynamically type check persisted data as it is loaded.

In our wolf example we would use the following code to initialize our process and the adaptives for each wolf.

```
public class Hunt {
  public static void main(String[] args){
    AdaptiveProcess
      hunt = AdaptiveProcess.init(new File(args[0]));
    Adaptive<Grid,Move>
      w1 = hunt.initAdaptive(Grid.class,Move.class),
      w2 = hunt.initAdaptive(Grid.class,Move.class);
```

We specify the aforementioned rewards of an adaptive process with the `reward` method. Positive values indicate positive feedback and tell the process that good choices were recently made, negative values indicate bad choices were recently made.

Upon receiving a reward, the adaptive process will consider the previous actions it has taken and adjust its view of the world accordingly. This permits later calls to `suggest` to generate better decisions. Details of the mechanics are described more formally in Section 3. We discuss the final method of `AdaptiveProcess`, `disableLearning`, later.

Continuing with the previous block of code, the body of our game we sketched out earlier in pseudo code could be implemented as follows.

```
    Rabbit rabbit = Rabbit.random();
    Grid g0 = Grid.INITIAL;
    while (true) {
      Move rabbitMove = rabbit.pickMove(g0);
      Grid g1 = g0.moveRabbit(rabbitMove);

      // ... pick move for wolf 1
      Move wolf1Move = w1.suggest(g1,Move.SET);
      Grid g2 = g1.moveWolf1(wolf1Move);

      // ... pick move for wolf 2
      Move wolf2Move = w2.suggest(g2,Move.SET);
      Grid g3 = g2.moveWolf2(wolf2Move);

      if (g3.rabbitCaught()) {
        // ... raise our score a large amount
        hunt.reward(CATCH_REWARD);
        break;
      }

      g0 = g3;
      // ... lower our score a small amount
      hunt.reward(MOVE_PENALTY);
    }
  }
}
```

The interesting pieces of this code are those near the comments where we filled in adaptive code and we discuss them here. First, the wolf strategies are as simple as calls to the adaptive variables' `suggest` methods. In each case, we pass in the current game state (the `Grid`) and the set of all moves `Move.SET`. Note that every move is legal; we simply translate moves into walls as `Move.STAY` for simplicity.

Second, where we referred to scores earlier, we place calls to the `reward` method of the adaptive process representing our hunting goal. After each unsuccessful round we assess a small penalty `MOVE_PENALTY`. Once the rabbit is captured we reward a large amount `CATCH_REWARD`. In our example we use -1 and 1000, respectively.

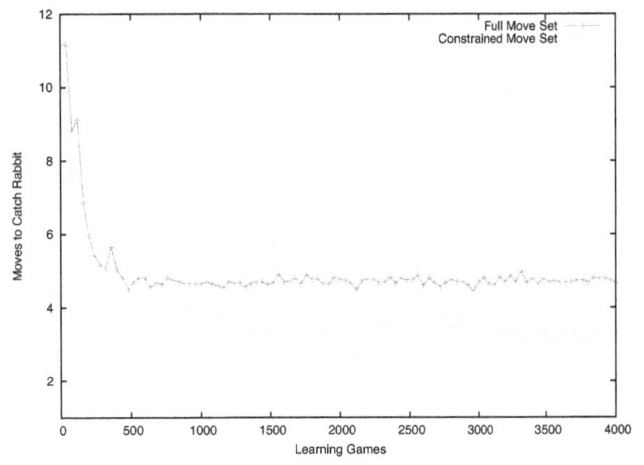

Figure 1. Average number of moves to catch the rabbit.

If we run the game over multiple iterations, the average number of moves for the wolves to catch the rabbit drops fairly quickly. After a few thousand runs the average is between 4 and 6 moves. With grid dimensions of 3×4 from the initial state, the worst-case optimal solution is 4 moves. That is, if the rabbit stays as far away from the wolves as possible each round, it will take up to 4 moves to capture it. With a random rabbit, we should expect smaller averages.

The reason for this initial discrepancy is two-fold. First, a few thousand iterations is not a long time for the adaptive process to learn an optimal strategy; indeed after a few thousand more games, the average drops lower. Second, and more importantly, even once an optimal strategy is found, the adaptive process will continue to search for better ones and may try suboptimal strategies. An initially bad looking move might lead to a better overall solution. Hence, it is necessary for the adaptive process to operate suboptimally as its adaptive variables try various move sequences.

Recall the `disableLearning` method of `AdaptiveProcess` whose description we deferred earlier. This method tells the adaptive process to suspend its search through suboptimal values and use only the best moves for every given world state. This is a means for the programmer to indicate to the adaptive process that it should stop searching and work deterministically with the knowledge it currently has. During practice we explore new strategies, but during the big game we use what we know works. If we transition to this optimal mode and run the wolf hunt program shown before, the average number of moves to catch the rabbit drops to around five after just a few thousand rounds.

In Figure 1 the plot titled "Full Move Set" shows the average number of rounds necessary to catch the rabbit as a function of the number of games learned when playing in this optimal mode. We discuss the second plot presently.

2.3 Optimizing the Adaptation Behavior

Recall in one extreme we consider algorithms that are fully specified, where the programmer completely describes how to solve the problem and manually handles all cases. Such algorithms can be complicated even for easy tasks. In an opposite extreme we offload the entire strategy to some function that we learn via machine learning algorithms. But in doing so we forfeit control over various aspects of it. Furthermore, debugging such algorithms is difficult.

One of the goals of our ABP library is to offer a middle ground; the programmer can specify some of the analytical solution, but leave small pieces to be learned. An example of this is shown by the `suggest` method of `Adaptive`. The second argument takes a set of permissible moves.

Let us suppose that our programmer implementing the wolf hunt game observed that any successful strategy would require the two wolves moving in opposite directions. In that case, we could easily specify this partial knowledge by passing in a subset of the permissible moves. We illustrate this by showing a slice of the earlier code inside the game loop.

```
// ... pick move for wolf 1
Move wolf1Mv = w1.suggest(g1,setOf(LEFT,DOWN,STAY));
Grid g2 = g1.moveWolf1(wolf1Mv);

// ... pick move for wolf 2
Move wolf2Mv = w2.suggest(g2,setOf(RIGHT,DOWN,STAY));
Grid g3 = g2.moveWolf2(wolf2Mv);
```

Including the above constraint gives the more efficient "Constrained Move Set" plot shown in Figure 1. (The `setOf` function just wraps a list into a `Set`.) This constrained learning permits a better solution, and one that can typically be learned faster since the adaptives must explore fewer alternatives.

2.4 Varying Context and Action Types

In general, different adaptives within a process may contain different context and action types. Recall the method from `AdaptiveProcess` to create a new adaptive.

```
public <C,A> Adaptive<C,A>
        initAdaptive(Class<C> contextClass,
                     Class<A> actionClass);
```

Hence, the type variables `C` and `A` for the context and action type are applied to the adaptives, not the process. For example, suppose our hunting game contained a lion and a wolf working together. These different animals might have completely different capabilities and different move types. Imagine that a lion can `POUNCE` as well as do the other basic moves. Then the adaptive representing the lion might have a `LionMove` as its action type and the wolf adaptive could have a `WolfMove`.

The parametric polymorphism here gives us some extra static type checking and saves us having to explicitly cast objects. We are less likely to ask the wrong adaptive for an incorrect move type.

3. Formalizing ABP: Semantics and Learning

In the previous section, we illustrated how an `AdaptiveProcess` allows a programmer to explicitly encode their uncertainty about a program via `Adaptive` objects, as well as the desired program behavior via `reward` statements. The intention is for the resulting adaptive program to learn, over repeated executions, to make choices for adaptive values that maximize reward. However, the notions of "learning" and "maximize reward" have not yet been made precise. In this section, we first formalize these notions by providing a semantics that defines how a program with an `AdaptiveProcess` defines a precise optimization problem that serves as the learning objective. Next, we describe how this semantics allows us to draw on work in the field of reinforcement learning (RL) to solve the optimization problem over repeated runs of the program. Finally, we describe some useful extensions beyond the basic semantics, which are supported by the library and provide the programmer with additional flexibility.

3.1 Induced Optimization Problem

For simplicity, and without loss of generality, we describe the semantics for programs that include a single `AdaptiveProcess` and where the set of adaptive objects appearing in the program is fixed and statically determined. We also assume that the context and action types of each adaptive are discrete finite sets. The relaxation of these assumptions is discussed at the end of this section. Recall that the Wolf-Rabbit program from Section 2 contains a single `AdaptiveProcess` and two adaptives, each responsible for selecting actions for a wolf via calls to the `suggest` method.

The programmer did not need to specify an implementation for `suggest`, but rather expects that the ABP machinery will optimize this method for each adaptive in order to produce good program behavior, that is, capture the rabbit quickly.

To specify the optimization problem induced by an adaptive program, we first introduce some definitions. A *choice function* for an adaptive with context-type C and action-type A is a function from C to A. A *policy* for an adaptive program is an assignment of a choice function to each adaptive that appears in the program. In the Wolf-Rabbit example, a policy is a pair of functions, one for each wolf, that returns a movement direction given the current game context.

Given an adaptive program P and a policy π, we define the execution of P on input x with respect to π to be an execution of P where each call to an adaptive's `suggest` method is serviced by evaluating the appropriate choice function in π. Each such execution is deterministic and results in a deterministic sequence of calls to the `reward` method, each one specifying a numeric reward value. The sum of these rewards is of particular interest and we will denote this sum by $R(P,\pi,x)$, noting that R is a deterministic function of its arguments. In our Wolf-Rabbit example, the program input x might correspond to an initial position of the wolves and rabbit or a random seed that determines those positions and $R(P,\pi,x)$ depends on whether the wolves catch the rabbit and if so how long it took when following π.

Intuitively, we would like to find a π that achieves a large value of total reward $R(P,\pi,x)$ for inputs x that we expect to encounter. More formally, let D be a distribution over possible inputs x in our intended application setting. For instance, in the Wolf-Rabbit example, D might be the uniform distribution over possible initial positions of the wolves and rabbit, or might assign probability one to a single initial position. Given such a distribution D and an adaptive program P, we can now define the induced optimization problem to be that of finding a policy π that maximizes the expected value of $R(P,\pi,x)$ where x is distributed according to D. That is, our goal is to find π^* as defined below.

$$\pi^* = \arg\max_{\pi\in\Pi} \mathbb{E}\left[R(P,\pi,x)\right],\; x \sim D \tag{1}$$

That is we wish to find the arguments that maximizes the expression where Π is the set of all policies, $\mathbb{E}[\cdot]$ is the expectation operator, and $x \sim D$ denotes that x is a random variable distributed according to distribution D. In order to make this a well defined objective we assume that all program executions for any π and x terminate in a finite number of steps so that $R(P,\pi,x)$ is always finite.[1]

In all but trivial cases finding an analytical solution for π^* will not be possible. Thus, the ABP framework attempts to "learn" a good, or optimal, π based on experience gathered through repeated executions of the program on inputs drawn from D. Intuitively, during these executions the learning process explores different possibilities for the choices of the various adaptives in order to settle on the best overall policy for the program. Once this policy is found, the learning process can be turned off and the policy can be used from that point onward to make choices for the adaptives.

3.2 Learning Policies

Now consider how we might learn a good, or optimal, policy via repeated program executions. First, note that given a particular policy π we can estimate the expected reward $\mathbb{E}\left[R(P,\pi,x)\right]$ by first sampling a set of inputs $\{x_1,\ldots,x_n\}$ from D, then executing the program on each x_i with respect to π to compute $R(P,\pi,x_i)$, and then averaging these values. A naive learning approach then is to estimate the expected reward for each possible policy and then return the policy with the best estimate. This, however, is not a practical alternative since in general there are exponentially many policies. For example, in our Wolf-Rabbit example, the number of choice functions for each of the wolf adaptives is equal to the number of mappings from contexts to the five actions, which is exponential in the number of contexts. Thus, this naive enumeration approach is only practical for problems where the number of adaptives and contexts for those adaptives is trivially small.

To deal with the combinatorial complexity we leverage work in the area of RL [18] for policy learning. RL studies the problem of learning controllers that maximize expected reward in controllable stochastic transition systems. Informally, such a system transitions among a set of control points with rewards possibly being observed on each transition. Each control point is associated with a set of actions, the choice of which influences (possibly stochastically) the next control point and reward that is encountered. An optimal controller for such a system is one that selects actions at the control points to maximize total reward. It is straightforward to view an adaptive program as such a transition system where the control points correspond to the adaptives in a program. In particular, each program execution can be viewed as a sequence of transitions between control points, or adaptives, with interspersed rewards, where the specific transitions and rewards depend on the actions selected by the adaptives.

More formally, it has been shown [2, 13] that state-machine or program-like structures that are annotated with control points are isomorphic to Semi-Markov Decision Processes (SMDPs), which are widely used models of controllable stochastic transition systems. The details of SMDP theory and this result are not critical to this paper. However, the key point is that there are well-known RL algorithms for learning policies for SMDPs based on repeated interaction with those systems. This means that we can use those algorithms as a starting point for the learning mechanisms of our ABP library. In particular, our first version of the library is based on an algorithm known as SMDP Q-learning [5, 12], which extends the Q-learning algorithm [22] from Markov Decision Processes to SMDPs. Below we describe SMDP Q-learning in terms of its implementation in our ABP library. Naturally, future work will investigate other learning approaches, both existing and new, to understand which approaches are best suited for optimizing the adaptive programs produced by end programmers.

In the context of ABP, SMDP Q-learning aims to learn a *Q-function* for each adaptive in a program. A Q-function for an adaptive with context-type C and action-type A is a function from $C \times A$ to real numbers. In our current library, the Q-function for each adaptive is simply represented as a table, where rows correspond to the possible contexts and columns correspond to possible actions. The Q-function entry for adaptive object o, context c, and action a will be denoted by $Q_o(c,a)$. Intuitively, SMDP Q-learning aims at learning values so that $Q_o(c,a)$ indicates the goodness of adaptive o selecting action a in context c. Thus, after learning a Q-function, the choice function for each adaptive o simply returns the action that maximizes $Q_o(c,a)$ for any given context. Accordingly, the policy for the program after learning is taken to be the collection of the choice functions induced by the learned Q-function. It remains to describe the formal semantics of the Q-function and the algorithm used to learn it from program executions.

The intended formal meaning of the Q-function entry $Q_o(c,a)$ is the expected future sum of rewards until program termination after selecting action a in context c for adaptive o and then assuming that all other adaptives act optimally. If the table entries satisfy this definition, then selecting actions that maximize the Q-functions results in an optimal policy. SMDP Q-learning initializes the Q-function tables arbitrarily (often to all zeros) and then incrementally updates the tables during program executions in a way that moves the tables toward satisfying the formal definition of the Q-function. Under certain technical assumptions the algorithm is guaranteed to

[1] If this does not hold, for example, for a continually running program, other standard objectives are available including temporally-averaged reward and total discounted reward. There are straightforward adaptations to the learning algorithm described below for both of these objectives [11].

converge to the true Q-function and hence the optimal policy. We now describe the simple updates performed by the algorithm.

SMDP Q-learning initializes the Q-table to all zeros and then iteratively executes the adaptive program P on inputs drawn from D while exploring different action choices for the adaptives that it encounters. In particular, when the adaptive process is in learning mode, each call to the `suggest` method of an adaptive is serviced by the Q-learning algorithm, which returns one of the possible actions for that adaptive and also updates the Q-table based on the observed rewards. Specifically, for the i'th call to `suggest` for the current program execution, let o_i denote the associated adaptive, c_i denote the associated context, and a_i denote the action selected by Q-learning for that call to suggest. Also let r_i denote the sum of rewards observed via calls to the `reward` method between o_i and o_{i+1}. Note that in some cases there will be no calls to `reward` between o_i and o_{i+1} in which case $r_i = 0$. After encountering the $(i+1)$'th call to `suggest`, SMDP Q-learning performs the following two steps:

(1) **Update Q-function.** Update $Q_{o_i}(c_i, a_i)$ based on r_i and the Q-table information for context c_{i+1} of adaptive o_{i+1} (see Equation 2 as detailed later).

(2) **Select Action.** Select an action to be returned by `suggest` for the adaptive o_{i+1}.

Notice that this learning algorithm does not require the storage of full trajectories resulting from the program executions, rather it only requires that we store information about the most recent and current adaptives encountered. It remains to provide details for each of these two steps.

Q-Function Update When the $(i+1)$'th call to `suggest` is encountered, the Q-learning algorithm performs an update to the Q-table entry $Q_{o_i}(c_i, a_i)$ according to the following equation,

$$Q_{o_i}(c_i, a_i) \leftarrow (1-\alpha)Q_{o_i}(c_i, a_i) + \alpha(r_i + \max_a Q_{o_{i+1}}(c_{i+1}, a)) \quad (2)$$

where α is a real-valued *learning rate* between 0 and 1. Intuitively, this update is simply moving the current estimate of $Q_{o_i}(c_i, a_i)$ toward a refined estimate given by $r_i + \max_a Q_{o_{i+1}}(c_{i+1}, a)$. Since the update for entry $Q_{o_i}(c_i, a_i)$ is done at the $(i+1)$'th call to suggest and references the Q-table for o_{i+1} via the max operation, the above update is not well defined for that last adaptive in the program execution. Thus, we adjust the update for the last adaptive as follows. Let t be the number of calls to `suggest` throughout the program execution until termination. When the program terminates we update $Q_{o_t}(c_t, a_t)$ according to,

$$Q_{o_T}(c_T), a_T) \leftarrow (1-\alpha)Q_{o_T}(c_T, a_T) + \alpha \cdot r_T \quad (3)$$

where r_T is the total reward observed after o_T until the program terminates.

Theoretically, the above update rule is guaranteed to converge to the true Q-value, provided that α is decayed according to an appropriate schedule. However, the theoretically correct decay sequences typically lead to impractically slow learning. Thus, in practice, it is common to simply select a small constant value for α. The default in our library is 0.01.

Action Selection After performing a Q-table update for a call to `suggest`, Q-learning selects an action to be returned by `suggest` for the adaptive. In theory, there are many options for this choice that all guarantee convergence of the Q-learning algorithm to the true Q-function. In particular, any action selection strategy that is *greedy in the limit of infinite exploration (GLIE)* suffices for convergence. A selection strategy is GLIE if it satisfies two conditions: (1) For every adaptive and context it tries each action infinitely often in the limit, and (2) In the infinite limit it selects actions that maximize the Q-function, that is, for adaptive o_i in context c_i select $a_i = \arg\max_a Q_{o_i}(c_i, a)$. One simple and common GLIE strategy is ε-greedy exploration [18] and is what is currently implemented in our library. This strategy selects the greedy action with probability $1-\varepsilon$ and selects a random action with probability ε for $0 < \varepsilon < 1$. If ε is decreased at an appropriate rate, this strategy will be GLIE. In practice, however, it is common to simply select a small constant value for ε, which is used throughout the learning period. The default value in our library is 0.3.

To summarize, the SMDP Q-learning algorithm implemented in our library has two parameters: the learning rate α and the exploration constant ε, which have small default values (0.01 and 0.3 respectively), but can also be set by the programmer if desired. The Q-function table is initialized to all zero values and updated each time a call to `suggest` is encountered. It is worth noting that, in addition to the conditions mentioned above, the convergence of Q-learning also requires that the adaptive contexts satisfy certain theoretical assumptions [12]. In practice these assumptions rarely hold, but nevertheless, Q-learning has proven to be a practically useful algorithm in many applications even when such conditions are not satisfied [7].

3.3 Extensions

Multi-Process Adaptive Programs Recall that the above semantics were defined for programs that include a single adaptive process. In some cases it is useful to include multiple adaptive processes in a program, and our library supports this. Each such process has its own set of adaptives and its own reward statements throughout the program. For example, in the Wolf-Rabbit example, a programmer might want to include one adaptive process for the wolves and a different adaptive process for the rabbit. The rabbit process could be used to learn avoidance behavior for the rabbit, with the reward structure for this process the opposite of that of the wolves. In particular, yielding positive rewards for each step the rabbit stays alive and a large negative reward for being caught.

As another example, it is sometimes the case that a program can be broken into independent components that can each be optimized independently yet still yield overall good program behavior. For example, suppose we are writing a controller for a video game character where we must control both high-level choices about which map location to move to next and lower-level choices about exactly how to reach those locations. The problems of selecting a good location and how to get to those locations often decouple and we could treat these as separate adaptive processes. The motivation for doing this is that it is possible that optimizing the individual processes is easier than attempting to optimize a single process that mixes all of the decisions together.

Our framework handles multi-process programs by simply running independent learning algorithms on each of them. Theoretically, this extension puts us in the framework of Markov Games [9], which are the game-theoretic extension of Markov Decision Processes. Such games can be either adversarial, where the objectives of the different processes are conflicting (such as the first example) or cooperative, where the objectives of the processes agree with one another as in the second example. Understanding the convergence properties of RL algorithms in such game settings is an active area of research [16] and is much less understood than the single process case. As such we do not pursue a characterization of the solution that will be produced by our library at this time, but note that in practice the type of independent training pursued by our library has often been observed to produce useful results [14, 19].

Multi-Episode Adaptive Programs In the above framework, learning occurred over many repeated executions of the adaptive program, each execution using a program input drawn from some distribution. In the Wolf-Rabbit example, each program execution corresponds to a single game. While it is possible to use scripts to "train" the program through repeated executions, this is often not convenient for a programmer. Rather, it may be preferable to be able to effectively run a large number of games via one execution of the program and learn from all of those games. In our Wolf-Rabbit example, one way this might be done is to simply have a high-level loop in the main program that repeatedly plays games, allowing the AdaptiveProcess to learn from the entire game sequence.

In concept, learning may be successful on such a multi-game program execution. However, this basic approach has a subtle flaw, which can result in some amount of confusion for the learning algorithm. In particular, the learning algorithm will observe a long sequence of calls to suggest and to reward. In the case where a single program execution corresponds to multiple games, the calls to suggest and reward do not all correspond to the same game, but rather are partitioned across multiple games. It is clear to the programmer that actions selected by adaptives in one game have no influence on the outcome or reward observed in future games. However, this is not made explicit to the learning algorithm and can result in a more difficult learning problem. In particular, the learning algorithm will spend time trying to learn how the actions choices in a previous game influence the rewards observed in the next and future games. After enough learning, the algorithm will ideally "figure out" that indeed the different games are independent, however, this may take a considerable amount of time depending on the particular problem.

In order to allow programmers to perform such multi-game training, while avoiding the potential pitfall above, we introduce the concept of an *episode* into the library. In particular, we give the programmer the ability to explicitly partition the sequence of suggest and reward calls into independent sub-sequences. Each such independent sub-sequence will be called an episode, which in the Wolf-Rabbit example corresponds to a single game. We instantiate this concept in our library by adding the following method to the AdaptiveProcess class.

```
public void endEpisode()
```

The programmer can then place calls to this method at the end of each episode, which make the episode boundaries explicit for the learning algorithm. Thus, the learning algorithm will now see a sequence of calls to suggest and reward between calls to endEpisode.

It is straightforward to exploit this episode information in the SMDP Q-learning algorithm. The only adjustment is that upon encountering a call to endEpisode an update based on Equation 3 is performed instead of Equation 2. Further, no update is performed when encountering the first call to suggest after any endEpisode. The effect of these changes is to avoid Q-table updates that cross episode boundaries. The formal semantics for the multi-episode setting is almost identical to the one described above. The only difference is that we define $R(P,\pi,x)$ to be the average total reward across episodes during the execution of P on input x with respect to policy π. With this change the overall optimization problem is as specified in Equation 1.

Finally, we note that the concept of multi-episode program executions can be particularly useful when combined with multi-process programs. For example, there can be cases where the natural episode boundaries of two different processes in a program do not coincide with one another. Since calls to endEpisode are associated with individual adaptive processes, our library can easily handle such situations. The above multi-process example involving navigation in a video game environment provides a good example of when this situation might arise. The adaptive process corresponding to the high level choice about which location to move to next may have episode boundaries corresponding to complete games. However, these boundaries are not natural for the process dedicated to the details of navigating from one location to another. Rather, the natural episode boundaries for that process correspond to the navigation sequences between the goal locations specified by the high-level process.

```
void yahtzeePlayer(AdaptiveProcess player,
                   Adaptive<GameCtx,Category> c1,
                   Adaptive<GameCtx,Category> c2,
                   GameState s1) {
 for (int i = 1; i <= 13; i++) {
     Category cat1 = c1.suggest(getCtx(s1),
                                s1.getEmpty());
     State s2 = rollFor(cat1);
     Category cat2 = c2.suggest(getCtx(s2),
                                s2.getEmpty());
     State s3 = rollFor(cat2);

     //out of rolls here
     State s4 = assignBest(s3.getEmpty());
     player.reward(s4.score - s3.score);
 }
}
```

Figure 2. An Adaptive Yahtzee Algorithm

4. Evaluation

In Section 2 we have already provided positive experimental results on our example Wolf-Rabbit program. It was shown that through the use of our library the wolves could effectively learn to capture the rabbit. In this section we describe two more substantial applications of our library to problems where encoding a full solution by hand is not trivial. The first domain is the dice game of Yahtzee, and the second domain is multi-unit tactical battles in a real-time strategy game. In each case, we write adaptive programs using our library and show that the learning mechanism is able to effectively optimize the program behavior.

4.1 Yahtzee

Yahtzee is a well-known dice game. Players roll some dice and then apply the combination of numbers given to some category such as "three of a kind". Each category can only be applied once. Additionally during a round, a subset of the dice may be re-rolled. The goal is to maximize one's score over 13 rounds.

Here we consider the problem of using our library to create a program that can achieve good performance in Yahtzee. The structure of our adaptive program is based on observing the fundamental decisions that are made in each round of play. Specifically, each round involves up to two rolls of the dice. The decision about which of the dice to re-roll can be decomposed into a decision about which category to apply and then selecting the dice to re-roll with the aim of achieving the target category. Given a particular target category, it is relatively easy for humans to select a good set of dice to re-roll and accordingly straightforward to write standard code to select that set of dice. However, the selection of the target category before each roll is a key source of uncertainty that is not straightforward to program. This motivates an adaptive program where the adaptives correspond to choices about target categories and where the selection of dice to re-roll is hand-coded by the programmer without the use of adaptive elements. Our program shown in figure 2 has two Adaptive objects c1 and c2 with identical contexts and actions. The actions selected from are simply the set of empty categories at a particular moment in the game. The context represents the die faces and the *number* of empty categories remaining. The first re-roll is executed by first obtaining the set of empty categories in the current game and then making a call to the suggest method of c1 to obtain a target category. This category is then passed as an argument to our hard-coded function rollFor which selects dice and re-rolls them based on the category. Next, this same process is repeated, but using the c2 adaptive instead of c1. After the second re-roll, which means that a category must be selected for scoring, we use a simple scoring function assignBest to pick the empty category that will result in the highest score. Finally, after each round the adaptive process receives a reward equal to the increase in score achieved in that round. Note that with this reward function the total reward over a game is equal to the game score. Thus a program that optimizes the expected reward also optimizes the expected Yahtzee score.

We trained the program by having it play several million games over a period of approximately 30 minutes. The results in Table 1 show that the average score for our program (labeled ABP) before learning was 119, while after learning the average score was 195. This shows that the learning process results in a significant improvement in the program performance.

Table 1 gives the performance of our adaptive Yahtzee player compared to a state-of-the-art Monte-Carlo planning algorithm [8] called UCT. We see that the slow version achieves an average score of 208 compared to the 195 achieved by our adaptive program. However, UCT requires 6 orders of magnitude more time per game to achieve this result. On the other hand, UCT-fast achieves an average score of 161, which is significantly worse than our adaptive program, while still requiring several orders of magnitude more computation time. Unlike UCT our approach does require a training period to gradually improve its performance, however, this is a one-time cost that UCT will incur for each move. More important to us than the timing comparison though is the score comparison. With very little programming effort we were able to use our adaptive library to achieve competitive results compared to a state-of-the-art planning algorithm.

Program	Avg. Score	Avg. Game Time (sec)
ABP (before learning)	119	0.001
ABP (after learning)	195	0.001
UCT-fast	161	0.8
UCT-slow	208	152.0

Table 1. Performance on Yahtzee. All results are averaged over 1000 games.

We also verified that our program is learning useful information by observing the score at regular intervals during learning. Figure 3 shows the improvement in performance for our Yahtzee program as the number of learning games increases. Each point in the graph represents the average score over 1000 games played by the adaptive program in non-learning mode. Note that after only a small number of learning games, performance jumps from 119 to approximately 145. After this the performance steadily improves.

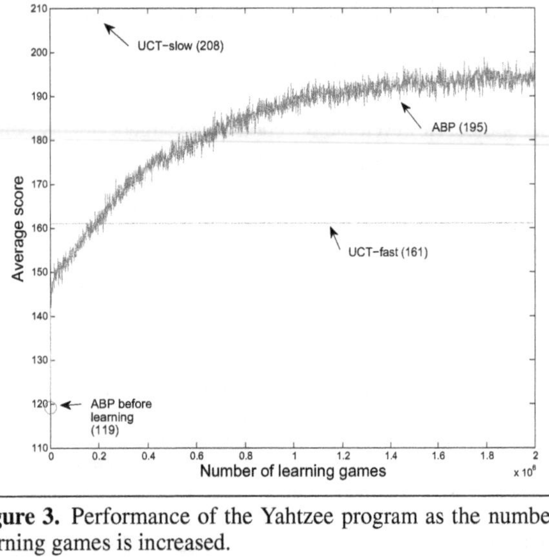

Figure 3. Performance of the Yahtzee program as the number of learning games is increased.

It is important to note that the context provided to the adaptives is not ideal. To make truly optimal decisions the contexts would need to encode the precise information about which categories are still empty. Rather our current contexts only include information about the number of empty categories (in addition to the values showing on the dice). Unfortunately, expanding the context to include exact information about which categories are open exceeds reasonable memory limitations. This is due to the fact that our current library requires the storage of Q-tables, which grow linearly in the number of contexts. There are 2^{13} possible combinations of open categories and expanding our context space by this factor was not practical. As mentioned in Section 6, this limitation can be removed using more advanced RL techniques which do not require storing Q-functions as explicit tables, but rather use more compact representations. We expect that including such techniques in future versions of the library will offer even better learning performance as more detailed contexts can then be used.

4.2 Tactical Battles in Wargus

Wargus [21] is a real-time strategy (RTS) game, which runs on the open-source RTS game engine Stratagus. RTS games involve controlling large numbers of game units in order to build an economy, a military, and to eventually overtake an opponent via military force. A major challenge for RTS game developers is developing the game AI. Unfortunately, current game AIs are relatively static and non-adaptive, which degrades their entertainment value for experienced human players. One of the reasons for this is that it is extremely difficult and time-consuming to hand-code flexible strategies for RTS games that can handle the breadth of situations that will eventually occur. Thus most approaches to game AI development centers around scripted behaviors. ABP offers an alternative paradigm for developing such strategies, allowing programmers to leave certain choices open to be optimized by the program automatically via repeated play. Here we consider the application of our library to the Wargus sub-problem of tactical battles.

Tactical battles are an important aspect of RTS games, where two groups of military units come into close contact and battle until one side is destroyed. Here we consider a tactical battle scenario in Wargus where we control 4 ground military units against 4 other ground military units controlled by the native Stratagus AI. The goal of the experiment is to write an adaptive program using our library that can learn to defeat the Stratagus AI by as large a margin as possible, where the margin of a win is measured with respect to the remaining hit points of our forces at the end of the game. For this purpose we have created a Java API to the Stratagus engine, that allows for Java programs to easily control units in the game.

Writing a good strategy even for this relatively small scenario can be challenging: Is it better to gang up on an enemy unit at any cost? Or is there some point after which we should attack the nearest enemy? How do we get our units to stay in formation? We are interested in writing an adaptive program using minimal effort that can learn to win this battle by automatically finding a good way to handle the above issues. More generally we are interested in using our library to learn a strategy that works well for any tactical battle, though that is beyond the scope of this work.

Our adaptive program must control the activities of each of our 4 military units. In this experiment we limit the actions that each unit considers to actions that attack one of the enemy units. After issuing an attack command to the Stratagus engine, the attacking unit pursues the target until coming into attack range and then continually inflicts damage on the target. Thus, the fundamental decision that must be made at each point in time is which enemy unit each of our units should attack. This is also the key source of uncertainty faced by the programmer when designing a control program for the units. With this motivation the structure of our adaptive program is as follows.

Our adaptive program contains a single adaptive process with a single adaptive that has a binary action set over the values `target` and `non-target`. The context of this adaptive will be specified later. After every 10 cycles of the Stratagus engine our program enters a decision phase where a target enemy unit is selected for each friendly unit. This decision phase contains nested loops over each of our friendly units and each enemy unit, which considers each pair of friendly and enemy units. For each pair (f, e), where f is a friendly unit and e is an enemy unit, the `suggest` method of our adaptive is called with a context that depends on (f, e). If the method returns `target` then e is set as the current target of f, otherwise the target of f remains unchanged. Thus, at the end of this phase, each friendly unit is assigned to attack the last enemy unit for which the adaptive returned `target`. A call to the `reward` method is made at the beginning of each decision phase with an argument equal to $\mathrm{HP}_e - \mathrm{HP}_f$, where HP_e and HP_f are the total hit points deducted from the enemy and friendly units respectively during the previous 10 game cycles. Thus the total reward over a single game is equal to the difference in total damage inflicted on the enemies minus the total damage inflicted on the friendly units, as desired.

It remains to specify the context of our adaptive. The context should capture useful information for making a decision about whether an enemy unit e is a good target for friendly unit f. Some of the key pieces of information relevant to this decision are: (1) the nearness of f to e, which we discretize to the values `CLOSE`, `NEAR`, `FAR`, (2) The number of other friendly units already targeting e, which can be one of four values, and (3) the health of e, which we discretize as `HEALTHY`, `MEDIUM`, `WEAK`. The context space for our adaptive is the cross-product of these three features, yielding a total of 36 possible contexts. These contexts are trivial to compute. The challenge is in selecting the best decision based on the context, which is a job we have left to the learning process.

We allowed our adaptive program to learn for 1000 repeated games of this 4 vs. 4 battle. Before training, our adaptive program achieved a health difference of -23, which indicates that the program was losing to the native Stratagus AI. By the end of training, the adaptive program learned to defeat the Stratagus AI by a hit point difference of 44, winning by a significant margin. For comparison purposes we wrote a deterministic program that implemented a simple strategy of attacking the nearest enemy unit. Initially, we expected this strategy to do reasonably well and at least win the game by a small margin based on our inspection of the map. Surprisingly, this deterministic program performs quite poorly and loses to the Stratagus AI by a margin of -22 hitpoints. This shows that the adaptive program is apparently learning a strategy that somehow trades-off proximity, the amount of "ganging up", and the enemy health. Overall these results are promising and suggest the investigation of ABP for more sophisticated scenarios and other aspects of RTS games.

5. Related Work

Our work is inspired by a variety of previous efforts in the field of reinforcement learning (RL). RL [18] is a subfield of artificial intelligence that studies algorithms for learning to control a system by interacting with the system and observing positive and negative feedback. RL is intended for situations where it is difficult to write a program that implements a high-quality controller, but where it is relatively easy to specify a feedback signal that indicates how well a controller is performing. Thus, pure RL can be viewed as an extreme form of ABP where the non-adaptive part of the program is trivial, requiring the RL mechanisms to solve the full problem from scratch. As such, successful applications of RL typically require significant expertise and experience. It is somewhat of an art to formulate a complex problem at the appropriate abstraction level so that RL will be successful.

The inherent complexity of pure RL led researchers to develop different mechanism for humans to provide natural forms of "advice" to RL systems, for example, in the form of a set of rules that specify hints about good behavior in various situations [10], or example demonstrations of good behavior by a domain expert [1]. However, these forms of advice still require an RL expert who is very familiar with the underlying algorithms for their successful application. In addition, the expressiveness of the types of advice that can be provided are quite limited, particularly in comparison with programming languages.

The desire to increase the expressiveness of advice provided to RL systems has resulted in research on hierarchical reinforcement learning [6, 13]. Here a human specifies behavioral constraints on the desired controller, or program, to be learned in the form of sub-task, or sub-procedure, hierarchies. The hierarchies specify potential ways that the high-level problem can be solved by solving some number of sub-problems, and in turn how those sub-problems can potentially be broken down and so on. Not all of the possibilities specified by the hierarchies will be successful or optimal, but the space of possible controllers can be dramatically smaller than the original unconstrained problem. Given these constraints, RL algorithms are often able to solve substantially more complex problems.

Provided with enough constraints the hierarchies described above can be viewed as defining programs. This idea was made explicit under the name partial programming, where a simple language based on hierarchical state machines was developed to provide guidance to an RL agent [2]. This language was soon replaced by the development of ALISP [3], which was a direct integration of RL with LISP. The key programming construct that ALISP adds to LISP is the choice point, which is qualitatively similar to `Adaptive` objects in our library. The primary focus of work on ALISP has been to develop adaptation rules for choice points and to understand the conditions under which learning in the infinite limit will result in controllers that achieve certain notions of optimality when executed in the world/environment. A more recent proposal for an adaptive programming language is $\mathrm{A^2BL}$ [17], which integrates RL with the agent behavior language (ABL). The proposal for $\mathrm{A^2BL}$ can be viewed as an instance of ABP for a language that is specialized to behavioral-based programming of software agents. Few details concerning a concrete syntax, implementation, semantics and learning rules are currently available for $\mathrm{A^2BL}$.

An important semantic distinction between the work in this paper and existing languages for partial programming in RL is that the semantics of languages such as ALISP are tightly tied to an interface to a world/environment that is external to the program. That is, an ALISP program by itself does not have a well defined semantics from a learning perspective until it is coupled with a world/environment, or more formally a Markov decision process (MDP). This requirement is most clearly reflected by the fact that the ALISP language does not include native reward statements. Rather rewards are assumed to be provided by an external MDP. A likely reason for the tight coupling to MDPs is that ALISP grew out of the area of RL where MDPs are already an assumed entity. However, this strict coupling to MDPs makes it difficult for a programmer who is not knowledgeable about RL to understand the semantics and exploit the potential power of the language.

On the other hand, the semantics provided for our ABP Java library are not tied to the notion of an external world, environment, or MDP in any way. Rather the semantics are defined completely in terms of just a program and a distribution over its inputs, which could be a constant input. In this sense, our library can be immediately applied in any context that Java programs might be written. Importantly, it is straightforward to write adaptive programs using our library that do interface to an external world, but this is not a native requirement of the library. Our work is arguably the first to develop an ABP framework for a language as widely used as Java. With the exception of ALISP, which is based on LISP, all other work on ABP that we are aware of has been in the context of non-mainstream and highly specialized languages, for example, $\mathrm{A^2BL}$ and PHAM [2], which greatly diminishes their potential impact. Our primary motivation was to develop a library for ABP that is highly flexible and has the potential for wide use by non-RL experts. We believe that our current library represents significant progress in identifying some of the key constructs needed to make this goal a reality in the object-oriented Java language.

There are numerous RL libraries and frameworks for Java and other object-oriented languages (e.g. Rl-Glue [20]). However, such libraries are designed for people with extensive experience in RL and their goal tends to be providing a test harness for experimenting with new algorithms. In contrast, ABP's goal is to provide a library that a non-expert can use to naturally describe adaptive constructs in their programs with.

6. Future Work

One of the immediate directions for future work is to support adaptives for which the number of possible contexts is enormous. For example, in Yahtzee we would have liked to have used a richer context for the adaptives that encoded the precise set of open categories. However, this was not practical due to the use of a table-based Q-function representation. To support such large context spaces we will implement support for compact representations of Q-functions and other related structures, which grow sub-linearly with respect to the number of contexts. This will also require developing learning algorithms that operate directly on these compact representations. The RL literature has studied a variety of such representations and learning algorithms [7], and we will initially draw on that work.

More fundamentally we believe that there is much work to be done with respect to understanding how different RL algorithms interact with different types of programming patterns involving adaptives. In particular, is it possible to analyze the structure of a program or its execution patterns in order to derive learning algorithms that learn more quickly? In addition, developing notions of equivalency-preserving transformations of adaptive programs might also be useful for automatically transforming programs to ones that are easier for learning. Some encouraging preliminary results are available in [15] where we use program analysis to automatically feed the learning algorithm better information. The resulting method achieves impressive results on a set of complex adaptive programs.

Finally, we are interested in understanding how programmers will think about and use ABP. In this direction, we plan to conduct studies where programmers use our library to write adaptive programs for problems where ABP appears beneficial. These studies will hopefully inform future library design decisions as well as direct research on the learning algorithms to better handle situations that are likely to arise with programmers.

7. Conclusion

For many problems, programmers have uncertainty about various choices to be made when solving a problem with a deterministic program. However, despite this uncertainty the programmer is still often able to specify a reward signal that indicates whether a program's run-time behavior is good or bad. The ABP paradigm is aimed at matching the programmer's knowledge in such situations, by allowing them to directly encode their uncertainty along with a reward signal. The goal then is for the resulting adaptive program to learn to optimize its decisions over repeated runs of the program.

The work in this paper has developed the first Java library for ABP and arguably the first ABP implementation for any language as widely used as Java. We provided examples of this library, specified a semantics for adaptive programs written using this library, and demonstrated its utility on non-trivial application problems. This work has set the stage for a more widespread use of the ABP paradigm by programmers that are not experts in machine learning.

Acknowledgments

This work is supported by the National Science Foundation under the grant CCF-0820286 "Adaptation-Based Programming".

References

[1] Pieter Abbeel and Andrew Y. Ng. Apprenticeship learning via inverse reinforcement learning. In *ICML*, pages 1–, 2004.

[2] David Andre and Stuart J. Russell. Programmable reinforcement learning agents. In *NIPS*, pages 1019–1025, 2000.

[3] David Andre and Stuart J. Russell. State abstraction for programmable reinforcement learning agents. In *AAAI/IAAI*, pages 119–125, 2002.

[4] Tim Bauer, Martin Erwig, Alan Fern, and Jervis Pinto. ABP. http://groups.engr.oregonstate.edu/abp/.

[5] Steven J. Bradtke and Michael O. Duff. Reinforcement learning methods for continuous-time markov decision problems. In *NIPS*, pages 393–400, 1994.

[6] Thomas G. Dietterich. The maxq method for hierarchical reinforcement learning. In *ICML*, pages 118–126, 1998.

[7] L.P. Kaelbling, M.L. Littman, and A.W. Moore. Reinforcement learning: A survey. *Journal of artificial intelligence research*, 4(237-285):102–138, 1996.

[8] Levente Kocsis and Csaba Szepesvári. Bandit based monte-carlo planning. In *ECML*, pages 282–293, 2006.

[9] Michael L. Littman. Markov games as a framework for multi-agent reinforcement learning. In *ICML*, pages 157–163, 1994.

[10] Richard Maclin, Jude W. Shavlik, Lisa Torrey, Trevor Walker, and Edward W. Wild. Giving advice about preferred actions to reinforcement learners via knowledge-based kernel regression. In *AAAI*, pages 819–824, 2005.

[11] S. Mahadevan. Average reward reinforcement learning: Foundations, algorithms, and empirical results. *Machine Learning*, 22(1):159–195, 1996.

[12] R.E. Parr. *Hierarchical control and learning for Markov decision processes*. PhD thesis, University of California, Berkeley, 1998.

[13] Ronald Parr and Stuart J. Russell. Reinforcement learning with hierarchies of machines. In *NIPS*, pages 1043–1049, 1997.

[14] Leonid Peshkin, Kee-Eung Kim, Nicolas Meuleau, and Leslie Pack Kaelbling. Learning to cooperate via policy search. In *UAI*, pages 489–496, 2000.

[15] Jervis Pinto, Alan Fern, Tim Bauer, and Martin Erwig. Robust learning for adaptive programs by leveraging program structure. In *ICMLA '10: Proceedings of the 2010 International Conference on Machine Learning and Applications*, Washington, DC, USA, to appear. IEEE Computer Society.

[16] Y. Shoham, R. Powers, and T. Grenager. Multi-agent reinforcement learning: a critical survey. In *AAAI Fall Symposium on Artificial Multi-Agent Learning*, 2004.

[17] Christopher Simpkins, Sooraj Bhat, Charles Lee Isbell Jr., and Michael Mateas. Towards adaptive programming: integrating reinforcement learning into a programming language. In *OOPSLA*, pages 603–614, 2008.

[18] Richard Sutton and Andrew Barto. *Reinforcement Learning: An Introduction*. MIT Press, 2000.

[19] Ming Tan. Multi-agent reinforcement learning: Independent versus cooperative agents. In *ICML*, pages 330–337, 1993.

[20] Brian Tanner and Adam White. RL-Glue : Language-independent software for reinforcement-learning experiments. *Journal of Machine Learning Research*, 10:2133–2136, September 2009.

[21] The Wargus Team. Wargus. http://wargus.sourceforge.net/.

[22] C.J.C.H. Watkins and P. Dayan. Q-learning. *Machine learning*, 8(3):279–292, 1992.

Calculating with Lenses

Optimising Bidirectional Transformations

Hugo Pacheco
DI-CCTC, Universidade do Minho, Braga, Portugal
hpacheco@di.uminho.pt

Alcino Cunha
DI-CCTC, Universidade do Minho, Braga, Portugal
alcino@di.uminho.pt

Abstract

This paper presents an equational calculus to reason about bidirectional transformations specified in the point-free style. In particular, it focuses on the so-called *lenses* as a bidirectional idiom, and shows that many standard laws characterising point-free combinators and recursion patterns are also valid in that setting. A key result is that uniqueness also holds for bidirectional folds and unfolds, thus unleashing the power of fusion as a program optimisation technique. A rewriting system for automatic lens optimisation is also presented, to prove the usefulness of the proposed calculus.

Categories and Subject Descriptors D.3.3 [*Programming Languages*]: Language Constructs and Features—Data Types and Structures,Recursion; D.3.4 [*Programming Languages*]: Processors—Optimization; F.3.2 [*Logics and Meanings of Programs*]: Semantics of Programming Languages—Algebraic approaches to semantics; I.1.1 [*Symbolic and Algebraic Manipulation*]: Expressions and Their Representation

General Terms Design, Languages, Theory

Keywords Program calculation, Bidirectional transformation, Point-free programming

1. Introduction

In an heterogeneous world of data formats and programming languages, data transformation frameworks play an essential role in facilitating the sharing of information among software applications. Modifications to the data often break the consistency between source and target data models; and a key problem with most of these frameworks is the lack of proper bidirectional mechanisms to synchronise them. Typically, we end up with ad-hoc solutions like manually engineering two unidirectional transformations together so that they are consistent according to the required synchronisation policy. This introduces a severe maintenance problem: any change in one of the data models implies a redefinition of both transformations and a new consistency verification.

In response to this problem, intrinsic *bidirectional transformation* [11] frameworks have become increasingly popular in various computer science domains, including heterogeneous data synchronisation [4, 14], software model transformation [12, 15, 29], graph transformations [16], schema evolution [2, 10], relational databases [3] and functional programming [21, 22, 25, 30, 31]. Most of these approaches encompass the design of domain-specific bidirectional languages in which one expression denotes a connected pair of transformations, whose consistency is guaranteed in the respective semantic space.

A distinctive contribution to the field is the *Focal* bidirectional tree transformation language, proposed by Foster *et al* [14], whose building blocks are the so-called *lenses*. A lens computes a view A from a concrete data model C, and encompasses three functions: $get : C \rightarrow A$, that abstracts details from a concrete model; $create : A \rightarrow C$, that enriches an abstract model into a new concrete model; and $put : A \times C \rightarrow C$, that synchronises a modified view with the original concrete model. As an example, consider that the concrete source data model is a list of people containing name and gender. A possible lens over this data type is the transformation that counts the number of women, whose get function could be trivially defined (for example, in *Haskell*) as follows:

$$
\begin{array}{ll}
\mathbf{type}\ Person = (Name, Gender) & \mathbf{data}\ Gender = M \mid F \\
\mathbf{data}\ Nat = Zero \mid Succ\ Nat & \mathbf{type}\ Name = String \\
get_w :: [Person] \rightarrow Nat & \\
get_w\ [\,] \qquad\qquad\qquad = Zero & \\
get_w\ ((nm, M) : ps) = get_w\ ps & \\
get_w\ ((nm, F) : ps)\ = Succ\ (get_w\ ps) &
\end{array}
$$

Using a traditional non-bidirectional approach, the programmer should now define the remaining functions according to sensible synchronisation requirements. For example, the $create$ function should, given a natural number, generate a list of women of that length, according to the lens properties (as formally presented in Section 2). Given that no other information is available, the only choice is to generate default names. A possible implementation is

$$
\begin{array}{l}
create_w :: Nat \rightarrow [Person] \\
create_w\ Zero \qquad = [\,] \\
create_w\ (Succ\ n) = (\texttt{"Eve"}, F) : create_w\ n
\end{array}
$$

Since put is expected to reconcile view updates with the source, it is reasonable to require that, likewise to $create$, the number of women in the output must be equal to the updated view. However, whenever possible, the names of women from the original list should also be restored. Men names should be restored at least up to the original length. Given these requirements, the definition of put is substantially more intricate. A possible implementation could be written as follows, but it is no longer trivial to check that it satisfies all above requirements.

$$
\begin{array}{ll}
put_w :: (Nat, [Person]) \rightarrow [Person] & \\
put_w\ (Zero, [\,]) & = [\,] \\
put_w\ (Zero, (nm, F) : ps) & = [\,] \\
put_w\ (Zero, (nm, M) : ps) & = (nm, M) : put_w\ (Zero, ps)
\end{array}
$$

PEPM'11, January 24–25, 2011, Austin, Texas, USA.

$$
\begin{aligned}
put_w\ (Succ\ n, [\,]) &= (\texttt{"Eve"}, F) : create_w\ n \\
put_w\ (Succ\ n, (nm, F) : ps) &= (nm, F) : put_w\ (n, ps) \\
put_w\ (Succ\ n, (nm, M) : ps) &= (nm, M) : put_w\ (Succ\ n, ps)
\end{aligned}
$$

These three functions could be packed together as a lens:

$$
\begin{aligned}
&\mathbf{data}\ Lens\ c\ a = Lens \\
&\quad \{get :: c \to a, put :: (a, c) \to c, create :: a \to c\} \\
&women = Lens\ get_w\ put_w\ create_w
\end{aligned}
$$

Given the requirements on *put*, it should be now clear that this conventional approach is bound for failure as model complexity increases. As such, *Focal* provides a rich set of lens combinators that allow users to combine primitive lenses into sophisticated bidirectional transformations, that are guaranteed to be consistent (or *well-behaved*) according to a precise synchronisation policy. In [25], we have taken a similar approach, by bidirectionalising some well-known point-free combinators and recursion patterns: any *get* function defined using those combinators specifies a *well-behaved* lens, where adequate *create* and *put* functions are generated for free. Using this language, we could redefine the above lens just as

$$women = length \circ filter\_l \circ map\ (out_G \circ {\pi_2}^{const\ \texttt{"Eve"}})$$

where *filter_l* filters all left-alternatives from a list, $out_G : Gender \to 1 + 1$ exposes the top-level structure of the *Gender* data type as a sum-of-products, and π_2 projects the second component of a pair (parameterised by the function *const* "Eve" to generate the other component whenever necessary).

Unfortunately, despite the convenience of these compositional approaches, the resulting transformation can suffer from poor efficiency, due to the cluttering of intermediate data structures; and if manual design of bidirectional transformations is tedious and error-prone, manual optimisation is a much more thankless (not to say impossible) task. Deeply related to this problem is the lack of an algebraic calculus to reason directly about lenses: proving bidirectional properties generally requires independent proofs for each of the three components. In particular, the lack of bidirectional *fusion* laws prevents the use of the typical optimisation techniques for functional programs. Quoting Foster et al [14]:

> "Is there an algebraic theory of lens combinators that would underpin optimisation of lens expressions in the same way that the relational algebra and its algebraic theory are used to optimise relational database queries? [...] This algebraic theory will play a crucial role in a more serious implementation effort."

The point-free style is characterised by a rich set of algebraic laws, making it very amenable for program calculation. Thus, we are particularly well positioned to answer this question: the first goal of this paper is precisely to determine which algebraic laws characterising the point-free combinators (and recursion patterns) can be lifted to lenses. Apart from few side-conditions to control the non-determinism in backward transformations, this algebraic theory will enable us to calculate with lenses using only the *get* point-free specification. For example, using the bidirectional fold fusion law presented in Section 3, we will be able to show that the map-fusion law is also valid on lenses, by performing the conventional proof:

$$map\ (\delta \circ \tau) = map\ \delta \circ map\ \tau \qquad map\text{-FUSION}$$

The second goal of this paper is to employ this bidirectional calculus as the kernel of an automatic optimisation tool for point-free lenses, thus combining the simplicity and elegance of a combinatorial approach with the efficiency of manually-crafted transformations. For instance, we can show that, after optimisation, the point-free specification of the *women* example performs neck-to-neck with the original handwritten definition. The implementation of this tool builds on a successful rewrite system for transformation of point-free programs [6, 9], extending it to support lenses. Of course, optimisation could be attempted independently at the three components of a lens, since they are also defined in the point-free style: we initially followed that approach but, unfortunately, the complexity of the *put* function prevented the automatic spotting of many optimisation opportunities. We ended up with a mixed approach: the bulk of optimisations is performed directly at the lens level (namely, all fusions involving recursion patterns), with some minor optimisations performed later at each component separately.

In the next section (Section 2), we briefly review the point-free lens combinators first presented in [25] and introduce the algebraic laws that characterise them. Section 3 reviews the construction of recursive lenses and studies the uniqueness properties of bidirectional folds and unfolds. In Section 4, we show how to harness these laws, in particular fusion, into an effective rewrite system for the simplification of bidirectional transformations and discuss the implementation of this rewrite system (using the functional programming language Haskell), together with the speedup results for a complex transformation scenario. Section 5 compares related work and Section 6 concludes the paper with a synthesis of the main contributions and directions for future work.

$$
\begin{aligned}
id\ &: A \to A \\
(\circ)\ &: (B \to C) \to (A \to B) \to (A \to C) \\
(\triangle)\ &: (A \to B) \to (A \to C) \to (A \to B \times C) \\
\pi_1\ &: A \times B \to A \\
\pi_2\ &: A \times B \to B \\
(\times)\ &: (A \to B) \to (C \to D) \to (A \times C \to B \times D) \\
(\nabla)\ &: (A \to C) \to (B \to C) \to (A + B \to C) \\
i_1\ &: A \to A + B \\
i_2\ &: B \to A + B \\
(+)\ &: (A \to B) \to (C \to D) \to (A + C \to B + D) \\
ap\ &: B^A \times A \to B \\
\bar{\cdot}\ &: (A \times B \to C) \to (A \to C^B) \\
\cdot^{\bullet}\ &: (B \to C) \to (B^A \to C^A) \\
!\ &: A \to 1 \\
\underline{\cdot}\ &: A \to (1 \to A)
\end{aligned}
$$

Figure 1. Point-free combinators

2. Point-free Combinators as Lenses

Before presenting the building blocks of our lens language, we need to set the semantic space where they exist. In this work, the semantic domain for functions will be the SET category, with sets (types) as objects and total functions as arrows. Being a "well-behaved" category, with products, co-products and terminal object, we immediately get a powerful set of point-free combinators for building complex functions out of simpler ones (Figure 1). Moreover, these constructs enjoy universal laws that enable reasoning by calculation. For example, the existence of categorical products ensures that there is a unique way to combine two functions with a shared domain into a function that applies both in order to produce a pair:

$$f = g \triangle h \Leftrightarrow \pi_1 \circ f = g \wedge \pi_2 \circ f = h$$

As expected, not every combination of *get*, *put* and *create* functions builds a reasonable lens. Several properties will be required of these functions in order to get a "well-behaved" lens (henceforward denoted just as "lens"). Using the point-free style, we can now give a precise definition of such properties.

Definition 1 (Lens). *A well-behaved lens δ, denoted by $\delta : C \trianglerighteq A$, is a bidirectional transformation that comprises three total functions $get_\delta : C \rightarrow A$, $put_\delta : A \times C \rightarrow C$ and $create_\delta : A \rightarrow C$, satisfying the following properties:*

$$get_\delta \circ create_\delta = id \qquad \text{CREATEGET}$$

$$get_\delta \circ put_\delta = \pi_1 \qquad \text{PUTGET}$$

$$put_\delta \circ (get_\delta \triangle id) = id \qquad \text{GETPUT}$$

Property CREATEGET guarantees that get is an abstraction function, this is, A contains at most as much information as C. PUTGET guarantees that the lens is *acceptable*, i.e., updates to a view cannot be ignored and must be translated exactly. Finally, GETPUT states that the lens should be *stable*, i.e, if the view does not change, then neither should the source.

In [25] our research question was: which morphisms in SET also denote lenses? In order to answer this question, each primitive function and combinator of Figure 1 was scrutinised and, whenever possible, bidirectionalised to a primitive lens or lens combinator. Being the point-free style so intertwined with algebraic calculation, the followup question must necessarily be: are the laws characterising the standard point-free combinators also valid in the lifted lenses? One of the objectives of this paper is precisely to answer this question. In the remaining of this section we will briefly recall the work presented in [25], but now stating for each bidirectionalised combinator the laws that characterise it. To avoid introducing a different notation, the lifted lens combinators are represented using the same notation but, to disambiguate lens laws from the standard point-free laws, lens variables will be denoted by greek letters ($\delta, \tau, \phi, \psi, \ldots$).

2.1 Basic lens combinators

The fundamental point-free combinators are identity and function composition. Both can be lifted to lenses as follows:

$$\begin{array}{ll} id : C \trianglerighteq A & \forall \delta : B \trianglerighteq A, \tau : C \trianglerighteq B.\ (\delta \circ \tau) : C \trianglerighteq A \\ get \ \ = id & get \ \ = get_\delta \circ get_\tau \\ put \ \ = \pi_1 & put \ \ = put_\tau \circ (put_\delta \circ (id \times get_\tau) \triangle \pi_2) \\ create = id & create = create_\tau \circ create_\delta \end{array}$$

The *identity* and *associativity* axioms that characterise these combinators are also valid for the lifted versions:

$$id \circ \delta = \delta = \delta \circ id \qquad id\text{-NAT}$$

$$\delta \circ (\tau \circ \phi) = (\delta \circ \tau) \circ \phi \qquad \circ\text{-ASSOC}$$

Since both these laws are valid, a category of lenses can be defined, whose objects are the same objects of SET and morphisms are well-behaved lenses.

Proof. Two lenses δ and τ are equal iff $get_\delta = get_\tau$, $put_\delta = put_\tau$, and $create_\delta = create_\tau$. The first equality is always trivially true because the get function has exactly the same point-free definition as the lens itself. The trickiest part is always proving that both $puts$ are equal (especially when involving lots of compositions). For example, for $\circ$-ASSOC such proof can done as follows:

$$\begin{array}{l} put_{\delta \circ (\tau \circ \phi)} \\ = \{\text{definition of } put\} \\ put_{\tau \circ \phi} \circ (put_\delta \circ (id \times get_{\tau \circ \phi}) \triangle \pi_2) \\ = \{\text{definition of } put\} \\ put_\phi \circ (put_\tau \circ (id \times get_\phi) \triangle \pi_2) \circ (put_\delta \circ (id \times get_{\tau \circ \phi}) \triangle \pi_2) \\ = \{\times\text{-FUSION}; \times\text{-ABSOR}; \times\text{-CANCEL}\} \\ put_\phi \circ (put_\tau \circ (put_\delta \circ (id \times get_{\tau \circ \phi}) \triangle get_\phi \circ \pi_2) \triangle \pi_2) \\ = \{\text{definition of } get\} \\ put_\phi \circ (put_\tau \circ (put_\delta \circ (id \times get_\tau \circ get_\phi) \triangle get_\phi \circ \pi_2) \triangle \pi_2) \\ = \{\times\text{-FUSION}; \times\text{-FUNCTOR-COMP}; \times\text{-CANCEL}\} \\ put_\phi \circ (put_\tau \circ (put_\delta \circ (id \times get_\tau) \triangle \pi_2) \circ (id \times get_\phi) \triangle \pi_2) \\ = \{\text{definition of } put\} \\ put_\phi \circ (put_{\delta \circ \tau} \circ (id \times get_\phi) \triangle \pi_2) \\ = \{\text{definition of } put\} \\ put_{(\delta \circ \tau) \circ \phi} \end{array}$$

Note that these equalities are proven using laws valid for functions on SET (see [25] for a compendium). Throughout the paper, we will use the same name to denote laws valid both on lenses and functions. Disambiguation should be trivial from the context. The proofs for $create$ of the law id-NAT are trivial and will be elided. Due to space constrains, the proofs of the remaining laws introduced in this section will not be presented. Although some of them are a bit more complex than the one above, they are still fairly easy, at least for someone experienced with the point-free style. □

The *bang* combinator is a lens that ignores all the concrete information:

$$\begin{array}{l} \forall_{f : 1 \rightarrow C}.\ !^f : C \trianglerighteq 1 \\ get \ \ = ! \\ put \ \ = \pi_2 \\ create = f \end{array}$$

Here, $f : 1 \rightarrow C$ is a function that generates default concrete values. Due to this parameter function, we cannot state that 1 is a proper terminal object of our category of lenses, because there is more than one lens with type $C \trianglerighteq 1$. Nonetheless, we can phrase a lifted version of the uniqueness law for !:

$$\delta = !^{create_\delta} \Leftrightarrow \delta : A \trianglerighteq 1 \qquad !\text{-UNIQ}$$

2.2 Products

Unfortunately, our category of lenses is not as "well-behaved" as SET. For example, as discussed in [25], there are no categorical products because in general it is not possible to define the split lens $\delta \triangle \tau : A \trianglerighteq B \times C$, given lenses $\delta : A \trianglerighteq B$ and $\tau : A \trianglerighteq C$; there are no lenses of type $A \trianglerighteq A \times A$ (unless A is the unit type 1), because the view is not an abstraction of the source. Thus, although $id : A \trianglerighteq A$ is a well-behaved lens, $id \triangle id : A \trianglerighteq A \times A$ is not. However, we do have the product bi-functor and projections as valid lenses, defined as follows:

$$\begin{array}{ll} \forall_{f : A \rightarrow B}.\ \pi_1{}^f : A \times B \trianglerighteq A & \forall_{f : B \rightarrow A}.\ \pi_2{}^f : A \times B \trianglerighteq B \\ get \ \ = \pi_1 & get \ \ = \pi_2 \\ put \ \ = id \times \pi_2 & put \ \ = swap \circ (id \times \pi_1) \\ create = id \triangle f & create = f \triangle id \end{array}$$

$$\begin{array}{l} \forall \delta : C \trianglerighteq A, \tau : D \trianglerighteq B.\ \delta \times \tau : C \times D \trianglerighteq A \times B \\ get \ \ = get_\delta \times get_\tau \\ put \ \ = (put_\delta \times put_\tau) \circ distp \\ create = create_\delta \times create_\tau \end{array}$$

In the projections, the parameter f is a function that generates default values for the deleted component of the pair. $swap : A \times B \rightarrow B \times A$ and $distp : (A \times B) \times (C \times D) \rightarrow (A \times C) \times (B \times D)$ are standard isomorphisms.

The following laws guarantee that the product lens is also a bi-functor in the category of lenses:

$$id \times id = id \qquad \times\text{-FUNCTOR-ID}$$

$$(\delta \times \tau) \circ (\phi \times \psi) = \delta \circ \phi \times \tau \circ \psi \qquad \times\text{-FUNCTOR-COMP}$$

Projections also enjoy a kind of naturality law, with a precise characterisation of how the default generation function must be adapted.

$$\pi_1{}^f \circ (\delta \times \tau) = \delta \circ \pi_1{}^{create_\tau \circ f \circ get_\delta} \qquad \pi_1\text{-NAT}$$

$$\pi_2{}^f \circ (\delta \times \tau) = \tau \circ \pi_2{}^{create_\delta \circ f \circ get_\tau} \qquad \pi_2\text{-NAT}$$

2.3 Sums

Similarly to products, categorical sums do not exist in the category of lenses, this time because the injections i_1, i_2 are not surjective functions and thus not definable as lenses. Notwithstanding, the sum bi-functor and either combinators denote valid lenses, as defined below:

$$
\begin{array}{l}
\forall_{p:A\to 2}, \delta : C \trianglerighteq A, \tau : B \trianglerighteq A.\ (\delta \nabla \tau)^p : C + B \trianglerighteq A \\
\begin{array}{lll}
get & = & get_\delta \nabla get_\tau \\
put & = & (put_\delta + put_\tau) \circ distr \\
create & = & (create_\delta + create_\tau) \circ p\,?
\end{array}
\end{array}
$$

$$
\begin{array}{l}
\forall_{f:A\times D\to C,\ g:B\times C\to D}, \delta : C \trianglerighteq A, \tau : D \trianglerighteq B. \\
\quad {}_{get_\delta \circ f = \pi_1\ \wedge\ get_\tau \circ g = \pi_1} \Rightarrow (\delta + \tau)^{f,g} : C + D \trianglerighteq A + B \\
\begin{array}{lll}
get & = & get_\delta + get_\tau \\
put & = & (put_\delta \nabla f + g \nabla put_\tau) \circ dists \\
create & = & create_\delta + create_\tau
\end{array}
\end{array}
$$

In these definitions, $distr : (A + B) \times C \to A \times C + B \times C$ and $dists : (A + B) \times (C + D) \to (A \times C + A \times D) + (A \times C + A \times D)$ are isomorphisms that distribute products over sums, while $(?)$ lifts a predicate of type $A \to 2$ to a more useful input-preserving function of type $A \to A + A$. The either combinator is parameterised by a predicate p that dictates the choice of left or right alternatives in $create$. We will denote by ${}_{\bullet}\nabla$ and $\nabla_{\bullet}$ the versions when the predicate always returns true or false, respectively. In the sum combinator, the parameter functions specify how to reconstruct concrete values whenever the abstract and concrete sums are "out of sync". The conditions $get_\delta \circ f = \pi_1$ and $get_\tau \circ g = \pi_2$ force these functions to be acceptable (likewise to put), i.e., the view cannot be ignored when computing the defaults. Useful candidates that satisfy these restrictions are $create_\delta \circ \pi_1$ and $create_\tau \circ \pi_1$, respectively, and when superscripts are omitted from the sum these are assumed to be the parameters.

Likewise to its functional counterpart, the either lens combinator also satisfies fusion and absorption laws:

$$\delta \circ (\tau \nabla \phi)^p = (\delta \circ \tau \nabla \delta \circ \phi)^{p \circ create_\delta} \qquad \text{+-FUSION}$$

$$(\delta \nabla \tau)^p \circ (\phi + \psi)^{f,g} = (\delta \circ \phi \nabla \tau \circ \phi)^p \qquad \text{+-ABSOR}$$

Note how the first law constrains the new predicate to be coherent with the $create$ of the fused lens. Compositions of sums can be fused according to the following law, that states how the new parameter functions can be deduced:

$$
\begin{array}{c}
(\delta + \tau)^{f,g} \circ (\phi + \psi)^{h,i} = (\delta \circ \phi + \tau \circ \psi)^{j,k} \\
\Leftrightarrow \\
{}_{j = h \circ (f \circ (id \times get_\psi) \triangle \pi_2)\ \wedge\ k = i \circ (g \circ (id \times get_\phi) \triangle \pi_2)}
\end{array}
\qquad \text{+-COMP}
$$

If the parameters are the standard $create \circ \pi_1$ we have the following simplified version:

$$(\delta + \tau) \circ (\phi + \psi) = \delta \circ \phi + \tau \circ \psi \qquad \text{+-FUNCTOR-COMP}$$

Together with the following law, this ensures that the sum combinator is also a bi-functor.

$$(id + id)^{f,g} = id \qquad \text{+-FUNCTOR-ID}$$

2.4 Isomorphisms as lens combinators

The simplest cases of bidirectional transformations are isomorphisms. Given a bijective function $f : A \to B$ (with inverse $f^{-1} : B \to A$), we can trivially define a *lens isomorphism* $f : A \trianglerighteq B$ as:

$$
\begin{array}{lll}
get & = & f \\
put & = & f^{-1} \circ \pi_1 \\
create & = & f^{-1}
\end{array}
$$

It is trivial to prove that $f \circ f^{-1} = f^{-1} \circ f = id$ is also valid at the lens level. There are many useful examples of such lens isomorphisms, such as the following:

$$
\begin{array}{ll}
swap & : A \times B \trianglerighteq B \times A \\
assoc & : A \times (B \times C) \trianglerighteq (A \times B) \times C \\
coswap & : A + B \trianglerighteq B + A \\
coassoc & : A + (B + C) \trianglerighteq (A + B) + C \\
distl & : (A + B) \times C \trianglerighteq A \times C + B \times C \\
distr & : A \times (B + C) \trianglerighteq A \times B + A \times C
\end{array}
$$

Since splits and injections are not valid lenses, these lens isomorphisms play an important role in extending the expressivity of our point-free lens language. For example, all lenses that rearrange nested pairs can be defined as compositions of $swap$, $assoc$, $assoc^{-1}$ and products [23].

A *natural lens* η between functors F and G, denoted by $\eta : F \dot{\trianglerighteq} G$, is a lens that transforms instances of F into instances of G, while preserving the inner instances of the polymorphic type argument. It assigns to each type A an arrow $\eta_A : F\ A \trianglerighteq G\ A$ such that, for any lens $\delta : A \trianglerighteq B$, the following naturality condition holds:

$$\eta \circ F\ \delta = G\ \delta \circ \eta \qquad \eta\text{-NAT}$$

This concept can be generalised to functors of higher arity. If a natural lens η is also an isomorphism, then it is called a *natural lens isomorphism*. Such is the case of all the above lenses. For example, the following bidirectional naturality laws are also valid:

$$swap \circ (\delta \times \tau) = (\tau \times \delta) \circ swap \qquad swap\text{-NAT}$$

$$coswap \circ (\delta + \tau)^{f,g} = (\tau + \delta)^{g,f} \circ coswap \qquad coswap\text{-NAT}$$

The naturality law for $distl$ is a bit more tricky:

$$
\begin{array}{c}
distl \circ ((\delta + \tau)^{f,g} \times \phi) = (\delta \times \phi + \tau \times \phi)^{h,i} \circ distl \\
\Leftrightarrow \\
{}_{h = (f \times put_\phi) \circ distp\ \wedge\ i = (g \times put_\phi) \circ distp}
\end{array}
\qquad distl\text{-NAT}
$$

Many other useful laws can be proved about these lens isomorphisms, such as the following cancelation laws:

$${\pi_1}^f \circ swap = {\pi_2}^f \wedge {\pi_2}^f \circ swap = {\pi_1}^f \qquad swap\text{-CANCEL}$$

$$(\delta \nabla \tau)^p \circ coswap = (\tau \nabla \delta)^{coswap \circ p} \qquad coswap\text{-CANCEL}$$

$$({\pi_2}^f \nabla {\pi_2}^g)^p \circ distl = {\pi_2}^{(f+g) \circ p?} \qquad distl\text{-SND-CANCEL}$$

2.5 Higher-order lens combinators

Higher-order lenses are also definable in our category of lenses through exponentiation. The exponentiation type B^A denotes all functions with domain A and codomain B, and is characterised by an operation $f^A : B^A \to C^A$, where $f : B \to C$. Replacing the type superscript by the symbol $\bullet$, the exponentiation lens can be defined as follows:

$$
\begin{array}{l}
\forall \delta : B \trianglerighteq C.\ \delta^\bullet : B^A \trianglerighteq C^A \\
get = {get_\delta}^\bullet \\
put = {put_\delta}^\bullet \circ \hat{\triangle} \\
create = {create_\delta}^\bullet
\end{array}
$$

Here $\hat{\triangle} = \overline{(ap \times ap) \circ ((\pi_1 \times id) \triangle (\pi_2 \times id))}$ denotes the uncurried version of the split combinator [7]. Again, exponentiation is a functor in the lens category:

$$id^\bullet = id \qquad \bullet\text{-FUNCTOR-ID}$$

$$(\delta \circ \tau)^\bullet = \delta^\bullet \circ \tau^\bullet \qquad \bullet\text{-FUNCTOR-COMP}$$

The ap combinator can also be lifted to a lens. The point-free definition is a bit tricky, and thus we just present the point-wise version for better comprehension:

$$
\begin{array}{ll}
\forall_{f:B\to A}.\ ap^f : B^A \times A \trianglerighteq B \\
get\ (g,x) & = g\ x \\
put\ (y,(g,x)) & = (\lambda z \to \mathbf{if}\ x = z\ \mathbf{then}\ y\ \mathbf{else}\ g\ x, x) \\
create\ y & = (const\ y, f\ y)
\end{array}
$$

Note how the put function updates the original function with a new result for the input value that was applied. The parameter function f is used in $create$ to choose a value of the domain A. Application cancels exponentiation, according to the law:

$$ap^f \circ (\delta^\bullet \times id) = \delta \circ ap^{f \circ get_\delta} \qquad \bullet\text{-CANCEL}$$

Unfortunately, we also do not have categorical exponentiation in the category of lenses because the curry of a well-behaved lens may not be a well-behaved lens. For example, note that, although $\pi_2 : A \times B \trianglerighteq B$ is a lens, $\overline{\pi_2} : A \to B^B$ is not surjective and thus cannot be made into a lens (given a value of type A it returns the function id).

3. Recursion Patterns as Lenses

Concerning recursion, most inductive datatypes can be defined as fixpoints of polynomial functors (sums of products). Each datatype comes equipped with an isomorphism $out_F : \mu F \to F\ \mu F$ that can be used to expose its top-level structure (in a sense, encoding pattern matching over that type), and its converse $in_F : F\ \mu F \to \mu F$ that determines how values of that type can be constructed. Being isomorphisms, these functions can trivially be lifted to lenses. Besides uniquely determining a type (up to isomorphism), a functor also dictates a unique way of consuming and producing values of that type: the well-known recursion patterns fold and unfold. For example, given an algebra $g : F\ A \to A$, the fold $(\!|g|\!) : \mu F \to A$ is the unique function satisfying the following universal law:

$$f = (\!|g|\!) \Leftrightarrow f \circ in_F = g \circ F\ f$$

From this we can derive the well known fold fusion law. As we will see in this section, this universal law is also valid for lenses: it will enable us to apply fusion directly to lenses, thus streamlining the optimisation process.

Building on the results of the previous section, we first define a polytypic (polynomial) functor map over lenses:

$$
\begin{array}{l}
\forall \delta : C \trianglerighteq A.\ F\ \delta : F\ C \trianglerighteq F\ A \\
Id\ \delta = \delta \\
\underline{T}\ \delta = id \\
(F \otimes G)\ \delta = F\ \delta \times G\ \delta \\
(F \oplus G)\ \delta = F\ \delta + G\ \delta \\
(F \odot G)\ \delta = F\ (G\ \delta)
\end{array}
$$

This definition trivially satisfies the following laws:

$$F\ id = id \qquad \text{FUNCTOR-ID}$$
$$F\ \delta \circ F\ \tau = F\ (\delta \circ \tau) \qquad \text{FUNCTOR-COMP}$$

In order to bidirectionalise recursion patterns, in [25] we introduced a polytypic functor zipping function $fzip_F : (A \to C) \to F\ A \times F\ C \to F\ (A \times C)$ that satisfies the following laws:

$$put_{F\ \delta} = F\ put_\delta \circ fzip_F\ create_\delta \qquad fzip\text{-PUT}$$
$$F\ \pi_1 \circ fzip_F\ f = \pi_1 \qquad fzip\text{-CANCEL}$$
$$fzip_F\ f \circ (F\ g \triangle F\ h) = F\ (g \triangle h) \qquad fzip\text{-SPLIT}$$

One of the key results in [25] is that the fold can be bidirectionalised using an unfold for the put function:

$$
\begin{array}{ll}
\forall \delta : F\ A \trianglerighteq A.\ (\!|\delta|\!)_F : \mu F \trianglerighteq A \\
get & = (\!|get_\delta|\!)_F \\
put & = \mathbf{let}\ g = put_\delta \circ (id \times F\ get) \triangle \pi_2 \\
 & \quad\ \mathbf{in}\ \ [\!(fzip_F\ create \circ g \circ (id \times out_F))\!]_F \\
create & = [\!(create_\delta)\!]_F
\end{array}
$$

In [25] we have also shown that this definition yields a well-behaved lens whenever the unfold terminates. We will now prove that it also has uniqueness:

$$\delta = (\!|\tau|\!)_F \Leftrightarrow \delta \circ in_F = \tau \circ F\ \delta \qquad (\!|\cdot|\!)\text{-UNIQ}$$

Proof. This proof can be factorised in the following three lemmas:

$$get_\delta = get_{(\!|\tau|\!)_F} \Leftrightarrow get_{\delta \circ in_F} = get_{\tau \circ F\ \delta}$$
$$create_\delta = create_{(\!|\tau|\!)_F} \Leftrightarrow create_{\delta \circ in_F} = create_{\tau \circ F\ \delta}$$
$$put_\delta = put_{(\!|\tau|\!)_F} \Leftrightarrow put_{\delta \circ in_F} = put_{\tau \circ F\ \delta} \quad \Leftarrow \quad {}^{get_\delta = get_{(\!|\tau|\!)_F}}_{create_\delta = create_{(\!|\tau|\!)_F}}$$

Again, the first follows directly from the unidirectional uniqueness. The proof of the remaining is presented in Figure 2. □

In [25] we have also shown how to bidirectionalise the unfold using an hylomorphism (a composition of a fold after an unfold) for put. Due to space constrains we will not present the definition. Likewise to the fold, it is possible to prove that the bidirectional version of unfold also has uniqueness:

$$\delta = [\!(\tau)\!]_F \Leftrightarrow out_F \circ \delta = F\ \delta \circ \tau \qquad [\!(\cdot)\!]\text{-UNIQ}$$

From uniqueness it is trivial to derive the following laws, more amenable for equational reasoning:

$$
\begin{array}{ll}
(\!|in_F|\!)_F = id & (\!|\cdot|\!)\text{-REFLEX} \\
(\!|\tau|\!)_F \circ in_F = \tau \circ F\ (\!|\tau|\!)_F & (\!|\cdot|\!)\text{-CANCEL} \\
\delta \circ (\!|\tau|\!)_F = (\!|\phi|\!)_F \Leftarrow \delta \circ \tau = \phi \circ F\ \delta & (\!|\cdot|\!)\text{-FUSION} \\
[\!(out_F)\!]_F = id & [\!(\cdot)\!]\text{-REFLEX} \\
out_F \circ [\!(\tau)\!]_F = F\ [\!(\tau)\!]_F \circ \tau & [\!(\cdot)\!]\text{-CANCEL} \\
[\!(\tau)\!]_F \circ \delta = [\!(\phi)\!]_F \Leftarrow \tau \circ \delta = F\ \delta \circ \phi & [\!(\cdot)\!]\text{-FUSION}
\end{array}
$$

3.1 Algebraic laws for lenses over lists

Lists are ubiquitous in functional programming. As a demonstration of the usefulness of our bidirectional calculus, we will now show how some standard operations over lists can be defined in our language and prove some properties about them. In particular, the lenses used in our introduction example can be defined as follows:

$$
\begin{array}{ll}
length^A & : [A] \trianglerighteq Nat \\
length^v & = (\!|in_N \circ (id + \pi_2{}^{\underline{v \circ !}})|\!)_L \\
map & : (A \trianglerighteq B) \to ([A] \trianglerighteq [B]) \\
map\ \delta & = (\!|in_L \circ (id + \delta \times id)|\!)_L \\
filter\_l & : [A + B] \trianglerighteq [A] \\
filter\_l & = (\!|(in_L \bullet\!\nabla\ \pi_2) \circ coassoc \circ (id + distl)|\!)_L
\end{array}
$$

The parameter in *length* is the default value of type A to be inserted in the source list when the target length increases. In the introductory example it was omitted because it was the sole inhabitant of type 1. Many more lenses over lists can be found in the Haskell `pointless-lenses` library introduced in [25]. Some of the usual laws that can be proved about these functions are presented in Figure 3. Since map is defined exactly as its unidirectional version, the following map fusion laws can be trivially proven from uniqueness.

$$(\!|\tau|\!) \circ map\ \delta = (\!|\tau \circ (id + \delta \times id)|\!) \qquad (\!|\cdot|\!)\text{-MAP-FUSION}$$
$$map\ \delta \circ [\!(\tau)\!] = [\!((id + \delta \times id) \circ \tau)\!] \qquad [\!(\cdot)\!]\text{-MAP-FUSION}$$

$$
\begin{aligned}
&\mathit{create}_\delta = \mathit{create}_{(\!|\tau|\!)_F}\\
&\Leftrightarrow \{\text{definition of } \mathit{create}\}\\
&\mathit{create}_\delta = [\!(\mathit{create}_\tau)\!]_F\\
&\Leftrightarrow \{[\!(\cdot)\!]\text{-}\textsc{Uniq}\}\\
&\mathit{out}_F \circ \mathit{create}_\delta\\
&= F\ \mathit{create}_\delta \circ \mathit{create}_\tau\\
&\Leftrightarrow \{\text{definition of } \mathit{create}\}\\
&\mathit{create}_{\mathit{in}_F} \circ \mathit{create}_\delta\\
&= \mathit{create}_{F\ \delta} \circ \mathit{create}_\tau\\
&\Leftrightarrow \{\text{definition of } \mathit{create}\}\\
&\mathit{create}_{\delta \circ \mathit{in}_F} = \mathit{create}_{\tau \circ F\ \delta}
\end{aligned}
$$

$$
\begin{aligned}
&\mathit{put}_\delta = \mathit{put}_{(\!|\tau|\!)_F}\\
&\Leftrightarrow \{\text{definition of } \mathit{put}\}\\
&\mathit{put}_\delta = \mathit{fzip}_F\ \mathit{create}_{(\!|\tau|\!)_F} \circ (\mathit{put}_\tau \circ (\mathit{id} \times F\ \mathit{get}_{(\!|\tau|\!)_F}) \triangle \pi_2) \circ (\mathit{id} \times \mathit{out}_F)\\
&\Leftrightarrow \{[\!(\cdot)\!]\text{-}\textsc{Uniq}\}\\
&\mathit{out}_F \circ \mathit{put}_\delta = F\ \mathit{put}_\delta \circ \mathit{fzip}_F\ \mathit{create}_{(\!|\tau|\!)_F} \circ (\mathit{put}_\tau \circ (\mathit{id} \times F\ \mathit{get}_{(\!|\tau|\!)_F}) \triangle \pi_2) \circ (\mathit{id} \times \mathit{out}_F)\\
&\Leftrightarrow \{\mathit{get}_{(\!|\tau|\!)_F} = \mathit{get}_\delta;\ \mathit{create}_{(\!|\tau|\!)_F} = \mathit{create}_\delta\}\\
&\mathit{out}_F \circ \mathit{put}_\delta = F\ \mathit{put}_\delta \circ \mathit{fzip}_F\ \mathit{create}_\delta \circ (\mathit{put}_\tau \circ (\mathit{id} \times F\ \mathit{get}_\delta) \triangle \pi_2) \circ (\mathit{id} \times \mathit{out}_F)\\
&\Leftrightarrow \{\mathit{fzip}\text{-}\textsc{Put};\ \text{definition of } \mathit{get}\}\\
&\mathit{out}_F \circ \mathit{put}_\delta = \mathit{put}_{F\ \delta} \circ (\mathit{put}_\tau \circ (\mathit{id} \times \mathit{get}_{F\ \delta}) \triangle \pi_2) \circ (\mathit{id} \times \mathit{out}_F)\\
&\Leftrightarrow \{\text{definition of } \mathit{put};\ \times\text{-}\textsc{Reflex}\}\\
&\mathit{out}_F \circ \mathit{put}_\delta = \mathit{put}_{\tau \circ F\ \delta} \circ (\mathit{id} \times \mathit{out}_F)\\
&\Leftrightarrow \{\mathit{in}\text{-}\textsc{Iso};\ \times\text{-}\textsc{Functor-Comp};\ \textsc{Leibniz}\}\\
&\mathit{out}_F \circ \mathit{put}_\delta \circ (\mathit{id} \times \mathit{in}_F) = \mathit{put}_{\tau \circ F\ \delta}\\
&\Leftrightarrow \{\times\text{-}\textsc{Cancel};\ \text{definition of } \mathit{put}\}\\
&\mathit{put}_{\mathit{in}_F} \circ (\mathit{put}_\delta \circ (\mathit{id} \times \mathit{in}_F) \triangle \pi_2) = \mathit{put}_{\tau \circ F\ \delta}\\
&\Leftrightarrow \{\text{definition of } \mathit{get};\ \text{definition of } \mathit{put}\}\\
&\mathit{put}_{\delta \circ \mathit{in}_F} = \mathit{put}_{\tau \circ F\ \delta}
\end{aligned}
$$

Figure 2. Proof of $(\!|\cdot|\!)$-UNIQ

$\mathit{map}\ \mathit{id} = \mathit{id}$	*map*-ID
$\mathit{map}\ \delta \circ \mathit{map}\ \tau = \mathit{map}\ (\delta \circ \tau)$	*map*-FUSION
$\mathit{map}\ \delta \circ \mathit{cat} = \mathit{cat} \circ (\mathit{map}\ \delta \times \mathit{map}\ \delta)$	*map*-CAT
$\mathit{map}\ \delta \circ \mathit{concat} = \mathit{concat} \circ \mathit{map}\ (\mathit{map}\ \delta)$	*map*-CONCAT
$\mathit{filter\_l} \circ \mathit{map}\ (\delta + \tau)^{f,g} = \mathit{map}\ \delta \circ \mathit{filter\_l}$	*filter_l*-MAP
$\mathit{length}^v \circ \mathit{cat} = \mathit{plus} \circ (\mathit{length}^v \times \mathit{length}^v)$	*length*-CAT
$\mathit{length}^v \circ \mathit{map}\ \delta = \mathit{length}^{\mathit{create}_\delta\ v}$	*length*-MAP
$\mathit{length}^v \circ \mathit{concat} = \mathit{sum} \circ \mathit{map}\ \mathit{length}^v$	*length*-CONCAT

Figure 3. Lens laws for common operations over lists.

For example, using $(\!|\cdot|\!)$-MAP-FUSION the proof of *length*-MAP can be done as follows:

$$
\begin{aligned}
&\mathit{length}^v \circ \mathit{map}\ \delta\\
&= \{\mathit{length}\text{-}\textsc{Def};\ (\!|\cdot|\!)\text{-}\textsc{Map-Fusion}\}\\
&(\!|\mathit{in}_N \circ (\mathit{id} + \pi_2{}^{\underline{v \circ !}}) \circ (\mathit{id} + \delta \times \mathit{id})|\!)_L\\
&= \{+\text{-}\textsc{Functor-Comp};\ \pi_2\text{-}\textsc{Nat}\}\\
&\quad \mathit{create}_\delta \circ \underline{v} \circ ! \circ \mathit{get}_{\mathit{id}}\\
&\quad = \{\underline{\cdot}\text{-}\textsc{Comp};\ \text{definition of } \mathit{get}\}\\
&\quad \underline{\mathit{create}_\delta\ v} \circ !\\
&(\!|\mathit{in}_N \circ (\mathit{id} + \pi_2{}^{\underline{\mathit{create}_\delta\ v \circ !}})|\!)_L\\
&= \{\mathit{length}\text{-}\textsc{Def}\}\\
&\mathit{length}^{\mathit{create}_\delta\ v}
\end{aligned}
$$

Some of these properties can be generalised for arbitrary recursive data types. For example, we can define generic mapping lens ([25]) for polymorphic types viewed as fixed points of bi-functors. In the next section, we will discuss how bidirectional laws can be harnessed into a rewrite system for lens optimisation. These list lenses and laws will be particularly useful in order to agilise the definition and optimisation of lenses over lists.

4. Implementation

The main difference between equational reasoning and term rewriting [1] is that bidirectional equations of the form $f = g$ are adapted into unidirectional rewrite rules of the form $f \rightsquigarrow g$ (read f leads to g), indicating that a term f can be substituted by a term g, but not otherwise. For the goal of simplification, the general idea is to substitute terms by simpler terms (for most cases). In our case, this corresponds to view the equational laws from Sections 2,3 as rules oriented from left-to-right. In this section, we explain the implementation (in Haskell) of the rewrite system that is in the core of our lens optimisation tool, walk through a complex transformation scenario, and compare the performance of optimised and non-optimised lenses to demonstrate the usefulness of the tool.

4.1 Mechanising Fusion

Laws like the ones presented in Figure 3 allow us to optimise lenses over recursive data types without using the fusion laws $(\!|\cdot|\!)$-FUSION and $[\!(\cdot)\!]$-FUSION directly. This is particularly useful because this fusion laws imply "guessing" the algebra (or co-algebra) of the resulting fold (or unfold). To be more specific, consider the bidirectional fold fusion law.

$$\delta \circ (\!|\tau|\!)_F = (\!|\phi|\!)_F \Leftarrow \delta \circ \tau = \phi \circ F\ \delta$$

Reading this law as a rewrite rule, in order to perform the reduction $\delta \circ (\!|\tau|\!)_F \rightsquigarrow (\!|\phi|\!)_F$, one must compute a lens ϕ such that $\delta \circ \tau = \phi \circ F\ \delta$ holds. Unfortunately, we cannot always avoid the need to use fusion, and thus some technique must be implemented in order to mechanise it. This research topic received some attention in the past: one of the most successful implementations is the MAG system [28], which views the guessing step as a *higher-order matching* problem. However, MAG is not fully automatic and thus not suitable for our optimisation tool: the user must have some idea of the steps of the proof to provide sufficient hints to proceed with the derivation.

Similarly to [27], our approach is to reduce the hard guessing step to a simple rewriting problem that, although not as general as MAG, is fully automatic and works in practice for many examples. In the above fusion law, if the converse of δ could be computed as δ°, then ϕ could trivially be defined as $\delta \circ \tau \circ F\ \delta^\circ$. Of course, this is just an alternative formulation of the guessing step and useless *per se*. However, if δ° is left opaque (just denoting the tagging of expression δ), and by applying our standard rewrite system, temporarily augmented with rules $\delta \circ \delta^\circ \rightsquigarrow \mathit{id}$ and $\delta^\circ \circ \delta \rightsquigarrow \mathit{id}$, we manage to get rid of δ°, then we get the desired algebra. This idea is embodied in the following rewrite rule, where we test that δ° does not occur in the normal form of $\delta \circ \tau \circ F\ \delta^\circ$.

$$\delta \circ (\!|\tau|\!)_F \rightsquigarrow (\!|\phi|\!)_F \Leftarrow \delta \circ \tau \circ F\ \delta^\circ \overset{*}{\rightsquigarrow} \phi \wedge \delta^\circ \notin \phi \quad (\!|\cdot|\!)\text{-FUSION}$$

As an example of this technique, Figure 4 presents the rewrite trace for one of the fusions needed to optimise the example in the introduction (indentation in the trace indicates the rewriting of side-conditions). To make the presentation clear, in this trace we mention the inverse of some rules (corresponding to the respective laws oriented from right-to-left). Obviously, to ensure termination, these rules are not encoded as such in our rewrite system. Instead, we have generalised rule versions that cover additional cases such as the following for *distl*-NAT (the definitions of f and g can be easily computed, but are omitted to simplify the presentation):

$$distl \circ (id \times \delta) \rightsquigarrow (id \times \delta + id \times \delta)^{f,g} \circ distl$$

$$distl \circ ((\delta + \tau) \circ \phi \times \psi) \rightsquigarrow (\delta \times \psi + \tau \times \psi)^{f,g} \circ distl \circ (\phi \times id)$$

4.2 Encoding in Haskell

In previous work [25], we have developed the `pointless-lenses` library for defining complex lens transformations as point-free lenses in Haskell. A straightforward method to optimise these lenses would be to specify the laws described in this paper as GHC rewrite rules [18], and allow their use by the GHC compiler. However, this approach provides little control over the rewrite strategy and is not capable of implementing laws such as !-UNIQ and $(\!|\cdot|\!)$-FUSION, since it does not support type-directed rewriting nor side-conditions. In order to harness the full power of our algebraic laws, we instead recover a successful type-safe, type-directed rewriting system for transformation of point-free programs [6, 9], and extend it to support bidirectional lenses. Instead of the *shallow embedding* of lenses as Haskell functions used in `pointless-lenses`, this rewrite system makes use of a *deep embedding*, where the objects and arrows of the target lens language are encoded as Haskell datatypes.

Representation of objects and arrows As defined in [9], the typed representation of objects (types and functors) uses *generalised algebraic data types* (GADTs) [19]:

```
data Type a where
  Int  :: Type Int
  One  :: Type 1
  ...
  Prod :: Type a → Type b → Type (a, b)
  Data :: String → Functor (F a) → Type a
  Fun  :: Type a → Type b → Type (a → b)
  Lens :: Type a → Type b → Type (Lens a b)
data Functor (f :: * → *) where
  I    :: Functor Id
  K    :: Type c → Functor c
  (⊠) :: Functor f → Functor g → Functor (f ⊗ g)
  (⊞) :: Functor f → Functor g → Functor (f ⊕ g)
  (⊡) :: Functor f → Functor g → Functor (f ⊙ g)
```

The above definitions provide value-level constructors for base types, sums, products, user-defined types, functions, lenses, and polynomial functors. For example, the value *Prod Int Int* represents the type *(Int, Int)*. Note that the *Functor* value in the definition of *Data* is not arbitrary: somehow, we must ensure that it is the base functor of the user-defined type a. This relation is established by the *type family* [26] $F\ a$, that acts as a type-level function from types to their base functors, as exemplified for lists:

```
type family F a :: * → *
type instance F [a] = 1 ⊕ a ⊗ Id
```

For example, *Data* `"[Int]"` $(K\ 1 \boxplus K\ Int \boxtimes I)$ is the representation of datatype $[Int]$. Moreover, when applying a functor to a type, we want to get an isomorphic sum-of-products type capable of being processed with point-free combinators. To this extent, we add the $Rep\ f\ a$ type family that, given a functor f and a type a, returns the equivalent "flat" type:

```
type family Rep (f :: * → *) a :: *
type instance Rep Id a = a
type instance Rep (g ⊗ h) a = (Rep g a, Rep h a)
...
```

Point-free expressions can also be represented in a type-safe manner using a GADT:

```
data PF f where
  Id    :: PF (c → c)
  Fst   :: PF ((a, b) → a)
  Bang  :: PF (a → 1)
  ...
  IdL   :: PF (Lens c c)
  FstL  :: PF (a → b) → PF (Lens (a, b) a)
  BangL :: PF (1 → c) → PF (Lens c One)
  CataL :: PF (Lens (Rep (F a) b) b) → PF (Lens a b)
  ...
```

Note that the inhabitants of type $PF\ f$ are the point-free representations of both unidirectional functions and bidirectional lenses.

Rewrite rules and systems In our implementation, rules are represented by monadic type-preserving functions that, given a type representation and a point-free expression, return a new expression of the same type:

```
type Rule = ∀f ∘ Type f → PF f → RewriteM (PF f)
```

RewriteM is a stateful monad that keeps a trace of the applied rules and is an instance of *MonadPlus*, thus modelling partiality in rule application: the monadic function *success* updates the *RewriteM* monad to keep trace of a successful reduction; failure is signalled with *mzero*. For example, we can encode a rewrite rule for !-UNIQ as follows:

```
bang_uniq :: Rule
bang_uniq (Lens _ _) (BangL f) = mzero
bang_uniq (Lens a One) l = do
  let createl = createof (Lens a One) l
  g ← optimise_fun (Fun One a) createl
  success "!-Uniq" (BangL g)
bang_uniq _ _ = mzero
```

The first case of this rule avoids a rewriting loop (application of *banqUniq* to ! itself. The third catch-all case indicates that the rule fails for any other input. The second case reveals the two-layered architecture of our rewrite system: the strategy *optimise_fun* simplifies function representations, of the form $PF\ (a \to b)$, and the strategy *optimise_lens* rewrites lens representations, of the form $PF\ (Lens\ a\ b)$. To mediate between these two classes, the procedures *getof*,*createof* and *putof* take the representation of a lens and return the representations of the corresponding *get*,*put* and *create* functions. As a general methodology, whenever a unidirectional function is created inside a lens rule, we apply *optimise_fun* to simplify it.

The rewrite systems themselves are built using strategic term rewriting [20], where the combination of a standard set of basic rules allows the simple design of flexible rewriting strategies. Some standard strategic combinators are $\otimes$, $\oslash$ and *nop*, that encode sequential composition, choice and identity. From these, other combinators can be derived, such as $try\ r = r \oslash nop$. Examples

$$
\begin{array}{l}
length \circ filter\_l \\
\rightsquigarrow \{ filter\_l\text{-}\textsc{Def};\ (\![\cdot]\!)\text{-}\textsc{Fusion};\ +\text{-}\textsc{Functor} \} \\
\quad length \circ (in_L \mathbin{{}_\bullet\nabla} \pi_2{}^{\underline{bo}!}) \circ coassoc \circ (id + distl) \circ (id + id \times length^\circ)) \\
\quad \rightsquigarrow \{ +\text{-}\textsc{Functor-Comp};\ +\text{-}\textsc{Functor-Id}^{-1};\ distl\text{-}\textsc{Nat};\ +\text{-}\textsc{Functor-Comp}^{-1} \} \\
\quad length \circ (in_L \mathbin{{}_\bullet\nabla} \pi_2{}^{\underline{bo}!}) \circ coassoc \circ (id + (id \times length^\circ + id \times length^\circ)^{(\pi_1 \times put_{length^\circ}) \circ distp, (\pi_1 \times put_{length^\circ}) \circ distp}) \circ (id + distl) \\
\quad \rightsquigarrow \{ coassoc\text{-}\textsc{Nat};\ +\text{-}\textsc{Absor} \} \\
\quad length \circ (in_L \circ (id + id \times length^\circ) \mathbin{{}_\bullet\nabla} \pi_2{}^{\underline{bo}!} \circ (id \times length^\circ)) \circ coassoc \circ (id + distl) \\
\quad \rightsquigarrow \{ +\text{-}\textsc{Fusion};\ length\text{-}\textsc{Def};\ (\![\cdot]\!)\text{-}\textsc{Cancel} \} \\
\quad (in_N \circ (id + \pi_2{}^!) \circ (id + id \times length) \circ (id + id \times length^\circ) \mathbin{{}_\bullet\nabla} length \circ \pi_2{}^{\underline{bo}!} \circ (id \times length^\circ)) \circ coassoc \circ (id + distl) \\
\quad \rightsquigarrow \{ +\text{-}\textsc{Functor-Comp};\ \times\text{-}\textsc{Functor-Comp};\ length \circ length^\circ \rightsquigarrow id \} \\
\quad (in_N \circ (id + \pi_2{}^!) \mathbin{{}_\bullet\nabla} length \circ \pi_2{}^{\underline{bo}!} \circ (id \times length^\circ)) \circ coassoc \circ (id + distl) \\
\quad \rightsquigarrow \{ \pi_2\text{-}\textsc{Nat};\ length \circ length^\circ \rightsquigarrow id \} \\
\qquad create_{id} \circ \underline{b} \circ ! \circ get_{length^\circ} \rightsquigarrow \{ \text{definition of } create;\ !\text{-}\textsc{Uniq} \}\ \underline{b} \circ ! \\
\quad (in_N \circ (id + \pi_2{}^!) \mathbin{{}_\bullet\nabla} \pi_2{}^{\underline{bo}!}) \circ coassoc \circ (id + distl) \\
(\![(in_N \circ (id + \pi_2{}^!) \mathbin{{}_\bullet\nabla} \pi_2{}^{\underline{bo}!}) \circ coassoc \circ (id + distl)]\!)_L
\end{array}
$$

Figure 4. Fusion mechanisation example

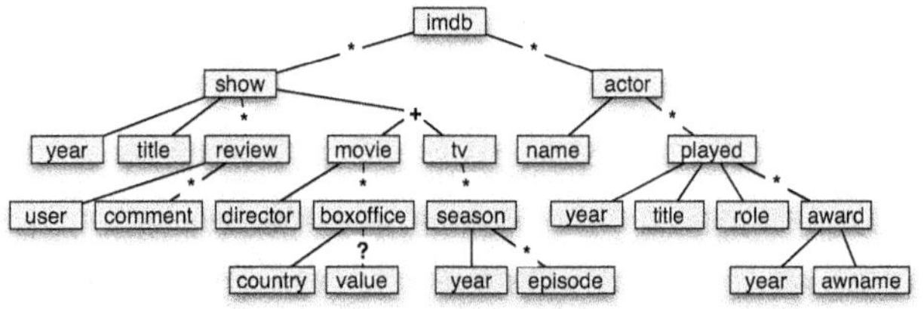

Figure 5. A movie database schema, inspired by IMDb.

of strategic combinators that traverse the structure of datatypes are *once*, that applies its argument rule exactly once according to a top-down traversal and *outermost*, that performs exhaustive rule application. Using these strategic combinators, we can construct complete transformation strategies, such as

$$
\begin{array}{rl}
optimise\_lens & = outermost\ opt \oslash rec \\
\textbf{where}\ opt & = nat\_id \oslash bang\_uniq \oslash \ldots \\
rec & = try\ (once\ fuse \oslash optimise\_lens) \\
fuse & = cata\_fusion \oslash ana\_fusion \oslash \ldots
\end{array}
$$

This strategy exhaustively applies the set of rewrite rules for lenses described across this paper, and some more. Some of these rules (particularly fusion rules) are evidently more expensive, due to the intermediate rewriting of side-conditions, and are deferred inside the strategy until no other rule can be applied.

4.3 Application scenario

We will now present some examples and compare the performance between automatically optimised lenses and their original point-free specifications. Consider the XML schema shown in Figure 5 for storing information about movies and actors in an IMDb like database. By representing this schema in Haskell (with sequences represented by left-nested tuples, multiple occurrences by lists, choices by left-nested *Either*s, and optional elements by *Maybe*), we can use our lens language to define views of the data. As an example, imagine that we want to summarise the information about movies and actors stored in our IMDb, according to the following lens transformation:

$$
\begin{array}{ll}
imdb & = shows \times actors \\
shows & = map\ ((id \times reviews) \times id) \circ filter\_l \\
 & \quad \circ\ map\ distr \circ map\ (id \times (movie + tv))
\end{array}
$$

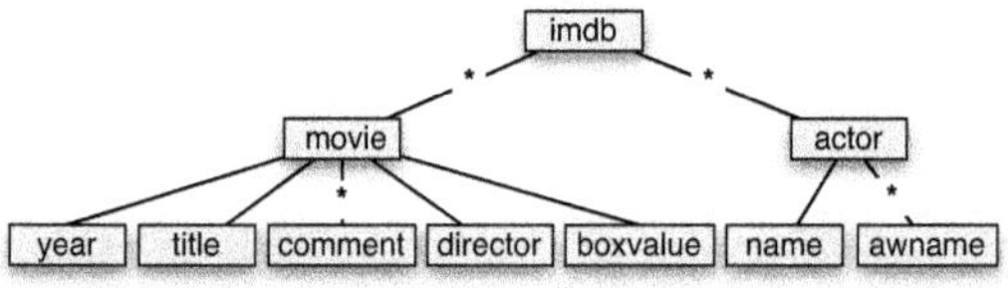

Figure 6. A view of the original schema.

$$
\begin{array}{ll}
reviews & = length^{creview} \circ concat \circ map\ \pi_2{}^{duser} \\
movie & = id \times boxoffices \\
boxoffices & = sum \circ filter\_r \circ map\ (out_M \circ \pi_2{}^{dcountry}) \\
tv & = concat \circ map\ \pi_2{}^{dyear} \\
actors & = map\ (id \times awards) \\
awards & = map\ \pi_2{}^{dyear} \circ concat \circ map\ \pi_2{}^{dytr}
\end{array}
$$

Here, *duser*, *dyear*, *creview*, ..., denote default functions and values, and *dytr* accounts for $(dyear \mathbin{\triangle} dtitle) \mathbin{\triangle} drole$; $out_M : Maybe\ A \rightarrow 1 + A$ is the deconstructor for the type $Maybe\ A$. The resulting schema is depicted in Figure 6. Our transformation comprises two main lenses applied in parallel to the lists of shows and actors. For each show, we first calculate the total box office value if it is a movie, or collect a list of episodes if it is a TV series. Then, we select only movies, count the number of comments for each review, and return the resulting list of movies. For each actor, we gather a list of all names of the awards he/she has won.

Obviously, the above specification is not very efficient: not only it relies on a heavily compositional style, but it also contains a redundant transformation. Fortunately, our rewrite system can apply several optimisations to this example. For instance, using fold fusion, it is able to reduce the *boxoffices* lens to a single traversal. Also, it can fuse consecutive mappings in *shows* and discard the redundant computation over TV series.

We have measured space and time consumption for this example, and the results are presented in Figure 7. Most of a lens inefficiency comes from the complex synchronising behaviour of its *put* function. Therefore, to better quantify the speedup achieved by our optimisation technique, we have compared the runtime behaviour of the *put* function before (`specification`) and after optimisation (`optimised`). We compiled each function using `GHC 6.12.1` with optimisation flag `O2`. Each example was tested with pre-compiled input databases of increasing size (measured in MBytes needed to store their Haskell definitions), randomly gener-

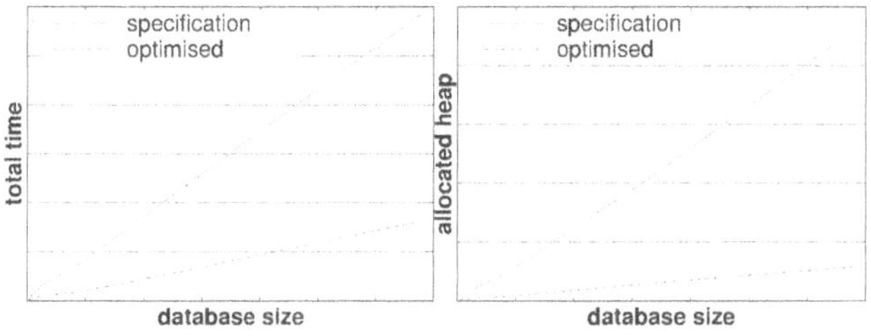

Figure 7. Benchmark results for the *imdb* example.

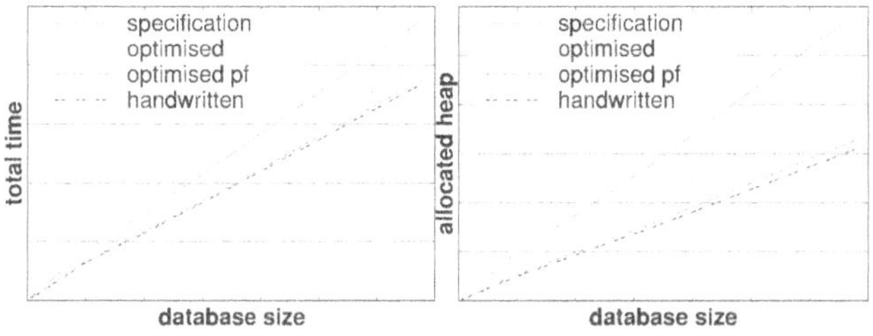

Figure 8. Benchmark results for the *women* example.

ated with the *QuickCheck* testing suite [5]. As expected, the original specification performs much worse than the optimised lens, by factors of 3.6 in time and 7.9 in space for the biggest sample, and the loss factor grows with the database size.

The reader may question why the benchmark results do not include a comparison with an handwritten definition. The answer is embarrassingly simple: it is extremely complex to hand-code the *put* function of the *imdb* lens, let alone an efficient version. However, we did compare the point-free (`specification`) and handwritten (`handwritten`) definitions for the *women* example from Section 1 and post the results in Figure 8. Below the optimised lens (`optimised`), we introduce another measure for the output of a second optimisation phase performed on the point-free definition of the *put* function (`optimised pf`). Even for this simple example, the optimised *put* allocates nearly half the memory and performs very close to the handwritten definition, both in time and space. This additional speedup reported in `optimised pf` is mainly due to the optimisation of expressions involving "opaque" lens isomorphisms, such as *assoc* or *distl*.

5. Related Work

This paper builds on the work first presented in [25], stating for each lens combinator the laws that characterise it and harnessing these into a lens optimisation framework. This quest for algebraic laws lead to pithy changes in the definitions of some combinators: we generalised the either combinator to subsume the left- and right-biased instances; the parameters of the sum combinator were also generalised but restricted to be *acceptable*, a desired property for calculation; the $i_1 \nabla id$ and $id \nabla i_2$ primitive combinators were eliminated because they can be defined as $(id \nabla id + id) \circ coassoc$ and $(id + id \nabla id) \circ coassoc^{-1}$, respectively. The exponentiation combinators are also new to this paper.

Unlike bidirectional interpreters, such as [21, 30], that execute the backward transformation by stepwise interpretation of the forward specification, algebraic bidirectionalisation techniques are concerned with deriving backward implementations by calculation. In [23], researchers from the University of Tokyo propose a point-free language of injective functions whose *put* functions can be calculated by inverting the specification of *get*. In [22], they bidirectionalise a restricted first-order functional language based on a notion of view-update under *constant complement*: after deriving a complement function get^c, put can be calculated from the specification $(get \triangle get^c)^{-1} \circ (id \times get^c)$, by resorting to tupling and inversion techniques. In principle, the inferred backward transformation could also be optimised using a rewrite system similar to ours, but that path was not explored and no clues are given about how to reason directly at the bidirectional level.

In the context of model-driven development, [29] discusses the inherent problems of existing bidirectional model transformation tools, and [12] proposes an algebraic framework for classifying the properties of bidirectional model transformations. Nevertheless, only consistency properties are considered, and no algebraic laws for calculation and optimization of bidirectional languages are discussed. A lens language for the bidirectionalisation of graph transformations is proposed in [16]. The key construct of this language is the structural recursion operation on graphs, that enjoys a fusion law on the underlying unidirectional graph algebra: two consecutive structural recursions $rec\ e_2 \circ rec\ e_1$ can be replaced by a single structural recursion $rec\ (rec\ e_2 \circ e_1)$ that avoids computing an intermediate result, if the expression e_2 does not depend on its argument graph. This calculational law is applied to the *get* transformation in [16], before bidirectionalisation. However, unlike in our setting, this optimisation is not stated bidirectionally and may yield different behaviours in the backward transformation.

In independent work, Hoffmann *et al* [17] study the fundamental properties of a symmetric generalisation of traditional lenses, from a category-theoretic perspective. Many of their results corroborate our own conclusions, such as the existence of tensor products and sums (but not categorical sums and products), and the ability to define recursive lenses with folds and unfolds that satisfy uniqueness (given certain termination considerations similar to [25]). Unlike us, categorical exponentiations were not studied and they have not shown how to harness their results into an effective lens optimisation framework.

In previous work, we have proposed a two-level bidirectional framework (2LT) for the point-free specification of *data refinement* transformations [2, 10]. Since the synchronisation behaviour is much simpler, optimisation of these bidirectional transformations can be done independently at the functional level for each component of the transformation [8, 9]. Here we not only tackle the dual problem of *data abstraction*, but also perform optimisation directly at the bidirectional level, due to the high complexity of composite *put* transformations. In the future, we intend to incorporate our results into the 2LT framework, thus enlarging the scope of model transformation scenarios to which it can be applied.

6. Conclusion

In this paper, we proposed an equational calculus to reason directly about lenses defined in the point-free style. This calculus allows us to hide the complexity of backward transformations, and calculate with lenses by reasoning only about the simple forward specification. The main result is the existence of uniqueness for bidirectional folds and unfolds, thus unleashing the power of fusion to optimise bidirectional programs, while preserving their semantics.

To prove the usefulness of this calculus, we have emloyed it at the kernel of an automatic optimisation tool for point-free lenses. This tool is implemented as an extension of a previous rewrite system [9], and both the updated lens library and the rewrite system for lens optimisation (including the encoding of the algebraic laws) are available through the Hackage package repository under the names `pointless-lenses` and `pointless-rewrite`, honouring a common joke about the point-free style.

In our current language, the nonexistence of splits and injections triggered the definition of several opaque primitive isomorphism combinators to regain expressiveness. In order to alleviate this problem, we are considering migrating to a point-free relational setting (as shown by Oliveira [24]). In particular, we intend to explore the calculation of invariants over target data structures, so that the above-mentioned combinators can be defined as total lenses for particular domains, with corresponding algebraic laws holding for such domains. Similarly, in *Focal* these restricted domains are built into the framework and enforced by a complex set-based type system, for each lens combinator. We also intend to use the powerful relational calculus to derive backward transformations that are correct by construction, thus avoiding the well-behavedness proofs (an approach similar to [22], but in a relational setting).

Lenses, as a framework for data abstraction, could also be of great value in scything through the complexity of large software systems [13]. However, in order to express transformations over these systems, structure-shyness of the specifications is imperative to reduce the specification cost and foster the reusability. To this extent, it would be interesting to extend our point-free bidirectional language with strategic lens combinators: this could enable the bidirectionalisation and subsequent optimisation of existing generic functional programs and structure-shy querying languages such as XPath.

References

[1] F. Baader and T. Nipkow. *Term rewriting and all that.* Cambridge University Press, 1998.

[2] P. Berdaguer, A. Cunha, H. Pacheco, and J. Visser. Coupled Schema Transformation and Data: Conversion for XML and SQL. In *Proceedings of the 9th International Symposium on Practical Aspects of Declarative Languages*, volume 4085 of *LNCS*, pages 290–304. Springer, 2007.

[3] A. Bohannon, B. C. Pierce, and J. A. Vaughan. Relational lenses: a language for updatable views. In *Proceedings of the 25th ACM SIGMOD Symposium on Principles of Database Systems*, pages 338–347. ACM, 2006.

[4] A. Bohannon, J. N. Foster, B. C. Pierce, A. Pilkiewicz, and A. Schmitt. Boomerang: resourceful lenses for string data. In *Proceedings of the 35th ACM SIGPLAN Symposium on Principles of Programming Languages*, pages 407–419. ACM, 2008.

[5] K. Claessen and J. Hughes. QuickCheck: a lightweight tool for random testing of Haskell programs. In *Proceedings of the 5th ACM SIGPLAN international conference on Functional programming*, pages 268–279. ACM, 2000.

[6] A. Cunha and H. Pacheco. Algebraic Specialization of Generic Functions for Recursive Types. In *Proceedings of the 2nd Workshop on Mathematically Structured Functional Programming*, 2008.

[7] A. Cunha and J. S. Pinto. Point-free program transformation. *Fundamenta Informaticae*, 66(4):315–352, 2005.

[8] A. Cunha and J. Visser. Strongly Typed Rewriting For Coupled Software Transformation. *Electronic Notes in Theoretical Computer Science*, 174(1):17–34, 2007.

[9] A. Cunha and J. Visser. Transformation of structure-shy programs with application to XPath queries and strategic functions. *Science of Computer Programming*, In Press, Corrected Proof, 2010.

[10] A. Cunha, J. N. Oliveira, and J. Visser. Type-safe Two-level Data Transformation. In *Proceedings of the 14th International Symposium on Formal Methods*, volume 4085 of *LNCS*, pages 284–299. Springer, 2006.

[11] K. Czarnecki, J. N. Foster, Z. Hu, R. Lämmel, A. Schürr, and J. F. Terwilliger. Bidirectional Transformations: A Cross-Discipline Perspective. In *Proceedings of the 2nd International Conference on Theory and Practice of Model Transformations*, volume 5563 of *LNCS*, pages 260–283. Springer, 2009.

[12] Z. Diskin. Algebraic Models for Bidirectional Model Synchronization. In *Proceedings of the 11th International Conference on Model Driven Engineering Languages and Systems*, volume 5301 of *LNCS*, pages 21–36. Springer, 2008.

[13] A. Egyed. Automated abstraction of class diagrams. *ACM Transactions on Software Engineering and Methodology*, 11(4):449–491, 2002.

[14] J. N. Foster, M. B. Greenwald, J. T. Moore, B. C. Pierce, and A. Schmitt. Combinators for bidirectional tree transformations: A linguistic approach to the view-update problem. *ACM Transactions on Programming Languages and Systems*, 29(3):17, 2007.

[15] S. Hidaka, Z. Hu, H. Kato, and K. Nakano. Towards a compositional approach to model transformation for software development. In *Proceedings of the 24th ACM Symposium on Applied Computing*, pages 468–475. ACM, 2009.

[16] S. Hidaka, Z. Hu, K. Inaba, H. Kato, K. Matsuda, and K. Nakano. Bidirectionalizing graph transformations. In *Proceedings of the 15th ACM SIGPLAN International Conference on Functional Programming*, pages 205–216. ACM, 2010.

[17] M. Hofmann, B. C. Pierce, and D. Wagner. Symmetric Lenses, 2010. Submitted for publication.

[18] S. P. Jones, A. Tolmach, and T. Hoare. Playing by the rules: rewriting as a practical optimisation technique in GHC. In *Proceedings of the 2001 ACM SIGPLAN Haskell Workshop*, pages 203–233. ACM, 2001.

[19] S. P. Jones, D. Vytiniotis, S. Weirich, and G. Washburn. Simple unification-based type inference for GADTs. In *Proceedings of the 11th ACM SIGPLAN international conference on Functional programming*, pages 50–61. ACM, 2006.

[20] R. Lämmel. Typed generic traversal with term rewriting strategies. *Journal of Logic and Algebraic Programming*, 54(1-2):1 – 64, 2003.

[21] D. Liu, Z. Hu, and M. Takeichi. Bidirectional interpretation of XQuery. In *Proceedings of the 2007 ACM SIGPLAN Symposium on Partial Evaluation and Semantics-based Program Manipulation*, pages 21–30. ACM, 2007.

[22] K. Matsuda, Z. Hu, K. Nakano, M. Hamana, and M. Takeichi. Bidirectionalization transformation based on automatic derivation of view complement functions. In *Proceedings of the 12th ACM SIGPLAN International Conference on Functional Programming*, pages 47–58. ACM, 2007.

[23] S.-C. Mu, Z. Hu, and M. Takeichi. An Algebraic Approach to Bi-Directional Updating. In *Proceedings of the 2nd Asian Symposium on Programming Languages and System*, volume 3302 of *LNCS*. Springer, 2004.

[24] J. N. Oliveira. Data Transformation by Calculation. In *Proceedings of the 2nd International Summer School on Generative and Transformational Techniques in Software Engineering*, volume 5235 of *LNCS*, pages 139–198. Springer, 2007.

[25] H. Pacheco and A. Cunha. Generic Point-free Lenses. In *Proceedings of the 10th International Conference on Mathematics of Program Construction*, volume 6120 of *LNCS*, pages 331–352. Springer, 2010.

[26] T. Schrijvers, S. M, S. P. Jones, and M. T. Chakravarty. Towards Open Type Functions for Haskell. In *Proceedings of the 19th International Symposium on Implementation and Application of Functional Languages*, pages 233–251, 2007.

[27] T. Sheard and L. Fegaras. A fold for all seasons. In *Proceedings of the 1993 conference on Functional Programming Languages and Computer Architecture*, pages 233–242. ACM, 1993.

[28] G. Sittampalam and O. de Moor. Mechanising Fusion. In J. Gibbons and O. de Moor, editors, *The Fun of Programming*, chapter 5, pages 79–104. Palgrave Macmillan, 2003.

[29] P. Stevens. Bidirectional model transformations in QVT: Semantic issues and open questions. In *Proceedings of the 10th International Conference on Model Driven Engineering Languages And Systems*, volume 4735 of *LNCS*, pages 1–15. Springer, 2007.

[30] J. Voigtländer. Bidirectionalization for free! (Pearl). In *Proceedings of the 36th Annual ACM SIGPLAN Symposium on Principles of Programming Languages*, pages 165–176. ACM, 2009.

[31] J. Voigtländer., Z. Hu, K. Matsuda, and M. Wang. Combining Syntactic and Semantic Bidirectionalization. In *Proceedings of the 15th ACM SIGPLAN International Conference on Functional Programming*, pages 181–192. ACM, 2010.

Calculating Tree Navigation with Symmetric Relational Zipper

Yuta IKEDA Susumu NISHIMURA

Department of Mathematics, Faculty of Science
Kyoto University
Kyoto 606-8502, Japan
{yuta-28,susumu}@math.kyoto-u.ac.jp

Abstract

Navigating through tree structures is a core operation in tree processing programs. Most notably, XML processing programs intensively use XPath, the path specification language that locates particular nodes in a given document structure.

This paper develops a theory for reasoning about equalities of tree navigation programs. In functional programming languages, tree navigation operations can be cleanly implemented as functions operating over the data structure known as Huet's zipper. The tree navigation functions are expected to have certain nice symmetric properties (e.g., a function going one-level down in the tree structure would be the inverse of another function coming back the other way around, and vice versa), but they are not indeed a perfect symmetry, due to partiality and non-injectivity of the functions.

In order to fully exploit the symmetry indicated by tree navigation operations, we model them by relations, instead of functions. The relational specification allows us to derive useful equations by simple calculations. We apply the calculational method to derive certain equalities of XPath expressions. The point-free relational reasoning not only leads to a concise justification of some known results but also establishes equations for a larger class of tree navigation operations, including those specified with negative constraints and those beyond XPath expressibility.

Categories and Subject Descriptors F.3.2 [*Logics and Meanings of Programs*]: Semantics of Programming Languages—Algebraic approaches to semantics; D.1.1 [*Programming Techniques*]: Applicative (Functional) Programming

General Terms Languages, Theory

Keywords Tree navigation, Zipper, XML path language, Relational calculus, Algebra of programming

1. Introduction

Huet's zipper [9] provides us a way to elegantly implement various operations for manipulating tree structures, including tree navigation, in functional programming languages. A zipper is a pair of a binary tree and a context, as specified below in the O'Caml syntax.[1]

```
type 'a tree =
  Leaf | Node of 'a tree * 'a * 'a tree
type 'a path =
    Top
  | L of 'a * 'a tree * 'a path
  | R of 'a * 'a tree * 'a path
type 'a zipper = 'a tree * 'a path
```

The context information is represented by a list-like structure, which records, in the reverse order, the path by which the current node is reached from the root. The constructor $\mathtt{L}(i,r,p)$ corresponds to a single traversal along a left branch of a tree node $\mathtt{Node}(l,i,r)$, where p is the path to reach the tree node from the root. The constructor $\mathtt{R}(i,l,p)$ has a role that simply interchanges the left and the right. The constructor `Top` stands for an empty path, indicating the root position of the whole tree. In Figure 1, we give four basic tree navigation functions on zippers. The function dn_L (resp., dn_R) descends the binary tree structure down by one level along a left (resp., right) branch, if possible. Conversely, the function up_L (resp., up_R) returns to its parent node by climbing up a left (resp., right) branch by one level, if possible.

The above definitions of tree navigation over zippers indicate that certain natural symmetric properties would hold: `dnL` and `upL` are inverses of each other and so are `dnR` and `upR`. This symmetry indicates that there could be many chances of simplification and optimization in tree navigation programs. We would be able to eliminate any symmetric pair of functions which are statically recognized as being executed successively.

The symmetry argued above, however, is not as perfect as one might expect. First, the above basic tree navigation operations and many other more complex ones as well are partial functions and hence a composition of a (seemingly) symmetric pair would work as a neutral operation only for limited inputs. (E.g., `dnL` ∘ `upL` is a *partial* identity.) Second, not every tree navigation operation necessarily has a corresponding inverse operation. For example, consider the following tree navigation function that climbs up any (left or right) branch by one level, if possible.

PEPM'11, January 24–25, 2011, Austin, Texas, USA.

[1] The choice of the implementation language is rather a matter of tastes and the results in this paper applies to any other suitable functional language such as Haskell, as long as trees and contexts involved are assumed to have finite structures. Although we will only consider binary trees in this paper, the fundamental techniques should successfully apply to zippers for other data strucutres.

```
let dnL = function
  | (Node(l,i,r),p) -> (l, L(i,r,p))
  | _ -> failwith "no way for dnL"

let upL = function
  | (l,L(i,r,p)) -> (Node(l,i,r),p)
  | _ -> failwith "no way for upL"

let dnR = function
  | (Node(l,i,r),p) -> (r, R(i,l,p))
  | _ -> failwith "no way for dnR"

let upR = function
  | (r,R(i,l,p)) -> (Node(l,i,r),p)
  | _ -> failwith "no way for upR"
```

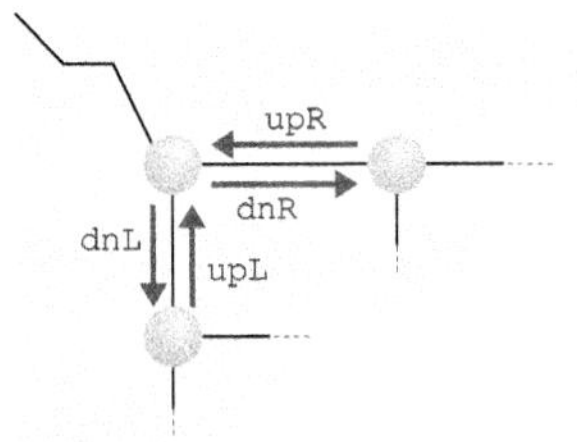

Figure 1. Tree navigation functions and a pictorial image of their operations. Left branches are drawn by vertical edges and right branches are drawn by horizontal edges.

```
let go_up = function
  | (l,L(i,r,p)) -> (Node(l,i,r),p)
  | (r,R(i,l,p)) -> (Node(l,i,r),p)
  | _ -> failwith "no way for go_up"
```

This function is not invertible, because it is not injective.

The aim of this paper is to develop a theory of tree navigation operations with perfect symmetric properties. For this, we leave the realm of functional programming paradigm and move to that of relational one [4]. The issue of partiality and non-injectivity discussed above is avoided by a relational modeling of zipper operations. By the relational modeling, the above mentioned basic navigation primitives have a perfect symmetry via relational converse, instead of functional inverse. A variety of tree navigation programs can be specified by combining these basic symmetric operations with a few composition operations on relations.

We also develop a set of algebraic laws that are useful for deriving the properties of relationally specified tree navigation. In order to demonstrate how our theory can be used to formally establish the properties of tree navigation operations via simple calculation, we consider equalities of given XPath [3] expressions that locate tree nodes in XML structured document trees. We will give a relational interpretation of XPath expressions, by which a range of equalities is instantly obtained by the symmetry intrinsic to our relational modeling. A more involved equalities on XPath predicates, which are an XPath construct that imposes further confinement to the set of located nodes, are also discussed both for positive (i.e., negation free) and negative fragments.

In the course of relational reasoning on XPath expressions, we introduce a new relational operation, called symmetric closure (Section 3), and develop several laws for calculating with that closure. This new closure operation is a key to the relational modeling of XPath expressions involving predicates (even including negatives) and the effective derivation of equalities on those XPath expressions.

1.1 Related work

The results presented in this paper is built on the foundation of the relational calculus (or algebra of programming, in other words) [4]. The point-free style calculation contributes to simplified derivations of equalities that we develop in later sections. It would be much harder to justify the same results in the pointwise style.

There are several studies that develop a set of laws for equational reasoning on XPath (or its relatives such as XQuery) [5, 6, 12, 13]. Each provides a particular set of reasoning laws for solving the problem in concern and henceforth the applicability of each proposal varies, depending on the particular choice of laws. Che et al. [5] proposed to use PAT-algebra and Cunha et al. [6] provided a set of laws for algebraic transformation of structure-shy programs, but both do not deal with reverse axes (i.e., upward tree navigation).

Olteanu et al. have extensively studied the laws for eliminating reverse axes [12, 13]. They provided an elegant set of equalities that exploit the symmetry we mentioned earlier. However, they did not give any equality for those XPath expressions that contain negative predicates. In Section 5, we will show that some XPath expression with negatives can be equated to a tree navigation specification which cannot be expressed in XPath language but in our relational language. This is due to our finer modeling of tree navigation via relational composition of a few navigation primitives, none of which cannot be expressed in XPath language. The finer granularity provides more opportunities for developing a larger set of equalities. Furthermore, our relational modeling allows point-free derivations that contribute to a simpler calculational reasoning. Some of simple equalities given in [12, 13] is an immediate consequence of relational converse. Also, the point-free style of derivations are more beneficial for reasoning about negative predicates. It would be hard and tend to be unmanageable to formally conduct justification of equalities on negatives in the pointwise style as in [12].

Genevès, et al. [8] provides an automatic procedure for various XPath decision problems, based on a modal μ-calculus. Though having different interpretation domains, theirs and ours are quite similar in their way of modeling tree navigation. Genevès, et al. encode tree navigation by existential modalities, which correspond to our tree navigation primitives. It should be however noted that they restrict their formulas to cycle-free fragments, which have no possible infinite iterations of a modality and its reverse. Though the cycle-free restriction is needed for designing an automatic decision procedure, the restriction does not matter for their development, as every XPath specification can be expressed by a cycle-free formula. When we do not care about automation and go beyond the XPath language, we claim that this restriction seems a bit restrictive. As we develop in later sections, a less strict well-foundedness condition is sufficient for our calculation. Nevertheless it is quite interesting that different formalizations via modal μ-calculus and relational calculus exhibit many similarities. A thorough comparison on this point would merit further investigation.

Outline. The rest of the paper is organized as follows. We first present our relational zipper operations that have symmetric properties, together with some basics on relational calculus in Section 2. Section 3 gives a relational semantics of XPath expressions, where a new closure operator is introduced. Thereafter we discuss XPath equalities for negation-free expressions in Section 4 and negative expressions in Section 5. Section 6 briefly describes the translation method for implementing relations in functional languages. Finally Section 7 concludes the paper.

2. Symmetric relational zipper operations

We introduce basic zipper operations that have symmetric properties. This section also contains a brief introduction to the relational calculus. For a more detailed introduction to this field, see standard references, e.g. [2, 4].

2.1 Relations

Given arbitrary sets A and B, a binary relation $R : A \leftarrow B$ is a subset of Cartesian product $A \times B$. We say R relates the input $b \in B$ to the output $a \in A$ if $(a,b) \in R$, written $a\,R\,b$. The relations of type $A \leftarrow B$ forms a complete lattice with $\subseteq$ as the ordering, where $\cup$ and $\cap$ are the join and meet operators, respectively. The largest relation in the lattice is the total relation, written $\Pi : A \leftarrow B$, and the smallest relation is the empty relation, written $\emptyset : A \leftarrow B$.

Two relations $R : A \leftarrow B$ and $S : B \leftarrow C$ can be composed into a single relation, written $R \circ S$, which is defined by $a(R \circ S)c \equiv \exists b \in B : a\,R\,b \wedge b\,S\,c$. The relational composition is associative and has the identity relation id as a unit element, where $a\;id\;b \equiv a = b$. It is also monotonic w.r.t. the ordering $\subseteq$, i.e., $R \circ S \subseteq R' \circ S'$ if $R \subseteq R'$ and $S \subseteq S'$. The relational composition distributes over the join (i.e., $R \circ (S \cup T) = (R \circ S) \cup (R \circ T)$), but it only semi-distributes over the meet (i.e., $R \circ (S \cap T) \subseteq (R \circ S) \cap (R \circ T)$).

A converse relation of $R : A \leftarrow B$, written $R^{\smile}$, is a relation that exchanges the inputs and outputs of R, that is, $b\,R^{\smile}\,a \equiv a\,R\,b$. The converse is self-dual (i.e., $R^{\smile\smile} = R$) and distributes over the join and meet (i.e., $(S \cup T)^{\smile} = S^{\smile} \cup T^{\smile}$ and $(S \cap T)^{\smile} = S^{\smile} \cap T^{\smile}$). We also have equality $(R \circ S)^{\smile} = S^{\smile} \circ R^{\smile}$ and the so called *modular law*: $(R \circ S) \cap T \subseteq (R \cap (T \circ S^{\smile})) \circ S$.

A relation $R : B \leftarrow A$ is called *simple* (resp., *injective*) if $R \circ R^{\smile} \subseteq id$. (resp., $R^{\smile} \circ R \subseteq id$). Dually, R is called *entire* (resp., *surjective*) if $R^{\smile} \circ R \supseteq id$. (resp., $R \circ R^{\smile} \supseteq id$).

A relation $R : A \leftarrow A$ is called *coreflexive* if $R \subseteq id$. Coreflexive relations are often used for checking membership of values. We write $C?$ for the coreflexive relation induced by a set C, that is, $x C? y \equiv x = y \wedge x \in C$. Thus a composed relation, say, $R \circ C?$ confines the input of R to the values that belong to C. Coreflexives are idempotent and commutative for relational composition. That is, $R \circ R = R$ and $R \circ S = S \circ R$ for any coreflexives $R, S : A \leftarrow A$.

Given two relations $R : A \leftarrow C$ and $S : B \leftarrow D$, we define a *relational product* $R \times S : (A \times B) \leftarrow (C \times D)$ by $(a,b)\; R \times S\; (c,d) \equiv a\,R\,c \wedge b\,S\,d$.

It is often convenient and instructive to characterize certain relational operators via Galois connection [2]. A Galois connection, in the present relational setting, is identified by a pair of operations f and g (called lower and upper adjoints, respectively) over relations that satisfy the equivalence $f(R) \subseteq S \equiv R \subseteq g(S)$ for any relations R and S.

Here we introduce two relational operators characterized by Galois connections, the relational difference operator $(-S)$ and the domain operator dom:

$$R - S \subseteq T \equiv R \subseteq S \cup T \qquad \text{(GC-DIFF)}$$

$$dom\ R \subseteq S \equiv R \subseteq \Pi \circ S, \quad \text{for all coreflexive } S. \qquad \text{(GC-DOM)}$$

The relational difference operator $(-S)$ is the left adjoint of the operator $(S \cup)$. The difference operator corresponds to the set difference, that is, $a\,(R - S)\,b$ if and only if $a\,R\,b$ but not $a\,S\,b$.

The domain operator dom is the left adjoint of the right conditional operator $(\Pi \circ)$. An explicit definition is given by $dom\ R = id \cap R^{\smile} \circ R$. Thus, for any relation $R : B \leftarrow A$, $dom\ R : A \leftarrow A$ is a coreflexive representing the set of inputs that have at least a single corresponding output.

By the Knaster-Tarski theorem, if f is a monotonic mapping on relations (i.e., $f(R) \subseteq f(S)$ whenever $R \subseteq S$), there exist the least fixpoint $\mu X.f(X)$ and the greatest fixpoint $\nu X.f(X)$, both of which are solutions of equation $X = f(X)$. The least and greatest fixpoints have the following properties useful for relational reasoning.[2, 10]

$$\mu X.f(X) = f(\mu X.f(X)) \qquad (\mu\text{-computation})$$

$$\mu X.f(X) \subseteq R \Leftarrow f(R) \subseteq R \qquad (\mu\text{-induction})$$

$$\nu X.f(X) = f(\nu X.f(X)) \qquad (\nu\text{-computation})$$

$$R \subseteq \nu X.f(X) \Leftarrow R \subseteq f(R) \qquad (\nu\text{-induction})$$

In particular, the reflexive transitive closure of a relation R is the least fixpoint $\mu X.id \cup R \circ X$, which we write R^* for short. The closure R^* satisfies the equations $S \circ R^* = \mu X.(S \cup X \circ R)$ and $R^* \circ S = \mu X.(S \cup R \circ X)$. Hence $R^* = \mu X.(id \cup X \circ R)$ and $R^* \circ R = R \circ R^*$ also hold. We will often write R^+ for $R \circ R^*$.

2.2 Relational zipper operations

In the rest of the paper, we assume the zipper data structure that we have given in Introduction. We also express the type of zippers by Zipper, rather than by `'a zipper` in the concrete O'Caml syntax, obfuscating the parametrized type `'a` of data stored in the tree nodes.

We first introduce a pair of relations representing generic operations for navigating up and down trees by one level, namely, the relations Dn : Zipper $\leftarrow$ Zipper and Up : Zipper $\leftarrow$ Zipper, which are defined as the smallest relations satisfying the following properties for any i, l, r, and p of appropriate types.

$$(l, \mathtt{L}(i,r,p))\ Dn\ (\mathtt{Node}(l,i,r), p)$$

$$(r, \mathtt{R}(i,l,p))\ Dn\ (\mathtt{Node}(l,i,r), p)$$

$$(\mathtt{Node}(l,i,r), p)\ Up\ (l, \mathtt{L}(i,r,p))$$

$$(\mathtt{Node}(l,i,r), p)\ Up\ (r, \mathtt{R}(i,l,p))$$

By definition, Up and Dn are a pair of symmetric operations, in the sense that they are converses of each other. It should be however noted that they are not inverses of each other. Neither $Up \circ Dn$ nor $Dn \circ Up$ is equal to id; We can only say that $Up \circ Dn = \mathtt{Node}? \times id \subseteq id$.

The four primitive operations introduced in Introduction can be defined in the relational setting as follows.

$$dn_L = (id \times \mathtt{L}?) \circ Dn \qquad dn_R = (id \times \mathtt{R}?) \circ Dn$$

$$up_L = Up \circ (id \times \mathtt{L}?) \qquad up_R = Up \circ (id \times \mathtt{R}?)$$

In abuse of notations, we use each constructor name `C` of a datatype to denote the set of values whose outermost constructor is `C`. E.g., `L` represents the set of all the paths in the form $\mathtt{L}(i,r,p)$. Thus `C?` denotes the coreflexive relation that checks if the outermost constructor is `C`. Hence dn_L and dn_R restrict the more general relation Dn to the navigation of the appropriate direction downward; up_L and up_R can move upward only if the direction moving upward matches that of the most recent downward navigation.

The four navigation operations exhibit clean symmetric properties, as we shall show below.

Each pair of dn and up of the same subscript are the converse of each other, i.e.,

$$dn_L{}^{\smile} = up_L \qquad dn_R{}^{\smile} = up_R \qquad \text{(UPDN-CONVERSE)}$$

Furthermore the composition of each converse pair is coreflexive.

$$dn_L \circ up_L \subseteq id \qquad up_L \circ dn_L \subseteq id$$

$$dn_R \circ up_R \subseteq id \qquad up_R \circ dn_R \subseteq id \qquad \text{(DNUP-COREFL)}$$

In other words, they are all simple and injective relations.

On the other hand, certain pairs of different subscripts induce empty relations.

$$up_L \circ dn_R = \emptyset \qquad up_R \circ dn_L = \emptyset \qquad \text{(UPDN-EMP)}$$

e ::=		XPath
	$/p$	absolute path
	$\mid p$	relative path
	$\mid e \cup e$	union
	$\mid e \cap e$	intersection
p ::=		Path
	$a :: *$	step
	$\mid a :: \beta$	step with node test
	$\mid p[q]$	predicate
	$\mid p/p$	path composition
a ::=		Axis
	self |	
	| child | foll-sibling | desc | desc-or-self | following	
	| parent | prec-sibling | anc | anc-or-self | preceding	
q ::=		Predicate
	q and q	conjunction
	| q or q	disjunction
	| not q	negation
	| p	path

Figure 2. XPath expression syntax

We notice that not every similar pair of relations necessarily induces an empty relation, e.g., $dn_R \circ up_L \neq \emptyset$.

From the fact that coreflexives derived from distinct constructors apparently have no intersection, e.g., $\mathtt{L?} \circ \mathtt{Top?} = \emptyset$, we also have additional pairs of relations that induce empty relations.

$$up_L \circ (id \times \mathtt{Top?}) = \emptyset \qquad up_R \circ (id \times \mathtt{Top?}) = \emptyset \qquad (\textsc{Up-Emp})$$

$$dn_L \circ (\mathtt{Leaf?} \times id) = \emptyset \qquad dn_R \circ (\mathtt{Leaf?} \times id) = \emptyset \qquad (\textsc{Dn-Emp})$$

We can also induce several properties:

$$S \subseteq T \circ \rho \implies S \circ \rho^{\smile} \subseteq T$$
$$S \subseteq \rho \circ T \implies \rho^{\smile} \circ S \subseteq T \qquad (\textsc{UpDn-Shunt})$$
$$\rho = \rho \circ \rho^{\smile} \circ \rho \qquad (\textsc{UpDn-Triple})$$

where ρ is either of dn_L, up_L, dn_R, or up_R.

3. Relational interpretation of XPath expressions

We give a relational modeling of tree navigation expressed by a core XPath language[2], whose syntax is given in Figure 2.

In Figure 3, we give the relational semantics of XPath expressions, in the style of denotational semantics [14].

An XPath expression e is either a relative path, an absolute path, or unions and intersections of them. Its formal meaning is given by a relation, written $I_e[\![e]\!]$, that relates each input (namely, a zipper recording the current tree node and context) to the (output) nodes that are located by e. A relative path p locates tree nodes reached from the current node via p, while an absolute path $/p$ locates tree nodes reached via p from the root node. The interpretation of the absolute path is thus appended with $(id \times \mathtt{Top?}) \circ (up_L \cup up_R)^*$ that navigates tree context to the root.

Step expressions $a :: *$ and $a :: \beta$ are a path that locates all nodes reached via the axis a. The former does not care about node labels but the latter locates only those β-labeled nodes. (In the rest of the paper, we will use small Greek letters for node labels.) The name of a node label is examined by a coreflexive $\beta?$, which is

[2] Some axis specifiers are shortened (descendant as desc; ancestor as anc). Also, XML attributes are omitted for the sake of simplicity, although they can be easily supported by enriching node tags with additional attribute information.

I_e : XPath $\to$ (Zipper $\leftarrow$ Zipper)

$$I_e[\![/p]\!] = I_p[\![p]\!] \circ (id \times \mathtt{Top?}) \circ (up_L \cup up_R)^*$$
$$I_e[\![p]\!] = I_p[\![p]\!]$$
$$I_e[\![e_1 \cup e_2]\!] = I_e[\![e_1]\!] \cup I_e[\![e_2]\!]$$
$$I_e[\![e_1 \cap e_2]\!] = I_e[\![e_1]\!] \cap I_e[\![e_2]\!]$$

I_p : Path $\to$ (Zipper $\leftarrow$ Zipper)

$$I_p[\![a :: *]\!] = (\mathtt{Node?} \times id) \circ I_a[\![a]\!]$$
$$I_p[\![a :: \beta]\!] = \beta? \circ I_a[\![a]\!]$$
$$I_p[\![p_1/p_2]\!] = I_p[\![p_2]\!] \circ I_p[\![p_1]\!]$$
$$I_p[\![p[q]]\!] = I_q[\![q]\!] \circ I_p[\![p]\!]$$

I_a : Axis $\to$ (Zipper $\leftarrow$ Zipper)

$$I_a[\![\text{self}]\!] = id$$
$$I_a[\![\text{child}]\!] = dn_R^* \circ dn_L \qquad I_a[\![\text{parent}]\!] = up_L \circ up_R^*$$
$$I_a[\![\text{foll-sibling}]\!] = dn_R^+ \qquad I_a[\![\text{prec-sibling}]\!] = up_R^+$$
$$I_a[\![\text{desc}]\!] = (dn_R^* \circ dn_L)^+ \qquad I_a[\![\text{anc}]\!] = (up_L \circ up_R^*)^+$$
$$I_a[\![\text{desc-or-self}]\!] = (dn_R^* \circ dn_L)^* \qquad I_a[\![\text{anc-or-self}]\!] = (up_L \circ up_R^*)^*$$
$$I_a[\![\text{following}]\!] = (dn_R^* \circ dn_L)^* \circ dn_R^+ \circ (up_L \circ up_R^*)^*$$
$$I_a[\![\text{preceding}]\!] = (dn_R^* \circ dn_L)^* \circ up_R^+ \circ (up_L \circ up_R^*)^*$$

I_q : Predicate $\to$ (Zipper $\leftarrow$ Zipper)

$$I_q[\![q_1 \text{ and } q_2]\!] = I_q[\![q_1]\!] \cap I_q[\![q_2]\!]$$
$$I_q[\![q_1 \text{ or } q_2]\!] = I_q[\![q_1]\!] \cup I_q[\![q_2]\!]$$
$$I_q[\![p]\!] = dom\ I_p[\![p]\!]$$

Figure 3. Relational interpretation of XPath expressions

```
<a>
  <b></b>
  <c>
    <d></d>
    <e></e>
    <f>
      <g><h></h></g><i></i>
    </f>
    <j></j>
    <k><l></l></k>
  </c>
</a>
```

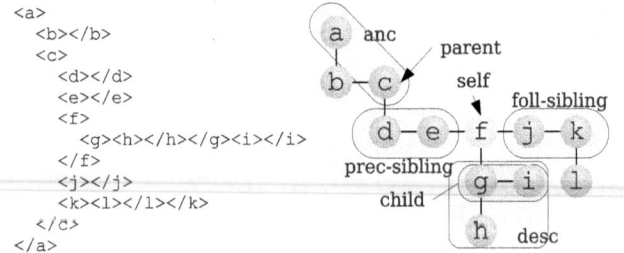

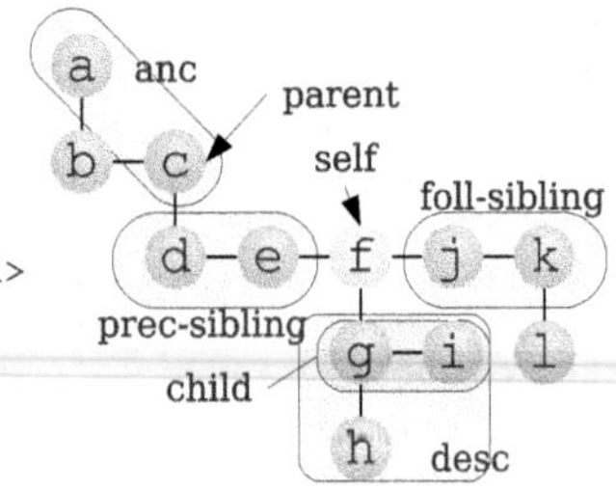

Figure 4. An XML document and its binary tree representation, with several axes relative to the `f` node

derived from the set of all zippers locating β-labeled nodes, i.e., $\{(\mathtt{Node}(l,i,r),p) \in \text{Zipper} \mid i = \beta\}$.

XPath provides various axes that can be classified into subgroups. The self axis is a neutral axis that navigates the current node solely to itself. The first half of the rest of the axes, i.e., child, foll-sibling, etc., are called forward axes, as they always navigate downward. Here we notice that we model XML document structure as shown in Figure 4. Every left branch connects a parent node and its first child; Every right branch connects adjacent sibling nodes. Thus the forward axes always proceed in the document order. If a node has no child or no sibling that follows, the corresponding branch is connected with `Leaf`, which is omitted from the figure. The other half of the axes, i.e., parent, prec-sibling, etc., are called reverse axes, as they always navigate upward. It is easy to observe that the forward and reverse axes are connected by the symmetry, e.g, $I_a[\![\text{child}]\!] = I_a[\![\text{parent}]\!]^{\smile}$.

Paths can be arbitrarily combined for successive navigation via $p_1/p_2/\cdots/p_n$.

Example 1 Let us show an example of relational interpretation of a simple XPath expression.

$$\begin{aligned} & I_e[\![\text{parent} :: */\text{foll-sibling} :: */\text{child} :: \alpha]\!] \\ = \ & I_p[\![\text{child} :: \alpha]\!] \circ I_p[\![\text{foll-sibling} :: *]\!] \circ I_p[\![\text{parent} :: *]\!] \\ = \ & \alpha? \circ dn_R^* \circ dn_L \circ (\texttt{Node?} \times id) \circ dn_R^+ \circ (\texttt{Node?} \times id) \circ up_L \circ up_R^* \end{aligned}$$

The XPath language allows us to further restrict the node set located by a path. A predicated path $p[q]$ confines the nodes located by p to those satisfying a predicate q, which is either a relative path or conjunctions, disjunctions, or negations of predicates. (We exclude negative predicates from our discussion for the moment. We will return to this topic in Section 5.)

We interpret the confinement via predicates by coreflexive relations. Conjunctions and disjunctions are trivially interpreted by the meets and joins. Given a predicated path $p[p']$, where p' is a path, the predicated path is interpreted as a path p whose located nodes are however confined to those nodes that have at least a single tree node reached via the path p'. Thus $p[p']$ is interpreted by the relation $(dom\ I_p[\![p']\!]) \circ I_p[\![p]\!]$.

For any coreflexive relations R and S, the following properties hold.

$$dom\ R = R \qquad \text{(COREFL-DOM)}$$

$$R \cup S \text{ and } R \cap S \text{ are coreflexive} \qquad \text{(COREFL-JOINMEET)}$$

$$R \cap S = R \circ S = S \circ R \qquad \text{(COREFL-COMP)}$$

Although we have given a formal specification of XPath expressions including predicates, it is not sufficient for effective calculation. As we have seen above, a predicate would be interpreted to a coreflexive relation of the form $dom\ R$, but its bare definitional expansion $id \cap R^{\smile} \circ R$ would not be suitable for calculation. (Recall that the meet $\cap$ operator only semi-distributes over relational compositions.) Below we develop a set of simplification laws that aid calculating predicated paths.

$$R = R \circ dom\ R \qquad \text{(DOM-DOMAIN)}$$

$$\Pi \circ dom\ R = \Pi \circ R \qquad \text{(DOM-RCOND)}$$

$$dom\ (R \circ S) = S^{\smile} \circ dom\ R \circ S, \quad \text{if } S \text{ is injective} \qquad \text{(DOM-COMP)}$$

The laws we have given so far are an easy exercise of relational calculation, which we leave to the reader.

Composition of (injective) relations can be calculated with (DOM-COMP). For calculation of the domain of a closure operator, we introduce another closure operator, called *symmetric closure*.

Definition 3.1 (Symmetric closure)

$$(R)[S_1, S_2, \ldots, S_n]^* = \mu X.(R \cup \textstyle\bigcup_{i=1}^n (S_i^{\smile} \circ X \circ S_i)) \quad (n \geq 1)$$

Suppose R is coreflexive and $S_1, S_2, \ldots, S_n$ are all injective. Then it is easy to see that $(R)[S_1, S_2, \ldots, S_n]^*$ is coreflexive.

Intuitively, $(R)[S_1, S_2, \ldots, S_n]^*$ is equivalent to the infinite union of relations of the form $S_{n_1}{}^{\smile} \circ S_{n_2}{}^{\smile} \circ \ldots \circ S_{n_k}{}^{\smile} \circ R \circ S_{n_k} \circ \ldots \circ S_{n_2} \circ S_{n_1}$, where $1 \leq n_i \leq n$ for all $i \in \{1, 2, \ldots, k\}$ $(k \geq 0)$. In words, $(R)[S_1, S_2, \ldots, S_n]^*$ intends a procedure that traverses zero or more navigation steps by S_i's, makes a test on the reached node via R, and then comes back to the original position along the reverse path.

Since the reverse traversal is always successful (provided the coreflexivity and injectivity above), the right condition of the symmetric closure satisfies the following equation.

$$\Pi \circ (R)[S_1, S_2, \ldots, S_n]^* = \Pi \circ R \circ (\textstyle\bigcup_{i=1}^n S_i)^*,$$
$$\text{for any coreflexive } R \text{ and injective } S_1, S_2, \ldots, S_n. \qquad \text{(SYMCLS-RCOND)}$$

This equation is derived as follows. Writing U for $\bigcup_{i=1}^n S_i$, we calculate:

$$\begin{aligned} & \Pi \circ (R)[S_1, \ldots, S_n]^* \subseteq \Pi \circ R \circ U^* \\ \Leftarrow \quad & \text{monotonicity} \\ & (R)[S_1, \ldots, S_n]^* \subseteq U^{\smile *} \circ R \circ U^* \\ \Leftarrow \quad & \mu\text{-induction; distributivity} \\ & R \cup (U^{\smile} \circ U^{\smile *} \circ R \circ U^* \circ U) \subseteq U^{\smile *} \circ R \circ U^* \\ \Leftarrow \quad & \mu\text{-computation; distributivity} \\ & \textbf{true} \end{aligned}$$

The converse inclusion follows as below.

$$\begin{aligned} & \Pi \circ R \circ U^* \subseteq \Pi \circ (R)[S_1, \ldots, S_n]^* \\ \Leftarrow \quad & \mu\text{-induction} \\ & \Pi \circ R \cup \Pi \circ (R)[S_1, \ldots, S_n]^* \circ U \subseteq \Pi \circ (R)[S_1, \ldots, S_n]^* \\ \Leftarrow \quad & \mu\text{-computation; distributivity; monotonicity} \\ & \Pi \circ (R)[S_1, \ldots, S_n]^* \circ S_i \subseteq \Pi \circ S_i^{\smile} \circ (R)[S_1, \ldots, S_n]^* \circ S_i, \text{ for all } i \\ \equiv \quad & \text{(DOM-RCOND); (DOM-COMP); (COREFL-DOM)} \\ & \textbf{true} \end{aligned}$$

□

We use the following law to calculate $dom(R \circ (\bigcup_{i=1}^n S_i)^*)$.

$$dom(R \circ (\textstyle\bigcup_{i=1}^n S_i)^*) = (dom\ R)[S_1, S_2, \ldots, S_n]^*,$$
$$\text{if } S_1, S_2, \ldots, S_n \text{ are all injective.} \qquad \text{(SYMCLS-DOM)}$$

To show this equation, we calculate:

$$\begin{aligned} & dom(R \circ (\textstyle\bigcup_{i=1}^n S_i)^*) \subseteq (dom\ R)[S_1, S_2, \ldots, S_n]^* \\ \equiv \quad & \text{(GC-DOM)} \\ & R \circ (\textstyle\bigcup_{i=1}^n S_i)^* \subseteq \Pi \circ (dom\ R)[S_1, S_2, \ldots, S_n]^* \\ \equiv \quad & \text{(SYMCLS-RCOND)} \\ & R \circ (\textstyle\bigcup_{i=1}^n S_i)^* \subseteq \Pi \circ dom\ R \circ (\textstyle\bigcup_{i=1}^n S_i)^* \\ \Leftarrow \quad & U \subseteq \Pi \circ dom\ U \text{ for any } U, \text{ by (GC-DOM)} \\ & \textbf{true} \end{aligned}$$

The converse inclusion is shown as below.

$$\begin{aligned} & (dom\ R)[S_1, S_2, \ldots, S_n]^* \subseteq dom(R \circ (\textstyle\bigcup_{i=1}^n S_i)^*) \\ \Leftarrow \quad & \mu\text{-induction; monotonicity} \\ & \textstyle\bigcup_{j=1}^n (S_j^{\smile} \circ dom(R \circ (\bigcup_{i=1}^n S_i)^*) \circ S_j) \subseteq dom(R \circ (\bigcup_{i=1}^n S_i)^*) \\ \equiv \quad & \text{Definition of } dom\text{; semi-distributivity} \\ & \textstyle\bigcup_{j=1}^n (S_j^{\smile} \circ S_j) \cap \bigcup_{j=1}^n (S_j^{\smile} \circ (\bigcup_{i=1}^n S_i)^{\smile *} \circ R^{\smile} \circ R \circ (\bigcup_{i=1}^n S_i)^* \circ S_j) \\ & \subseteq id \cap ((\textstyle\bigcup_{i=1}^n S_i)^{\smile *} \circ R^{\smile} \circ R \circ (\bigcup_{i=1}^n S_i)^*) \\ \Leftarrow \quad & S_j\text{'s are injective; monotonicity} \\ & \textbf{true} \end{aligned}$$

□

Example 2 Let us show an interpretation of a predicated XPath expression.

$$
\begin{aligned}
& I_e[\![\text{child} :: \beta[\text{parent} :: \alpha]]\!] \\
= \;& \text{by definition} \\
& dom\,(\alpha? \circ up_L \circ up_R^*) \circ \beta? \circ dn_R^* \circ dn_L \\
= \;& (\textsc{SymCls-Dom});\ (\textsc{Dom-Comp});\ (\textsc{Corefl-Dom}) \\
& (dn_L \circ \alpha? \circ up_L)[up_R]^* \circ \beta? \circ dn_R^* \circ dn_L
\end{aligned}
$$

In Section 5, where we examine negative XPath predicates, we need the fact that the least fixpoint of a relational closure $S \circ R^*$, i.e., the least solution of the equation $X = S \cup X \circ R$ in X, coincides with the greatest fixpoint for a certain class of R. This is equivalent to the unique extendability property of relational closures, which has been proved by Doornbos et al. [7].

They have shown that the unique extendability property holds under the well-foundedness condition:

Definition 3.2 (well-foundedness, [7]) *We call a relation* R well-founded, *if* $S \subseteq S \circ R$ *implies* $S \subseteq \emptyset$ *for any relation* S.

This definition echoes the usual definition found in the order theory: There is no infinite chain $a_0, a_1, a_2, \ldots$ satisfying $a_{i+1}\ R\ a_i$ for every i.

Since we model our tree navigation by relations over the zippers of finite trees and contexts, our tree navigation primitives up_L, dn_L, etc. are apparently well-founded and so are some of their unions, e.g., $dn_L \cup dn_R$ and $up_L \cup up_R$. Note that not every union is well-founded. (For instance, $dn_L \cup up_L$ is not.)

Thus we can use the following law in calculation.

$$S \circ R^* = \nu X.(S \cup X \circ R) \qquad (\textsc{Closure-UEP})$$

We can also prove that the symmetric closure also has the unique extendability property and hence the coincidence of the least and greatest fixpoints. Nevertheless we do not include this result to the present paper, as it is not needed for the development below.

4. Relational reasoning of XPath expressions

We examine how equalities of negation-free XPath expressions can be established by calculation. All the XPath equalities examined in this section are taken from [12, 13] but the proofs are much different, as we derive the equations in the point-free style.

4.1 The child/parent symmetry

Let us show the equalities of the following expressions:

child :: β[parent :: α] and self :: α/child :: β.

This is equivalent to showing the following equation over relations.

$$(dn_L \circ \alpha? \circ up_L)[up_R]^* \circ \beta? \circ dn_R^* \circ dn_L = \beta? \circ dn_R^* \circ dn_L \circ \alpha? \quad (4.1)$$

To show this equation, let us write Q for $(dn_L \circ \alpha? \circ up_L)[up_R]^*$. By the commutativity of coreflexives, it suffices to show the equation $Q \circ dn_R^* \circ dn_L = dn_R^* \circ dn_L \circ \alpha?$.

We first show next two lemmas.

(i) $up_R^* \circ dn_R^* \subseteq up_R^* \cup dn_R^*$

(ii) $dn_R \circ Q \subseteq Q \circ dn_R$

The inclusion (i) is justified as follows.

$$
\begin{aligned}
& up_R^* \circ dn_R^* \subseteq up_R^* \cup dn_R^* \\
\Leftarrow \;& \mu\text{-induction} \\
& dn_R^* \cup up_R \circ (up_R^* \cup dn_R^*) \subseteq up_R^* \cup dn_R^* \\
\equiv \;& \mu\text{-computation; distribution} \\
& dn_R^* \cup up_R \circ up_R^* \cup up_R \circ dn_R \circ dn_R^* \subseteq up_R^* \cup dn_R^* \\
\Leftarrow \;& up_R \circ dn_R \subseteq id;\ up_R \circ up_R^* \subseteq up_R^* \\
& \textbf{true}
\end{aligned}
$$

The inclusion (ii) is shown as follows.

$$
\begin{aligned}
& dn_R \circ Q \subseteq Q \circ dn_R \\
\equiv \;& \mu\text{-computation; distributivity; } up_L \circ dn_R = \emptyset \\
& dn_R \circ Q \subseteq dn_R \circ Q \circ up_R \circ dn_R \\
\equiv \;& \text{commutativity of coreflexives} \\
& dn_R \circ Q \subseteq dn_R \circ up_R \circ dn_R \circ Q \\
\equiv \;& dn_R \circ up_R \circ dn_R = dn_R \\
& \textbf{true}
\end{aligned}
$$

Now we show the equation (4.1). From lemma (i) we derive as follows.

$$
\begin{aligned}
& Q \circ dn_R^* \circ dn_L \subseteq dn_R^* \circ dn_L \circ \alpha? \\
\Leftarrow \;& (R)[S]^* \subseteq S^{\smile *} \circ R \circ S^* \text{ for all } R, S \\
& dn_R^* \circ dn_L \circ \alpha? \circ up_L \circ up_R^* \circ dn_R^* \circ dn_L \subseteq dn_R^* \circ dn_L \circ \alpha? \\
\Leftarrow \;& \text{monotonicity} \\
& up_L \circ up_R^* \circ dn_R^* \circ dn_L \subseteq id \\
\Leftarrow \;& \text{lemma (i)} \\
& up_L \circ (up_R^* \cup dn_R^*) \circ dn_L \subseteq id \\
\equiv \;& \mu\text{-computation; distributivity} \\
& up_L \circ dn_L \cup \\
& up_L \circ up_R^* \circ up_R \circ dn_L \cup up_L \circ dn_R \circ dn_R^* \circ dn_L \subseteq id \\
\Leftarrow \;& up_L \circ dn_L \subseteq id;\ up_R \circ dn_L = \emptyset;\ up_L \circ dn_R = \emptyset \\
& \textbf{true}
\end{aligned}
$$

The converse inclusion is a consequence of lemma (ii).

$$
\begin{aligned}
& dn_R^* \circ dn_L \circ \alpha? \subseteq Q \circ dn_R^* \circ dn_L \\
\Leftarrow \;& \mu\text{-induction} \\
& dn_L \circ \alpha? \cup dn_R \circ Q \circ dn_R^* \circ dn_L \subseteq Q \circ dn_R^* \circ dn_L \\
\Leftarrow \;& \text{lemma (ii)} \\
& dn_L \circ \alpha? \cup Q \circ dn_R \circ dn_R^* \circ dn_L \subseteq Q \circ dn_R^* \circ dn_L \\
\equiv \;& dn_R \circ dn_R^* \subseteq dn_R^* \\
& dn_L \circ \alpha? \subseteq Q \circ dn_R^* \circ dn_L \\
\Leftarrow \;& dn_L \circ \alpha? \circ up_L \subseteq Q;\ id \subseteq dn_R^* \\
& dn_L \circ \alpha? \subseteq dn_L \circ \alpha? \circ up_L \circ dn_L \\
\equiv \;& \text{commutativity of coreflexives; } dn_L \circ up_L \circ dn_L = dn_L \\
& \textbf{true}
\end{aligned}
$$

□

4.2 The descendant/ancestor symmetry

By analogy to the previous example, one might expect that two XPath expressions desc :: β[anc :: α] and desc-or-self :: α/desc :: β are equivalent, but not indeed. The former expression enumerates all the descendant β nodes which have an α node as its ancestor, but the latter enumerates only such β nodes whose α ancestor node is found as the current node or its descendant. They are nevertheless equated when they are prefixed by the absolute path '/', that is,

/desc :: β[anc :: α] and /desc-or-self :: α/desc :: β

are equivalent.

To establish this equivalence, we begin with a finer comparison between the relative path expressions. Let us show that

desc :: β[anc :: α] is equal to
(desc-or-self :: α/desc :: β) ∪ (self :: ∗[anc :: α]/desc :: β),

which amounts to showing the following equality of relations.

$$\begin{aligned} & dom\ (\alpha? \circ (up_L \circ up_R^*)^+) \circ \beta? \circ (dn_R^* \circ dn_L)^+ \\ = \ & \beta? \circ (dn_R^* \circ dn_L)^+ \circ \alpha? \circ (dn_R^* \circ dn_L)^* \cup \qquad (4.2) \\ & \beta? \circ (dn_R^* \circ dn_L)^+ \circ dom\ (\alpha? \circ (up_L \circ up_R^*)^+) \circ (\mathtt{Node}? \times id) \end{aligned}$$

Let us write C for $dn_R^* \circ dn_L$ and Q for $(dn_L \circ \alpha? \circ up_L)[up_L, up_R]^*$. Since $(up_L \circ up_R^*)^+ = up_L \circ (up_L \cup up_R)^*$, we have $dom\ (\alpha? \circ (up_L \circ up_R^*)^+) = Q$ by (SYMCLS-DOM) and hence, by the commutativity of coreflexives, monotonicity, and the fact that $dom\ dn_L \subseteq \mathtt{Node}? \times id$, it suffices to show the following inclusions.

$$C^+ \circ \alpha? \circ C^* \subseteq Q \circ C^+ \qquad (4.3)$$
$$C^+ \circ Q \subseteq Q \circ C^+ \qquad (4.4)$$
$$Q \circ C^+ \subseteq C^+ \circ \alpha? \circ C^* \cup C^+ \circ Q \qquad (4.5)$$

We first show a few subsidiary lemmas:

(i) $C \circ Q \subseteq Q \circ C$

(ii) $Q \circ C \subseteq C \circ (Q \cup \alpha?)$

Lemma (i) follows from the facts that $dn_L \circ Q \subseteq Q \circ dn_L$ and $dn_R \circ Q \subseteq Q \circ dn_R$. We will show $dn_L \circ Q \subseteq Q \circ dn_L$. (The other inclusion is similarly derived.)

$$\begin{aligned} & dn_L \circ Q \subseteq Q \circ dn_L \\ \equiv \quad & \mu\text{-computation; distributivity} \\ & dn_L \circ Q \subseteq dn_L \circ \alpha? \circ up_L \circ dn_L \cup dn_R \circ Q \circ up_R \circ dn_L \cup \\ & \qquad dn_L \circ Q \circ up_L \circ dn_L \\ \Leftarrow \quad & up_R \circ dn_L = \emptyset \\ & dn_L \circ Q \subseteq dn_L \circ Q \circ up_L \circ dn_L \\ \Leftarrow \quad & \text{commutativity of coreflexives; } dn_L = dn_L \circ up_L \circ dn_L \\ & \mathbf{true} \end{aligned}$$

We calculate as follows for lemma (ii).

$$\begin{aligned} & Q \circ C \subseteq C \circ (Q \cup \alpha?) \\ \Leftarrow \quad & Q \circ dn_R^* \subseteq dn_R^* \circ Q \ (\dagger) \\ & dn_R^* \circ Q \circ dn_L \subseteq C \circ (Q \cup \alpha?) \\ \Leftarrow \quad & \mu\text{-induction} \\ & Q \circ dn_L \cup dn_R \circ C \circ (Q \cup \alpha?) \subseteq C \circ (Q \cup \alpha?) \\ \equiv \quad & dn_R \circ C \subseteq C \\ & Q \circ dn_L \subseteq C \circ (Q \cup \alpha?) \\ \equiv \quad & \mu\text{-computation} \\ & dn_L \circ \alpha? \circ up_L \circ dn_L \cup \\ & \quad dn_L \circ Q \circ up_L \circ dn_L \cup dn_R \circ Q \circ up_R \circ dn_L \subseteq C \circ (Q \cup \alpha?) \\ \equiv \quad & up_R \circ dn_L = \emptyset;\ up_L \circ dn_L \subseteq id;\ dn_L \subseteq C \\ & \mathbf{true} \end{aligned}$$

In the above calculation, the fact (†) is derived as below.

$$\begin{aligned} & Q \circ dn_R^* \subseteq dn_R^* \circ Q \\ \Leftarrow \quad & \mu\text{-induction} \\ & Q \cup dn_R^* \circ Q \circ dn_R \subseteq dn_R^* \circ Q \\ \Leftarrow \quad & \mu\text{-computation; monotonicity} \\ & Q \circ dn_R \subseteq dn_R \circ Q \\ \equiv \quad & \mu\text{-computation; distributivity} \\ & dn_L \circ \alpha? \circ up_L \circ dn_R \cup \\ & \quad dn_L \circ Q \circ up_L \circ dn_R \cup dn_R \circ Q \circ up_R \circ dn_R \subseteq dn_R \circ Q \\ \Leftarrow \quad & up_L \circ dn_R = \emptyset;\ up_R \circ dn_R \subseteq id \\ & \mathbf{true} \end{aligned}$$

The inclusion (4.3) is calculated as follows.

$$\begin{aligned} & C^+ \circ \alpha? \circ C^* \subseteq Q \circ C^+ \\ \equiv \quad & C^+ = C^* \circ C \\ & C^* \circ C \circ \alpha? \circ C^* \subseteq Q \circ C^+ \\ \Leftarrow \quad & \mu\text{-induction} \\ & C \circ \alpha? \circ C^* \cup C \circ Q \circ C^+ \subseteq Q \circ C^+ \\ \Leftarrow \quad & C \circ Q \subseteq Q \circ C \\ & C \circ \alpha? \circ C^* \subseteq Q \circ C^+ \\ \Leftarrow \quad & \mu\text{-induction} \\ & C \circ \alpha? \cup Q \circ C^+ \circ C \subseteq Q \circ C^+ \\ \Leftarrow \quad & C^+ \circ C \subseteq C^+ \\ & dn_R^* \circ dn_L \circ \alpha? \subseteq Q \circ C \\ \Leftarrow \quad & \mu\text{-induction} \\ & dn_L \circ \alpha? \cup dn_R \circ Q \circ C \subseteq Q \circ C \\ \Leftarrow \quad & dn_R \circ Q \subseteq Q \circ dn_R \\ & dn_L \circ \alpha? \cup Q \circ dn_R \circ C \subseteq Q \circ C \\ \Leftarrow \quad & dn_R \circ C \subseteq C;\ dn_L \circ \alpha? \circ up_L \circ dn_L \subseteq Q \circ C \\ & dn_L \circ \alpha? \subseteq dn_L \circ \alpha? \circ up_L \circ dn_L \\ \Leftarrow \quad & \text{commutativity of coreflexives; } dn_L = dn_L \circ up_L \circ dn_L \\ & \mathbf{true} \end{aligned}$$

The inclusion (4.4) follows from lemma (i). The inclusion (4.5) is derived as follows.

$$\begin{aligned} & Q \circ C^+ \subseteq C^+ \circ \alpha? \circ C^* \cup C^+ \circ Q \\ \Leftarrow \quad & \mu\text{-induction; distributivity} \\ & Q \circ C \cup C^+ \circ \alpha? \circ C^* \circ C \cup C^+ \circ Q \circ C \subseteq C^+ \circ \alpha? \circ C^* \cup C^+ \circ Q \\ \equiv \quad & C^* \circ C \subseteq C^* \\ & Q \circ C \cup C^+ \circ Q \circ C \subseteq C^+ \circ \alpha? \circ C^* \cup C^+ \circ Q \\ \equiv \quad & \text{lemma (ii)} \\ & C^+ \circ Q \circ C \subseteq C^+ \circ \alpha? \circ C^* \cup C^+ \circ Q \\ \Leftarrow \quad & \mu\text{-induction} \\ & C \circ Q \circ C \cup C \circ (C^+ \circ \alpha? \circ C^* \cup C^+ \circ Q) \subseteq C^+ \circ \alpha? \circ C^* \cup C^+ \circ Q \\ \Leftarrow \quad & \text{distributivity; } C \circ C^+ \subseteq C^+\text{; lemma (ii)} \\ & C \circ C \circ (Q \cup \alpha?) \subseteq C^+ \circ \alpha? \circ C^* \cup C^+ \circ Q \\ \Leftarrow \quad & \text{distributivity; } C \circ C \subseteq C^+;\ id \subseteq C^* \\ & \mathbf{true} \end{aligned}$$

□

As a corollary to the equation (4.2), we establish the equality between the absolute path expressions:

$$I_p[\![/\text{desc} :: \beta[\text{anc} :: \alpha]]\!] \ = \ I_p[\![/\text{desc-or-self} :: \alpha/\text{desc} :: \beta]\!].$$

This follows from the fact that the absolute path /self :: ∗[anc :: α]/desc :: β is interpreted as the empty relation, which is a consequence of the following lemma:

$$(dn_L \circ \alpha? \circ up_L)[up_L, up_R]^* \circ (id \times \mathtt{Top}?) \subseteq \emptyset. \qquad (4.6)$$

This lemma is shown by the following calculuation.

$$
\begin{aligned}
& (dn_L \circ \alpha? \circ up_L)[up_L, up_R]^* \circ (id \times \mathtt{Top}?) \subseteq \emptyset \\
\equiv \quad & \mu\text{-computation; distributivity} \\
& dn_L \circ \alpha? \circ up_L \circ (id \times \mathtt{Top}?) \cup \\
& dn_L \circ (dn_L \circ \alpha? \circ up_L)[up_L, up_R]^* \circ up_L \circ (id \times \mathtt{Top}?) \cup \\
& dn_R \circ (dn_L \circ \alpha? \circ up_L)[up_L, up_R]^* \circ up_R \circ (id \times \mathtt{Top}?) \subseteq \emptyset \\
\equiv \quad & up_L \circ (id \times \mathtt{Top}?) = \emptyset;\ up_R \circ (id \times \mathtt{Top}?) = \emptyset \\
& \mathbf{true} \qquad \square
\end{aligned}
$$

5. Calculating with negative predicates

So far we have dealt with positive fragments of XPath expressions only. It is not difficult to give a relational specification for negative predicates. We interpret negative predicates by

$$I_q[\![\text{not } q]\!] = \neg I_q[\![q]\!],$$

where $\neg$ is the complement on coreflexive relations R, which is defined by $\neg R = id - R$.

Some basic properties of negation is listed below. (As usual, $\neg$ binds tighter than the others.)

For any coreflexive relations R and S, we have:

$\neg R$ is coreflexive	(NEG-COREFL)
$\neg R$ is anti-monotonic in R	(NEG-ANTIMONO)
$\neg\emptyset = id$ and $\neg id = \emptyset$	(NEG-CMPL)
$\neg\neg R = R$	(NEG-DBLNEG)
$\neg(R \cup S) = \neg R \cap \neg S$ $\neg(R \cap S) = \neg R \cup \neg S$	(NEG-DEMORGAN)
$R \cup \neg R = id$ and $R \cap \neg R = \emptyset$	(NEG-EXMDL)

These properties allow us to treat negations as those in propositional logic formulas.

5.1 Calculating relational negations

For effective calculation of negative predicates, we make use of the following laws for simplifying expressions of the form $\neg\, dom\ R$.

$$\neg dom\ (R \circ S) = \neg dom\ S \cup S^{\smile} \circ (\neg dom\ R) \circ S, \quad \text{if } S \text{ is simple and injective.} \qquad \text{(NEG-DOM)}$$

$$\neg dom\ (R \circ S) = \neg S \cup (\neg dom\ R) \circ S, \quad \text{if } S \text{ is coreflexive.} \qquad \text{(NEG-DOMCOREFL)}$$

Let us show (NEG-DOM). (The law (NEG-DOMCOREFL) immediately follows from (NEG-DOM).)

For one inclusion, we derive:

$$
\begin{aligned}
& \neg dom\ (R \circ S) \subseteq \neg dom\ S \cup S^{\smile} \circ (\neg dom\ R) \circ S \\
\equiv \quad & \text{(GC-DIFF), twice} \\
& \neg\neg dom\ S \subseteq dom\ (R \circ S) \cup S^{\smile} \circ (\neg dom\ R) \circ S \\
\equiv \quad & \text{(NEG-DBLNEG); (DOM-COMP)} \\
& S^{\smile} \circ S \subseteq S^{\smile} \circ (dom\ R) \circ S \cup S^{\smile} \circ (\neg dom\ R) \circ S \\
\equiv \quad & \text{monotonicity; distributivity} \\
& id \subseteq dom\ R \cup \neg dom\ R \\
\equiv \quad & \text{(NEG-EXMDL)} \\
& \mathbf{true}
\end{aligned}
$$

For the other inclusion, we show both $\neg dom\ S \subseteq \neg dom\ (R \circ S)$ and $S^{\smile} \circ (\neg dom\ R) \circ S \subseteq \neg dom\ (R \circ S)$.

$$
\begin{aligned}
& \neg dom\ S \subseteq \neg dom\ (R \circ S) \\
\Leftarrow \quad & \text{anti-monotonicity} \\
& dom\ (R \circ S) \subseteq dom\ S \\
\Leftarrow \quad & S \text{ is injective} \\
& S^{\smile} \circ dom\ R \circ S \subseteq S^{\smile} \circ S \\
\Leftarrow \quad & dom\ R \text{ is coreflexive} \\
& \mathbf{true}
\end{aligned}
$$

$$
\begin{aligned}
& S^{\smile} \circ (\neg dom\ R) \circ S \subseteq \neg dom\ (R \circ S) \\
\equiv \quad & \text{(NEG-DBLNEG); (GC-DIFF); (DOM-COMP)} \\
& id \subseteq \neg(S^{\smile} \circ (\neg dom\ R) \circ S) \cup \neg(S^{\smile} \circ dom\ R \circ S) \\
\equiv \quad & \text{anti-monotonicity; de Morgan's law; } \neg id = \emptyset \\
& S^{\smile} \circ (\neg dom\ R) \circ S \cap S^{\smile} \circ dom\ R \circ S \subseteq \emptyset \\
\Leftarrow \quad & \text{modular law, twice} \\
& S^{\smile} \circ (\neg dom\ R \cap S \circ S^{\smile} \circ dom\ R \circ S \circ S^{\smile}) \circ S \subseteq \emptyset \\
\Leftarrow \quad & S \text{ is simple} \\
& S^{\smile} \circ (\neg dom\ R \cap dom\ R) \circ S \subseteq \emptyset \\
\equiv \quad & \text{(NEG-EXMDL)} \\
& \mathbf{true} \qquad \square
\end{aligned}
$$

Example 3 An XPath expression with a negative predicate is interpreted as follows.

$$
\begin{aligned}
& I_e[\![\text{desc} :: \beta[\text{not anc} :: \alpha]]\!] \\
= \ & \neg(dn_L \circ \alpha? \circ up_L)[up_L, up_R]^* \circ \beta? \circ (dn_R^* \circ dn_L)^+
\end{aligned}
$$

5.2 The descendant/ancestor symmetry with negation

As an example of calculation with negative predicates, we try to find a relational tree navigation that is equal to the following absolute XPath expression:

$$/\text{desc} :: \beta[\text{not anc} :: \alpha].$$

Similar to the calculation conducted in Section 4.2, we first show another equation corresponding to the relative path.

$$
\begin{aligned}
& \neg(dn_L \circ \alpha? \circ up_L)[up_L, up_R]^* \circ \beta? \circ (dn_R^* \circ dn_L)^+ \\
= \ & \beta? \circ (dn_R^* \circ dn_L \circ \neg\alpha?)^+ \circ \neg(dn_L \circ \alpha? \circ up_L)[up_L, up_R]^*
\end{aligned} \qquad (5.1)
$$

Let us write C for $dn_R^* \circ dn_L$ and Q for $(dn_L \circ \alpha? \circ up_L)[up_L, up_R]^*$. It is easy to show that the equations $C^+ = (dn_R \cup dn_L)^* \circ dn_L$ and $(C \circ \neg\alpha?)^+ = (dn_R \cup dn_L \circ \neg\alpha?)^* \circ dn_L \circ \neg\alpha?$ hold.

By the commutativity of coreflexives, it suffices to show the equality $(C \circ \neg\alpha?)^+ \circ \neg Q = \neg Q \circ C^+$.

We first show the following lemmas.

(i) $\neg Q \circ dn_R = dn_R \circ \neg Q$

(ii) $\neg Q \circ dn_L = dn_L \circ \neg\alpha? \circ \neg Q$

(iii) $\neg Q \circ C = C \circ \neg\alpha? \circ \neg Q$

By applying μ-computation, de Morgan's law, and (NEG-DOM), we obtain the equation $\neg Q = R_1 \cap R_2 \cap R_3$ where

$$
\begin{aligned}
R_1 &= \neg(dom\ up_L) \cup dn_L \circ \neg\alpha? \circ up_L, \\
R_2 &= \neg(dom\ up_L) \cup dn_L \circ \neg Q \circ up_L, \text{ and} \\
R_3 &= \neg(dom\ up_R) \cup dn_R \circ \neg Q \circ up_R.
\end{aligned}
$$

We will prove (ii). (Lemma (i) can be shown in a similar way.) Since $dn_L \circ \neg\alpha? \circ up_L \circ dn_L = dn_L \circ \neg\alpha?$ because of coreflexivity and $dn_L = dn_L \circ up_L \circ dn_L$, we have $R_1 \circ dn_L = \neg(dom\ up_L) \circ dn_L \cup dn_L \circ \neg\alpha?$. Further we calculate by the laws (DOM-DOMAIN), (COREFL-COMP), and (NEG-EXMDL):

$$\begin{aligned}\neg(dom\ up_L) \circ dn_L &= \neg(dom\ up_L) \circ (dom\ up_L) \circ dn_L \\ &= (\neg(dom\ up_L) \cap (dom\ up_L)) \circ dn_L = \emptyset.\end{aligned}$$

Thus we have $R_1 \circ dn_L = dn_L \circ \neg\alpha?$. Similarly, we can derive $R_2 \circ dn_L = dn_L \circ \neg Q$. Further we have $R_3 \circ dn_L = dn_L$ because $up_R \circ dn_L = \emptyset$ and also $dn_L \subseteq \neg(dom\ up_R) \circ dn_L$, as shown below.

$$\begin{aligned}& dn_L \subseteq \neg(dom\ up_R) \circ dn_L \\ \Leftarrow\ & \quad \text{(DOM-DOMAIN); monotonicity} \\ & dom\ up_L \subseteq \neg(dom\ up_R) \\ \equiv\ & \quad \text{(NEG-DBLNEG); (GC-DIFF); de Morgan} \\ & id \subseteq \neg(dom\ up_L \cap dom\ up_R) \\ \equiv\ & \quad dom\ up_L \cap dom\ up_R = dn_L \circ up_L \circ dn_R \circ up_R = \emptyset \\ & \mathbf{true}\end{aligned}$$

Therefore (ii) can be shown as follows.

$$\begin{aligned}\neg Q \circ dn_L &= (R_1 \cap R_2 \cap R_3) \circ dn_L = R_1 \circ R_2 \circ R_3 \circ dn_L \\ &= R_1 \circ R_2 \circ dn_L = R_1 \circ dn_L \circ \neg Q = dn_L \circ \neg\alpha? \circ \neg Q\end{aligned}$$

Lemma (iii) is a consequence of (i) and (ii), as shown below. (The other inclusion is proved in a similar way using μ-induction.)

$$\begin{aligned}& \neg Q \circ C \subseteq C \circ \neg\alpha? \circ \neg Q \\ \equiv\ & \quad \text{(CLOSURE-UEP)} \\ & \neg Q \circ C \subseteq \nu X.(dn_L \circ \neg\alpha? \circ \neg Q \cup dn_R \circ X) \\ \Leftarrow\ & \quad \nu\text{-induction} \\ & \neg Q \circ C \subseteq dn_L \circ \neg\alpha? \circ \neg Q \cup dn_R \circ \neg Q \circ C \\ \equiv\ & \quad \text{(i) and (ii)} \\ & \neg Q \circ C \subseteq \neg Q \circ dn_L \cup \neg Q \circ dn_R \circ C \\ \equiv\ & \quad \text{distributivity; } \mu\text{-computation} \\ & \mathbf{true}\end{aligned}$$

Now we show the inclusion $(C \circ \neg\alpha?)^+ \circ \neg Q \subseteq \neg Q \circ C^+$.

$$\begin{aligned}& (C \circ \neg\alpha?)^+ \circ \neg Q \subseteq \neg Q \circ C^+ \\ \Leftarrow\ & \quad \mu\text{-induction} \\ & C \circ \neg\alpha? \circ \neg Q \cup C \circ \neg\alpha? \circ \neg Q \circ C^+ \subseteq \neg Q \circ C^+ \\ \equiv\ & \quad \text{(iii)} \\ & \neg Q \circ C \cup \neg Q \circ C \circ C^+ \subseteq \neg Q \circ C^+ \\ \equiv\ & \quad \mu\text{-computation} \\ & \mathbf{true}\end{aligned}$$

For the other inclusion, we calculate:

$$\begin{aligned}& \neg Q \circ C^+ \subseteq (C \circ \neg\alpha?)^+ \circ \neg Q \\ \Leftarrow\ & \quad \mu\text{-induction} \\ & \neg Q \circ C \cup (C \circ \neg\alpha?)^+ \circ \neg Q \circ C \subseteq (C \circ \neg\alpha?)^+ \circ \neg Q \\ \equiv\ & \quad \text{(iii)} \\ & C \circ \neg\alpha? \circ \neg Q \cup (C \circ \neg\alpha?)^+ \circ C \circ \neg\alpha? \circ \neg Q \subseteq (C \circ \neg\alpha?)^+ \circ \neg Q \\ \equiv\ & \quad \text{monotonicity; } \mu\text{-computation} \\ & \mathbf{true} \qquad \square\end{aligned}$$

The absolute path specification we consider is then equated to a relational specification as follows.

$$\begin{aligned}& I_e[\![/\text{desc} :: \beta[\text{not anc} :: \alpha]]\!] \\ &= \beta? \circ (dn_R^* \circ dn_L \circ \neg\alpha?)^+ \circ (id \times \mathtt{Top?}) \circ (up_L \cup up_R)^*\end{aligned} \tag{5.2}$$

To establish this equation via (5.1), it is sufficient to show the equation:

$$\neg(dn_L \circ \alpha? \circ up_L)[up_L, up_R]^* \circ (id \times \mathtt{Top?}) = id \times \mathtt{Top?}.$$

Writing Q for $(dn_L \circ \alpha? \circ up_L)[up_L, up_R]^*$, we derive this equation as follows.

$$\begin{aligned}& \neg Q \circ (id \times \mathtt{Top?}) = id \times \mathtt{Top?} \\ \equiv\ & \quad \text{(COREFL-COMP); monotonicity} \\ & id \times \mathtt{Top?} \subseteq \neg Q \\ \equiv\ & \quad \text{(NEG-DBLNEG); (GC-DIFF); de Morgan} \\ & id \subseteq \neg(Q \cap (id \times \mathtt{Top?})) \\ \equiv\ & \quad \text{anti-monotonicity; } \neg id = \emptyset\text{; (COREFL-COMP)} \\ & Q \circ (id \times \mathtt{Top?}) \subseteq \emptyset \\ \equiv\ & \quad (4.6) \\ & \mathbf{true} \qquad \square\end{aligned}$$

Here we notice that the resulting relational specification in (5.2) is implementable as a functional program (see the next section) but not expressible by an XPath expression.

6. Translating relations to programs

This section briefly describes how relational specifications of tree navigation can be translated into functional programs. As most of the translation process comprises of standard techniques such as power transpose (see e.g. [4]), we elaborate mainly on what are specific to the present work.

To fill the gap between relational specifications and functional programs, we need a few rearrangements on the former. First, we rewrite the relation into an equivalent one that has no nested closures and more explicit conditional choices. For this, we rewrite, e.g., the relation $(dn_R^* \circ dn_L \circ \neg\alpha?)^+$ derived in Section 5 into $(dn_R \cup dn_L \circ \neg\alpha?)^* \circ dn_L \circ \neg\alpha?$. Second, assuming coreflexivity of R and injectivity of S_1, ..., S_n, we deal with every symmetric closure $(S_1, \cdots, S_n)[R]^*$ or its negation, which is derived from an XML predicate, according to (SYMCLS-RCOND). For example, the XPath negative predicate [not anc :: α] in Section 5 is regarded as (the negation of) $\Pi \circ dn_L \circ \alpha? \circ up_L \circ (up_L \cup up_R)^*$, which is a right condition derived from $(dn_L \circ \alpha? \circ up_L)[up_L, up_R]^*$. This use of right conditions in place of coreflexives is intended for efficiency, where (SYMCLS-RCOND) allows us to skip almost half of the tree navigation in the symmetric closure.

Once prepared as above, we proceed the translation as below. We treat every coreflexive R as its right condition $\Pi \circ R$ and translate it to a boolean-valued function whose output is true if and only if something is related by R with the input. The relational meets, joins, and negation should be interpreted as corresponding operations on boolean values. Relational compositions of coreflexives should be treated as conjunction, as indicated by (COREFL-COMP). Every atomic predicate, which is derived from an XPath step path, should be replaced with a suitable node test. For the other (not coreflexive) relations, we interpret them to its power transpose [4]: Given a relation R over zippers, the power transpose of R, written ΛR, is a function that takes a zipper and returns a set of zippers related by R. Adopting lists as the conventional representation for sets, we can implement ΛR by a function that returns a list of zippers that are related by R to the input zipper and we also replace each relational union with the list append.

```
let rec root z =
  match z with
    (_,Top) -> z
  | (_,L _) -> root (upL z)
  | (_,R _) -> root (upR z)

let node a =
  function (Node(l,i,r),p) -> a=i | _ -> false

let rec pred_anc a z =
  match z with
    (Leaf,_) | (_, Top) -> false
  | (Node _, L _) ->
      let u = upL z in node a u || pred_anc a u
  | (Node _, R _) -> pred_anc a (upR z)

let desc b z =
  let rec dn z =
    match z with
      (Node _,_) ->
        List.append (if node b z then [z] else [])
          (List.append (dn (dnL z)) (dn (dnR z)))
    | (Leaf,_) -> []
  in match z with
    (Node _,_) -> dn (dnL z)
  | _ -> []

let abs_desc_npred_anc a b z =
  let npred_anc a z = not (pred_anc a z)
  in List.filter (npred_anc a) (desc b (root z))

let nadesc a z =
  let rec nadcsf z =
  match z with
    (Leaf,_) -> [z]
  | (Node _, _) ->
      List.append [z]
        (List.append (nadcsf (dnR z))
          (if not (node a z)
           then nadcsf (dnL z) else []))
  in match z with
       (Leaf,_) -> []
     | (Node _,_) ->
         if not (node a z)
         then nadcsf (dnL z) else []

let abs_b_nadesc a b z =
  List.filter (node b) (nadesc a (root z))
```

Figure 5. A translation result

The translation procedures described above are mostly mechanical, but it would be difficult to fully automate the whole tranlation process because human insights are required in some translation steps, e.g., closure unnesting.

Figure 5 gives the result of translation of the relations that we examined in Section 5, namely, `abs_desc_npred_anc` for the relation corresponding to the negatively predicated absolute path expression /desc :: β[not anc :: α] and `abs_b_nadesc` for its equivalent relation $\beta? \circ (dn_R^* \circ dn_L \circ \neg\alpha?)^+ \circ (id \times \mathtt{Top}?) \circ (up_L \cup up_R)^*$ derived by calculation. Although the given program has chances of further optimization by other transformation techniques such as fusion [4], we leave them unexploited for readability.

7. Conclusion

We have proposed a theory for reasoning about equalities of relationally specified tree navigation. A small number of relational elements, tree navigation primitives and a few operations such as the symmetric closure, suffice for reasoning about both positive and negative XPath expressions and even those navigation beyond XPath expressibility.

There are several directions for future research based on the present work. First, we have not considered data updates in zippers at all. Developing primitive operations for data updates and a set of laws for reasoning would make our result more widely applicable. The result on negative predicates in Section 5 suggests that the XPath language is missing some symmetry induced from negative predicates. Identifying an extended path language that is closed under this symmetry would provide a fruitful merit with the language design. Although the present paper concerns only binary trees, we believe that the present work can be generalized to more varieties of data structures, based on the general zipper-like data structures as investigated in [1, 11]. Developing a theory for navigation in such general zipper-like data structures would also be an interesting topic to pursue.

Acknowledgments

The second author was partly supported by KAKENHI 20500001.

References

[1] M. Abbott, T. Altenkirch, C. McBride, and N. Ghani. δ for data: Differentiating data structures. *Fundamenta Informaticae*, 65(1–2): 1–28, 2004.

[2] R. Backhouse, R. Crole, and J. Gibbons, editors. *Algebraic and Coalgebraic Methods in the Mathematics of Program Construction: International Summer School and Workshop*, volume 2297 of *LNCS*. Springer, 2002.

[3] A. Berglund, S. Boag, D. Chamberlin, M. F. Fernández, M. Kay, J. Robie, and J. Siméon. *XML Path Language (XPath) 2.0, W3C Recommendation*, 2007. `http://www.w3.org/TR/xpath20/`.

[4] R. Bird and O. de Moor. *Algebra of Programming*, volume 100 of *International Series in Computer Science*. Prentice Hall, 1997.

[5] D. Che, K. Aberer, and M. T. Özsu. Query optimization in XML structured-document databases. *The VLDB Journal*, 15(3):263–289, 2006.

[6] A. Cunha and J. Visser. Transformation of structure-shy programs: Applied to XPath queries and strategic functions. In *Proceedings of the 2007 ACM SIGPLAN Workshop on Partial Evaluation and Semantics-based Program Manipulation*, pages 11–20. ACM, 2007.

[7] H. Doornbos, R. Backhouse, and J. van der Woude. A calculational approach to mathematical induction. *Theoretical Computer Science*, 179(1–2):103–135, 1997.

[8] P. Genevès, N. Layaïda, and A. Schmitt. Efficient static analysis of XML paths and types. In *PLDI '07: Proceedings of the 2007 ACM SIGPLAN Conference on Programming Language Design and Implementation*, pages 342–351. ACM Press, 2007.

[9] G. Huet. The zipper. *Journal of Functional Programming*, 7(5):549–554, 1997.

[10] Mathematics of Program Construction Group. Fixed-point calculus. *Information Processing Letters*, 53(3):131–136, 1995.

[11] C. McBride. The derivative of a regular type is its type of one-hole contexts. Available electronically `http://www.cs.nott.ac.uk/~ctm/diff.ps.gz.`, 2001.

[12] D. Olteanu, H. Meuss, T. Furche, and F. Bry. XPath: Looking forward. Technical Report PMS-FB-2001-17, University of Munich, 2001.

[13] D. Olteanu, H. Meuss, T. Furche, and F. Bry. XPath: Looking forward. In *XML-Based Data Management and Multimedia Engineering — EDBT 2002 Workshops*, volume 2490 of *LNCS*, pages 109–127. Springer, 2002.

[14] P. Wadler. A formal semantics of patterns in XSLT and XPATH. *Markup Languages: Theory and Practice*, 2(2):183–202, 2000.

A Program Transformation for Returning States in Functional-Logic Programs

Rafael Caballero *
University Complutense of Madrid
rafa@sip.ucm.es

Abstract

This paper studies the conditions necessary to safely introduce new values as part of the results of function rules in functional-logic programs. The idea is to consider an initial functional-logic program and to produce, by means of a program transformation, a new program including states. Each rule of the new program returns pairs of values, with the first value the same as in the original program, and the second one a new value that can be defined in terms of the values returned by the function calls occurring in the rule. We prove that the transformation ensures the equivalence of the two programs with respect to the Constructor-based ReWriting Logic, a suitable semantics for functional-logic programs.

Categories and Subject Descriptors F [*3*]: 3

General Terms Languages

Keywords Functional-Logic languages, stateful computations, program transformation

1. Introduction

Functional-Logic programming (see [12]) has been proposed as a suitable combination of both Logic and Functional Programming. Programs in this paradigm can combine features like logic variables, higher order functions, non-deterministic computations, and laziness. As explained in [4], the combination proposed by this paradigm is conservative: programs that do not use the features of one paradigm behave as programs of the other paradigm. However, most functional-logic programs combine characteristics of both Logic and Functional Programming. It is known that the behavior of these programs is not well-described by usual approaches like ordinary term rewriting systems or λ-calculus. The presence of higher order features makes things more difficult. Reasoning principles that are essential in a standard deterministic functional setting (like extensionality) become incorrect in functional-logic programs [15].

Therefore, a new semantic framework called constructor-based ReWriting Logic (CRWL) was proposed in [8, 9] in order to allow reasoning in this paradigm. CRWL proves *approximations* of the form $e \to t$. In particular we will use the notation $\mathcal{P} \vdash e \to t$ to indicate that in CRWL $e \to t$ can be proven with respect to $\mathcal{P}$, i.e. that the partial pattern t *approximates* the result of evaluating e with respect to some program $\mathcal{P}$. For instance, consider the following program written in the syntax of the functional-logic language $\mathcal{TOY}$[1], where variables start with uppercase letters and the rest of the syntactic symbols with lowercase letters:

EXAMPLE 1. *Simple arithmetic with Peano numbers*

```
data nat          = zero | s nat

plus zero Y       = Y
plus (s X) Y      = s(plus X Y)

multi zero Y      = zero
multi (s X) Y     = plus Y (multi X Y)
```

Calling $\mathcal{P}$ to this program we expect for instance that

$$\mathcal{P} \vdash \texttt{plus (s zero) (s zero)} \to \texttt{s (s zero)}$$

and also that $\mathcal{P} \vdash$ `plus (s zero) (s zero)` $\to$ `s` $\bot$, and even that $\mathcal{P} \vdash$ `plus (s zero) (s zero)` $\to \bot$. The symbol *bottom* ($\bot$) approximates any expression, and it is useful for representing laziness. CRWL also allows one to prove that two expressions can be approximated by the same total term (i.e. by a term without $\bot$) by using strict equalities. For example,

$$\mathcal{P} \vdash \begin{array}{l}\texttt{plus (s zero) (s zero) ==} \\ \texttt{multi (s (s zero)) (s zero)}\end{array}$$

holds because both $\mathcal{P} \vdash$ `plus (s zero) (s zero)` $\to$ `s (s zero)` and $\mathcal{P} \vdash$ `multi (s (s zero)) (s zero)` $\to$ `s (s zero)` hold. In this paper we use this semantics for proving the correctness of a transformation that introduces pairs of results in functional-logic program rules. For instance, consider the program of the previous example and suppose that we also wish to know the number of calls to `plus` that have been performed in any computation. Then we could transform the program into a new one of the form:

EXAMPLE 2. *Obtaining the number of calls to* `plus`

```
plusT zero Y      = (Y,1)
plusT (s X) Y     = (s A,  B+1)
                    where (A,B)= plusT X Y

multiT zero Y     = (zero,0)
multiT (s X) Y    = (A2,B1+B2 )
                    where
                     (A1,B1) = multiT X Y
                     (A2,B2) = plusT Y A1
```

* This work has been partially supported by the Spanish projects FAST-STAMP(TIN200 8-06622- C03-01/TIN), PROMETIDOS-CM (S2009TIC-1465) and GPD-UCM (UCM-BSCH-GR58/ 08- 910502).

PEPM'11, January 24–25, 2011, Austin, Texas, USA.

We have used the suffix T in the transformed version of the functions. Now each rule returns a pair, where the first value is the same result as in Example 1, and the second one is the number of calls to `plus`. The schema followed for transforming a rule is simple:

- Each function call occurring in the rule is now a local definition returning a pair.
- The function rule itself returns a pair. The first value is obtained by replacing the function calls occurring in the body of the original rule by the corresponding variables (like `(plus X Y)` by `A` in the second rule for `plusT`).
- The second value in the result pair is the addition of the second values of the function calls, incremented by one in the case of rules for `plusT`.

For instance, now we can prove:

$$\mathcal{P} \vdash \texttt{plusT}\,(\texttt{s}\,\texttt{zero})\,(\texttt{s}\,\texttt{zero}) == (\texttt{s}(\texttt{s}\,\texttt{zero}),\,2)$$

It is worth noticing that we are in fact introducing a *state monad* [16, 19] in disguise. However, the language $\mathcal{TOY}$ does not incorporate lambda abstractions explicitly, and from the point of view of the simplicity of the theoretical results and proofs it will be convenient to avoid the explicit introduction of monadic combinators in this paper.

One may wonder if the underlying transformation that yields the code of Example 2 can be formalized and generalized, and moreover, if the semantic equivalence of the two programs can be established. This is the purpose of this paper. To begin with, it is easy to see that the semantic equivalence only occurs under certain circumstances, as shown in the next example:

EXAMPLE 3. *Suppose we add the two following functions to those of Example 1:*

```
undef   = undef
f       = multi zero undef
```

Following the same ideas used for obtaining the code of Example 2, we obtain the following transformed functions:

```
undefT   = (X,Y)
           where (X,Y) = undefT
fT       = (A2, B1+B2)
            where
            (A1,B1) = undefT
            (A2,B2) = multiT zero A1
```

However, now we have that $\mathcal{P} \vdash$ `f == zero`, *but* $\mathcal{P} \vdash$ `fT == (zero,` t`)` *does not hold for any term* t. *Although we have not introduced the CRWL calculus yet, it is easy to see that evaluating* `f` *does not require evaluating the loop* `undef`. *However, the evaluation of* `fT` *will require the evaluation of* `undefT` *to obtain the value* `B1`, *which is required to obtain the result* `B1+B2`. *In fact the goal* `f == zero` *succeeds in the functional-logic languages* $\mathcal{TOY}$ *[1] or Curry [11], but* `fT == (zero,N)` *will loop.*

The solution to this problem will be to introduce an impure primitive `dVal` that allows the transformed program to check if a function call is necessary for obtaining the result of the initial program rule or not. This function will be introduced in Section 3.1.

Another complication arises when higher-order functions like `map` are introduced, as the next example shows.

EXAMPLE 4. *Consider the* `map` *function and its transformation following the schema above:*

```
map F []            = []
map F [X | Xs]      = [F X | map F Xs]

mapT F []           = ([],0)
mapT F [X | Xs]     = ([A1 | A2],B1+B2)
                      where
                       (A1,B1) = F X
                       (A2,B2) = mapT F Xs
```

And the following two new functions, and their transformations:

```
g    = map (plus (s zero)) [s zero]
h    = map (plus) [s zero]

gT   = (A1,B1)
        where
         (A1,B1) = mapT (plusT (s zero)) [s zero]

hT   = (A1,B1)
        where (A1,B1) = mapT (plus) [s zero]
```

The first function `g` *and its transformation* `gT` *behave equivalently. However, in the case of* `h` *and* `hT` *it is possible to prove* $\mathcal{P} \vdash$ `h ==` [`plus (s zero)`] *but it is not possible to prove* $\mathcal{P} \vdash$ `hT == ([plus (s zero)],` N`)` *for any value* N. *In fact in a typed language like* $\mathcal{TOY}$ *or Curry (or in the corresponding version in Haskell [13]), the function* `hT` *will produce a type error, although* `h` *is correctly typed.*

Therefore, the schema not only can produce non-equivalent computations, it can even produce ill-typed programs! The problem is that in the transformed version of `map`, `mapT`, it is assumed that the functional argument `F` applied to one argument will return a pair of values. This is true in the case of `(plusT (s zero))`, the argument of `mapT` in `gT`. But in `hT` the argument `(plus)` is still a partial application after applied to one argument (the program arity of `plus` is two, and therefore it needs two arguments to become evaluable). The solution, presented in Section 3 will consist of introducing new function rules for replacing partial applications of functions and constructors.

In the rest of the paper we will see a transformation schema that produces equivalent programs, thus solving these difficulties. The transformation generalizes a transformation used for producing computation trees in declarative debuggers [6]. The contributions of this work, in particular with respect to [6] are:

- It generalizes the particular case of declarative debugging, where a computation tree was associated to every function, to the case of a state accompanying each rule result. This generalization is not trivial. In particular we discuss the properties that the expression associated to each rule must fulfill in order to produce the state values, something which was not necessary in [6].
- We introduce formal rules that defined this general program transformation, which makes the process of implementing the transformation and the proof of its correctness simpler and clearer. In [6] the transformation did not use explicit rules and was difficult to implement.
- An uniform treatment of the problem of partial applications (Example 4) and of the problem of undefined function calls (Example 3).

In [10] M. Hamana presented a direct semantic characterization of states in functional-logic programs. The proposal uses a computational meta-language for representing programs, and presents a translation of the axioms of the metalanguage into a conditional term rewriting system. The main difference with respect to the approach of this paper is that we do not propose a new semantics for stateful functional-logic programs. Instead, this work presents a source-to-source transformation which shows how a functional-logic program can be transformed safely into an equivalent program without changing the basic underlying semantics (the only change is the addition of a non-declarative primitive).

The transformation rules and the main theoretical results of this paper corresponds to a generalization and adaptation of the author's PhD Thesis [7], which was supervised by Mario Rodríguez-Artalejo.

The next section introduces the basics of the theoretical framework we use in the rest of the paper, including the syntax and semantic functional-logic programs.

2. Functional-Logic Programs

First we define the basic pieces used both in programs and in their semantics. Then we introduce the syntax of functional-logic programs, and finally the semantic calculus that supports these languages.

2.1 Expressions, Patterns and Substitutions

The *signature* of a functional-logic program will be denoted as $\Sigma = \langle\, DC,\ FS\rangle$, where $DC = \bigcup_{n\in\mathbb{N}} DC^n$ and $FS = \bigcup_{n\in\mathbb{N}} FS^n$ are respectively sets of data constructors $c, d, \ldots$, and of function symbols $f, g, \ldots$. Each symbol must have a fixed arity $n \geq 0$, and in this case we say for instance that $f \in FS^n$. We assume the existence of an infinite set Var of variables. Then we can define the set of the partial expressions, $e \in Exp_\perp$ as:

$$e ::= \perp \mid X \mid h \mid (e\, e')$$

where $X \in Var$, $h \in DC \cup FS$. Expressions of the form $(e\,e')$ represent the application of expression e (acting as a function) to e' (representing an argument). As usual we assume that the expression $(e_0\, e_1 \ldots\, e_n)$ abbreviates $((\ldots(e_0\, e_1)\ldots)\, e_n)$. The set of variables in e is represented by $var(e)$. An expression e is called *ground* when $var(e) = \emptyset$. *Flexible expressions* are of the form $X\, e_1 \ldots e_m$ with $X \in Var, m > 0$, while *rigid expressions* are of the form $h\, e_1 \ldots e_m$ with $m \geq 0, h \in DC \cup FS$. Rigid expressions can be further divided into *active* if $h \in FS^n$ with $m \geq n$, or *passive* otherwise. *Partial patterns* $t \in Pat_\perp \subset Exp_\perp$ are defined as: $t ::= \perp \mid X \mid c\, t_1\, \ldots\, t_m \mid f\, t_1\, \ldots\, t_{m'}$ where $X \in Var$, $c \in DC^n$, $0 \leq m \leq n$, $f \in FS^{n'}$, $0 \leq m' < n'$ and the t_i represent partial patterns. The value $\perp$ is useful for representing lazy computations. The approximation order $\sqsubseteq$ is defined as the least partial order in $Pat_\perp$ verifying that $\perp \sqsubseteq t$, for $t \in Pat_\perp$, and that $h\, \overline{t}_m \sqsubseteq h\, \overline{s}_m$ iff $t_i \sqsubseteq s_i$ for $1 \leq i \leq m$. Total patterns are patterns without any occurrence of $\perp$. The set of total patterns is denoted by Pat. A *total substitution* is an application $\theta : Var \to Pat$ with an unique extension $Exp \to Exp$ represented also by θ. $Subst$ represents the set of the total substitutions, and $Subst_\perp$ the set of the partial substitutions $\theta : Var \to Pat_\perp$ analogously defined. The *domain* of a substitution θ, $dom(\theta)$, is the set of variables X such that $\theta(X) \neq X$, and *range* of θ, $ran(\theta)$, to $\bigcup_{X\in dom(\theta)} var(\theta(X))$. As usual $\theta = \{X_1 \mapsto t_1, \ldots, X_n \mapsto t_n\}$ will represent the substitution with domain $\{X_1, \ldots, X_n\}$ verifying $\theta(X_i) = t_i$ for $1 \leq i \leq n$. We will write $e\theta$ instead of $\theta(e)$, and $\theta\sigma$ for representing the composition of θ and σ such that $e(\theta\sigma) = (e\theta)\sigma$ for any e. We also define the *disjoint union* $\theta_1 \uplus \theta_2$ of two substitutions θ_1 and θ_2 with disjoint domains as the substitution θ such that $dom(\theta) = dom(\theta_1) \cup dom(\theta_2)$, $\theta(X) = \theta_1(X)$ for every $X \in dom(\theta_1)$, and $\theta(Y) = \theta_2(Y)$ for every $Y \in dom(\theta_2)$.

The mapping $id(X) = X$ for every $X \in Var$ is called *identity substitution*, and any substitution ρ bijective from Var to itself is called a *renaming*. Two expressions e and e' are *variants* when there is some renaming ρ such that $e\rho = e'$. We say $\theta \leq \theta'$ iff $\theta' = \theta\sigma$ for $\sigma \in Subst_\perp$.

2.2 Syntax of Functional-Logic Programs

We assume functional-logic programs composed of data type declarations, type alias, infix operators, function type declarations and defining rules for functions symbols. The reader is referred to [1] and [11] for detailed descriptions of the syntax of the functional languages $\mathcal{TOY}$ and Curry respectively. The rules defining a function can be written as: $f\ t_1 \ldots t_n \to r \Leftarrow C$, where $f \in FS^n$, r is an expression (that can contain new extra variables) and t_i are patterns. The condition C is a (possibly empty) sequence of *atomic conditions* $C_1, \ldots, C_k$, where each C_i can be either a *strict equality* $e == e'$, with $e, e' \in Exp$, or an *approximation* $d \to s$, with $d \in Exp$ and $s \in Pat$.
The examples in this paper are written in the concrete syntax of the lazy functional-logic language $\mathcal{TOY}$, but the code can be easily adapted to other similar languages like Curry. In $\mathcal{TOY}$ the program rules are written in a slightly different way:

$$\underbrace{f\ t_1 \ldots t_n}_{\text{left-hand side}} \quad \to \quad \underbrace{r}_{\text{right-hand side}} \quad \Leftarrow \quad \underbrace{EI}_{\text{strict equalities}} \quad \text{where} \quad \underbrace{LD}_{\text{local def.}}$$

Thus, the condition C of the program rule is split into two parts: A first part EI of strict equalities $e == e'$, and another part LD with the approximations $d \to s$, written as *local definitions*.

Without loss of generality, we assume *normalized* programs. A program is normalized if all its program rules are normalized:

DEFINITION 1. *A program rule is normalized iff:*

- *Every active expression occurs in a local definition of the form $f\ \overline{t}_n \to X$ with $f \in FS^n$ and $t_i \in Pat$ for $i = 1 \ldots n$. Therefore no nested active expressions are allowed.*
- *Every flexible expression occurs in a local definition of the form $X\ t \to Y$, with t a pattern.*

It is easy to check that given a functional-logic program it is possible to define an equivalent, normalized program introducing additional local definitions. This previous phase is also assumed in works about the definition of operational semantics for functional-logic languages like [3], and in semantics for the partial evaluation of functional-logic programs [2].

2.3 The CRWL calculus

The Constructor-based ReWriting Logic (CRWL) [8, 9] has been proposed as suitable declarative semantics for functional-logic programming with lazy non-deterministic functions. The calculus is defined by five inference rules: (BT) that indicates that any expression can be approximated by bottom, (RR) that establishes the reflexivity over variables, the decomposition rule (DC), the (JN) (join) rule that indicates how to prove strict equalities, and the function application rule (FA):

BT $\quad e \to \perp$

RR $\quad X \to X \quad$ with $X \in Var$

DC $\quad \dfrac{e_1 \to t_1\ \ldots\ e_m \to t_m}{h\ \overline{e}_m \to h\ \overline{t}_m} \quad h\ \overline{t}_m \in Pat_\perp$

JN $\quad \dfrac{e \to t \quad e' \to t}{e == e'} \quad t \in Pat$ (total pattern)

FA $\quad \dfrac{e_1 \to t_1\ \ldots\ e_n \to t_n \quad C \quad r \to t}{f\ \overline{e}_n \to t}$
if $(f\ \overline{t}_n \to r \Leftarrow C) \in [P]_\perp, t \neq \perp$

In every inference rule, $e, e_i \in Exp_\perp$ are partial expressions $t_i, t, s \in Pat_\perp$ are partial patterns, and $h \in DC \cup FS$. The notation $[P]_\perp$ of the inference rule *FA* represents the set $\{(l \to r \Leftarrow C)\theta \mid (l \to r \Leftarrow C) \in P,\ \theta \in Subst_\perp\}$ of partial instances of the rules in program P. The most complex inference rule is FA (Function Application), which formalizes the steps for computing a *partial pattern* t as approximation of a function call $f\ \overline{e}_n$:

1. Obtain partial patterns t_i as suitable approximations of the arguments e_i.
2. Verify the condition C, and check that t approximates the right-hand side r.

Observe that in FA we can suppose that $f \in FS^n$ is applied to exactly n arguments because we are assuming normalized programs.

3. Program Transformation

In this Section we present the program transformation that will produce equivalent stateful programs. First, we introduce the primitive `dVal`, and then the functions that will substitute for the partial applications. These two basic pieces are used in the transformed program presented in Subsection 3.3.

3.1 The primitive `dVal`

In order to define the program transformation we need a new primitive function for detecting function calls that have not been evaluated. The primitive will be called `dVal` (from defined value) in our setting, and is based on a primitive used in the first declarative debugger for functional programs like Haskell [17] (where it is named `dirt`).

We will assume that `dVal` has type $A \to string$, indicating that it takes a value of any type and returns a string. The value returned will represent the argument as a string if it is in *head normal form*, that is, if it is not an active expression, and "_" in every other case. Observe that the primitive is impure because it cannot be defined as a normal functional-logic function. In fact the value of `dVal` will depend on whether the argument contains some function call that has not been been evaluated *before* the evaluation of `dVal`. The concept of *being evaluated before* is unclear in the general context of pure declarative programming, where the evaluation order is usually irrelevant. However, for convenience we assume that in a sequence of conditions the implementations proceed checking the atomic conditions from left to right, as shows the following example in $\mathcal{TOY}$:

EXAMPLE 5. *Relevance of evaluation order in* `dVal`
The goal:

`dVal X == Y, X==zero where X = plus zero zero`

will produce the computed answer `Y` $\mapsto$ `"_"` *in* $\mathcal{TOY}$ *since* `X` *contains the function call* `plus zero zero`, *which has not been evaluated before (observe that local definitions like* `where X = plus zero zero` *are* lazy *in the sense that they do not require evaluating the expression at the right-hand side). The function is evaluated by the strict equality* `X==zero`, *but only after the evaluation of* `dVal`. *However, if we change the order of the atomic conditions:*

`X==zero, dVal X == Y where X = plus zero zero`

we obtain `Y` $\mapsto$ `"zero"`, *because now the strict equality* `X==zero` *requires the evaluation of* `plus zero zero` *before* `dVal` *is applied.*

The implementation of this primitive is not difficult in systems based on the schema defined in [14] for translating functional-logic programs into Prolog. In this schema, function calls correspond to Prolog terms representing *suspensions*. Each suspension contains one variable indicating if the term has been evaluated, and another one indicating the result of the evaluation. Observe also that we have considered *strings* for representing terms, but any other datatype that can 1) distinguish terms containing unevaluated function calls, and 2) obtain the name of the outer functor of terms (this will be necessary to recognize the auxiliary functions obtained in next Subsection), can be employed. In $\mathcal{TOY}$ `dVal` is defined returning a structured datatype `pVal` that satisfies these requirements. In general we will use the notation $\ulcorner s \urcorner$ to indicate the representation of s returned by `dVal`.

3.2 Auxiliary Functions

In order to deal with partial applications in the transformed program, we will use a set of auxiliary functions defined as followed:

DEFINITION 2. *Given a program* $\mathcal{P}$, *the program* $\mathcal{P}_{aux}$ *contains the following program functions:*

1. $\mathcal{P}_{aux}$ *includes a new function* `bottom` *defined by the following rule* `bottom = bottom`.
2. *For each* $f \in FS^n$ *defined in* $\mathcal{P}$, $\mathcal{P}_{aux}$ *includes* $n-1$ *new functions defined as:*

$$f_0^{\mathcal{T}}\ X_1 \quad \to (f_1^{\mathcal{T}}\ X_1,\quad \texttt{bottom})$$
$$\dots$$
$$f_{n-2}^{\mathcal{T}}\ \overline{X}_{n-1} \quad \to (f\ \overline{X}_{n-1},\quad \texttt{bottom})$$

3. *For each* $c \in DC^n$ *defined in* $\mathcal{P}$, $\mathcal{P}_{aux}$ *includes* n *new functions defined as:*

$$c_0^{\mathcal{T}}\ X_1 \quad \to (c_1^{\mathcal{T}}\ X_1,\quad \texttt{bottom})$$
$$\dots$$
$$c_{n-1}^{\mathcal{T}}\ \overline{X}_n \quad \to (c\ \overline{X}_n,\quad \texttt{bottom})$$

4. *A function* `isAuxiliary` *with type* $string \to bool$, *such that the function call* (`isAuxiliary` $\ulcorner s \urcorner$) *returns* `true` *iff* s *is a pattern rooted by an auxiliary function in* $\mathcal{P}_{aux}$.
5. *A function* `isBottom` *with type* $string \to bool$, *such that the function call* (`isBottom` $\ulcorner s \urcorner$) *returns* `true` *iff* $s = \perp$.

Observe that we assume that the auxiliary functions are defined using new function names different from those occurring in $\mathcal{P}$.

EXAMPLE 6.
Possible implementations of `isBottom` *and* `isAuxiliary`, *assuming that auxiliary functions begin with the prefix* `aux$`

```
isBottom X    = X=="_"
isAuxiliary X = X==['a','u','x','$' | R]
```

Each auxiliary function $f_m^{\mathcal{T}}$ needs $m+1$ arguments to be evaluated and returns a pair $(A, \texttt{bottom})$ with A a partial application of function $f_{m+1}^{\mathcal{T}}$. The only exception is $f_{n-2}^{\mathcal{T}}$ which returns a partial application of f. The auxiliary functions $c_m^{\mathcal{T}}$ are analogously defined, except for $c_{n-1}^{\mathcal{T}}$, which returns a total application of c. The purpose of these new functions will be to substitute for the partial applications of functions and constructors. In the transformed program these partial applications must return pairs when applied to an argument, as shown in the introduction (see Example 4). Function `bottom` represents a value that can only be reduced to $\perp$.

3.3 Transformation Rules

Figure 1 introduces the transformation rules for adding states to (normalized) functional-logic programs. Given a program rule $(f\ \overline{t}_n \to r \Leftarrow C)$ defining a function f, the transformed rule $f^{\mathcal{T}}$ is obtained applying rule (TR_1). The premises of this transformation rule transform the patterns $\overline{t}_n$, the right-hand side r, and the conditions C. The transformation of C consists of a transformed

Program rules:

$$(\mathbf{TR_1})\quad \frac{t_1 \Rightarrow^{\mathcal{T}} s_1 \ \dots\ t_n \Rightarrow^{\mathcal{T}} s_n \quad r \Rightarrow^{\mathcal{T}} s \quad C \Rightarrow^{\mathcal{T}} (C^{\mathcal{T}} \,;\, (r_1,T_1),\dots,(r_m,T_m))}{\begin{array}{l} f\,\overline{t}_n \to r \Leftarrow C \ \Rightarrow^{\mathcal{T}} \\ \quad f^{\mathcal{T}}\,\overline{s}_n \to (s,T) \Leftarrow C^{\mathcal{T}},\ \text{process}_{f_k}\ (\texttt{clean}\ [(\texttt{dVal}\ r_1,T_1),\dots,\ (\texttt{dVal}\ r_m,T_m)]) \to T \end{array}}$$

with $f\,\overline{t}_n \to r \Leftarrow C$ the k-th program rule for f, T a new variable

Patterns:

$$(\mathbf{TR_2})\quad \frac{}{\bot \Rightarrow^{\mathcal{T}} \bot} \qquad (\mathbf{TR_3})\quad \frac{}{X \Rightarrow^{\mathcal{T}} X}\ \text{If X} \in \text{Var} \qquad (\mathbf{TR_4})\quad \frac{t_1 \Rightarrow^{\mathcal{T}} s_1 \ \dots\ t_m \Rightarrow^{\mathcal{T}} s_m}{h\,\overline{t}_m \Rightarrow^{\mathcal{T}} h\,\overline{s}_m}\ \text{If } h \in DC^m$$

$$(\mathbf{TR_5})\quad \frac{t_1 \Rightarrow^{\mathcal{T}} s_1 \ \dots\ t_m \Rightarrow^{\mathcal{T}} s_m}{h\,\overline{t}_m \Rightarrow^{\mathcal{T}} h^{\mathcal{T}}_m\,\overline{s}_m}\ \text{If } h \in DC^n \text{ with } n > m, \text{ or } h \in FS^n \text{ with } n > m+1 \qquad (\mathbf{TR_6})\quad \frac{t_1 \Rightarrow^{\mathcal{T}} s_1 \ \dots\ t_m \Rightarrow^{\mathcal{T}} s_m}{f\,\overline{t}_m \Rightarrow^{\mathcal{T}} f^{\mathcal{T}}\,\overline{s}_m}\ \text{If } f \in FS^{m+1}$$

Conditions:

$$(\mathbf{TR_7})\quad \frac{C_1 \Rightarrow^{\mathcal{T}} (D_1 \,;\, (r_1,T_1),\dots,(r_k,T_k)) \quad C_2 \Rightarrow^{\mathcal{T}} (D_2 \,;\, (r_{k+1},T_{k+1}),\dots,(r_m,T_m))}{C_1, C_2 \ \Rightarrow^{\mathcal{T}} \ (D_1, D_2 \,;\, (r_1,T_1),\ \dots,\ (r_m,T_m))}$$

$$(\mathbf{TR_8})\quad \frac{l \Rightarrow^{\mathcal{T}} u \quad r \Rightarrow^{\mathcal{T}} v}{l == r \Rightarrow^{\mathcal{T}} (u == v \,;\,)} \qquad (\mathbf{TR_9})\quad \frac{e \Rightarrow^{\mathcal{T}} u \quad t \Rightarrow^{\mathcal{T}} v}{e \to t \Rightarrow^{\mathcal{T}} (u \to v \,;\,)}\ \text{If } e \in Pat_\bot$$

$$(\mathbf{TR_{10}})\quad \frac{s \Rightarrow^{\mathcal{T}} u \qquad t \Rightarrow^{\mathcal{T}} v}{X\ s \to t \ \Rightarrow^{\mathcal{T}} \ (X\ u \to (v,T) \,;\, (v,T))}\quad \text{If } X \in Var,\ T \text{ new variable}$$

$$(\mathbf{TR_{11}})\quad \frac{t_1 \Rightarrow^{\mathcal{T}} s_1 \ \dots\ t_n \Rightarrow^{\mathcal{T}} s_n \quad t \Rightarrow^{\mathcal{T}} v}{f\,\overline{t}_n \to t \ \Rightarrow^{\mathcal{T}} \ (f^{\mathcal{T}}\,\overline{s}_n \to (v,T) \,;\, (v,T))}\quad \text{If } f \in FS^n,\ T \text{ new variable}$$

Figure 1. Program transformation

condition $C^{\mathcal{T}}$ followed by a lists of pairs (r_i, T_i). The idea is that each (r_i, T_i) corresponds to the transformation of a function call occurring in C. In particular T_i is a new variable that will contain the state associated to the function call whose result is r_i. Finally, (TR_1) introduces a new local definition

$$\text{process}_{f_k}\ (\texttt{clean}\ [(\texttt{dVal}\ r_1,T_1),\dots,\ (\texttt{dVal}\ r_m,T_m)]) \to T$$

This local definition combines the states $T_1,\dots,T_m$, but only after filtering those states that correspond to non-evaluated function calls. This is done by function `clean`, which is defined as follows:

DEFINITION 3. *The function* `clean`.

```
clean []          = []
clean [(A,B)|Xs] =
  if (isBottom A) 'or' (isAuxiliary A)
  then Rest else [B | Rest]
  where Rest = clean Xs
```

The input argument of `clean` is a list of pairs (A, B), where A is the result of applying `dVal` to the result of a function call, and B is the state associated with the same function call. Thus, clean eliminates all the states corresponding to auxiliary functions and also to non-evaluated function calls. The function $process_{f_k}$ must have type $[\tau] \to \tau$, meaning that it takes a list of states of type τ and returns a state of the same type. We use the double subindex to indicate that different rules of the same function can have different associated processing functions. The definition of the *process* functions is not provided by the transformation, they depend on each particular problem, and must be supplied by the user. When codifying $process_{f_k}$, the user must take into account that the size of its input list can change in the presence of higher-order variables or non-strict computations. We require the following *completeness property* for $process_{f_k}$: for every list L of type τ, $\mathcal{P} \vdash (process_{f_k}\ L) == s$ holds for some total pattern s.

Observe that Figure 1 does not include transformation rules for general expressions. This is because we are considering normalized programs, which limits the form of the possible expressions. In particular we only need to consider approximations either of the form $X\ s \to t$ with $X \in Var$ and $t, s \in Pat_\bot$, or of the form $f\,\overline{t}_n \to t$ with $f \in FS^n$ and $t_i \in Pat_\bot$ for $1 \le i \le n$. These two forms correspond to rules (TR_{10}) and (TR_{11}), respectively. The purpose of the transformation rules for patterns (TR_2)-(TR_6) is only the substitution of partial applications by the new auxiliary functions introduced in Subsection 3.2.

DEFINITION 4. *Given a normalized functional-logic program $\mathcal{P}$ such that* `dVal` *is not in the signature of P, the transformed program $\mathcal{P}^{\mathcal{T}}$ is defined as a new program containing:*

- *The same datatype and infix operator declarations as in $\mathcal{P}$.*
- *The* `clean` *function defined above.*
- *The functions in $\mathcal{P}_{aux}$.*
- *For each program rule in $\mathcal{P}$, its corresponding transformed rule obtained applying the transformation defined in Figure 1.*

We use the notation $P \Rightarrow^{\mathcal{T}} \mathcal{P}^{\mathcal{T}}$ to indicate that $\mathcal{P}^{\mathcal{T}}$ is the transformed of $\mathcal{P}$.

Finally, it is necessary to define the transformation of normalized goals (a goal is normalized is satisfies the two conditions of Definition 1). Although syntactically a goal has the form of a program condition, its transformation requires a different treatment.

DEFINITION 5. *Let G be a normalized goal. Suppose that applying the rules of Figure 1 we have*

$$G \Rightarrow^{\mathcal{T}} (G^{\mathcal{T}} ; (r_1, T_1), \ldots, (r_m, T_m))$$

Then we define the transformation of G as the goal

$$G^{\mathcal{T}}, T_1 == R_1, \ldots, T_n == R_n$$

with R_i new variables for $i = 1 \ldots n$.

The idea is that we obtain the states T_i *after* the transformed goal has been computed. This ensures that the evaluation of `dVal`, which is associated with the computation of the T_i, will find in head normal form exactly all the expressions that are needed by the initial computation, and as active expressions the function calls whose states must be ignored to keep the laziness.

4. Examples Revisited

Now we can apply the transformation to the examples presented in the introduction of the paper. Since our purpose was to count the number of calls to rules of function `plus` the states will represent integers, and the functions `process` will represent the sum of all the integers in a list. This can be defined as usual in functional programming: `process = foldl (+) 0`. A variation of this function is used in the second rule for `plus`, indicating that the result must be incremented by one (to count the computation of the own rule).

EXAMPLE 7. *Transformed program.*

```
data nat = zero | s nat

plusT zero  Y = (Y,1)
plusT (s X) Y = (s(A), T)
                where
                  (A,B)= plusT X Y
                  T = processOne (clean [(dVal A,B)])

multiT zero Y = (zero,0)
multiT (s X) Y =
   (A2,process (clean [(dVal A1,B1),(dVal A2,B2)]))
   where
     (A1,B1) = multiT X Y
     (A2,B2) = plusT Y A1

undefT = (X,process (clean [(dVal X,Y)]))
         where (X,Y) = undefT

fT = (A2,process (clean [(dVal A1,B1),(dVal A2,B2)]))
     where
       (A1,B1) = undefT
       (A2,B2) = multiT zero A1

mapT F []      = ([],0)
mapT F [X | Xs] =
  ([A1 | A2],process (clean [(dVal A1,B1),(dVal A2,B2)]))
    where
       (A1,B1) = F X
       (A2,B2) = mapT F Xs

gT = (A1,process (clean [(dVal A1,B1)]))
    where (A1,B1) = mapT (plusT (s zero)) [s zero]


hT = (A1,process (clean [(dVal A1,B1)]))
     where (A1,B1) = lmapT (auxPlus0) [s zero]

auxPlus0 X = (plus X, bottom)

process    = foldl (+) 0
processOne = foldl (+) 1
```

In the example we only include one auxiliary function, `auxPlus0`, because it is the only one required by the examples (in general all of them must be included because they can be used in some goal).

Next we apply the Definition 5 for transforming the goals tried in the introduction.

EXAMPLE 8. *Goal* `plus (s zero) (s zero)==R`.
First the goal is normalized, obtaining: `A==R where A=plus (s zero) (s zero)`. *Now we apply the Definition 5 obtaining the transformed goal:*

```
A == R, T == R1
    where  (A,T) = plusT (s zero) (s zero)
```

which in $\mathcal{TOY}$ yields the expected result: `{R -> s (s zero), R1 -> 2 }` *, meaning that the result is* `(s (s zero))` *and that the computation has used the function* `plus` *twice.*

EXAMPLE 9. *Goal* `f == zero`.
After normalizing the goal we obtain `F == zero where F = f`. *Applying the Definition 5 we have the transformed goal:* `F == zero, T==R1 where (F,T) = fT`.

In Example 3 it was shown that the first, naive, transformation produced a non-terminating computation. However, now the computation is terminating, and we obtain the solution `{ R1 -> 0 }` *meaning that no rule of* `plus` *was needed during the computation.*

EXAMPLE 10. *Goal* `h == [plus (s zero)]`
Normalizing we have `H == [plus (s zero)] where H = h`, *and applying Definition 5:* `H == [plus (s zero)], T==R1 where (H,T) = hT` . *In our first attempt in Example 4 the transformed program could not compute any result (in fact it was ill-typed). Now the goal is well-typed and yields the solution* `R1 -> 0` *, meaning again that no rules of* `plus` *have been needed to solve the goal.*

5. Theoretical Results

In this section we introduce the theoretical result that supports our framework, including proof sketches. The main goal is to prove that the original program $\mathcal{P}$ and the transformed program $\mathcal{P}^{\mathcal{T}}$ are somehow equivalent. This will be achieved in the last two theorems at the end of the section. First we introduce some auxiliary results.

5.1 Computations involving `dVal`

The first difficulty when reasoning about the transformed program is that computations in $\mathcal{P}^{\mathcal{T}}$ do not admit CRWL proofs due to the presence of the impure primitive `dVal`. Therefore, we define a variant of CRWL that includes a specific rule for dealing with this primitive:

DEFINITION 6.

1. *The* reversible patterns *over $\Sigma^{\mathcal{T}}$ are the members of the set $Pat_{\text{inv}} \subset Pat_{\perp}^{\mathcal{T}}$ defined as:*

   $$Pat_{\text{inv}} = \perp \mid X \mid h_m^{\mathcal{T}}\, \bar{t}_m \mid c\, \bar{t}_m \mid f^{\mathcal{T}}\, \bar{t}_m$$

   where $X \in Var$, $h_m^{\mathcal{T}}$ is an auxiliary function introduced during the transformation $\mathcal{P} \Rightarrow^{\mathcal{T}} \mathcal{P}^{\mathcal{T}}$, $t_i \in Pat_{\text{inv}}$ for $i = 1 \ldots m$, $c \in DC^m$, and $f \in FS^{m+1}$.
2. *The* reversible substitutions *are the members of the set $Subst_{\text{inv}} \subset Subst_{\perp}^{\mathcal{T}}$ defined as:*

   $$Subst_{\text{inv}} = \{\theta \in Subst_{\perp}^{\mathcal{T}} \mid \theta(X) \in Pat_{\text{inv}}, X \in dom(\theta)\}$$

3. *Given a program rule (R) $\in \mathcal{P}^{\mathcal{T}}$, we denote by $NV_{(R)}$ the set of new variables introduced during the transformation that yielded (R), and by $OV_{(R)}$ the rest of variables in (R) (which correspond to variables in the original rule).*
4. *The set of* admitted instances *of $\mathcal{P}^{\mathcal{T}}$ is*

$$\{ (R)(\theta_1 \uplus \theta_2) \mid \begin{array}{l} (R) \in \mathcal{P}^{\mathcal{T}}, \\ dom(\theta_1) \subseteq OV_{(R)},\ \theta_1 \in Subst_{\text{inv}}, \\ dom(\theta_2) \subseteq NV_{(R)},\ \theta_2 \in Subst_{\perp}^{\mathcal{T}} \ \} \end{array}$$

5. *Given $s \in Pat_{\text{inv}}$, the transformation $s^{\mathcal{T}^{-1}}$ is defined as follows:*

$$\begin{array}{lll} (INV_1)\ s^{\mathcal{T}^{-1}} & = s & \text{if } s \in Pat_{\perp}. \\ (INV_2)\ (h_m^{\mathcal{T}}\ \overline{t}_m)^{\mathcal{T}^{-1}} & = h\ \overline{t}_m^{\mathcal{T}^{-1}} & \text{if } h \in DC \cup FS. \\ (INV_3)\ (f^{\mathcal{T}}\ \overline{t}_m)^{\mathcal{T}^{-1}} & = f\ \overline{t}_m^{\mathcal{T}^{-1}} & \text{if } f \in FS. \\ (INV_4)\ (c\ \overline{t}_m)^{\mathcal{T}^{-1}} & = c\ \overline{t}_m^{\mathcal{T}^{-1}} & \text{if } c \in DC,\ c\ \overline{t}_m \notin Pat_{\perp}. \end{array}$$

6. *We define the semantic calculus $dValSC$ including the rules of CRWL described in Subsection 2.3, plus the following additional rule:*

   DV `dVal` $s \rightarrow u$ *with* $u \sqsubseteq \ulcorner s^{\mathcal{T}^{-1}} \urcorner$ *and* $s \in Pat_{\text{inv}}$

   Moreover, the inference rule FA of $dValSC$ will employ admitted instances instead general instances. We use the notation $P \vdash_{dValSC} \varphi$ to indicate that φ admits a proof in $dValSC$.

Thus, the $dValSC$ calculus is an extension of CRWL with an additional rule for `dVal`, and with the restriction of limiting FA to admitted instances. It is easy to check that CRWL and $dValSC$ define the same semantics for programs without `dVal`, since:

i) The inference rule **DV** will not be employed.

ii) It is possible to check that any CRWL-proof can be transformed into an equivalent one using only admissible instances.

The set of the reversible patterns Pat_{inv} represent to the set of patterns in $\mathcal{P}^{\mathcal{T}}$ that can be obtained as the transformation of a pattern in $\mathcal{P}$. Observe that $Pat_{inv} \neq Pat_{\perp}^{\mathcal{T}}$, since the signature of the transformed program contains new symbols as `dVal`,or `clean`. The definition also introduces the transformation $^{\mathcal{T}^{-1}}$, which converts reversible patterns in Pat_{inv} into values of $Pat_{\perp}^{\mathcal{T}}$. The following proposition indicates that $^{\mathcal{T}^{-1}}$ behaves as expected:

PROPOSITION 1. *Let $\mathcal{P}, \mathcal{P}^{\mathcal{T}}$ be such that $\mathcal{P} \Rightarrow^{\mathcal{T}} \mathcal{P}^{\mathcal{T}}$. Let $\Sigma = \langle DC, FS \rangle$ be the signature of $\mathcal{P}$, $Pat_{\perp}$ the set of partial patterns over Σ and Pat_{inv} as in Definition 6. Then:*

1. *For every $t \in Pat_{\perp}$, $t^{\mathcal{T}} \in Pat_{\text{inv}}$ and $(t^{\mathcal{T}})^{\mathcal{T}^{-1}} = t$.*
2. *For every $t \in Pat_{\text{inv}}$, $t^{\mathcal{T}^{-1}} \in Pat_{\perp}$ and $(t^{\mathcal{T}^{-1}})^{\mathcal{T}} = t$.*

Proof sketch: The first point can be proven using structural induction on $t \in Pat_{\perp}$, and checking in each case the transformation rule (TR_2)-(TR_6) of Figure 1 can be applied to t for obtaining $t^{\mathcal{T}}$. Analogously, the second part can be proven using structural induction on the form of $t \in Pat_{inv}$ and checking that in each case only one rule among (INV_1)-(INV_4) is applicable. □

The next result indicates `dVal` is always applied to patterns, as expected by the inference rule (DV):

PROPOSITION 2. *Let $\mathcal{P}, \mathcal{P}^{\mathcal{T}}$ be programs such that $\mathcal{P} \Rightarrow^{\mathcal{T}} \mathcal{P}^{\mathcal{T}}$. Suppose that the symbol `dVal` is not in the signature of $\mathcal{P}$. Then all the expressions of the form (`dVal` e) in $\mathcal{P}^{\mathcal{T}}$ verify $e \equiv t^{\mathcal{T}}$ for some t, and therefore $e \in Pat_{\text{inv}}$.*

Proof sketch: We check the occurrences of `dVal` in the transformation rule (TR_1), since only this rule introduces `dVal` in $\mathcal{P}^{\mathcal{T}}$. All the occurrences of `dVal` will have the form `dVal` r_i, with r_i obtained in the premise of (TR_1) corresponding to the condition transformation. Then it is easy to check that the r_i are obtained by rules (TR_{10}) and (TR_{11}), and that in both cases they correspond to the transformation of patterns. □

The next result extends this result to proofs of atomic conditions in $dValSC$

PROPOSITION 3. *Let $\mathcal{P}, \mathcal{P}^{\mathcal{T}}$ be programs such that $\mathcal{P} \Rightarrow^{\mathcal{T}} \mathcal{P}^{\mathcal{T}}$. Let $c, c^{\mathcal{T}}$ be atomic conditions such that c is normalized and that $c \Rightarrow^{\mathcal{T}} (c^{\mathcal{T}}\ ;\ seq)$ for some value sequence seq. Let $\theta \in Subst_{\perp}^{\mathcal{T}}$ be of the form $\theta \equiv \theta_1 \uplus \theta_2$, with $dom(\theta_1) \subseteq Var(c)$ and $\theta_1(X) \in Pat_{\text{inv}}$ for every $X \in dom(\theta_1)$. Suppose that $\mathcal{P}^{\mathcal{T}} \vdash_{dValSC} c^{\mathcal{T}}\theta$.*

Then all the expressions of the form (`dVal t`) *occurring in a proof of $\mathcal{P}^{\mathcal{T}} \vdash_{dValSC} c^{\mathcal{T}}\theta$ verify* `t` *$\in Pat_{inv}$.*

Proof sketch: First observe that $c^{\mathcal{T}}\theta$ cannot contain any expression of the form (`dVal t`) since `dVal` was not in c and thus it is not in $c^{\mathcal{T}}$. Moreover, θ only can introduce `dVal` substituting some new variable, but examining the transformation we can check that new variables are never applied to any other value t and thus an expression of the form `dVal t` cannot occur. From Proposition 2, we have that in the rules of $\mathcal{P}^{\mathcal{T}}$ the calls to `dVal` are always of the form `dVal` s for $s \in Pat_{inv}$. This expressions will appear in the proof with the form (`dVal s`)$(\theta_1 \uplus \theta_2)$ due to the use of admitted instances in $dValSC$. Since s does not include new variables (it has been obtained transforming a pattern), we have $s(\theta_1 \uplus \theta_2) = s\theta_1$. Then using structural induction on $s\theta_1$ it can be proved that $s\theta_1 \in Pat_{inv}$. □

5.2 Goal Solving Systems

The purpose of functional-logic systems is to solve *goals* with respect to a given program $\mathcal{P}$. This is done by *goal solving systems* which find solutions for goals. In our setting we consider goals G which have the same syntax as program rule conditions, with the requirement that G must contain at least one strict equality $e_1 == e_2$. We assume that we use a *reasonable goal solving system*:

DEFINITION 7. *Reasonable Goal Solving Systems.*

A goal solving system (GSS in short) produces solutions *for a user goal G. A solution is a substitution θ with domain the variables occurring in the strict equalities of G. We say that a Goal Solving System is:*

- Correct w.r.t. `dVal` *if for every solution θ of G, there is a substitution ν with domain the variables occurring in the local definitions of G such that $\mathcal{P} \vdash_{dValSC} G(\theta \uplus \nu)$.*
- Complete w.r.t. `dVal` *if $\mathcal{P} \vdash_{dValSC} G(\theta \uplus \nu)$ with $dom(\theta)$ the variables not defined by local definitions in G, then θ is a solution for G in GSS.*
- Reasonable *if its complete and correct w.r.t.* `dVal`.

Thus, we assume that we have a GSS that correctly implements `dVal`. It is worth noticing that although real systems like $\mathcal{TOY}$ or Curry are correct (and correct w.r.t. `dVal` if the primitive is included), usually they are not complete but *weakly* complete, meaning that in general they produce more general solutions than those used in the semantic calculus.

5.3 Soundness and Correctness of the Technique

In this Subsection we establish the main theoretical results of the paper. We start establishing the correctness of the transformation for strict equalities and approximations involving only patterns.

LEMMA 1. *Let $\mathcal{P}, \mathcal{P}^{\mathcal{T}}$ be programs such that $\mathcal{P} \Rightarrow^{\mathcal{T}} \mathcal{P}^{\mathcal{T}}$. Let $Pat_{\perp}$ be the set of partial patterns over the signature of $\mathcal{P}$. Then for every $t, s \in Pat_{\perp}$:*

1. $\mathcal{P} \vdash s \rightarrow t$ *iff* $\mathcal{P}^{\mathcal{T}} \vdash_{dValSC} s^{\mathcal{T}} \rightarrow t^{\mathcal{T}}$.
2. $\mathcal{P} \vdash s == t$ *iff* $\mathcal{P}^{\mathcal{T}} \vdash_{dValSC} s^{\mathcal{T}} == t^{\mathcal{T}}$.

Proof sketch: First observe that $t^{\mathcal{T}}$ and $s^{\mathcal{T}}$ are patterns because t and s are patterns. Therefore, neither the inference (DV) nor the inference (FA) can be used in the semantic proofs. Then the result can be proved directly in CRWL:

1. $\mathcal{P} \vdash s \rightarrow t$ iff $\mathcal{P}^{\mathcal{T}} \vdash s^{\mathcal{T}} \rightarrow t^{\mathcal{T}}$.
2. $\mathcal{P} \vdash s == t$ iff $\mathcal{P}^{\mathcal{T}} \vdash s^{\mathcal{T}} == t^{\mathcal{T}}$.

The first result can be proven using complete induction on the size of a proof for $\mathcal{P} \vdash s \rightarrow t$, distinguishing cases depending on the form of s for the 'if' part, and on the form of $s^{\mathcal{T}}$ for the 'only if' part.

For proving the result over strict equalities, observe that the proof of $\mathcal{P} \vdash s == t$ must have at the root a (JN) inference of the form

$$\frac{s \rightarrow u \quad t \rightarrow u}{s == t}$$

with $u \in Pat$, and analogously for the proof of $\mathcal{P}^{\mathcal{T}} \vdash s^{\mathcal{T}} == t^{\mathcal{T}}$. Then the result follows as a consequence of the previous item. □

The following lemma show the relationship between the transformation and patterns affected by substitutions.

LEMMA 2. *Let $\mathcal{P}, \mathcal{P}^{\mathcal{T}}$ be such that $\mathcal{P} \Rightarrow^{\mathcal{T}} \mathcal{P}^{\mathcal{T}}$. Let $\Sigma = \langle DC,\ FS\rangle$ be the signature of $\mathcal{P}$. Let $Pat_\perp$ and $Subst_\perp$ be, respectively, the set of partial patterns and of partial substitutions over Σ. Let $Pat_\perp^{\mathcal{T}}$, $Subst_\perp^{\mathcal{T}}$ be, respectively, the set of partial patterns and of partial substitutions in $\mathcal{P}^{\mathcal{T}}$. Then for every $t \in Pat_\perp$:*

1. *For every $\theta \in Subst_\perp$, $(t\theta)^{\mathcal{T}} = t^{\mathcal{T}}\mu$, with $\mu \in Subst_{\text{inv}}$ such that:*
   - *(a) $dom(\mu) = dom(\theta)$.*
   - *(b) $\mu(X) = \theta(X)^{\mathcal{T}}$ for every $X \in dom(\mu)$.*
2. *For every $\mu \in Subst_{\text{inv}}$, $t^{\mathcal{T}}\mu = (t\theta)^{\mathcal{T}}$, with $\theta \in Subst_\perp$ such that:*
   - *(a) $dom(\theta) = dom(\mu)$.*
   - *(b) $\theta(X) = \mu(X)^{\mathcal{T}^{-1}}$ for every $X \in dom(\theta)$.*

Proof sketch:

1. By the definition of μ, $\mu \in Subst_{inv}$ since for each $X \in dom(\mu)$ we have $\mu(X) = \theta(X)^{\mathcal{T}}$, with $\theta(X) \in Pat_\perp$ and $t^{\mathcal{T}} \in Pat_{inv}$ for $t \in Pat_\perp$ (first item of Proposition 1). Then we can prove that $(t\theta)^{\mathcal{T}} = t^{\mathcal{T}}\mu$ using structural induction on t.
2. From the definition of θ we have $\theta \in Subst_\perp$, since for every $X \in dom(\theta)$, $\theta(X) = \mu(X)^{\mathcal{T}^{-1}}$, and for each $t \in Pat_{inv}$, $t^{\mathcal{T}^{-1}} \in Pat_\perp$ (by the second item of Proposition 1). Then $(t\theta)^{\mathcal{T}} = t^{\mathcal{T}}\mu$ can be checked using structural induction on t.

□

The following result is an immediate consequence of the previous lemmata:

COROLLARY 1. *Let $\mathcal{P}$, $\mathcal{P}^{\mathcal{T}}$, $Pat_\perp$, $Pat_\perp^{\mathcal{T}}$, $Subst_\perp$, θ and μ be as in the previous lemma. Let $a, b \in Pat_\perp$ and $a^{\mathcal{T}}, b^{\mathcal{T}} \in Pat_\perp^{\mathcal{T}}$ be such that $a \Rightarrow^{\mathcal{T}} a^{\mathcal{T}}$ and $b \Rightarrow^{\mathcal{T}} b^{\mathcal{T}}$. Then:*

- *$\mathcal{P} \vdash a \rightarrow b\theta$ iff $\mathcal{P}^{\mathcal{T}} \vdash_{dValSC} a^{\mathcal{T}} \rightarrow b^{\mathcal{T}}\mu$.*
- *$\mathcal{P} \vdash a\theta \rightarrow b$ iff $\mathcal{P}^{\mathcal{T}} \vdash_{dValSC} a^{\mathcal{T}}\mu \rightarrow b^{\mathcal{T}}$.*

Proof sketch:

- By Lemma 1 $\mathcal{P} \vdash a \rightarrow b\theta$ iff $\mathcal{P}^{\mathcal{T}} \vdash a^{\mathcal{T}} \rightarrow (b\theta)^{\mathcal{T}}$, and by Lemma 2 $(b\theta)^{\mathcal{T}} = b^{\mathcal{T}}\mu$, which proves the result.
- Analogously, by Lemma 1 $\mathcal{P} \vdash a\theta \rightarrow b$ iff $\mathcal{P}^{\mathcal{T}} \vdash (a\theta)^{\mathcal{T}} \rightarrow b^{\mathcal{T}}$, and by Lemma2 $(a\theta)^{\mathcal{T}} = a^{\mathcal{T}}\mu$, which proves the result.

□

Now we can extend the result to general approximations.

THEOREM 1. *Let $\mathcal{P}$ be a normalized program and f a function of arity n defined in $\mathcal{P}$. Let $\mathcal{P}, \mathcal{P}^{\mathcal{T}}$ be programs such that $\mathcal{P} \Rightarrow^{\mathcal{T}} \mathcal{P}^{\mathcal{T}}$. Let $\overline{t}_n, t$ be partial patterns in the signature of $\mathcal{P}$, with $t \neq \perp$. Then*

(i) If $P \vdash f\,\overline{t}_n \rightarrow t$ then $\mathcal{P}^{\mathcal{T}} \vdash_{dValSC} f^{\mathcal{T}}\,\overline{t_n^{\mathcal{T}}} \rightarrow (t^{\mathcal{T}}, s)$, with s a total pattern.

(ii) If $\mathcal{P}^{\mathcal{T}} \vdash_{dValSC} f^{\mathcal{T}}\,\overline{t_n^{\mathcal{T}}} \rightarrow (t^{\mathcal{T}}, s)$ with s a total pattern, then $P \vdash f\,\overline{t}_n \rightarrow t$.

Proof sketch:

In this proof sketch we represent the sets of partial patterns, constructors and function symbols in $\mathcal{P}$ by $Pat_\perp$, DC and FS, respectively.

We first establish a relation between the two parts of the result. This will be useful for proving both parts simultaneously.

(i) If $\mathcal{P} \vdash f\,\overline{t}_n \rightarrow t$ holds such as (i) indicates, the last step of its CRWL proof must be a FA inference rule application of the form:

(1) $$\frac{t_1 \rightarrow t'_1\theta \ \dots\ t_n \rightarrow t'_n\theta \quad C'\theta \quad r'\theta \rightarrow t}{f\,\overline{t}_n \rightarrow t}$$

with $(f\,\overline{t'}_n \rightarrow r' \Leftarrow C') \in \mathcal{P}$ and $\theta \in Subst_\perp$. Suppose that

(2) $$(f\,\overline{t'}_n \rightarrow r' \Leftarrow C') \Rightarrow^{\mathcal{T}} (f^{\mathcal{T}}\,\overline{s}_n \rightarrow (s, T) \Leftarrow C)$$

i.e., $(f^{\mathcal{T}}\,\overline{s}_n \rightarrow (s, T) \Leftarrow C)$ is the transformation of the program rule employed in this case. Then we prove that $\mathcal{P}^{\mathcal{T}} \vdash_{dValSC} f^{\mathcal{T}}\,\overline{t}_n^{\mathcal{T}} \rightarrow (t^{\mathcal{T}}, s)$ allows a CRWL proof, with a (FA) inference step at the root of the form:

(3)

$$\frac{(t_i^{\mathcal{T}} \rightarrow s_i(\mu \uplus \nu))_{i=1\dots n} \quad C(\mu \uplus \nu) \quad (s,T)(\mu \uplus \nu) \rightarrow (t^{\mathcal{T}}, u)}{f^{\mathcal{T}}\,\overline{t}_n^{\mathcal{T}} \rightarrow (t^{\mathcal{T}}, u)}$$

using a program instance

$$(f^{\mathcal{T}}\,\overline{s}_n \rightarrow (s, T) \Leftarrow C)(\mu \uplus \nu)$$

where

- $\mu \in Subst_{inv}$ such that $dom(\mu) = dom(\theta)$, with θ the substitution employed in (1), and $\mu(X) = \theta(X)^{\mathcal{T}}$ for each $X \in dom(\theta)$.
- $\nu \in Subst_\perp$ such that $dom(\nu) = \{T_1, \dots, T_m\}$, with $T_1, \dots, T_m$ the new *state* variables introduced during the transformation (2). The precise definition of $\nu(T_i)$ for $i = 1 \dots m$ is defined during the proof.

Notice that the definition of $(\mu \uplus \nu)$ ensures that the instance employed in (3) is an admitted instance, such as the definition of the $dValSC$ calculus (Def. 6) requires.

(ii) Suppose that $\mathcal{P}^{\mathcal{T}} \vdash_{dValSC} f^{\mathcal{T}}\,\overline{t_n^{\mathcal{T}}} \rightarrow (t^{\mathcal{T}}, s)$ holds as (ii) indicates. Then the last inference step of the proof must be an (FA) inference of the form (3), using an admitted instance $(\mu \uplus \nu)$ of a rule $(f^{\mathcal{T}}\,\overline{s}_n \rightarrow (s, T) \Leftarrow C)$ of the transformed program $\mathcal{P}^{\mathcal{T}}$. This program rule must be the transformed of a program rule in $\mathcal{P}$ as indicated in (2). By the definition of admitted instance ν and μ have the same form as in the previous case. Then we can prove that $\mathcal{P} \vdash f\,\overline{t}_n \rightarrow t$ with a proof in

CRWL that applies at the root the inference (1), using the rule whose transformed version was employed in (3), and with an instance θ such that

- $dom(\theta) = dom(\mu)$
- $\theta(X) = \mu(X)^{\mathcal{T}^{-1}}$

From the previous reasoning it is enough to prove that (1) admits a CRWL proof iff (3) admits a CRWL proof, thus proving (i) and (ii) simultaneously.

Thus, it is enough to prove that each premise (3) has a proof in CRWL iff the corresponding premise (1) can be proven in CRWL as well.

1. Premises $t_i \rightarrow t'_i\theta$ of (1) and their corresponding premises in (3).

   We must check that for each $i = 1 \ldots n$

   $$\mathcal{P}^{\mathcal{T}} \vdash_{dValSC} t_i^{\mathcal{T}} \rightarrow s_i(\mu \uplus \nu)$$

   iff

   $$\mathcal{P} \vdash t_i \rightarrow t'_i\theta$$

   Since $s_i \in Pat_\perp$ we have that its transformation rules (TR_2)-(TR_6)) does not introduce new variables, and therefore $s_i(\mu \uplus \nu) = s_i\mu$. Moreover, by ($TR_1$) we have that $s_i \equiv (t'_i)^{\mathcal{T}}$. Thus, we must prove that $\mathcal{P}^{\mathcal{T}} \vdash_{dValSC} t_i^{\mathcal{T}} \rightarrow (t'_i)^{\mathcal{T}}\mu$. By Corollary 1 this holds iff $\mathcal{P} \vdash t_i \rightarrow t'_i\theta$ (observe that θ and μ satisfy the form of the Corollary).

2. Premises corresponding to conditions $C'\theta$ in (1), and their corresponding premises $\mathcal{P}^{\mathcal{T}} \vdash_{dValSC} C(\theta \uplus \nu)$ in (3).

   By the transformation rule (TR_1) C is of the form

   $$\begin{array}{l} f^{\mathcal{T}}\, \overline{s}_n \rightarrow (s, T) \\ \quad \Leftarrow C^{\mathcal{T}}, \\ \quad\quad \text{process}_{f_k}\ (\texttt{clean}\ [(\texttt{dVal}\ r_1, T_1), \\ \quad\quad\quad \ldots, \\ \quad\quad\quad (\texttt{dVal}\ r_m, T_m)]) \rightarrow T \end{array}$$

   Thus, the first atomic conditions are obtained by the transformation of condition the condition C', and we have an additional condition corresponding to the local declaration for T.

2.a) $\mathcal{P}^{\mathcal{T}} \vdash_{dValSC} c^{\mathcal{T}}(\theta \uplus \nu)$ for $c^{\mathcal{T}}$ atomic, $c^{\mathcal{T}} \in (C')^{\mathcal{T}}$. In this case there must exist $c' \in C'$ atomic such that $c' \Rightarrow^{\mathcal{T}} c^{\mathcal{T}}$, since the rules ($TR_7$)-($TR_{11}$) transform atomic conditions into atomic conditions. Moreover, for each $c'\theta$ we have

$$\textbf{(4)} \qquad \mathcal{P} \vdash c'\theta$$

since $\mathcal{P} \vdash C'\theta$ by (1). By the sake of space we omit the proof of the subcases of this case, which are not complicated but tedious. The subcases are obtained examining the possible forms of c', which can be in a normalized program:

2.a.1) $c' \equiv a == b$ with $a, b \in Pat_\perp$.

2.a.2) $c' \equiv a \rightarrow b$, with $a \in Pat_\perp, b \in Pat_\perp$.

2.a.3) $c' \equiv X\ a \rightarrow b$, with $X \in Var, a \in Pat_\perp, b \in Pat_\perp$. By the transformation rule (TR_9) we have that

$$X\ a \rightarrow b \Rightarrow^{\mathcal{T}} (X\ a^{\mathcal{T}} \rightarrow (b^{\mathcal{T}}, T_X)\,;\,(b^{\mathcal{T}}, T_X))$$

that is,

$$c^{\mathcal{T}} \equiv X\ a^{\mathcal{T}} \rightarrow (b^{\mathcal{T}}, T_X)$$

From (4) we have that $\mathcal{P} \vdash (X\ a \rightarrow b)\theta$ with a proof included in the proof of (1). There are two possibilities depending in the possible forms of $\theta(X) \in Pat_\perp$:

- $\theta(X) = g\ \overline{a}_m$ with $g \in DC^{m+1}$, $a_i \in Pat_\perp$ for $i = 1 \ldots m$.
- $\theta(X) = g\ \overline{a}_m$ with $g \in DC^n$, $n > m + 1$, $a_i \in Pat_\perp$ for $i = 1 \ldots m$.

Observe that other forms for $\theta(X)$ like $\theta(X) = g\ \overline{a}_m$ with $g \in DC^m$, $a_i \in Pat_\perp$ for $i = 1 \ldots m$ are not possible, since then (1) will include a proof for $(g\ \overline{a}_m\ a \rightarrow b)\theta$. However, this is not possible because then we will have a constructor of arity m applied to $m + 1$ arguments.

2.a.4) $c' \equiv g\ \overline{a}_m \rightarrow b$ with $g \in FS^m$, $a_i \in Pat_\perp$ for $i = 1 \ldots m$, and $b \in Pat_\perp$.

2.b) The remainder condition is:

$$\begin{array}{l} \mathcal{P}^{\mathcal{T}} \vdash_{dValSC} \\ \quad (\text{process}_{f_k}\ (\texttt{clean} \\ \quad [(\texttt{dVal}\ r_1, T_1), \ldots, (\texttt{dVal}\ r_m, T_m)]) \rightarrow T)(\mu \uplus \nu) \end{array}$$

This case does not correspond to any premise in the original proof, but it is a consequence of the application of the completeness property for the user functions $process_{f_k}$ required in Subsection 3.3.

3. $\mathcal{P}^{\mathcal{T}} \vdash_{dValSC} (s, T)(\mu \uplus \nu) \rightarrow (t^{\mathcal{T}}, u)$ in (3) iff $P \vdash r'\theta \rightarrow t$ in (1).

   By (TR_1) we have that $r' \Rightarrow^{\mathcal{T}} (s\,;\,)$, that is $s \equiv (r')^{\mathcal{T}}$, with r' the body of the program rule (2). Then s cannot contain new variables, and we must prove

   $$\mathcal{P}^{\mathcal{T}} \vdash_{dValSC} (((r')^{\mathcal{T}})\mu, \nu(T)) \rightarrow (t^{\mathcal{T}}, u)$$

   Since we have defined ν such that $\nu(T) = u$ this corresponds to proving

   $$\mathcal{P}^{\mathcal{T}} \vdash_{dValSC} (((r')^{\mathcal{T}})\mu, u) \rightarrow (t^{\mathcal{T}}, u)$$

   The proof of this approximation, if exists, must have a DC inference at the root with premises $((r')^{\mathcal{T}})\mu \rightarrow t^{\mathcal{T}}$ and $u \rightarrow u$. The proof of $u \rightarrow u$ is obtained applying decomposition DC and reflexivity, RR. The proof of $\mathcal{P}^{\mathcal{T}} \vdash_{dValSC} ((r')^{\mathcal{T}})\mu \rightarrow t^{\mathcal{T}}$. By the Corollary 1 this holds iff

   $$\mathcal{P}^{\mathcal{T}} \vdash_{dValSC} r'\theta \rightarrow t$$

   which corresponds to the premise in (1).

Regarding the definition of ν, from of the observation of rules (TR_1)-(TR_{11}) we have that $T_1, \ldots, T_m$ occur in the right-hand side of exactly one approximation of the transformed rule conditions. Thus, there is no $\nu(T_i)$ undefined and neither of them have two different definitions for $i = 1 \ldots m$. □

THEOREM 2. *Let $\mathcal{P}, \mathcal{P}^{\mathcal{T}}$ be programs such that $\mathcal{P} \Rightarrow^{\mathcal{T}} \mathcal{P}^{\mathcal{T}}$. Let $C, C^{\mathcal{T}}$ be a conditions such that C is normalized, contains at least one strict equality, and $C \Rightarrow^{\mathcal{T}} (C^{\mathcal{T}}\,;\,(r_1, T_1), \ldots, (r_m, T_m))$. Let $G \equiv C$ a normalized goal, and let $G' \equiv C^{\mathcal{T}}, T_1 == R_1, \ldots, T_m == R_m$ be a goal where the R_i are new variables for $i = 1 \ldots m$. Let GSS be some reasonable functional-logic goal solving system. Then*

1. *If θ_1 is a solution for G then there is some substitution θ_2 such that $\theta_1 \uplus \theta_2$ is a solution for G' with $dom(\theta_2) = \{R_1, \ldots, R_m\}$.*
2. *If $\theta_1 \uplus \theta_2$ is a solution for G' with $dom(\theta_2) = \{R_1, \ldots, R_m\}$ and θ_1, then θ_1 and is a solution for G in GSS.*

Proof sketch:

The two results are consequences of Theorem 1, and of the properties of reasonable goal solving systems. We show the basic ideas proving the first result (the second one is analogous). Let θ_1 be a solution for G. Since GSS is reasonable, it is correct w.r.t. dVal and therefore $\mathcal{P} \vdash_{dValSC} G(\theta_1 \uplus \nu_1)$ for some ν_1. Since neither $\mathcal{P}$ nor G include dVal, this means $\mathcal{P} \vdash G(\theta_1 \uplus \nu_1)$. Now using Theorem 1 it is possible to obtain that $\mathcal{P}^{\mathcal{T}} \vdash_{dValSC} C^{\mathcal{T}}((\theta_1 \uplus \nu_1) \uplus \nu_2)$ with ν_2 a substitution such that $\nu_2(T_i) = s_i$ with s_i a total pattern (this result is not obvious and requires a lemma proving the relation between CRWL proofs for conditions in $\mathcal{P}$ and in $\mathcal{P}^{\mathcal{T}}$). Then defining $\theta_2(R_i) = s_i$ for $i = 1 \ldots m$ we have $\mathcal{P} \vdash_{dValSC} (C^{\mathcal{T}}, T_1 == R_1, \ldots, T_m == R_m)((\theta_1 \uplus \theta_2) \uplus (\nu_1 \uplus \nu_2))$, and the result is obtained by the completeness of GSS defining $\theta = (\theta_1 \uplus \theta_2)$ and $\nu = (\nu_1 \uplus \nu_2)$. □

In the case of weakly complete systems the proof will be analogous, but to each θ_1 solution of G will correspond a θ_1' such that $\theta_1' \leq \theta_1$ and $\theta_1' \uplus \theta_2$ is a solution for G'. Conversely, if $\theta_1 \uplus \theta_2$ is a solution for G', we will have that there is some θ_1' which is a solution for G with $\theta_1' \leq \theta_1$. The restriction to ground terms is due to the characteristics of the semantic calculus.

6. Conclusions and Future Work

We have presented a program transformation that introduces states accompanying function results in functional-logic programs. We have shown that this transformation is not trivial, in particular higher-order applications and lazy computations must be taken into account in order to achieve an equivalent transformed program. Although similar approaches have been considered in the definition of declarative debuggers for functional and functional-logic languages, the proposal presented here generalizes the results in a broader context. The transformation has been defined through a set of transformation rules, and the correctness of the results has been established.

Most functional-logic languages are typed languages. However, in this work we have omitted considerations about types in the transformation. The reason is that this problem was already addressed in detail in [6] for the particular case of computation trees. The generalization to a different type is straightforward. In particular if the type of every $\texttt{process}_{f_k}$ function occurring in the transformed program is the same, then we can prove that the transformation of a well-typed program is always well-typed, with the proof analogous to the proof of Theorem 4.2 in [6].

Regarding future work this proposal has two possible application fields:

- In techniques/tools that rely on states for obtaining results about computations, such as the introduction of attribute grammars [18] in functional-logic parsers [5], Theorem 2 can be used as auxiliary result for proving soundness results.
- A different possibility will be to implement the transformation, leaving the definition of the *process* functions to the user. In this way the technique could be used as a "functional-logic pattern" for introducing states.

It would also be interesting to study the transformation in the context of functional-logic programming, and in particular to study the relationship between the transformation and the state monad [16, 19].

References

[1] M. Abengózar-Carneros et al. Toy: A multiparadigm declarative language. version 1.0. Technical Report SIP-119/00, Universidad Complutense de Madrid, Departamento de Sistemas Informáticos y Programación, UCM, February 2002.

[2] E. Albert, M. Hanus, and G. Vidal. A residualizing semantics for the partial evaluation of functional logic programs. *Inf. Process. Lett.*, 85 (1):19–25, 2003.

[3] E. Albert, M. Hanus, F. Huch, J. Oliver, and G. Vidal. Operational semantics for declarative multi-paradigm languages. *Journal of Symbolic Computation*, 40:795–829, 2005.

[4] S. Antoy and M. Hanus. Functional logic programming. *Commun. ACM*, 53(4):74–85, 2010.

[5] R. Caballero and F. Lpez-Fraguas. A functional-logic perspective of parsing. In A. Middeldorp and T. Sato, editors, *Functional and Logic Programming*, volume 1722 of *Lecture Notes in Computer Science*, pages 85–99. Springer Berlin / Heidelberg, 1999.

[6] R. Caballero and M. Rodríguez-Artalejo. A Declarative Debugging System for Lazy Functional Logic Programs. *Electronic Notes in Theoretical Computer Science*, 64:113 – 175, 2002.

[7] R. Caballero-Roldán. *Técnicas de Diagnóstico y Depuración Declarativas para lenguajes lógico-funcionales.* PhD thesis, Departamento de Sistemas Informáticos y Programación, Universidad Complutense de Madrid, 2004.

[8] J. González-Moreno, M. Hortalá-González, F. López-Fraguas, and M. Rodríguez-Artalejo. A rewriting logic for declarative programming. In *Proc. European Symposium on Programming (ESOP'96)*, volume 1058 of *LNCS*, pages 156–172. Springer, 1996.

[9] J. González-Moreno, M. Hortalá-González, F. López-Fraguas, and M. Rodríguez-Artalejo. An approach to declarative programming based on a rewriting logic. *Journal of Logic Programming*, 40(1): 47–87, 1999.

[10] M. Hamana. *Semantics for Interactive Higher-order Functional-Logic Programming.* PhD thesis, University of Tsukuba, 1998.

[11] M. Hanus. Curry: An Integrated Functional Logic Language (version 0.8.2, 2006). Available at: http://www.curry-language.org, 2006.

[12] M. Hanus. Multi-paradigm declarative languages. In *ICLP'07: Proceedings of the 23rd international conference on Logic programming*, pages 45–75, Berlin, Heidelberg, 2007. Springer-Verlag.

[13] S. P. Jones, editor. *Haskell 98 Language and Libraries: The Revised Report.* http://haskell.org/, September 2002. URL `http://haskell.org/definition/haskell98-report.pdf`.

[14] R. Loogen, F. J. López-Fraguas, and M. Rodríguez-Artalejo. A demand driven computation strategy for lazy narrowing. In *PLILP '93: Proceedings of the 5th International Symposium on Programming Language Implementation and Logic Programming*, pages 184–200, London, UK, 1993. Springer-Verlag.

[15] F. López-Fraguas, J. Rodríguez-Hortalá, and J. Sánchez-Hernández. Rewriting and call-time choice: The ho case. In J. Garrigue and M. Hermenegildo, editors, *Functional and Logic Programming*, volume 4989 of *Lecture Notes in Computer Science*, pages 147–162. Springer Berlin / Heidelberg, 2008.

[16] E. Moggi. Notions of computation and monads. *Information and Computation*, 93:55–92, 1989.

[17] L. Naish and T. Barbour. A declarative debugger for a logical-functional language. In *Eight International Conferencie on Industrial and Engineering Applications of Artificial Intelligence and Expert System - Invited and Additional Papers*, volume 2, pages 91–99. DSTO General Document 51, 1995.

[18] J. Paakki. Attribute grammar paradigmsa high-level methodology in language implementation. *ACM Comput. Surv.*, 27:196–255, June 1995.

[19] P. Wadler. Comprehending monads. In *LFP '90: Proceedings of the 1990 ACM conference on LISP and functional programming*, pages 61–78, New York, NY, USA, 1990. ACM.

Type Classes in Functional Logic Programming

Enrique Martin-Martin
Dpto. Sistemas Informáticos y Computación, Universidad Complutense de Madrid, Madrid, Spain
emartinm@fdi.ucm.es

Abstract

Type classes provide a clean, modular and elegant way of writing overloaded functions. Functional logic programming languages (FLP in short) like Toy or Curry have adopted the Damas-Milner type system, so it seems natural to adopt also type classes in FLP. However, type classes has been barely introduced in FLP. A reason for this lack of success is that the usual translation of type classes using *dictionaries* presents some problems in FLP like the absence of expected answers due to a bad interaction of dictionaries with the call-time choice semantics for non-determinism adopted in FLP systems.

In this paper we present a *type-passing* translation of type classes based on *type-indexed functions* and *type witnesses* that is well-typed with respect to a new liberal type system recently proposed for FLP. We argue the suitability of this translation for FLP because it improves the dictionary-based one in three aspects. First, it obtains programs which run as fast or faster—with an speedup from 1.05 to 2.30 in our experiments. Second, it solves the mentioned problem of missing answers. Finally, the proposed translation generates shorter and simpler programs.

Categories and Subject Descriptors D.3.3 [*Language Constructs and Features*]: Polymorphism; D.3.2 [*Language Classifications*]: Multiparadigm languages

General Terms Languages, Design, Performance.

Keywords Type Classes, Functional Logic Programming, Type-indexed functions.

1. Introduction

Type classes [10, 30] are one of the most successful features in Haskell. They provide an easy syntax to define overloaded functions—*classes*—and the implementation of those functions for different types—*instances*. Type classes are usually implemented by means of a source-to-source transformation that introduces extra parameters—called *dictionaries*—to overloaded functions [10, 30], generating Damas-Milner [7] correct programs. Dictionaries are data structures containing the implementation of overloaded functions for specific types and dictionaries for the superclasses. The efficiency of translated programs—using several optimizations [4, 11]—and the fact that the translation handles correctly multiple modules and separate compilation, have resulted in that nowadays it is the most used technique for implementing type classes in functional programming (FP). Another scheme for translating type classes is passing type information as extra arguments to overloaded functions [29]. In this scheme, overloaded functions use a *typecase* construction in order to pattern-match types and decide which concrete behavior—*instance*—to use. Although it is possible to encode it using *generalized algebraic data types* (GADTs) [6, 14] or Guarded Recursive Datatype Constructors [31], this translation scheme has not succeeded in the FP community.

Functional logic programming (FLP) [12] aims to combine the best of declarative paradigms (functional, logic and constraint languages) in a single model. FLP languages like Toy [22] or Curry [13] have a strong resemblance to lazy functional languages like Haskell [15]. However, a remarkable difference is that functional logic programs can be non-confluent, giving raise to so-called *non-deterministic functions*, for which a *call-time choice* semantics [8] is adopted. The following program is a simple example, using Peano natural numbers given by the constructors z and s[1]: $coin \to z$, $coin \to s\ z$, $dup\ X \to pair\ X\ X$—where *pair* is the constructor symbol for pairs. Here, *coin* is a non-deterministic function (*coin* evaluates to z and $s\ z$) and, according to call-time choice, *dup coin* evaluates to *pair z z* and *pair (s z) (s z)* but not to *pair z (s z)* or *pair (s z) z*. Operationally, call-time choice means that all copies of a non-deterministic subexpression (*coin* in the example) created during reduction share the same value.

Functional logic languages have adopted the Damas-Milner type system, although it presents some problems when applied directly [9, 21]. However, with the exception of some preliminary proposals as [26]—presenting some ideas about type classes and FLP not further developed—and [23]—showing some problems that the dictionary approach produces when applied to FLP systems—type classes have not been incorporated in FLP. From the point of view of the systems, only an experimental branch of [1] and the experimental systems [2, 3] have tried to adopt type classes. One reason for this limited success is the problems presented in [23]. In addition to them, another important issue to address is the lack of expected answers when combining non-determinism and *nullary*[2] overloaded functions [24]. This problem is shown in the program in Fig. 1, taken from [24]. We use a syntax of type classes and instances similar to Haskell but following the mentioned syntactic convention adopted in the Toy system. The program contains an overloaded function `arb` which is a non-deterministic generator, and its instance for booleans. It also contains a function `arbL2` which returns a list of two elements of the same instance of `arb`. Fig. 1-b) contains the translated program following the standard translation using dictionaries [10, 30]. The `arb` type class generates a data declaration for `arb` dictionaries—`dictArb`—and a projecting function `arb` to extract the concrete implementation from the dictionary. The instance `arb bool` gen-

PEPM'11, January 24–25, 2011, Austin, Texas, USA.

[1] We follow the syntactic conventions of Toy where identifiers are lowercased and variables are uppercased.

[2] i.e. of arity 0.

```
class arb A where
  arb :: A

instance arb bool where
  arb → false
  arb → true

arbL2 :: arb A => list A
arbL2 → [arb, arb]
```

a) Original program

```
data dictArb A = dictArb A

arb :: dictArb A -> A
arb (dictArb F) → F

arbBool :: bool
arbBool → false
arbBool → true

dictArbBool :: dictArb bool
dictArbBool → dictArb arbBool

arbL2 :: dictArb A -> list A
arbL2 DA → [arb DA, arb DA]
```

b) Translated program using dictionaries

Figure 1. Program containing a type class with a constant non-deterministic overloaded function

erates a concrete dictionary—`dictArbBool`—and the `arbL2` function is transformed to accept an `arb` dictionary as first argument and pass it to the `arb` functions in its right-hand side. Expected results for the expression `arbL2::(list bool)` are `[true, true]`, `[true, false]`, `[false, true]` and `[false, false]`, however its evaluation in the translated program only produces `[true, true]` and `[false, false]`. The reason is the call-time choice semantics. The translated expression `arbL2 dictArbBool` reduces to `[arb dictArbBool, arb dictArbBool]`, but both copies of `dictArbBool` must share their value. Therefore they cannot be reduced to `dictArb true` and `dictArb false` in the different occurrences of the right-hand side, losing two expected solutions.

In this paper we propose and evaluate a type-passing translation of type classes for FLP based on type-indexed functions—functions with a different behavior for different types [14]—and type witnesses—representations of types as data values—that is well-typed in a new liberal type system recently proposed for FLP [20]. The proposed translation is not integrated in the type checking phase as in [10, 30], but it is a separated phase after type checking. This previous type checking phase is assumed to use a standard type system supporting type classes [5, 27], and decorates the function symbols with the inferred types.

We show that the proposed translation is a suitable option for FLP compared to the classical dictionary-based translation because of three reasons. First, it obtains programs which run as fast or faster—with and speedup ranging from 1.05 to 2.30 in our experiments. When we apply optimizations to both translated programs the speedup still remains favorable to the proposed translation. Second, it solves the mentioned problem of missing answers when combining non-determinism and nullary overloaded functions. Finally, the proposed translation has a similar complexity to the dictionary-based one, but generates shorter and simpler programs.

The following list summarizes the main contributions of the paper and at the same time presents the structure of the paper.

- We formalize a type-passing translation for type classes in FLP in Sect. 3. Although the broad idea of using such kind of translation is not a novelty [29], its concrete realization and the application to FLP, relying in a new type system [20], are new. In particular, the liberality of the type system avoids the need of a *typecase* construction in the target language, resulting in that translated programs do not need to enhance the syntax of FLP systems with that construction.
- We have measured the execution time of a collection of different programs involving overloaded functions that can be part of bigger real FLP programs—see Sect 4.1. Some of these programs have been adapted from the *nobench* suite of benchmark programs for Haskell. The speedup results—from 1.05 to 2.30—show that when no optimizations are applied, programs translated using the proposed type-passing scheme perform faster than those translated using the dictionary-based translation.
- There are several well-known optimizations than can be applied to translated programs using the dictionary-based scheme [4, 11]. In Sect. 4.1 we present some optimizations to the proposed type-passing translation. We have repeated the execution time measurements to the optimized programs, and we have checked that the proposed translation still obtains faster programs even when optimizations are applied.
- We study how the proposed translation solves the problem of missing answers that appears when combining non-determinism and nullary overloaded functions—see Sect. 4.2.
- In Sect. 5 we discuss some additional aspects—including some problems—that arise with the translations of type classes in FLP.

Type variable	$\alpha, \beta, \gamma \ldots$		
Type constructor	C		
Class name	κ , $\kappa^\bullet$		
Simple type	τ	$::= \alpha \mid \tau \rightarrow \tau'$	
		$\mid C\ \overline{\tau_n}$	with n = arity(C), n ≥ 0
Context	θ	$::= \langle \overline{\kappa_n\ \alpha_n} \rangle$	with n ≥ 0
Saturated context	ϕ	$::= \langle \overline{\kappa_n\ \tau_n} \rangle$	with n ≥ 0
Overloaded type	ρ	$::= \phi \Rightarrow \tau$	
Type scheme	σ	$::= \forall \overline{\alpha_n}.\tau$	with n ≥ 0

Figure 2. Syntax of types

2. Preliminaries

This section introduces the syntax of types, the source language and the target language of the proposed translation. It also introduces the liberal type system in which the translated programs are well-typed.

2.1 Syntax

Fig. 2 gives the syntax of types, which are the usual ones when using type classes [10]. The only difference is that class names can have a mark $^\bullet$. We use this mark in the translation to distinguish between which class constraints generate a type information to pass to overloaded functions, as we will explain in Sect. 3. Overloaded types are simple types enclosed with a *saturated* context. Notice that in a saturated context class restrictions not only affect type variables but they can affect simple types as *list bool* or *pair int (list nat)*. Contexts, which express class constraints over type variables, will be used in class and instance declarations. Type schemes are the same as in the Damas-Milner type system [7], and play the usual role to handle *parametric* polymorphism.

The syntax of source programs of the translation is shown in Fig. 3. It is the usual syntax for programs with type classes of one argument [10] adapted to Toy's syntax. We assume a denumerable set of data variables (X), and a set of function symbols

$$
\begin{array}{rl}
\text{function symbol} & f \\
\text{constructor symbol} & c \\
\text{data variable} & X \\
\\
\text{program} ::= & \overline{data}\ \overline{class}\ \overline{inst}\ \overline{type}\ \overline{rule} \\
\text{data} ::= & \texttt{data}\ C\ \overline{\alpha} = c_1\ \overline{\tau} \mid \ldots \mid c_k\ \overline{\tau} \\
\text{class} ::= & \texttt{class}\ \theta \Rightarrow \kappa\ \alpha\ \texttt{where}\ \overline{f :: \tau} \\
\text{inst} ::= & \texttt{instance}\ \theta \Rightarrow \kappa\ (C\ \overline{\alpha})\ \texttt{where} \\
 & \quad \overline{f\ \overline{t} \to e} \quad \text{with } \overline{t} \text{ linear} \\
\text{type} ::= & f :: \theta \Rightarrow \tau \\
\text{rule } r ::= & (f :: \rho)\ \overline{t} \to e \quad \text{with } \overline{t} \text{ linear} \\
\text{pattern } t ::= & X \mid c\ \overline{t_n} \quad \text{with n} \le \text{arity(c)} \\
 & \mid f\ \overline{t_n} \quad \text{with n} < \text{arity(f)} \\
\text{expression } e ::= & X \mid c \mid f :: \rho \mid e\ e \mid let\ X = e\ in\ e
\end{array}
$$

Figure 3. Syntax of source programs

(f) and constructor symbols (c), all them with associated arity. We say that a function is a *member* of a type class if it is declared inside that type class declaration, and it is an *overloaded function* if its inferred type has class constraints in the context. Notice that member function are overloaded functions, since they have exactly one class constraint in the context of its type. Patterns—our notion of values—are a subset of expressions. Notice that constructor and function symbols partially applied to patterns—called HO-patterns—are considered as patterns in our setting, the HO Constructor-based conditional ReWriting Logic (HO-CRWL) approach to FLP [25] followed by the Toy system. This corresponds to an intensional view of functions, i.e., different descriptions of the same 'extensional' function can be distinguished by the semantics. In program rules (r) the set of patterns $\overline{t}$ is linear (there is not repetition of variables) and there are not extra variables in the right-hand side. However we do not support HO-patterns made with overloaded function symbols in the left-hand side of rules, due to some complications that arise during translation—see Sect 5.3. A particularity of the syntax is that function symbols in rules and expressions are always decorated with an overloaded type. We assume that this decoration comes from a previous type checking phase, and reflects to which types are functions applied. In the type checking stage the type checker decorates function symbols with a variant of its type, and instantiate it with the proper type of the application. For example if `eq` has the usual type $\langle eq\ A\rangle \Rightarrow A \to A \to bool$, a rule for a function `g`:

```
g X → eq X [true]
```

will have the decoration

$$\texttt{g::}\langle\rangle \Rightarrow (list\ bool) \to bool\ \ \texttt{X}\ \to$$
$$\quad \texttt{eq::}\langle eq\ (list\ bool)\rangle \Rightarrow (list\ bool) \to (list\ bool) \to bool\ \ \texttt{X [true]}$$

In the right-hand side of `g`, the saturated context $\langle eq\ (list\ bool)\rangle$ indicates that the overloaded `eq` function is applied to elements of type $list\ bool$, so it needs that type information. The function `g` in the left hand side does not have any context because its context is *reduced* during type checking—see Sect. 3.3—and became empty, so it does not appear in the inferred type for `g`.

The syntax of target programs is similar to source programs, except that there are not class or instance declarations, function symbols in rules and expressions are not decorated with type information and type declarations for functions are only simple types.

2.2 Liberal type system for FLP

The type system considered for the target language is a new simple extension of the Damas-Milner type system recently proposed for FLP [20]. The typing rules for expressions correspond to the well-known variation of Damas-Milner type system [7] with syntax-directed rules. The type inference algorithm $\Vdash$ follows the same

```
size :: A -> nat
size false → s z
size true → s z
size z → s z
size (s X) → s (size X)

eq :: A -> A -> bool
eq true true → true
eq false false → true
eq z z → true
eq (s X) (s Y) → eq X Y
```

Figure 4. Examples of type-indexed functions

ideas that algorithm $\mathcal{W}$ [7], however we have given the type inference a relational style $\mathcal{A} \Vdash e : \tau|\pi$. This algorithm accepts a set of type scheme assumptions $\mathcal{A}$ over symbols s_i which can be variables or constructor/function symbols—$\{\overline{s_n : \sigma_n}\}$—and an expression e, returning a simple type τ and a type substitution π—$[\overline{\alpha_n/\tau_n}]$. Intuitively, τ is the "most general" type which can be given to e, and π the "most general" substitution we have to apply to $\mathcal{A}$ in order to be able to derive any type for e. The difference is that, unlike FP, we cannot write programs as expressions—we do not have λ-abstractions—so we need an explicit method for checking whether a program is well-typed. We will say that a program is well-typed wrt. a set of assumptions if all the rules are well-typed:

DEFINITION 1. *A rule $f\ \overline{t} \to e$ is well-typed wrt. to a set of assumptions $\mathcal{A}$ iff:*

- $\mathcal{A} \oplus \{\overline{X_n : \alpha_n}\} \Vdash f\ \overline{t} : \tau_L|\pi_L$
- $\mathcal{A} \oplus \{\overline{X_n : \beta_n}\} \Vdash e : \tau_R|\pi_R$
- $\exists\pi.(\tau_L, \overline{\alpha_n\pi_L}) = (\tau_R, \overline{\beta_n\pi_R})\pi$

where $\overline{X_n}$ are the variables in $\overline{t}$, $\oplus$ is the symbol for the usual union of sets of assumptions and $\overline{\alpha_n}$, $\overline{\beta_n}$ are fresh type variables.

Intuitively, a rule is well-typed if the types $(\tau_R, \overline{\beta_n\pi_R})$ inferred for the right-hand side and its variables are more general than the types $(\tau_L, \overline{\alpha_n\pi_L})$ inferred for its left-hand side and its variables. Notice that programmers must provide an explicit type for every function symbol, otherwise the first point of the definition fails to infer the type for the expression $f\ \overline{t}$. Therefore Def. 1 cannot be used to infer the types of the functions, but to check that the types provided for the functions are correct.

The most remarkable feature of this new system is its liberality, that allows the programmer to define type-indexed functions in a very easy way, but still assuring essential safety properties like *type preservation* and *progress*—see [20] for more details. Consider the type-indexed functions `size` and `eq` defined over natural and booleans that appear in Fig. 4. The first three rules for `size` are well-typed because the type inferred for the right-hand side (nat) is more general than the inferred in the left-hand side (nat again). In the fourth rule the types inferred for the left-hand side and the variable `X` are both nat, and in the right-hand side the inferred types are nat and β resp., so the rule is well typed since (nat, β) is more general than (nat, nat). The same happens in the fourth rule of `eq`, where $(bool, \beta, \beta)$ inferred for the right-hand side is more general than $(bool, nat, nat)$ inferred for the left-hand side. The rest of rules for `eq` are well-typed for similar reasons.

3. Translation

As we have said in Sect. 1, the translation follows a type-passing scheme [29] and uses type-indexed functions and type witnesses. Instead of passing dictionaries containing the concrete implementation of the overloaded functions to use, in this scheme we pass data values—type witnesses—representing the types to which overloaded functions are applied. In the source program, saturated contexts that decorate function symbols show what types are they applied to, so we use that information to generate the concrete type witnesses. Member functions are translated into type-indexed functions that pattern-match on the type witness and decide which instance of the overloaded function to use. Due to the liberality of the type system, these type-indexed functions are encoded with type witnesses without the need of a special *typecase* constructions as in [29], so translated programs are usual FL programs.

3.1 Type witnesses

Type witnesses are data values that represent types. In [6, 14] these *type representations* are encoded using a GADT containing all the type representations. We follow a slightly different approach: we extend every data declaration with a new constructor in order to represent the type of the declared data. For example, a data declaration for Peano naturals `data nat = z | s nat` is extended with the constructor **#nat**, resulting in `data nat = z | s nat | #nat`; and a data declaration for lists `data list A = nil | cons A` is extended to `data list A = nil | cons A | #list A`. This extension of data declarations can be easily performed by the system. An interesting point of type witnesses defined this way is that they have exactly the same type they represent. In the previous example, `#nat` has type nat, and `#list (#list #nat)` has type *list (list A)*. This link between types and type witnesses allows us to generate automatically the type witness of a given simple type, fact that is used during translation.

DEFINITION 2 (Generation of type witnesses).

- $testify(\alpha) = X_\alpha$
- $testify(C\ \tau_1 \ldots \tau_n) = \#C\ testify(\tau_1) \ldots testify(\tau_n)$

The function testify returns the same data variable X_α for the same type variable α. Notice that the testify function is not defined for functional types $\tau \rightarrow \tau'$. This is because we consider a source language where instances over functional types are not possible, so in the translation we will not need to generate type witnesses for that types. However, in our liberal type system it would be simple to create type witnesses for those types using a special data constructor `#arrow` of type $\alpha \rightarrow \beta \rightarrow (\alpha \rightarrow \beta)$.

3.2 Translation

In the classical dictionary-based scheme [10, 30], the translation is integrated in the type checking phase so that it uses the inferred type information. In this paper we follow a different approach, supposing that the translation from type classes to type-indexed functions comes after a type checking phase that has inferred the types to the whole program [5, 27]. Since the inferred type information is needed for the translation, we assume that the type checking phase has decorated the function symbols with their corresponding types. The idea of the translation is simple: we inspect the context of the types that decorate function symbols and extract from them the concrete type witnesses that we need to pass to the functions. We define a set of translation functions for the different constructions (whole programs, data declarations, classes, instances, type declarations, rules and expressions):

DEFINITION 3 (Translation functions).

$$trans_{prog}(\overline{data}\ \ \overline{class}\ \ \overline{inst}\ \ \overline{type}\ \ \overline{rule}) = \overline{trans_{data}(data)}\ \overline{trans_{class}(class)}\ \overline{trans_{inst}(inst)}\ \overline{trans_{type}(type)}\ \overline{trans_{rule}(rule)}$$

$$trans_{data}(\mathtt{data}\ C\ \overline{\alpha} = c_1\ \overline{\tau} \mid \ldots \mid c_k\ \overline{\tau}) = \mathtt{data}\ C\ \overline{\alpha} = c_1\ \overline{\tau} \mid \ldots \mid c_k\ \overline{\tau} \mid \#C\ \overline{\alpha}$$

$$trans_{class}(\mathtt{class}\ \theta \Rightarrow \kappa\ \alpha\ \mathtt{where}\ \overline{f :: \tau}) = \overline{f :: \alpha \rightarrow \tau}$$

$$trans_{inst}(\ \mathtt{instance}\ \theta \Rightarrow \kappa\ (C\ \overline{\alpha})\ \mathtt{where}\ \overline{f\ \overline{t} \rightarrow e}) = \overline{f\ testify(C\ \overline{\alpha})\ \overline{trans_{expr}(t)} \rightarrow trans_{expr}(e)}$$

$$trans_{type}(f :: \theta \Rightarrow \tau) = f :: \alpha_1 \rightarrow \ldots \rightarrow \alpha_n \rightarrow \tau$$
where $\alpha_1 \ldots \alpha_n$ *appear in* θ *constrained by a class marked with* $^\bullet$

$$trans_{rule}((f :: \rho)\ \overline{t} \rightarrow e) = trans_{expr}(f :: \rho)\ \overline{trans_{expr}(t)} \rightarrow trans_{expr}(e)$$

$$trans_{expr}(X) = X$$
$$trans_{expr}(c) = c$$
$$trans_{expr}(f :: \rho) = f\ testify(\tau_1) \ldots testify(\tau_n)$$
where $\rho \equiv \phi \Rightarrow \tau$ *and* $\tau_1 \ldots \tau_n$ *appear in* ϕ *constrained by a class marked with* $^\bullet$
$$trans_{expr}(e\ e') = trans_{expr}(e)\ trans_{expr}(e')$$
$$trans_{expr}(let\ X = e\ in\ e') = let X = trans_{expr}(e)\ in\ trans_{expr}(e')$$

The translation of a program is simply the translation of its components. Data declarations are extended with the constructor of its type witness as explained in Sect. 3.1. Class declarations generate type declarations for the type-indexed functions. The generated type is the same as the one declared in the class but it has an extra first argument for the type witness. Consider the class declaration for the class `foo`:

```
class foo A where
  foo :: A → bool
```

This declaration generates a type declaration for the type-indexed function `foo` adding an extra first argument A to the type of the member function. This argument A is the type variable of the type class:

```
foo :: A → A → bool
```

Type declarations are treated in a similar way, with the difference that we only add new arguments to the translated type if they are constrained by a class with a $^\bullet$ mark, i.e., if the corresponding type witnesses are needed. Consider the type declaration for `f`:

```
f :: ⟨eq• A, ord A, eq• B⟩ ⇒ A → B → bool
```

This declaration generates a type declaration with the extra arguments A and B—and in that order—which are the type variables constrained by marked class names in the context:

```
f :: A → B → A → B → bool
```

Rules in an instance declaration are translated one by one. These rules generate the rules of type-indexed functions, so we add a type witness of the concrete instance as the first argument so they dispatch on it. Notice that a rule generated from an instance do not need any extra type-witness, since the type declared in the class declaration is a simple type and does not have a context. Consider the instance declaration `foo` for $list\ A$:

```
instance foo (list A) where
  foo X → false
```

This declaration generates a rule for the type-indexed function `foo` whose first argument is the type witness `(#list` X_A`)`, the result of the testify function for the type $list\ A$ of the instance declaration:

```
foo (#list X_A) X → false
```

To translate a rule, we translate all its components. Notice that according to our source syntax, patterns $\overline{t}$ do not contain overloaded function symbols, so they are decorated with types with empty contexts $\langle\rangle$. Therefore type witnesses will not be added to patterns, and the translation function $trans_{expr}$ will only erase the type decorations. The most important case of $trans_{expr}$ is the translation of a function symbol. When we have an overloaded function, we have to provide the type witnesses it needs. In this case we inspect the saturated context ϕ, collecting those types constrained by a marked class name and adding their associated type witnesses. The order in which these type witnesses are supplied is important, and must be the same for all the occurrences of the same overloaded function. Consider a possible occurrence of the previous function `f` applied to concrete types:

`f` :: $\langle eq^{\bullet}\ bool, ord\ bool, eq^{\bullet}\ (list\ int)\rangle \Rightarrow bool \rightarrow (list\ int) \rightarrow bool$

The translation of this decorated function symbol adds type witnesses for booleans and lists of integers, which are the types constrained by marked class names in the context:

```
f #bool (#list #int)
```

Notice that in expressions not containing overloaded functions, the result of the translation is the original expression without type decorations in functions symbols. The same happens with programs no containing overloaded functions. Therefore in these cases the translation does not introduce any overhead in the program.

As the reader can notice, the translation does not need the complete decoration of function symbols but only the types marked with a $^{\bullet}$ in the context. We have decided to use the complete inferred decorations to make more notable the close link between the translation and the type checking phase.

3.3 Important issues for the translation

The type checking phase is very important for this translation, since the information it provides in the contexts of the types that decorates function symbols directs the translation. There are two important issues that the type checker must address: context reduction and the marking of class names in contexts.

Context reduction

When performing the type checking of functions, the type checker infers a type τ and a context of class constraints. Consider the non-deterministic function `f`, where `gt` is the *greater* function with type $\langle ord\ A\rangle \Rightarrow A \rightarrow A \rightarrow bool$ and `eq` the equality function with type $\langle eq\ A\rangle \Rightarrow A \rightarrow A \rightarrow bool$:

```
f (X:Xs) Z → gt X Z
f (X:Xs) Z → and (eq X Z) (eq Xs [Z])
```

For these rules, the inferred type is $(list\ A) \rightarrow A \rightarrow bool$ and the context is $\langle ord\ A, eq\ A, eq\ (list\ A)\rangle$. The constraint $ord\ A$ comes from the order comparison in the first rule `gt X Z`, the constraint $eq\ A$ from the equality comparison between Z and the head of the list X, and the constraint $eq\ (list\ A)$ from the equality comparison `eq Xs [Z]`. However, this context contains some redundant information and could be reduced. There are three rules for context reduction:

- *Eliminating duplicate constraints.* We can reduce the context $\langle eq\ A, eq\ A\rangle$ to $\langle eq\ A\rangle$ and no information is lost.
- *Using instance declarations.* The usual instance declaration for equality on lists is `instance eq A ⇒ eq (list A) where (...)`, specifying how to use the equality on values A to define an equality on $list\ A$. Therefore, we can reduce the context $\langle eq\ A, eq\ (list\ A)\rangle$ to $\langle eq\ A\rangle$. This reduction is not a problem from the point of view of type witnesses, because given a type witness for A we can generate a type witness for $list\ A$.
- *Using class declarations.* The class declaration for `ord` is `class eq A ⇒ ord A where (...)`, specifying that any instance of `ord` is also an instance of `eq`. Therefore we can reduce the context $\langle ord\ A, eq\ A\rangle$ to $\langle ord\ A\rangle$. From the point of view of type witnesses this is not a problem, because we still know that we need a type witness of A.

Therefore, the previous context for function `f` would be reduced to $\langle ord\ A\rangle$ using all the previous rules. In [17] they explore different choices about how much context reduction to apply. Haskell's choice is to reduce the context completely before generalization, and this choice is necessary in our translation. Otherwise, the translation could generate rules that violate the restriction of linear left-hand sides. Consider the instance declaration for equality on pairs **instance** $\langle eq\ A, eq\ B\rangle \Rightarrow$ `eq (pair A B)` **where** `(...)`, and the rule `g P1 P2 → ([fst P1, snd P2], eq P1 P2)`—where `fst` and `snd` project the first and second component of a pair respectively. If we do not use the instance declaration to reduce the context, the type decoration obtained for `g` is $\langle eq^{\bullet}\ (pair\ A\ A)\rangle \Rightarrow (pair\ A\ A) \rightarrow (pair\ A\ A) \rightarrow (pair\ (list\ A)\ bool)$. Then the left-hand side of the translated rule would be `g (#pair` X_A X_A`) P1 P2`. This is not syntactically valid in our target language as the data variable X_A appears twice. Applying two steps of context reduction using the instance and eliminating duplicates we obtain $\langle eq\ A\rangle$. With this new context the left-hand side of the translated rule is `g` X_A `P1 P2`, which now is valid in the target language.

Marking of class names

We have used marked class names in contexts to know which type witness to pass to functions. The task of marking class names is an easy task that must be done after type checking, when the types of all the functions are inferred. At this point, contexts will have only constraints on type variables due to context reduction. There can be more than one class constraint over the same type variable, however we do not want to pass duplicate type witnesses for the same type. That is the reason why we mark with a $^{\bullet}$ only one constraint per type variable, defining the order in which type witnesses must be passed. Consider a Fibonacci function that accepts any numeric argument and returns an integer:

```
fib N = if N<2 then 1 else fib (N-1) + fib (N-2)
```

Its inferred type is $\langle num\ A, ord\ A\rangle \Rightarrow A \rightarrow int$. However, we do not need to pass two identical type witnesses to the rule. Therefore we mark one of the constraints over A, obtaining the type $\langle num^{\bullet}\ A, ord\ A\rangle \Rightarrow A \rightarrow int$. Then in every call of the `fib` function we will only pass one type witness. Moreover, if we do not use the $^{\bullet}$ marks the left-hand side of the `fib` rule would be translated into `fib` X_A X_A `N`, with two occurrences of the data variable X_A, violating the syntactic constraint that patterns in a left-hand side of a rule are linear.

3.4 Case study: equality and order

Fig. 5 contains the translation of a complete program using equality and order. Fig. 5-a) shows the source program with type declarations in the function symbols. These decorations are introduced by the type checker so the user does not need to write them in the source program. We suppose that usual booleans functions `and`, `or`::$\langle\rangle \Rightarrow bool \rightarrow bool \rightarrow bool$ and the conditional function `ifthen`::$\langle\rangle \Rightarrow bool \rightarrow A \rightarrow A \rightarrow bool$ are defined. We also assume that functions for equality and ordering are defined for booleans and integers: `eqBool`, `eqInt`, `gtBool` and `gtInt`. Notice that the type checker has marked with a $^{\bullet}$ the classes *eq* and *ord* in the types of `eq` and `gt` respectively, as can be seen in the decorations of the different occurrences of these functions. We have defined the `eq` and `gt` functions for booleans and integers using two variables `X` and `Y` as arguments so that the rules have arity 2, instead of defining them as `eq = eqBool`, `eq = eqInt`, etc. The reason for this is that because of HO-patterns, we need that all the rules for overloaded functions have the same arity, as we will discuss in Sect. 5.3. Notice how the type checker decorates function symbols with the corresponding type instantiated to the concrete type used in the application. This is the case of the second occurrence of `eq` in the last rule of the instance *eq (list A)*, which has the decoration $\langle eq^{\bullet}\ (list\ A)\rangle \Rightarrow (list\ A) \rightarrow (list\ A) \rightarrow bool$ since `eq` is applied to lists. Fig. 5-b) shows the result of applying the translation of Def. 3 to the source program. Notice how the same

```
class eq A where
  eq :: A → A → bool

instance eq bool where
  eq X Y = eqBool::⟨⟩ ⇒ bool → bool → bool X Y

instance eq int where
  eq X Y = eqInt::⟨⟩ ⇒ int → int → bool X Y

instance ⟨eq A, eq B⟩ ⇒ eq (pair A B) where
  eq (U,V) (X,Y) = and::⟨⟩ ⇒ bool → bool → bool
    (eq::⟨eq• A⟩ ⇒ A → A → bool U X)
    (eq::⟨eq• B⟩ ⇒ B → B → bool V Y)

instance ⟨eq A⟩ ⇒ eq (list A) where
  eq [] [] = true
  eq [] (Y:Ys) = false
  eq (X:Xs) [] = false
  eq (X:Xs) (Y:Ys) = and::⟨⟩ ⇒ bool → bool → bool
    (eq::⟨eq• A⟩ ⇒ A → A → bool X Y)
    (eq::⟨eq• (list A)⟩ ⇒ (list A) → (list A) → bool Xs Ys)

member :: ⟨eq• A⟩ ⇒ (list A) → A → bool
member::⟨eq• A⟩ ⇒ (list A) → A → bool [] Y = false
member::⟨eq• A⟩ ⇒ (list A) → A → bool (X:Xs) Y =
    or::⟨⟩ ⇒ bool → bool → bool
    (eq::⟨eq•A⟩ ⇒ A → A → bool X Y)
    (member::⟨eq• A⟩ ⇒ (list A) → A → bool Xs Y)

class ⟨eq A⟩ ⇒ ord A where
  gt :: A → A → bool

instance ord bool where
  gt X Y = gtBool::⟨⟩ ⇒ bool → bool → bool X Y

instance ord int where
  gt X Y = gtInt::⟨⟩ ⇒ int → int → bool X Y

memberOrd :: ⟨ord• A⟩ ⇒ (list A) → A → bool
memberOrd::⟨ord• A⟩ ⇒ (list A) → A → bool [] Y = false
memberOrd::⟨ord• A⟩ ⇒ (list A) → A → bool (X:Xs) Y = ifthen
  (gt::⟨ord• A⟩ ⇒ A → A → bool X Y) false
memberOrd::⟨ord• A⟩ ⇒ (list A) → A → bool (X:Xs) Y = ifthen
  (eq::⟨eq• A⟩ ⇒ A → A → bool X Y) true
memberOrd::⟨ord• A⟩ ⇒ (list A) → A → bool (X:Xs) Y = ifthen
  (gt::⟨ord• A⟩ ⇒ A → A → bool Y X)
  (memberOrd::⟨ord• A⟩ ⇒ (list A) → A → bool Xs Y)
```

a) Source program with type decorations

```
eq :: A → A → A → bool
eq #bool X Y = eqBool X Y
eq #int X Y = eqInt X Y
eq (#pair X_A X_B) (U,V) (X,Y) = and
  (eq X_A U X)
  (eq X_B V Y)
eq (#list X_A) [] [] = true
eq (#list X_A) [] (Y:Ys) = false
eq (#list X_A) (X:Xs) [] = false
eq (#list X_A) (X:Xs) (Y:Ys) = and
  (eq X_A X Y)
  (eq (#list X_A) Xs Ys)

member :: A → (list A) → A → bool
member X_A [] Y = false
member X_A (X:Xs) Y = or
    (eq X_A X Y)
    (member X_A Xs Y)

gt :: A → A → A → bool
gt #bool X Y = gtBool X Y
gt #int X Y = gtInt X Y

memberOrd :: A → (list A) → A → bool
memberOrd X_A [] Y = false
memberOrd X_A (X:Xs) Y = ifthen
  (gt X_A X Y) false
memberOrd X_A (X:Xs) Y = ifthen
  (eq X_A X Y) true
memberOrd X_A (X:Xs) Y = ifthen
  (gt X_A Y X)
  (memberOrd X_A Xs Y)
```

b) Translated program

Figure 5. Translation of a program using equality and order

type variable A in the decorations generates the same data variable X_A in the translated program—see for example the second rule for `member`. This is important since all these occurrences represent the same type witness that is passed as an argument.

4. Advantages of the Translation

In this section we show some of the benefits of the proposed translation compared to the classical dictionary-based one in FLP.

4.1 Efficiency

To test the efficiency of the proposed translation against the classical translation using dictionaries [10, 30], we have elaborated 7 different programs using type classes. We have chosen programs that can be part of real functional-logic programs and use the standard type classes *eq*, *ord* and *num*:

- *eqlist*: equality comparison between lists of integers.
- *fib*: Fibonacci function that accepts numeric arguments.
- *galeprimes*: sieve of prime numbers using a function of difference of sorted lists.
- *memberord*: member function in sorted lists.
- *mergesort*: John von Neumann's sorting algorithm.
- *permutsort*: sorting by selecting a sorted permutation of the original list.
- *quicksort*: C.A.R. Hoare's sorting algorithm.

The programs *fib, galeprimes, mergesort* and *quicksort* have been adapted from the suite of benchmark programs for Haskell implementations *nobench* [28]. Although *permutsort* is an inefficient sorting algorithm, we have included it in the set of tests because it is an example of the *generate-and-test* scheme, a kind of programs combining non-determinism and lazy evaluation, for which FLP obtains better results than functional or logic programs [8].

For each program we have measured in Toy the elapsed time in the evaluation of 100 random expressions in both translations. Translated programs using dictionaries are valid programs in Toy since it has a Damas-Milner type system. However, Toy has not integrated the liberal type system for FLP presented in [20]. In order to compile and execute the translated programs with type-indexed functions and type witnesses—which are not correct with respect to a Damas-Milner type system—we have used a especial version of Toy without the type checking phase. This does not distort the

Program	Speedup	Speedup (Optimized)
eqlist	1.6414	1.3627
fib	2.3063	2.3777
galeprimes	1.4885	1.0016
memberord	2.2802	2.2386
mergesort	1.0476	1.0453
permutsort	1.7186	1.7259
quicksort	1.0743	1.0005

Figure 6. Speedup of the proposed translation over the classical translation using dictionaries

measures since once compiled Toy programs do not carry any type information at run time, so compiled programs are the same regardless the type system. For each expression we have calculated the speedup: the elapsed time in the translated program with dictionaries divided by the elapsed time in the translated program using type-indexed functions and type witnesses, and we have computed the mean speedup of the 100 tests. The results appear in the second column of Fig. 6. The biggest speedups are obtained in *fib* and *memberord*. The reason for the speed gain in *fib* is that the function `fib` needs two dictionaries—*ord* and *num*—but only one type witness, which means one extra matching each time `fib` is called. In *memberord* the reason is that it uses the overloaded function `eq` with every element. This function is contained in the *eq* dictionary which is inside the *ord* dictionary, so before apply it we have to extract the *eq* dictionary. This projection is not needed with type witnesses. The programs *permutsort*, *eqlist* and *galeprimes* also obtain a good speedup. In the case of *eqlist*, the reason of the speedup is that the `eq` function builds the dictionary of equality on lists in each recursive call. However, the same type witness argument for lists is passed to the recursive call. The rest of programs—*mergesort* and *quicksort*—do not obtain any improvement and run as fast as with dictionaries.

There are some well-known optimizations that can be applied to the translation using dictionaries [4, 11]. However, in the translation using type-indexed functions and type witnesses there is also room for optimizations. Therefore we have measured the speedup of the same programs when optimizations are applied to both translations. For the dictionary-based translation we have considered those optimizations from [4] applicable to our set of tests. For each test program, the following optimizations have been applied in sequence:

- *Flattening of dictionaries*: expand class dictionaries to contain both the methods of the class and all its superclasses. The dictionary of the superclasses is kept as well as flatting it, because it is sometimes needed.
- *Constant folding*: eliminate the method projection from a dictionary when the concrete dictionary is known. For example, `arb dictArbBool` is replaced by `arbBool`—see Fig. 1-b).
- *Automatic function specialization*: generate an specialized version of a function when it is applied to a concrete dictionary. This optimization has been only applied to `galeprimes`, since it is the only tested program whose code contains a function that is applied to a concrete dictionary.

The rest of optimizations presented in [4] have not been considered because they are dependent on the underlying architecture, which is different between Haskell and Toy, or because they address specific problems which do not appear in our test programs—as programming with complex numbers.

For the proposed translation using type-indexed functions and type witnesses the considered optimizations are:

- *Specialized version from instances*: Apart from the generated rules for the type-indexed functions, instances also generate specialized versions of the overloaded functions. For example, the instance **instance** $\langle eq\ A\rangle \Rightarrow eq\ (list\ A)$ from Fig. 5-a) generates the function `eq_list`:

```
eq_list :: A → (list A) → (list A) → bool
eq_list X_A [] [] = true
eq_list X_A [] (Y:Ys) = false
eq_list X_A (X:Xs) [] = false
eq_list X_A (X:Xs) (Y:Ys) =
   and (eq X_A X Y) (eq_list X_A Xs Ys)
```

  Any occurrence of an overloaded symbol applied to a concrete type witness is replaced by the specialized version: `eq (#list bool)` is replaced by `eq_list #bool`, `ord #nat` by `ord_nat`, etc.

- *Automatic function specialization*: The same optimization explained before, but used when a function is applied to a concrete type witness. This optimization has been only applied to `galeprimes` for the same reasons as before.

The speedup results of the optimized versions appear in the third column of Fig. 6. For the programs *fib*, *memberord*, *mergesort*, *permutsort* and *quicksort*, the speedup does not change substantially. The reason is that dictionary optimizations do not affect the target program—with the exception of a constant folding in the definition of the `ord` dictionaries that is used once per test—and the specialized version of the type-indexed functions are not used. For the program *eqlist* the optimizations avoid the creation of the equality dictionary for lists—in the dictionary-based translation—and make use of the specialized version of equality for list—in the type-passing translation. The speedup decreases but the program with type-indexed functions and type witnesses still runs faster. For the *galeprimes* program there is no speedup since after applying the optimization to both translations the resulting code is similar because of the automatic function specialization.

The code of the tested programs and detailed results of the tests can be found in `http://gpd.sip.ucm.es/enrique/publications/pepm11/testPrograms.zip`.

4.2 Adequacy to call-time choice

Apart from the improvement in efficiency, the proposed translation also solves the problem of missing answers when combining non-determinism and overloading presented in Sect. 1. The problem is that dictionaries are shared, and non-deterministic nullary member functions inside them are evaluated to the same value in all the copies. With the proposed translation this problem does not arise because member function are not projecting functions that extracts from dictionaries but type-indexed functions that accepts a type witness as an argument. This type witness is shared as dictionaries, but each occurrence of the member function is a different application so they can generate different values.

The translation using type-indexed functions and type witnesses of the program containing the `arb` class appeared in Fig. 1-a) is:

```
arb :: A → A
arb #bool → false
arb #bool → true

arbL2 :: A → (list A)
arbL2 X_A → [arb X_A, arb X_A]
```

The class and instance declaration have generated the type-indexed `arb` function with two rules for booleans, and `arbL2` is translated to accept a type witness and pass it to the `arb` functions in its right-hand side. In this case the translation of the expression `arbL2::(list bool)` is `arbL2 #bool`, which can be reduced to `[arb #bool, arb #bool]` using the rule for `arbL2`. Here the first occurrence of `arb #bool` in the list can be reduced to `false` and the second to `true` using the different rules for `arb`, so it produces the answer `[false, true]` that was missing. In a similar way `arbL2 #bool` can be reduced to `[true, false]`.

The problem with non-deterministic nullary member functions and the dictionary-based translation could be solved if they are automatically replaced by functions of arity 1. This way, dictionaries do not contain functions that can be evaluated but HO-patterns—functions partially applied—that are values and can be shared without problem. However this solution presents some problems that are further discussed in Sect. 5.2.

4.3 Simplicity

From the point of view of difficulty, both translations—the dictionary-based and the proposed one—have a similar complexity: a type checking phase and a translation that uses the obtained type information. However, translated programs using the proposed translation are simpler than those obtained using the dictionary-based one. They are shorter, since they declare less data types and functions. Besides, type witnesses are first-order data, unlike dictionaries which are higher-order data containing functions. Finally, type witnesses have in most cases a simpler structure and are smaller than dictionaries.

With the two translations, obtained programs are the result of an automatic procedure integrated in the compiler, so the simplicity of obtained programs is not so important from the point of view of the user. However, it might be useful for later analyses or manipulations of translated programs. Furthermore, as we have seen in Sect. 4.1 and Sect. 4.2, this simplicity comes with an improvement of the efficiency and a better adequacy to call-time choice.

5. Discussion

In this section we discuss some additional aspects, including some problems, that arise with the translations of type classes in FLP.

5.1 Multiple modules and separate compilation

The dictionary-based translation combines well with multiple modules and separate compilation. A class declaration defines a datatype and some projecting functions, and instances define concrete values of the dictionary type. Therefore different instances can be compiled separately and joined later. With the proposed translation using type-indexed functions and type witnesses this seems more difficult. The problem is that generated type-indexed functions are *open* functions [18]: there is *one* type-indexed function per member function, but the rules can be spread in several modules. However, this is not a problem in Toy due to its code generation method and the demand of the type-indexed functions generated from member functions of classes. Toy programs use a demand driven strategy [19] for evaluating function applications. Consider a `leq` function on Peano natural numbers defined as:

```
leq z Y            = true
leq (s X) z        = false
leq (s X) (s Y) = leq X Y
```

In this case, the first argument is demanded in all the rules, and the second argument is demanded only in the second and third rules. Then the strategy is to evaluate the first argument to *head-normal form*. If it is the constructor `z`, then we apply the first rule. If it is the constructor `s` we evaluate the second argument of the rule. If the evaluation of that argument is the constructor `z` we apply the second rule. Otherwise if it is the constructor `s` we apply the third rule. The Prolog code generated for this function is[3]:

[3] This is not the exact code generated by the Toy compiler. We have simplified it for the sake of conciseness.

```
leq(A,B,H) :- hnf(A,HA), leq_1(HA,B,H).

leq_1(z,B,true).
leq_1(s(X),B,H) :- hnf(B,HB), leq_1_2(s(X),HB,H).

leq_1_2(s(X),z,false).
leq_1_2(s(X),s(Y),H) :- leq(X,Y,H).
```

The predicate `hnf` is a built-in predicate that computes *head normal forms*. The predicate `leq` is the main predicate to evaluate the `leq` function. It uses the predicates `leq_1` and `leq_1_2`, where the numbers represent in which positions a head normal form has been previously obtained. Notice that the last argument of the predicates represents the result. It is easy to see that these predicates follow the demand driven strategy explained before.

The peculiarity of translated member functions is that they always have a constructor in their first argument: the type-witness. Therefore their first argument is always demanded in all the rules translated from the instances, so the strategy is to evaluate it to head normal form. Consider the `eq` function in Fig. 5-b). Since the first argument is demanded in all the rules, we generate the predicate to evaluate the type witness to head normal form:

```
eq(W,A,B,H) :- hnf(W,HW), eq_1(HW,A,B,H).
```

We also generate the predicate `eq_1` with clauses for the different instances:

```
eq_1(#bool,A,B,H) :- eqBool(A,B,H).
eq_1(#int,A,B,H) :- eqInt(A,B,H).
eq_1(#pair(WA,WB),A,B,H) :- (...)
eq_1(#list(WA),A,B,H) :- (...)
```

If each instance of `eq` is in a different module, we compile them separately. However, in each translated module the first argument of `eq` is uniformly demanded, so we generate the predicate `eq/4` as before and the corresponding clauses for `eq_1/4` and the rest of predicates. Notice that in the translated rules for equality on pairs and list, the three arguments are uniformly demanded. In these cases we chose from left to right, so we always generate the same clause for `eq/4` that computes the head-normal form of the first argument and calls to `eq_1/4`. In the compilation of a program that imports the different modules with the instances, the code for the `eq` function is obtained by simply joining the predicates `eq/4`, `eq_1/4` ... from the compiled modules. Each compiled module contains a clause for `eq/4`, so it is important to remove those duplicates in the final compiled program.

Notice that this solution is not valid for arbitrary open functions, since the demand of the arguments is unknown and the code generation would require an analysis with the rules from all the modules.

5.2 Possible solution for non-deterministic nullary member functions in the dictionary-based translation

The loss of expected answers that arises in the dictionary-based translation when non-deterministic nullary member functions are used could be solved if they are automatically replaced by unary functions. Fig. 7 shows the program translated with dictionaries from Fig. 1-a) where `arb` has been extended to an unary function accepting unit as argument. The translation of `arbL2::(list bool)` is `arbL2 dictArbBool` as in the original case, but now it reduces to `[arb dictArbBool (), arb dictArbBool ()]`. Although both copies of the dictionary are shared, now they can only be reduced to `dictArb arbBool`. It is now a value—notice that `arbBool` is a HO-pattern—so it cannot be reduced further. After the extraction of the `arbBool` function from the dictionary the expression is `[arbBool (), arbBool ()]`, which can be reduced to `[false, true]` or `[true, false]` applying the rule for `arbBool` for twice.

Since being non-deterministic is a typically undecidable property, the technique of adding the unit argument should be applied to every nullary member function, even if it is indeed determinis-

```
data dictArb A = dictArb (unit → A)

arb :: dictArb A -> (unit → A)
arb (dictArb F) → F

arbBool :: unit → bool
arbBool () → false
arbBool () → true

dictArbBool :: dictArb bool
dictArbBool → dictArb arbBool

arbL2 :: dictArb A -> list A
arbL2 DA → [arb DA (), arb DA ()]
```

Figure 7. Translation of the program in Fig. 1-a) extending `arb` to have one argument

tic. This will introduce an unnecessary overhead—apart from the inevitable overhead caused by dictionaries—to nullary deterministic member functions. We could consider an analysis to detect (in some cases) if the definition of a nullary member function in a concrete instance is deterministic. In those cases the extra unit argument could in principle be avoided. However this solution makes difficult separate compilation. The reason is that a later inclusion of a new module with an instance where the considered nullary member function is non-deterministic will force the recompilation of all the related modules: it will be necessary to change the dictionary declaration—now it contains a member function whose first argument is of type *unit*—and add the unit argument to the rules in the previous instances.

The translation using type-indexed functions and type witnesses proposed in this paper treats non-deterministic nullary member functions and the rest of member functions in a homogeneous way. Furthermore, it does not require recompilation and it does not add any extra overhead to deterministic nullary member functions—apart from the type-witness. Therefore, we believe that the proposed translation is a better option than the dictionary-based translation when dealing with the combination of non-determinism and nullary member functions.

5.3 Problems with arities and HO-patterns

In our FLP setting the arity of function symbols plays an important role to identify whether a function application forms a HO-pattern or it is totally applied and can be reduced. Therefore all the rules of the same function must have the same arity, and this property must be ensured in the target program. In FP the compiler checks that all the rules of a function have the same number of arguments, but this is not checked for the rules of member functions in different instances. However, this property must be checked if the proposed translation is used. The reason is that the rules of the same member function in different instances are translated to be the rules of the same type-indexed function. If the original rules from the instances have different arities, then the rules for the type-indexed functions will have different arities and the translated program will not be a valid FL program. To solve this problem we propose to annotate the arity of member functions in the class declaration. For example the class declaration for `eq` in Fig. 5-a) is changed to:

`class` $eq\ A$ `where`
  `eq/2 ::` $A \rightarrow A \rightarrow bool$

Using this arity declaration the compiler will be able to check if all the rules for `eq` have the same arity even if they belong to instances in different modules. Notice that this problem with arities does not appear in the dictionary-based translation since the rules of a member function in an instance generates a specialized function—see `arbBool` in Fig. 1-b)—and the member function itself is transformed into a function which projects from the dictionary.

Another problem to address is the occurrence of HO-patterns containing overloaded functions in the patterns of the left-hand side of rules. If this kind of functions appear in the patterns, the type checking stage will decorate them with an overloaded type. Besides, class constraints coming from the overloaded function could remain after context reduction, so the defined function symbol will have an overloaded type containing them. In this situation the proposed translation will generate non-linear functions. Consider the program from Fig. 5-a) and the rule that uses the HO-pattern `eq`:

`f eq` $\rightarrow$ `true`

After the type checking stage the rule is decorated as:

`f::`$\langle eq^\bullet\ A\rangle \Rightarrow (A \rightarrow A \rightarrow bool) \rightarrow bool$
  `eq::`$\langle eq^\bullet\ A\rangle \Rightarrow A \rightarrow A \rightarrow bool$ $\rightarrow$ `true`

so the translated rule would be:

`f` X_A `(eq` X_A`)` $\rightarrow$ `true`

This rule is invalid in our setting, since the variable X_A appears twice in the left-hand side so the patterns are non-linear. Notice that this problem also appears in the dictionary-based translation since the same variable representing the dictionary would be passed as the extra argument of `f` and `eq`.

A possible solution to this problem might be not to translate the patterns in the left-hand sides of the rules, so no type witnesses would be added to the overloaded functions in patterns. Since the class constraints from these functions remain in the context of the defined function, they will generate the type witnesses as the first arguments of the defined function. However, this solution leads to a loss of expected answers. Consider the same function rule for `f`. If we do not translate the patterns, the translated rule would be:

`f` X_A `eq` $\rightarrow$ `true`

which now is linear. The value `true` is an expected answer of the evaluation of `f eq::`$bool \rightarrow bool \rightarrow bool$—we have added the type decoration to `eq` to avoid ambiguity. The type checker would extend this expression with complete type decorations:

`f::`$\langle eq^\bullet\ bool\rangle \Rightarrow (bool \rightarrow bool \rightarrow bool) \rightarrow bool$
  `eq::`$\langle eq^\bullet\ bool\rangle \Rightarrow bool \rightarrow bool \rightarrow bool$

and the translation of this expression would be:

`f #bool (eq #bool)`

However this translated expression does not match with the head of the rule `f` X_A `eq`, so it cannot be reduced to `true`. Notice that it also happens with the dictionary-based translation. The translation of the rule would be the same, as `f` needs an extra argument containing the dictionary of equality. The translation of the expression would add two dictionaries for the equality on booleans:

`f dictEqBool (eq dicEqBool)`

This translated expression cannot be reduced to the value `true` either. It does not match with the head of the rule for `f`, but the subexpression `eq dicEqBool` can be reduced to `eqBool`—assuming that `eqBool` is the function inside the dictionary of equality for booleans. However the resulting expression `f dictEqBool eqBool` cannot be reduced to `true` using the rule `f` X_A `eq` $\rightarrow$ `true` because it does not match with its head.

Considering the problems that HO-patterns containing overloaded functions in the left-hand side of rules cause in both translations, it seems a good design choice to prohibit the occurrence of overloaded functions in the patterns in the left-hand side of rules. However HO-patterns are a very expressive feature of FLP, so this problem must be further studied in order to find a solution.

6. Concluding Remarks and Future Work

In this paper we have proposed a translation for type classes in FLP following a type-passing scheme [29]. The translation uses type-indexed functions and type witnesses, and translated programs are well-typed wrt. a new liberal type system for FLP [20]. We argue that the proposed translation is a good design choice to implement type classes in FLP because it improves on the standard dictionary-based translation in some points:

- Our tests show that translated programs using type-indexed functions and type witnesses perform faster—in general—than those using the dictionary-based translation [10, 30]. The tests also show that if we apply optimizations to both translated programs, those using type-indexed functions and type witnesses still perform faster, although the difference in this case is smaller.
- It does not present the problem of missing answers which appears with the dictionary-based translation in programs that use non-deterministic nullary member functions [24].
- The proposed translation consists in simple steps that make use of type decorations for function symbols obtained by usual type checking algorithms supporting type classes [5, 27], so it does not add extra complications over the standard dictionary-based translation. Besides, translated programs using the proposed translation are shorter and simpler than those generated using the dictionary-based translation.
- Although it needs some special treatment, the proposed translation supports multiple modules and separate compilation in an easy way.

We consider some lines of future work. The first is the implementation of the complete translation into the Toy system. Since the translation rules are pretty simple, the hard step is implementing the standard type checker supporting type classes and place the type decorations in the function symbols. Once the translation is implemented, we will be able to test the efficiency results with a larger set of programs. We also want to study if the proposed translation supports easily well-known extensions of type classes like *multi-parameter type classes* [17] or *constructor classes* [16] for FLP. According to [29], these extensions fit easily in a type-passing translation scheme. Finally, we intend to study in further detail the problematic of HO-patterns using overloaded functions in the left-hand sides of rules, so that we can find better solutions than prohibit them.

Acknowledgments

This work has been partially supported by the Spanish projects TIN2008-06622-C03-01, S2009TIC-1465, UCM-BSCH-GR58/08-910502. We also want to acknowledge to Francisco López-Fraguas and Juan Rodríguez-Hortalá for their useful comments and ideas.

References

[1] Münster Curry compiler. `http://danae.uni-muenster.de/~lux/curry/`.

[2] Sloth Curry compiler. `http://babel.ls.fi.upm.es/research/Sloth/`.

[3] Zinc compiler. `http://zinc-project.sourceforge.net/`.

[4] L. Augustsson. Implementing Haskell overloading. In Proc. *FPCA '93*, pages 65–73, 1993.

[5] S. Blott. Type inference and type classes. In *Proc. of the 1989 Glasgow FP Workshop*, pages 254–265, 1990.

[6] J. Cheney and R. Hinze. First-class phantom types. Technical Report TR2003-1901, Cornell University, July 2003.

[7] L. Damas and R. Milner. Principal type-schemes for functional programs. In Proc. *POPL '82*, pages 207–212, 1982.

[8] J. C. González-Moreno, M. T. Hortalá-González, F. J. López-Fraguas, and M. Rodríguez-Artalejo. An approach to declarative programming based on a rewriting logic. *Journal of Logic Programming*, 40(1):47–87, 1999.

[9] J. C. González-Moreno, M. T. Hortalá-González, and M. Rodríguez-Artalejo. Polymorphic types in functional logic programming. *Journal of Functional and Logic Programming*, 2001(1), July 2001.

[10] C. V. Hall, K. Hammond, S. L. Peyton Jones, and P. L. Wadler. Type classes in Haskell. *ACM Trans. Program. Lang. Syst.*, 18(2):109–138, 1996.

[11] K. Hammond and S. Blott. Implementing Haskell type classes. In *Proc. of the 1989 Glasgow FP Workshop*, pages 266–286, 1990.

[12] M. Hanus. Multi-paradigm declarative languages. In Proc. *ICLP 2007*, volume 4670 of *LNCS*, pages 45–75. Springer, 2007.

[13] M. Hanus (ed.). Curry: An integrated functional logic language (version 0.8.2). Available at `http://www.informatik.uni-kiel.de/~curry/report.html`, March 2006.

[14] R. Hinze and A. Löh. Generic programming, now! In *Datatype-Generic Programming 2006*, volume 4719 of *LNCS*, pages 150–208. Springer, 2007.

[15] P. Hudak, J. Hughes, S. P. Jones, and P. Wadler. A history of Haskell: being lazy with class. In Proc. *HOPL III*, pages 12–1–12–55, 2007.

[16] M. P. Jones. A system of constructor classes: overloading and implicit higher-order polymorphism. In Proc. *FPCA '93*, pages 52–61, 1993.

[17] S. P. Jones, M. Jones, and E. Meijer. Type classes: An exploration of the design space. In *Haskell Workshop*, 1997.

[18] A. Löh and R. Hinze. Open data types and open functions. In Proc. *PPDP '06*, pages 133–144, 2006.

[19] R. Loogen, F. J. López-Fraguas, and M. Rodríguez-Artalejo. A demand driven computation strategy for lazy narrowing. In Proc. *PLILP '93*, pages 184–200, 1993.

[20] F. J. López-Fraguas, E. Martin-Martin, and J. Rodríguez-Hortalá. Liberal Typing for Functional Logic Programs. *To appear APLAS 2010*. Available at `http://gpd.sip.ucm.es/enrique/publications/liberalTypingFLP/aplas2010.pdf`.

[21] F. J. López-Fraguas, E. Martin-Martin, and J. Rodríguez-Hortalá. New results on type systems for functional logic programming. Volume 5979 of *LNCS*, pages 128–144. Springer, 2010.

[22] F. J. López-Fraguas and J. Sánchez-Hernández. $\mathcal{TOY}$: A multiparadigm declarative system. In Proc. *RTA'99*, volume 1631 of *LNCS*, pages 244–247. Springer, 1999.

[23] W. Lux. Adding Haskell-style overloading to Curry. In *Workshop of Working Group 2.1.4 of the German Computing Science Association GI*, pages 67–76, 2008.

[24] W. Lux. Type-classes and call-time choice vs. run-time choice - Post to the Curry mailing list. `http://www.informatik.uni-kiel.de/~curry/listarchive/0790.html`, 2009.

[25] J. C. González-Moreno, M. T. Hortalá-González, and M. Rodríguez-Artalejo. A higher order rewriting logic for functional logic programming. In Proc. *ICLP'97*, pages 153–167, 1997.

[26] J. J. Moreno-Navarro, J. Mariño, A. del Pozo-Pietro, Á. Herranz-Nieva, and J. García-Martín. Adding type classes to functional-logic languages. In *1996 Joint Conf. on Declarative Programming, APPIA-GULP-PRODE'96*, pages 427–438, 1996.

[27] T. Nipkow and C. Prehofer. Type reconstruction for type classes. *Journal of Functional Programming*, 5(2):201–224, 1995.

[28] D. Stewart. nobench: Benchmarking Haskell implementations. `http://www.cse.unsw.edu.au/~dons/nobench.html`.

[29] S. R. Thatté. Semantics of type classes revisited. In Proc. *LFP '94*, pages 208–219, 1994.

[30] P. Wadler and S. Blott. How to make ad-hoc polymorphism less ad hoc. In Proc. *POPL '89*, pages 60–76, 1989.

[31] H. Xi, C. Chen, and G. Chen. Guarded recursive datatype constructors. *SIGPLAN Not.*, 38(1):224–235, 2003. ISSN 0362-1340.

Strictification of Circular Programs *

João Paulo Fernandes
Universidade do Porto &
Universidade do Minho, Portugal
jpaulo@fe.up.pt

João Saraiva
Universidade do Minho,
Portugal
jas@di.uminho.pt

Daniel Seidel Janis Voigtländer
Universität Bonn,
Germany
{ds,jv}@iai.uni-bonn.de

Abstract

Circular functional programs (necessarily evaluated lazily) have been used as algorithmic tools, as attribute grammar implementations, and as target for program transformation techniques. Classically, Richard Bird [1984] showed how to transform certain multi-traversal programs (which could be evaluated strictly or lazily) into one-traversal ones using circular bindings. Can we go the other way, even for programs that are not in the image of his technique? That is the question we pursue in this paper. We develop an approach that on the one hand lets us deal with typical examples corresponding to attribute grammars, but on the other hand also helps to derive new algorithms for problems not previously in reach.

Categories and Subject Descriptors D.3.3 [*Programming Languages*]: Language Constructs and Features; D.1.1 [*Programming Techniques*]: Applicative (Functional) Programming

General Terms Design, Languages

Keywords program transformation

1. Introduction

Circular programs were first introduced by Bird [1984] to avoid multiple traversals originating from nested function calls. He fuses several traversals of the same input data structure by tupling their results and applying *unfold/fold*-transformation steps [Burstall and Darlington 1977]. Possible intra-traversal dependencies—if information gathered in one traversal is used in another—are captured by circular definitions in the transformed program, which given certain conditions are well-behaved under a lazy evaluation strategy. Subsequently, this kind of transformation was recast in terms of attribute grammars [Johnsson 1987; Kuiper and Swierstra 1987], and indeed circular programs have become one successful implementation technique for attribute grammars [de Moor et al. 2000; Saraiva 1999]. Circular programs have also been used as an algorithmic tool [Jones and Gibbons 1993; Okasaki 2000] and as target for transformation techniques other than pure elimination of multiple traversals [Fernandes et al. 2007; Pardo et al. 2009; Voigtländer 2004].

In this paper, we are interested in transforming circular programs into non-circular ones. In essence, we want to go in the opposite direction of the transformation that Bird [1984] proposed (and that Chin et al. [1999] systematized, and made more effective by exploiting strictness analysis). Why would we be interested in that, other than out of curiosity? We do care about efficiency: it is well known that circular programs, while nominally avoiding multiple traversals, can actually lead to high space and time costs through introduction of extra thunks, countermanding any potential benefit. Specifically, when looking for an implementation strategy for attribute grammar systems, lazily evaluated circular programs are an easy, but not necessarily the most practical route. Instead, one may ultimately want to go for a strict functional language as target. An early approach for such strictification is already inherent in the work of Kuiper and Swierstra [1987]. They provide two mappings from attribute grammars to functional programs: one that leads to a possibly multi-traversal, non-circular program and one that leads to a single-traversal, typically circular program. To get from a circular program to a non-circular one, it may be possible to apply the second mapping in reverse and then the first mapping in forward mode. Actually, that is exactly the opposite of the use that Kuiper and Swierstra propose to make of their mappings, and of course, it will only work if the circular program at hand is indeed the image of some non-circular program under the respective mappings in the opposite directions. Similarly, trying to somehow "simply" invert the original transformation technique of Bird [1984] would up front limit the class of programs we could hope to deal with. Hence, we are instead looking for an independent approach to eliminating circular definitions.

The latter also sets our work here apart from earlier work of Fernandes and Saraiva [2007]. They used attribute grammar techniques to transform lazy circular programs into programs executable both lazily (e.g., in Haskell) and strictly (e.g., in OCaml). Essentially, they recover the attribute grammar (dependencies) that correspond to a given circular program, ostensibly only evaluable in a lazy language, via syntactic analysis. Then, they use a (complex) scheduling algorithm from the attribute grammar world [Kastens 1980] to statically determine an admissible evaluation order, and implement it via a non-circular functional program. Thus, the need for a lazy evaluation engine to determine an admissible evaluation order dynamically at runtime is avoided. Again, this approach only works for circular programs that already correspond to an attribute grammar in a rather direct way. Instead, our aim here is to deal more generally with circular programs, however arising, also ones which do not correspond to an attribute grammar or are images of some non-circular program under any of the known techniques for going from non-circular to circular. A case in point is our dealing with a circular breadth-first tree numbering program due to Jones and Gibbons [1993] and Okasaki [2000].

* This work was supported as a joint project by Fundação para a Ciência e Tecnologia (FCT), grant No. FCT/Proc 441.00, and Deutscher Akademischer Austausch Dienst (DAAD), grant No. 50106501. The Portuguese partners are also supported under the SSaaPP research project, PTDC/EIA-CCO/108613/2008. Additionally, João Paulo Fernandes was supported by FCT, grant No. SFRH/BPD/46987/2008, and Daniel Seidel was supported by Deutsche Forschungsgemeinschaft (DFG), grant No. VO 1512/1-1.

PEPM'11, January 24–25, 2011, Austin, Texas, USA.

We start in Section 2 by considering the classical *repmin* example and using it to introduce our approach to transforming circular programs into non-circular ones. We employ type-based analysis and general program transformation techniques. Our transformation in this example could be completely automatic, and indeed this is the case for typical examples that would also be in the reach of attribute grammar techniques. To emphasize this point, we consider a practical example from a programming language environment in Section 3. But automation, or even just formal presentation of a fixed transformation technique, is not our goal here. Rather, we are interested in the interplay and connection of program manipulation techniques with the aim of transforming circular into non-circular programs. Indeed, we perform an extended case study in Section 4 for an algorithmic circular programming idea originally due to Jones and Gibbons [1993] and then used by Okasaki [2000] in a comparison of breadth-first numbering algorithms. The circular program considered there is particular in that it does not correspond to an attribute grammar, nor can it be seen as an image of a multi-traversal program under the transformation of Bird [1984]. Instead, it embodies an independent algorithmic use of circular definitions. As such, it poses a challenging problem, and it turns out that in deriving a non-circular version from it we have to invest some creativity. The overarching approach, however, will still be the one from Section 2, and the bits of creativity we invest will pay off in terms of interesting algorithmic variations we arrive at. Interestingly, Okasaki [2000] discussed various implementations, in a strict language, of breadth-first numbering that he and others had come up with. He only gave the circular program for comparison, without relating it in any way to any of the strict algorithms. With our derivations, we can actually bridge the gap and get, from the circular program, new alternatives for strict implementation of breadth-first numbering.

As languages in this paper, we use Haskell and—to emphasize when programs are non-circular and can be evaluated strictly—OCaml. To also be able to make concrete statements about efficiency, we provide measurements and discussion in Section 5. We conclude in Section 6 and give a perspective for using our transformation approach from this paper as a facilitator for further optimization techniques.

Before we start, it seems worth pointing out that our approach here is orthogonal to the lambda-abstraction strategy of Pettorossi and Proietti [1988]. They avoid circular definitions by transforming multi-traversal, non-circular programs into single-traversal, non-circular programs that use higher-order. We instead go from single-traversal, circular programs to multi-traversal, non-circular programs that stay first-order. Of course, one could envision combining these transformation routes to replace circularity by higher-orderness while preserving single-traversal behavior.

2. Our General Strategy, and an Example

Our general strategy for transforming a lazy circular into a strict non-circular program is:

1. Find out which parts of the output of a circular call depend on which parts of its input. (Several approaches would be possible to do so, for example classical syntactic dependency analysis. Our main approach will be type-based.)
2. Naively split the circular call into several ones, each computing only one of the outputs, and exploit the information gained in the first step to decouple these different calls.
3. Specialize the different calls (using slicing, partial evaluation, ...) to work only with those pieces of input and output that are actually relevant in each case.

We demonstrate it based on the following circular program, due to Bird [1984]:

$$\textbf{data}\ \mathsf{Tree}\ a = \mathsf{Leaf}\ a \mid \mathsf{Fork}\ (\mathsf{Tree}\ a)\ (\mathsf{Tree}\ a)$$

$$\begin{aligned}
&repmin :: \mathsf{Tree\ Int} \to \mathsf{Int} \to (\mathsf{Tree\ Int}, \mathsf{Int})\\
&repmin\ (\mathsf{Leaf}\ n)\quad m = (\mathsf{Leaf}\ m, n)\\
&repmin\ (\mathsf{Fork}\ l\ r)\ m = (\mathsf{Fork}\ l'\ r', min\ m_1\ m_2)\\
&\qquad\qquad\qquad\textbf{where}\ (l', m_1) = repmin\ l\ m\\
&\qquad\qquad\qquad\qquad\quad\ (r', m_2) = repmin\ r\ m
\end{aligned}$$

$$\begin{aligned}
&run :: \mathsf{Tree\ Int} \to \mathsf{Tree\ Int}\\
&run\ t = \textbf{let}\ (nt, m) = repmin\ t\ m\ \textbf{in}\ nt
\end{aligned}$$

Our goal is to remove the circularity in *run*. So we need to find out which parts of the output of the circular call

$$(nt, m) = repmin\ t\ m$$

depend on which parts of its input. For this example, there is a very easy way to exploit type information. Note that the type $\mathsf{Tree\ Int} \to \mathsf{Int} \to (\mathsf{Tree\ Int}, \mathsf{Int})$ assigned to *repmin* above is not the most general one that would be possible. Indeed, if we omit the explicit type signature and ask Haskell to infer a type from the defining equations of *repmin*, the answer will be:

$$repmin :: \mathsf{Ord}\ a \Rightarrow \mathsf{Tree}\ a \to b \to (\mathsf{Tree}\ b, a)$$

If we had used a non-polymorphic version *min* specialized to type Int, the answer would have been:

$$repmin :: \mathsf{Tree\ Int} \to b \to (\mathsf{Tree}\ b, \mathsf{Int})$$

In any case, we can see that the second output of *repmin* cannot possibly depend on the second input of *repmin* (unless Haskell's arguably impure strict evaluation primitive *seq* would be used, which we assume not to be the case for the programs we transform). The argument is that there is no way how the polymorphic input of unknown type b could be used to influence the computation of an Int. (We will later make use of a more precise formulation of this kind of reasoning.) What we can deduce from this is that for any $t :: \mathsf{Tree\ Int}$ and m_1, m_2 of the same (but arbitrary) type,

$$snd\ (repmin\ t\ m_1) \equiv snd\ (repmin\ t\ m_2)$$

Indeed, for any t and m,

$$snd\ (repmin\ t\ m) \equiv snd\ (repmin\ t\ \bot) \qquad (1)$$

for the undefined value $\bot$.

This information comes in very useful. Note that we could always equivalently (but less efficiently, with two traversals, and still circular) have written the definition of *run* above as:

$$\begin{aligned}
&run :: \mathsf{Tree\ Int} \to \mathsf{Tree\ Int}\\
&run\ t = \textbf{let}\ (nt, _) = repmin\ t\ m\\
&\qquad\qquad\quad\ (_, m) = repmin\ t\ m\\
&\qquad\quad\ \textbf{in}\ nt
\end{aligned}$$

But now we can use (1) to deduce that this is equivalent to:

$$\begin{aligned}
&run :: \mathsf{Tree\ Int} \to \mathsf{Tree\ Int}\\
&run\ t = \textbf{let}\ (nt, _) = repmin\ t\ m\\
&\qquad\qquad\quad\ (_, m) = repmin\ t\ \bot\\
&\qquad\quad\ \textbf{in}\ nt
\end{aligned}$$

which is a non-circular program.

It is not a particularly efficient program, of course, because it twice uses the full *repmin* though only parts of the inputs and outputs are actually relevant in each case. Let us try to remedy this. First for the second call, namely $(\_, m) = repmin\ t\ \bot$. Clearly, it would be beneficial to have a more specialized function, $repmin_{snd}$, which takes only a tree argument and produces only the second output of the original $repmin$. Of course, we can easily define such a function:

$$\begin{aligned}&repmin_{snd} :: \mathsf{Tree\ Int} \to \mathsf{Int}\\&repmin_{snd}\ t = snd\ (repmin\ t\ \bot)\end{aligned}$$

and then replace the above call by simply $m = repmin_{snd}\ t$. Moreover, using standard techniques (general unfold/fold-transformations [Burstall and Darlington 1977], or even an algorithmic variant [Pettorossi and Proietti 1996]), one can derive from the above a direct definition of $repmin_{snd}$:

$$\begin{aligned}&repmin_{snd} :: \mathsf{Tree\ Int} \to \mathsf{Int}\\&repmin_{snd}\ (\mathsf{Leaf}\ n) \quad = n\\&repmin_{snd}\ (\mathsf{Fork}\ l\ r) = min\ (repmin_{snd}\ l)\ (repmin_{snd}\ r)\end{aligned}$$

Similarly, we can replace the other call in the above definition of run, namely $(nt, \_) = repmin\ t\ m$, by $nt = repmin_{fst}\ t\ m$ with:

$$\begin{aligned}&repmin_{fst} :: \mathsf{Tree\ Int} \to b \to \mathsf{Tree}\ b\\&repmin_{fst}\ (\mathsf{Leaf}\ n) \quad m = \mathsf{Leaf}\ m\\&repmin_{fst}\ (\mathsf{Fork}\ l\ r)\ m = \mathsf{Fork}\ (repmin_{fst}\ l\ m)\\&\qquad\qquad\qquad\qquad\qquad\quad (repmin_{fst}\ r\ m)\end{aligned}$$

Ultimately, by simple inlining, this leads to a program consisting of $repmin_{fst}$, $repmin_{snd}$, and:

$$\begin{aligned}&run :: \mathsf{Tree\ Int} \to \mathsf{Tree\ Int}\\&run\ t = repmin_{fst}\ t\ (repmin_{snd}\ t)\end{aligned}$$

which is non-circular, can be evaluated strictly, and indeed corresponds exactly to the program from which Bird [1984] derived the circular version that we started this section with. It can trivially be rewritten in OCaml as:

```
type 'a tree = Leaf of 'a | Fork of ('a tree) * ('a tree)

let rec repmin_fst t m =
  match t with
    Leaf n      -> Leaf m
  | Fork (l, r) -> Fork (repmin_fst l m, repmin_fst r m)

let rec repmin_snd t =
  match t with
    Leaf n      -> n
  | Fork (l, r) -> min (repmin_snd l) (repmin_snd r)

let run t = repmin_fst t (repmin_snd t)
```

Our plan is to apply the approach demonstrated on the $repmin$ example to more complicated programs. As seen above, the key is the discovery of dependencies between inputs and outputs, in a preferably lightweight manner. In the example, we have used a type-based argument, namely that from the inferred function type

$$repmin :: \mathsf{Tree\ Int} \to b \to (\mathsf{Tree}\ b, \mathsf{Int})$$

we can see that the second output cannot depend on the second input. We also promised that there is a precise formulation for such reasoning. Indeed, we next review work in short that provides the desired information systematically.

2.1 Type-Based Useless-Variable Elimination

Kobayashi [2001] proposed a method for detecting dead code via type inference. The basic idea is that if some subexpression in a program can be replaced by a special value () of a special type () without affecting the type of the "$main$-expression" of the program, then it is guaranteed that the subexpression in question has no impact whatsoever on the result computed by the program. Instead of the special value () of the special type () we employ the undefined value $\bot$ of polymorphic type, otherwise our procedure is exactly as Kobayashi's. Our intended use is a bit different: rather than detecting dead code as such, we want to discover input-output-dependencies. But, of course, the latter problem can be reduced to the former: we simply surround a function call of interest with a projection onto some of its output components, pose the resulting expression as $main$-expression, and any pieces of the input that will be detected as useless then are known to not influence the part of the output we are interested in. Concretely, for the $repmin$ example we invoke Kobayashi's method on both

$$\begin{aligned}&\mathbf{let}\ repmin\ (\mathsf{Leaf}\ n)\quad m = (\mathsf{Leaf}\ m, n)\\&\quad repmin\ (\mathsf{Fork}\ l\ r)\ m = (\mathsf{Fork}\ l'\ r', min\ m_1\ m_2)\\&\qquad\qquad\qquad\mathbf{where}\ (l', m_1) = repmin\ l\ m\\&\qquad\qquad\qquad\qquad\quad (r', m_2) = repmin\ r\ m\\&\mathbf{in}\ fst\ (repmin\ t\ m)\end{aligned}$$

and

$$\begin{aligned}&\mathbf{let}\ repmin\ (\mathsf{Leaf}\ n)\quad m = (\mathsf{Leaf}\ m, n)\\&\quad repmin\ (\mathsf{Fork}\ l\ r)\ m = \ldots\\&\mathbf{in}\ snd\ (repmin\ t\ m)\end{aligned}$$

The output (with $\bot$ instead of (), as mentioned above) is:

$$\begin{aligned}&\mathbf{let}\ repmin\ (\mathsf{Leaf}\ n)\quad m = (\mathsf{Leaf}\ m, \bot)\\&\quad repmin\ (\mathsf{Fork}\ l\ r)\ m = (\mathsf{Fork}\ l'\ r', \bot)\\&\qquad\qquad\qquad\mathbf{where}\ (l', m_1) = repmin\ l\ m\\&\qquad\qquad\qquad\qquad\quad (r', m_2) = repmin\ r\ m\\&\mathbf{in}\ fst\ (repmin\ t\ m)\end{aligned}$$

and

$$\begin{aligned}&\mathbf{let}\ repmin\ (\mathsf{Leaf}\ n)\quad m = (\bot, n)\\&\quad repmin\ (\mathsf{Fork}\ l\ r)\ m = (\bot, min\ m_1\ m_2)\\&\qquad\qquad\qquad\mathbf{where}\ (l', m_1) = repmin\ l\ m\\&\qquad\qquad\qquad\qquad\quad (r', m_2) = repmin\ r\ m\\&\mathbf{in}\ snd\ (repmin\ t\ \bot)\end{aligned}$$

respectively. That is how we learn that the second output of $repmin$ does not depend on its second input. Also, Kobayashi's method comes with an optimality statement, in the sense that it finds the maximum of what is possible in terms of replacing subexpressions with () while preserving the type of the overall expression. So from the above result we can also deduce that the first output of $repmin$ indeed depends on both its inputs.

Moreover, Kobayashi [2001] also presents an algorithm that actually eliminates the detected dead code. Basically, it simply removes all function arguments and results that were singled out as special during type inference. Continuing our example, this leads exactly to the functions $repmin_{fst}$ and $repmin_{snd}$ shown earlier in Section 2, for use in replacements of the calls $fst\ (repmin\ t\ m)$ and $snd\ (repmin\ t\ \bot)$.

We see that much of what we need for our strictification toolbox does already exist. We add the ideas of splitting a circular call into separate ones, decoupling, and putting all the pieces together. In fact, our contribution is a way of combining known approaches for general program analysis and transformation such that strictification of circular programs becomes possible. As we will see with more complicated examples later on, one cannot always use Kobayashi's method and/or unfold/fold-transformations "out of the box", though.

3. A Simple Programming Environment

In this section, we apply our approach to a circular program of practical interest, one that deals with the scope rules of a simple programming language.[1] A program in that language consists of a sequence of instructions, where each instruction may either be the declaration or the use of a variable, e.g., $p = [\mathbf{use}\ x; \mathbf{decl}\ x; \mathbf{decl}\ x; \mathbf{use}\ y;]$. Such programs may be described by the following data type:

$$\begin{aligned}&\mathbf{type}\ \mathsf{Prog} = [\mathsf{It}]\\&\mathbf{data}\ \mathsf{It} = \mathsf{Decl\ Var} \mid \mathsf{Use\ Var}\\&\mathbf{type}\ \mathsf{Var} = \mathsf{String}\end{aligned}$$

Now, in order to be well formed, programs in the language, or Prog values, should obey the following scope rules:

1. all variables used must be declared. The declaration of a variable, however, may occur after its first use.
2. a variable must be declared at most once.

We aim to develop a semantic function that analyzes a sequence of instructions and computes a list containing the variable identifiers of the instructions which do not obey the above rules. We require that the list of invalid identifiers follows the sequential structure of the input program. Thus, the semantic meaning of processing the example sentence is $[x, y]$: variable x has been declared twice, and the use of variable y has no binding occurrence at all.

The list of semantic errors encountered in a program (representable as **type** Errors = [Var]), is obtained by checking, for each variable declaration, whether it has already appeared or not. For this, our implementation needs to go on accumulating (in an element of **type** Env = [Var]) the variables that are declared in a program. Furthermore, each variable that is used must be declared somewhere in the program, so we need to know the global environment of the program (the list of all variables declared in it).

The following program implements the desired semantic analysis. A circular call is defined in *run* so that the global environment of an instruction sequence is used while still being constructed.

$$\begin{aligned}&sem :: \mathsf{Prog} \to \mathsf{Env} \to \mathsf{Env} \to (\mathsf{Errors}, \mathsf{Env})\\&sem\ []\quad dcls\ \_ = ([\,], dcls)\\&sem\ (\mathsf{Decl}\ var : p)\ dcls\ env_g\\&\quad = \mathbf{let}\ (errs_p, env_p) = sem\ p\ (var : dcls)\ env_g\\&\qquad\quad errs_{prog} = \mathbf{if}\ var \in dcls\ \mathbf{then}\ var : errs_p\ \mathbf{else}\ errs_p\\&\qquad \mathbf{in}\ (errs_{prog}, env_p)\\&sem\ (\mathsf{Use}\ var : p)\ dcls\ env_g\\&\quad = \mathbf{let}\ (errs_p, env_p) = sem\ p\ dcls\ env_g\\&\qquad\quad errs_{prog} = \mathbf{if}\ var \in env_g\ \mathbf{then}\ errs_p\ \mathbf{else}\ var : errs_p\\&\qquad \mathbf{in}\ (errs_{prog}, env_p)\end{aligned}$$

$$\begin{aligned}&run :: \mathsf{Prog} \to \mathsf{Errors}\\&run\ prog = \mathbf{let}\ (errs, env) = sem\ prog\ [\,]\ env\ \mathbf{in}\ errs\end{aligned}$$

Our goal is now to transform this program into a non-circular one. We follow the same derivation procedure as in the previous section, and obtain:

$$\begin{aligned}&sem_{snd} :: \mathsf{Prog} \to \mathsf{Env} \to \mathsf{Env}\\&sem_{snd}\ [\,]\quad dcls = dcls\\&sem_{snd}\ (\mathsf{Decl}\ var : p)\ dcls = sem_{snd}\ p\ (var : dcls)\\&sem_{snd}\ (\mathsf{Use}\ var : p)\ \ dcls = sem_{snd}\ p\ dcls\end{aligned}$$

$$\begin{aligned}&sem_{fst} :: \mathsf{Prog} \to \mathsf{Env} \to \mathsf{Env} \to \mathsf{Errors}\\&sem_{fst}\ [\,]\quad \_\ \ \_ = [\,]\\&sem_{fst}\ (\mathsf{Decl}\ var : p)\ dcls\ env_g\\&\quad = \mathbf{let}\ errs_p = sem_{fst}\ p\ (var : dcls)\ env_g\\&\qquad \mathbf{in}\ \mathbf{if}\ var \in dcls\ \mathbf{then}\ var : errs_p\ \mathbf{else}\ errs_p\\&sem_{fst}\ (\mathsf{Use}\ var : p)\ \ dcls\ env_g\\&\quad = \mathbf{let}\ errs_p = sem_{fst}\ p\ dcls\ env_g\\&\qquad \mathbf{in}\ \mathbf{if}\ var \in env_g\ \mathbf{then}\ errs_p\ \mathbf{else}\ var : errs_p\end{aligned}$$

$$\begin{aligned}&run :: \mathsf{Prog} \to \mathsf{Errors}\\&run\ prog = sem_{fst}\ prog\ [\,]\ (sem_{snd}\ prog\ [\,])\end{aligned}$$

As we see, the strictification procedure was able to realize that in a non-circular setting the global environment needs to be available (totally, due to the use-before-declare discipline) before semantic errors can be computed; it also tells us *how* that environment can be obtained.

The above program makes no essential use of lazy evaluation, and can be rewritten as an OCaml program (which we omit here due to space restrictions). In the next section we show that the principles we have been using so far still apply to circular programs that do not correspond directly to attribute grammars.

4. Breadth-First Numbering

Inspired by the work of Jones and Gibbons [1993] on breadth-first labelling, Okasaki [2000] gives the following circular program for numbering the inner nodes of a tree in breadth-first order:[2]

$$\mathbf{data}\ \mathsf{Tree}\ a = \mathsf{Empty} \mid \mathsf{Fork}\ a\ (\mathsf{Tree}\ a)\ (\mathsf{Tree}\ a)$$

$$\begin{aligned}&bfn :: \mathsf{Tree}\ a \to [\mathsf{Int}] \to (\mathsf{Tree\ Int}, [\mathsf{Int}])\\&bfn\ \mathsf{Empty}\quad ks\quad = (\mathsf{Empty}, ks)\\&bfn\ (\mathsf{Fork}\ \_\ l\ r)\ \tilde{}(k : ks) = (\mathsf{Fork}\ k\ l'\ r', (k+1) : ks'')\\&\qquad \mathbf{where}\ (l', ks') = bfn\ l\ ks\\&\qquad\qquad\quad (r', ks'') = bfn\ r\ ks'\end{aligned}$$

$$\begin{aligned}&run :: \mathsf{Tree}\ a \to \mathsf{Tree\ Int}\\&run\ t = \mathbf{let}\ (nt, ks) = bfn\ t\ (1 : ks)\ \mathbf{in}\ nt\end{aligned}$$

4.1 A First Approach: Offsets

As mentioned in the introduction, a bit of creativity is needed to deal with the above circular program. Driven by the observation that the second output of *bfn* is "somehow" obtained from its second input by incrementing list elements, potentially repeatedly, we first derive a variant of *bfn* which in its second output returns just those increments/offsets, rather than the result of actually adding them to the second input. The desired relationship between the two functions is:

$$bfn\ t\ ks \equiv \mathbf{let}\ (nt, ds) = bfn_{Off}\ t\ ks\ \mathbf{in}\ (nt, zipPlus\ ks\ ds)$$

where

$$\begin{aligned}&zipPlus :: [\mathsf{Int}] \to [\mathsf{Int}] \to [\mathsf{Int}]\\&zipPlus\ [\,]\quad ds\quad = ds\\&zipPlus\ ks\quad [\,]\quad = ks\\&zipPlus\ (k : ks)\ (d : ds) = (k + d) : (zipPlus\ ks\ ds)\end{aligned}$$

The desired function is obtained pretty straightforwardly as follows:

$$\begin{aligned}&bfn_{Off} :: \mathsf{Tree}\ a \to [\mathsf{Int}] \to (\mathsf{Tree\ Int}, [\mathsf{Int}])\\&bfn_{Off}\ \mathsf{Empty}\quad ks\quad = (\mathsf{Empty}, [\,])\\&bfn_{Off}\ (\mathsf{Fork}\ \_\ l\ r)\ \tilde{}(k : ks) = (\mathsf{Fork}\ k\ l'\ r',\\&\qquad\qquad\qquad 1 : (zipPlus\ ds\ ds'))\\&\quad \mathbf{where}\ (l', ds) = bfn_{Off}\ l\ ks\\&\qquad\qquad (r', ds') = bfn_{Off}\ r\ (zipPlus\ ks\ ds)\end{aligned}$$

[1] Due to space limitations, we consider a simplified version of the Algol 68 rules only. The complete definition is given by de Moor et al. [2000], and is used in the Eli attribute grammar-based system [Kastens et al. 2007].

[2] We use a lazy pattern match (notation: $\tilde{}(k : ks)$) in the second equation of *bfn*, where Okasaki uses a strict one. The lazy version is more convenient for our derivation later on.

and can be used inside *run* as follows:

$$
\begin{array}{l}
run :: \mathsf{Tree}\ a \rightarrow \mathsf{Tree\ Int} \\
run\ t = \mathbf{let}\ (nt, \sim ds) = bfn_{Off}\ t\ (1 : ks) \\
\qquad\qquad\quad ks \qquad\ \ = zipPlus\ (1 : ks)\ ds \\
\qquad\quad \mathbf{in}\ nt
\end{array}
$$

We see that there are now essentially two apparent circular dependencies: ds appears to depend on ks and ks on ds, plus ks depends on itself. Let us first deal with the former. Splitting the call to bfn_{Off} as follows:

$$
\begin{array}{l}
run :: \mathsf{Tree}\ a \rightarrow \mathsf{Tree\ Int} \\
run\ t = \mathbf{let}\ (nt, \_) = bfn_{Off}\ t\ (1 : ks) \\
\qquad\qquad\quad (\_, ds) = bfn_{Off}\ t\ (1 : ks) \\
\qquad\qquad\quad ks \qquad = zipPlus\ (1 : ks)\ ds \\
\qquad\quad \mathbf{in}\ nt
\end{array}
$$

and applying the "type-based analysis plus specialization" approach from Section 2 (more specifically, involving Kobayashi's analysis as discussed in Section 2.1, since pure Haskell type inference is not enough to provide the required information here, due, e.g., to the call $zipPlus\ ks\ ds$ in bfn_{Off}) leads to:[3]

$$
\begin{array}{l}
run :: \mathsf{Tree}\ a \rightarrow \mathsf{Tree\ Int} \\
run\ t = \mathbf{let}\ nt = fst\ (bfn_{Off}\ t\ (1 : ks)) \\
\qquad\qquad\quad ds = bfn_{Off,snd}\ t \\
\qquad\qquad\quad ks = zipPlus\ (1 : ks)\ ds \\
\qquad\quad \mathbf{in}\ nt
\end{array}
$$

$$
\begin{array}{l}
bfn_{Off,snd} :: \mathsf{Tree}\ a \rightarrow [\mathsf{Int}] \\
bfn_{Off,snd}\ \mathsf{Empty} \qquad\quad = [\,] \\
bfn_{Off,snd}\ (\mathsf{Fork}\ \_\ l\ r) = 1 : (zipPlus\ ds\ ds') \\
\quad \mathbf{where}\ ds\ \ = bfn_{Off,snd}\ l \\
\qquad\qquad ds' = bfn_{Off,snd}\ r
\end{array}
$$

Note that it was not possible to specialize the call $fst\ (bfn_{Off}\ t\ (1 : ks))$ to some function $bfn_{Off,fst}$ with fewer input dependencies. On the good side, we have managed to eliminate the circularity between ks and ds, being left with only the circular dependency of ks on itself in the equation $ks = zipPlus\ (1 : ks)\ ds$. Let us look at that equation in a bit more detail, in particular "expanding" the lists to see how their elements relate to each other:

$$
\begin{array}{l}
\quad [k_0, k_1, \ldots] \\
\equiv\ zipPlus\ [1, k_0, k_1, \ldots]\ [d_0, d_1, \ldots, d_n] \\
\equiv\ (1 + d_0) : (zipPlus\ [k_0, k_1, \ldots]\ [d_1, \ldots, d_n]) \\
\equiv\ (1 + d_0) : ((1 + d_0) + d_1) : (zipPlus\ [k_1, \ldots]\ [d_2, \ldots, d_n]) \\
\equiv\ (1 + d_0) : ((1 + d_0) + d_1) : (((1 + d_0) + d_1) + d_2) : \\
\quad (zipPlus\ [k_2, \ldots]\ [d_3, \ldots, d_n]) \\
\equiv\ \ldots \\
\equiv\ (tail\ (scanl\ (+)\ 1\ [d_0, d_1, \ldots, d_n])) \\
\quad +\!\!+\ (zipPlus\ [k_n, \ldots]\ [\,]) \\
\equiv\ (tail\ (scanl\ (+)\ 1\ ds))\ +\!\!+\ [k_n, \ldots] \\
\equiv\ (tail\ (scanl\ (+)\ 1\ ds))\ +\!\!+\ [last\ (scanl\ (+)\ 1\ ds), \ldots] \\
\equiv\ (tail\ (scanl\ (+)\ 1\ ds))\ +\!\!+\ (repeat\ (last\ (scanl\ (+)\ 1\ ds)))
\end{array}
$$

Note that the last line contains no elements from $[k_0, k_1, ...]$, so we have discovered a non-circular definition for ks. Using it instead of the equation $ks = zipPlus\ (1{:}ks)\ ds$ leads to a version of *run* that does not anymore contain circular definitions at all. Admittedly, arriving at the above takes some creativity. But since both *scanl* and *zipPlus* / *zipWith* are pretty well known functions, the discovery that the circular binding involving *zipPlus* can be replaced with straight calls to *scanl* is actually not all too far-fetched.

The only thing that now seems to prevent us from executing *run* in a strict language is the call to *repeat*, which creates an infinite list. Actually, in OCaml this is not a real problem, because despite being strict, OCaml has some simple support for infinite lists. However, we can actually do away with infiniteness completely, because it is easy to see that this part of the list ks will not actually ever be needed. After all, bfn_{Off} never consumes more elements from its second argument than $bfn_{Off,snd}$ produces (for the same input tree, in the list ds). Hence, we can finally rewrite *run* into:

$$
\begin{array}{l}
run :: \mathsf{Tree}\ a \rightarrow \mathsf{Tree\ Int} \\
run\ t = \mathbf{let}\ nt = fst\ (bfn_{Off}\ t\ (1 : ks)) \\
\qquad\qquad\quad ks = tail\ (scanl\ (+)\ 1\ (bfn_{Off,snd}\ t)) \\
\qquad\quad \mathbf{in}\ nt
\end{array}
$$

where bfn_{Off} and $bfn_{Off,snd}$ are the functions shown earlier in this subsection.

The version of the program that we have now arrived at reads as follows when transliterated to OCaml:

```
open List

type 'a tree = Fork of 'a * ('a tree) * ('a tree) | Empty

let rec zipPlus ks ds =
  match ks with
    []          -> ds
  | (k :: ks') -> match ds with
                    []          -> ks
                  | (d :: ds') -> (k + d) :: zipPlus ks' ds'

let rec bfnOff t ks =
  match t with
    Empty          -> (Empty, [])
  | Fork (_, l, r) ->
      let ks' = tl ks in
      let (l', ds) = bfnOff l ks' in
      let (r', ds') = bfnOff r (zipPlus ks' ds) in
      (Fork (hd ks, l', r'), 1 :: (zipPlus ds ds'))

let rec bfnOff,snd t =
  match t with
    Empty          -> []
  | Fork (_, l, r) ->
      let ds  = bfnOff,snd l and
          ds' = bfnOff,snd r
      in 1 :: (zipPlus ds ds')

let rec scanl f n xs =
  match xs with
    []          -> [n]
  | (x :: xs') -> n :: (scanl f (f n x) xs')

let run t = fst (bfnOff t (scanl (+) 1 (bfnOff,snd t)))
```

While having succeeded in turning a lazy, circular into a strict, non-circular program, there is an unpleasant thing about the result: we see recomputation of the same intermediate results $zipPlus\ ds\ ds'$ in $bfn_{Off,snd}$ and bfn_{Off}. That is the price so far of replacing a single (though circular) traversal by two separate ones. Fortunately,

[3] Here is why we used a lazy pattern match above. Without it, we would have a bogus dependency of the second output of bfn_{Off} on its second input (namely requiring that the second input is not the empty list when the first input is a Fork). It would be possible to work around that by using that bfn_{Off} is never called with the empty list inside *run* and ensuing recursive calls. But working with a lazy pattern match right away is more convenient.

it is easy to avoid the recomputations by changing $bfn_{Off,snd}$ to store all the relevant intermediate results:

```
let top t =
  match t with
    Empty           → []
  | Fork (ds, _, _) → ds

let rec bfn_{Off,snd} t =
  match t with
    Empty           → Empty
  | Fork (_, l, r)  →
      let tds  = bfn_{Off,snd} l and
          tds' = bfn_{Off,snd} r
      in Fork (1 :: (zipPlus (top tds) (top tds')), tds, tds')
```

and then reusing them in bfn_{Off}. The latter means that the tree result of $bfn_{Off,snd}$ should be passed as an additional argument to bfn_{Off}. But since that tree has exactly the same shape as the input tree, and since bfn_{Off} already recurses over that input tree *while completely ignoring its content* (only using the tree's *shape*), it is actually possible to avoid introducing an extra argument, instead directly using the result of $bfn_{Off,snd}$ to drive the computation of bfn_{Off}:

```
let rec bfn_Off t ks =
  match t with
    Empty            → (Empty, [])
  | Fork (ds'', l, r) →
      let ks' = tl ks in
      let (l', ds) = bfn_Off l ks' in
      let (r', _) = bfn_Off r (zipPlus ks' ds) in
      (Fork (hd ks, l', r'), ds'')

let run t = let tds = bfn_{Off,snd} t
            in fst (bfn_Off tds (scanl (+) 1 (top tds)))
```

or, alternatively:

```
let rec bfn_Off t ks =
  match t with
    Empty           → Empty
  | Fork (_, l, r)  →
      let ks' = tl ks in
      let l'  = bfn_Off l ks' and
          r'  = bfn_Off r (zipPlus ks' (top l)) in
      Fork (hd ks, l', r')

let run t = let tds = bfn_{Off,snd} t
            in bfn_Off tds (scanl (+) 1 (top tds))
```

Efficiency-wise, we have found that (the Haskell analogons of) these two alternatives just given are on a par. But an interesting difference between the two is that the second one, as opposed also to the original, circular program, has very good potential for parallel evaluation: in it, the two bfn_{Off}-calls are independent of each other. However, we have not explored this aspect further, yet.

A completely different alternative for avoiding *zipPlus*-recomputations, instead of introducing an intermediate data structure to store results, is to use the relationship

$$bfn\ t\ ks \equiv \textbf{let}\ (nt, ds) = bfn_{Off}\ t\ ks\ \textbf{in}\ (nt, zipPlus\ ks\ ds)$$

with which we started the derivation in this subsection. Through it, we can rewrite the Haskell definition of *run* above the transliterated OCaml program (starting with **open** List) into:

```
run :: Tree a → Tree Int
run t = let nt = fst (bfn t (1 : ks))
            ks = tail (scanl (+) 1 (bfn_{Off,snd} t))
        in nt
```

After all, we have by the above relationship that *bfn* and bfn_{Off} compute the same value in the first component of their output pair. The essence with this solution (which would equally well be possible in OCaml, of course) is that we have originally refactored *bfn* into bfn_{Off} to facilitate the removal of the circular dependency, but after we have done the specialization to/for $bfn_{Off,snd}$, we can, for the other traversal, switch back to the original function.

In either case (using *bfn* or bfn_{Off} for the second traversal in *run*, without or with employing an intermediate structure), we have now a two phase solution instead of the original circular definition. The first phase computes a list of "level beginnings", e.g., with

```
t = Fork 'a' (Fork 'b' Empty Empty)
      (Fork 'c' (Fork 'd' (Fork 'e' Empty Empty) Empty)
       (Fork 'f' Empty Empty))
```

we get:

$$scanl\ (+)\ 1\ (bfn_{Off,snd}\ t) \equiv [1,2,4,6,7]$$

The second phase uses such a list to do the actual numbering, either relying on *zipPlus*-calls (but with potential for independent, parallel processing of subtrees) or without (but with a necessarily more sequential processing). In the next subsection now, we derive an alternative for the *first* phase.

4.2 A Second Approach: Prefixes

Instead of using, as in the previous subsection, that the second output of the original *bfn* is obtained from its second input (*ks*) by element-wise adding a finite list (*ds*) to a finite prefix (of *ks*), we can also start from just the observation that exactly a finite prefix will be changed, without taking into account that this happens by repeatedly incrementing. So we now start again from the original *bfn* and first derive a variant which in its second output returns that finite prefix, rather than the whole second input with that prefix changed. The desired relationship between the two functions is:

$$bfn\ t\ ks \equiv \textbf{let}\ (nt, ps) = bfn_{Pre}\ t\ ks\ \textbf{in}\ (nt, merge\ ks\ ps)$$

where

```
merge :: [Int] → [Int] → [Int]
merge []       ps       = ps
merge ks       []       = ks
merge (_ : ks) (p : ps) = p : (merge ks ps)
```

The desired function is obtained pretty straightforwardly as follows:

```
bfn_Pre :: Tree a → [Int] → (Tree Int, [Int])
bfn_Pre Empty        ks         = (Empty, [])
bfn_Pre (Fork _ l r) ~(k : ks) = (Fork k l' r',
                                   (k + 1) : (merge ps ps'))
  where (l', ps)  = bfn_Pre l ks
        (r', ps') = bfn_Pre r (merge ks ps)
```

and can be used inside *run* as follows:

```
run :: Tree a → Tree Int
run t = let (nt, ps) = bfn_Pre t (1 : ks)
            ks       = merge (1 : ks) ps
        in nt
```

Similar expansion and calculation as for the equation $ks = zipPlus\ (1 : ks)\ ds$ in Section 4.1 establishes that the equation $ks = merge\ (1{:}ks)\ ps$ means $ks = ps \mathbin{+\!\!+} (repeat\ (last\ (1{:}ps)))$.

Moreover, since bfn_{Pre} never consumes more elements from its second argument than it produces in its second output, we know that no element of list ks beyond those from ps will ever be needed, so we can directly write:

```
run :: Tree a → Tree Int
run t = let (nt, ps) = bfn_Pre t (1 : ks)
            ks       = ps
        in nt
```

Inlining, and splitting the call to bfn_{Pre} as follows:

```
run :: Tree a → Tree Int
run t = let (nt, _) = bfn_Pre t (1 : ps)
            (_, ps) = bfn_Pre t (1 : ps)
        in nt
```

leaves us with a circular dependency of ps on itself. Applying the "type-based analysis plus specialization" approach from Section 2 leads to:

```
bfn_Pre,snd :: Tree a → [Int] → [Int]
bfn_Pre,snd Empty        ks       = []
bfn_Pre,snd (Fork _ l r) ~(k : ks) = (k + 1) : (merge ps ps')
  where ps  = bfn_Pre,snd l ks
        ps' = bfn_Pre,snd r (merge ks ps)

run :: Tree a → Tree Int
run t = let nt = fst (bfn_Pre t (1 : ps))
            ps = bfn_Pre,snd t (1 : ps)
        in nt
```

but *fails* to discover any limits on input-output-dependencies. In particular, the circular dependency of ps on itself persists. Our best bet now is to again expand the list ps and try to discover internal relationships between list elements from

$$[p_0, p_1, \ldots, p_n] \equiv bfn_{Pre,snd}\ t\ [1, p_0, p_1, \ldots, p_n]$$

However, this clearly depends dynamically on the concrete tree t (in a certain way which we do not want to simply take for granted, though). So what can we do?

Well, conceptually at least we can still apply our approach of splitting a circular equation into several ones in the hope of discovering limited dependencies. The equation $ps = bfn_{Pre,snd}\ t\ (1{:}ps)$ thus becomes:

$$\begin{aligned}
[p_0, _, \ldots, _] &= bfn_{Pre,snd}\ t\ [1, p_0, p_1, \ldots, p_n]\\
[_, p_1, \ldots, _] &= bfn_{Pre,snd}\ t\ [1, p_0, p_1, \ldots, p_n]\\
&\ldots\\
[_, _, \ldots, p_n] &= bfn_{Pre,snd}\ t\ [1, p_0, p_1, \ldots, p_n]
\end{aligned}$$

By inspection, in particular observing the behavior of $merge$, we find that the ith position of the output list of $bfn_{Pre,snd}$ only ever depends on the ith position of its second argument. Hence, the above becomes:

$$\begin{aligned}
[p_0, _, \ldots, _] &= bfn_{Pre,snd}\ t\ [1, \bot, \bot, \ldots, \bot]\\
[_, p_1, \ldots, _] &= bfn_{Pre,snd}\ t\ [\bot, p_0, \bot, \ldots, \bot]\\
&\ldots\\
[_, _, \ldots, p_n] &= bfn_{Pre,snd}\ t\ [\bot, \ldots, p_{n-1}, \bot]
\end{aligned}$$

Note that this is of course not something we could write in the program, because even the length n of the target list can and will vary dynamically with t. But assume we had a function h which given an i and p_{i-1} (or 1 if $i = 0$) gives us the value bound to p_i in the relevant (if even existing) line above. More specifically, we seek a function

$$h :: \mathsf{Tree}\ a \to (\mathsf{Int}, \mathsf{Int}) \to \mathsf{Maybe\ Int}$$

such that $h\ t\ (i, p_{i-1})$ is Nothing if $bfn_{Pre,snd}\ t\ (1 : ps)$ contains no p_i, otherwise is Just p_i. Then we could rewrite run as follows:

```
run :: Tree a → Tree Int
run t = let go (i, p) = case h t (i, p) of
                          Nothing → []
                          Just p' → p' : (go (i + 1, p'))
            ps = go (0, 1)
        in fst (bfn_Pre t (1 : ps))
```

The desired h-function can be derived from $bfn_{Pre,snd}$ by using that:

1. Instead of an input list we only need to pass in the single value that would have resided in the ith position (starting counting from zero). That is, an input (i, p) to h corresponds to an input list to $bfn_{Pre,snd}$ consisting of i occurrences of $\bot$, then p, then filled up with further $\bot$s.
2. Instead of an output list we only need to return information about whether an ith position exists in it, and if so, the value of that list element.
3. Lookup in lists interacts in a very simple way with the $merge$-function. Namely, an ith position exists in $merge\ xs\ ys$ if and only if it is so in at least one of xs and ys; and moreover, if both xs and ys contain an ith position, then the value from ys takes precedence.

The resulting function looks as follows:

```
h :: Tree a → (Int, Int) → Maybe Int
h Empty        (_, _) = Nothing
h (Fork _ l r) (0, k) = Just (k + 1)
h (Fork _ l r) (i, k) = case h l (i − 1, k) of
                          Nothing → case h r (i − 1, k) of
                                      Nothing → Nothing
                                      Just p' → Just p'
                          Just p  → case h r (i − 1, p) of
                                      Nothing → Just p
                                      Just p' → Just p'
```

Its first equation corresponds to the first equation of $bfn_{Pre,snd}$. Its second equation corresponds to the second equation of $bfn_{Pre,snd}$ in the case that we are focussed on the 0th position in input and output. Finally, its third equation corresponds to the second equation of $bfn_{Pre,snd}$ in the case that we are focussed on a later position, i.e., the k in (i, k) corresponds to some element of the tail ks in $bfn_{Pre,snd}$'s equation, and correspondingly the output, if any, is to come from the call $merge\ ps\ ps'$ with $ps \equiv bfn_{Pre,snd}\ l\ ks$ and $ps' \equiv bfn_{Pre,snd}\ r\ (merge\ ks\ ps)$. Then, of the four branches of the nested **case**-expressions in the definition of h,

- the first corresponds to the case where neither ps nor ps' (which is actually equivalent to $bfn_{Pre,snd}\ r\ ks$ in this case as far as the $(i-1)$st position is concerned) contains an $(i-1)$st position;
- the second corresponds to the case where ps does not contain an $(i-1)$st position, but ps' (essentially equivalent to $bfn_{Pre,snd}\ r\ ks$ as before) does;
- the third corresponds to the case where ps does contain an $(i-1)$st position, with value p, but ps' (now equivalent to $bfn_{Pre,snd}\ r\ ps$ as far as the $(i-1)$st position is concerned) does not; and
- the fourth corresponds to the case that both ps and ps' (again essentially equivalent to $bfn_{Pre,snd}\ r\ ps$) contain values in the $(i-1)$st position, of which the one from the call on r takes precedence due to the call $merge\ ps\ ps'$.

Thus, we have arrived at a non-circular program suitable for use in OCaml. However, this time we right away replace, via the relationship

$$bfn\ t\ ks\ \equiv\ \mathbf{let}\ (nt, ps) = bfn_{Pre}\ t\ ks\ \mathbf{in}\ (nt, merge\ ks\ ps)$$

from the beginning of this subsection, bfn_{Pre} by the original bfn (for computing the first component of the output pair):

```
let rec bfn t ks =
  match t with
    Empty          → (Empty, ks)
  | Fork (_, l, r) →
      let (k, ks') = (List.hd ks, List.tl ks) in
      let (l', ks'') = bfn l ks' in
      let (r', ks''') = bfn r ks'' in
      (Fork (k, l', r'), (k + 1) :: ks''')

let rec h t ip =
  match t, ip with
    Empty, _                → None
  | Fork (_, l, r), (0, k) → Some (k + 1)
  | Fork (_, l, r), (i, k) → match h l (i − 1, k) with
                                 None   → h r (i − 1, k)
                               | Some p →
                                   (match h r (i − 1, p) with
                                       None    → Some p
                                     | Some p' → Some p')

let run t = let rec go (i, p) =
              match h t (i, p) with
                None    → []
              | Some p' → p' :: (go (i + 1, p')) in
            let ps = go (0, 1) in fst (bfn t (1 :: ps))
```

Essentially, we have arrived at an implementation of a breadth-first task via iterative deepening! Note that the Haskell version of it also works well on infinite trees, just as the Haskell versions from Section 4.1 do.

5. Analysis

Being able to transform circular into non-circular programs is certainly nice on a conceptual level, but ultimately of course the question is what such a transformation does to program efficiency. The two major factors of interest are runtime and heap consumption. We have performed a whole range of experiments in Haskell and OCaml. In order to really compare the impact of strictification (rather than the power of different compilers), we decided to plot here the results of systematic measurements in Haskell only. To simulate strict evaluation, rather than only evaluating a non-circular program in a lazy fashion, we employed Haskell's strict evaluation primitives (*seq* and friends). So generally we compare three program versions: a circular one, a non-circular one derived from it (and evaluated lazily), and an explicitly strictified version of the latter (with strictness primitives judiciously added where Haskell would otherwise deviate from OCaml's evaluation order). Measurements were performed on a Dell Precision Workstation T3400 with an Intel® Core™2 Q9550 processor (4 x 2.83GHz) and 3.8GB memory available. Programs were compiled with ghc-6.12.3, optimizing with `-O2`. The Criterion library (`http://hackage.haskell.org/package/criterion`) was used for runtime measurements and GHC's built-in profiler for heap measurements (for the latter, with stack size increased to 500 MBytes via the runtime option `-K500M`). Where appropriate and interesting, we also comment on the relative efficiency of OCaml vs. Haskell, as observed via wall-clock measurements. (For OCaml we used native-code compilation via `ocamlopt` version 3.11.2, stack size set with `ulimit -s 500000`.) We analyze the programs from Sections 2 and 4, and variants/algorithms that have come up in the literature [Chin et al. 1999; Okasaki 2000; Pettorossi and Skowron 1987]. We do not show results for the programs from Section 3, even though we have measured them as well. Those measurements show that the non-circular versions are on a par with, or better than (sometimes considerably, depending on the distribution of variable declarations and uses in the input sequence), the circular version.

5.1 Repmin

First the relation between circular and non-circular variants of the simple *repmin*-example is measured using three program versions: the circular program we started from in Section 2, the non-circular program we ended up with in Section 2, and a completely strict version of the latter. It turns out that the circular version is slowest, despite the fact that it ostensibly saves traversal work compared to the two non-circular versions. The relative efficiency of the two non-circular versions depends on the shape of trees. On fully balanced trees we find that the lazily evaluated version is better (also than the OCaml version, which has about the same performance as the strict Haskell version):

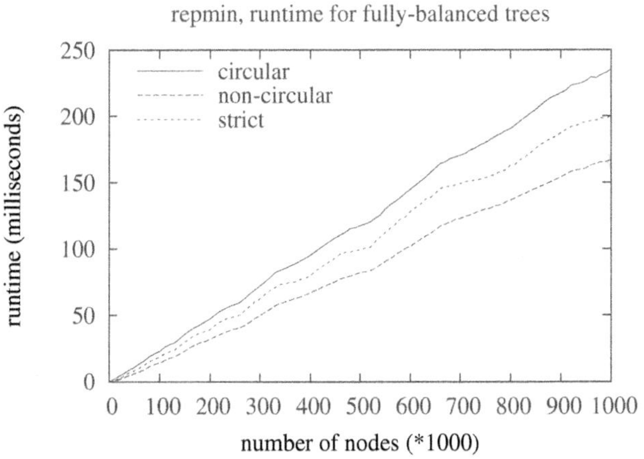

while for strongly left-leaning trees we observed that the completely strict version had a small advantage.

An interesting point of comparison is the results of Chin et al. [1999]. They consider *strictness-guided tupling* to prevent the introduction of extra thunks, and also look at circular tupling. In particular, they perform measurements for various versions of *repmin* (which they call *mintip*) in their Section 6. It turns out that, possibly due to changes/advances in compiler technology for lazy languages, our findings today differ from what they observed. In a nutshell, their results are summarized in Table 3 on page 127, replicated here in part:[4]

100 times of *mintip* on a tree of depth 12					
	Heap	Time(s)			
	(bytes)	INIT	MUT	GC	Total
No Tupling (!)	29,679,824	0.02	19.49	0.57	20.08
Tupling with (!)	52,620,228	0.01	27.81	4.14	31.96
No Tupling (⋆)	24,762,928	0.03	14.51	0.57	15.11
Tupling with (⋆)	18,211,728	0.02	11.95	0.34	12.31

[4] Of the six lines of measurements there, we consider only the first two and the last two, because the middle two concern a "medium-strict" version of *repmin* that we do not have otherwise present in our repertoire.

The first line here corresponds to our non-circular version. The second line corresponds to our circular version. The third line corresponds to our completely strictified non-circular version. And finally, the fourth line is the outcome of Chin et al.'s strictness-guided, circular tupling, i.e., a circular program with extra strictness annotations to prevent the detrimental effects of tupling on efficiency. In contrast to Chin et al.'s measurements, our plot above situates "No Tupling (⋆)" between "No Tupling (!)" and "Tupling with (!)", and if we include "Tupling with (⋆)" in the picture, we find that it performs almost identically to "No Tupling (⋆)" (actually, slightly worse).

We have also run lazily and strictly evaluated versions of *repmin* that Pettorossi and Skowron [1987] obtained by applying the lambda-abstraction strategy [Pettorossi and Proietti 1988]. We found them to perform worse than all the program versions considered above. In OCaml, the multi-traversal and the single-traversal, higher-order program had almost indistinguishable performance, and were not considerably faster than the original circular version in Haskell. As in the case of the results of Chin et al. [1999], we do not really have a ready explanation for these differences we observed from what the literature suggests about the relative performance to be expected when comparing different flavors of circular and non-circular programs.

5.2 Breadth-First Numbering

Here, let us begin by studying the programs from Section 4.1. We measure five program versions:

- the circular program we started from in Section 4;
- the non-circular Haskell program we finally ended up with in Section 4.1, with bfn_{Off} replaced by the original *bfn*, and with the main call in *run* changed to fit with the OCaml versions;
- a completely strict version of the latter;
- a Haskell version of the last OCaml program in Section 4.1, using an intermediate structure; and
- a completely strict version of the latter.

It turns out that the versions using an intermediate structure are not really a consistent/substantial runtime improvement over the original, circular program (but recall that we identified parallelization potential for these versions, which might ultimately change the picture), while the versions doing without an intermediate structure (but coming without potential for parallelization) do quite well in sequential evaluation:

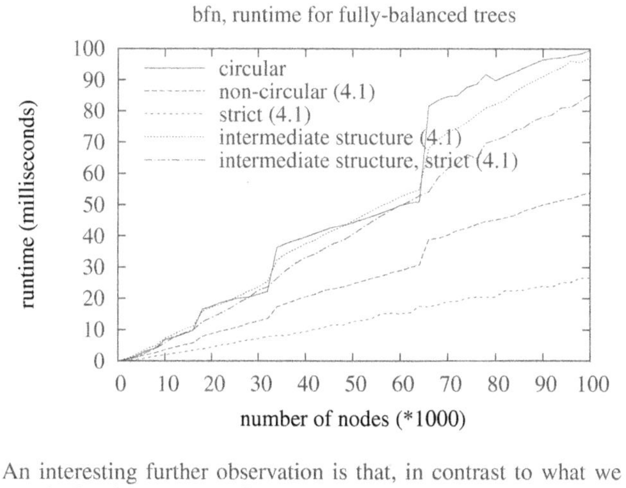

An interesting further observation is that, in contrast to what we saw in Section 5.1, use of Haskell's strictness primitives pays off here, as both the strict programs perform faster than their corresponding non-strict versions.[5] Moreover, if we look at Haskell heap consumption even the program versions using an intermediate structure are better than the original, circular program:

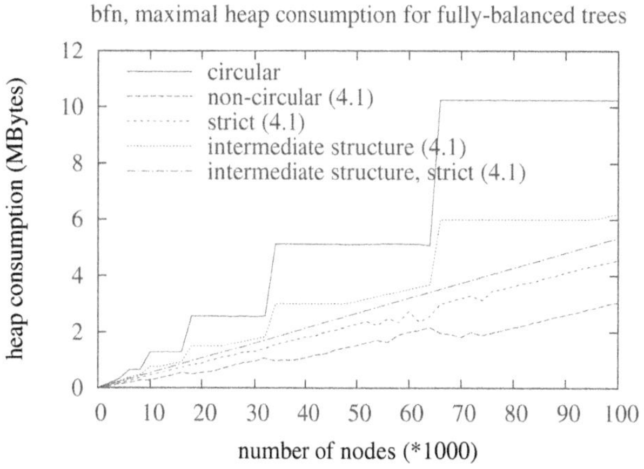

We also measured the final non-circular Haskell program derived in Section 4.2, with bfn_{Pre} replaced by the original *bfn* (and with *h* changed slightly to fit with the OCaml version), and a completely strict version of it. We found that the strictified version is about equally good as the completely strict version arising from Section 4.1 (which was the best one above), and that the same relative statement holds for wall-clock measurements in OCaml. In terms of Haskell heap consumption, we found that the lazily evaluated non-circular program arising from Section 4.2 performs almost exactly like the corresponding one from Section 4.1, and similarly for the completely strict Haskell versions.

We have already mentioned that Okasaki [2000] studied breadth-first numbering from an algorithmic perspective. As non-circular programs, he presents two different algorithms, one level-oriented (his Figure 5), the other forest/queue-based (his Figure 3). If we run a Haskell implementation of the level-oriented solution and a completely strict version of it against the circular breadth-first numbering program and against our own best version, we get the following timings (showing that our own program still performs the best; the same holds in OCaml):

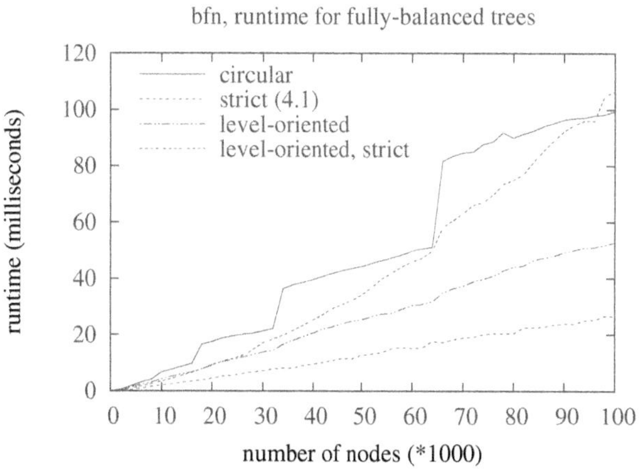

[5] And if we move to OCaml, the runtimes of the strict versions are cut by about another half.

For Haskell heap consumption, the situation is similar:

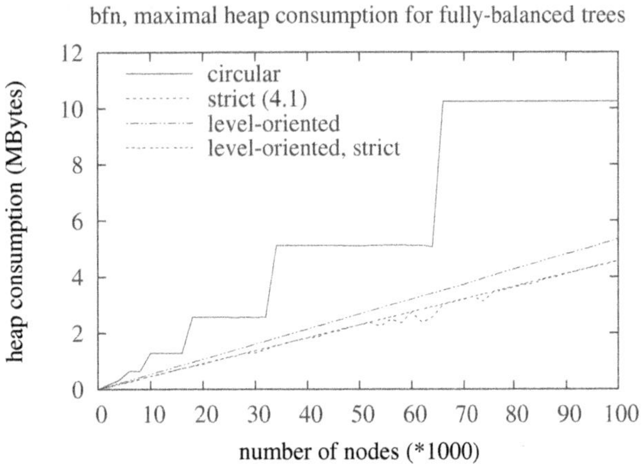

Measuring a Haskell implementation of Okasaki's forest/queue-based solution and a completely strict version of it, we found that both perform similarly to the original, circular program in terms of runtime:

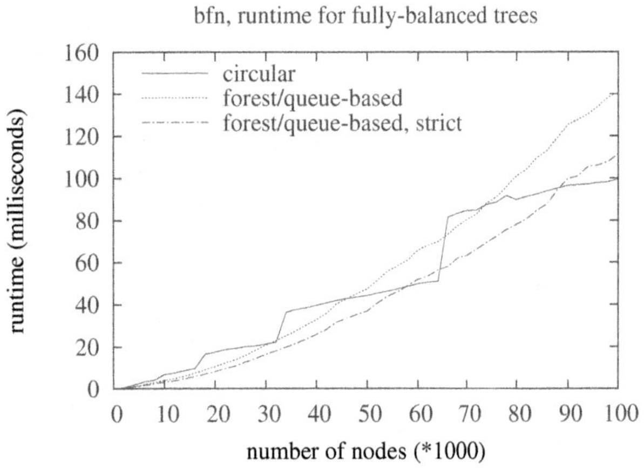

while the heap consumption lines are similar to those for the level-oriented programs above. Surprisingly, we observed the forest/queue-based solution in OCaml to take about 50% more time than the corresponding strict Haskell version. (We have not tried to fine-tune Okasaki's OCaml version to potentially invert the situation, which might well be possible.)

6. Conclusion

We have proposed an approach to eliminating circular definitions from traversal programs in a lazy functional language, and performed benchmarking that shows it effective in practice. One further potential use of this kind of transformation is as a preprocessing step for other optimization techniques. For example, elimination of intermediate results (deforestation) from compositions of circular programs (with other, circular or non-circular) programs is a challenging problem. By first eliminating circularity, we could reduce this problem to one in a more standard setting. Using techniques like those of Voigtländer [2004] and Fernandes et al. [2007] we could even end up with circular programs again in the end. Similarly, we could try to benefit from the technique of Chin et al. [1999] for the optimization of circular programs. As developed, that technique applies to a non-circular program as a starting point. In fact, the authors emphasize that the same effects cannot be obtained by directly applying strictness analysis to a circular program. But using our approach, a possible route for optimization of circular programs would be to first transform into a non-circular program and then use Chin et al.'s technique.

Acknowledgments

We thank the anonymous reviewers for their comments and suggestions, and Chris Okasaki for remarks on *bfn* and our variants.

References

R.S. Bird. Using circular programs to eliminate multiple traversals of data. *Acta Informatica*, 21(3):239–250, 1984.

R.M. Burstall and J. Darlington. A transformation system for developing recursive programs. *Journal of the ACM*, 24(1):44–67, 1977.

W.N. Chin, A.H. Goh, and S.C. Khoo. Effective optimisation of multiple traversals in lazy languages. In *Partial Evaluation and Semantics-Based Program Manipulation, Proceedings*, Technical Report, University of Aarhus, pages 119–130, 1999.

O. de Moor, S.L. Peyton Jones, and E. Van Wyk. Aspect-oriented compilers. In *Generative and Component-Based Software Engineering 1999, Revised Papers*, LNCS 1799:121–133. Springer, 2000.

J.P. Fernandes and J. Saraiva. Tools and libraries to model and manipulate circular programs. In *Partial Evaluation and Semantics-Based Program Manipulation, Proceedings*, pages 102–111. ACM, 2007.

J.P. Fernandes, A. Pardo, and J. Saraiva. A shortcut fusion rule for circular program calculation. In *Haskell Workshop, Proceedings*, pages 95–106. ACM, 2007.

T. Johnsson. Attribute grammars as a functional programming paradigm. In *Functional Programming Languages and Computer Architecture, Proceedings*, LNCS 274:154–173. Springer, 1987.

G. Jones and J. Gibbons. Linear-time breadth-first tree algorithms: An exercise in the arithmetic of folds and zips. Technical Report 71, Department of Computer Science, University of Auckland, 1993.

U. Kastens. Ordered attribute grammars. *Acta Informatica*, 13:229–256, 1980.

U. Kastens, A.M. Sloane, and W.M. Waite. *Generating Software from Specifications*. Jones & Bartlett Publishers, 2007.

N. Kobayashi. Type-based useless-variable elimination. *Higher-Order and Symbolic Computation*, 14(2–3):221–260, 2001.

M.F. Kuiper and S.D. Swierstra. Using attribute grammars to derive efficient functional programs. In *Computing Science in the Netherlands, Proceedings*, pages 39–52. SION, 1987.

C. Okasaki. Breadth-first numbering: lessons from a small exercise in algorithm design. In *International Conference on Functional Programming, Proceedings*, pages 131–136. ACM, 2000.

A. Pardo, J.P. Fernandes, and J. Saraiva. Shortcut fusion rules for the derivation of circular and higher-order monadic programs. In *Partial Evaluation and Program Manipulation, Proceedings*, pages 81–90. ACM, 2009.

A. Pettorossi and M. Proietti. Importing and exporting information in program development. In *Partial Evaluation and Mixed Computation 1987, Proceedings*, pages 405–425. North-Holland, 1988.

A. Pettorossi and M. Proietti. Rules and strategies for transforming functional and logic programs. *ACM Computing Surveys*, 28(2):360–414, 1996.

A. Pettorossi and A. Skowron. Higher order generalization in program derivation. In *Theory and Practice of Software Development, Proceedings*, LNCS 250:182–196. Springer, 1987.

J. Saraiva. *Purely Functional Implementation of Attribute Grammars*. PhD thesis, Utrecht University, Department of Computer Science, 1999.

J. Voigtländer. Using circular programs to deforest in accumulating parameters. *Higher-Order and Symbolic Computation*, 17(1–2):129–163, 2004.

A Semantics for Lazy Assertions

Olaf Chitil
University of Kent, UK
O.Chitil@kent.ac.uk

Abstract

Lazy functional programming languages need lazy assertions to ensure that assertions preserve the meaning of programs. Examples in this paper demonstrate that previously proposed lazy assertions nonetheless break basic semantic equivalences, because they include a non-deterministic disjunction combinator. The objective of this paper is to determine "correct" definitions for lazy assertions. The starting point is our formalisation of basic properties such as laziness, taking them as axioms of our design space. We develop the first denotational semantics for lazy assertions; assertions denote subdomains. We define a weak disjunction combinator and together with a conjunction combinator assertions form a bounded distributive lattice. From the established laws we derive an efficient prototype implementation of lazy assertions for Haskell as a library.

Categories and Subject Descriptors D.1.1 [*Programming Techniques*]: Applicative (Functional) Programming; F.3.2 [*Semantics of Programming Languages*]: Denotational semantics

General Terms Languages, Reliability, Theory

1. Introduction

Assertions have been used by programmers for a long time to express within their programming language properties of parts of their programs [20]. Assertions document expected properties. They are usually checked at runtime; if a fault occurs, the assertion raises an exception and thus helps locating the cause of the fault [21].

Assertions look like the perfect match for lazy functional programming languages: Because assertions are side-effect free functions, inserting or removing an assertion should not change the meaning of a program, except when the violation of an assertion is reported by an exception. Let us consider a simple example of an assertion in Haskell:

```
assert nats [4,2]
```

Here `nats` shall be an assertion expressing that a given list is a list of natural numbers. The function `assert` applies the assertion[1] to the list `[4,2]`. The expression evaluates to `[4,2]`. In contrast, the expression

```
assert nats [4,-2]
```

raises an exception, because the assertion is violated. The function `assert nats` is a partial identity on integer lists.

A lazy functional language allows the definition of infinite data structures. We should be allowed to insert our assertion directly into the recursive definition of the infinite list of Fibonacci numbers:

```
fibs :: [Integer]
fibs = assert nats
         (0 : 1 : zipWith (+) fibs (tail fibs))
```

Here `zipWith` combines the Fibonacci list and the Fibonacci list without its first element via element-wise addition.

For this definition to work, just as it does without the application of `assert nats`, the assertion must be lazy. An assertion is lazy, if the argument of assertion application is evaluated always only as far as it is demanded by the context of the assertion application. In denotational terms this means that the assertion has to accept not just total lists of natural numbers, but also any partial approximation of such a list:

```
assert nats (0:1:⊥)        ⇝   0:1:⊥
assert nats (0:1:1:⊥)      ⇝   0:1:1:⊥
assert nats (0:1:1:2:⊥)    ⇝   0:1:1:2:⊥
```

In general, any approximation of an acceptable value has to be accepted by an assertion to ensure that the programmer can insert assertions anywhere without changing the meaning of the program. Lazy languages need lazy assertions.

Several lazy assertion systems have been proposed [5–7], but they turn out to be unacceptable, because they break basic semantic equivalences that are used by any optimising compiler. Consider an assertion `equal` for tuples of Booleans which asserts that the two values of the tuple are equal. This assertion can easily be defined in all previously proposed systems. As expected, the program snippet

```
let x = assert equal (True,False)
in (fst x, snd x)
```

raises an exception when evaluated. However, let us apply the basic program transformation of let-inlining and we get

```
(fst (assert equal (True,False)),
 snd (assert equal (True,False)))
```

Evaluating this snippet yields `(True,False)`. No assertion exception is raised! The simple reason is that each of the two assertions only sees a partial value and both `(True,⊥)` and `(⊥,False)` have to be accepted by a lazy assertion as they are approximations of the

[1] We follow common practise of separating the assertion and the assertion application function `assert`. In practise `assert` also takes additional arguments to name the error location in case the assertion is violated. Some assertion systems [9] fuse `assert` with the assertion though refunctionalisation, which can improve performance. However, considering assertions as data that is interpreted by `assert` makes the implementation design easier, because definitions of interpreters are generally easier to understand than higher-order functions.

PEPM'11, January 24–25, 2011, Austin, Texas, USA.

evidently acceptable values (True,True) and (False,False) respectively.

The nub of the problem is that `assert equal` is not a function, it is non-deterministic. The value of `assert equal (True,False)` is either `(True, error "assertion violated")` or `(error "assertion violated", False)`, depending on which part of the tuple is demanded first. Previously proposed assertion systems use non-pure extensions such as `unsafePerformIO` to step outside the pure functional language to enable the implementation of `assert equal`. Allowing such "non-deterministic functions" whose results depend on the context requires a complex, non-standard language semantics. As we have just seen, it also breaks standard equivalences.

We do not want to repeat the experience of first implementing a new assertion system and later finding that it does not meet basic semantic requirements. Instead we start with defining a simple denotational semantics, ensuring that lazy assertions will have the expected semantics. We formalise requirements such as laziness and take them as axioms that determine our design space. From the axioms we derive many further properties of lazy assertions. In particular we establish that lazy assertions with a conjunctive and a disjunctive combinator form a bounded distributive lattice. We see that disjunction has to be weaker than we might expect and that assertions do not allow for a general negation operator. Only after establishing these general properties we finally consider assertions for specific type structures, mainly algebraic data types. We use the previously proved properties to derive an efficient implementation in Haskell.

The example of Boolean tuples demonstrated that proper lazy assertions by their very nature cannot express properties that relate different parts of a data structure. Hence we start in Section 2 with a number of examples showing that despite this limitation many useful applications of the lazy assertions, which we derive in this paper, exist. Then Section 3 sets out our denotational semantics and motivates and formalises axioms. Subsequently Section 4 derives central properties of lazy assertions and develops a less intuitive, but smaller set of axioms for future use. Section 5 is the core of the paper, defining general assertion combinators and proving their properties. In Section 6 we then instantiate the general semantics for specific data types, prove type-specific laws and derive the implementation. Section 7 discusses related work and Section 8 concludes.

2. Examples for Assertions

Which kind of properties can we express with lazy assertions? For primitive built-in types such as `Integer` and `Char` we have a combinator that allows any Boolean predicate to check the desired property:

```
pred :: Prim t => (t -> Bool) -> Assert t
```

For algebraic data types lazy assertions are mainly patterns. For the list data type with its two constructors

```
(:) :: t -> [t] -> [t]
[]  :: [t]
```

we have two corresponding assertion combinators

```
pCons :: Assert t -> Assert [t] -> Assert [t]
pNil  :: Assert [t]
```

Furthermore, the assertion combinator

```
(<|>) :: Assert t -> Assert t -> Assert t
```

combines two assertions disjunctively, a value may fulfil the first or the second assertion. With these combinators we can define the assertion of the introduction:

```
nats :: Assert [Integer]
nats = pNil <|> pCons (pred (>=0)) nats
```

So a list of natural numbers is either an empty list or a non-empty list with a natural number as first element and a list of natural numbers as the tail. The definition reads similar to an algebraic data type definition in Haskell.

Many language features are useful for better defining assertions. For example, we may want to separate the reusable idea of asserting a property for all elements of a list:

```
nats :: Assert [Integer]
nats = pList (pred (>=0))

pList :: Assert t -> Assert [t]
pList a = pNil <|> pCons a (pList a)
```

We also have a lazy assertion combinator

```
pAny :: Assert t
```

that accepts any value of any type a.

We can easily define an assertion that accepts only infinite lists:

```
infinite :: Assert [t]
infinite = pCons pAny infinite
```

The assertion accepts also all partial approximations, such as $7:\bot$, but not any list ending with the constructor `[]`.

We can also define assertion combinators with parameters that are not assertions. For example, we can define assertions that only accept lists of a given minimal length:

```
lengthAtLeast :: Int -> Assert [t]
lengthAtLeast 0     = pAny
lengthAtLeast (n+1) = pCons pAny (lengthAtLeast n)
```

If the given length is 0, any list is accepted. If it is greater, then the list must be non-empty and the tail must be of a length 1 shorter. This assertion might be used in a definition such as

```
initAv :: [Int] -> Int
initAv = assert (lengthAtLeast 5 |-> pAny) initAv'

initAv' xs = sum (take 5 xs) 'div' 5
```

Here

```
(|->) :: Assert s -> Assert t -> Assert (s->t)
```

wraps assertions for a pre- and a post-condition around a function. The assertion `lengthAtLeast` guarantees that `initAv` always determines the average of the first 5 list elements; it raises an exception if the list is too short.

The assertion `lengthAtLeast` is strict in its numeric argument. Using it with a constant argument is safe, but otherwise it could turn a terminating into a non-terminating program.

Let us consider a bigger example. Assume we have a program manipulating propositional formulae with functions computing various normal forms. The data type for representing a propositional formula is

```
data Form = Imp Form Form | And Form Form |
            Or Form Form | Not Form | Atom Char
```

Now we want to assert that some function produces a conjunctive normal form. The assertion `conjNF` defined below accepts the set of conjunctive normal forms:

```
conjNF, disj, lit, atom :: Assert Form

conjNF = pAnd conjNF conjNF <|> disj
disj = pOr disj disj <|> lit
```

```
lit = pNot atom <|> atom
atom = pAtom pAny
```

Again these definitions look similar to several algebraic data type definitions or a context-free grammar.

Another function may transform a formula such that all binary operations are left-associated. The assertion `left` can check for this property:

```
left, noImp, noAnd, noOr, nonBind :: Assert Form

left = noImp <|> noAnd <|> noOr
noImp = pAnd left noAnd <|> pOr left noOr <|> nonBin
noAnd = pImp left noImp <|> pOr left noOr <|> nonBin
noOr = pImp left noImp <|> pAnd left noAnd <|> nonBin
nonBin = pNot left <|> pAtom pAny
```

These definitions contain repeated code. Easier to read is an equivalent definition that uses the combinator `<\>` that subtracts a given constructor from the set of accepted values, that is, any term with the given constructor at the top is not accepted.

```
left = pImp left (left <\> cImp) <|>
       pAnd left (left <\> cAnd) <|>
       pOr left (left <\> cOr) <|>
       pNot left <|> pAtom pAny
```

If we want to ensure that a formula is both in conjunctive normal form and all binary operators left-associated, we just use the conjunction combinator `<&>`:

```
leftConjNF :: Assert Form
leftConjNF = conjNF <&> left
```

3. Semantics and Axioms

Every assertion asserts a property for values of a given domain, such as the values of type `Form`. For our denotational semantics of lazy assertions we make the standard assumption that a domain D is a directed complete partial order with least element $\bot$ [1]. So every directed subset has a least upper bound. For simplicity we also assume that the exception raised by assertion violation is represented by the least element $\bot$ of the domain; it is not distinct.

What exactly is an assertion? An assertion a divides the domain D into a set of accepted values $[\![a]\!]$ and the remaining non-accepted values. The function `assert` turns any assertion a into a function that maps from the domain into the domain. From now on we write $\langle a \rangle : D \to D$ for the semantics of the expression `assert` a. From $\langle a \rangle$ we obtain the acceptance set $[\![a]\!]$:

DEFINITION 1 (Acceptance set of an assertion).
Let a be an assertion. Then

$$[\![a]\!] := \{v \in D \mid \langle a \rangle\, v = v\}$$

is the acceptance set of a.

Our axioms for lazy assertions are the following:

DEFINITION 2 (Axioms for lazy assertions).
a is a lazy assertion, *if it meets the following axioms:*

1. *$\langle a \rangle : D \to D$ is a continuous function.*
2. *a is* trustworthy, *that is, $\langle a \rangle\, v \in [\![a]\!]$ for any value v.*
3. *$\langle a \rangle$ is a* partial identity, *that is, $\langle a \rangle\, v \sqsubseteq v$ for any value v.*
4. *$[\![a]\!]$ is a lower set.*

A lower set is a set that contains all approximations of its elements, that is, S is lower if and only if $v \in S$ and $v' \sqsubseteq v$ imply $v' \in S$.

We require the four axioms for the following reasons:

1. We want to ensure that the addition of assertions does not change the semantics of the lazy language in any way. Hence we require $\langle a \rangle$ to be a function. To be sure and for ease of implementation we also aim to define lazy assertions as a library within the lazy language itself. Consequently $\langle a \rangle$ has to be a continuous function.
2. A purpose of an assertion is to protect the context of the assertion-wrapped expression, and thus the remainder of the programme, from ever seeing a value that is unacceptable for the assertion. Trustworthiness captures this property.
3. To preserve the semantics of a program when introducing assertions, an assertion has to be the identity on all values of the acceptance set. Even for values outside the acceptance set an assertion should not return an arbitrary value, but some approximation of the original value.
4. We already argued in the introduction, that any approximation v' of a value v that is evidently acceptable must be accepted as well. When the context of the assertion application forces evaluation only up to v', the demanded parts of v' have to be returned. Raising an exception would be wrong, because v' may later be evaluated further to v. When only v' is demanded the assertion may not evaluate further to check whether v' is actually v, because that would be eager evaluation and could cause non-termination.

Any acceptance set of a lazy assertion is a domain. Trivially, any subset A of a domain D is a partial order and the least upper bound of any directed subset in D is also a least upper bound in A. However, we have to prove that these least upper bounds are in A. We also need $\bot \in A$.

THEOREM 1 (Acceptance sets are domains).
If a is a lazy assertion, then $[\![a]\!]$ is a domain.

Proof: Let $X \subseteq [\![a]\!]$ be directed. With the definition of $[\![a]\!]$ follows $\langle a \rangle\, X = X$; hence $\bigsqcup(\langle a \rangle\, X) = \bigsqcup X$. Because $\langle a \rangle$ is continuous, $\langle a \rangle\, (\bigsqcup X) = \bigsqcup(\langle a \rangle\, X)$. Both together give $\langle a \rangle\, (\bigsqcup X) = \bigsqcup X$. Hence $\bigsqcup X \in [\![a]\!]$.

There is at least one element to which all assertion arguments are mapped. Partial identity tells us that $\bot$ must be mapped to $\bot$ (in that sense our lazy assertions are strict), and hence any acceptance set must contain $\bot$. □

So assertions really describe subtypes; their acceptance sets are subdomains.

Trustworthiness is clearly desirable, but it is just a different way of stating that the assertion function should be idempotent:

LEMMA 2 (Trustworthiness and idempotency).
$\forall v \in D.\ \langle a \rangle\, v \in [\![a]\!]$ *if and only if* $\forall v \in D.\ \langle a \rangle\, (\langle a \rangle\, v) = \langle a \rangle\, v$.

Proof: Because $[\![a]\!] = \{w \mid \langle a \rangle\, w = w\}$. □

Findler and Blume [9] previously proposed projections as a semantics for contracts.

DEFINITION 3. *A function $p : D \to D$ on a domain D is a* projection *if*

- *it is continuous,*
- *it is idempotent, and*
- *it is a partial identity.*

LEMMA 3 (The image of a projection is an acceptance set).
If p is a projection, then $\{p\, v \mid v \in D\} = \{v \in D \mid p\, v = v\}$.

Proof: Let $v' \in \{p\, v \mid v \in D\}$. Hence exists $\hat{v} \in D$ with $v' = p\, \hat{v}$. Idempotency gives $p\, (p\, \hat{v}) = p\, \hat{v}$. Hence $v' = p\, \hat{v} \in \{v \in D \mid p\, v = v\}$.

Let $v' \in \{v \in D \mid p\, v = v\}$. So $p\, v' = v'$. Hence $v' \in \{p\, v \mid v \in D\}$. □

So if $\langle a \rangle$ is a projection, then its image is $[\![a]\!]$. Together with Lemma 2 we conclude:

THEOREM 4 (Assertions are lower projections).
a is a lazy assertion if and only if $\langle a \rangle$ is a projection and its image is a lower set.

Our axioms do not explicitly demand that assertion application raises an exception for unacceptable values. However, it is a consequence of the axioms that the result is a partial value and thus "contains" $\bot$, which represents our exception.

LEMMA 5 (Assertions are prompt). *$\langle a \rangle\ v \sqsubset v$, for all $v \notin [\![a]\!]$.*

Proof: Let $v \notin [\![a]\!]$. Because $\langle a \rangle$ is a partial identity, $\langle a \rangle\ v \sqsubseteq v$. Because $v \notin [\![a]\!]$, but according to trustworthiness $\langle a \rangle\ v \in [\![a]\!]$, we get $\langle a \rangle\ v \sqsubset v$. □

4. Revised Axioms

We already have two characterisations of lazy assertions: Through the well-motivated axioms of Definition 2 and as lower projections (Theorem 4). Now we aim to determine an alternative set of axioms which require us to check fewer properties and that will make it easier to find concrete assertions.

We cannot simply drop any of our axioms. None is implied by the others, for each axiom we can easily construct some pseudo-assertion that does not meet this axiom but all others. Instead we note that we defined the acceptance set $[\![a]\!]$ of an assertion through assertion application $\langle a \rangle$. We consider doing the opposite: Given a suitable acceptance set $[\![a]\!]$, its assertion application $\langle a \rangle$ is uniquely determined.

First we define the lower set for a given value v and a set $A \subseteq D$ with respect to a given value:

$$\downarrow\{v\} := \{v' \mid v' \sqsubseteq v\}$$
$$A_v := \downarrow\{v\} \cap A$$

With these we define assertion application:

THEOREM 6. *Let a be a lazy assertion. For any value $v \in D$*

$$\langle a \rangle\ v \in [\![a]\!]_v \quad \text{and} \quad \langle a \rangle\ v = \bigsqcup [\![a]\!]_v$$

Proof: Partial identity yields $\langle a \rangle\ v \sqsubseteq v$ and trustworthiness $\langle a \rangle\ v \in [\![a]\!]$. Together we have $\langle a \rangle\ v \in \downarrow\{v\} \cap [\![a]\!] = [\![a]\!]_v$.

Let $w \in [\![a]\!]_v$. So $w \sqsubseteq v$ and with monotonicity follows $\langle a \rangle\ w \sqsubseteq \langle a \rangle\ v$. Also $w \in [\![a]\!]$ and thus $\langle a \rangle\ w = w$. Together we get $w \sqsubseteq \langle a \rangle\ v$ and hence $\langle a \rangle\ v$ is an upper bound for $[\![a]\!]_v$. Because $\langle a \rangle\ v \in [\![a]\!]_v$, it is the least upper bound of $[\![a]\!]_v$. □

We now have a complete definition for assertion application. Our axioms did not leave us any freedom of choice. But we do not have yet a complete definition of assertions, because there is an infinite number of sets we might choose as acceptance set, and for each of these we need to check our axioms.

So let us examine acceptance sets more closely.

COROLLARY 7. *$[\![a]\!]_v$ is an ideal for any value v.*

Proof: As the intersection of two lower sets, $[\![a]\!]_v$ is a lower set. Because $[\![a]\!]_v$ contains an upper bound for all elements according to Theorem 6, it is directed. □

So $[\![a]\!]_v$ has to be an ideal, but $[\![a]\!]$ does *not* have to be an ideal! For an example of an acceptance set that is not an ideal, consider an assertion that accepts all values of a domain. It trivially meets all our axioms. Domains are generally not directed. For instance, the domain of Boolean values contains both `True` and `False` which have no common upper bound.

Do we really need to check all our axioms for any assertion we come up with? Indeed, we only have to ensure that our acceptance set meets certain properties:

DEFINITION 4 (Lazy domain). *A set $A \subseteq D$ is a* lazy domain *if*

- *A is lower,*
- *A contains the least upper bound of any directed subset, and*
- *A_v is directed for all values $v \in D$.*

For any lazy assertion a its acceptance set $[\![a]\!]$ is a lazy domain, but also the reverse is true:

THEOREM 8 (A lazy domain determines an assertion). *Let $A \subseteq D$ be a lazy domain. Let assertion application be defined as*

$$\langle a \rangle\ v := \bigsqcup A_v$$

Then a is a lazy assertion with acceptance set $[\![a]\!] := A$.

Proof: First we show $A = [\![a]\!]$.

Let $v \in A$. Then $\downarrow\{v\} \cap A = \downarrow\{v\}$. Hence $\langle a \rangle\ v = \bigsqcup A_v = \bigsqcup \downarrow\{v\} = v$. So $v \in [\![a]\!]$.

Let $v \in [\![a]\!]$. So $\langle a \rangle\ v = v$. Thus $\bigsqcup A_v = v$. Because A_v is directed and A contains the least upper bound of any directed subset, $v \in A$.

Next we check the assertion axioms:

1. Because $\langle a \rangle$ is defined through the continuous operations lower set, intersection with a fixed set and least upper bound, it is continuous itself.
2. Trustworthiness: Because A_v is directed and A contains the least upper bound of any directed subset, $\langle a \rangle\ v = \bigsqcup A_v \in A$.
3. Partial identity: Let $v \in D$ be any value. v is an upper bound of $\downarrow\{v\}$. Thus it is an upper bound of $\downarrow\{v\} \cap A$. Hence the least upper bound $\langle a \rangle\ v$ is less or equal the upper bound v.

□

So in this section we have shown that our old, intuitive axioms are equivalent to fewer, less intuitive axioms, which however are easier to check. In the future we just make sure that we chose acceptance sets that are lazy domains.

5. Assertion Combinators

For any value v we can easily define an assertion called v that accepts v and all its approximations:

$$[\![v]\!] := \{w \mid w \sqsubseteq v\}$$

This acceptance set is a lazy domain and thus gives us a lazy assertion. However, what we really are looking for is a set of combinators for building interesting assertions from very simple ones. These combinators should have a useful algebra.

5.1 Minimal and maximal assertions

The canonical partial ordering of assertions is the subset relationship of their acceptance set.

All acceptance sets are domains. Hence the minimal acceptance set contains just the least element $\bot$. The assertion that accepts any value of the domain is trivially the maximal assertion.

$$[\![\texttt{pNone}]\!] = \{\bot\}$$
$$[\![\texttt{pAny}]\!] = D$$

These two acceptance sets are lazy domains. Implementing assertion application for either assertion is straightforward:

$$\langle \texttt{pNone} \rangle\ v = \bigsqcup [\![\texttt{pNone}]\!]_v = \bigsqcup\{\bot\} = \bot$$
$$\langle \texttt{pAny} \rangle\ v = \bigsqcup [\![\texttt{pAny}]\!]_v = \bigsqcup \downarrow\{v\} = v$$

For `pNone` the assertion function constantly returns $\perp$, for `pAny` it is the identity.

5.2 Conjunction

The definition for conjunction of two assertions is straightforward:

DEFINITION 5 (Conjunction of assertions).

$$[\![a \,\texttt{<\&>}\, b]\!] := [\![a]\!] \cap [\![b]\!]$$

Conjunction is well-defined, because the intersection of two lower sets $[\![a]\!]$ and $[\![b]\!]$ is a lower set, intersection preserves least upper bounds, and the intersection of two directed sets is a directed set, so

$$\begin{aligned}[\![a \,\texttt{<\&>}\, b]\!]_v &= \downarrow\{v\} \cap ([\![a]\!] \cap [\![b]\!]) \\ &= (\downarrow\{v\} \cap [\![a]\!]) \cap (\downarrow\{v\} \cap [\![b]\!]) \\ &= [\![a]\!]_v \cap [\![b]\!]_v\end{aligned}$$

is directed.

LEMMA 9. *Conjunction of assertions is commutative and associative and has the assertion `pAny` as neutral element.*

Proof: The defining intersection operator is commutative and associative with the full set (domain) as neutral element. □

LEMMA 10. *Conjunction equals two assertions* $\langle a \,\texttt{<\&>}\, b\rangle\; v = \langle a\rangle\; (\langle b\rangle\; v)$ *for any value* v.

Proof:

$$\begin{aligned}&\langle a\rangle\;(\langle b\rangle\; v) \\ =&\text{(definition)} \\ &\langle a\rangle\;(\bigsqcup(\downarrow\{v\} \cap [\![b]\!])) \\ =&(\langle a\rangle \text{ continuous}) \\ &\bigsqcup\{\langle a\rangle\; w \mid w \in (\downarrow\{v\} \cap [\![b]\!])\} \\ =&\text{(definition)} \\ &\bigsqcup\{\bigsqcup(\downarrow\{w\} \cap [\![a]\!]) \mid w \in (\downarrow\{v\} \cap [\![b]\!])\} \\ =&(\downarrow\{v\} \cap [\![b]\!] \text{ is already lower}) \\ &\bigsqcup(\downarrow\{v\} \cap [\![b]\!] \cap [\![a]\!]) \\ =&\text{(definition)} \\ &\langle a \,\texttt{<\&>}\, b\rangle\; v\end{aligned}$$

□

5.3 Disjunction

The cause of the semantic problems of previous lazy assertion contract systems is the presence of standard disjunction in these systems. Disjunction in these systems cannot be given a simple denotational semantics, because it is non-deterministic. Here we see that defining

$$[\![a \vee b]\!] := [\![a]\!] \cup [\![b]\!]$$

does not work, because in general

$$\begin{aligned}[\![a \vee b]\!]_v &= \downarrow\{v\} \cap ([\![a]\!] \cup [\![b]\!]) \\ &= (\downarrow\{v\} \cap [\![a]\!]) \cup (\downarrow\{v\} \cap [\![b]\!])\end{aligned}$$

is not directed, because ideals are not closed under unions, and this union hence generally does not have a least upper bound.

Defining a disjoint disjunction is an option. If $[\![a]\!]$ and $[\![b]\!]$ are disjoint, except for the element $\perp$, then $(\downarrow\{v\} \cap [\![a]\!]) \cup (\downarrow\{v\} \cap [\![b]\!])$ is directed and thus an ideal. For most of our examples in Section 2 disjoint union would be sufficient. The main problem is that there is no easy way to statically (e.g. in the type system) ensure that the acceptance sets of two assertions are disjoint and partially defined operations complicate any algebra.

Instead we take inspiration from ideal completion. The least ideal containing a given set X is given by intersecting all ideals that contain the set X: $\bigcap\{Y | X \subseteq Y, Y \text{ is ideal}\}$. Similarly we define a new disjunction operator `<|>`:

DEFINITION 6 (Disjunction of assertions).

$$[\![a \,\texttt{<|>}\, b]\!] := \bigcap\{Y \mid [\![a]\!] \cup [\![b]\!] \subseteq Y, Y \textit{ lazy domain}\}$$

There always exists at least one Y fulfilling the required properties, namely the domain itself. In the extreme case the disjoint union returns `pAny`.

Our disjunction combinator is well-defined: $[\![a \,\texttt{<|>}\, b]\!]$ is a lazy domain, because it is the intersection of lazy domains Y. In particular, $[\![a \,\texttt{<|>}\, b]\!]_v$ is directed for any $v \in D$ by definition.

Let us consider a few simple examples. Let `fstTrue` and `sndTrue` be assertions on Boolean tuples that determine that the first, respectively the second component of a tuple is `True`. The assertion `fstTrue <|> sndTrue` accepts any tuple! That may be surprising, but if we expected it to reject `(False,False)`, what result should it return for `(False,False)`? Both $(\perp$`,False)` and `(False,`$\perp)$ are suitable candidates in the acceptance set. Neither of them is better than the other, we need a common upper bound and hence `(False,False)` was added to the acceptance set.

Note that `fstTrue <&> sndTrue` is the assertion that requires both components of a tuple to be `True`. Similarly we can define a `fstFalse <&> sndFalse`. Combining these disjunctively, `(fstTrue <&> sndTrue) <|> (fstFalse <&> sndFalse)`, again yields the assertion that accepts *every* tuple. We cannot express that the two components of the tuple should be equal. Relationships between components are not expressible.

LEMMA 11. *Disjunction of assertions is commutative and associative and has the assertion `pNone` as neutral element.*

Proof: The union operator in the definition of disjunction is commutative and associative with the set $\{\perp\}$ (included in any acceptance set) as neutral element. □

5.4 Conjunction & Disjunction

LEMMA 12 (Absorption laws).

$$\begin{aligned}a \,\texttt{<\&>}\, (a \,\texttt{<|>}\, b) &= a \\ a \,\texttt{<|>}\, (a \,\texttt{<\&>}\, b) &= a\end{aligned}$$

Proof:
First law:

$$\begin{aligned}&[\![a \,\texttt{<\&>}\, (a \,\texttt{<|>}\, b)]\!] \\ =&[\![a]\!] \cap \bigcap\{Y \mid [\![a]\!] \cup [\![b]\!] \subseteq Y, Y \text{ lazy domain}\} \\ =&\bigcap\{[\![a]\!] \cap Y \mid [\![a]\!] \cup [\![b]\!] \subseteq Y, Y \text{ lazy domain}\} \\ =&\bigcap\{Y \mid [\![a]\!] \cap ([\![a]\!] \cup [\![b]\!]) \subseteq Y, Y \text{ lazy domain}\} \\ =&\bigcap\{Y \mid [\![a]\!] \subseteq Y, Y \text{ lazy domain}\} \\ =&[\![a]\!]\end{aligned}$$

Second law:

$$
\begin{aligned}
&[\![a \texttt{<|>} (a \texttt{<\&>} b)]\!] \\
&= \bigcap\{Y \mid [\![a]\!] \cup ([\![a]\!] \cap [\![b]\!]) \subseteq Y, Y \text{ lazy domain}\} \\
&= \bigcap\{Y \mid [\![a]\!] \subseteq Y, Y \text{ lazy domain}\} \\
&= [\![a]\!]
\end{aligned}
$$

□

The two binary combinators are related via distributive laws:

LEMMA 13 (Distributive laws).

$$a \texttt{<|>} (b \texttt{<\&>} c) = (a \texttt{<|>} b) \texttt{<\&>} (a \texttt{<|>} c)$$

$$a \texttt{<\&>} (b \texttt{<|>} c) = (a \texttt{<\&>} b) \texttt{<|>} (a \texttt{<\&>} c)$$

Proof:
First law:

$$
\begin{aligned}
&[\![a \texttt{<|>} (b \texttt{<\&>} c)]\!] \\
&= \bigcap\{Y \mid [\![a]\!] \cup ([\![b]\!] \cap [\![c]\!]) \subseteq Y, Y \text{ lazy domain}\} \\
&= \bigcap\{Y \mid ([\![a]\!] \cup [\![b]\!]) \cap ([\![a]\!] \cup [\![c]\!]) \subseteq Y, Y \text{ lazy domain}\} \\
&= \bigcap\{Y \mid [\![a]\!] \cup [\![b]\!] \subseteq Y, [\![a]\!] \cup [\![c]\!] \subseteq Y, Y \text{ lazy domain}\} \\
&= \bigcap\{Y \mid [\![a]\!] \cup [\![b]\!] \subseteq Y, Y \text{ lazy domain}\} \\
&\quad \cap \bigcap\{Y \mid [\![a]\!] \cup [\![c]\!] \subseteq Y, Y \text{ lazy domain}\} \\
&= [\![(a \texttt{<|>} b) \texttt{<\&>} (a \texttt{<|>} c)]\!]
\end{aligned}
$$

The second distributive law is known to be equivalent to the first.
□

COROLLARY 14. *Lazy assertions form a bounded distributive lattice with meet* `<&>`, *join* `<|>`, *least element* `pNone` *and greatest element* `pAny`. *The ordering is the subset-relationship on acceptance sets.*

Thus all laws of bounded distributive lattices hold for lazy assertions, for example the idempotency laws:

$$a \texttt{<\&>} a = a$$

$$a \texttt{<|>} a = a$$

5.5 Negation

We cannot define any negation for lazy assertions that would turn them into a Boolean algebra. Let a be an assertion with $[\![a]\!] = \{\bot, (\bot, \bot)\}$. From the first complement law of Boolean algebra, $a \texttt{<\&>} \neg a = \texttt{pNone}$, follows that $[\![a]\!] \cap [\![\neg a]\!] = \{\bot\}$. Laziness requires that $[\![\neg a]\!]$ is a lower set. So $[\![\neg a]\!] = \{\bot\}$. Hence $[\![a \texttt{<|>} \neg a]\!] = [\![a]\!]$. This contradicts the second complement law of Boolean algebra $a \texttt{<|>} \neg a = \texttt{pAny}$.

We will see that we can still define a useful, weaker variation of negation for constructor terms.

6. Implementing Assertions

In the previous section we developed a general semantics for lazy assertions for any domain. We have not yet said much about any concrete acceptance sets $[\![a]\!]$. For that we have to consider the concrete domains of specific types. We currently only have `pNone`, pAny and the combinators `<&>` and `<|>`, which on their own make for a rather boring set of assertions. Every domain needs its specific set of additional assertions and that is where we have design choices. Also, our semantic definitions are non-constructive. They just define acceptance sets, not algorithms for evaluating assertions. In particular our definition of `<|>` in terms of an intersection of a usually infinite set is hardly a good basis for an implementation.

6.1 Primitive Data Types

Every programming language includes some primitive data types such as number and characters that are flat domains, that is, $v \sqsubseteq w$ implies $v = \bot$. If a value of such a primitive data type is demanded in the computation, the whole atomic value is demanded. Hence like for strict assertions we can use predicates, Boolean-valued functions ϕ of our programming language, as assertions. This choice gives us maximal expressibility. We can for example define an assertion requiring a number to be prime.

We define the acceptance set of a predicate assertion for flat domains as

$$[\![\phi]\!] := \{\bot\} \cup \{v \mid \phi\, v\}$$

We have to explicitly include $\bot$ to ensure that the acceptance set is lower, as we may have $\phi\ \bot = \bot$ or $\phi\ \bot = \texttt{False}$. Predicate assertions meet our revised axioms: $[\![\phi]\!]$ is lower and $[\![\phi]\!]_v$ is directed for any v, because the domain is flat and these sets include $\bot$.

From the definition of the predicate acceptance set and our general assertion application definition we can derive an implementation of predicate assertion application:

$$
\begin{aligned}
\langle\phi\rangle\, v &= \bigsqcup \downarrow\!\{v\} \cap [\![\phi]\!] \\
&= \bigsqcup \{\bot, v\} \cap (\{\bot\} \cup \{w \mid \phi\, w\}) \\
&= \bigsqcup \{\bot\} \cup (\texttt{if}\ \phi\, v\ \texttt{then}\ \{v\}\ \texttt{else}\ \{\bot\}) \\
&= \texttt{if}\ \phi\, v\ \texttt{then}\ v\ \texttt{else}\ \bot
\end{aligned}
$$

The implementation works also for $v = \bot$, and no matter whether $\phi\bot = \bot$ or not.

Choosing $[\![\phi]\!] := \{\bot\} \cup \{v \mid \phi\, v \neq \texttt{False}\}$ looks like a good alternative definition for predicate assertions; it would also include all values v with $\phi\, v = \bot$. However, if we try to derive the assertion application, then we find it un-implementable.

The least and greatest predicate assertions are

$$\texttt{pNone} := \lambda x.\texttt{False}$$

$$\texttt{pAny} := \lambda x.\texttt{True}$$

and the canonical definitions for conjunction and disjunction

$$\phi \texttt{<\&>} \psi = \lambda x.\phi\, x \wedge \psi\, x$$

$$\phi \texttt{<|>} \psi = \lambda x.\phi\, x \vee \psi\, x$$

do indeed meet our previous definitions:

$$
\begin{aligned}
[\![\phi \texttt{<\&>} \psi]\!] &= [\![\phi]\!] \cap [\![\psi]\!] \\
&= \{v \mid \phi\, v \wedge \psi\, v\} \\
[\![\phi \texttt{<|>} \psi]\!] &= \bigcap\{X \mid [\![\phi]\!] \cup [\![\psi]\!] \subseteq X, X \text{ lazy domain}\} \\
&= \bigcap\{X \mid [\![\phi]\!] \cup [\![\psi]\!] \subseteq X\} \\
&= [\![\phi]\!] \cup [\![\psi]\!] \\
&= \{v \mid \phi\, v \vee \psi\, v\}
\end{aligned}
$$

The latter proof works, because in flat domains any set X including $\bot$ is lower, least upper bounds are trivial, and $\downarrow\!\{v\} \cap X$ is always directed.

Although negation is not generally available for lazy assertions, we could define it for flat domains:

$$\neg\phi := \lambda x.\neg(\phi\, x)$$

Its semantics meets our revised axioms, but it is unclear whether this combinator is useful in practise, as the programmer can manipulate the predicate directly.

6.2 Algebraic Data Types

Our main focus are data types whose values are constructor terms, such as the type `Form` for representing propositional formulae. Data constructors are symbols with an arity, including arity 0, and terms are built from full applications of a finite number of different data constructors to terms, and the value $\bot$. The domain is not flat. Often it even allows for infinite values (least upper bounds of a countable directed set of finite, partial approximations). The domain is usually not directed.

Like in our introductory example, we use constructors as patterns to describe assertions. A pattern assertion is built by applying a constructor to as many assertions as the arity of the constructor specifies. Thus constructor terms are a subset of constructor assertions, but together with other assertion combinators the assertion language becomes richer. Let C be a data constructor of the programming language and $a_1, \ldots, a_n$ lazy assertions for its argument domains.

$$[\![C\ a_1 \ldots a_n]\!] := \{\bot\} \cup \{C\ v_1 \ldots v_n \mid v_1 \in [\![a_1]\!] \ldots v_n \in [\![a_n]\!]\}$$

This definition meets our revised axioms of lazy assertions: Because $a_1, \ldots, a_n$ are lazy assertions, $[\![a_1]\!], \ldots, [\![a_n]\!]$ are lower and $[\![a_1]\!]_{v_1}, \ldots, [\![a_n]\!]_{v_n}$ are directed for any $v_1, \ldots v_n$ of the respective domains. Hence $[\![C\ a_1 \ldots a_n]\!]$ is lower and $[\![C\ a_1 \ldots a_n]\!]_v$ is directed for all v.

Now we look for constructive definitions of our two combinators `<&>` and `<|>`. For `<&>` we easily find the following two laws:

LEMMA 15 (Conjunction of constructor assertions).

$$(C\ a_1 \ldots a_n)\ \mathtt{<\&>}\ (C\ b_1 \ldots b_n) = C(a_1\ \mathtt{<\&>}\ b_1) \ldots (a_n\ \mathtt{<\&>}\ b_n)$$
$$(C\ a_1 \ldots a_n)\ \mathtt{<\&>}\ (C'\ b_1 \ldots b_n) = \mathtt{pNone} \qquad \textit{if } C \neq C'$$

Proof:
First law:

$$\begin{aligned}
&[\![(C\ a_1 \ldots a_n)\ \mathtt{<\&>}\ (C\ b_1 \ldots b_n)]\!]\\
=&[\![C\ a_1 \ldots a_n)]\!] \cap [\![C\ b_1 \ldots b_n]\!]\\
=&(\{\bot\} \cup \{C\ v_1 \ldots v_n \mid v_1 \in [\![a_1]\!], \ldots, v_n \in [\![a_n]\!]\}) \cap\\
&(\{\bot\} \cup \{C\ v_1 \ldots v_n \mid v_1 \in [\![b_1]\!], \ldots, v_n \in [\![b_n]\!]\})\\
=&(\{\bot\} \cup \{C\ v_1 \ldots v_n \mid v_1 \in [\![a_1]\!] \cap [\![b_1]\!], \ldots, v_n \in [\![a_n]\!] \cap [\![b_n]\!]\})\\
=&[\![C(a_1\ \mathtt{<\&>}\ b_1) \ldots (a_n\ \mathtt{<\&>}\ b_n)]\!]
\end{aligned}$$

Second law:

$$\begin{aligned}
&[\![(C\ a_1 \ldots a_n)\ \mathtt{<\&>}\ (C'\ b_1 \ldots b_n)]\!]\\
=&(\{\bot\} \cup \{C\ v_1 \ldots v_n \mid v_1 \in [\![a_1]\!], \ldots, v_n \in [\![a_n]\!]\}) \cap\\
&(\{\bot\} \cup \{C'\ v_1 \ldots v_n \mid v_1 \in [\![b_1]\!], \ldots, v_n \in [\![b_n]\!]\})\\
=&\{\bot\}\\
=&[\![\mathtt{pNone}]\!]
\end{aligned}$$

□

Our general definition of `<|>` is more complicated than our definition of `<&>`. So let us look at some of its details to see what happens for constructor terms. Consider the set

$$\begin{aligned}
S := \{\bot\} \cup \{C\ v_1\ v_2 \mid &(v_1 \in [\![a_1]\!] \wedge v_2 \in [\![a_2]\!]) \vee\\
&(v_1 \in [\![b_1]\!] \wedge v_2 \in [\![b_2]\!])\}
\end{aligned}$$

In general $\downarrow\{v\} \cap S$ is not directed for all values v. Consider for example the elements $C\ v_1 \perp$ and $C \perp v_2$ of S, with $v_1 \in [\![a_1]\!]$ and $v_2 \in [\![b_2]\!]$. Their least upper bound is $C\ v_1\ v_2$, which is not in S by definition. So any (lower) Y with $S \subseteq Y$ and $\downarrow\{v\} \cap Y$ directed must include these least upper bounds. In other words, any such Y must be a superset of

$$\begin{aligned}
\{\bot\} \cup \{C\ v_1\ v_2 \mid &(v_1 \in [\![a_1]\!] \vee v_1 \in [\![b_1]\!]) \wedge\\
&(v_2 \in [\![a_2]\!] \vee v_2 \in [\![b_2]\!])\}
\end{aligned}$$

Hence the following holds:

$$\begin{aligned}
&[\![(C\ a_1 \ldots a_n)\ \mathtt{<|>}\ (C\ b_1 \ldots b_n)]\!]\\
=&\bigcap\{Y \mid \{\bot\} \cup \{C\,\overline{v} \mid (v_1 \in [\![a_1]\!] \wedge \ldots \wedge v_n \in [\![a_n]\!]) \vee\\
&\qquad (v_1 \in [\![b_1]\!] \wedge \ldots \wedge v_n \in [\![b_n]\!])\} \subseteq Y,\\
&\quad Y \text{ lazy domain}\}\\
=&\bigcap\{Y \mid \{\bot\} \cup \{C\,\overline{v} \mid (v_1 \in [\![a_1]\!] \vee v_1 \in [\![b_1]\!]) \wedge \ldots \wedge\\
&\qquad (v_n \in [\![a_n]\!] \vee v_n \in [\![b_n]\!])\} \subseteq Y,\\
&\quad Y \text{ lazy domain}\}\\
=&\{\bot\} \cup \{C\,\overline{v} \mid v_1 \in \bigcap\{Y_1 \mid [\![a_1]\!] \cup [\![b_1]\!] \subseteq Y_1,\\
&\qquad Y_1 \text{ lazy domain}\}, \ldots,\\
&\quad v_n \in \bigcap\{Y_n \mid [\![a_n]\!] \cup [\![b_n]\!] \subseteq Y_n,\\
&\qquad Y_n \text{ lazy domain}\}\}\\
=&\{\bot\} \cup \{C\,\overline{v} \mid v_1 \in [\![a_1\ \mathtt{<|>}\ b_1]\!], \ldots, v_n \in [\![a_n\ \mathtt{<|>}\ b_n]\!]\}\\
=&[\![C\ (a_1\ \mathtt{<|>}\ b_1) \ldots (a_n\ \mathtt{<|>}\ b_n)]\!]
\end{aligned}$$

So we find that for constructor terms the first law for `<|>` is surprisingly similar to that for `<&>`:

LEMMA 16 (Disjunction of constructor assertions).

$$(C\ a_1 \ldots a_n)\ \mathtt{<|>}\ (C\ b_1 \ldots b_n) = C\ (a_1\ \mathtt{<|>}\ b_1) \ldots (a_n\ \mathtt{<|>}\ b_n)$$

For different constructors no simple law exists, but we note that if $C \neq C'$, then $Y := [\![C\ a_1 \ldots a_n]\!] \cup [\![C'\ b_1 \ldots b_n]\!]$ is lower. Least upper bounds are preserved and $\downarrow\{v\} \cap Y$ is directed for any value v, because $[\![C\ a_1 \ldots a_n]\!] \cap [\![C'\ b_1 \ldots b_n]\!] = \{\bot\}$. Hence

$$\begin{aligned}
&[\![(C\ a_1 \ldots a_n)\ \mathtt{<|>}\ (C'\ b_1 \ldots b_n)]\!]\\
=&\bigcap\{Y \mid [\![C\ a_1 \ldots a_n]\!] \cup [\![C'\ b_1 \ldots b_n]\!] \subseteq Y,\\
&\quad Y \text{ lazy domain}\}\\
=&[\![C\ a_1 \ldots a_n]\!] \cup [\![C'\ b_1 \ldots b_n]\!]
\end{aligned}$$

Altogether we see that although the general definition of `<|>` in terms of an infinite intersection is not simple, its incarnation for constructors is easy to use. In our introductory examples and most applications the two assertions combined by `<|>` have either disjoint acceptance sets, in which case we get a simple union of acceptance sets, or they have the same acceptance sets, in which case idempotency gives us as expected $a\ \mathtt{<|>}\ a = a$. For the general case of a partial overlap we have Lemma 16.

Lazy assertions form a bounded distributive lattice, there is no general negation. However, in our initial example we noted that it is very useful to be able to express that an assertion does not accept certain top-level constructors. Hence we introduce a specific subtraction combinator on assertions that removes a constructor. Let a be a lazy assertion and c be a constructor of its domain.

$$[\![a\mathtt{<\backslash>}C]\!] := [\![a]\!] \backslash \{C\ v_1 \ldots v_n \mid v_1, \ldots, v_n \text{ any domain values}\}$$

This definition meets our revised axioms, $[\![a\mathtt{<\backslash>}C]\!]$ is lower and $[\![a\mathtt{<\backslash>}C]\!]_v$ directed for any v if a meets the axioms.

The combinator meets distribution laws:

$$(a \;\texttt{<\&>}\; b) \;\texttt{<\textbackslash>}\; C = (a\texttt{<\textbackslash>}C) \;\texttt{<\&>}\; (b\texttt{<\textbackslash>}C)$$

$$(a \;\texttt{<|>}\; b) \;\texttt{<\textbackslash>}\; C = (a\texttt{<\textbackslash>}C) \;\texttt{<|>}\; (b\texttt{<\textbackslash>}C)$$

More important for an implementation is that the following laws trivially hold:

LEMMA 17 (Subtraction for constructor assertions).

$$C\,\overline{a} \;\texttt{<\textbackslash>}\; C = \texttt{pNone}$$

$$C\,\overline{a} \;\texttt{<\textbackslash>}\; C' = C\,\overline{a} \qquad \textit{if } C \neq C'$$

6.3 Implementation

We have not yet actually given a complete implementation of the assertion combinators for constructor terms. However, the laws of our lemmas and the general distributive lattice laws are sufficient to derive an efficient implementation.

The laws allow us to represent any constructor assertion of any algebraic data type as a finite disjunction

$$C_1\,\overline{a}_1 \;\texttt{<|>}\; C_2\,\overline{a}_2 \;\texttt{<|>}\; \ldots \;\texttt{<|>}\; C_m\,\overline{a}_m$$

where $\{C_1, \ldots, C_m\}$ is a subset of the constructors of the algebraic data type.

Clearly any simple constructor assertion $C\,\overline{a}$ is already in that form. The least assertion `pNone` is represented as the empty disjunction and

$$\texttt{pAny} = C_1\,\overline{\texttt{pAny}} \;\texttt{<|>}\; \ldots \;\texttt{<|>}\; C_n\,\overline{\texttt{pAny}}$$

The definition of assertion application for our representation is straightforward:

$$\langle C_1\,\overline{a}_1 \;\texttt{<|>}\; \ldots \;\texttt{<|>}\; C_m\,\overline{a}_m\rangle\,(C\,\overline{v}) = \begin{cases} C\,(\langle\overline{a}_j\rangle\,\overline{v}) & \text{if } C = C_j \\ \bot & \text{otherwise} \end{cases}$$

$$\langle C_1\overline{a}_1 \;\texttt{<|>}\; \ldots \;\texttt{<|>}\; C_m\,\overline{a}_m\rangle\;\bot = \bot$$

Here $\langle\overline{a}_j\rangle\,\overline{v}$ is an abbreviation for component-wise assertion application.

Using our laws for constructor assertions we can define conjunction and disjunction on our representation:

$$(C_{i_1}\,\overline{a}_{i_1}\texttt{<|>}\ldots\texttt{<|>}C_{i_m}\,\overline{a}_{i_m}) \;\texttt{<\&>}\; (C_{j_1}\,\overline{b}_{j_1}\texttt{<|>}\ldots\texttt{<|>}C_{j_l}\,\overline{b}_{j_l})$$

$$= C_{k_1}\,(\overline{a}_{k_1}\texttt{<\&>}\overline{b}_{k_1})\texttt{<|>}\ldots\texttt{<|>}C_{k_o}\,(\overline{a}_{k_o}\texttt{<\&>}\overline{b}_{k_o})$$

where

$$\{k_1, \ldots, k_o\} = \{i_1, \ldots, i_m\} \cap \{j_1, \ldots, j_l\}$$

and

$$(C_{i_1}\,\overline{a}_{i_1}\texttt{<|>}\ldots\texttt{<|>}C_{i_m}\,\overline{a}_{i_m}) \;\texttt{<|>}\; (C_{j_1}\,\overline{b}_{j_1}\texttt{<|>}\ldots\texttt{<|>}C_{j_l}\,\overline{b}_{j_l})$$

$$= C_{k_1}\,\overline{z}_{k_1}\;\texttt{<|>}\ldots\texttt{<|>}\;C_{k_o}\,\overline{z}_{k_o}$$

where

$$\{k_1, \ldots, k_o\} = \{i_1, \ldots, i_m\} \cup \{j_1, \ldots, j_l\}$$

$$z_{k_s} = \begin{cases} \overline{a}_{k_s}\texttt{<|>}\overline{b}_{k_s} & \text{if } k_s \in \{i_1, \ldots, i_m\} \cap \{j_1, \ldots, j_l\} \\ \overline{a}_{k_s} & \text{if } k_s \in \{i_1, \ldots, i_m\} \backslash \{j_1, \ldots, j_l\} \\ \overline{b}_{k_s} & \text{if } k_s \in \{j_1, \ldots, j_l\} \backslash \{i_1, \ldots, i_m\} \end{cases}$$

In these equations $\overline{a}\texttt{<|>}\overline{b}$ and $\overline{a}\texttt{<\&>}\overline{b}$ are abbreviations for the component-wise combinations.

The definition of `<\>` for this representation is simple: it just removes one of the elements of the disjunction.

This implementation is efficient, because the disjunctive representation of an assertion is computed only once, afterwards assertion application for constructor terms requires linear time in the size of the checked data structure. By introducing an additional representation of `pAny` we can also avoid doing any checking work on a data structure that is accepted anyway. The efficiency of the function assertions for primitive types fully depends on the efficiency of the predicates that the programmer chooses.

A prototype implementation using this representation, including predicate assertions for primitive types, exists in Haskell and has been used in several examples, including the propositional formulae of Section 2. Associated types [3, 4] enable providing a single class with functions `assert`, `<|>`, etc. with different implementations for each type.

6.4 What about Function Types?

The domain of functions over a domain D and codomain D' is the set of continuous functions $[D \rightarrow D']$ from the domain to the codomain.

We follow previous work on assertions for strict functional languages [10] and define a function assertion as a tuple $a \mapsto b$ of an assertion a for the domain, the pre-condition, and an assertion b for the codomain, the post-condition. We can define the standard function assertion application [10] simply by composing existing assertion applications:

$$\langle a \mapsto b\rangle\,\delta = \lambda x.\langle b\rangle\,(\delta\,(\langle a\rangle\,x))$$

Thus the assertion correctly checks both the pre- and the post-condition. Function arguments and results are checked lazily, only as far as they are demanded by the context. We can compose function assertions to build assertions for higher-order functions.

However, our definition of the acceptance set yields

$$[\![a \mapsto b]\!] = \{\delta \in [D \rightarrow D'] \mid \langle b\rangle \circ \delta \circ \langle a\rangle = \delta\}$$

which is not a lazy domain! It is not even a lower set.

Instead, comparison with the eager quotient model [2] suggests

$$[\![a \mapsto b]\!] = \{\delta \in [D \rightarrow D'] \mid \forall v \in [\![a]\!].\, \delta\,v \in [\![b]\!]\}$$

and comparison with the eager projection model [9] suggests

$$[\![a \mapsto b]\!] = \{\delta \in [D \rightarrow D'] \mid \forall v \in D.\, \delta\,v \in [\![b]\!]\}$$

Both these sets are lazy domains. However, both acceptance sets describe only half of the assertion application. Neither of them expresses that if the function argument is not within the acceptance set $[\![a]\!]$, then an exception should be raised, because the pre-condition is violated.

Function assertions are different from first-order assertions in that they describe properties of both the assertion argument, the function, and the context of the assertion application (which provides the argument for the function).

Findler and Blume solved this problem in their projection model [9] by interpreting an eager function assertion as a *pair* of projections. One projection restricts the assertion argument, the other restricts the context. For first-order assertions the context projection is just the identity function. Similarly we could use either pairs of lazy projections (cf. Theorem 4) or introduce a second acceptance set restricting the context. We believe that the definitions and lemmas of previous sections can be transferred.

There is still more potential for lazy function assertions: For eager functional languages there exist dependent function assertions, where the assertion of the function result depends on the argument passed to the function. For algebraic data types lazy assertions cannot relate different subterms of constructor terms, because the subterms can be demanded in any order. Relating argument and result of a function is different, because only after the result of a function has been demanded, the argument may be demanded. Hence it should be possible to express non-strictness properties such that only when a certain part of the result of a function is demanded, the function demands a certain part of its argument.

7. Discussion of Related Work

There is an extensive literature on assertions and contracts for non-functional programming languages. A contract combines several assertions. A contract consists of a pre-condition that a function caller or client has to meet and a post-condition that the function or server promises in return [19]. When the contract is violated, one of the parties is blamed. In this paper we discussed only assertions. Contracts with blaming can be built on top of them.

Assertion-based contracts became popular in eager functional programming languages with Findler and Felleisen's seminal paper on contracts for higher-order functions [10]. All interesting properties of functional values, which are passed around by higher-order functions, are undecidable; it is impossible to check a function contract for all argument-result-pairs. However, Findler and Felleisen realised that it is sufficient to check both the pre- and the post-condition of a functional value only when this function is applied. The resulting contract system is sound.

This "lazy" checking of contracts for functional values in eager languages provides another argument for using lazy assertions in lazy languages: A lazy data type `T` is isomorphic to the function type `Unit -> T` in an eager language. Demanding a value of the lazy type `T` corresponds to applying the function of the eager type `Unit -> T`. Hence because an assertion for a function is checked only when the function is applied to an argument, an assertion for a lazy value should only be checked when the value is demanded.

Other contributions of Findler and Felleisen's paper, a system for correctly attributing blame in case of contract violation and an implementation as an extension of a Scheme runtime system are not relevant for this paper, as the implementation approach is different. The work also provides dependent function contracts, where the assertion for the codomain can use the actual argument value.

Hinze et al. [17] transferred contracts for higher-order functions to Haskell, implementing it as a library instead of modifying the runtime system. Thus it will provide a good model for building contracts and blame assignment on top of our assertions. However, their semantics is a seemingly random mixture of eager and lazy assertion evaluation.

Lazy assertions were first discussed and several implementations presented in 2004 [7]. That paper makes the point that while eager assertions must be `True`, lazy assertions must not be `False`, which lead us here to require that acceptance sets are lower. The paper uses predicates on values of all types and hence, despite some technical tricks using concurrency, the assertions are lazy but neither trustworthy nor prompt. The paper itself gives examples of where assertion violations are noticed too late. This problem was later rectified [5, 6]. Both these papers implement lazy assertions as libraries that require only the commonly provided non-pure function `unsafePerformIO`, which performs side effects within a purely functional context. The first lazy and trustworthy implementation [6] uses patterns similar to those in this paper to express assertions over algebraic data types. However, a non-deterministic implementation of disjunction leads to the semantic problems described in the introduction. Later [5] provided a more user-friendly language for expressing assertions and improved the internal structure of the implementation, but the implementation principles were identical and hence the non-deterministic disjunction remained. The axioms of our Definition 2 are inspired by this previous work, but there was no formal semantics and the implementation derived here is completely different.

Degen et al. [8] classify all existing assertion systems for Haskell as eager (straight translation of [10]), semi-eager [17] and lazy [5–7]. They check whether the systems meet their four desirable properties of meaning reflection, meaning preservation, faithfulness and idempotency. Sadly, none of the assertion systems meets all four properties. In particular, they note that lazy assertions are not faithful. Hence, although eager assertions are not meaning preserving for lazy languages, they prefer them and conclude with the slogan "Faithfulness is better than laziness". The lazy assertions presented in this paper are idempotent and also meaning reflecting and meaning preserving, as far as the informal definitions of the latter properties allow such a statement. To demonstrate that lazy assertions are not faithful, Degen et al. consider the expression

```
assert (pred (==0) |-> pAny) (\x -> 42) 5
```

Evaluating it yields `42` in all lazy assertion systems, including the one presented in this paper. However, faithfulness would require evaluation to yield an exception, complaining that `5` is unequal `0`. Faithfulness is similar to trustworthiness, but stricter for function assertions. In this paper, the semantic value passed as argument to the function `(\x -> 42)` is the exception $\perp$. So the function gets an argument within the acceptance set and hence the assertion is trustworthy. The expression above is equivalent to

```
(\x -> 42) (assert (pred (==0)) 5)
```

It is important to know what an assertion guarantees and what not. The semantics defined in this paper provides an answer. Faithfulness seems to be unnecessarily too strong a requirement. Faithfulness conflicts with laziness, because acceptance sets are lower. Trustworthiness suffices.

Blume et al. proposed and studied several semantic models of Findler and Felleisen's higher-order contracts [2, 9, 11]. These semantic models are based on operational semantics. The quotient model [2] equates a contract with the set of terms satisfying the contract. The property of safety, that is, whether a term contains a blame exception that can be raised by a context, plays a major role. The projection model [9, 11] interprets a contract as a pair of projections and defines a suitable ordering on these pairs of projections. The papers do not discuss algebraic data types, because in strict languages these domains are flat and hence contracts for algebraic data types are predicates like for other primitive types. Instead the papers focus on higher-order functions and correct blame assignment. They are more complex than our simple semantics of lazy assertions. To define a semantics for lazy assertions incorporating higher-order functions we probably have to combine ideas from both worlds.

For lazy functional logic languages Hanus [16] proposed to allow the user to choose for each assertion whether it should be eager or lazy, depending on whether meaning preservation or faithfulness are essential. Assertion checking can even be delayed until a point in the program execution, e.g. just before an important output action. The prototypical implementation combines ideas from eager [10] and early lazy assertions [7], taking advantage of some logical language features. The semantics is not studied, but as functional logic languages permit non-deterministic functions, older — more expressive — lazy assertions may still fit within the semantics of the language [18]. It would be interesting to determine whether that is the case, or the fact that the non-determinism of an assertion depends on its context would still break the language semantics.

The original idea of assertions is that they are checked at runtime. However, there exist several proposals for doing at least part of the checking statically, like type checking [12, 22]. The main challenge is to handle the intrinsic undecidability of assertions. The proposal for Haskell [22] is not lazy in the sense of this paper; acceptance sets are not lower. That is fine; we require our laziness only because our assertions are checked at runtime.

Work on improving the implementation of eager higher-order contracts for Scheme are ongoing [13]. These ideas are closely linked to the eager semantics of Scheme.

Our semantics uses basic domain theory. Acceptance sets are *inclusive* subsets as they are often used to interpret types [14]. Assertions are *finitary* projections, widely used for defining domains [14, 15]. Our assertion sets with respect to a given value, $[\![a]\!]_v$, are *normal* in $[\![a]\!]$ [15]. The definition of $[\![a]\!]_v$ also reminds of *bases of domains* [1]. Still, the specific combination of axioms for lazy assertions made it hard to reuse many standard theorems of domain theory.

8. Conclusions

We have defined a semantics for lazy assertions. Our semantics is simple; it is based on the acceptance set $[\![a]\!]$ of an assertion a as the subset of the domain that contains all accepted values. Our axioms are few and clarify what lazy assertions are. The axioms yield a beautiful algebra of assertions, a bounded distributive lattice. It turns out that for primitive and algebraic data types the axioms leave little freedom in choosing suitable assertion combinators. From the semantics we derived an efficient prototype implementation of lazy assertions for Haskell. The implementation is just a library, thus requiring no specific runtime system support and guaranteeing to preserve the language semantics.

Associated type classes provide a simple interface to lazy assertions, but in the future we have to find a suitable generic programming framework to enable us to define lazy assertions once for all types, without any tedious repetition for pattern combinators and even combinators such as conjunction for every type.

Previous lazy assertions, which break standard semantic equivalences, can express properties such as a list being ordered. However, checking such an assertion can take time that is exponential in the length of the list. Hence there is an advantage in that the lazy assertions presented here are limited to properties of algebraic data types that can be checked in linear time. It is a limitation that simple equality checks like for the Boolean tuple in the introduction cannot be expressed. However, such assertions can only be violated when data structures are fully evaluated, which may happen less frequently in programs that work with many partial data structures (cf. the Pasta interpreter application in [7]) and thus may be less useful. Lazy assertions for algebraic data types are, however, quite different from those for eager functional languages. Existing functions and predicates cannot be reused but instead the pattern matching assertion combinators have to be used; the definition of lazy assertions is similar to the definition of algebraic data types. Thus lazy assertions for algebraic data types are less like eager assertions but more like subtypes expressing context-free properties, underlined by the fact that acceptance sets are subdomains. In principle, variants of the original algebraic data type could be used instead. For example, each intermediate abstract syntax tree in a multi-pass compiler could be specified as a separate algebraic data type, but subtypes are far more convenient to write and read.

The aim of this paper was to study *lazy* assertions. Laziness mainly influences the semantics of algebraic data types, hence these were the focus of our studies. It is reassuring that predicate-based assertions for primitive types seamlessly fit into this framework. Lazy assertions for functions still require further work. We are confident that the established implementation of non-dependent function assertions for eager functional languages can also be fitted within our lazy semantic framework. More exciting but yet unanswered is the prospect of developing a form of dependent function assertions. These function assertions will go far beyond standard subtypes.

Acknowledgments

I thank Colin Runciman and Frank Huch for many earlier discussions about lazy assertions.

References

[1] S. Abramsky and A. Jung. Domain theory. In S. Abramsky, D. M. Gabbay, and T. S. E. Maibaum, editors, *Handbook of Logic in Computer Science*, volume 3, pages 1–168. Clarendon Press, 1994.

[2] M. Blume and D. McAllester. Sound and complete models of contracts. *J. Funct. Program.*, 16(4-5):375–414, 2006.

[3] M. M. T. Chakravarty, G. Keller, and S. P. Jones. Associated type synonyms. In *ICFP '05: Proceedings of the tenth ACM SIGPLAN international conference on Functional programming*, pages 241–253. ACM, 2005.

[4] M. M. T. Chakravarty, G. Keller, S. P. Jones, and S. Marlow. Associated types with class. In *POPL '05: Symposium on Principles of programming languages*, pages 1–13. ACM, 2005.

[5] O. Chitil and F. Huch. Monadic, prompt lazy assertions in Haskell. In *APLAS 2007*, LNCS 4807, pages 38–53, 2007.

[6] O. Chitil and F. Huch. A pattern logic for prompt lazy assertions in Haskell. In *Implementation and Application of Functional Languages: 18th International Workshop, IFL 2006*, LNCS 4449, 2007.

[7] O. Chitil, D. McNeill, and C. Runciman. Lazy assertions. In *Implementation of Functional Languages: 15th International Workshop, IFL 2003*, LNCS 3145, pages 1–19. Springer, November 2004.

[8] M. Degen, P. Thiemann, and S. Wehr. True lies: Lazy contracts for lazy languages (faithfulness is better than laziness). In *4. Arbeitstagung Programmiersprachen (ATPS'09)*, Lübeck, Germany, October 2009.

[9] R. B. Findler and M. Blume. Contracts as pairs of projections. In *International Symposium on Functional and Logic Programming (FLOPS)*, LNCS 3945, pages 226–241, 2006.

[10] R. B. Findler and M. Felleisen. Contracts for higher-order functions. In *ICFP '02: Proceedings of the seventh ACM SIGPLAN international conference on Functional programming*, pages 48–59, 2002.

[11] R. B. Findler, M. Blume, and M. Felleisen. An investigation of contracts as projections. Technical report, University of Chicago Computer Science Department, 2004. TR-2004-02.

[12] C. Flanagan. Hybrid type checking. In *POPL '06: Symposium on Principles of programming languages*, pages 245–256. ACM, 2006.

[13] M. Greenberg, B. C. Pierce, and S. Weirich. Contracts made manifest. In *POPL '10: Symposium on Principles of programming languages*, pages 353–364. ACM, 2010.

[14] C. A. Gunter. *Semantics of programming languages: structures and techniques*. MIT Press, 1992.

[15] C. A. Gunter and D. S. Scott. Semantic domains. In *Handbook of Theoretical Computer Science, Volume B: Formal Models and Sematics (B)*, pages 633–674. MIT Press, 1990.

[16] M. Hanus. Lazy and faithful assertions for functional logic programs. In *Proc. of the 19th International Workshop on Functional and (Constraint) Logic Programming (WFLP 2010)*, pages 50–64. Universidad Politécnica de Madrid, 2010.

[17] R. Hinze, J. Jeuring, and A. Löh. Typed contracts for functional programming. In *Proceedings of the 8th International Symposium on Functional and Logic Programming, FLOPS 2006*, LNCS 3945, pages 208–225, 2006.

[18] F. J. López-Fraguas, J. Rodríguez-Hortalá, and J. Sánchez-Hernández. A simple rewrite notion for call-time choice semantics. In *PPDP '07*, pages 197–208, 2007.

[19] B. Meyer. Applying "design by contract". *Computer*, 25(10):40–51, 1992.

[20] D. L. Parnas. A technique for software module specification with examples. *Commun. ACM*, 15(5):330–336, 1972.

[21] D. S. Rosenblum. A practical approach to programming with assertions. *IEEE Trans. Softw. Eng.*, 21(1):19–31, 1995.

[22] D. N. Xu, S. Peyton Jones, and K. Claessen. Static contract checking for Haskell. In *POPL '09: Symposium on Principles of programming languages*, pages 41–52. ACM, 2009.

iTasks for a Change

Type-Safe Run-Time Change in Dynamically Evolving Workflows

Rinus Plasmeijer[1] Peter Achten[1] Pieter Koopman[1]
Bas Lijnse[1,2] Thomas van Noort[1] John van Groningen[1]

[1] Institute for Computing and Information Sciences, Radboud University Nijmegen
P.O. Box 9010, 6500 GL, Nijmegen, The Netherlands

[2] Faculty of Military Sciences, Netherlands Defence Academy
P.O. Box 10000, 1780 CA, Den Helder, The Netherlands

{rinus, p.achten, pieter, b.lijnse, thomas, johnvg}@cs.ru.nl

Abstract

Workflow management systems (WFMS) are software systems that coordinate the tasks human workers and computers have to perform to achieve a certain goal based on a given workflow description. Due to changing circumstances, it happens often that some tasks in a running workflow need to be performed differently than originally planned and specified. Most commercial WFMSs cannot deal with the required run-time changes properly. These changes have to be specified at the level of the underlying Petri-Net based semantics. Moreover, the implicit external state has to be adapted to the new task as well. Such low-level updates can easily lead to wrong behaviour and other errors. This problem is known as the dynamic change bug. In the iTask WFMS, workflows are specified using a radically different approach: workflows are constructed in a compositional style, using pure functions and combinators as self-contained building blocks. This paper introduces a change concept for the iTask system where self-contained tasks can be replaced by other self-contained tasks, thereby preventing dynamic change bugs. The static and dynamic typing system furthermore guarantees that these tasks have compatible types.

Categories and Subject Descriptors D.3.3 [*Programming Languages*]: Language Constructs and Features

General Terms Design, Languages

Keywords combinators, type-safe run-time change, workflow

1. Introduction

Workflow management systems (WFMS) are software systems that coordinate, generate, and monitor tasks performed by human workers and computers. Such systems are interesting to study because they are nontrivial representatives of how contemporary distributed software systems are manufactured. A concrete workflow ensures that essential actions are performed in the right order. Workflows have potentially long running times (in the order of months and years) during which many workers and computers can be involved. It is well known from literature (Van der Aalst, 2001) that during its life cycle, a workflow needs to adapt to handle changing requirements, ad-hoc situations, evolutionary concerns, and so on. It also illustrates that adapting a running workflow system easily leads to incorrect behaviour. This phenomenon is known as the dynamic change bug (Ellis et al., 1995). Most traditional WFMSs are affected by this issue because their semantics is based on Petri Nets. Changes are made on the level of individual places and transitions, which is a too low level of abstraction. Making an arbitrary change in a Petri Net while the tokens are moving around often leads to errors. Moreover, the tasks have an implicit external state which is often stored in a database. This state has to be adapted to the changed task without corrupting the state of other tasks stored in the same database.

The iTask system (Plasmeijer et al., 2007) distinguishes itself from traditional WFMSs. First, iTask is actually a monadic combinator library in the pure and lazy functional programming language Clean. It defines a WFMS, embedded in Clean where the combinators are used to combine tasks. Tasks are defined by higher-order functions which are pure and self contained. Second, most WFMSs take a workflow description specified in a workflow description language (WDL) and generate a partial workflow application that still requires substantial coding effort. An iTask specification on the other hand denotes a full-fledged, web-based, multi-user workflow application. It strongly supports the view that a WDL should be considered as a complete specification language rather than a partial description language. Third, despite the fact that an iTask specification denotes a complete workflow application, the workflow engineer is not confronted with boilerplate programming (e.g., data storage and retrieval, GUI rendering, form interaction) because this is all dealt with using generic programming techniques. Fourth, an iTask workflow evolves dynamically; depending on user-input and results of subtasks. Fifth, in addition to the host language features, the iTask system adds higher-order tasks (i.e., tasks that create and accept other tasks) and recursion to the modelling repertoire of workflow engineers. Sixth, in contrast with the large catalogue of common workflow patterns (Van der Aalst et al., 2002), iTask workflows are captured by means of a small number of core combinator functions.

In this paper we show how type-safe run-time changes are incorporated in iTask. Together with the compositionality and self-containedness of tasks, this prevents dynamic change bugs. Type-safe run-time change is challenging for several reasons. First, an iTask workflow dynamically evolves. This implies that the set of

PEPM'11, January 24–25, 2011, Austin, Texas, USA.

```
edit                 :: String a                  → Task a   | iTask a
(@:)    infixr 5 :: p (Task a)                → Task a   | property p
                                                          & iTask a
return               :: a                          → Task a   | iTask a
(≫=)   infixl 1 :: (Task a) (a → Task b) → Task b   | iTask b
(-||-)  infixr 3 :: (Task a) (Task a)      → Task a   | iTask a
(-&&-) infixr 4 :: (Task a) (Task b)      → Task (a, b)
                                               | iTask a & iTask b
```

Figure 1. The iTask core combinator functions

tasks that may require replacement is not known in advance and that a change must take both the current workflow state into account as well as its future. Second, all tasks are typed and include context restrictions for ad-hoc polymorphic and generic functions. This implies that a single change is really about changing a set of functions. Third, iTask workflows are constructed using combinators. We show that we can handle all changes by modifying only one single combinator drastically. For the sake of clarity, we emphasize that in this paper we concentrate on the change mechanism and its semantics. There are still many challenging research questions to be answered with respect to validation and formal reasoning of changes, but this remains future work.

This paper is organized as follows. First, we describe the core iTask system and explain its usage by means of a running example: a paper review workflow (Section 2). Next we explain the concept of change functions and illustrate how it is used to alter the paper review workflow (Section 3). We capture the semantics by first giving a reference implementation of the core combinator functions (Section 4) after which we extend it with type-safe run-time change (Section 5). Finally, we compare our approach with related work (Section 6) and conclude and discuss future work (Section 7).

2. The iTask core system

In this section we give a brief overview of the iTask system. We restrict ourselves, without loss of generality, to the core combinator functions (Section 2.1), which we then use in the running example (Section 2.2). The actual iTask system offers a couple of additional combinators for advanced task structures, workflow process management, and exception handling. The change mechanism is orthogonal to these features.

2.1 The core combinator functions

The core combinator functions of the iTask system are displayed in Figure 1. (Note that in Clean the arity of functions is shown explicitly by separating argument types by spaces instead of →.) A task has an opaque type Task a: the type parameter a is the type of the result value that is committed once the task finishes.

One primitive task concerns editors: an editor is created with edit prompt va. When applied to an initial va of type a, it creates a GUI in which the worker can inspect and alter the given value arbitrarily many times. An editor can create and handle such a GUI for any first-order type a. It uses a set of generic functions (hence the context restriction | iTask a) which are derived by the compiler automatically. The iTask system guarantees that only values of type a are created. This continues until the worker decides to commit the value to the workflow, which terminates the task. The prompt argument provides the worker with information about the purpose of this task.

Tasks are assigned properties using the @: combinator. For now, we restrict the properties to an identification label and the user who has to work on the task (of the opaque types Label and User respectively). If u :: User and l :: Label, then u @: ta, l @: ta, and (u, l) @: ta sets the worker, label, and both respectively of the task ta. In general, properties that can be set are captured by the type class property, which is discussed later in Section 3.1. We call tasks annotated using the @: combinator, *main tasks*. As we will see later on, such tasks are subject to change once the workflow is running.

To compose tasks sequentially, the monadic combinators return and ≫= (Wadler, 1990) are provided. The task return va succeeds immediately and emits its value va. In ta ≫= atb, the task ta is evaluated first. When this task returns its value, say va, it is passed to atb to compute the next task to be executed.

To compose tasks in parallel, the combinators -||- and -&&- are provided. A task constructed using -||- is finished as soon as either one of its subtasks is finished, returning the result of that task. The combinator -&&- is finished as soon as both subtasks are finished, and pairs their results.

2.2 Running example: a paper review workflow

In this section we illustrate the use of the iTask system by designing a workflow for reviewing papers that can be part of a conference management system.

We start by defining the types that determine the universe of discourse. For conciseness, we use very simple types: a paper is represented by some opaque type Paper for which two access functions are available to display the title and full content:

```
:: Paper
title :: Paper → String
full  :: Paper → String
```

We define two label-generating functions, using a constructor function label :: String → Label, to identify the tasks for reviewing and bidding for papers:

```
reviewLabel :: Paper → Label
reviewLabel p = label ("review " + title p)

bidLabel :: Paper → Label
bidLabel p = label ("bid " + title p)
```

The chair and other members are synonyms of the opaque type User:

```
:: Chair     :== User
:: PC        :== [Reviewer]
:: Reviewer:== User
```

Programme committee members bid for papers to review, and for those papers that they are in charge of, they make a decision. A decision is either to Reject, Discuss, or Accept a paper:

```
:: Bid       :== (Reviewer, [Paper])
:: Review    :== (Paper, (Reviewer, Decision))
:: Decision  = Reject | Discuss | Accept
```

This settles the universe, we proceed with the tasks. First we design a task that lets all programme committee members bid for papers. We proceed in a bottom-up fashion and first create another main task to ask a programme committee member whether she would like to review a specific paper (the value True is the default value):

```
choosePaper :: Paper → Task Bool
choosePaper p = bidLabel p @: edit (title p) True
```

We present the choice for each paper and obtain the selected papers using a parallel list comprehension that filters the chosen papers:

```
choosePapers :: [Paper] → Task [Paper]
choosePapers ps = all (map choosePaper ps) ≫= λds →
                  return [p \\ p←ps & True←ds]
```

The function all guarantees that all tasks in the list are evaluated to completion, and collects and returns their results:

```
all :: ([Task a] → Task [a]) | iTask a
all = foldr (λta tas → ta -&&- tas ≫= λ(va, vas) →
                        return [va : vas]) (return [])
```

Next, we request the bid of all programme committee members:

```
assignPapers :: PC [Paper] → Task [Bid]
assignPapers pc ps = all [ member @: (choosePapers ps ≫= λs →
                                      return (member, s))
                         \\ member ← pc
                         ]
```

The resulting list tells us which papers the programme committee members want to review. In a real system, the chair verifies the number of reviewers per paper, which is not modelled here due to limited space.

Now we design a single paper review for some reviewer, identified by the title of the paper. The reviewer either reviews the paper or delegates the task to another reviewer. Hence, this task is modeled as a choice between two alternatives:

```
reviewPaper :: Paper Reviewer → Task Review
reviewPaper p r = reviewLabel p @:
                  (plainReview p r -||- delegateReview p r)
```

A plain review of a paper shows the paper to the reviewer, who decides to reject, discuss (the initial value), or accept the paper:

```
plainReview :: Paper Reviewer → Task Review
plainReview p r = edit (full p) Discuss ≫= λd →
                  return (p, (r, d))
```

Alternatively, a reviewer may decide to delegate the review of a paper to another reviewer. Hence, reviewPaper is an example of a recursive workflow. The original reviewer remains responsible for reviewing the paper, which explains why she is still passed as an argument to reviewPaper:

```
delegateReview :: Paper Reviewer → Task Review
delegateReview p r = edit "Delegate review" r ≫= λother →
                     other @: reviewPaper p r
```

Given this assignment, we ask all members to perform their tasks:

```
reviewPapers :: [Bid] → Task [Review]
reviewPapers bids = all [ r @: reviewPaper p r
                        \\ (r, ps) ← bids, p ← ps
                        ]
```

The entire workflow of first making a selection of papers, followed by reviewing all papers by all reviewers, is a simple succession:

```
reviews :: PC [Paper] → Task [Review]
reviews pc ps = assignPapers pc ps ≫= reviewPapers
```

A conference management system can use this result to automatically separate all clear cases (i.e., all reject and all accept) from the papers that require discussion.

The final step is to turn this specification into an executable application. The main function in Clean is called Start and must accept and return a unique *World value in order to interact with the external world. The type attribute * is due to Clean's uniqueness typing (Barendsen and Smetsers, 1993) to ensure single-threaded use of the corresponding value, which allows us to model side-effects in a pure functional language. The library function startEngine takes a list of workflow specifications, using the constructor function workflow that are made available to the workers:

```
Start :: *World → *World
Start world = startEngine [workflow "Review" reviewWF] world

reviewWF :: Task [Review]
reviewWF = getUsersWithRole "chair"    ≫= λchairs →
           getUsersWithRole "reviewer" ≫= λpc     →
           readDB "papers"             ≫= λpapers →
           (hd chairs, label "reviews") @: reviews pc papers
```

To complete the example, the proper workers and papers need to be loaded. The iTask system supports several functions to obtain information about its workers. The library function getUsersWithRole takes a role and yields all currently registered workers who have that role, readDB takes an identifier and reads the information from the corresponding database. Finally, we assign the main review tasks reviews to the chair with the label "reviews".

3. Type-safe run-time change

The iTask system includes many features to define workflows. Despite this expressive power, it is cumbersome to anticipate on every possible future way of working in a workflow specification. Moreover, it is too much work to anticipate on all changes that can happen simply because the workflow would become much too complicated. The ability to make changes at run time helps to keep workflow specifications concise. When specifying the workflow, we define the current way of working. At run time it is determined when and where a change in the way of working is needed.

In order to keep the system simple, we only allow main tasks to be changed, meaning, tasks explicitly labelled using the @: combinator. This is not a fundamental restriction since any task can be promoted to a main task. Moreover, other combinators can be made aware of changes in the same fashion.

In the remainder of this section we first explain what properties of a task are (Section 3.1) and what a change function is (Section 3.2). We create an API for often occurring change patterns (Section 3.3). Next we use this API in the running example (Section 3.4) to show a number of changes.

3.1 Properties

As alluded to in Section 2.1, tasks can have several properties. These are captured by the opaque type Properties. The type class property defines the properties that can be set and get:

```
class property p where
  setProperty :: p Properties → Properties
  getProperty :: Properties → p

instance property Label, User
```

Instances for the types Label and User are used in this paper.

3.2 Dynamic change

A workflow under execution consists at any time of at least one main task. The mechanism of change that we propose in this paper is as follows. A change is a function that is applied to a main task if it fits the properties and type of that task. Based on the properties of the main task to be changed, the change function decides whether or not to change the properties, the entire main task, and also how to continue changing in the future. This is performed for all current main tasks, as well as for the future main tasks in the workflow. Hence, a change that alters main tasks of type Task a is a function of type Change a:

```
:: Change a :== Properties (Task a) (Task a)
                → ( Maybe Properties
                  , Maybe (Task a)
                  , Maybe ChangeContinuation
                  )
```

Its arguments are the current properties p of the main task and expressions corresponding to the current task current and the original description of the task original, both of type Task a.

If the change function yields new properties np, these are used instead of the current properties p. Such a change establishes for instance that a specific task is moved from one worker to another.

If the change function yields a new task new, the old task current is aborted and replaced by new. Naturally, new has to be of the same type as current. It can be constructed from the task current, representing the task possibly under current evaluation, as well as the original task description original, representing the same task before people were working on it. So, we can either construct a complete new task, or continue with the work but let it for example be followed by a supervising task inspecting its result, or restart the main task from scratch if necessary. By changing the task, a worker might be faced with the fact that her work is no longer needed or that something else has to be performed. The iTask system informs the user about such issues.

If the change function yields a continuation cf, the type of which is discussed below, then the change function wants to alter another main task, but now it will use the change function cf. This allows the change function to alter its behaviour, making use of the knowledge it obtained from inspecting the main tasks so far. When the change function yields no continuation, the change is said to be *exhausted*. After changes have been applied to every current main task, any remaining continuations are stored in order such that they can be applied to future main tasks. Stored continuations are removed automatically when the corresponding change is exhausted, or manually by an authorized user.

The type of the ChangeContinuation deserves special attention. The type Change a is too restrictive since only main tasks of the same type can be changed. Returning a change of type ∀ a: Change a is too liberal, with this type we cannot limit changes to tasks of a specific type. The dynamic typing system of Clean (Pil, 1999) solves this problem by defining a change continuation as a dynamic type:

```
:: ChangeContinuation :== Dynamic
```

The dynamic value contains a change function of some type Change a. The iTask system can only apply this function to a main task of type Task b if the types a and b can be unified at run time, as we will see in Section 5.3. Changes of a type that cannot be unified with a main task are ignored.

3.3 Change combinators

For convenience, we define a set of change combinators to create proper change functions, as shown in Figure 2. We give examples of their use in Section 3.4.

The initial change change0 terminates change handling immediately and alters neither properties nor tasks. Changes that only concern properties, tasks, or the change continuation are expressed preferably as functions over Properties, Task, and Change functions. These functions are lifted to change functions with newProps, newTask, and newChange respectively. In the definition of newChange we have to make sure that the provided function over change functions fits the value stored in the change continuation. We use a type-dependent dynamic pattern match (Pil, 1999) with the type attribute ^ to check that their types unify. Another useful variant is forceChange ncf, which forces the change continuation to always become ncf; even if the current change is exhausted.

Switching between two alternative change functions tf and ef is achieved by switch cond tf ef, using a predicate cond on the properties of the main task. Two frequently occurring patterns are expressed in terms of switch: the function when cond cf applies its change only when cond holds, and once cond cf applies its change exactly once to the first task that satisfies cond and terminates.

A change function is applied to exactly one task, and then determines how to proceed by returning a change continuation function. Iteration of the same change is captured with repeat cf, which makes sure that cf is applied from now on.

Sometimes it is desirable to overrule the result of a main task, depending on its current properties. We introduce two overruling functions: overruleOne cond vf overrules the first task that satisfies the predicate cond, and overruleAll cond vf overrules all of them.

3.4 Running example: changing the paper review workflow

We use the change combinators of Figure 2 to construct change functions for the paper reviewing workflow example.

Suppose that reviewer r1 is no longer able to perform her duties, and the symposium chair decides that all her work must be handed over to reviewer r2. This is realized by the change function handOver:

```
handOver :: Reviewer Reviewer → Change a | iTask a
handOver r1 r2 = repeat (delegate r1 r2)

delegate :: Reviewer Reviewer → Change a | iTask a
delegate r1 r2 = newProps changeProp change0
where changeProp p | getProperty p == r1 = setProperty r2 p
                   | otherwise            = p
```

A slightly more involved example is to delegate the work of the member to a list of members $[pc_1 \, .. \, pc_n]$ in round-robin order:

```
distribute :: Reviewer [Reviewer] → Change a | iTask a
distribute r []       = change0
distribute r [pc:pcs] = forceChange (distribute r (pcs ++ [pc]))
                                    (delegate r pc)
```

As another example, suppose that the symposium chair decides that a reviewing task has to be supervised by someone identified as super. The result of a completed task ta is offered to super, who decides to edit this result and commit it or redo the entire task:

```
check :: String Reviewer (Task a) (Task a) → Task a | iTask a
check s super ta t0 = ta >>= λva → super @: (edit s va -||- t0)
```

The symposium chair can now conditionally supervise tasks:

```
supervise :: (Properties → Bool) String Reviewer → Change a
                                                  | iTask a
supervise cond s super = repeat (when cond (newTask (check s super)
                                                     change0))
```

Such kind of overruling can be performed to the extreme: suppose that the symposium chair decides that the result of a certain main task (e.g., a review) must be a specific value. If the chair knows the label of the task, then this action is formalized as:

```
overrule :: Label a → Change a | iTask a
overrule l x = overruleOne (λps → getProperty ps == l) (const x)
```

Suppose that a late paper p arrives and the programme chair decides to enter this paper in the reviewing workflow. She needs to extend the main workflow, identified by the label "reviews" as used in Section 2.2, with a new instance of an entire review for the single paper p:

```
late :: PC Paper → Change [Review]
late pc p = once (λps → getProperty ps == label "reviews") add
where add = newTask
              (λta _ → ta -&&- reviews pc [p] >>= λ(old, new) →
                       return (old ++ new))
              change0
```

Conversely, suppose that an author withdraws her paper. In that case, programme committee members should stop bidding or reviewing that particular paper. Such tasks are identified by their bidLabel and reviewLabel:

```
noBid :: Paper → Change Bool
noBid p = overruleAll (λps → getProperty ps == bidLabel p)
                      (const False)

noReview :: Paper → Change Review
noReview p = overruleAll (λps → getProperty ps == reviewLabel p)
                         (λps → (p, (getProperty ps, Reject)))
```

After the manager has applied these two change functions to the workflow, every bid is converted to not selecting it, and a review is

```
change0              :: Change a
change0              =λp ta t0 → (Nothing, Nothing, Nothing)

newProps             :: (Properties → Properties) (Change a) → Change a        | iTask a
newProps fp cf       =λp ta t0 → case cf p ta t0 of (Nothing, nta, ncf) → (Just (fp  p), nta, ncf)
                                                    (Just np, nta, ncf) → (Just (fp np), nta, ncf)

newTask              :: ((Task a) (Task a) → Task a) (Change a) → Change a    | iTask a
newTask fta cf       =λp ta t0 → case cf p ta t0 of (np, Nothing,  ncf) → (np, Just (fta  ta t0), ncf)
                                                    (np, Just nta, ncf) → (np, Just (fta nta t0), ncf)

newChange            :: ((Change a) → Change a) (Change a) → Change a          | iTask a
newChange fcf cf     =λp ta t0 → case cf p ta t0 of (np, nta, Just (ncf :: Change a^)) → (np, nta, Just (dynamic (fcf ncf)))
                                                    (np, nta, ncf)                     → (np, nta, ncf)

forceChange          :: (Change a) (Change a) → Change a                       | iTask a
forceChange ncf cf   =λp ta t0 → case cf p ta t0 of (np, nta, _) → (np, nta, Just (dynamic ncf))

switch               :: (Properties → Bool) (Change a) (Change a) → Change a | iTask a
switch cond tf ef    =λp ta t0 → if (cond p) (tf p ta t0) (ef p ta t0)

when                 :: (Properties → Bool) (Change a) → Change a              | iTask a
when cond cf         = switch cond cf change0

once                 :: (Properties → Bool) (Change a) → Change a              | iTask a
once cond cf         = switch cond cf (forceChange (once cond cf) change0)

repeat               :: (Change a) → Change a                                  | iTask a
repeat cf            = forceChange (repeat cf) cf

overruleOne          :: (Properties → Bool) (Properties → a) → Change a       | iTask a
overruleOne cond vf = once cond (λp → newTask (λ_ _ → return (vf p)) change0 p)

overruleAll          :: (Properties → Bool) (Properties → a) → Change a       | iTask a
overruleAll cond vf = repeat (when cond (λp → newTask (λ_ _ → return (vf p)) change0 p))
```

Figure 2. The iTask change combinators

changed to reject it. As a consequence, the programme committee members do not perform redundant work.

The above functions are all examples of change functions. They can be stored and loaded as dynamic values in arbitrary Clean programs. To actually apply such a change function to an iTask workflow, an authorized user loads such a dynamic change function, identifies it with a label, and adds it to the workflow. The label is required to allow the user to remove the change function at any later time.

With these examples, we demonstrate that realistic changes can be modelled concisely with a set of combinators. Each of these changes could have been anticipated within the original workflow, but this would have resulted in an unwieldy workflow specification.

4. The iTask core reference implementation

In this section we first capture the semantics of the iTask core system as defined in Section 2. Change handling as described in Section 3, is treated in Section 5. As we will see, change handling is defined in such a way that it only affects the @: combinator. The semantic definitions of all other combinators remain the same.

We express the semantics in terms of a reference implementation, using Clean as modeling language. There are several advantages to this approach. First, using a strongly typed programming language with an expressive type system gives static type checking of the semantic model for free. Second, it allows the model to be executed to verify if it behaves as expected. Execution of a carefully designed set of unit tests appeared to be crucial in order to validate various versions of the semantics. Third, use of Clean creates no artificial gap between the modeling language and actual implementation, which would occur had we used Agda, Coq, or other means.

The semantic description we present here for the iTask core system is different from an earlier version (Koopman et al., 2009). The main goal of that work was to establish an initial semantics and investigate its properties using model-based testing. In that approach, we make use of an algebraic datatype to model combinators and are forced to use a closed universe of task types. Here we define the semantics of the combinators using semantic functions; there are no restrictions on the types being used. Instead of semantic functions, the use of generalised algebraic data types (Peyton Jones et al., 2006) would have been an alternative approach, but this requires an integration with dynamic types (Van Noort et al., 2010a).

The signatures of the semantic functions correspond closely to the original signatures of the modeled combinator functions. The semantic function of a combinator function of type Task a has type STask a (Section 4.1) and describes a one-step reduction of a task given a worker event and current state of the workflow.

In the reference implementation we abstract from all details that involve boilerplate programming, such as data storage and retrieval, GUI rendering, and form interaction. For this reason, the semantic functions do not include the iTask context restriction, but do require Dynamic to handle input of arbitrary type.

Although workers are assumed to work in a distributed setting, the events they produce are collected and sequentially offered to the iTask system. It handles events one by one in a single event-handling loop (Section 4.2) such that we do not have to worry about concurrency. The reduction of tasks with respect to event sequences describes a term-rewriting system. It is a fixed-point computation that eventually may lead to a task in normal form. The effect of one reduction step is a reduced term which, if the fixed point is not reached, is capable of handling the next event. Additionally, the set of next possible input events is calculated, which is used by the real iTask system to generate proper feedback and a GUI for the workers.

4.1 Semantic types

A semantic function performs a one-step reduction based on the current identification and properties of the task, as well as the worker event and state of the system. Its type is defined as follows:

```
:: STask a:== TaskId Properties Event State → *(Reduct a, State)
```

As a notational convention, semantic functions use the formal parameters λi p e s. Next, we explain the individual components of the STask type.

Stable task identifiers Several workers can work on tasks at the same time. Since each worker has her own GUI, the state of the workflow system can be changed by someone else while a worker is working on a task. Meanwhile, new tasks can be created while others are no longer needed. Hence, we have to guarantee that a task someone is working on is uniquely identified and that this identification remains the same over time under all conditions. To enforce such stable unique task identifiers, we impose an identification scheme that encodes the path from the root of the task expression to the given combinator function by a list of integers:

```
:: TaskId:== [Int]

taskId0 :: TaskId
taskId0 = [0]
```

We use taskId0 as the initial TaskId. A combinator with unique identification i identifies its subexpressions uniquely as [0 : i], [1 : i], and so on, as specified by subIds:

```
subIds :: TaskId → [TaskId]
subIds i = [[n : i] \\ n←[0 .. ]]
```

Properties As described earlier in Section 3.1, tasks can have several properties. Hence, the semantic function of a task takes such properties. The initial properties are defined by props0, which we do not define in this paper since the Properties type is opaque.

Events The generic foundation of the iTask system permits us to abstract from GUI programming, and instead refer to GUI elements in terms of the value of their editors. The value of an editor can be of any type, hence we use a dynamic to store its value.

A worker who terminates an editor, emits a Commit tid event. A worker who manipulates the GUI that is generated by an edit task with identification value tid, updates a new value of the corresponding type and emits an Update tid (dynamic value) event. Not all worker events are related to editor tasks: examples of other events are when a worker signs into the system or requests to refresh (part of) the GUI:

```
:: Event  = Commit TaskId | Update TaskId Value | Refresh
:: Value:== Dynamic
```

Reductions of subtasks (e.g., return) can cause further reduction which needs to be triggered as well. We model this behaviour also using a Refresh event.

State The combinator library of the iTask system is a monadic state transformer. The unique state consists of two components: the values of all currently active, nonterminated editors, and the unique external world that links the iTask workflow with its environment:

```
:: *State        = {es :: [EditorValue], world :: *World}
:: EditorValue:== (TaskId, User, Value)
```

Note that by including the type attribute * in the definition of State, any occurrence of that type is attributed unique automatically.

While handling an event, every nonterminated editor accumulates its current value in the collection of editor values. As a result, after the workflow has entirely handled the event, the state has an exact and complete record of the values of all currently active editors. The presence of the external world in the state demonstrates that the workflow engineer can, in principle, create custom tasks with side-effects. It should be noted that we do not discuss this further in this paper. In addition, it makes the connection between the workflow and the external world explicit, using the following two functions:

```
showGUI      :: State → State
getNextEvent :: State → (Event, State)
```

The function showGUI renders the values of the current active editors (which are collected in the es field of the state), and displays them in the external world. The function getNextEvent retrieves an event from the external world. Their definitions are not relevant to this paper. Finally, the initial state is created with state0:

```
state0 :: *World → State
state0 world = {world = world, es = []}
```

Reducts The reduction semantics describes the reduction behaviour for each combinator of the iTask system with a semantic function. A task combinator expression reduces to either task normal form or to a new task combinator expression:

```
:: Reduct a = NF a | Redex (STask a)
```

A task is in normal form when it is terminated and has committed its final value; its reduct is NF value. Note that the committed value is lazy like any other value in Clean and hence not necessarily in normal form. The reduct of a task that is not yet terminated, is a new task expression. Such a value nta has type STask a, and the reduct has value Redex nta.

4.2 Task normalization

The evaluation of a combinator expression is defined by the function normalize which is a fixed-point computation that terminates when a normal form is reached:

```
1  normalize :: (STask a) *World → (a, *World)
2  normalize ta world = toNF (startTask ta Refresh (state0 world))
3
4  toNF :: (Reduct a, State) → (a, *World)
5  toNF (NF va,     s) = (va, s.world)
6  toNF (Redex ta, s) = toNF (reduce ta (getNextEvent (showGUI s)))
7
8  reduce :: (STask a) (Event, State) → (Reduct a, State)
9  reduce ta (e, s)
10     | valid e s.es = startTask ta e s
11     | otherwise    = (Redex ta, showError "Invalid event" e s)
12
13 startTask :: (STask a) Event State → (Reduct a, State)
14 startTask ta e s = ta taskId0 props0 e {s & es = []}
```

All current editor values that are accumulated in the state are offered to the workers using showGUI. They either update or commit an arbitrary editor with an arbitrary (but type-preserving) new value which generates an event that is collected using getNextEvent. Only valid events cause a reduction of the workflow (line 10). When evaluating a new event, the task is provided with the proper initial values of task identification, properties, and an empty accumulator of editor values, as defined by startTask (lines 13-14).

Invalid events can be generated by workers who are looking at old versions of the workflow in their GUI and generate events corresponding to tasks which are no longer needed. Due to the consistent naming of tasks, we can determine if an event belongs to an editor that is still active by comparing its identifier to the identifiers of active editors collected in the state:

```
valid :: Event [EditorValue] → Bool
valid (Commit tid)   es = isMember tid [ j \\ (j, _, _)←es ]
valid (Update tid _) es = isMember tid [ j \\ (j, _, _)←es ]
valid _              _  = True
```

In case of an invalid event, an error message is shown using the helper function showError (line 11).

4.3 Combinator semantics

We now define the semantic functions for the iTask core system shown in Figure 1. Each occurrence of Task is replaced by STask in the original signatures.

We start with the edit combinator, which is the only semantic function that inspects Commit and Update events:

```
1  edit :: String a → STask a | Dynamic a
2  edit _ va = λi p e s →
3    case e of
4      Commit tid
5        | tid == i → (NF va, s)
6      Update tid (nva :: a^)
7        | tid == i → (Redex (edit nva), addES i p nva s)
8      _            → (Redex (edit va),  addES i p va s)
9
10 addES :: TaskId Properties a State → State | Dynamic a
11 addES i p va s = {s & es = [(i, getProperty p, dynamic va) : s.es]}
```

An event matches an editor when the task identifications values are equal (lines 5 and 7). Although we know ourselves that the type of an updated value is identical to the type of the value of an editor, we need to guarantee this using a type-dependent dynamic pattern match (line 6), as seen earlier in Section 3.3. The three kinds of events, as defined in Section 4.1, each inflict different behaviour of edit. First, if the worker has terminated an editor task, it reduces to normal form with the current value stored in the editor (line 5). Second, if the worker has changed the current value of the editor task to nva (line 6), then it reduces to an editor task with the nva value (line 7). In any other case the current value of the editor is not changed (line 8). Except when the task normal form is reached, the current value is accumulated in the workflow state.

The semantic function of @: assigns a new property to the given task. This is achieved straightforwardly by updating the old properties with the new property as long as this combinator is a redex:

```
(@:) infixr 5 :: p (STask a) → STask a | property p
(@:) np ta  = λi p e s →
  case ta i (setProperty np p) e s of
    (Redex nta, s) → (Redex (np @: nta), s)
    reduct         → reduct
```

The new properties set by np @: ta are inherited by all subtasks within ta until overruled by another @: combinator.

The monadic combinators are return and ≫=:

```
1  return :: a → STask a
2  return va = λi p e s → (NF va, s)
3
4  (≫=) infixl 1 :: (STask a) (a → STask b) → STask b
5  (≫=) ta atb = λi p e s →
6    case ta (subIds i !! 0) p e s of
7      (NF va,    s) → setTaskId (λi → subIds i !! 1) (atb va)
8                                i p Refresh s
9      (Redex nta, s) → (Redex (nta ≫= atb), s)
```

The semantic function of return immediately emits its argument value as normal form without modifying the state (line 2). The semantic function of ≫= is the bind operator of a state monad. In ta ≫= atb, the task ta is reduced one step first (line 6). (The expression xs !! i selects the ith element of xs.) If a task normal form is reached, then the committed value va of that task is provided to the second argument of ≫= (line 7). A Refresh event is applied to the newly created task in order to collect its events in the state (line 8). If the task is still a redex, then a new redex is constructed (line 9). Note that caution is advised in numbering subexpressions since the one-step reduction can change the shape by transforming ta ≫= atb to atb va, where va is the task normal form value of ta. The function setTaskId is used to warrant the correct identification of new subtasks:

```
setTaskId :: (TaskId → TaskId) (STask a) → STask a
setTaskId fi ta = λi p e s →
  case ta (fi i) p e s of
    (Redex nta, s) → (Redex (setTaskId fi nta), s)
    reduct         → reduct
```

When given a function that generates a correct task identification value, setTaskId will always start numbering with this identification value. In case of ≫=, the second subtask needs to receive the second subidentification value at index 1 (line 7).

The semantic function of -||- is defined as follows:

```
1  (-||-) infixr 3 :: (STask a) (STask a) → STask a
2  (-||-) ta ua = λi p e s →
3    case ta (subIds i !! 0) p e s of
4      (NF va,     s) → (NF va, s)
5      (Redex nta, s) →
6        case ua (subIds i !! 1) p e s of
7          (NF wa,     s) → (NF wa, s)
8          (Redex nua, s) → (Redex (nta -||- nua), s)
```

When reduction of the left subtask ta yields a normal form, the corresponding value is the result of this expression (line 4). Otherwise the right task, ua, is reduced. If that yields a normal form the entire reduction is also finished (line 7). When neither subtask is finished a new instance of the combinator is constructed using the updated subtasks (line 8).

The semantic function of -&&- is defined similarly:

```
1  (-&&-) infixr 4 :: (STask a) (STask b) → STask (a, b)
2  (-&&-) ta tb = λi p e s →
3    let (reducta, s1)  = ta (subIds i !! 0) p e s
4        (reductb, s2)  = tb (subIds i !! 1) p e s1
5    in case (reducta, reductb) of
6         (NF va,     NF vb    ) → (NF (va, vb),                 s2)
7         (NF va,     Redex ntb) → (Redex (return va -&&- ntb),  s2)
8         (Redex nta, NF vb    ) → (Redex (nta -&&- return vb),  s2)
9         (Redex nta, Redex ntb) → (Redex (nta -&&- ntb),        s2)
```

First, the left subtask, ta, is reduced. Then, the right subtask, tb is reduced using the state of the first reduction. When both tasks are in normal form, reduction is finished and the results are paired and returned (line 6). Otherwise, a new instance of the combinator is constructed using the updated tasks (lines 7-9). If only one of the subtasks is in normal form, return is used to create a trivial redex.

5. Change handling reference implementation

In this section, we discuss what it takes to extend the reference implementation of the iTask core system with change handling. We first describe the changes to the elements of the semantic types (Section 5.1). We then proceed with the normalization of tasks (Section 5.2) and show how changes that enter a workflow during reduction are added and can be removed. Handling current and pending changes is performed only by the change-aware @: combinator (Section 5.3).

5.1 Semantic types

The type of a semantic function remains the same (we repeat it for easy reference), only the types for events and state are altered:

```
:: STask a:== TaskId Properties Event State → *(Reduct a, State)
```

Events As discussed in Section 3.4, authorized users can add and remove changes. This is captured by two new worker events to add (AddChange) and remove (RemoveChange) changes:

```
:: Event           = Commit TaskId | Update TaskId Value | Refresh
                   | AddChange LabeledChange
                   | RemoveChange (ChangeLabel → Bool)
:: LabeledChange:== (ChangeLabel, ChangeContinuation)
:: ChangeLabel   :== String
```

State The state is extended with change administration:

```
:: *State   = { es :: [EditorValue], world :: *World
              , cc :: Maybe LabeledChange
              , cq :: Queue LabeledChange
              }
:: Queue a:== [a]
```

Changes are stored in the state for two reasons. First, a change function modifies itself via its continuation, which is stored in the cc field of the state. Second, when all current main tasks have been changed and we still have a continuation, then the change needs to be applied to future main tasks. This change is appended to the change queue cq. Whenever new tasks are created this queue of change functions is applied in the same order as they have been issued. We define several access functions:

```
setChange :: (Maybe LabeledChange) State → State
setChange nc s = {s & cc = nc}

queueChange :: (Maybe LabeledChange) State → State
queueChange (Just c) s = {s & cq = s.cq ++ [c]}
queueChange _        s = s

storeChange :: State → State
storeChange s=:{cc} = setChange Nothing (queueChange cc s)
```

The function setChange updates the current change of the state, queueChange appends a change function to the queue of pending changes, and storeChange moves the current change to the queue of pending changes.

5.2 Task normalization

As we have seen in Section 4.2, a running workflow is characterized by the semantic functions normalize and reduce. We only need to adapt reduce to add and remove changes.

```
1  reduce :: (STask a) (Event, State) → (Reduct a, State)
2  reduce ta (e, s) =
3    case e of
4      AddChange c
5        → let (reduct, s2) = startTask ta Refresh
6                                        (setChange (Just c) s)
7          in (reduct, storeChange s2)
8      RemoveChange p
9        → (Redex ta, {s & cq = filter (not o p o fst) s.cq})
10     _ | valid e s.es = startTask ta e s
11       | otherwise    = (Redex ta, showError "Invalid event" e s)
```

Nonchange events are handled exactly as before (lines 10-11). Adding a change causes reduction of the task with the given change set as current change (lines 5-6). After this reduction, the (potentially updated) change is stored in the queue of pending changes (line 7). Removing a change is a matter of keeping changes that do not satisfy the removal predicate p (lines 8-9).

5.3 Change-handling semantics

The key challenge is to adapt the @: combinator to make it aware of changes. This is a complex operation for several reasons. First, when np @: t0 is reduced, t0 is the initial subtask description that is required as third argument of any matching change function. As a consequence, t0 needs to be memorized during further reductions. Second, as soon as a new main task is created, all pending changes need to be applied to it in the order of their occurrence. When the task changes, we change the identification value of the subtask (by incrementing its index in the list of subidentification values that is generated with subIds, see Section 4.1). Third, any matching change produces either a continuation which should be used next time or it is exhausted.

For clarity of presentation, we have collected the necessary definitions in Figure 3. In contrast to the earlier semantic function definitions, the reduction behaviour of the @: combinator that includes changes consists of two stages. First, all pending changes are handled exactly once (line 3). Naturally, if this results in a task in task normal form, we are done (line 5). Otherwise, the second step is to reduce to the internal combinator ((nn, np, t0) @:+ nta) (line 4). It keeps track of the correct subtask identification index, properties, and the initial task, together with the result of the earlier reduction. The internal combinator @:+ keeps rewriting to itself as long as its subtask is not in task normal form (line 10). Note that the initial task t0 remains constant. If there is a current change, it is handled as described by doOneChange (line 12). If there is no current change, we only need to reduce its subtask (line 13).

Handling pending changes one by one amounts to folding doOneChange over the queue of pending changes. This is expressed concisely by doPendingChanges (line 18-19).

Finally, doOneChange is the pivotal function that actually applies a change to a task. It does not matter whether this change is a pending change or a new change. The only difference is that a pending change, if not exhausted, needs to be restored in the queue of pending changes, whereas a current change needs to be restored as current change. Hence, doOneChange is parameterized with a restore function of type RestoreChange (line 16) that restores the altered change function in the state. In case of @:+ this is the function setChange and in case of pending changes this is function queueChange (both functions were introduced earlier in Section 5.1). To make doOneChange suited for handling pending changes as well as current changes, it alters a structure of type ChangeResult a (line 15) which keeps track of the subtask identification index, properties, task (as a redex), and state. Required additional information is passed as the first three arguments: the initial task description, the current subtask identification index, and the means to restore the continuation in the state (line 22). A change can be applied without compromising type safety when either its type can be unified with the type of the task (line 24) or if the change function itself is sufficiently generic to handle the task (line 25). Both cases require extensions to standard dynamic typing: type-dependent dynamic pattern matching as seen earlier in Sections 3.3 and 4.3, and ad-hoc polymorphic functions in dynamic values (Van Noort et al., 2010b). If the checks fail, then we only need to restore the change function in the state (line 26). Handling a matching change is described by the change function (lines 27-32). We apply the change to the required arguments (line 29) and obtain the next subtask identification index, task, and change continuation (line 30). (The function fromMaybe removes the Just constructor from its second argument if it has one, and returns the first argument otherwise.) A new reduct is computed (line 32), the change continuation is restored, and possibly altered subtask identification index and properties are returned (line 27).

```
(@:) infixr 5 :: p (STask a) → STask a | property p & Dynamic a
(@:) np t0 =λi p e s →
  case doPendingChanges t0 i (setProperty np p) s of
    (nn, np, (Redex nta, s)) → ((nn, np, t0) @:+ nta) i np e s
    (_ , _, reduct)          → reduct

(@:+) infixr 5 :: (Int, Properties, STask a) (STask a) → STask a | Dynamic a
(@:+) (n, p, t0) ta =λi _ e s →
  case doCurrentChange i e s of
    (nn, np, (Redex nta, s)) → (Redex ((nn, np, t0) @:+ nta), s)
    (_, _, reduct)           → reduct
where doCurrentChange i Refresh s=:{cc = Just c} =doOneChange t0 i setChange (n, p, (Redex ta, {s & cc = Nothing})) c
      doCurrentChange i e       s                = (n, p, ta (subIds i !! n) p e s)

:: *ChangeResult a:== (Int, Properties, *(Reduct a, State))
:: RestoreChange  :== (Maybe LabeledChange) State → State

doPendingChanges :: (STask a) TaskId Properties State → ChangeResult a | Dynamic a
doPendingChanges t0 i np s=:{cq} = foldl (doOneChange t0 i queueChange) (0, np, (Redex t0, {s & cq = []})) cq

doOneChange :: (STask a) TaskId RestoreChange (ChangeResult a) LabeledChange → ChangeResult a | Dynamic a
doOneChange t0 i restoreChange (n, p, (r, s)) (ci, d) =
  case (r, d) of
    (Redex ta, cf :: Change a^)                → change ta cf
    (Redex ta, cf ::∀b: Change b | Dynamic b) → change ta cf
    (reduct,   _)                              → (n, p, (reduct, restoreChange (Just (ci, d)) s))
where change ta cf = (nn, np, (reduct, restoreChange nc s2))
      where
        (mbnp, mbnt, mbcf) = cf i p ta t0
        (np, nta, nc)      = (fromMaybe p mbnp, fromMaybe ta mbnt, mapMaybe (λcf → (ci, cf)) mbcf)
        nn                 = if (isJust mbnt) (n + 1) n
        (reduct, s2)       = nta (subIds i !! nn) np Refresh s
```

Figure 3. The change-handling reference implementation of the @: combinator

6. Related work

There are three kinds of related work. First there are other WFMSs that recognized the need for dynamic changes of the workflow executed. Second, there are other constructs to change programs at run time. Finally, there are programming languages that have support for run-time change of code under execution.

The need for run-time changes in workflow systems has been recognized early (Ellis and Keddara, 2000; Ellis et al., 1995). These changes describe dynamic modification of both the specification of the workflow as well as any running instantiation of this specification. Several change patterns have been described (Weber et al., 2008), classifying types of changes that should be supported by a WFMS in two categories: adaption patterns and patterns for changes to predefined regions. The former describes changes to instantiations in which parts are either inserted, deleted, moved, replaced, and so on. The latter allows to defer the full specification of a workflow to run time, by predefining regions which are eligible to change at run time. Finally, in the untyped imperative ADEPT (Reichert and Dadam, 1998) workflow system, changes can only be applied if they satisfy preconditions imposed on global parameters or side-effects. Preconditions allow properties to be checked other than type correctness as in the iTask system. It is interesting to investigate how conditions can be added to the iTask system in general. Each of these approaches are confronted with the dynamic change bug. The Petri Nets representing the workflow is changed during its execution. Because these changes directly manipulate the structure of the Petri Net, this can quickly lead to inconsistencies. As the described reference implementation shows, a task is a pure and self-contained function which can only be replaced by another pure function of the same type.

The standard approach to changing behaviour at run time is known as the strategy pattern (Gamma et al., 1995). Here, the behaviour that can potentially be changed is insulated and the object possessing this behaviour is equipped with an explicit way to change it. In the context of this paper this would imply that we have to equip each task with such a hook. We believe our solution using change events that replaces a task by a new task is more elegant.

Finally, a number of programming languages offer support for run-time change of code. Erlang (Armstrong and Virdin, 1990) supports hot code swapping which is not type safe. ML (Duggan, 2001; Gilmore et al., 1997; Walton et al., 1998) offers type-safe dynamic module swapping. Imperative languages have been the subject of run-time change of code as well (Hicks, 2001; Stoyle et al., 2007). Aspect-oriented programming (Dantas et al., 2008; Kiczales et al., 1997) is another way to change programs dynamically. All these language-based approaches complicate the semantics significantly, our system possesses a plain rewrite semantics which we expect to make reasoning about changes considerably easier.

7. Conclusions and future work

In this paper we have demonstrated how running workflows can be changed type safely. This is a very important feature because deviations from the standard way of working is very common in daily practice. Yet, most commercial WFMS do not support making such changes properly and are subject to dynamic change bugs. This means that they are not of any help when their help is actually needed most. Adding the ability to perform type-safe run-time changes is difficult because their implementation commonly relies on Petri Nets and an implicit external state. Their focus is on control flow while the flow of information between tasks is realized as a side-effect storing information in databases.

In the iTask system, tasks are described by typed, pure, and self-contained functions which explicitly pass information to each other. Replacing a task means type-safe replacement of one pure function by another one. The type system ensures that the values passed between task have the correct type in the initial workflow as well as after any number of changes in this workflow.

Not only tasks under current execution can be changed type safely, also tasks generated in the future by the workflow can be changed. This is quite powerful, since tasks are evaluated dynamically and it is not known in advance which tasks come into existence. The change function can use what it has seen so far to decide how to act in the future.

We have captured the semantics of this powerful construct by giving a reference implementation in Clean. This enabled us to test its behavior. We have proven the practical applicability of the new feature by implementing it in the real iTask system, using the reference implementation as a lead. In the real system, tasks rely on the availability of generic functions. Hence we needed to be able to replace ad-hoc polymorphic functions in a type-safe fashion.

There are numerous possibilities for future work. For instance, the end user needs to be well informed about which work is not taken place as planned, which alternatives exist, and what their effects are. We want to investigate how the change concept can be used to resolve unexpected situations in the context of workflow support for crisis management. Since crisis situations are very unpredictable, it is essential that a WFMS is capable of run-time change in order to be of any use. Also, we plan to look at how we can reason more precisely about the effects of changes to a running workflow.

Acknowledgements

The authors would like to thank the anonymous reviewers for their helpful comments and suggestions, and Jan Martin Jansen for scrupulously reading earlier versions of the paper. This research is supported by the Technology Foundation STW, applied science division of NWO, and the Technology Program of the Ministry of Economic Affairs.

References

Wil van der Aalst. Exterminating the dynamic change bug: A concrete approach to support workflow change. *Information Systems Frontiers*, 3:3:297–317, 2001.

Wil van der Aalst, Arthur ter Hofstede, Bartek Kiepuszewski, and Ana Barros. Workflow patterns. Technical Report FIT-TR-2002-02, Queensland University of Technology, 2002.

Joe Armstrong and Robert Virdin. Erlang - An experimental telephony programming language. In *Proceedings of the International Switching Symposium, ISS '90, Stockholm, Sweden*, pages 2–7, 1990.

Erik Barendsen and Sjaak Smetsers. Conventional and uniqueness typing in graph rewrite systems (extended abstract). In Rudrapatna Shyamasundar, editor, *Proceedings of the Conference on the Foundations of Software Technology and Theoretical Computer Science, FSTTCS '93, Bombay, India*, volume 761 of *Lecture Notes in Computer Science*, pages 41–51. Springer-Verlag, 1993.

Daniel Dantas, David Walker, Geoffrey Washburn, and Stephanie Weirich. Aspectml: a polymorphic aspect-oriented functional programming language. *ACM Transactions on Programming Languages and Systems*, 30 (3):1–60, 2008.

Dominic Duggan. Type-based hot swapping of running modules. In *Proceedings of the International Conference on Functional Programming, ICFP '01, Florence, Italy*, pages 62–73. ACM Press, 2001.

Clarence Ellis and Karim Keddara. A workflow change is a workflow. In Wil van der Aalst, editor, *Business Process Management*, volume 1806 of *Lecture Notes in Computer Science*, pages 201–217. Springer-Verlag, 2000.

Clarence Ellis, Karim Keddara, and Grzegorz Rozenberg. Dynamic change within workflow systems. In *Proceedings of the Conference on Organizational Computing Systems, COOCS '95, Milpitas, CA, USA*, pages 10–21. ACM Press, 1995.

Erich Gamma, Richard Helm, Ralph Johnson, and John Vlissides. *Design patterns: elements of reusable object-oriented software*. Addison-Wesley, 1995.

Stephen Gilmore, Dilsun Kirli, and Christopher Walton. Dynamic ML without dynamic types. Technical Report ECS-LFCS-97-378, University of Edinburgh, 1997.

Michael Hicks. *Dynamic software updating*. PhD thesis, University of Pennsylvania, 2001.

Gregor Kiczales, John Lamping, Anurag Mendhekar, Chris Maeda, Cristina Lopes, Jean-Marc Loingtier, and John Irwin. Aspect-oriented programming. In Mehmet Aksit and Satoshi Matsuoka, editors, *Proceedings of the European Conference on Object-Oriented Programming, ECOOP '97, Jyväskylä, Finland*, pages 220–242. Springer-Verlag, 1997.

Pieter Koopman, Rinus Plasmeijer, and Peter Achten. An executable and testable semantics for iTasks. In Sven-Bodo Scholz, editor, *Revised Selected Papers of the International Symposium on the Implementation and Application of Functional Languages, IFL '08, Hertfordshire, UK*, volume 5836 of *Lecture Notes in Computer Science*. Springer-Verlag, 2009.

Thomas van Noort, Peter Achten, and Rinus Plasmeijer. A typical synergy - Dynamic types and generalised algebraic datatypes. In Marco Morazán and Sven-Bodo Scholz, editors, *Revised Selected Papers of the International Symposium on the Implementation and Application of Functional Languages, IFL '09, South Orange, NJ, USA*, volume 6041 of *Lecture Notes in Computer Science*, pages 179–197. Springer-Verlag, 2010a.

Thomas van Noort, Peter Achten, and Rinus Plasmeijer. Ad-hoc polymorphism and dynamic typing in a statically typed functional language. In Bruno Oliveira and Marcin Zalewski, editors, *Proceedings of the Workshop on Generic Programming, WGP '10, Baltimore, MD, USA*, pages 73–84. ACM Press, 2010b.

Simon Peyton Jones, Dimitrios Vytiniotis, Stephanie Weirich, and Geoffrey Washburn. Simple unification-based type inference for GADTs. In Julia Lawall, editor, *Proceedings of the International Conference on Functional Programming, ICFP '06, Portland, OR, USA*, pages 50–61. ACM Press, 2006.

Marco Pil. Dynamic types and type dependent functions. In Kevin Hammond, Tony Davie, and Chris Clack, editors, *Proceedings of the International Workshop on the Implementation of Functional Languages, IFL '98, London, UK*, volume 1595 of *Lecture Notes in Computer Science*, pages 169–185. Springer-Verlag, 1999.

Rinus Plasmeijer, Peter Achten, and Pieter Koopman. iTasks: executable specifications of interactive work flow systems for the web. In Ralf Hinze and Norman Ramsey, editors, *Proceedings of the International Conference on Functional Programming, ICFP '07*, pages 141–152, Freiburg, Germany, 2007. ACM Press.

Manfred Reichert and Peter Dadam. ADEPT$_{\mathsf{flex}}$ - Supporting dynamic changes of workflows without losing control. *Journal of Intelligent Information Systems*, 10(2):93–129, 1998.

Gareth Stoyle, Michael Hicks, Gavin Bierman, Peter Sewell, and Iulian Neamtiu. Mutatis Mutandis: safe and predictable dynamic software updating. *ACM Transactions on Programming Languages and Systems*, 29(4), 2007.

Philip Wadler. Comprehending monads. In *Proceedings of the Conference on Lisp and Functional Programming, LFP '90, Nice, France*, pages 61–77, 1990.

Christopher Walton, Dilsun Kirli, and Stephen Gilmore. An abstract machine for module replacement. In Stephan Diehl and Peter Sestoft, editors, *Proceedings of the Workshop on Principles of Abstract Machines, PAM '98, Pisa, Italy*, 1998.

Barbara Weber, Manfred Reichert, and Stefanie Rinderle-Ma. Change patterns and change support features - Enhancing flexibility in process-aware information systems. *Data and Knowledge Engineering*, 66(3): 438–466, 2008.

www.ingramcontent.com/pod-product-compliance
Lightning Source LLC
Chambersburg PA
CBHW080553220326
41599CB00032B/6461